The Vietnam Run

The Vietnam Run

*American Merchant Mariners
in the Indochina Wars,
1945–1975*

MICHAEL GILLEN

McFarland & Company, Inc., Publishers
Jefferson, North Carolina

LIBRARY OF CONGRESS CATALOGUING-IN-PUBLICATION DATA

Names: Gillen, Michael, 1948– author.
Title: The Vietnam run : American merchant mariners
in the Indochina wars, 1945–1975 / Michael Gillen.
Other titles: American merchant mariners in the Indochina wars, 1945–1975
Description: Jefferson, North Carolina : McFarland & Company, Inc., Publishers, 2023 |
Includes bibliographical references and index.
Identifiers: LCCN 2022052215 | ISBN 9781476688152 (paperback : acid free paper) ∞
ISBN 9781476646367 (ebook)
Subjects: LCSH: Vietnam War, 1961-1975—Transportation. | Merchant marine—
United States—History—20th century. | Indochinese War, 1946–1954—
Transportation. | Military sealift—United States—History—20th century. |
Vietnam War, 1961–1975—Naval operations, American. | Indochinese War,
1946–1954—United States. | BISAC: HISTORY / Wars & Conflicts /
Vietnam War | HISTORY / Military / Naval
Classification: LCC DS559.8.T7 G55 2023 | DDC 959.704/345—dc23/eng/20221123
LC record available at https://lccn.loc.gov/2022052215

BRITISH LIBRARY CATALOGUING DATA ARE AVAILABLE

ISBN (print) 978-1-4766-8815-2
ISBN (ebook) 978-1-4766-4636-7

Front cover: *top* An American merchant ship moves down the Long Tau channel
to the sea after unloading cargo in Saigon, 1969 (U.S. Navy/Military Sea
Transportation Service); *bottom* Merchant seamen aboard SS *Beaver Victory*,
Saigon, 1966. Pictured far right: Ben Mignano, Bosun
(courtesy National Maritime Union).

Printed in the United States of America

*McFarland & Company, Inc., Publishers
Box 611, Jefferson, North Carolina 28640
www.mcfarlandpub.com*

For Fern
with all my love,

and to the memory of American merchant seamen
who perished while serving on the Vietnam Run.

Table of Contents

Acknowledgments

It takes a crew, and though this has largely and typically been a solo endeavor over many years, there have been many who in various ways have made valuable and much appreciated contributions to it. I wish to express my gratitude in particular to the following:

John Gorley Bunker, maritime historian and Merchant Marine veteran of World War II, for the innumerable clippings and articles related to this project he handed to me in the early goings, and who was a mentor if there ever was one.

Marilyn B. Young, preeminent historian of the Vietnam War and much more, my advisor as I completed graduate work at New York University, for whom I worked there as a teaching assistant, who also was a mentor if there ever was one, and whose friendship I cherished.

Rear Admirals Thomas A. King and Thomas J. Patterson, senior officials with the Maritime Administration in the 1960s (later at the U.S. Merchant Marine Academy), one on the East Coast and the other the West Coast, for their interest, encouragement, sitting for interviews, providing access to archives, and valuable information relating to their experiences with the "break out" of ships from reserve fleets for the Vietnam Run.

W.D. "Bill" Ehrhart, poet (*Thank You for Your Service: Collected Poems*), essayist, and memoirist of the Vietnam War, for his interest, support, and encouragement all along the line, his friendship, and steering me to the right publisher some years ago.

Roger S. Durham, friend, historian of the American Civil War, memoirist of the Vietnam War, for his interest and encouragement as I worked on this project, and who would have seen and benefited from deliveries made by merchant ships during his year-long tour at Cam Ranh Bay.

Those I traveled with on my two return trips to Vietnam after the war, for sharing their experiences with me, appreciating my own, and who in a number of cases have become some of my best and lifelong friends.

Among those I traveled with to Vietnam on Project Hearts and Minds medical supply missions, two in particular—Frank Corcoran and Dayl Wise—have not only become good friends, but shown interest in and given encouragement for this project over many years. Some of their photographs appear in this book.

The many Merchant Marine veterans of the Vietnam War—far too many to name here individually, though many names do appear in this book—some who became lifelong friends, who contributed recollections in writing or interviews, documents, photographs, clippings, and articles.

Those in maritime labor organizations for whom I worked or otherwise had meaningful contact with over the years, who took interest in and supported this project in early goings, provided photographs, access to archived materials, and printed my appeals to members for information in their publications.

Many members of my family, and good friends, for their support and interest in this project all along the line.

Jan Dickler, my brother-in-law, and "brother" otherwise, for his interest and encouragement, and providing valuable tech support at crucial points along the way.

And for Fern, for her love, tremendous support, an occasional timely "swift kick" to keep me on course with this project, her own creative spirit and good work, and so many other things that enrich my life. In addition to my heartfelt appreciation, this book as noted elsewhere is also dedicated to her.

Abbreviations and Acronyms

AB . . . . Able Seaman
ACTOV . . . . Accelerated Turnover to the Vietnamese
APL . . . . American President Lines
ARA . . . . American Radio Association
ARVN . . . . Army of the Republic of Vietnam
AT&B . . . . Alaska Tug & Barge
CASL . . . . Committee of American Steamship Lines
CHICOM . . . . Chinese Communist
CINCPAC . . . . Commander in Chief Pacific
DOD . . . . Department of Defense
DMZ . . . . Demilitarized Zone
DRV . . . . Democratic Republic of Vietnam (North Vietnam)
FOWT . . . . Fireman-Oiler-Watertender
GAA . . . . General Agency Agreement
GVN . . . . Government of Vietnam (Saigon)
ILA . . . . International Longshoremen's Association
IOMM&P . . . . International Organization of Masters, Mates & Pilots
KIA . . . . Killed in Action
LCM . . . . Landing Craft, Mechanized ("Mike" Boat)
LCU . . . . Landing Craft, Utility
LST . . . . Landing Ship, Tank
MAAG . . . . Military Assistance Advisory Group
MACV . . . . Military Assistance Command, Vietnam
MARAD . . . . Maritime Administration
MEBA . . . . Marine Engineers Beneficial Association
MSC . . . . Military Sealift Command
MSTS . . . . Military Sea Transportation Service
MT . . . . Measurement Ton
NDRF . . . . National Defense Reserve Fleet
NLF . . . . National Liberation Front
NMU . . . . National Maritime Union
NSA . . . . National Shipping Authority
NSAM . . . . National Security Action Memorandum
OPLAN . . . . Operations Plan
OS . . . . Ordinary Seaman
OSS . . . . Office of Strategic Services

PAVN . . . . People's Army of Vietnam
PBR . . . . Patrol Boat, River
PLAF . . . . People's Liberation Armed Forces (South)
PSYOPS . . . . Psychological (warfare) Operations
QMED . . . . Qualified Man in the Engine Department
RPG . . . . Rocket Propelled Grenade
RSSZ . . . . Rung Sat Special Zone
RVN . . . . Republic of Vietnam
SEAL . . . . Sea, Air and Land (U.S. Navy Special Ops Force)
SEATO . . . . Southeast Asia Treaty Organization
SIU . . . . Seafarers International Union
SUP . . . . Sailors' Union of the Pacific
USAID . . . . U.S. Agency for International Development
USNFVMHS . . . . U.S. Naval Forces Vietnam Monthly Historical Summary
USNS . . . . United States Naval Ship (civilian crew)
USL . . . . United States Lines
USS . . . . United Seamen's Service/United States Ship (Navy crew)
VC . . . . Viet Cong
VCI . . . . Viet Cong Infrastructure

Preface

Not Just "Minding Their Own Business"

All was quiet shortly after midnight on June 7, 1969, as I stood a security watch on the SS *Fairport* as the ship lay at anchor in the harbor of Da Nang, South Vietnam. The World War II–vintage cargo ship had arrived in-country a few days before, and most of her cargo of some 8,000 tons of 250- and 500-pound bombs still remained to be offloaded into barges. Several members of the ship's crew were ashore enjoying a much-deserved shore leave after the long trans-Pacific crossing. In the darkness little could be seen looking shoreward, and little could be heard except the gentle lapping of the waters of the bay against the hull of ship.[1]

The peace of night was suddenly transformed by flashes of light, followed quickly by sounds of explosions coming from the vicinity of Da Nang's deepwater piers a few miles away. Flames, and what dawn would reveal as a huge cloud of black billowing smoke drifting seaward toward Da Nang's iconic Monkey Mountain, would continue through the morning and well into the day as a U.S. Navy fire-suppression team fought to save what we would later learn was one of many civilian-crewed merchant ships in the harbor at that time.[2]

But their efforts would ultimately end in failure. In what had been a periodic rocket attack by the enemy on targets in Da Nang, which for good reason had come to be known in those days as "rocket city" for the regularity of those attacks, a butane tanker had been hit. As our liberty launch, a World War II–vintage LCM "Mike" boat landing craft, passed by the place where the tanker had been upright only a day earlier, all that could now be seen following the ship's capsizing in place at the pier was its bottom.[3]

Most merchant seamen came to understand well before their initial arrival in-country, and certainly after witnessing the destruction of another ship by rocket attack, the reality of it: that they and their war-cargo-laden ships might also be subject to attack and possible destruction while serving on the Vietnam Run. They were often, in fact, prime targets of an enemy that did not discriminate between those in military or civilian service, whether American, South Vietnamese, South Korean, Australian, or any other nationals who came to oppose them.

As word of ships attacked, damaged, and in some cases sunk, and seamen injured and in many cases killed, began to make its way around the stateside hiring halls and to other venues where seamen spent their time, the understanding that their future voyages to Vietnam meant venturing into "harm's way" as much as it might for anyone else going there under whatever circumstance was taken as a given.

1

Dark smoke drifts seaward from a merchant ship after being hit by Viet Cong rockets, Da Nang, June 1969 (Author photo).

Many merchant seamen were to learn, often the hard way, that one's status as a "civilian non-combatant" involved in logistical support operations in-country made no difference to those against whom this involvement was deployed.

Bill Stephenson, an assistant engineer who had been issued an identification card indicating his civilian non-combatant status, would later ask, "What was I supposed to do, wave the card at the VC and expect they wouldn't shoot at me?"[4]

As it was, Stephenson would narrowly escape death in August 1968 as his ship made its way up the river channel to Saigon. Five minutes after leaving a shop area where he had been working, an RPG round entered through the porthole and exploded, leaving "a pile of splinters" in place of the box on which he had been sitting.

The "Viet Cong" or "VC"—as fighters of the National Liberation Front were commonly known—certainly would not have been aware of the actual extent to which American merchant seamen were involved in the transportation of war materiel and other supplies brought into their country to be used against them. (By most accounts, government or otherwise, ships crewed by merchant seamen transported about 95 percent of all such cargoes brought into South Vietnam during the war.[5]) But what they could plainly see with their own eyes moving along their inland waterways, entering their coastal port cities, and being offloaded onto piers and into barges for transshipment to other locations in-country was all they needed to know.

And if the Viet Cong could not obtain American-made war materiel by capture in the field, theft along the piers and from nearby warehouses, or by other means—such as purchase on the black market—they would attempt to destroy it using artillery, long-range rockets, floating and limpet mines, mortars, recoilless rifle, RPGs, and by whatever means possible, as it sat in ships prior to unloading in harbors, moved along the inland waterways, or by overland transportation in convoy before it reached its intended destination in-country.

Merchant seamen working their way along the Vietnam Run in the 1960s and early 1970s, moving their ammunition-laden ships into position for offloading in Saigon, Da Nang, Cam Ranh Bay, and other ports all along the coast of South Vietnam, knew they were not "just minding their own business" in contrast to a strictly commercial-driven peacetime context.

What American merchant seamen were about—whether transporting thousands of French troops back to Vietnam in the closing months of 1945; moving military rolling stock, weapons, and ammunition to Saigon in support of the French in the late 1940s and early 1950s; or providing logistical support for American advisors, and then large-scale combat units in Vietnam in later years—was war.[6]

As such, and as had been the case in previous wars—whether "declared" or not—the U.S. Merchant Marine would be transformed, visually and otherwise, becoming an indispensable auxiliary to the armed forces, known commonly in that context as "the Fourth Arm of Defense."

In the case of Vietnam, more than 170 government-owned, mothballed ships—largely painted gray—would be withdrawn from National Defense Reserve Fleets (NDRF) for Vietnam Service, and placed under operation by privately owned shipping companies under General Agency Agreement (GAA). Many other ships would be withdrawn from commercial service and placed under contract—and also government control—with the Military Sea Transportation Service (later renamed Military Sealift Command). Thus, the complexion of the ships running along the Vietnam Pipeline, as well as the ultimate control of the ships transporting military supplies into the war zone, would be changed.

What most seamen did not understand, however, was the series of events—the historical context—for their own service to and in Vietnam during the war, and how long the U.S. Merchant Marine had been involved there specifically in support, first, of French efforts to reclaim and maintain control of Vietnam following World War II, and then, following the French defeat, the role it played in the effort by the United States to buttress South Vietnam, despite formal agreements ending the "French War" at the Geneva Conference, as a key point along the Cold War containment line in East Asia.

An opportunity presented itself to me many years after my service to Vietnam as a merchant seaman, and now well along in a career in academia, to speak at an educational conference about the role of American civilian merchant seamen in the war. This would be a good chance to shed light on what has generally been, and continues to be, a little-known, little-understood, and under-appreciated aspect of that history. Some months later I headed down the line from New York to the conference venue, the Vietnam War Era Educational Center, in Holmdel, New Jersey.[7]

After arriving at the educational center, a short walk from the impressive New Jersey Vietnam Veterans Memorial, I began looking for the location of the particular session in which I would make my presentation. I was surprised to find it grouped into a catch-all category of sorts having to do with "business interests." This, I thought, would surely cause those looking for a hot topic to turn hard to starboard in another direction.

But, more importantly, this categorization was not only lamentable for possibly convincing conference attendees to look elsewhere, but for essentially if unintentionally misleading conference attendees at the outset in terms of the history of the Merchant Marine and its transformation in wartime.

By the time I returned later to take my place at the presenter table, I had re-written the opening remarks for the paper, feeling that the well-intentioned but ill-informed placement of my topic within a session with its misleading title required some response—some clarification—up front. I was certainly grateful for the work of conference organizers, making it happen in the first place, but explained that the categorization used for the Merchant Marine, while appropriate in a peacetime context, was not correct for the situation in which the United States had increasingly become involved in Vietnam, and even if at times it contained elements of peacetime trade activity.

Without the logistical support—a reference that might have worked well in fact for the conference session—enhanced by the "breakout" and addition of some 170 once-mothballed government-owned cargo ships to the Vietnam Run, the war, simply put, could not have been waged. As General William C. Westmoreland, commander of American forces in Vietnam between 1964 and 1968, would put it, "We were utterly dependent upon the sea logistical line."[8]

But there was much more to it even than that. American merchant ships were called upon to transport, sometimes under hostile fire, hundreds of thousands of refugees, during both the French and American War periods, from one area in-country to another, and also as South Vietnam itself was on the verge of collapse, in 1975, before the onrushing armies of North Vietnam.

Thousands of Vietnamese were taken aboard merchant ships—well beyond normal and even "emergency" overload capacity, in many cases—and transported to other countries within Southeast Asia, where they were disembarked for temporary holding and processing as refugees before making their way to the United States and other countries that would have them.

The role of the Merchant Marine did not, however, end there. For years following the end of the Vietnam War, American merchant mariners took their ships out of their way—forsaking, as it were, the best business interests of their owners—to rescue thousands of Vietnamese "boat people" after they, the lucky ones, set out in the South China Sea in small boats not designed for such journeys—especially not when grossly overloaded, as many were—until spotted either adrift or still under power by a sharp-eyed seaman.

Many thousands of other Vietnamese, it is believed, either perished as their boats sank in heavy seas, were set upon by pirates, or drifted without power until water, supplies, and their lives ran out.

Those fortunate to be spotted and rescued by American merchant ships or naval ships crewed by merchant seamen, while the many ships of many other countries passed them by—were under orders to do so—would live to see another day, settled safely ashore elsewhere, and even, years later, return again to the motherland of Vietnam they had once forsaken.

Having taught university courses relating to the Vietnam War for many years in New York, it was with much interest that I awaited the release and airing in 2017 of the television documentary series *The Vietnam War* directed by Lynn Novick and Ken Burns. As I began viewing the 10-part, 18-hour-long series I had a number of questions in mind that I hoped would be answered to my satisfaction, though I had some doubts from the start. First, and despite flaws that were sure to become evident, would it truly stimulate a resurgence of interest, reflection, and discussion about what was a major defining moment in our nation's history? Would it, or some episodes of it at least, be useful as teaching aids to underscore aspects of the "Vietnam Experience" that need to be emphasized and remembered? And could it possibly convey any sense, for someone who had not experienced combat in Vietnam (or elsewhere) as to the nature and short- and long-term impact of such an experience? And also, relating to my own brief experience in Vietnam during the war, and longtime interest in maritime history otherwise, would it have anything to say specifically about the three-decades-long role of the U.S. Merchant Marine in the Vietnam War? Would the series acknowledge the American merchant seamen who, engaged once again after the war in peacetime commerce and passing through the South China Sea where many had been before, rescued Vietnamese "boat people" while operators of ships from other (though not all) nations had explicit orders to avoid and certainly not stop to assist them?

While the much anticipated Burns and Novick documentary series certainly did stimulate serious commentary, discussion—and debate—relating in general to the Vietnam War, did contain much compelling testimony relating to the Vietnam Experience, and would be useful, I concluded, as an aid to instruction, many, myself included, concluded that it had once again taken the easy way out—perhaps to make it more palatable (and marketable) for general audiences—rather than confront and dig more deeply into certain inconvenient truths. As for my particular interest in its inclusion of material relating to the role of the U.S. Merchant Marine in the war and its aftermath, it failed miserably to do so. This was, I thought, a sorry and major omission.

Was I really surprised at this omission? No, not really. The task of filling in some of the gaping spaces—the references to logistical support for the French during their phase of the war; the role of the merchant marine in providing the major logistical support (and suffering its own casualties in the process) for the millions of American military personnel who would serve in Vietnam; and its role in evacuating Vietnamese out of country in the end, and then aiding in the rescue of thousands of "boat people" in later years—that would still be left to others to do.

Because of the numbers of them—some 170 added to the Vietnam logistical pipeline following their breakout from Reserve Fleets along the West, East, and Gulf Coasts in the mid–1960s—the World War II–vintage "Victory ship," with its distinctive well deck profile and smoke stack, stands, for me, as the iconic ship of the Vietnam Run. More than 400 were constructed in American shipyards in the last two years of World War II, and because they were faster than the more numerous Liberty ships built during the war, they would prove to be better suited for postwar commercial use. Many, transferred to private shipping companies, would be seen along international trade routes for decades as others, still owned by the government that had ordered their construction, were placed in storage in National Defense Reserve Fleets (NDRF) to be "broken out" in times of national emergency, such as during the Korean War.

It was one of these ships—the *Baton Rouge Victory*—that would be sunk by a command-detonated floating mine in the river channel to Saigon, in 1967, with the greatest number of merchant seamen killed of any such incident during the war.

In addition to the Victory ships broken out of reserve for Vietnam, many others, some turned into ammunition carriers for the Navy's Military Sea Transportation Service (MSTS)—and as such still crewed by merchant seamen—and still others in commercial service and privately owned, would be pulled off commercial runs and entered into contract with the MSTS, thus making this type of ship the most common operating on the Vietnam Run until the last years of the war.

There were of course many other merchant ship types seen in Vietnam during the war, and increasing numbers of a particular new and revolutionary ship type— the containership (most were conversions of other break-bulk types in the early goings)—began to play an important role as they were added to the fleet in later years and Victory ships began to be removed from the Vietnam Run.

Having reached retirement age by 1970, and unable to compete with newer, faster ships built in postwar years, most of those Victory ships would make one final one-way voyage, not in return to reserve fleets but to ship breakers in Taiwan and elsewhere, as most of the reserve fleets—fondly known as "boneyards"—that had once held them in mothballs were themselves phased out of existence.

I saw many of those Victory ships, loading cargoes for war in stateside ports, making their way westward through the Panama Canal—headed for "The Nam"— and swinging at anchor out in the harbor of Da Nang, as our ship was, waiting or in process of offloading munitions into barges for conveyance ashore.

They too, and tankers carrying aviation gasoline also anchored out, would have had patrol boats circling them through the night, dropping concussion grenades into the water to discourage Viet Cong "swimmers" from getting too close and attaching "limpet" mines to the ships' hulls in attempts to destroy what they knew would eventually be used against them.

Those days are long past now— more than 50 years for me, as I write this—but the history of it, and the lessons learned, hopefully, and the fact that merchant seamen were not "just minding their own business" in Vietnam during the war, must still be taught and written. Those involved, and the ships that were involved along the Vietnam Run, should and must be remembered as part of that history.

This then is my contribution to that end.

The author as he appears on his merchant mariner's identification card, issued in Philadelphia in 1967 (Author photo).

PART ONE

The First Indochina (French) War

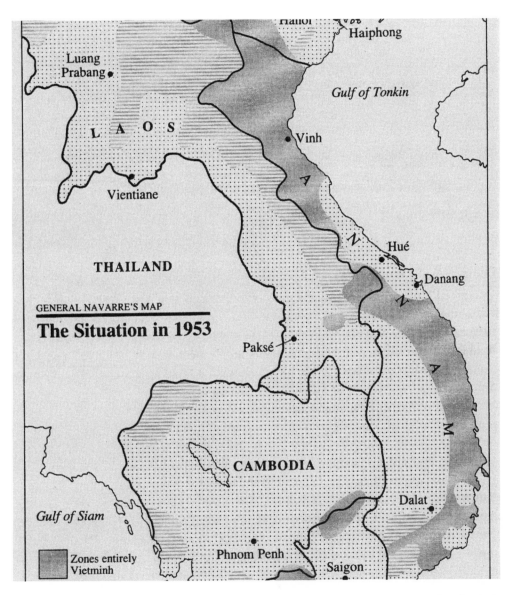

General Navarre's map of French Indochina showing major port areas providing logistical support, 1953.

1

For Want of a Ship

"So far, we have been unable to find any ships [for the French]."
—President Franklin D. Roosevelt,
Yalta Conference, 1945

"Indochina from one day to the next became accessible to us again."
—General Charles de Gaulle, *War Memoirs*

The French had their own name for what American merchant seamen would later call the Vietnam Run. With Vietnam having been seized in stages and incorporated into what would become known as French Indochina, *Indochine* would certainly have been part of a French seaman's own reference for what was in any case the steady flow of merchant ships from France to and from the geographical area of the world roughly between India and China.[1] For nearly a century, and even as French control of Vietnam was interrupted with the arrival of the Japanese early in World War II, merchant ships continued nonetheless to transport the goods of commerce, war, and empire, except that much of it now became destined, until August 1945, for support of the Japanese Empire.[2] By whatever name it was called, that pipeline of merchant ships was intended for and served a similar purpose: to provide continuous logistical support for a massive military, commercial, and—for France and Japan at least—colonial undertaking many thousands of ocean miles from the home countries.

From the time France first landed troops in Vietnam in 1858 in the central Vietnamese port city of Da Nang, which they would come to call *Tourane* for as long as they were in Vietnam (and which would later become an important deepwater port for American merchant ships involved in another war), France began a long campaign to establish and build upon its initial foothold in Southeast Asia, adding by increments areas that would become additional parts of its vast empire.[3] Great numbers of merchant ships sailing the many thousands of miles from France not only to this area but to and from other areas that supplied colonial troops—notably Senegal, Morocco, and Algeria—would be required for that endeavor.

While often protected by warships, especially when organized into convoy groups, the cargo and troopships crewed by these French civilian seamen were at the heart of its *Indochine* Run. Sailing on a regular basis in support of their operations in Indochina, ships transported the raw materials and other fruits of empire that would sustain, underwrite, and hopefully turn a profit from it.

And, of course, these ships transported the thousands of French nationals who

Churchill, Roosevelt and Stalin at the Yalta Conference in February 1945. It was there that FDR told Stalin of a French request for ships to transport troops back to Vietnam (U.S. Army).

settled with their families in and oversaw development and exploitation of their Indochina colonies and what would fondly be known as their "Balcony on the Pacific" from the Red River Delta in the north to the Mekong Delta in the south, the extremities of modern Vietnam.[4]

French missionaries and traders had first arrived in Vietnam in the early decades of the seventeenth century.[5] They, as well as other French nationals in commercial, military, or religious undertakings, began making concerted and impassioned pleas early on for greater support and involvement from the French government for an enterprise that would, they argued without sparing hyperbole, be extremely beneficial in time not only for their intended missions to Christianize and civilize—the so-called *mission civilisatrice*—but for the good of the treasury of the French empire in general.

As one French military commander argued in the late eighteenth century during a period of civil war in Vietnam, giving support to one particular side in that conflict would enable France "to become ... the real rulers of the country under the name of the legitimate ruler," thus gaining "exclusive control over one of the richest branches of commerce outside of India."[6]

It would not be until 1858, however, before the French, along with a Spanish force out of the Philippines, entered the splendid natural harbor of Da Nang with a fleet of ships to influence release of a Catholic priest, a Spaniard. The mission ultimately failed in its outward purpose, and the French garrison departed less than two years later. One French historian would write that as the "sole trace of their passage, the French and Spanish left in Tourane a graveyard with 1,000 graves."[7] That failed expedition was soon followed by another French force that went ashore further to the south, in Saigon, from which it established a more lasting foothold in Vietnam and from which it would eventually, and after decades of Vietnamese resistance, lead to full colonization and incorporation of Vietnam into the French empire as Tonkin, in the north, Annam in the center, and Cochin-China in the south.[8]

These ships, the means for the arrival of French missionaries, traders, sailors, and soldiers to Vietnam in the first place, would remain a huge and indispensable part of the equation as long as the French remained as masters of the area.

While temporarily supplanted by new masters—the Japanese—the French never gave up on Vietnam. As World War II entered its final phase, they began to plan for an eventual return to Vietnam and what had become, after an initial lengthy period of suppression of nationalist resistance, very much a paying proposition.[9] But this return would only be possible if the ships and supplies could be found to reassert control over the *Annamien*, their typical reference for the Vietnamese.[10]

The French fleet was, however, in a shambles, and they were in no position to accomplish this task without significant help from others. General Charles de Gaulle, leader of the Free French forces, understood this simple logistical reality: without ships, Vietnam and its resources would be out of reach, and waging war there, if it came to that, would be equally impossible.

So, de Gaulle turned to the United States, and President Franklin Delano Roosevelt. Roosevelt knew about ships. Though his was not the technical and intimate familiarity of a seaman, born over the course of a professional seagoing career, it was that of a master geopolitical strategist who understood the role of ships as instruments of foreign policy. As a former Assistant Secretary of the Navy, and now leader of a nation that had produced an unprecedented number of naval and merchant ships in the struggle to defeat fascist powers, FDR understood that ships—war ships as well as merchant ships—were as much a key to victory in war as they would be in the shaping of the peace to follow.

By the end of World War II, in fact, the United States would build some 5,600 new ocean-going merchant ships, including more than 2,700 of the slower but reliable Liberty ships, 700 tankers, and more than 400 of the faster Victory-type cargo ships that would play such a role in the postwar period, and in support of the 30-year-long war soon to begin in Vietnam.[11]

Roosevelt had strong feelings about the future of Vietnam, and whether or not the United States should assist the French to return there to pick up where they had left off before the arrival of the Japanese in the early 1940s.

"Indo-China should not go back to the French," Roosevelt had confided to his Secretary of State, Cordell Hull, "but should be administered by an international trusteeship. France has milked it for 100 years. The people of Indo-China are entitled to something better than that."[12]

And so, when de Gaulle approached him several months before the Japanese were finally defeated, and asked about the availability of ships for moving French troops to Vietnam, Roosevelt balked. Then, at the Yalta Conference in February 1945, FDR told Soviet leader Joseph Stalin about de Gaulle's request for ships. He was reported to have told Stalin: "So far, we have been unable to find any ships."[13]

While there might have been some shortage of troopships in certain theaters of the war, Roosevelt's reluctance to help the French was no doubt more a reflection of his dream for the postwar world and the status of colonial peoples than it was a true indication of the availability of transport ships.[14]

But Roosevelt's dream for the postwar world died with him in April 1945. His successor, Harry Truman, had none of FDR's knowledge of and therefore appreciation for the Vietnamese. And his priorities took on new form as visions and fears of "cold war" and of a perceived Soviet menace loomed close on the horizon even before the final salvos were fired in World War II.

The significance of Roosevelt's death in this regard was not lost on Lord Louis Mountbatten, Supreme Commander of the Southeast Asian Theater of operations, who told de Gaulle that France had "a good chance of getting satisfaction, for Roosevelt is no longer around."[15]

Within a week of the Japanese surrender in the field, in mid–August 1945, Charles de Gaulle once again approached the now new president of the United States in Washington, D.C., for ships to transport French troops back to Vietnam. Truman told de Gaulle that the United States would offer, as de Gaulle recalled in his war memoirs, "no opposition to the return of the French army and authority in Indo-China. Indo-China from one day to the next became accessible to us once again."[16]

Within a few weeks of de Gaulle's visit, word of the new American position regarding the French return to Vietnam had begun to take form in real terms. In one report through diplomatic channels, the American ambassador to France reported that France had "expressed deep appreciation for the shipping the United States had agreed to make available in the Pacific."[17]

De Gaulle had finally succeeded in securing what he knew would be a key to the future of France in Vietnam. And, within only a few weeks of his visit to Washington, D.C., U.S.-owned troopships, crewed by American merchant seamen, began departing from American ports for France—not to load returning American troops, as many believed would be the case—but to embark French troops for a return to Vietnam.[18]

Though it will long be debated, it can be argued that what would eventually become known as the Vietnam War began in a real sense with the arrival of those first American ships, carrying French troops, to Saigon in the closing months of 1945. And American merchant seamen would not only bear witness to these unfolding events, but would contribute significantly to them as well.[19]

2

Sailing into War (1945)

"[The Vietnamese] all spoke to us of their hatred of the French and their wonderment at the Americans [for] bringing the French invaders back."

—Henry Dooley, SS *Winchester Victory*

"As the French band assembled on [the ship's] no. 3 hatch, 2 Jap soldiers in full uniform stood at the bottom of the gangway with fixed bayonets. I was one of the first ashore, and they snapped to attention as we left the ship."

—David Boylan, SS *Stamford Victory*

The war was finally over.

As word spread of the Japanese surrender in the field that mid–August day in 1945, church bells rang throughout the country, and spontaneous demonstrations—outpourings in the streets—broke out as the realization of war's end, nearly four years after it had begun for the United States, started to sink in.[1]

David R. Boylan, a 21-year-old Merchant Marine officer who had recently arrived by train from Providence, Rhode Island, where he had been home on leave, was among those caught up in the wild celebration taking place in New York City's Times Square that day as news of the Japanese surrender spread throughout the city.[2]

Boylan had come to New York to ship out again, but on this particular day he and thousands of others found themselves passionately participating in what was a day of celebration and thanksgiving.

By then, Boylan had played his part in the war effort, working his way up "through the hawespipe" from ordinary seaman to second mate sailing in ships providing logistical support for troops in such places as New Caledonia, New Hebrides, and Guadalcanal in the Pacific, and later in the Atlantic. In a few weeks he would have his next ship, the *Stamford Victory*, and find himself involved as the ship's second mate in the gratifying task of carrying, not war materiel, but American troops for their return at long last to the United States.

The formal surrender of the Japanese to the Allied forces under the command of General Douglas MacArthur took place aboard the battleship *Missouri* in Tokyo Bay on September 2, 1945, while Boylan was still in New York waiting for his next ship. On that same day in Vietnam's northern capital city of Hanoi, hundreds of thousands of nationalists under the leadership of Ho Chi Minh gathered in *Place Puginier*— soon to be renamed Ba Dinh Square—and declared their independence from France in a massive gathering and emotional outpouring of their own. This historic event

French musicians assembled on the deck of SS *Stamford Victory* prior to their debarking in Saigon in November 1945 (courtesy David R. Boylan).

was attended by American representatives of the Office of Strategic Services (OSS) who had arrived from southern China within days of the Japanese surrender in the field a few weeks before.[3] Speaking into a microphone from a large wooden platform built for the occasion, Ho, borrowing from and inspired by the American Declaration of Independence, proclaimed: "All men are created equal. They are endowed by their creator with certain inalienable rights; among these are life, liberty, and the pursuit of happiness."

At one point in his speech Ho paused and asked the assembled crowd a simple but profound question: "My fellow countrymen, have you understood?"[4]

The reply, coming in unison from a crowd estimated by some to be a million people, was a resounding "Yes!"

Boylan finally signed voyage papers a few weeks after these events, joining SS *Stamford Victory* on September 19, 1945, about a week before the ship departed New York for Le Harve, France, to load returning units of the 48th Armored Infantry Battalion and the 707th Tank Battalion for the return to Boston.[5] The ship was under the command of Captain W.A. Hutchens, whom Boylan would later describe as a "seventy-seven year old rascal from Casco Bay, Maine" who had been "born on a sailing vessel and returned to sea at the age of nine."[6]

Arriving too late on October 7 to make the Sunday papers, smiling GIs were pictured in the Monday edition of the *Boston Herald* as having disembarked from *Stamford Victory* the day before.[7]

The next day, Boylan signed on *Stamford Victory* again for what would be his last voyage as a merchant seaman, and for what he and most other members of the crew had every reason to expect would be a voyage much like the last. The ship was, after all, bound again for France. But instead of a return to Le Harve to embark American troops, the ship was diverted to Marseilles, where French troops began embarking for Indochina. It was only then apparently that Boylan and his shipmates were told of the ship's actual destination. "I don't think we really learned what we were going to do," Boylan recalled, "until we got to Marseilles."[8]

Another seaman arriving on a troopship not long after Boylan and *Stamford Victory* recalled: "Everybody thought we were going to France and back; we knew it was just going to be a three-week trip. But they lied to us."[9]

Some 2,000 French troops, described as "seasoned veterans with career officers," boarded *Stamford Victory* before it proceeded, on or about October 23, first, to Algiers in North Africa, "to pick up giant kegs of wine," recalled Boylan, "and in Aden, Arabia to take on water. There were a few French nurses on board who kept the officers amused by tossing coins between their breasts."[10]

It was while *Stamford Victory* was underway to Suez from North Africa that President Truman made what is generally considered his first major foreign policy speech in New York, and which reflected an attitude in contrast to the apparent reality of an American troopship movement steaming to Indochina in support of the French return to one of its colonial domains. He said that his government would oppose recognition of "any government imposed upon any nation by the force of any foreign power" and emphasized his support for "all peoples who are prepared for self-government" to "choose their own form of government ... without interference from any foreign power."[11]

Truman's words did not apply, it was clear, to the Democratic Republic of Vietnam (DRV), which had declared its independence from France the previous month. And some observers soon discerned a distinct gap between the rhetoric of "no assistance" for the French in Indochina, and the reality.[12]

After transiting the Suez Canal, *Stamford Victory* rendezvoused with the French warship *Richelieu* in the Indian Ocean to secure medicine for a seriously ill soldier. "To my surprise," Boylan recalled, "it was penicillin from Terre Haute, Indiana."[13]

Merchant seaman aboard *Stamford Victory*, Saigon, November 1945 (courtesy David R. Boylan).

"Our next stop was Singapore," he recalled, "where we enjoyed a drink at the Raffles Hotel. The

When *Stamford Victory* arrived with French troops in Vietnam soon after the Japanese surrender in World War II, it appeared with its deck guns still in place, as in this wartime publicity photograph of an unidentified Victory ship.

British ambassador joined us as a passenger to begin his service in Saigon. We picked up the pilot as we entered the Saigon River. He and the Captain hit it off well at the beginning, but were soon calling each other a 'blue nose' and jickey S.O.B."[14]

Several weeks before Boylan's ship arrived at Cap St. Jacques (later renamed Vung Tau) at the mouth of the river approaches to Saigon, the British had arrived in Saigon to disarm and begin repatriation of the Japanese. The anchorage at Cap St. Jacques and the 40-mile deep-draft river channels to Saigon had been surveyed and swept for mines. The *Stamford Victory* traversed the length of the Long Tau Channel without incident to its voyage destination.[15]

Stamford Victory docked in Saigon in mid–November 1945, just under a month after leaving France, and was believed to be the first American ship to arrive there since the Japanese occupation. It carried the first contingent of French troops—approximately 2,000—brought in by this first of what would be as many as a dozen American Victory-type troopships arriving by the end of the year.[16]

Upon arriving in Saigon, the crew of *Stamford Victory* were among the first Americans to witness the peculiar sight of fully armed Japanese soldiers, only weeks after Japan's formal surrender at the end of World War II, being deployed by the British in Vietnam. Boylan described the spectacle years later:

> We docked in Saigon sometime in November. As we tied up at the dock I was surprised to see Japanese soldiers in 3 towers about 25 ft. high with mounted machine guns. As the French band assembled on the [ship's] no. 3 hatch, 2 Jap soldiers in full uniform stood at the bottom of the gangway with fixed bayonets. I was one of the first ashore, and they snapped to attention as we left the ship.[17]

The use of Japanese troops by the British in Vietnam underscores the extent to which, and how rapidly, the Allied powers yielded to expediency in the weeks and months following the end of World War II.[18] Implementation of policies in the early aftermath of World War II soon revealed both newly emerging Cold War attitudes as well as a return, as movements of French troops dramatically illustrated, to the *status quo ante bellum* in Indochina; France had no intention other than to pick up where it had left off there. And the British, charged with sorting things out in the southern half of Vietnam, seemed just as committed to paving the way for the French return there.[19] The policy of the United States was, in turn, to assist its allies while attempting to minimize the visibility of its own involvement in fostering the perpetuation of colonialism in the area.

On October 20, 1945—a few weeks before the arrival of *Stamford Victory* in Saigon with French troops—the Truman administration attempted to clarify its policy regarding East Asia and Indochina in particular. Speaking before the Foreign Policy Association in New York, the director of the State Department's Far Eastern Affairs Office, John Carter Vincent, reiterated what Charles de Gaulle had been told in Washington, D.C., in August. "With regard to the situation in Indochina," he said, "this government does not question French sovereignty in that area." Vincent was careful to add—though events would soon contradict his words—that it was also not the intention of the United States government to "assist or participate in forceful measures for the imposition of control by territorial sovereigns."[20]

Less than a week after Vincent's speech, President Truman, as noted above, publicly stated in general terms his government's opposition to the forceful imposition of rule "by any foreign power" upon other nations. At the moment Truman was speaking in New York about the self-determination of peoples, American troopships, crewed by American merchant seamen, were already underway to France to begin embarking French troops for Indochina. And by the end of December as many as 18,000 soldiers—perhaps a third or more of the total force of 50,000 French troops in Vietnam by the end of 1945—had arrived there in American civilian-crewed transports.[21]

That the United States was involved, as the troopship movement and subsequent events and actions revealed, was clear, if not generally known. It was, simply put, a matter of shifting geopolitical priorities on the part of the U.S. government: it was willing to help France in Indochina, and expected a *quid pro quo*—cooperation in Europe to counter Soviet influence—in return.[22]

The use of Japanese troops to maintain order, and put down early manifestations of anti-colonial revolt—often reported as acts of "terrorism" in the mainstream American press—as the British did in Vietnam and elsewhere, went against the grain of many who regarded it as a sell-out of stated American and Allied principles for which World War II had ostensibly been fought. "If there is anything that makes my blood boil," even General Douglas MacArthur was moved to observe, "it is to see our allies in Indochina and Java deploying Japanese troops to reconquer these little people we promised to liberate. It is the most ignoble kind of betrayal."[23]

American military personnel on the ground in Hanoi and Saigon were equally critical not only of the use of Japanese troops in Vietnam at this time, but of providing support for the return of French military forces to the area. Major Patti of the OSS had written to General Albert Wedemeyer, his superior in Kunming, China, that "this former French colony no longer looks to France for tutelage and protection and will in all probability resist with all means available the return of the *status quo ante*."[24]

Following the *Stamford Victory* to Vietnam in the closing months of 1945 were the American troopships *Pachaug Victory, Taos Victory, Winchester Victory,* and *Amherst Victory,* with as many as seven additional American troopships participating in the operation. The merchant mariners who crewed these ships were among the first Americans to see the transition of power taking place in Vietnam in the weeks and months following World War II, and they were witness not only to the use of Japanese troops by the British but to reactions of the Vietnamese themselves to the "ignoble betrayal" in which even the Americans seemed to be participating. As one seaman who had been there later observed, the Vietnamese "all spoke to us of their hatred of the French and their wonderment at the Americans [for] bringing the French invaders back."[25]

American merchant seamen bore witness to what they saw in Vietnam in the closing months of 1945, and many of them neither liked what they saw, nor quietly accepted their unexpected roles in the French troop lift. While there is no indication that crewmembers of *Stamford Victory* said anything publicly about it at the time, such was not the case with at least five of the vessels that converged on Saigon in late November, and following the *Stamford Victory*'s departure.

Pachaug Victory and *Taos Victory* had sailed from the United States within a week of the *Stamford Victory,* and were reported leaving Marseilles on October 31. Each carried more than 1,000 French troops. Two days after departing Marseilles the crew of *Pachaug Victory* decided something had to be done to protest the very operation in which they were engaged. On November 2 while still underway to Suez, a memorandum was drawn up for posting to the National Maritime Union, in which most of the ship's unlicensed personnel (non-officers) were members. A copy was also prepared and later sent, presumably from Suez, to the War Shipping Administration (WSA) in Washington, DC. It read, in part:

> At this time, while servicemen are waiting in foreign countries to be transported to the United States for a discharge ... we the 88 members of the troopship S.S. *Pachaug Victory* protest the use of American ships to transport foreign Troops and war equipment [guns and ammunition].[26]

Seamen aboard another ship, *Winchester Victory,* also found a means to protest the operation while still underway to Vietnam. At a meeting held aboard ship on November 21 a report was presented by an elected committee regarding action already taken to protest the troopship movement. It reported that cablegrams had been sent to both President Truman and Senator Robert Wagner of New York, which read:

> We, the unlicensed personnel of the SS *Winchester Victory,* vigorously protest the use of this and other American vessels for carrying foreign combat troops to foreign soil for the purpose of engaging in hostilities to further the imperialist policies of foreign governments when there are American soldiers waiting to come home. Request immediate congressional investigation of this matter.[27]

The ship's committee also reported that an airmail registered letter had been sent to Admiral Emory Land of the War Shipping Administration in Washington, D.C.

Some days later, presumably in the last week of November 1945, committees from four American troopships—*Winchester Victory, Taos Victory, Georgetown*

Victory, and *Kings Point Victory*—gathered in Saigon to draw up a joint resolution protesting the operation. According to minutes kept by the recording secretary of *Winchester Victory*, the resolution "condemned the policy of the U.S. Government in chartering ships, flying the American flag" to transport troops "in order to subjugate the native population" of Vietnam.[28] Later, on December 1, 1945, the ship's committee from *Winchester Victory* composed a letter in Singapore that it addressed "to various senators and congressman [*sic*]." It stated:

> At this writing, our ship, along with other American-owned and manned ships, are laying at anchor in Singapore, preparatory to being assigned to a similar mission by the British government; in this instance, the carrying of more foreign combat troops to Batavia, Netherlands East Indies, where the British are supporting the Dutch government in their imperialist policy of ruthlessly suppressing the native populations of these countries.[29]

The letter ended with an observation as to the impact of the troopship movement on the reputation of the United States in Southeast Asia, a common theme among those concerned with the direction of U.S. policy towards the area following World War II. "The native populations," the letter noted, "are under the impression that our government is sponsoring these punitive campaigns; the faith and prestige that the U.S. has enjoyed in this part of the world during the Japanese occupation has suffered tremendous and irreparable loss."[30]

At least one additional troopship has been positively identified as having participated in the Vietnam troopship operation at this time, the *Amherst Victory*. Spotted in Marseilles on November 11, 1945, some two weeks after *Stamford Victory*, the *Amherst Victory* probably arrived in Saigon during the first week of December, after the meeting there of other ships committees. While there is no indication that her crew also protested the operation, her presence in Marseilles, where she reportedly loaded 1,900 French troops, prompted at least one American soldier who observed the ship to register his own protest. "We have read many explanations for the lack of shipping," the GI wrote to *Stars and Stripes*, "but today we saw an incident [sailing of *Amherst Victory* with French troops] that demands some explanation. This is the first trip for this ship since being converted for troop transport. It is still under our control. How many more ships are being deployed from deployment?"[31]

Word of the American troopship movement to Southeast Asia began filtering back to the United States in November, perhaps as a result of the letter writing campaign initiated by the seamen involved in the operation. Though there were no indications that the story was picked up by the mainstream press, one liberal-left newspaper in New York, *PM Daily*, ran a brief article in its November 12, 1945, issue, before most of the ships had even reached Saigon. With a Marseilles dateline, *PM* noted that "American troop transports are ferrying French colonial troops to French Indo-China" while "GI veterans … are impatiently awaiting transportation back to the States."[32]

Additional if limited coverage of the troopship movement also appeared in the *NMU Pilot*, the monthly publication of the National Maritime Union. One article in the *Pilot* was accompanied by a cartoon showing a merchant ship bearing the words "American shipping" on its side, and flying a skull and crossbones flag with the word "imperialism" emblazoned upon it. And *The Militant*, a publication of the Socialist Workers Party, gave credit to *PM* for bringing word of the troopship movement to its attention, observing that "the reality of the Atlantic Charter" was "visible in the blood-soaked soil of the colonial lands."[33]

The small number of Americans on the ground in Indochina in the closing months of 1945 began to be recalled, and Major Patti of the OSS, who had warned against providing assistance for the French return there, departed on September 30.[34] While he was not aware until after the fact, therefore, of the American troopship movement, at least one other American, Arthur Hale, a State Department representative presumably assigned to observe and subsequently report on the situation, received word of the troopship movement, though from the vantage point of Hanoi where he was from October 15 to 28. "Incidents such as the recent shipment of French troops in American vessels," he noted in his lengthy report, "must have impaired considerably the great prestige in the eyes of the Annamites we enjoyed at the cessation of hostilities with Japan."[35]

Hale's report concluded by saying that the United States was "in danger of losing completely the immense good will towards America which has already been assailed by our own equivocal conduct in regard to Indochina."[36]

Perhaps in partial response to all those who did express themselves in telegrams, letters, editorials, articles, books, floor debate, and speeches before various citizens groups and elsewhere, the American troopship movement to Vietnam came to an end as 1945 came to a close. On January 15, in fact, the Department of State informed the Secretary of War that it was against United States policy to "employ American flag vessels or aircraft to transport troops of any nationality to or from the Netherlands East Indies or French Indochina, nor to permit the use of such craft to carry arms, ammunition or military equipment to these areas."[37]

It was a little like closing the proverbial barn door after letting the horse out. The deed was done, the troops had been moved, and France had been helped significantly by the United States to regain a footing in its one-time "balcony on the Pacific" in Vietnam. And as those concerned about U.S. foreign policy relating to Vietnam suspected, and in some cases proved in the next and subsequent years, American policy makers would find other ways to help France, quietly, before once again, and soon enough, sending merchant ships fully loaded with military materiel, and crewed by American merchant seamen, to Vietnam.

Once the United States sailed into war in Vietnam in late 1945, it remained there to one degree or another, to the bitter end, nearly 30 years later. American merchant seamen would not only witness and participate significantly in those early events, but also be among the first to protest the very policies and actions of the United States that had sent them to Vietnam in the first place.[38]

3

A Curious "Neutrality" (1946–1949)

"Whether the French like it or not, independence is coming to Indochina. Why, therefore, do we tie ourselves to the tail of their battered kite?"

—Raymond D. Fosdick, November 1949

"We are organizing the machinery through which we can make effective help [to Southeast Asia] possible."

—Secretary of State Dean Acheson, January 1950

It was like closing the proverbial barn door after letting the horse out. But in this case, despite public protestations and declarations, and even internal policy directives to the contrary, the door through which logistical support for the French in Vietnam moved in the late 1940s and early 1950s only continued to open—slowly and quietly at first, and then more openly for all to see—until the final French defeat at the hands of the Viet Minh in 1954.

That meant, of course, that merchant ships, one way or another, would have to be made available and actively deployed in support of French fortunes in Vietnam and wider Indochina.

Despite public statements the previous October that "it was not the policy of the United States to assist the French to reestablish their control over Indochina"— even as ships moved from the United States to load and then transport French soldiers to Vietnam—the dawning of 1946 in the area revealed a reality that belied such claims. By then some 50,000 French troops had been transported back to Vietnam, as many as a third of them moved in American troopships crewed by American merchant seamen.[1]

As noted previously, Secretary of War Robert Porter Patterson would be informed by the Department of State at this time that it was the policy of the United States to remain neutral, which precluded the use of American ships for transporting either foreign troops or military supplies to French Indochina or the Dutch East Indies.[2] The directive not to employ American flag vessels on behalf of the French, though not widely known, might well have been influenced by public backlash— including that of seamen inadvertently involved in the actual troopship movement itself—against what was perceived precisely as "re-imposition of control" by a colonial power in the immediate aftermath of a world war in which many of those who fought—and sailed ships—against fascism were guided by principles enunciated in

President Harry S. Truman, left, was less sympathetic towards Ho Chi Minh, right, and the Vietnamese nationalist cause, than was his predecessor, Franklin D. Roosevelt. The emerging Cold War had everything to do with that (Library of Congress).

such things as the Atlantic Charter, principles which at the same time had inspired and given hope to those long denied self-determination by their colonial overlords.[3]

Emerging postwar geopolitical realities—namely, the so-called Cold War between the United States and the Soviet Union, along with their respective allies—were quickly overshadowing "promises" of support for colonial peoples made during World War II. Efforts continued to be made, however, to at least pay lip service to such pledges while providing real material and economic support to those very colonial powers. As one historian would note some years later in a published study about American aid to Southeast Asia in the late 1940s, "in Indochina the United States had vacillated, making noises of sympathy for 'self-determination' but putting its dollars behind the French."[4]

While State and Defense Department directives appeared to clearly preclude for the time being further flagrant use of troop and cargo ships crewed by American seamen in logistical support of the French in Vietnam—enabling them to pick up in effect where they had left off prior to World War II—other means were quickly found and used from the get-go to circumvent the spirit if not the letter of existing directives and those guiding principles of the Second World War that had finally and successfully been brought to an end not long before.

Fighting had for all intents and purposes broken out between the French and Ho Chi Minh's nationalist forces—the Viet Minh—within a few weeks of the September 2, 1945, declaration of independence from French rule in Hanoi's Ba Dinh Square. Some 1,200 French soldiers had been released from prisons in the south soon after, and others would arrive by troopship from France in the last three months of the year.[5] They were crucial for French plans to secure a foothold in Vietnam—their "balcony on the Pacific"—once again, and to forestall efforts by the Viet Minh to secure and expand their own stake in Vietnam's future.

In addition to the deployment of the aforementioned American troopships, a significant amount of surplus American-made military equipment, including some 800 tanks, trucks, and other types of rolling stock that had originally been part of "lend-lease" shipments to the British in the China-Burma-India (CBI) theater of operations prior to entry of the United States in the war, was transferred to the French for use in Indochina.[6] This was in addition to a large quantity of military equipment turned over to them late in World War II for use in the anticipated invasion of the Japanese home islands.

However, with the war ended sooner than expected following the atomic-bombing of Hiroshima and Nagasaki, the French were, as historian George McTurnan Kahin has put it, "permitted to keep [the] equipment without payment [and were later] free to use these arms as they saw fit."[7]

The British had assumed responsibility for disarming and repatriating Japanese soldiers in the southern portion of Vietnam immediately following V-J Day, and it was to them that the request was made by Secretary of State James Byrnes in October of 1945 for the transfer of military equipment to the French for their own purposes in Indochina. The formal transfer of that rolling stock did not actually take place until early in 1946, following the declaration by the State Department that it was not the policy of the United States to "carry arms, ammunition, or military equipment" to Southeast Asia in support of France and other colonial powers seeking to pick up where they had left off in that area prior to World War II.[8]

The Look of "Neutrality"

It would be argued by U.S. policy makers—who might well have been feeling the heat from American critics—that the use of troopships and conveyance of military equipment was simply a practical expedient, and part of mutual assistance agreements hammered out among Allied nations in the closing months of World War II for dealing with the immediate postwar period. Nonetheless, it provided for "bad optics," so an order came down for the removal of American markings from military equipment—a request "the French frequently neglected to observe," according to one account—and public declarations of "neutrality" continued to be made regarding support for the French in Vietnam and throughout greater French Indochina during this period.

Other means were also found by the United States, however, while still keeping as low a "hands off" profile as possible, to significantly assist France in conducting its own logistical support operations for reoccupation, control, and the exploitative activities of empire that would hopefully make their return to the area once again worthwhile.

The Merchant Ship Sales Act

Under provisions of the Merchant Ship Sales Act of 1946, for example, some 75 merchant ships built by the United States during World War II—including 30 that were described as capable of carrying large numbers of troops—were sold to France. And to help expedite the sale, the U.S. government also deposited a credit of $17 million with the U.S. Maritime Commission expressly for that purpose.[9] In those days that sum could buy a small fleet of merchant ships, and that's exactly what France needed in order to rebuild its own fleet following World War II. How and where those ships would be used certainly did not have to be spelled out in sales agreements, but it would not have taken much thought to conclude that many of them would be used in direct logistical support operations—military and otherwise—in Indochina.

Clearly, as some American operatives on the ground in Vietnam—and many others—would note during this period, "existing directives [regarding Vietnam] were being bent."[10]

The willingness to bend policy directives on behalf of the French while at least maintaining an appearance of neutrality was in keeping with emergent Cold War attitudes and agendas of the times. Despite the difficulty of dealing with Charles de Gaulle, leader of Free French forces during World War II, France was nonetheless regarded potentially as a key player in the overall plan to counter Soviet power and influence in Europe.[11] As a 1948 State Department official put it, the United States considered support of France "vital" to its interests and aims in Europe, and more important than "the realization of our objectives in Indo-china."[12] De Gaulle, well aware of American concerns that France might "drift" closer to the Soviet Union, had already shown he was not above playing upon American priorities, and anti–Communist fears, to further his own objectives in Europe as well as Southeast Asia.[13]

Publicly, however, the Truman administration, while maintaining its "hands off" position in the emerging Franco-Vietnamese conflict, also expressed hope that France would eventually allow the Vietnamese a greater degree of autonomy, if still within the French Union. These expressions of hope, however, were usually stated in such a way as to minimize alienation of the French. Privately, the Truman administration not only bent directives regarding such things as the disposition of surplus military equipment, but also encouraged some field operatives to assist the French in other ways, as in negotiations with the Chinese, who had been given the responsibility for disarming and repatriating Japanese from northern Vietnam, to pave the way for their military reoccupation of Vietnam's northern sector.[14]

As their attitude regarding the French revealed, American policy makers were increasingly concerned about Soviet influence not only in Europe but in Asia as well. And to an increasingly large extent, therefore, Indochina policy in 1946 and subsequent years was determined and justified by this propensity to understand the world in terms of a Soviet and a communist threat.[15] It was certainly the basis for writing off Ho Chi Minh, despite his popularity and reputation as a nationalist that long pre-dated emerging postwar geopolitical realities, as a "tool" of the Soviet Union.[16]

If American policy makers failed to respond positively enough to the spirit of nationalism sweeping across Southeast Asia following World War II, as many critics charged, the developing tactics of countering Soviet power, coupled with an often blinding anti-communist ideology, explains the lack of response and failure to take advantage of the opportunity presented by Vietnam in the late 1940s.[17]

The missed opportunity, as many have regarded it, was personified by Ho Chi Minh himself. He had appealed to the United States for at least moral support on a number of occasions, including at least twice to President Truman between late 1945 and late 1946. Other appeals were made indirectly through officials and operatives connected with the Southeast Asia Division or "desk" of the Department of State. At a meeting in Hanoi in early 1946 its director, Abbot Low Moffat, had a face-to-face with Ho Chi Minh in Vietnam during which Ho made a surprising offer involving the large deepwater harbor at Cam Ranh Bay that would become so well known to American merchant seamen in later years.[18]

Cam Ranh Bay: A Plum for the Picking?

Located some 200 miles north of Cap St. Jacques (Vung Tau) along the southern coast of Vietnam, Cam Ranh Bay is one of the finest deepwater natural harbors in East Asia, providing protection from the elements that blow in from the South China Sea while offering ample anchorage space in both an inner and outer harbor for deep-draft ocean-going ships that would come to call. Configured with those anchorage areas, it stretches some 20 miles from north to south, and up to 10 miles at its widest point.

Cam Ranh Bay had sheltered Russia's Black Sea Fleet in 1905 before it continued northward for its ill-fated encounter with Japan's modern, well-trained and skillfully handled naval force in the Straits of Tsushima. It would in turn be used by the Japanese decades later during World War II to assemble and launch its own naval operations in Southeast Asia, including in support of an invasion of Malaysia in 1942. Its merchant ships, including many tankers so crucial for the maintenance of its empire and home islands, would put in there throughout the war. And many of those ships would increasingly face destruction there and in adjacent waters as American and Allied aircraft gained control of the skies overhead and sought them out.[19]

The subject of Cam Ranh Bay entered a conversation between Ho Chi Minh and Abbot Low Moffat during Moffat's visit to Hanoi in December 1946. He reported back to Washington soon afterwards that "Vietnam [has] no navy and [has] no intention of being warlike, but would be glad to cooperate with the U.S. in developing Cam Ranh Bay as a naval base" and that it was "a very important location between Singapore and Hong Kong and opposite the P[hilippine] I[slands]."[20]

Moffat went on to report that he had replied to Ho that he knew "nothing of the military plans" of the U.S. government, but doubted if the United States would "be interested in such a base." Moffat concluded his remarks to his superior in the State Department regarding this offer from Ho as follows: "Cam Ranh Bay, as you know, is in South Annam and is presently controlled by the French."[21]

Moffat also described a separate conversation held afterwards with Hoang Minh Giam, the Deputy Foreign Minister of the DRV, in which, seemingly as a further enticement to the Truman administration, he brought up the subject of trade relations and possible future visits to Vietnam's major northern port of Haiphong by American merchant ships. "Then he [Giam] started to explain," wrote Moffat, "how Vietnam wanted free ports, and the right to trade freely; to get foreign capital where they would; they wanted American capital, commerce; they hoped an American airline would use Hanoi; an American ship line [would] use Haiphong regularly."[22]

Not surprisingly, nothing was to come of the apparent offers by Ho Chi Minh for the use of Cam Ranh Bay as a naval base, nor Giam's follow-up regarding the use of Hanoi for commercial aircraft landings and Haiphong for merchant ships. Once again, though Moffat and others understood what Ho Chi Minh represented for the Vietnamese, and still regarded him as worth listening to and continuing dialogue with, this offer of the Cam Ranh Bay "plum" might well have been the last time he would make such an offer.[23]

Realistically, the Cam Ranh Bay "plum" had little chance to ripen for the harvesting despite Ho's apparent offer, even considering the terms of the Franco-Vietnamese Agreement in 1946, which, while resulting in a reduction if not a full stop in hostilities, called for the phased withdrawal of French forces from Vietnam within a five-year period.[24]

Moffat was among those who were quite convinced that Ho Chi Minh "was a nationalist first, and then a communist" and should not be summarily written off for the ideology he had come to embrace for his anti-colonialist movement. But Moffat and the Southeast Asia desk of the State Department he presided over since its creation during World War II were overshadowed by the more well-established and influential European desk, to which President Truman, it became clear, was more inclined to turn for advice in the charged atmosphere of an emerging Cold War.[25]

Ho Chi Minh was never given the courtesy of a reply from Washington. For various reasons, not the least of which was the threat he and the Viet Minh posed to the *status quo* in Vietnam and the French presence there, and the underlying American priorities in Southeast Asia. Ho—despite his popularity and reputation as a staunch nationalist—was simply not their man. By the summer of 1946, Archimedes Patti, who had been with the OSS in Vietnam in the closing months of 1945, would later note, "the word had reached Washington, and all official references to Ho were prefixed 'communist.'"[26]

Despite his continued efforts to communicate with the Truman administration, Ho Chi Minh came to the disappointing but realistic conclusion by 1946 that the United States would offer no help to the Viet Minh in their struggle against the French. "We apparently stand quite alone," he remarked, "[and] shall have to depend on ourselves."[27] This realization, coupled with the overriding concern of continued occupation in the north by some 150,000 Chinese troops, as well as other considerations, caused Ho to agree, in March, to the temporary reintroduction of French troops in that area. The March 6 accord placed a time limit on this French military presence and was designed, among other things, to ensure the withdrawal of the Chinese, a goal both the Vietnamese and French were anxious to accomplish. Ho was called to task by other Vietnamese nationalists for opening the door once again to French troops in the north but felt he had no choice in the matter, preferring, as he put it, "to sniff French shit for five years than eat Chinese shit for the rest of my life."[28]

The March 6 accord also provided for a plebiscite that would determine the future of Cochin-China, the French name for Vietnam's rice-rich southernmost area that included Saigon and the bulk of profitable rubber plantations.[29] It would be another three years before the matter of Cochin-China would be resolved, resulting in the discontinuance of the name and the area's incorporation into a newly-configured "State of Vietnam."

Further attempts to negotiate details of a peaceful settlement to the Franco-Vietnamese dispute were made in 1946, the last being the Fontainebleau

Conference, which resulted in a *modus vivendi* that lasted for only 70 days.[30] As has been generally agreed to, France never intended to grant full independence to the Vietnamese; rather, French negotiators entered into agreements with the Viet Minh to secure whatever advantage could be gained, never living up to what, on paper at least, appeared to be significant concessions to the Vietnamese.[31]

Any progress that might have been made in 1946 towards a peaceful solution of the conflict quickly evaporated in late November in the vicinity of the northern port of Haiphong. After some skirmishing between the French navy and Viet Minh troops over the question of customs control, French High Commissioner for Indochina Georges d'Argenlieu sent word from Paris to his deputy in Saigon to "teach those insolent Annamites a lesson."[32] The lesson was administered in the form of a naval bombardment by the French cruiser *Suffern* in Haiphong, resulting—by French estimate—in some 25,000 casualties, including 6,000 killed.[33] Ho Chi Minh and his government fled Hanoi the following month, after an attack by Vietnamese militia on the city's power station. The war, which for all intents and purposes had begun in the south in September 1945, was very much on again.

While France, China, and the Viet Minh had jockeyed for position and haggled over terms regarding Vietnam in 1946, the United States, having ended its troop-ship movement and declared its non-involvement, adopted a lower profile in the conflict. This reduced visibility, a misleading indicator of actual American support for the French, created an illusion of American neutrality in the conflict, one that was to endure for some four years until it finally came "out of the closet" for all to see. Indochina policy was overshadowed by American involvement in the developing Chinese civil war, which had resumed with a will in the wake of World War II. But as the Nationalist Chinese position deteriorated, Indochina—and United States policy toward the region—took on new importance.[34]

By 1947 the table for continued support of the French in Indochina—if largely still in the closet—was increasingly being set as the anti-communist language and attitudes of the Cold War gained the day both in public discourse as well as in back-channel government communications and classified policy directives that defined the tone and set the course for the U.S. role in the early phase of what would become the nearly 30-year-long Vietnam War.[35]

Abbot Low Moffat himself, reflective of the trend, was gone from the Southeast Asia desk by early 1947, shipped off to a series of diplomatic posts far removed from an area he had come to know and understand well, and where he might have continued to make valuable input on policy. In such places as Greece, Great Britain, Burma, and Ghana, he would have little if any of the influence he might have had on U.S. Indochina policy during his few years with the Southeast Asia desk.[36]

While it was not official policy in these years to openly support the French campaign against the nationalist Viet Minh forces, ways continued to be found to do so, quietly, as has been noted. And when legislation was passed in Congress in 1947 to fund a program that would assist countries in Western Europe to rebuild in the wake of World War II—it was formally designated the European Recovery Act, known more commonly as the Marshall Plan after the Secretary of State who had championed it—funds from that also found their way for use by the French in Indochina.[37]

While those concerned about the developing drift of Indochina and specifically Vietnam policy in the years immediately following World War II could only suspect its true nature at times due to U.S. government efforts to describe and obfuscate otherwise, the truth about what was actually taking place would periodically surface. Such had happened in the closing months of 1945, as noted with the arrival of American ships loaded to the gills with French troops. Harold R. Isaacs, one of the few American reporters in-country to actually witness the arrival of those ships in 1945, would continue to monitor and write about U.S. Indochina policy in subsequent years. In his 1947 book *No Peace for Asia*, for example, he would note the hypocrisy of American policy toward Vietnam, and the reaction of Vietnamese towards it, when he drew attention to "the stunning announcement of an American deal with France for the purchase of $160 million worth of vehicles and miscellaneous industrial equipment for the French in Indo-China. The Americans were democrats in words but no help [to the Vietnamese nationalist cause] in fact."[38]

And, to cite another example, the misallocation of Marshall Plan funds for use by France in Vietnam was also suspected by critics of U.S. Vietnam policy at that time, and came to public attention as fact by late 1948. It was noted in *Far East Spotlight*, a publication of the Committee for a Democratic Far Eastern Policy, that the French had been "permitted to divert $35,000,000 from their Marshall Plan allotment for the same purpose [as the Dutch in Indonesia] in Indochina."[39]

American merchant ships of various types and under various contractual arrangements, both subsidized and non-subsidized berth liners as well as tramp ships, would call regularly on Vietnam throughout the late 1940s. Military cargoes destined for the French were loaded with as little attention and fanfare as possible— certainly not visible on deck—and consisting of "partial" rather than full cargo loads of various sizes. But the size of these loads, and the numbers of ships carrying them, increased as the commitment of American support for the French increased during these years.

Merchant seamen got a good look at the two principal ports of call in Vietnam in those years—Saigon in the south and Haiphong in the north—as well as the complexion of French military forces engaged in the growing war against the Viet Minh. Sometimes encountered ashore or while transiting the 40-mile-long deep-draft river channel from its mouth at Cap St. Jacques (later reverting to the Vietnamese name, Vung Tau), these troops were at various times either French, French colonial—such as Senegalese, Moroccan, or Algerian—and those of the French Foreign Legion who often spoke with German accents and had prior service not long before with the German SS and *Wehrmacht*.

Fred Killingback, bosun in the SS *African Dawn* during a typical voyage to Vietnam in 1948—when cargoes destined for the French would not have been displayed on deck to call undue attention to them—recalled years later some encounters with some such French military personnel[40]:

> We went up the river [to Haiphong] and docked [and] were only there for a few days, and then two days in Saigon. We did not have much cargo for either port. One night we were in a gin mill having a few—there were about five of us—and it seemed that all the rest of the patrons that were in this bar were French Foreign Legion. And, oddly enough, about 90 percent of 'em were German. And although they were very friendly towards us, and several of 'em emplored [sic] us to join the French Foreign Legion, which we took a dim view of ... but at any rate we later found out that most of 'em were war criminals; they had fought in the German army—most of them were in the SS—and after the war in Europe, they had

gotten into North Africa because they were wanted by Allied military officials ... and these guys were right off the wall....

And then down in Saigon I ran into a few French officers. It was along one of the main drags, and I was having a drink at an outdoor café and they were at the next table and they asked me to join them—several of them could speak English—and I did. They seemed like nice guys. We didn't get into any politics, and I was with 'em maybe an hour and then I drifted on.

I do remember the French coming aboard and telling us very explicitly that if we went ashore at night time to be extremely careful where we went because the Vietminh—which they were called in those days—all they knew was that you were Caucasian.[41]

The extent to which American merchant ships like *African Dawn* would be calling on Haiphong and Saigon in the late 1940s and beyond would clearly not be determined by the United States entering into trade relations with Ho's DRV, but by Cold War imperatives and policy decisions that had favored—and would continue to favor—French fortunes in Vietnam, and in cooperation with emergent pro–French elements identified as non-communist and "nationalist" though limited to autonomous rule with the French Union. Year by year, as such policy continued to be made public, articulated in classified interdepartmental memoranda, or introduced as legislation to be debated and voted upon, it moved the country inexorably towards deeper and deeper involvement in the Vietnam conflict.

The movement toward greater involvement in what the French citizens would begin to call "la sale guerre"—or "dirty war"—and Americans would come to know soon enough as a "quicksand war" in Vietnam, was by no means without its critics, however, as was seen in the immediate aftermath of World War II, and at every step along the way in the years and decades to come.

Two key developments surfaced in 1949—one a legislative matter having to do with appropriations specifically designed to underwrite military support for the French in Indochina, and another having to do with the installation of a non-communist alternative to Ho Chi Minh in Vietnam, the former Emperor Bao Dai. Coming at a pivotal stage in the Cold War—and hot war in Vietnam—they would be hotly debated within the halls of Congress, in the mainstream American press, and, increasingly, in the homes and along the Main Streets of urban and rural America.

The Mutual Defense Assistance Act (MDAA) of 1949

The introductory wording of the Mutual Defense Assistance Act of 1949, signed into law by President Truman on October 6, 1949, reaffirmed the policy of the United States "to achieve international peace and security through the United Nations so that armed force shall not be used except in the common interest."[42]

Clearly, an area of "common interest" identified long before in the Cold War context of the day was Vietnam, and funds needed to be made available in response to urgent French appeals to support its war against the Viet Minh, which, by 1949, was depleting stocks of war materiel and producing casualties running into the tens of thousands.[43]

Passage of the MDAA of 1949 had not come without a fight, as indicated by a final vote count of 238–122 on September 28 in the U.S. House of Representatives.[44] There were many reasons why the legislation had been opposed—in both the House and Senate—and that was reflected in part in an opinion piece written by the journalist Walter Lippmann while debate was still ongoing in Congress. He was concerned, as were many others, that the pending legislation would support "a general license to intervene and to commit the United States all over the globe, as, when, and how the President and his appointees decide secretly that they deem it desirable to intervene."[45]

Intervention in the Vietnam War, dating back to late 1945, had already been taking various forms, and it would continue to increase throughout the "French War" by whatever name that war would come to be known. Funds appropriated under provisions of the MDAA began to be applied in 1950, and most of what it bought—more than 530,000 tons of war materiel in the initial three-year period, by one account—would find its way into the ports of Saigon and Haiphong in the cargo holds and on the decks of ships crewed by American merchant seamen.

The Bao Dai "Solution"

While efforts continued to be made by American policy makers to portray and dismiss Ho Chi Minh as little more than a tool of the Soviet Union, saying his broad popular support was the product of his manipulative ways, internal, classified policy statements were still painting a different picture of him in order to guide future policy making and counter his actual strength and appeal. A State Department "Policy Statement on Indochina" issued on September 27, 1948, for example, pointed out: "We are all too aware of the unpleasant fact that Communist Ho Chi Minh is the strongest and perhaps the ablest figure in Indochina and that any suggested solution which excludes him is an expedient of uncertain outcome."[46]

If Ho "was not their man" as former OSS agent Archimedes Patti said was the case by mid–1946, and others believed before then, then who was? In his seminal history of American involvement in the Vietnam War, historian George McTurnan Kahin explains: "In their search for a Vietnamese collaborator, the French finally fell back on the same expedient resorted to by the Japanese some two years before. They turned to the ex-emperor Bao Dai, conveniently forgetting that he had abdicated [on August 25, 1945], publicly rallied to the Viet Minh, and then, at Ho's invitation, served on the DRV's advisory council for some seven months."[47]

Having developed a reputation as the "nightclub emperor" during his self-imposed if comfortable exile in France (he spent much of his time on the French Riviera), Bao Dai did return to Vietnam as the French wished. He would serve in the new State of Vietnam according to the Élysée Agreement, agreed to in Paris on March 8, 1949, for what would become known as the "Bao Dai Solution" for providing an alternative to Ho Chi Minh.[48]

Soon enough, classified policy statements would be stressing the need for support of Bao Dai, and to do whatever could be done, in the face of a dawning and concerning reality, for building his base of support. "Particular attention should be given," one memorandum of the National Security Council urged in December 1949, "to bring home to the French the urgency of removing barriers to the obtaining by Bao Dai ... of the support of a substantial proportion of the Vietnamese."[49]

But even within the U.S. State Department, as the cautionary presence of Abbot Low Moffat and others suggested, not all subscribed to the formula of rejecting Ho Chi Minh outright in favor of the less popular former emperor of Vietnam. "My belief," State Department consultant for Far Eastern policy Raymond B. Fosdick would submit in a memorandum in early November 1949, "is that Bao Dai is doomed. The compromises which the French are so reluctantly making cannot possibly save it. The Indochinese are pressing toward complete nationalism and nothing is going to stop them. They see all too clearly that France is offering them a kind of semi-colonialism." Fosdick, who had come to the State Department after years as head of the Rockefeller Foundation, argued that the support of the United States for this qualified and incomplete independence would "cost us our standing and prestige in all of Southeast Asia." He concluded: "The rest [of what prestige might still remain for the U.S. in this area] will go down with the Bao Dai regime if we support it."[50]

Despite the consolidation of the three former divisions of Vietnam—Tonkin, Annam, and Cochin-China—into one entity, and measures that might have looked good otherwise to many on paper, they did not go far enough. France was never willing to grant full independence to the Vietnamese. In reality, George McTurnan Kahin has noted, "many of the substantive attributes of sovereignty were retained in French hands." Despite the hopes of U.S. foreign policy makers and others in setting up former emperor Bao Dai as a viable alternative to Ho Chi Minh, reality fell far short of expectations. "His regime," Kahin has concluded, "remained an unconvincing façade for a continuing French military rule that excluded Vietnamese from roles of political significance."[51]

The Bao Dai "solution" nonetheless served its purpose in the context of the Cold War; though never gaining the widespread public support of Ho Chi Minh, and having his role as an effective political leader curtailed by the French, Bao Dai would serve little more than a figurehead role, until he relinquished that position soon after the French defeat in 1954.

The establishment of the State of Vietnam—what would also be referred to as the Republic of Vietnam—controlled as it was by the French, and with increasing economic and material support provided by the United States, would serve another significant purpose, George McTurnan Kahin and others would argue, in providing the pretext for claiming that a colonial war had been transformed into a civil war, in which France was simply supporting one of the two contestants. As the chief political adviser to the French viceroy in Indochina put it, the objective was to transfer France's own direct confrontation with the Viet Minh to "the internal Annamite level." And the Truman administration soon participated in this charade, Secretary of State Acheson in particular helping to ensure that one of the most perduring myths of the Vietnam War gained popular acceptance in the United States—if not in France.[52]

While historians such as George McTurnan Kahin have provided valuable critical analysis of the context, events, and policy decisions leading up to full-scale American involvement in the Vietnam War, more credit should be given as well to those who contemporaneously, despite the attitudes and rhetoric of Cold War, urged caution, pointed out policies that seemed to contradict principles that guided those who went off to fight in World War II, and appeared otherwise contrary to the best practical and economic interests of the United States. Those who, for a multitude of reasons spanning the ideological and political spectrum, questioned the wisdom of being drawn more deeply into a conflict between France and the Viet Minh, which, it also seemed obvious to many, had no real end in sight.[53]

Raymond B. Fosdick, in his role as a consultant to the Secretary of State on matters relating to Southeast Asia, expressed his concerns about the situation in Vietnam in a November 1949 memorandum to the DOS. "Certainly," he wrote in part, "we should not play our cards in such a way that once again, as in China, we seem to be allied with reaction. Whether the French like it or not, independence is coming to Indochina. Why, therefore, do we tie ourselves to the tail of their battered kite?"[54]

The answer to Fosdick's question would come soon enough, and in no uncertain terms, as the U.S. Secretary of State, Dean Acheson, spoke his mind publicly in response to a series of new geopolitical developments in the next few months.

That merchant ships, as well as naval types specifically designed for war, could be considered instruments of foreign policy had been understood and articulated long before the French ever arrived in Indochina. But their crucial role in reestablishing the hegemony of the French there following World War II was understood only too well by General Charles de Gaulle, who had approached President Roosevelt for ships for that purpose many months before the war ended. It was understood too that in addition to transporting troops and supplies, without which wars overseas could not be waged, their presence as a factor of intimidation was also taken into account by the makers of policy.

The Griffin Mission

On January 12, 1950, Secretary of State Acheson delivered a major speech before the National Press Club having to do with the "Crisis in China" and which would offer an "examination of United States Policy" in the area. The "fall" of the Nationalist Chinese regime of Chiang Kai-shek and the establishment of the People's Republic of China led by Mao Zedong only weeks before had immediately escalated concern not only for the situation in China but in other areas of East Asia that might well come under the influence if not the control of China.

Speaking for the Truman administration, Acheson assured those in attendance—and his words would soon be spread far and wide—of measures the United States was prepared to take to counter the Communist threat in the area. With specific reference to Southeast Asia he said: "We are organizing the machinery through which we can make effective help possible."[55]

That "machinery" would of course take different forms and be fueled by whatever financial, economic, and material resources could be mustered within existing constraints, and as quickly as possible. For the purpose of assessing the immediate nature and extent of the "effective help" envisioned, and given the new sense of urgency in the wake of the "fall" of China, a Survey Mission to Southeast Asia, as one participant would later put it, was "rather hastily thrown together and dispatched to the area."[56]

As Vietnam took on ever more importance, especially after the defeat of the

Nationalist Chinese paved the way for the establishment of the People's Republic of China (PRC) in 1949, and as both the PRC and the Soviet Union formally recognized Ho Chi Minh's Democratic Republic of Vietnam, it was viewed as a key link in the Cold War "containment" line, first articulated by George Kennan in 1947, which stretched southward along the Pacific Rim from Japan.[57] The availability and use of merchant ships as they related to this policy sometimes entered into conversations and reports of those tasked with gathering information in the field and making recommendations for the application of strategies and tactics that could be useful for maintaining and perhaps extending those "containment" lines.

The Survey Mission to Southeast Asia was headed by Robert A. Griffin, an official with the Economic Cooperation Administration who had previously been involved with the China aid program.[58] Departing for Southeast Asia in February 1950, the Griffin Mission, as it came to be called, paid particular attention to Indochina and was, according to its leader, intended to gather information about which decisions could be made to forestall "a repetition of the circumstances leading to the fall of China."[59] But the mission, as Heath would later put it, "was going to have to ride two somewhat incompatible horses." These would be a "fire horse" that would "troubleshoot" and respond quickly with aid "to help combat Communist pressures" in the area, and a "plow horse" that would engage in the long term for positive political development.[60]

In the end, the Griffin Mission made strong recommendations for increased military aid for the French in Vietnam, and envisioned among other things the "psychological shock" that American merchant ships would have—presumably upon the Viet Minh—as they sailed to Vietnam "with military aid material in the immediate future."[61]

If there wasn't already enough of a growing sense of urgency following developments in China, as reflected in Acheson's speech to the National Press Club, a series of diplomatic development in the days immediately following that speech ratcheted up the alarm even further. Ho Chi Minh's Democratic Republic of Vietnam (DRV) broadcast an international appeal on January 14, 1950, for diplomatic recognition. That was followed the next day by recognition of the PRC by the DRV, and that formal recognition was reciprocated in turn on January 18 by the PRC. Then, on January 30 the DRV was formally recognized by the Soviet Union.[62]

Though many would continue to believe, as Abbot Low Moffat had concluded, that Ho Chi Minh was "a nationalist first, and then a Communist" these developments in January 1950, and what was to come later in the year, made it just that much more difficult to make those arguments, and easier to support those—such as the French in Vietnam—who were perceived as expending their treasure and blood along the expanded East Asian containment line.

Secretary of State Acheson, one of the principle architects of American post–World War II Cold War foreign policy, and one of the so-called "wise men" who would advise a young, newly elected president from Massachusetts a decade later, would react quickly and strongly to the exchanges of diplomatic recognition between the DRV, PRC, and the Soviet Union on January 1, 1950, saying it "should remove any illusions as to the 'nationalist' nature of Ho Chi Minh's aims and reveals Ho in his true colors as the mortal enemy of native independence in Indochina."[63] The meaning of "independence" for the Vietnamese was by then subject to interpretation, and those formulating and implementing policy to counter the threat of a "red tide" in Vietnam and throughout Southeast Asia offered their own definition for that within the Cold War context.

Not too many months after the developments, diplomatic recognition declarations, and reaction of January 1950 by Acheson and others, one particular American merchant ship—the *Steel Rover*—visibly loaded with military supplies on deck as well as in her holds and headed out of the port of San Francisco on a trans-Pacific voyage for Southeast Asia, would presumably represent just what the Griffin Mission had in mind when it called for that "fire horse"[64] to make its presence known in Vietnam.

4

"America was with the French" (1950–1953)

"I walked down to the Majestic [Hotel] and stood a while watching the unloading of the American bombers. The sun had gone, and they worked by the light of arc lamps."

—Graham Greene, *The Quiet American*

"The day the *Steel Rover* arrived in Saigon was a date of the very first importance."

—Lucien Bodard, *The Quicksand War*

"It wasn't likely [the French] would have armed guards aboard a vessel just to pass the time of day."

—*West Coast Sailors*, 1951

A few days after the outbreak of the Korean War on June 25, 1950, the American merchant ship *Steel Rover* (Isthmian) finished crewing up in San Francisco for a round-the-world voyage.[1] "When we readied to leave the States from Oakland, California," recalled John Santos, the ship's carpenter, a few months later, "it seemed like the war days all over again, except for one thing: television cameramen were everywhere taking pictures of our cargo of army gear as it was loaded overhead from cranes, and they made sweeping shots of our deck, which was loaded with jeeps and crated supplies in such quantities that the catwalk ran from bow to stern."[2]

The *Steel Rover*, a C-3 type cargo ship put in service during World War II, was not destined for Korea, as many observers might have assumed, but heading instead for French Indochina, specifically Saigon in the southern area of Vietnam that had until late the previous year been known as Cochin-China.[3] This was in fact the first full load of U.S. military aid for the French in Vietnam—with much in plain sight on deck—after a public directive by President Truman earlier that month removed any veil of secrecy and restraint that might still have been in place over U.S. support for French fortunes in that area.[4]

"We got away all right," Santos recalled, "and had an uneventful [trans-Pacific] crossing." After calling initially on Manila in the Philippines, *Steel Rover* continued to Hong Kong. "It was as we were leaving Hong Kong," he continued, "that trouble came our way. On Sunday morning, August 2, we left Hong Kong for Saigon. As we left the lighthouse we took a course close along the shore. We were about 15 miles from Hong Kong and still skirting the shore when the first shell was fired."[5]

The ship's radio operator, Fred Huntley, remembered many years later that it was mid-morning and the *Steel Rover*'s cargo booms were topped in preparation for discharging cargo at its next port—Saigon. "The sea was smooth as glass and the weather was pleasant with a slight morning haze. We were sailing five or six miles offshore and land was not visible."[6]

"I was in the radio operator's quarters," Huntley continued, "which was located in the radio shack housing aft of the smoke stack on the top deck of the SS *Steel Rover*.... It was after breakfast and I was in my bathroom enjoying a quiet shave when all at once—whamm! Then another whamm! I thought [that] one of the cargo booms must have broken loose and started flapping around."[7]

While Huntley was still shaving, John Santos was working on deck on the number two hatch cover. He later recalled: "The first shell landed about 20 yards off to our starboard. When I heard the explosion I looked back at number one house [where] we had a box of hand grenades and I thought they had gone off. But while I was turning to look, number two shot was fired and landed in line with our bow. I knew then what it was and said to myself 'this is no place for me.'"[8]

Santos continued:

> I made a dash for the midship house, and the rest of the deck gang joined me. As we neared the midship house I said to the First Assistant [Engineer], 'Someone is firing on us!' And as if to prove it, shell number three came whistling in. We all ducked inside and the shell landed about 20 yards off the port side. While we waited inside, number four and five came over. One of the shells, I learned later, struck close to our stern and sent fragments through our flag and into the stern.[9]

While Santos and the rest of the deck gang headed for cover in the mid-ship house, radio operator Huntley had a job to do: he hurried into the radio shack and pushed the start button of a Navy medium-frequency 500-watt radio transmitter. "In a minute the generator got up to speed," Huntley recalled, "and I tapped out in international Morse code 'SOS SOS SOS DE KIWP SS STEEL ROVER BEING SHELLED OUTSIDE HONG KONG SEND AIRCRAFT.' There was no reply so I repeated the message several times. Meanwhile, the ship's vibration increased noticeably as Captain Preble signaled the engine room for every ounce of speed as he ordered the helm hard over to port."[10]

The shelling, presumably from Chinese shore batteries, was all the persuasion Captain Preble needed to steam back to Hong Kong, where a naval attaché came aboard to speak with him, and to assess any damage. The ship was inspected the next morning and *Steel Rover* got underway again for Saigon. "But this time," Santos recalled, "we headed straight out away from the port and then made our way southward."[11]

Fred Huntley also remembered that the ship "kept well clear of the coast," reporting: "While all crew members experienced some trepidation, we reached the coast of Indo-China without further incident."[12] *Steel Rover* arrived off Cap St. Jacques, at the entrance to the channel leading to Saigon, on August 9, 1950. This was less than a week following the arrival of the first contingent of U.S. military personnel with the Military Assistance Advisory Group (MAAG), the "advisors" tasked with monitoring the distribution, training for, and use of newly authorized shipments of military hardware and supplies for the French in Vietnam.[13]

Getting from Cap St. Jacques (Vung Tau) on the coast to Saigon was another matter. The mangrove swamps along the winding 40-mile river approach had already established a reputation for providing Viet Minh snipers with prime cover, and given the chance to pop off at one of the despised French or colonial soldiers, or anyone else in league with their enemy, they would do so, and often did. Though American merchant seamen would find the situation along the Long Tau River that much worse some 15 years later as more powerful and sophisticated weaponry was brought to bear, there was still more than enough cause for concern in 1950, and for taking appropriate precautions.

"All of us felt that if any trouble arose it would be in the Saigon River," said John Santos. "Several of the men said that we wouldn't be so lucky as there were people who wanted to prevent this first shipment of arms from reaching their destination."[14]

> We arrived in Saigon [actually Cap St. Jacques on the coast] on August 9, and when we reached the pilot station we were given an armed guard aboard the ship, and river gunboats patrolled the waters alongside the ship. We were told to stay inside while making the run, just to be on the safe side. Maybe the small armada escorting us changed someone's mind because we had no trouble. When the ship tied up, a contingent of soldiers came down to the ship and stood guard all the time the cargo was being worked.[15]
>
> Next to us was a British ship that had left Hong Kong a few hours before we did. We heard that she had been damaged slightly and two officers wounded. We spent little time in Saigon and everyone heaved a sigh of relief when the ship pulled out and headed for less troubled parts of the world.[16]

While the United States had already found significant ways to support the French effort in Vietnam, and American merchant ships had been calling on Vietnam since 1945 with a variety of cargoes, certainly including military materiel, the *Steel Rover*'s full and openly displayed military cargo did represent a shift the significance of which was not lost on the French. Lucien Bodard, a French reporter who had witnessed the arrival of the ship to Saigon, later wrote that the day on which *Steel Rover* arrived "was a date of the very first importance—America was with the French."[17]

With the onset of the Korean War, Bodard noted, in somewhat overstated and misleading fashion, that a change had occurred in both attitude and policy on the part of the United States, and as represented by the arrival of *Steel Rover*. "The change is plain to see," he wrote. "America was no longer calling for the expulsion of the Expeditionary Force but for alliance with it. The whole American machine had put itself in reverse, for now instead of rejecting France the United States was helping her."[18]

"The Viets too," Bodard noted, "were aware of what [pending] arrival of the ship meant and on their radio they said they would blow up the *Steel Rover*."

> Because of this the French took the most elaborate precautions: they dragged the fifty miles [*sic*] of the Saigon River (a little while before, the *Saint Loup Pervia*, an ordinary trading vessel, had been mined there). On the appointed day the *Steel Rover* steamed slowly up through the muddy, winding channel in the midst of the labyrinthine mangroves, surrounded by a remarkable escort—a mine-sweeper in front, guard boats all around, planes above, and both banks lined with troops. Precautions in the port itself were even stricter. When the *Steel Rover* had tied up and the jeeps, already in their gray-green war paint, were being unloaded, there was a policeman with a revolver and a Moroccan with a machinegun for every coolie.[19]

While Bodard's description of "both banks lined with troops" was perhaps limited to the immediate vicinity of Saigon, his description of overall security arrangements for this one ship would seem to be accurate, and in contrast with those provided most other arrivals of American merchant ships with military cargoes, which were limited to an armed guard detail boarded for the river transit at Cap St. Jacques.

Bodard's description of American merchant seamen he came in contact with on the *Steel Rover* is amusing if not entirely flattering. "I went on board and looked at the crew," he noted, "healthy, broad-shouldered, coarse, well-fed sailors stripped to the waist, with peaked caps on their heads. The Captain was a huge man with an Irish name [Preble], and his red hair blazed in the sun. He offered me a drink—a Negro brought whiskey—and very cheerfully told me that he had little notion of why he was there in Saigon, and that he did not give a damn. I gazed at all these big tattooed uncaring men and I realized that America had really swung into action and that she was backing the Expeditionary Force for good and all."[20]

Though not then bound for Korea, the highly publicized voyage of *Steel Rover* to Vietnam—which might not have raised much attention otherwise—immediately underscored the increased linkage between the two areas as key points along the Cold War containment line. As George McTurnan Kahin would describe it many years later, Korea

> sharpened overnight our thoughts and actions with respect to Southeast Asia. The American military response symbolized in the most concrete manner possible the basic belief that holding the line in Southeast Asia was essential to American security interests. The French struggle in Indochina came far more than before to be seen as an integral part of the containment of communism in that region of the world. Accordingly, the United States intensified and enlarged its programs of aid in Indochina. Military aid shipments to Indochina acquired in 1951 the second highest priority, just behind the Korean War program.[21]

President Truman had given public endorsement to this link when he declared on June 27, 1950, that he had "directed acceleration in the furnishing of military assistance to the forces of France and the Associated States in Indochina and the dispatch of a military mission to provide close working relations with those forces."[22]

A few months after the outbreak of war in Korea, and the arrival of SS *Steel Rover* with its highly visible deck load of military supplies for the French in Indochina, a contingent of U.S. military personnel, whose number is generally put at 35, were deployed from the United States to Vietnam with the stated purpose of monitoring the use of funds and related shipments of military supplies sent to the French in Indochina. They would also be tasked, as Ronald Spencer has put it, to "evaluate French tactical efficiency in the use of U.S. equipment."[23] These were the first "advisers" of the Military Assistance Advisory Group (MAAG) whose number would reach nearly 100 by the end of that first year, about 350 by the end of the French War in 1954, and ultimately more than 17,000 by the end of the Kennedy administration in November 1963.[24]

Increased and speeded up shipments of military supplies for the French in Indochina could not, in light of reverses on the ground to that point, and what was to come later in the year, come to soon. The Viet Minh had developed its fighting forces significantly by 1950. As Bernard Fall has explained, "the guerilla groups of 1946–1949 had transformed themselves into battalions, then into regiments, and now began to take their final shape as 10,000-man divisions. The first series of five divisions—the Divisions 304, 308, 312, 316, and 320—was created in 1950."[25] That growth of organized units of varying size had contributed to Viet Minh successes against the French, and a reduction of military hardware, vehicles, and ammunition stocks, as well as in the morale of French forces suffering at the hands of well-led and motivated Viet Minh forces.

A turning point in the war, reflecting the Viet Minh's effective deployment of its new battalion, regimental, and division-sized units, came in the weeks of early October 1950 when a line of French forts in the extreme northern area of Vietnam around Lang-son were attacked with disastrous and telling results for the French, and massive losses in both personnel and equipment stocks.[26] As Bernard Fall would later describe it, "Lang-son itself ... was abandoned in an almost-panic with 1,300 tons of ammunition, food, equipment and artillery still intact. When the smoke cleared the French had their greatest colonial defeat since Montcalm had died at Quebec."[27]

The losses at Lang-son and elsewhere would have to be replaced, and that would eventually involve increased shiploads of replenishment cargoes making their way along the seaborne pipeline from ports in the United States in ships crewed by American merchant seamen. In addition to the loss of some 6,000 troops at Lang-son, military supplies left behind by French forces who escaped the Viet Minh to fight again included the following:

- 450 trucks and three armored platoons
- 13 artillery pieces and 125 mortars
- 940 machineguns
- 1,200 sub-machineguns
- 8,000+ rifles

The magnitude of these losses was put into perspective later by Bernard Fall when he wrote in *Street Without Joy* that "their abandoned stocks [at Lang-son] alone sufficed for the equipment of a whole additional Viet-Minh division."[28]

The task of turning things around for the French in Vietnam—devising more successful strategies and tactics, raising the dispirited morale of French forces, and pressuring for additional and speeded-up shipments of military hardware and ammunition from the United States—would fall to famed General Jean de Lattre de Tassigny, who arrived in Vietnam in December 1950 just two months after the debacle at Lang-son.[29] During a barnstorming tour to the U.S. in September and October 1951, de Lattre made reference to the wars in Korea and Indochina to bolster his arguments, declaring, "If you lose Korea, Asia is not lost; but if you lose Indochina, Asia is lost."[30] This was an indirect reference to the "domino theory," suggesting that countries in Southeast Asia would "fall" one after the other like dominoes to communism if Vietnam and the rest of Indochina could not be held by the French, with American support.[31]

De Lattre's pitch to U.S. policy makers, and the American public, seemed to have the desired impact as pledges for enhanced commitment were soon followed by an upsurge in shipments of military supplies flowing to Vietnam. "The most dramatic effect of de Lattre's visit," military historian Ronald Spector would later note, "was a marked increase in the size and speed of American aid deliveries to Saigon."[32] In the four months following de Lattre's appeal for increased deliveries of American-made military goods, more than 130,000 tons of rolling stock, aircraft, weapons, ammunition, and other supplies would arrive, mostly in ships crewed by American merchant seamen. These shipments included the following[33]:

- 8,000 general purpose vehicles
- 650 combat vehicles
- 200 aircraft
- 3,500 radio sets
- 14,000 automatic weapons
- 53 million rounds of ammunition

De Lattre's leadership in Vietnam would be marked by a series of notable successes on the ground, especially in the northern reaches of Tonkin in 1951, in great part due, as Bernard Fall would later describe it, to "a new offensive spirit" of French forces, supported "by the ever-mounting influx of American equipment."[34] Though de Lattre and other French military commanders in-country would express annoyance at requirements for what they termed "excessive justification" required by the MAAG for additional shipments of equipment and resented the very presence of American military personnel—de Lattre had complained in April 1951, for example, that there were "entirely too many Americans in Indochina"—the benefit of American military supplies for his operations was given the credit that it was due.[35]

In the aftermath of fighting at Vinh Yen in June 1951 in the northern Red River Delta area of Tonkin, some 30 miles northeast of Hanoi in June 1951, it was noted by American Consul Edmund Gullion that "recent Viet Minh assaults were repulsed only with [availability of] American weapons."[36] There had actually been dangerous shortages of American-made ammunition during some of the fighting in the north at that time—notably that of 105-millimeter howitzer rounds—but some of the difference was made up, it seems, by cannisters filled with a highly flammable gel-like substance that were dropped on Viet Minh forces by American-made aircraft. In *Street Without Joy* Bernard Fall provides one eyewitness account:

> All of a sudden a sound can be heard in the sky and strange birds appear, getting larger and larger. Airplanes. I order my men to take cover from the bombs and machinegun bullets. But the planes dived upon us without firing their guns. However, all of a sudden, hell opens in front of my eyes. Hell comes in the form of large, egg-shaped containers, dropping from the first plane. Immense sheets of flames, extending over hundreds of meters, it seems, strike terror in the ranks of my soldiers. This is *napalm*, the fire which falls from the skies.[37]

Despite de Lattre's efforts and accomplishments both on the ground in Vietnam, and in the stateside venues where he made his appeals for support, his prediction that he would achieve "decisive victory" over the Viet Minh within 15 months—that is, by mid–1952—would not come to pass. By January 1952, in fact, he would be dead, having succumbed not to a Viet Minh bullet in Vietnam, but to cancer after having returned to France sooner than anticipated. His promise of victory was in any case highly doubtful. He would be but one of a dozen French commanders-in-chief in Indochina in less than nine years, none of whom would be able to achieve the desired outcome there as he had envisioned it.[38]

Another linkage between the wars in Korea and Vietnam in the early 1950s, though not generally explored by historians comparing the one situation with the other, involved basic logistics and the vital support provided by the fleet of merchant ships required to haul war materiel to both areas. Some 750 government-owned cargo ships built during World War II—mostly of the EC2 "Liberty" type, but also including dozens of the faster "Victory" ships, and other types—would be withdrawn from stateside National Defense Reserve Fleets (NDRF) for the Korean "emergency."[39] And many of those ships, including Victory ships highlighted in this chapter, would be used to provide logistical support for the French war in Indochina as well. American merchant seamen manning ships in those years might typically find themselves shipping out for the "coldest war" in Korea, only to be headed for a far different clime in the tropical latitudes of Vietnam.[40]

Weather could be dealt with well enough, but more of a threat for those making the 40-mile river transit from Cap St. Jacques to Saigon was the occasional pot shot from within the dense mangrove cover along the way (not yet affected by massive defoliant applications) and floating mines that did serious damage to some ships. Fortunately, there were few casualties reported among the ranks of American merchant seamen during this period, in contrast to later years. Nonetheless, reports involving seamen from ships of other countries, and the image of at least one mined ship being unloaded while beached at Cap St. Jacques, suggested that dangerous and life-threatening encounters were a distinct possibility.[41] Warnings were certainly carried back stateside for the benefit, hopefully, of other seamen who would also be making their way along the Vietnam Run in those years. In a letter published in a maritime labor publication in July 1950, for example, the crew of SS *Steel Admiral* advised: "Crewmen [in Saigon] should watch their step. The night before our arrival, two Greek seamen were killed just outside the gate. The natives have been having some big demonstrations so the crews going ashore should not make any stops at local bars around the gate."[42]

A typical voyage to Vietnam in those days was experienced by the crew of SS *Southwestern Victory* (Shepard Lines), which arrived in Saigon in April or May 1952 with a mixed military cargo that included 6×6 trucks, jeeps, small arms ammunition, and creosoted telephone poles.[43] Francis J. Dooley, the ship's second assistant engineer, recalled some years later that the Viet Minh "had succeeded in getting some mines in the water at the mouth of the Saigon River." He remembered: "A Greek-registered Liberty ship struck one in the week preceding our arrival and was beached at Cape St. Jacques. One could observe her cargo being removed while her bow was pointed beachward, approximately 50 yards offshore."[44]

"When the river pilot boarded our vessel," Dooley remembered, "he was accompanied by Vietnamese soldiers of the French Army and Foreign Legionnaires. They were, indeed, a tough-looking crowd, and typical of the members of the Legion, post–World War II. The Legionnaires set up small caliber air-cooled machine guns on the boat deck and on the bridge deck, and opened boxes of hand grenades. Most of them sat behind the windscreen as we went up the river, and about a half dozen kept a lookout on both sides of the vessel."[45]

Other onboard security measures were also taken, as Dooley explained:

> All of the dead eyes were dogged down behind the porthole glasses so that the vessel had to rely on its bulkhead fans for cooling; it was, consequently, an extremely hot trip up the Saigon River. The crew was not allowed on deck or outside the house. The anchor party stayed in the foc'sle head shelter deck.[46]

The voyage up the river was uneventful. The vessel was steered from the flying bridge.

There was no telegraph on the flying bridge so signals to and from the engine room by the mechanical telegraph had to be transmitted from inside the wheelhouse, one deck below; one sound-powered phone was on the flying bridges and it confirmed the telegraph's orders.

When Francis Dooley arrived aboard *Southwestern Victory* in 1952, he encountered some of these early advisers with MAAG. "When we arrived in Saigon," he remembered, "we tied up in an area ... downtown, since it was close to the heart of the city."

The U.S. Military Mission in Saigon was a most unusual one. All of the soldiers with whom I had contact spoke excellent French and I was advised that they were selected especially for this duty since it was not anticipated that the French or Vietnamese encountered in Indochina would speak English. Interesting, too, the military personnel at that time were paid approximately three times the regular rate in the U.S. Army to maintain parity with their counterparts in the French army.[47]

"Saigon at that time," Dooley also noted, "was an interesting city, and quite accurately named 'The Paris of the Far East.' The boulevards were wide, there were sidewalk cafes where it was safe to sit and watch the crowds go by, the restaurants were superb, and the nightclubs were everything a sailor could look for after a long voyage across the Pacific." Dooley also noted: "In the evening there were many areas of the city that were off limits, but other than that, I know of no instances where the crew encountered any difficulties with the locals while we were there."[48]

When we maneuvered down the river, the same conditions pertained aboard the vessel as when we went up. I did note, however, that there were several fast water craft in the river, each containing about a dozen French Legionnaires that sped past us and beached themselves in the weeds on the east bank of the river where the Legionnaires went ashore. The firing of weapons could be heard. The trip down the river, other than that, was uneventful. When we got to Cape St. Jacques, the Legionnaires and the pilot left the vessel.[49]

"The 150th Ship"

Someone, presumably a clerk attached to the MAAG office in Saigon, was keeping track of the number of shiploads of American-made military supplies arriving in that port since the SS *Steel Rover* made its way there—with great fanfare and security measures—back in 1950. Aside from security details, often comprised of French Foreign Legionnaires assigned to each ship making its way up, and back down, to the coast again, not every ship would be accorded the pomp and ceremony marking a significant milestone, as *Steel Rover* had been.

But on June 1, 1952, another milestone was reached with the arrival of what was recognized as the 150th ship loaded with military supplies for the French Union forces in Indochina.[50] (Francis Dooley's ship, *Southwestern Victory*, had arrived a few weeks too early to have been accorded this recognition.) Once again, in addition to those Legionnaires on board, there would be proper ceremony and no doubt speeches and toasts, made by dignitaries and other guests invited to mark the occasion.

"This is a practical demonstration," a reporter from *The New York Times* would write, "that our help is really going forward."[51]

Curiously, either due to poor reporting or perhaps security considerations, the name of the ship referred to in that back-page item in *The New York Times* was not mentioned, nor the names of any involved, nor any details relating to the ship's cargo. Aside from underscoring, in the fashion of a Cold War era publicist, the role this ship and others had made in the fight for "a society that has a chance to be free [from Communist domination]" the only real details provided related to the numbers of ships that had arrived heretofore, and the increased pace of those arrivals.

"An important factor right now," the article posited, "is the stepped-up tempo of the arrivals. Fifty of those ships have unloaded in Saigon since January as compared to the hundred that reached the embattled area in the course of the preceding sixteen months."

"The answer to the pressure and the threat [posed by a Viet Minh offensive]," the article concluded, "is more help speedily delivered. With that in mind, the arrival of the 150th ship is good news."[52]

Word of the arrival of this 150th ship in Saigon did not go unnoticed, it seems, by speech writers in Washington, D.C., who seized upon it as a useful indication of commitment, and sign of progress, being made in the French War. Speaking publicly to assembled reporters at a press conference a few weeks later about current reports from the field, Secretary of State Dean Acheson remarked:

> We in the United States are aware of the vital importance of the struggle in Indochina to the cause of the free world. We have earmarked for Indochina economic and materiel aid to a considerable amount during the past two years. We are doing our best to activate deliveries: as you are aware the 150th ship bearing American arms and munitions to Indochina arrived in Saigon within the past two weeks.[53]

Acheson spoke of "favorable developments" and having "checked" Communist aggression in Indochina, in part by the quantity and timely arrival of American merchant ships in Saigon and elsewhere. But vast quantities of military supplies arriving in ports providing logistical support, as is all too well known, does not always translate directly, for a variety of reasons, into the success of military operations. His positive words, in fact, and those of a nameless reporter writing about the arrival of a nameless ship in Saigon, were at best misleading, and actually belied to a great extent the reality of what was happening in 1952, and into the next year, in Vietnam and other areas of French Indochina.

In addition to Saigon the other principal port of call for American seamen in Vietnam in the early 1950s, as noted earlier, was Haiphong in the north. Eugene Kauder was a seaman in SS *Greeley Victory* (South Atlantic Steamship Co.), which arrived in Haiphong with a cargo of military supplies in 1953.[54] "Security as I remember it," he wrote several years later, "wasn't too tight. The town was occupied by French forces and Senegalese troops. We were there about two weeks, and I had a marvelous time as bars [and] restaurants were in operation, and no untoward incidents were happening in or around Haiphong. It was like a miniature Saigon [which was] similar to Paris."[55]

Kauder was also in Saigon about a year later, in SS *Virginia City Victory* (Cuba Mail Lines), and recalled: "Senegalese armed troops had come aboard the vessel at Vung Tau and stayed aboard the vessel the entire transit of the Saigon River to Saigon City. No problems. I remember taking a taxi from Saigon to Vung Tau in order to go to the beach. Things seemed to be OK; no one bothered me."[56]

Making the run to Vietnam in the early 1950s as well as in later years, Kauder recalled one difference between the two periods: "We were welcome at all the French clubs; I can't say the same for the Merchant Marine when the U.S. forces were in Viet Nam."[57]

That the war in Vietnam was escalating from north to south, and from one month to the next, there seemed little doubt. As casualties mounted among French forces it became known at home and in the field as *la sale guerre*, the "dirty war." The United States increasingly upped its commitment—from an initial pledge of $15 million in 1950 to 20 times that by 1953—and there seemed no end in sight despite the investment of treasure, the changes in command and strategy, and the increase in the steady presence of ships on the Vietnam Run.[58]

War Risk Insurance

Though it is not believed that American merchant seamen had suffered casualties in the early years of the First Indochina (French) War, the importance of their ships' cargoes to the French war effort, and proximity to hostilities, made it inevitable that the subject of war zone compensation would eventually enter discussions between ship owners and maritime labor organizations. Arguments made by ship owners that the situation on the ground was "becoming better instead of worse" flew in the face of reality, and it was pointed out in rebuttal, as one maritime union publication reported it, that "it wasn't likely the French Government, which can ill spare the guards or the money they cost, would have armed guards aboard a vessel just to pass the time."[59]

Despite initial disagreement as to its need, discussions early in this new phase of war between the owners of ships and the labor organizations that crewed them resulted in contractual agreements by mid–July 1951 for "five and ten" that extended the war zone bonus area for American merchant seamen, paid out an additional five dollars a day for service in those areas, and provided $10,000 war risk insurance coverage respecting loss of life and disability due to war-related causes in-country. Additionally, the war zone was extended to include a ship within a 60-mile radius of the mouth of the Saigon River.[60]

The specific wording of the agreement worked out between the Pacific Maritime Association ship operators and West Coast–based maritime labor organizations, which would be similar to agreements negotiated with Gulf and East Coast ship operators, was as follows:

"The Pacific Maritime Association hereby agrees to further amend paragraph (4) of the Supplementary Agreement entered into between Pacific Maritime Association, on behalf of its members therein stated, and your Association on June 29, 1950, to read in its entirety as follows:

> 4. (a) War Risk Insurance Coverage respecting loss of life and disability in the form prescribed by the Second Seamen's War Risk Policy shall be provided in the maximum sum of $10,000 for each member of the crew employed on and aboard such a vessel while in waters described in Areas I, II, III, IV, and V above, and in the waters within and bounded by the following lines:

(b) Beginning at a point on the China Coast at 23° north latitude, thence easterly to a point 22°30' north latitude and 118° east longitude thence westerly to Gap Rock thence due west along the 21°50' line north latitude to the China Coast.

(c) Within a sixty (60) mile radius of the mouth of the Donnai River or Cape St. Jacques.

2. Each member of the Licensed Deck Department shall be entitled to a bonus of $5 for each day the vessel is within a sixty (60) mile radius of the mouth of the Donnai River or Cape St. Jacques.

The foregoing amendment of paragraph (4) shall become effective on July 18, 1951."

The approved amendment document was signed by W.J. Clark, representing the P.M.A. and Captain C.F. May, president of the National Organization of Masters, Mates & Pilots of America on July 31, 1951.[61]

Hazards and potential or actual casualty associated with service in the war zone was not always that which might have resulted, of course, from direct contact with the Viet Minh. The very nature of highly explosive cargoes—ammunition of various types, for example—carried its own risk in the very handling of it, and sometimes it was not entirely clear if shipboard mishaps involving such cargoes were the function of carelessness, Murphy's Law, or the ultimate allegiance of hired stevedores who gained access to cargo holds loaded with such materiel. An incident involving the SS *Lynn Victory* in Saigon in early February 1952 is a case in point.[62]

Unloading while anchored out, billows of smoke began appearing from number three cargo hold that contained many cases of phosphorous hand grenades (each case containing 16 metal-cased grenades) which were packed tightly to the top of the hold. Members of the crew rushed into the affected area after French and local stevedores fled the ship and fought a blaze for about an hour before it was brought under control. It was reported that other small fires broke out "for the rest of the night" but were extinguished quickly. Except for excessive smoke inhalation suffered by some of the crew, there was no greater harm done to crew or ship. The cause of the fire was not determined, but sabotage was not ruled out.[63]

It was as if the death of General de Lattre, given the honorific title of Marshall of France (Marechal de France) posthumously in January 1952, had taken the wind out of the sails of the fighting spirit of French forces in Indochina. But there was much more to it than that. The overall commander of Viet Minh forces opposing the French, Vo Nguyen Giap, had learned hard-won lessons in 1951 in set-piece engagements with French forces, notably at Lang-son in northern Tonkin.[64] His strategy in 1952 and going forward would reflect that, much to the detriment of the French, now without the inspiring leadership of de Lattre. The Viet Minh were ably led, fighting with that age-old *doc lap*—"spirit of independence"—that had motivated resistance to foreign intervention for many centuries. It now seemed undiminished. As much as the French had been increasingly supplied and funded by the United States, so too were the Viet Minh increasingly being supplied, provided with advisers, and trained by the People's Republic of China (PRC), soon to be freed of the burden and drain of Korea to focus even more fully on developments closer to its southern border.[65]

Despite the infusion of funds, military hardware, and ammunition, things were not going well for the French as they waded deeper and deeper into their "quicksand war" in Indochina through 1952 and into the following year. During the first year following the election of Eisenhower to the American presidency there was, as one historian would note, a "rapid erosion of the French military position" in Vietnam.[66] That, in turn, would force the issue in terms of evolving U.S. policy towards Vietnam, the process of approving additional financial and material support for French fortunes there, and corresponding pressure put upon the French to more effectively prosecute the war in Indochina, or else. Negative reports about the progress of the war, coupled with the reality of the expense increasingly being borne by the American taxpayer, gave rise to increased opposition in Congress and the editorial pages of periodicals read by American citizens across the country.[67]

The end of the war in Korea, which by early 1953 had resulted in the deaths of more than 36,000 Americans due mostly to battle-related causes, came not by decisive action wrought by one side against the other on the ground but by negotiated settlement—an armistice—in July 1953, that resulted in partition of the Korean Peninsula virtually where it had been when the war began more than three years earlier.[68] This would impact the situation in Indochina in different ways, and also lead to increased questioning of *la sale guerre* by French politicians and citizens who asked why, if such a settlement could be achieved in Korea, it could not be accomplished for Indochina as well.[69]

The best that could be said was that it had come to a stalemate between the opposing forces in 1952. Yet, such developments as the defeat at and retreat from Hoa Binh early in the year, after it had been occupied in force by General de Lattre the previous November, suggested a momentum shift to others, not just a stalemate.[70] "What Washington did know," Ronald Spector has written, "was discouraging. All American observers agreed that in operations during 1952 the French had, at best, achieved a stalemate."[71] Others, however, even those sympathetic to the French cause, put it another way at the time. According to General Trapnell, then in command of the MAAG in Vietnam, the Viet Minh, despite their disadvantages caused by "heterogeneous equipment, long supply lines, and inadequate transport" when compared to French forces in Indochina, had actually gained and "retained the initiative."[72]

Despite the best efforts of U.S. policy makers—as well as the mainstream American press, which largely still supported the French in Indochina—to put a positive spin on it, as when Secretary of State Dean Acheson declared at a press conference on June 18, 1952, that the "tide is in our favor" in Indochina, the reality on the ground painted a different picture.[73]

Much of what optimism had been regenerated under General de Lattre's command in 1951 had dissipated, and there was a turn for the worse when, in April 1953, General Vo Nguyen Giap sent three Viet Minh divisions headlong into Laos, an area of French Indochina that had been a relative backwater in the war until that point.[74] In attempting to meet the new challenge the French reduced their strength in various garrisons throughout Vietnam, no doubt precisely what Giap had hoped and planned for.

This turn of events caused some policy makers in Washington, and many watching from France, to conclude that an initiative on the ground might never be regained. What could be done at least to regain enough initiative and ground to put France in a better position for the negotiated settlement that increasing numbers— especially in France—were now advocating?[75]

"Improve port facilities as early as practicable"

Much of what was considered wrong, and in need of improvement as soon as possible to turn a failing situation around in Indochina, was spelled out to the Secretary of Defense in a memorandum from the Joint Chiefs of Staff on March 13, 1953.[76] Emphasis was placed up front, in an oft-repeated refrain in and outside of government circles in those days, on "speeding and improving the development of indigenous combat forces" to replace losses and increase the number of troops available for operations against the Viet Minh. This was part of a process typically referred to by the French in racist terms as the "yellowing" of their forces in Indochina.

Also emphasized up front and potentially benefiting those, such as merchant seamen, involved in logistical support operations, was reference to "supporting logistical and operating facilities." Specific recommendations included "steps ... to improve the port and air facilities in the Tonkin [Red River] Delta area as early as possible" and to provide material and financial support to accomplish these improvements.[77]

The primary port intended for improvements in the area would have been Haiphong, but specific needs for infrastructure enhancements there or elsewhere were not spelled out. What neither the French nor the American taxpayers footing the bill could have known, however, is that the sands of time required for significant improvements along those lines were already fast running out.

The memorandum from the Joint Chiefs noted that the formation of "effective Vietnamese forces" was "handicapped by deficient Vietnamese incentive and lack of qualified indigenous military leadership." It concluded by underscoring, as others had been doing, the need to "impress upon the French the necessity and desirability for granting the Associated States greater responsibility and economic and political potentials," and to grant increased autonomy to Vietnamese forces.[78]

Many had and would continue to echo sentiments seen here regarding the need to grant greater autonomy to the Vietnamese.[79] A newly minted senator from Massachusetts by the name of John F. Kennedy, for example, would declare on the floor of the Senate a few months later:

> It is because we want the war to be brought to a successful conclusion that we should insist on genuine independence.... Regardless of our united effort, it is a truism that the war can never be successful unless large numbers of the people of Vietnam are won over from their sullen neutrality and open hostility to it and fully support its successful conclusion.... I strongly believe that the French cannot succeed in Indochina without giving concessions necessary to make the native army a reliable and crusading force.[80]

Could an adequate native force be recruited, trained, equipped, and added to the existing French forces for effectively countering the Viet Minh in the time envisioned, and, if so, who would provide the inspiring leadership that President Eisenhower and others had been calling for since the death of General de Lattre more than a year before?

The answer, at least to the leadership question, came with the appointment in May 1953 of yet another French commander—the seventh of nine in the space of less than nine years by the time all was said and done—Lieutenant General Philip Navarre.[81]

Very much a different type, and without the legendary military career of de Lattre, Navarre would present something that de Lattre also had: a plan, one to which would be given his name.[82] It was upon that plan now that all hopes for victory, or at least a much more favorable position for a negotiated settlement, were placed by the French who continued to play an increasingly unacceptable price in blood and treasure, and the United States, which was increasingly covering the majority share of the financial cost of the war.

Despite optimistic public statements to the contrary by government officials and publicists attempting to shore up support for the French in Indochina, that policy, and authorization of additional funding for the policy, was increasingly called into question as French fortunes after a period of setbacks on the ground appeared in jeopardy.

A National Intelligence Estimate (NIE-91) in early June 1953, just a few weeks after Navarre's appointment as commander-in-chief of French forces in Indochina, provided a grim assessment of performance by French Union forces to that point,[83] including its "failure to attack [Viet Minh] supply lines" during Giap's successful incursion into Laos. The expansion of the war into that area had other serious ramifications in terms of the overall military situation since it "caused the French to commit large forces throughout Indochina to static defense, this seriously reducing French ability to take the offense."[84]

Not only had the Viet Minh demonstrated its ability to effectively move larger-scale units—now better equipped by the Chinese—as it had done in Laos, its prestige, the NIE report argued, "has been increased" in so doing. The failure of French forces to respond effectively seemed to ensure, as NIE-91 also suggested, that "popular apathy will probably continue to prevent a significant increase in Indochinese will and ability to resist the Viet Minh."[85]

The Navarre Plan

Eisenhower had suggested that what the French needed as a replacement commander-in-chief in Indochina was someone who would be both "forceful and inspirational," and high hopes—what many would consider the last great hope for a military victory—were placed on General Navarre and the plan of action he devised and which would be given his name.[86] Delivered in writing to General John W. O'Daniel, in charge of a fact-finding mission sent to Vietnam, and then submitted in a report dated July 14, 1953, to the Joint Chiefs of Staff, the plan called for

taking the initiative immediately with local offensives, emphasizing guerilla warfare, (b) initiating an offensive (utilizing the equivalent of three [3] divisions) in Tonkin by 15 September 1953, (c) recovering a maximum number of units from areas not directly involved in the war, (d) reorganizing battalions into regiments and regiments into divisions, with necessary support units and (e) developing the armies of the Associated States and giving them greater leadership responsibility in the conduct of operations.[87]

What Navarre was offering seemed to be what Eisenhower and other members of his administration had been insisting upon.[88] But the proof would be in the proverbial pudding. Would there be adequate time in which to implement all aspects of that plan?

Eisenhower's new Secretary of State, John Foster Dulles, was soon hyping the Navarre Plan, saying it would break "the organized body of Communist aggression by the end of the 1955 fighting season."[89]

The French government made it known that additional funds—a formal request would be submitted by them for $385 million—beyond what had already been approved by the U.S. Congress, would be required specifically for implementation of the Navarre Plan.[90] Funds were recommended by the Department of State—presumably not long after the French government suggested the planned offensive could not move forward without said funding—and this was also supported by the NSC, and the Joint Chiefs of Staff would argue that "the Navarre concept offers a promise of success sufficient to warrant appropriate additional U.S. aid."[91]

In late June 1953, a month following Navarre's arrival in Saigon, the U.S. Congress began consideration of the Eisenhower administration's request for additional funds for the French in Indochina. This moved fairly quickly through both the House Foreign Affairs and the Senate Foreign Relations Committees until it reached the floor of the Senate, where, as one history has described it, "there occurred, for the first time since the Indochina War began ... a very frank and realistic debate about the situation and about the dilemma facing the United States."[92]

While approval of funds never really seemed in doubt, the debate raised other issues regarding the granting of full independence for Vietnam, and prospects for deeper involvement by the United States in the war. Passionate debate stemmed in large part from amendments proposed for the funding bill in slightly differing versions submitted by freshman Senator John F. Kennedy (D–MA) and Barry M. Goldwater (R–AZ), revealing in itself a degree of bipartisan concern for Indochina policy in general. Their amendments made approval for additional funding contingent upon French commitment to granting full independence to the Associated States of Indochina.[93]

Goldwater spoke eloquently, quoting the American Declaration of Independence, and warning that unless the French delivered on an independence promise, "as surely as day follows night our boys will follow this $400 million" to "the jungles of Southeast Asia."[94] Other senators—Republican and Democrat, liberal and conservative—shared his point of view, and Everett McKinley Dirksen (R–IL), recently returned from Vietnam, suggested that without granting true and full independence the war could go on "endlessly" and might require the sending of U.S. troops. "But if it spoils too long, look out," he said. "Then we shall indeed have a potential and a problem which can harass and embarrass this country as nothing else."[95]

While many members of the Senate basically agreed with Goldwater and Kennedy that France needed to make greater political concessions, most were unwilling to put it in writing—even in Kennedy's watered-down version—as an attachment to the funding bill. It was defeated by a vote of 64–17.[96]

The supplementary aid agreement to fund the Navarre Plan went forward, with the requested and approved amount and U.S. expectations for its use spelled out in an exchange of letters between Ambassador Douglas Dillon and French Foreign Minister Bidault on September 29, 1953. This coincided with the projected beginning of Navarre's highly anticipated campaign against the Viet Minh in the far-northern reaches of Vietnam.[97]

In declaring what Eisenhower and his Indochina policy advisers expected—and required if funds were to be released—Foreign Minister Bidault stated up front in his letter that "the strategic plan of the French command" consisted "essentially of retaking the offensive with a view to breaking up and destroying the regular enemy forces." He emphasized that his government intended "to carry forward vigorously and promptly the execution" of that offensive. This would have been music to the ears of Ambassador Dillon, and to those to whom this letter would quickly be transmitted. So too was the pledged "buildup of the Associated States forces" as well as the intention "to dispatch French reinforcements to General Navarre."[98]

In confirming the supplemental aid amount of $385 million, Dillon in turn stated it would be provided "with a view to helping to bring hostilities in Indo-China to a satisfactory conclusion within the forseeable future" and "to bring this long struggle to an early and victorious conclusion."

The additional funds for underwriting Navarre's planned offensive, Dillon concluded in his letter to Bidault, were to be made available "in the conviction that the heroic efforts and sacrifices of France and the Associated States to prevent the engulfment of Southeast Asia by the forces of international Communism, and to permit thereby the emergence of the free and independent states of Cambodia, Laos and Vietnam, are in the interest of the entire free world."[99]

As would be revealed all too soon, well before in fact the deadline for supplemental funding for the Navarre Plan came to pass and all military supplies intended for Navarre had been offloaded in Haiphong for transshipment to his forces in Tonkin, the hoped-for victory in set-piece battle would have already turned to a bitter and decisive defeat at the hands of the Viet Minh.

The "desperate search for the set-piece battle" with the Viet Minh, as Bernard Fall would characterize it, had become "an obsession of the successive French commanders-in-chief in Indochina until the end of the war."[100] This was reflected in Navarre's plan, which to some extent had been influenced by General O'Daniel's strong recommendation during his visits with the French commander-in-chief, and was in turn supported by President Eisenhower, the Joint Chiefs of Staff, and key policy makers who also generally agreed with the more aggressive approach, involving the large-scale force it represented.

General Vo Nguyen Giap, on the other hand, in adjusting his own strategy and tactics after the costly Lang-son campaign in 1951, had made a point of avoiding another such costly set-piece engagement. However, he would deign to risk that again in early 1954 in a bowl-shaped valley in the far northwestern corner of Vietnam some seven miles from the Laotian border, which while of some strategic importance for connecting routes between China, Laos, and Thailand passing through it, had not been given much attention to that point.

Located within the valley was a collection of hamlets serving as the seat of government for this isolated area, and which were known collectively as Dien Bien Phu.[101]

The French forces gathering at Dien Bien Phu under command of General Christian de Castries, with Navarre and Cogny making repeated visits during the months of preparation involved, were confident—overly so—despite inherent disadvantages to the location which, it seems, were obscured by their overconfidence and failure to acknowledge the capabilities the Viet Minh could bring to bear there. What would take place at Dien Bien Phu starting in March 1954, Bernard Fall has noted, "took place in the same hazardous tactical situation and terrain as the costly battle for the pocket of Hoa-Binh, with the sole difference that the French air supply handicap had been lengthened by 200 miles and the enemy's firepower had increased by 300 percent."[102]

The French would come to realize all too soon, once the reality of what they were up against—including the Viet Minh's ability to move artillery into place on high ground above them—dawned on them, that there was no escape from that rice bowl-shaped valley short of suicidal attempts to break out.

Whether or not improvements in the logistical infrastructure in the Red River Delta area had been accomplished to any significant degree in the months following the recommendation made by the Joint Chiefs of Staff to do so is not entirely clear. There was not, in fact, as it turned out, much time left for that, and what funds had been authorized and made available would have been distributed on a priority basis that would not necessarily have included additions of or improvements to piers to which ships would arrive to disgorge their precious cargoes of military supplies. Regardless, the major northern port of Haiphong, and any other areas that could accommodate ocean-going shipping, if only as they lay at anchor in mid-stream or off-shore, and were serviced by barge and lighter, would be kept busy in late 1953 and the first half of 1954. What was to come, as far as the role Haiphong and ships calling there would play, could not have been imagined by most. As the situation grew steadily grimmer while more drastic contingency plans were considered and debated during the closing weeks of the battle, hope still sprung eternal among those who refused to give up on the French and what they represented in the throes of the larger Cold War.

Those facilities, the ships, and the crews who operated them would be put to another kind of use—and test—as hundreds of thousands of Vietnamese refugees, opting to relocate southward following the settlement that ended the French War, made their way by whatever means they could, hauling what belongings they could, to board merchant and naval vessels arriving to transport them away.

5

Passage to Freedom (1954–1955)

"We went up there [Haiphong] and picked up about 3,000 of them. It was a straight shot, and they were all waiting when we got there.

We went right alongside the dock, I recall that. They just walked right aboard. It was all very orderly. They just loaded 'em, and out we went."

—Charles A. Welch, deck engineer, SS *Beauregard*

The Liberty ship *Jose Marti* was in Japan's Inland Passage in August 1954, homeward bound after discharging a cargo of wheat to Hiroshima, when it received orders to change course back to Yokosuka, Japan. Once there it was to fit out for transporting refugees to, as one of her crew put it, "some god-forsaken place in Asia that few [of us] had ever heard of."[1]

The place was Haiphong in northern Vietnam, and *Jose Marti* and her crew were to become part of Task Force 90—code-named Operation Passage to Freedom—which had been formed in the aftermath of the French defeat at Dien Bien Phu, in May 1954, and the final agreement ending hostilities at the Geneva Conference in Switzerland in July.[2]

French commander General Henri Navarre had bragged to an American official in February 1954 that he expected to be able to "inflict a substantial, if not decisive defeat" upon the Viet Minh in the battle shaping up at Dien Bien Phu.[3] But under the leadership of General Vo Nguyen Giap, who would have high ground, numerical advantage, and the determined will of troops as exemplified by the positioning of artillery where the French never dreamed they could be placed, it would be the Viet Minh instead who, in the end, would win the decisive victory over the French at Dien Bien Phu. When all was said and done the overconfident French, underestimating the Viet Minh's capabilities, would leave some 2,000 dead on the Muong Thanh Plain, as another 7,000 were marched off under guard to prison camps some 500 miles away, many perishing en route, and many more in the camps themselves.[4]

Aside from any real prospect of outright military victory, whatever chips for bargaining the French might have hoped to gain as a result of the strategic Navarre Plan were left in the mud around Dien Bien Phu along with their dead. The Geneva Conference and resultant accords would prove a rude awakening for the French, and nothing gained but the end of an era—and its nearly 100-year-long extension of the French Empire into Indochina.

Comprised of more than 100 merchant and naval vessels of various types ranging from large troopships, attack transports, EC2 "Liberty" ships, and C1-type cargo ships, to various types of the smaller landing craft, Task Force 90 was rushed into service for the massive naval evacuation operation that would remain in effect for the 300-day period specified by the Geneva Declaration, and ending in mid–May 1955.[5]

Jose Marti was one of some 25 ships—nearly one quarter of the total task force fleet—crewed by American merchant seamen. Of that number a dozen were privately owned merchant cargo ships of different types, while the remainder—including the big troopships—were USNS-designated vessels of the Navy's Military Sea Transportation Service (MSTS) "nucleus" fleet.[6]

Not designed as a troopship, nor converted beforehand for carrying troops—as many Liberty and Victory-type cargo ships had been during World War II—*Jose Marti* was nonetheless directed to a Yokosuka shipyard for quick conversion to accommodate hundreds of Vietnamese refugees.

After the installation of steel ladders to the lower holds, horseshoe-shaped latrines overhanging the ship's stern, and large cooking kettles on deck, tons of rice were brought aboard *Jose Marti* for the yet undetermined number of refugees who

American merchant seamen were greeted by Vietnamese refugees, as they appear here in Haiphong, waiting in orderly fashion to board ships for the "Passage to Freedom" south in 1954 and 1955 (U.S. Navy).

were to be transported from embarkation points in and near Haiphong to Saigon and other points south of the 17th parallel regrouping line specified by the Geneva Accords.[7]

The Agreement on the Cessation of Hostilities in Vietnam dated July 20, 1954, had called for a "provisional military demarcation line" to be fixed "on either side of which the forces of the two parties shall be regrouped after their withdrawal, the forces of the People's Army of Viet Nam to the north of the line and the forces of the French Union to the south." The agreement further specified that "the period within which the movement of all forces of either party into its regrouping zone on either side of the provisional military demarcation line shall be completed shall not exceed three hundred (300) days from the date of the present Agreement's entry into force."[8] That would give signatory parties to the agreement until the following May to complete their regrouping movements.

In addition to the two zones, north and south, a narrow demilitarized buffer zone not more than five kilometers wide on either side—and which would long thereafter be known simply as the "DMZ"—was established to help "avoid any incidents which might result in the resumption of hostilities." Furthermore, it was stipulated that "all military forces, supplies and equipment" were to be "withdrawn from the demilitarized zone within twenty-five (25) days of the present Agreement's entry into force."[9]

Jose Marti deck engineer Francis Davis recalled years later, "This project of a freighter carrying passengers was aborted since there were so many [refugees], and we became involved in hauling military equipment and vehicles instead. We first took tents for a city of 50,000 from Pusan [Korea] to Saigon for about six months."[10]

Though her intended purpose in the operation had changed, *Jose Marti* would spend those months shuttling between the major northern port of Haiphong and Saigon in the south. "It was only a three-day run to Saigon," Davis recalled, "but there was always a lot of waiting—in Along Bay or in the Saigon River."[11]

Who Boarded the Ships

There were a variety of factors contributing significantly to the number of Vietnamese choosing to make their way south of the 17th parallel in the wake of the Geneva Accords and, therefore, to the number boarding ships of Task Force 90, mostly in Haiphong and the vicinity, but "off the beach" as well, in the closing months of 1954 and early months of 1955. Some factors—fear of reprisal, for example, among those who had fought with the French against the Viet Minh—were understandable and would account for much of the regrouping movement that took place from north to south. An estimated 132,000 French Union troops, at least half of which were described as Vietnamese auxiliaries, made their way south of the line during the 300-day period allowed for in the Geneva Accords. (Between 130,000 and 150,000 southern-based Viet Minh, with family members and administrative cadres, made their way north during this period.[12])

The vast majority of Vietnamese civilians making their way south by whatever means—but mostly by ship—were from Vietnam's Catholic religious minority. While many of them would remain behind—the figure for those leaving is generally put at about half of the Catholic population known to have been in northern Vietnam at that time—many were particularly fearful of reprisal—or of "at least a dim future if they remained"—as a result of their association with the French Union military forces. Pastors from a number of northern parishes, such as those in districts of Phat Diem and Bui Chu Provinces, had organized militias composed of their members and obligated to operate under French command for local defense if called upon to do so.[13] So in this way they were marked as collaborators and were more easily convinced to make their way by whatever means south of the DMZ.

"By planned coincidence": Loading refugees "off the beach"

Not all Vietnamese refugee evacuations to the south were as "neat and orderly" as experienced by many whose ships arrived alongside piers in Haiphong, embarked those assembled with their belongings below, and then got underway again relatively easily. What the crew of USNS *General Brewster* experienced off Van Ly, Bui Chu Province, about halfway into the 300-day re-grouping period specified in the Geneva Accord, is a case in point.[14]

On the moonlit evening of November 30, 1954, out from the fishing village of Van Ly, Bui Chun Province just beyond the three-mile limit, the large French repair ship *Jules Verne* stood along with four French LCMs that had arrived ostensibly for maintenance and repair work. They were soon joined by the USNS *General Brewster*, a civilian-crewed transport of the Navy's Military Sea Transportation Service (MSTS) that was en route from Saigon after having delivered Vietnamese refugees brought down from Haiphong. She arrived, one account suggested, by "planned coincidence" in order to minimize attention and prevent interference by Viet Minh authorities with what was about to take place.[15]

Shortly before the pre-arranged hour the scene on the beaches and waters directly offshore from Van Ly began to be transformed. As Dr. Tom Dooley, a U.S. Navy medical officer then working in temporary refugee camps near Haiphong would later describe it in his published account of those days: "At the escape hour minus ten, the sea was uneasy. On the three-mile stretch of churning water from the ships to the shore there was nothing to be seen but the moonlight, and that was too bright ... too dangerous. Then the escape hour arrived, eight o'clock. Within minutes the sea was a veritable mass of bumboats, barks, and bamboo rafts."[16]

The four shallow-draft French LCMs began moving quickly toward the shore and the thousands of Vietnamese suddenly appeared "on the beach [dragging] their boats across the sands into the tide out to the small French craft which were speedily spreading in toward them." "French and Vietnamese met," Dooley continued, "and the French craft opened their bow doors wide and silently engulfed the refugees, many times raft and all. Then the French craft turned around and raced out to the [*Jules*] *Verne* and [*General*] *Brewster*. They disgorged their loads of pitiful people and returned to pick up more."

According to Dooley's account some 6,000 refugees would be taken aboard the two ships by dawn. "Then [they] set out for Haiphong," he reported. "There they discharged their loads into our camps and returned to Bui Chu for more." After two days and nights, Dooley also recorded, more than 18,000 refugees had been embarked and transported north to Haiphong in this way.[17]

Much of the movement of Vietnamese refugees from Bui Chu, including those who went "over the beach" at Van Ly and others who boarded fishing boats and other small craft, proceeded northward at first to Haiphong and Ha Long Bay below that point, before eventually being taken aboard large transports for the journey down the coast to Cap St. Jacques. This movement was clearly driven to a large extent by fear of active association with the French, while many others were induced by what has been described as "dramatic" and "black" propaganda generated by American special operatives who had arrived in Vietnam almost before the ink was dry on the Geneva Accords.[18]

Movement from north to south was encouraged by American policy makers and covert operatives who not only played up the concept of freedom (*tu do*) in banners that greeted evacuees as they boarded some ships, but also appealed to their Catholic faith—the vast majority of refugees were described as devotees of Catholicism, a minority religion in Vietnam—with leaflets that stated, for example, that "Christ has gone to the south" and "the Virgin Mary has departed from the north." The American psychological warfare operatives were apparently not unwilling to suggest the possibility of nuclear conflagration—such as that used upon the Japanese cities of Hiroshima and Nagasaki scarcely 10 years before—to add to the fears of any Vietnamese, especially those in or near Haiphong, still wavering about whether they would join the exodus southward or not.[19]

As Bernard Fall would put it, "the mass flight was admittedly the result of an extremely intensive, well-conducted, and, in terms of its objective, very successful American psychological warfare operation."[20]

Contemporaneous accounts would describe the movement of civilians to below the 17th parallel as largely spontaneous, but as Chester Cooper, a former CIA operative and White House Indochina policy specialist would later put it, "the vast movement of Catholics to South Vietnam was not spontaneous."[21] Rather, it was driven by the Catholic Church, the French, the Americans, and Bao Dai's prime minister, soon to be installed as president of South Vietnam: the Catholic nationalist and non-communist alternative to Ho Chi Minh, Ngo Dinh Diem. All warned of a loss of religious freedom if they remained in the north.[22]

On August 17, less than a month following the conclusion of the Geneva Conference, and about a week after Task Force 90 Operation Passage to Freedom got underway, the attack transport USS *Menard* (APA 201) became the first of the American ships to embark Vietnamese refugees—some 1,924—and then depart from the vicinity of Haiphong for the south. The second ship to do so was reportedly USS *Montrose*, another attack transport, which departed Haiphong the following day with 2,100 refugees aboard.[23] Francis Davis and the crew of SS *Jose Marti* arrived in Haiphong about two weeks later, after having delivered its load of tents from Pusan, Korea to Saigon.

Not long after the final agreement was reached at Geneva, word began to filter down to American merchant ships then in various locations in Vietnam as to the movement of combatants and civilians within the temporarily designated zones north and south of the 16th parallel. In Saigon "with the Communist threat still hanging heavily over the city," as one maritime labor newspaper would put it for the benefit of its members, representatives from at least four ships—*Alcoa Pioneer*, *Beauregard*, *Seacomet*, and *Steel Admiral*—gathered at the Continental Palace Hotel to discuss the implications of the Geneva Agreement for themselves and other mariners who would be arriving in Vietnam in the future.[24]

At Cat Lai, just downriver from the city, *Beauregard* was in the process of unloading its full load of ammunition intended for the French and their allied forces. The ship's deck engineer, Charles A. Welch, had heard of the scheduled meeting of ships' representatives in Saigon but, because of his involvement in unloading operations, was unable to attend. Nonetheless, his ship, built initially as an attack transport for the Navy during World War II and acquired by Waterman Steamship Company in 1947, was well represented.[25]

The *Beauregard* had loaded cargo at the Naval Ammunition Depot in Leonardo, New Jersey, and then proceeded to Oakland, California, where it arrived in June to top off with additional cargo. From there she would continue to Cat Lai to unload ammunition originally intended for the French. As events unfolded in the wake of Geneva, however, *Beauregard* received orders to put in at Subic Bay in the Philippines, where she would then be outfitted for embarking and accommodating Vietnamese refugees as part of Task Force 90. Cargo holds were fitted with ladders, and one was prepared for food preparation and storage. She then proceeded to Cap St. Jacques (Vung Tau).

Typically for those days *Beauregard* had taken on an armed guard of a dozen Senegalese colonial troops, under command of a French officer, prior to making its way up the river channel from Cap St. Jacques to Cat Lai, a few miles down from Saigon. "We didn't go to any dock," Welch recalled years later, "[but] unloaded in the stream. We spent about three weeks there."[26]

Plans for regrouping within the two designated zones were well underway, and a date for final movements according to Geneva had been specified for the following May, by the time *Beauregard* finished unloading at Cat Lai. While a couple of readily available naval vessels had initially been dispatched from Task Force 90 to commence involvement by the United States in refugee evacuation and relocation, *Beauregard* would become one of the first American merchant ships re-routed for the purpose. Unlike *Jose Marti*, the role of which was changed from transporting refugees to hauling supplies, *Beauregard* would soon begin embarking refugees in Haiphong, possibly becoming the first American merchant ship to arrive there—on September 1, 1954— as part of the operation after re-fitting at Subic Bay for her specific role in support of evacuations.[27]

As Welch explained, "We went [from Cat Lai] to the Philippines [where] we got orders to go and fit out. The Navy did [the work]. [In those] Waterman type ships everybody lived back aft, except myself, the engineers and the mates, and a couple of the stewards and the cooks. Well, one of the problems was [that] they rigged up all those toilets all around [and extending out from] the stern, and that's [near] where the crew slept. And they put waterlines all along the deck."[28]

M.C. Cooper, deck maintenance on the *Beauregard*, recalled later that the ship's number four cargo hatch "was used for stores to cook for [the refugees]. They had a lot of rice—sacks of rice—and canned goods, all kinds of canned meats, and particularly a lot of canned fish. And they put big steam kettles, two of them, after in the number four hatch, and underneath the overhang of the housing, and they hooked those up to the deck steam lines. She had steam winches, so she had a deck steam line."[29]

Cooper also remembered that "jury toilets" had been constructed around the ship's stern: "Just like a horseshoe ... one right after the other, and they were covered, they were real nice, made out of real beautiful timber and everything. But it was hard to get them to use it. Also, they didn't want to go down in those holds. They were afraid we would close [it] on them, close the hatch on them. They were told by the communists that we'd take them out to sea and dump them. That's what I was told by this Catholic priest."[30]

"We went up there [to Haiphong]," Charles Welch recalled, "and picked up I guess about 3,000 of them. It was a straight shot, and they were all waiting when we got there. We went right alongside, I recall that. They just walked right aboard. It was all very orderly. They just loaded 'em, and out we went."[31]

"They'd bring everything they owned," M.C. Cooper would recall years later. "They'd have bicycles and pots and pans, [and] a couple of chickens."[32]

"They were all supposedly Catholics," Charles Welch remembered.

And we brought 'em down, and then we discharged them right by the Majestic Hotel in Saigon. And then the Red Cross made a big to-do and came and gave 'em each a can of evaporated milk. I was never thrilled with the Red Cross, ever since I made the North Africa deal in World War II. They would come and scrounge everything off the ships, and then they'd go up there [to Red Cross station] and they'd sell it [back] to ya. I would never give a nickel to the Red Cross. The Salvation Army, yes, but the Red Cross, they can go [expletive deleted].[33]

Nearly a quarter of the more than 100 American ships participating in Operation Passage to Freedom were crewed by merchant seamen. These included 11 cargo ships under time charter to the MSTS, and 14 of the MSTS "nucleus" ships including the large troopships *General A.W. Brewster, General R.L. Howze, General W.M. Black, Marine Adder,* and *Marine Serpent,* each of which had an overload capacity for carrying 3,000 troops or refugees as the case might be, and an emergency overload capacity for carrying as many as 5,000 to 7,000. They and other ships in the fleet were put to the test in this case, with some embarking numbers well into the "emergency overload" realm.

On one run between Haiphong and Saigon, for example, USNS *Black* carried 5,224 refugees. While referred to as a record number for the operation by some sources, another of the MSTS troopships, USNS *Marine Serpent*—again with a crew largely comprised of merchant seamen—was given credit for a record lift of some 6,289 refugees, who were transported to Saigon in May 1955, the final month of the operation.[34]

During *Marine Adder*'s four-month involvement in the operation, some 14 births were recorded to have taken place on the ship. *Howze* had arrived in Saigon on one occasion, in January 1955, with some 4,300 refugees on board, many of whom were greeted by Cardinal Francis Spellman—the long-serving Catholic Archbishop of New York—who walked the ship's deck after its arrival. By March 1955 *Howze* had transported some 37,315 refugees, and some 38 births were recorded during her several runs between the north and south.[35]

In the first three months of the operation, ships of Task Force 90, Operation Passage to Freedom had transported some 173,311 refugees southward along with thousands of military and other vehicles.[36] In one month alone—September 1954—it was estimated that some 3,000 refugees a day had been transported to the south, initially to Saigon and then, to reduce the bottleneck there, to Cap St. Jacques.

By the end of the 300-day operation the following May, some 587,000 refugees and troops of the French Union had been transported from the north to south, and of these more than 52 percent—a figure put at 310,848 men, women, and children— had been transported in American naval and merchant ships. While the number carried in ships crewed by American merchant seamen would be difficult if not impossible to precisely determine, given that about 20 percent of the ships involved in transporting this number were crewed by merchant seamen, the figure could well be in the range of 60,000 that were carried in vessels manned by American merchant seamen.

As for Francis Davis and the crew of the Liberty ship *Jose Marti*, who had been diverted to Vietnam after delivering wheat to Hiroshima late the previous year, they would spend four months shuttling resettlement cargo between Haiphong and Saigon after delivering an initial load of tents from Pusan to Saigon. "With the exception of getting sniped at steaming up the Saigon River," Davis recalled years later, "my most memorable experiences during that cruise were the several times that we lay at anchor, awaiting berth, in Along Bay outside the port of Haiphong. We spent our off-duty hours skin-diving in the crystal-clear water among the chimney rocks that towered above the bay. These distinctive formations resemble those seen on Chinese scrolls, and were a tourist site during the French presence."[37]

Unsung Workhorses of Task Force 90

While ships such as *Jose Marti* did not receive the attention of others carrying refugees to various destinations in the south—the most compelling stories and images were, quite understandably, those of the refugees themselves—the tents, equipment, medical supplies, foodstuffs, and myriad of other items required for providing temporary shelter, support, and sustenance for those relocated refugee populations was vitally important. Several of the merchant and naval ships involved with Task Force 90 would make run after run, month after month, from north to south and to other areas where those much-needed supplies were manufactured, stock-piled, and made ready for shipment by sea transport.

At least a half-dozen of the smaller, civilian-crewed C1-M-AV1 type ships— diesel-powered and 388 feet in length—were among those workhorse ships that, while not engaged in transporting refugees, hauled precisely those cargoes soon to be giving shape to and delivering supplies for refugee encampments of tens of thousands that were rising around Saigon, Tourane (Da Nang), and Cap St. Jacques (Vung Tau). Notable among these ships, all of which had been built during World War II, were USNS *Fentress*, USNS *Hennepin*, USNS *Herkimer*, USNS *Muskingum*, USNS *Pembina*, and USNS *Captain Arlo L. Olson*.[38]

Probably the first of the C1-M-AV1s to reach Haiphong at the start of Passage to Freedom was USNS *Hennepin*, whose operational history, profiled here, was not untypical. Launched in a Superior, Wisconsin, shipyard in June 1944, and named after a county in Minnesota, *Hennepin* began her career as a U.S. Navy cargo ship (AK) operating in the Pacific before being transferred to the U.S. Army for service, as USAT *Hennepin*, in the immediate postwar period. Then, in 1950 and for the rest of her operational career, *Hennepin*, crewed by merchant seamen, would serve with the

Navy's Military Sea Transportation Service (MSTS), most notably in logistical support of the war in Korea and with refugee evacuation operations in Vietnam.[39]

USNS *Hennepin* was in Yokohama, Japan when, on August 30, 1954—around the same time that SS *Jose Marti* received word to return to Japan to fit out for Task Force 90—she got underway for Haiphong, where she arrived on September 7. *Hennepin* then spent three months shuttling from northern areas of Vietnam to Saigon and Cap St. Jacques. Finally, on December 22, 1954, she departed Cap St. Jacques for Japan, ending at that point her involvement with Passage to Freedom. *Hennepin* would continue to sail between Japan and Korea, and to South—and Southeast Asia—including the Yokohama to Saigon Run between late 1957 and April 1958. Finally, inactivated by the Navy in July 1958, *Hennepin* was transferred to the U.S. Maritime Administration in 1959, and then sold for scrapping in 1960.[40]

While the precise movements of many of the other C1-M-AV1 types with Task Force 90 are not known, those of at least one other involved in the operation besides *Hennepin* have come to light. Arriving much later than *Hennepin* was the USNS *Herkimer*, which departed from Yokohama for Vietnam on November 6, 1954, arriving at Haiphong on November 15. After that she spent the next two months shuttling between the north and south with supplies—but without taking on refugees—making a total of three runs from Haiphong to Cap St. Jacques and Saigon. Then, on January 23, 1955, having completed service with Task Force 90, *Herkimer* departed once again for Japan. However, *Herkimer*'s time in Vietnamese waters was by no means over as she would return again years later, in February 1962, resuming "intermittent" runs to South Vietnam during the later "American" phase of the war. While it's not clear when those runs to Vietnam ended for *Herkimer*, her long service with MSTS—by then renamed Military Sealift Command (MSC)—would finally come to an end in 1973. At that point, as would be the case for other C1-M-AV1s that would continue to fulfill the promise of their original design, *Herkimer* would continue in service with the U.S. Department of the Interior, Trust Territory of the Pacific Islands (TTPI), hauling cargoes and passengers between the islands of Micronesia.[41]

The C1s, and other ships such as the Liberty *Jose Marti* not transporting refugees during Operation Passage to Freedom, were not as high-profile, but were crucial nonetheless in not only providing support for those refugees but for the fledgling nation of South Vietnam and its first president. Those ships would be followed by hundreds of others, making thousands of runs between the United States and South Vietnam during the country's brief lifespan of just under two decades.

Much can be said about the role played by makers of policy, and those who implement the policy in its many forms, diplomatically, and tactically, to bring about change in target areas. In the case of northern Vietnam following Geneva, American covert operatives engaged in psychological operations (psyops) to encourage fearful Vietnamese civilians to leave all behind—including the most important graves of ancestors—to relocate, largely by sea transportation, to the far southern reaches of Vietnam. There, despite expectations of those who had signed the Geneva Accords to reunify Vietnam within two years, a new nation would be created for the express purpose of preventing implementation of those Accords and reunification of Vietnam under a Communist regime under the leadership of Ho Chi Minh. The crucial role played by those manning the ships involved in transporting refugees from north to south, significantly adding to the political base of support of new leadership in the south, would not go unnoticed or unrewarded by those who were the beneficiaries of their efforts.

In 1957, two years after completion of Operation Passage to Freedom, several ships involved in the operation, crewed by American merchant seamen, were awarded the Vietnamese Presidential Unit Citation. By then the nationwide election mandated by the Geneva Accords for bringing the "temporarily" divided nation together again under one duly elected president had come and gone, blocked by those who understood that if actually held it would not go their way. The Republic of Vietnam (South Vietnam) and its first president—created and installed largely through the efforts and with material and economic support of the United States—saw fit to recognize the significant role played by ships operated by its sponsor nation. The role played by these ships and crews in creating a political base of support for the new president in the south should not be underestimated. So, from different standpoints, the awarding of the Presidential Unit Citations was certainly appropriate in giving credit where credit was due.[42]

Of the more than 100 American ships that comprised Task Force 90, Operation Passage to Freedom, 16 ships crewed by merchant seamen were so recognized, including five of the large troop transports of the MSTS "nucleus" fleet: USNS *General A.W. Brewster*, USNS *General R.L. Howze*, USNS *General W.M. Black*, USNS *Marine Adder*, and USNS *Marine Lynx*.

Seven privately owned cargo ships time-chartered to the MSTS, including the Liberty ship *Jose Marti*, which, while homeward bound after delivering wheat to Hiroshima, had been diverted to join Task Force 90 and Operation Passage to Freedom, also received the Presidential Unit Citation.

Also included in the list of ships honored by South Vietnam were four of the smaller C1-M-AV1 cargo ships, all also part of the MSTS "nucleus" fleet, and therefore crewed by American merchant seamen. They were: USNS *Fentress*, USNS *Hennepin*, USNS *Muskingum*, and USNS *Pembina*.

Steering around the Geneva Accords

A revealing assessment of the outcome of the Geneva Conference, as well as a framework for a future course of action by the United States towards Vietnam, was spelled out in a secret policy statement generated by the National Security Council (NSC) on August 20, 1954, as Task Force 90 was just getting underway to transport hundreds of thousands of Vietnamese military personnel and civilians from the northern sector to the southern. NSC 5492/2—"Review of U.S. Policy in the Far East" as it would be known—was created at the urging of Secretary of State John Foster Dulles—himself a member of the NSC—and approved by other key members of the NSC and Eisenhower administration. For what it recommended, most of which would be approved, funded, and put into action, this should be viewed as a key—if not generally known—policy statement that guided Vietnam policy—moved the United States deeper and deeper into the "quagmire" there, as some would put it—for many years to come.[43]

The NSC document called for negotiation of "a Southeast Asia security treaty with the UK, Australia, New Zealand, France, the Philippines, Thailand and, as appropriate, other free South and Southeast Asian countries willing to participate." The organization, the acronym of which would come to be S.E.A.T.O., by which it would be commonly known, would indeed be born, but with signatory nations limited to only two actually from Southeast Asia.

Somewhat shocking was the NSC document's assertion that the proposed new security organization would "not limit the U.S. freedom to use nuclear weapons, or involve a commitment for local defense or for stationing U.S. forces in Southeast Asia."

While the use of nuclear weapons would never be taken off the table, had been considered as an option while the French were being battered by Viet Minh artillery at Dien Bien Phu, and would enter discussions again in later years, they would never be resorted to as a viable option. However, as would become all too well known, the "stationing of U.S. forces in Southeast Asia" was just a matter of time as the number of "advisors" would increase more than sixfold in South Vietnam by the end of 1963, and large-scale units were introduced beginning in early 1965 until more than 500,000 U.S. military personnel would be in-country at its peak by the middle of 1969.

With reference to the "advisory" period of U.S. involvement in the late 1950s and early 1960s, the increased presence of American military advisors—and merchant seamen making their way along the Vietnam Run—and commitment to supply South Vietnam in the years following the French defeat and withdrawal would be reflected in the NSC policy statement of August 1954 that the United States "would continue to provide a limited military assistance and training missions, wherever possible, to the states of Southeast Asia in order to bolster their will to fight, to stabilize legal governments, and to assist them in controlling subversion."[44]

In a telling statement under the heading "Political and Covert Action" the NSC policy document argued that the United States should "conduct covert operations on a large and effective scale in support of the foregoing policies." What most citizens would not learn until the publication of the *Pentagon Papers* more than a decade later was that such operations had already begun, and for the benefit of its newly tapped "non–Communist" alternative to Ho Chi Minh, and its emerging client state in South Vietnam.[45]

"Geneva did not leave two separate states," historian George McTurnan Kahin has noted,

> but, rather two contesting parties within a single national state. These two rivals—the Viet Minh (the Democratic Republic of Vietnam) and the Bao Dai Regime (the State of Vietnam)—each continued after Geneva, just as each had done before, to lay claims to the whole country. The difference was that whereas prior to Geneva the contending parties had sought to enforce their claim through military means, now these agreements had transferred their contest to the political level, with the resolution dependent upon the outcome of the scheduled national elections.[46]

The Last Ship Out

Evacuation of refugees by ship from northern Vietnam—Task Force 90 operations code-named Passage to Freedom—came to an end in mid–May 1955, 300 days after movement southward and to the north of the DMZ had begun as specified by the Geneva Accords. The last American ship to depart with refugees from Haiphong was reportedly the *General A.W. Brewster*, an MSTS transport crewed by civilian merchant seamen. The *Brewster* had made multiple runs between north and south, and had been involved in successful dark-of-night, over-the-beach evacuations from the fishing village of Van Ly, south of Nam Dinh, in late October, loading refugees from French LCMs and transporting them to Haiphong where they would be placed in camps, processed, and given medical treatment before eventually boarding ships again for the voyage south to the Saigon area.

Brewster would return to Haiphong multiple times until, on May 13, 1955, she would be the last American ship to leave Haiphong and the northern zone during the relocation period.

From there she moved first to the Do Son Peninsula to take on more refugees on May 15, and then to the Bay of Lan Ha—down coast from the iconic beauty of Ha Long Bay—before finally departing the area for the south.[47]

But there would be one last ship to depart from Haiphong, on May 15, after the *Brewster*. As Bernard Fall would later describe it, and the significance of that last ship's sailing for the south: "The First Indochina War ended as the last French ship left the outer harbor of Haiphong [and either] by accident or design its name was *Esperance*—Hope."[48]

With choices and policy decisions already having been made as to whether or not the "road map" provided by the Geneva Accords would actually be followed in the near- and long-term aftermath of the First Indochina (French) War, and where and behind whom the United States would put its support in the ongoing context of the Cold War, the seeds of the Second Indochina (American) War were being sown even as—if not before—the last ship pulled away from that pier in Haiphong with its charges of Vietnamese refugees. They would be heading south towards, and despite the clear mandate of Geneva, what would become a newly created country, South Vietnam, under the leadership of America's choice for better or for worse, Ngo Dinh Diem.

Once again, as events were soon to unfold, American merchant seamen would be witness to, reflective by their very presence of, and integral participants in what was to come, drawing the United States deeper and deeper into what would soon come to be referred to as a "quagmire" of its own making, for many years to come, in Vietnam.

The Ships: One Phase to the Next

While the Liberty ship *Jose Marti* is not believed to have called on Vietnam again, at least some members of her former crew, including Francis Davis, certainly did. And several of the other civilian-crewed ships either under contract to or part of the MSTS fleet involved in Task Force 90, Operation Passage to Freedom—including *Beauregard*—would return, in both commercial service, and in support of military operations during the Second Indochina (American) War.

As fate would have it, at least six of the ships crewed by American merchant seamen in Passage to Freedom would return to Vietnam again at different points during the next 20 years. The troopships USNS *Brewster*, *Howze*, and *Black* would later be taken off the European troopship run in support of the American buildup in Vietnam in 1965 and 1966. And *Beauregard*, one of the first American cargo ships to be fully transformed into a new type—the containership—would make regular runs to Vietnam in that capacity in the early 1970s.

The SS *Marine Adder*, later reworked and with her name changed to *Transcolorado*, would complete several voyages to Vietnam with military cargoes throughout the Vietnam War period, and would play an important role in the evacuations of Vietnamese refugees before the final offensive by the North Vietnamese Army (NVA) and ultimate surrender of the South Vietnamese government at the end of April 1975. Charles A. Welch, a seaman who had witnessed the "orderly" manner in which Vietnamese refugees had boarded his ship, *Beauregard*, in Haiphong in late 1954, would return to Vietnam numerous times after that. And when the *Transcolorado* steamed in support of refugee evacuations between Da Nang and Cam Ranh Bay in the final days of the Vietnam War, he would be aboard—now as an assistant engineer—to witness and participate in something that, in contrast to the 1954–55 evacuation experience, would be horrific, desperate, panicked—sometimes under hostile fire—and far from orderly.

Task Force 90 (Passage to Freedom) Evacuation Totals

	French (Air)	French (sea)	USN	Self	Total
Vietnamese (Civilian)	172,783	101,239	293,002	41,328	608,352
French (Civilian)	11,206	26,818	0	0	38,024
Vietnamese military	6,187	37,838	14,868	0	58,893
French Military	23,459	69,080	2,978	0	95,517

Source: Ronald Bruce Frankum, *Operation Passage to Freedom: The United States Navy in Vietnam, 1954–1955* (Lubbock: Texas Tech University Press, 2007).

American Civilian-Crewed Ships Participating in Task Force 90 (Operation Passage to Freedom, 1954–1955)

MSTS "Nucleus" Vessels	Time-Chartered to MSTS
USNS *General Black*	SS *Beauregard*
USNS *General Brewster*	SS *George Culucundis*
USNS *Fentress*	SS *Hawaiian Bear*
USNS *Generalw Howze*	SS *Hurricane*
USNS *Hennepin*	SS *Jose Marti*
USNS *Marine Adder*	SS *Seaborne*
USNS *Marine Lynx*	SS *Sea Splendor*
USNS *Muskingum*	
USNS *Pembina*	

PART TWO

The Second Indochina (American) War

6

Signing on with Diem
(1956–1959)

"If we are not the parents of little Vietnam, then surely we are the god parents. We presided at its birth, we gave assistance to its life, [and] we have helped to shape its future."
—Senator John F. Kennedy, 1956

"His faith is made less of the kindness of the apostles than of the ruthless militancy of the Grand Inquisitor; his view of government less of the constitutional strength of a president of the republic than of the petty tyranny of a tradition-bound mandarin."
—Bernard Fall, *The Two Viet-Nams* (1963)

The nationalist Ngo Dinh Diem returned to Vietnam on June 26, 1954, after having been away from his country during the final years of the war against the French.[1] Waiting for him upon his arrival at Tan Son Nhut Airport in Saigon that day was a crowd of some 500 Vietnamese who were described as largely from the city's Catholic minority community. This made sense since Diem was a devout Catholic himself, from a family whose original conversion to the faith dated well back to the seventeenth century, and it was the Catholic population in and around Saigon who would constitute his political base in the months and years to come.[2]

Making his way from downtown Saigon in what was described as a "battered Citroen" to greet Diem that morning at Tan Son Nhut, and be part of an official American welcoming delegation, was Colonel Edward Lansdale, an experienced special operative who had served with the Office of Strategic Services (OSS) during World War II and was now with the Central Intelligence Agency (CIA).[3] His arrival in Saigon on June 1, 1954, a few weeks ahead of Diem, also signaled the arrival of the Saigon Military Mission (SMM), which had been conceived for the express purpose of advising and supporting Diem as Vietnam's alternative to the popular communist nationalist Ho Chi Minh.[4]

Other members of the SMM were soon to arrive to launch various covert operations in the northern reaches of Vietnam, and cover would be provided for this CIA-operated group by the Military Assistance Advisory Group (MAAG), which had sent its first small group of advisors to Vietnam in 1950.[5]

As Lansdale later described it in a lengthy report that would remain classified for many years: "The SMM was to enter into Vietnam quietly and assist the Vietnamese, rather than the French, in unconventional warfare. The French were to be kept as

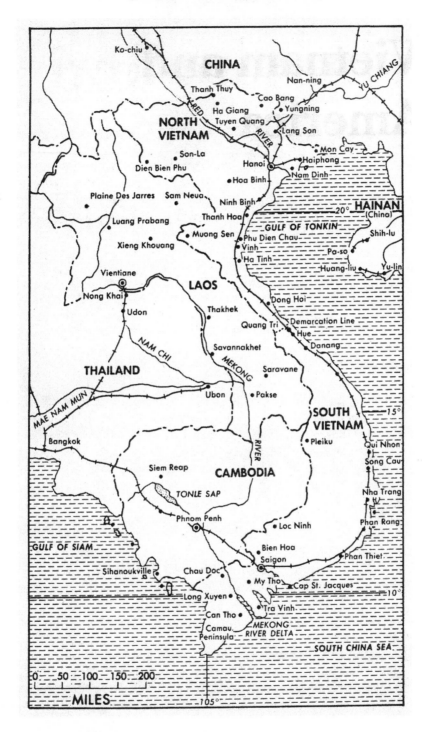

After nationwide elections mandated by Geneva were prevented from taking place in 1956 largely by machinations of the United States, maps such as these showing South Vietnam as a newly created nation became more prevalent. Distributed around 1959 in the transition period following the French defeat, this particular map still indicates the French name, Cap St. Jacques, for the coastal area that would later appear as Vung Tau.

friendly allies in the process, as far as possible." The broad mission of the VMM team furthermore "was to undertake paramilitary operations against the enemy and to wage political-psychological warfare."[6]

The operatives of newly organized SMM teams would, in addition to planning and executing various forms of sabotage in Hanoi and other northern areas prior to the withdrawal from those areas by French and their indigenous allied forces according to terms agreed upon at Geneva, would conduct various "black propaganda" and psychological operations (psyops) to encourage civilians in the northern areas to relocate below the demilitarized zone (DMZ) separating the two relocation zones at the 17th parallel in the south.[7] Within weeks of Diem's arrival in Saigon, merchant and naval vessels of Task Force 90, Operation Passage to Freedom, began arriving in northern port areas to embark and provide transportation southward. During the course of a 300-day period designated by Geneva for relocations, some 600,000 refugees made their way south, mostly by ship, and nearly half that number would be transported by American merchant and naval vessels.[8]

Though the Catholic population in and around Saigon would more than double in the months during which Passage to Freedom operations took place, it would still very much remain a minority population in a Buddhist-dominated country.[9] Therein would lie perhaps the greatest challenge, not only for Diem but for those intent on installing and maintaining him in power as the non-communist alternative to Ho Chi Minh: expanding a narrow, mostly Catholic base of support.

Despite early optimism expressed upon his return to Vietnam after his period of self-imposed exile, it remained to be seen how Diem's predominantly Catholic base in the south would in fact be expanded in order for him to truly represent a viable political majority that would carry him forward. How well Diem, despite his particular personality and style of leadership could and would succeed in reaching out beyond his narrow base to draw others into it, remained to be seen.

The son of a scholar-official, Diem had also risen to the higher ranks of the educated mandarinate ruling class, and had served the emperor Bao Dai in Hue before resigning in protest against French influence upon the court.[10] Diem seems to have avoided collaboration with the Japanese during World War II, though some accounts suggest that he had in fact offered his services to the Japanese. He and an older brother, Khoi, were actually arrested—charged with collaboration—after the Japanese defeat. But while Diem was released, his brother was executed for the charges.[11]

Not wanting to cooperate with French authorities after the Japanese surrender, Diem went into self-imposed exile in 1950, spending some three years between two Maryknoll Catholic seminaries in the United States, and more briefly in France, before returning to Vietnam.[12]

While clearly of another stripe when compared to Diem, the nationalist Ho Chi Minh was also well educated and in some ways a throwback, as Diem himself, to authoritarian rulers typical throughout "Confucian" East Asia. Shortly before Diem was assassinated in 1963, for example, Bernard Fall described him in the following way:

> His faith is made less of the kindness of the Apostles than of the ruthless militancy of the Grand Inquisitor; his view of government less of the constitutional strength of a president of the republic than of the petty tyranny of a tradition-bound mandarin.[13]

However, and in the context of the late twentieth-century Cold War, they were easily perceived and presented, if somewhat misleadingly, as polar opposites. Ho had not only formed the *Vietnam Doc Lap Dong Minh* (Viet Minh) in 1941 to oppose Japanese occupation; he had also cooperated with the United States from his base in Southern China by supplying intelligence and assisting with the rescue of downed American pilots.[14] Ho successfully led the Viet Minh to victory over the French by 1954, thus adding to his popularity and reputation as a nationalist—in contrast to Diem, who had no experience as a leader of nationalist forces.[15]

Diem's appeal to his American supporters and policy makers in those early years of the Cold War was precisely because of his uncompromising anti-communist attitude, which had caused him to resist association with nationalists considered too radical. Diem's brand of nationalism would allow—indeed, would require for his very existence and survival—for the growing presence in his country of yet another Western power, the United States, for the more than nine years he remained in power.[16] And during his time in the United States he had come to know and impress various political and religious leaders, including a young Democratic senator from Massachusetts, John F. Kennedy, and the influential conservative Catholic archbishop Francis Spellman, who befriended Diem and welcomed him as a resident guest at the Maryknoll Seminary in Lakewood, New Jersey.[17] Much of the nearly three years Diem would spend in the United States prior to his return to Vietnam would be spent living either there or in another Maryknoll Seminary in Ossining, New York.[18]

Months later, as a reflection of his support for Diem and interest in the movement of Catholic refugees southward during refugee relocation operations, Spellman would make his way to Saigon and be seen greeting and blessing refugees aboard at least one of the civilian-crewed ships involved in the operation, USNS *General Howze*. As reported a few months after his visit to Saigon:

> In January [1955] Francis Cardinal Spellman boarded [*General*] *Howze* in Saigon as 4,300 refugees prepared to debark. Accompanied by Chaplain J.L. Ramias, the ship's Catholic chaplain, the Cardinal walked about the decks and talked to and blessed the Vietnamese.[19]

It did not take long for Kennedy, Spellman, and other influential American supporters to believe that Diem just might have the right credentials to become the non-communist alternative to Ho Chi Minh that they and others were seeking.[20]

Diem clearly had gained influential supporters in the United States during his years in self-imposed exile there, and this would be manifested in various ways leading up to, and soon after his arrival back in Vietnam. The roles played by Lansdale, the VMM, MAAG, and soon those—including merchant seamen—involved in transporting hundreds of thousands of refugees from the northern areas of Vietnam to the south, was proof enough of that. But for those intent on establishing Diem firmly in power in South Vietnam—despite the mandate of Geneva—more clearly needed to be done to legitimize and ensure that his rule would not only extend to the date agreed upon at Geneva for nationwide elections in Vietnam, but well beyond.[21]

A new regional treaty organization, formally dubbed the Manila Pact but more commonly referred to as the South East Asia Treaty Organization (SEATO), would go a long ways to achieving that end of providing legal and other forms of support for Diem after it was approved by the U.S. Congress in February 1955.[22] And while its eight signatory nations would be limited to only two actually located within

Southeast Asia, it nonetheless would provide what its designers had in mind for it within the context of Cold War policy-making.[23]

As historian Marilyn B. Young would characterize it, U.S. Vietnam policy after Geneva would consist of two "pillars" largely of its own creation: Ngo Dinh Diem as the non-communist alternative to Ho Chi Minh, and SEATO, the regional security arrangement that would enable, with some dubious interpretations of the specific organizational statutes, increased military and material support to flow to its new client state of Vietnam.[24] This would not only provide a legal justification for intervening militarily in support of Diem's Vietnam, but become, as Young has put it, "part of the early definition of such a state, since at the time it was signed there was only one Vietnam [which was] explicitly banned from participation in any military agreement, whose political shape would be determined by elections to be held in 1956."[25]

The creation of SEATO not long after the return of Diem to Vietnam was one thing, and its application for the sake of South Vietnam's viability as a separate entity beyond a reunified Vietnam envisioned by the Geneva Accords, was to be revealed soon enough.

Of immediate concern for the purpose of shoring up Diem's fledgling regime was the condition of the Vietnamese military and police forces under his control and which would be in place by the time the French withdrawal from Vietnam was completed by May 1955.[26]

To that end instructions were issued by the U.S. State Department to the American embassy in Saigon for purposes of establishing a program "for training that number of Vietnamese armed forces necessary to carry out internal security missions."[27] Retired Air Force General J. Lawton Collins was tapped to head up this effort in Vietnam, and was instructed to proceed to Vietnam as the special representative of President Eisenhower. With the rank of ambassador, Collins was given "broad authority to direct, utilize and control all agencies and resources of the U.S. government with respect to Vietnam."[28]

Ceiling limits had been placed by the Geneva Accords on the number of U.S. military personnel allowed to be in-country during this period; the Military Assistance Advisory Group (MAAG) ceiling, for example, was set at its operating number (350) at the time of the signing of the Accords.[29] Monitoring of, and consideration of any adjustments made to these ceiling limits, fell within the purview of the International Control Commission (ICC) established at Geneva. The United States found it increasingly difficult to operate under such ceiling constraints, and ways were soon found to augment the number of military personnel in-country either overtly or covertly, with or without the approval of the ICC.

Despite the public praise bestowed upon Diem as the impressive and best alternative to the communist Ho Chi Minh, not all those sent to Vietnam initially in support of Diem remained, in the face of reality on the ground as they saw it, quite convinced. In fact, General Collins himself, within weeks of his own arrival in-country, had come to the conclusion that Diem "does not have the capacity to unify the divided factions in Vietnam" and should be replaced. Feeling that Diem "lacked good judgement, was unable to work with other men of ability, and was isolated politically," Collins argued in a meeting with President Eisenhower the following April that there would be no viable solution to the situation in Vietnam "as long as Diem remains."[30]

Since the United States had never signed the Geneva Accords, tasking its representative with the uncomfortable task of sitting quietly throughout and without otherwise participating other than "taking note" of the proceedings, and South Vietnam did not even exist as a separate country at that point, both could later claim as a justification for their actions that neither were obligated to abide by them. Nonetheless, when and as possible, the United States would choose, at least in the immediate aftermath of Geneva, to avoid certain situations and implementation of policy that might appear in flagrant violation of the letter if not the spirit of the accords.[31]

It became obvious in light of early U.S. support for both Diem and SEATO that emerging U.S. post–Geneva Vietnam policy would have nothing to do with—indeed would undermine to the extent possible—both the mandated nationwide elections as well as any possibility of allowing that the two zones, one north and one south of the 17th parallel, might eventually choose the life-long nationalist and communist Ho Chi Minh as its sole leader, no matter how popular he might be in having successfully led a war against a western colonial power, France. As one historian would subsequently note, reflecting the opinion of many others, "the 17th parallel was beginning to assume the dimensions of a national boundary rather than the temporary cease-fire line negotiated only two months before at Geneva."[32]

Those in southern Vietnam who might have been looking for a sign after Geneva as to the direction that Diem would take the country had only to wait until August 1, 1954, for that, but it was not what many might have hoped. "Our first great shock came twelve days after the Ceasefire Agreements were signed," recalled Nguyen Huu Tho, then a lawyer in Saigon, some years later. "There was a monster demonstration of gay, cheering people in Saigon, mainly to hail and celebrate the signing of the Geneva Agreements, but resolutions were also passed asking for the immediate release of political and military prisoners, as provided for in the Agreements." The response, added Nguyen Huu Tho, "came in a volley of rifle fire. Several people were injured. That this, the first demonstration in peace and freedom, as we thought, should be brutally suppressed, acted as a cold douche on the most ardent spirits. The same day we set up a Committee of Defense and Peace and the Geneva Agreements, and I was elected president."[33]

American Friends of Vietnam (AFV)

Having consolidated his control by successfully taking on the religious sects and organized crime, Diem silenced many of his in-country and stateside critics who had believed him incapable of achieving what he had, with American military support, achieved by the middle of 1955.[34] By the end of the year an organized pro–Diem lobby, the American Friends of Vietnam (AFV), had been formed in the United States, and would support Diem for as long as he remained in power, and, barring that, for as long as South Vietnam remained viable.[35]

One of the AFV's early members was a first-term senator from the state of Massachusetts, John F. Kennedy. Addressing the organization's convention in June 1956 regarding "America's stake in Vietnam" Kennedy praised the accomplishments of Diem in the two years since his arrival back in Vietnam, saying he had met "firmly with determination the major political and economic crises which had heretofore continually plagued Vietnam."[36] His words regarding Vietnam were reflective of central tenets of containment policy first articulated in the late 1940s, as well a key rationale—the "domino theory"—articulated by those making and otherwise supporting Vietnam policy at the core of which was the need for maintaining South Vietnam as a non-communist bulwark in Southeast Asia. "Vietnam represents," Kennedy argued to his sympathetic AFV audience, "the cornerstone of the free world in Southeast Asia, the keystone in the arch, the finger in the dike. Burma, Thailand, India, Japan, the Philippines and obviously Laos and Cambodia are among those whose security would be threatened if the Red Tide of Communism overflowed into Vietnam."[37]

Not only would nationwide elections never be held, but they would also be preempted by some four months by elections limited to the southern zone only, clearly controlled—rigged, as some would express it—by the Diem regime. When the results of the election were made known, the number of votes for Diem appeared to exceed the number of actual registered voters.[38] The reaction by his supporters in the United States was expectedly positive and effusive for that period of South Vietnam nation-building, and before sentiment eventually turned against Diem both at home and abroad.

"Perhaps no more eloquent testimony to the new state of affairs in Viet-Nam could be counted," declared Assistant Secretary of State Robertson in June 1956, "than the voice of the people themselves as expressed in their free election of last March. At that time the last possible question as to the feeling of the people was erased by an overwhelming majority for President Diem's leadership."[39]

Overwhelming majority, indeed, but anyone actually believing that the people of Vietnam in general—and in the majority—would be content with these particular election results would be surprised soon enough by the growing movement against Diem whose behavior and reaction to any form of dissent would suggest that South Vietnam was anything but "free" and "democratic" but reflected instead an authoritarian reality more typical of traditional East Asian leadership.

By early 1956 the die had been cast—well ahead of the July date set by Geneva for nationwide elections in Vietnam. That would have resulted in an easy win, no doubt—so American intelligence reports suggested—for the communist Ho Chi Minh. And even if that somehow fit into some pre–Cold War notion of "freedom" and "self-determination" for colonial peoples who had been long deprived of these things, it simply could not be allowed to happen in the Cold War context of those times.

Diem, a Catholic in a Buddhist-dominated country, would never be popular much beyond that Catholic base; he had been installed and would remain in power as long as he did because of backing received from foreign and western power. That was deemed largely irrelevant, as lamentable as those facts might have been, by American foreign policy makers.

As an earlier president of the United States was reported to have said regarding support for a particular Central American dictator, "he might be a bastard, but at least he's *our* bastard."[40] That seemed to be the operative attitude as well towards Diem. While there was guarded optimism and hope that he, with American support, might pull it off, his regime grew increasingly dictatorial, repressive against dissent and South Vietnam's Buddhist majority, and removed from any notion of a democratic ideal.

Operation Passage to Freedom was long over, and forces aligned with one side or the other had found their way by various means—and many thousands in American merchant and naval ships—to areas north or south of the temporarily designated parallel and demilitarized zone (DMZ)—as designated by the Geneva Accords. The date for nationwide elections to reunify the country under one leader was mandated for two years hence. Ho Chi Minh's nationalists, who, it was generally believed, would no doubt be the winner in such an election, had bowed to pressure from China and Russia to delay the reunification process; this compromise was difficult to swallow, but the arbitrary division of the country was considered a military expedient that was, according to Geneva's final agreement, only temporary. It didn't, as is all too well known, turn out as those who signed the Accords expected.

Temporary Equipment Recovery Mission (TERM)

While the United States pointed out that since it had not been a signatory to and had only "taken note" of proceedings at Geneva—this argument was put forward most notably as national elections were undermined by the United States with concurrence from Diem, who had every reason to maintain himself in power in South Vietnam—attempts were made otherwise to avoid flagrant violations of the Geneva Accords as possible, and if other means could be employed for achieving the desired ends in any case. Here is where the clandestine operatives, paramilitary activities, and employment of proxies—especially Vietnamese trained covertly or otherwise by American military advisors—would make up much of the difference.

The design, planning, and implementation of such programs as the Temporary Equipment Recovery Mission (TERM), which would involve deployment of American civilian seamen and merchant ships, would prove particularly useful during the early years of the Ngo Dinh Diem regime.[41] Introduced in early 1956 and involving hundreds of additional military personnel on the ground ostensibly for the exclusive purpose of recovering, inventorying, and removing military equipment and rolling stock from the country that had been brought to the French by ship, is a case in point. As its name clearly suggested, this was to be a temporary operation for such things as equipment recovery and activities related to the training of Vietnamese military and police personnel. But its operative parameters appear to have been increasingly ignored without ramification.

To the degree it did live up to its initial stated purpose, and what those who signed off on it might have expected, the involvement of merchant seamen in its implementation would have been central to achieving its objectives.

When the Geneva Conference and Accords formally ended the First Indochina (French) War in Vietnam in July 1954, the number of American advisory personnel in place in Vietnam as part of the Military Advisory Assistance Group (MAAG) was put at 342. This number was expected, under the terms of Geneva, to remain constant or decrease if and when deemed appropriate. But the withdrawal of French forces from Vietnam—something that the president of the newly established Republic of Vietnam insisted be achieved as quickly and fully as possible—resulted in a logistical crisis, putting increased pressure upon an already under-strength MAAG to continue not only its advisory training mission for building an independent South Vietnamese military, but also to manage such things as the task of equipment recovery.[42]

The United States had provided France and the Associate States of Vietnam with vast quantities of military rolling stock—such things as tanks, jeeps, and personnel carriers—as well as weapons and ammunition, some of which first appeared openly on the decks of American cargo ships such as *Steel Rover* soon after the outbreak of war in Korea in 1950.

As per the Pentalateral Agreement of late December 1950, title to such equipment was to revert back to the United States at the conclusion of hostilities in Vietnam. That, of course, came in 1954. Then, in December of that year with the Collins-Ely Agreement, France and the United States formally agreed that they would survey and inventory military equipment of American origin to ascertain which of it should either be returned to the United States, transferred to the South Vietnamese military, or be retained by France.[43]

The South Vietnamese leadership was by then greatly interested in retaining as much military equipment as it could for use against the insurgency in the south, and France, which was faced with the prospect of waging another war, in North Africa, was hopeful of receiving or re-directing as much equipment as possible for its own purposes. The United States, in part to justify the very existence of TERM, expected to load its rightful share of this equipment onto ships for return homeward or to other areas in its vast military base network where they could be put to work.

It was not until February 1956, however, that France finally agreed to enter into a joint inventory of such military equipment with the United States. That same month, and following an earlier refusal by the ICC to support an American plan to increase the size of its advisory contingent in Vietnam—that would have been a violation of agreements coming out of Geneva—a plan was devised by the DOS and DOD to send, on a "temporary" basis and for purposes of equipment recovery and removal, as well as to assist the South Vietnamese in improving its logistics capability. Despite continued opposition, but without any final position taken by the ICC, the plan for a Temporary Equipment Recovery Mission (TERM) was authorized and soon began to take shape for implementation.[44]

In light of the constraints imposed by the Geneva Accords, the plan for implementation of the TERM had taken some finagling. But, by describing the additional 350 members of the mission that would be sent to Vietnam as part of a "temporary" measure and separate from (but still subordinate to) the MAAG, the mission, which would be sent over in increments over a 120-day period, commenced operation in-country in June 1956. There was cautionary advice given, however, by the Department of State, to have the mission appear as legitimate as possible in the eyes of the world. Thus, it was suggested that "training [by TERM personnel] should in no case be allowed to become the single or even the primary duty" of those involved with the mission. And it was expected, a DOS communication further stated, that a significant yet unspecified amount of recovered equipment would actually be shipped out of Vietnam "so as to implement in good faith the promise made to other governments whose benevolent acquiescence to the operation we have obtained."[45]

The increase of American military personnel at this time was not, in the end, "temporary" as it turned out. While TERM did end as an independent mission in 1959—the amount of recovered equipment actually loaded aboard ships and returned to the United States will probably never be known—those added personnel simply became part of the MAAG, bringing the total number of advisors by the end of the year to some 692, with another 48, a reserve for TERM personnel on leave or in transit, presumably still available now for the MAAG.[46]

This had been part of a numbers game of sorts, a ploy to circumvent the Geneva Accords and to add to the advisory personnel regardless of what they might have been called, and into which bucket they had been placed. But that ploy would pale in comparison to what was to come, when the Geneva Conference–mandated nationwide elections, intended to reunify Vietnam under the leadership of that election's winner, were prevented from taking place by the regime of Ngo Dinh Diem, backed by the United States, neither of which, they would point out, had been party to—i.e., had signed—the agreements coming out of the Geneva Conference.

That the Merchant Marine had played a significant role in the equipment recovery program there can be little doubt, though references to it in other historical accounts and official communications are virtually nonexistent. This is not surprising, but that role can be surmised, and should be noted to set the record straight. During times such as this, when a prohibition existed otherwise on the presence of foreign warships in Vietnamese waters, the civilian-crewed ships of the Merchant Marine could always be called upon.

In early 1956, still several months before the mandated nationwide elections were scheduled to take place in Vietnam, all seemed peaceful enough to merchant seamen arriving in the southern port of Saigon. Typical of visits at that time was that experienced by the crew of the Isbrandtsen Line's C-2 *Flying Clipper* (Captain Mountain), which arrived in January and anchored off Cap St. Jacques after a long voyage from New York via the Red Sea and Indian Ocean ports. They waited for enough tide to cross the bar for the northward river transit to Saigon. A pilot came aboard in the early afternoon, anchor was weighed, and the *Flying Clipper* proceeded without incident to Saigon, arriving just after sunset. The scene was described years later by Donald L. Merchant, the ship's third assistant engineer[47]:

> The sides of the river were covered with a dense low growth of foliage growing right into the water. Further up the river large flat areas were dyked off to permit the growing of rice. As we approached Saigon the river traffic increased. Mostly small sampans propelled by a person standing with one oar on a platform in the stern. The oar was held by a short post in the gunwale and was pushed with a rhythmic sculling motion in which a step forward was taken to put the whole body into the propelling stroke. Other vessels on the river were unpowered barges moving along when the tide served, and anchoring near the bank when the tide changed direction.
>
> As Saigon was approached numerous wrecks half out of the water appeared along the river bank, and other derelict small tugs were perched on the levee. These may have been left from the 2nd World War and from the French occupation.
>
> The wharves and warehouses were aligned along the left side of [the] river. On the right side were mooring buoys for vessels working cargo into barges. The right bank was covered with many tiny houses built on pilings right down into the river.
>
> The city of Saigon proper started on the right just after a small river joined the main stream. Most ships were turned around at this point and headed downstream before docking. The ship proceeded slowly past the berths on the flooding tide, dropped the anchor at the turning place, then by backing and filling swung around on the anchor with the bow practically into the houses on the bank. Then the anchor would be picked up again and the vessel would go back down the stream to its assigned berth.

Merchant further recalled that in his early visits to Saigon, beginning with the January 1956 arrival of *Flying Clipper* and continuing later that year in the *Steel Scientist*, an Isthmian Line C-3, a number of ships in port were French.[48]

The Vietnamese had recently achieved their independence but French influence was everywhere. The dock area was well laid [out] with wide spaces between the warehouses and next to the ships. The cargo could move swiftly to and from the vessels.

There were currency restrictions and all foreign money had to be locked up and sealed by the Customs. The agent gave a draw in Vietnamese *dong*. I drew $10 worth, as I remember, and went ashore. I seemed to be able in those days and just out of school, to get by on tiny amounts of money. I caught a bus outside the gate and rode across the bridge by the yacht club and got out near the Majestic Hotel on the river front. A large boulevard with a tree-lined mall ran into the city center. The streets at that time were French named and most had trees planted along them. I went to a movie that was an American western with dubbed in French and Vietnamese subtitles.

The streets were almost deserted from 1 p.m. to 5 p.m. Then the stores opened up again and life picked up. Traffic was not heavy in those days; more bicycles and motor scooters than autos. Tiny French cars made from what looked like corrugated metal [Citroens], ancient trucks, swaybacked from years of overloading, and an occasional fat American car could be seen.

The language barrier was substantial. Most everyone spoke Vietnamese and French but English had not become common as it had in most seaports. The French apparently had educated the Vietnamese to some degree as most everyone I encountered was quite literate in French.

The only military presence in evidence around Saigon was a few members of the Foreign Legion. Some of our stalwart crew met some in a bar, got into some argument and came out second best.

Next I was on the *Steel Scientist* [Capt. Meyer], an Isthmian C-3 that called there June 16, 1956. I believe we loaded rice and sailed within a couple of days. This was one of the last trips Isthmian had ships going eastbound around the world. The next voyage I made to Saigon was on the westbound around the world service. They planned to have a ship in Saigon every two weeks on a regular basis. Three days were usually scheduled but varied according to the cargo.[49]

In August 1958 [and three occasions in 1959] I was there aboard the *Steel Flyer*.[50] We carried mostly manufactured goods from the U.S. and occasionally loaded rubber in Saigon. The company agent at that time was

Societe Fiducare du Vietnam
Union Fianciere D'Extreme Orient
35 Boulevard Charner
Saigon, Viet Nam

The Captain on the *Steel Flyer* was usually Capt. Janiche, and I was 12-4 3rd Assistant and later 1st asst. The tempo of life in Saigon was still relatively quiet, altho the port area was busy.

The river transit and docking went much as before. The edge of the quay was a stone wall carefully made and very flat. There were no fender pilings or camels to keep the ship off and the space between the ship and the wharf would close to nothing when the ship was breasted in tight to hold it against the current. This would effectively restrict the overboard discharge of the generator circulating water. The generators would be running near their limit anyway, first because of the 90 degree river temperature, and also the longshoremen worked so hard it would take all three generators to keep up with the demand. Shortly after docking the vacuum would drop and the lights start to get dim. The engineers would be running around like mad trying to find the problem when someone would remember that we had done this last trip. Then the mate would have to be found, and he also was having problems of his own getting the cargo started, and he in turn would get the deck gang to slack the lines and put out some fenders to hold the ship off the dock. Later Isthmian put huge grader tires aboard their ships to be rigged as fenders before docking.

On the trip in May 1959 there were as passengers three families of missionaries going to do five year hitches in Vietnam. One family [was] going back for the third time.

The voyages to Vietnam of *Flying Clipper*, *Steel Scientist*, and *Steel Flyer* to which Donald Merchant refers occurred in the period immediately following and extending by some three years beyond the date on which nationwide elections were supposed to have been held for reunification of Vietnam under one duly elected president according to terms agreed upon at Geneva. That there would have been few if any attacks upon merchant vessels making their way to and from Saigon in the period leading up to July 1956, when elections were intended to take place, was understandable, in part because those most eager for the elections to take place—clearly Ho Chi Minh and his followers—would have wished to avoid any incidents, including an attack on merchant shipping, that might have undermined the elections. While it's clear United States policy makers never intended for those elections to take place, such an incident might well have been used to further justify the delay or prevention altogether of the elections.

While Ho Chi Minh and the DRV leadership did perhaps retain some expectation that the elections would still be held, despite continuing declarations to the contrary by Diem and his American supporters that neither South Vietnam—which did not actually exist at the time the Geneva Accords were concluded—nor the United States had signed those Accords, they were obliged to see the date come and go before determining a course of action in the aftermath of the failed promise of Geneva for national reunification.[51]

Nonetheless, commencing in 1957—the year following the date for elections—and continuing well into the next year, a series of communications were sent to Diem by the DRV, appealing to his sense of nationalism, and inviting him to work with them for the purpose of national reunification and ridding Vietnam once and for all of foreign interference in their internal affairs.

In one of a series of letters sent to Ngo Dinh Diem from North Vietnamese leadership in the late 1950s, appealing to his nationalist tendencies and suggesting they still retained some hope that he might come around to their point of view for the sake of a reunified country precluding further involvement from the United States, Prime Minister Pham Van Dong began:

"Since the victorious conclusion of the heroic resistance war waged by all our people [against France], all our compatriots, from north to south, have been nurturing the same ardent desire to see peace consolidated and our Fatherland rapidly reunified."

Pham argued that the failure to achieve reunification was due to "the policy of intervention of American imperialism in the southern part of our country" and having "set up the military alliance bloc of SEATO to interfere ever more deeply in the internal affairs of other countries including the southern part of our country."[52]

Diem, with the assistance of the United States, had made it quite clear that he had no intention of stepping down from power in South Vietnam. Pham Van Dong's letter, in which he also pointed specifically to significant airfield, road, and port development for military purposes (whatever he had been told by his operatives on the ground was a far cry from what was to come in the decade to follow) may well have been simply a statement for the historical record, with little real belief that Diem would take it seriously. Indeed, he never even replied to any of these letters.

The Incident at Bien Hoa

The air and logistical support base at Bien Hoa, about 16 miles northeast of Saigon, had first been developed by the French in the early 1950s. Now, in 1959, and after further development more recently with American support for South Vietnam, it may well have been one of the bases to which Pham Van Dong had referred in his letter to Ngo Dinh Diem the year before. This base, regularly receiving truck convoy deliveries of supplies that had been brought to Saigon by merchant ship, was the location of one of the American advisory detachments part of the Military Assistance Advisory Group (MAAG).[53] On a weekly basis for entertainment the detachment of some 13 military advisory personnel would gather together in their mess hall to enjoy one of the latest feature films from the United States. On the evening of July 8, 1959, the men were enjoying *The Tattered Dress* and perhaps a form of favorite libation.[54]

During a brief pause with the lights turned on to switch film reels there was suddenly an outburst of automatic weapons fire coming from the windows of the building. Within a very short space of time two of the American advisors—Major Dale R. Buis and Master Sergeant Chester M. Ovnand—lay dead on the floor, with another advisor wounded. These were the first American advisors killed by enemy action during the Vietnam War.[55]

With the routine of the American advisory detachment clearly established beforehand, quite possibly with help from one of the Vietnamese women who were invited, this raid, also aided by a lax security arrangement for the occasion (including two Vietnamese soldiers who typically watched the movies through the windows), marked a transition, as military historian Ronald Spector has described it, "from the serious yet scattered and sporadic Viet Cong activities of 1958 and early 1959 to a sustained campaign of terrorism and military action which was to increase steadily in size and intensity through the early 1960s."[56]

As the decade came to a close, there were ominous signs as reflected in the attack on Bien Hoa that the stakes of having signed on with Diem were only going to be increasing and more deadly. Ho Chi Minh and his followers had hoped initially that nationwide elections within two years of the Geneva Accords might actually be held, as specified. But that date had come and gone with only "free elections"—in which Diem would win 98.2 percent of the votes cast—held in the southern zone, what American intelligence and others had come to refer to as "Free Vietnam" despite the authoritarian controls clearly having been introduced by Diem.[57]

By the end of the decade, and after efforts to appeal to Diem had been made by DRV leadership for cooperation for the sake of peaceful reunification without interference from the United States, a new phase in the long Vietnam War—as reflected by the attack on Bien Hoa, which had resulted in what are generally considered the first Americans killed by southern Vietnamese insurgents—was about to be unveiled.

A newly elected American president who, as a U.S. senator had declared that the Vietnamese, with American material support, would have to win their struggle for themselves, would soon take the oath of office, declaring that Americans would have to "bear any burden in the pursuit of liberty" around the world. Vietnam was clearly viewed as an important link in the East Asian containment line at which point liberty, as defined in the Cold War context, would be defended against all foes.[58]

Making its way up the river channel from Vung Tau to Saigon early in the term of the new president, crewed by American merchant seamen, and of a type not generally associated with civilian seamen but rather sailors of the U.S. Navy, would be a large ship that had not been in Vietnam before: an aircraft carrier that had seen service as a convoy escort during World War II. Its flight deck was crowded with fixed-wing aircraft and helicopters, many destined for shipment to the base at Bien Hoa upon their arrival in Saigon.[59]

Here again was an example of American merchant seamen arriving as instruments of developing American foreign policy, representing in this case another phase of a war that would soon turn much more deadly, and see many of them—and their ships, including the "escort" or "Jeep" aircraft carriers—made targets of an increasingly determined, more numerous, and well-armed enemy.

7

Kennedy's Burden (1960–1963)

"We have increased our training mission, have increased our logistics support, and are attempting to prevent a communist takeover of Vietnam, which is in accordance with policy."

—John F. Kennedy, 1962

"...the American people do not want to use troops to remove a Communist regime only 90 miles away [in Cuba], how can I ask them to use troops to remove one 9,000 away?"

—John F. Kennedy, 1963

The mangrove swamps and jungle along the river approaches to Saigon were, at least in late 1960, still green. American merchant seamen who had been there before were still using French names, now officially changed to Vietnamese, for places along the way. But at the time of John Fitzgerald Kennedy's election to the American presidency in November 1960, at the age of 43, Vietnam was in transition, the war against a growing insurgency there had taken on a greater sense of urgency, and the green of the mangrove along the Saigon River would soon be turning to shades of black.[1]

Kennedy's election meant, and would soon reveal, that support for the fledgling Republic of South Vietnam and its leader Ngo Dinh Diem, begun scarcely six years before during the Eisenhower administration, would continue. In his inaugural address, delivered in January 1961, Kennedy pledged to "pay any price, bear any burden, meet any hardship, support any friend, oppose any foe, in order to assure the survival and the success of liberty."[2] While his words were generally well received in the Cold War context of the times, and would inspire many Americans to serve and

John F. Kennedy, shown here in 1961, would increase the number of U.S. advisors significantly in South Vietnam during his abbreviated term in office, but evidence suggests he had actually begun the process of their withdrawal within a few months of his assassination in 1963 (Library of Congress).

The USNS *Core*, crewed by merchant seamen, was the first of the World War II–built "escort" or "jeep carriers" that arrived, beginning during the Kennedy administration, for transporting fixed-wing aircraft and helicopters to Vietnam throughout the war (U.S. Navy / Military Sea Transportation Service).

sacrifice for that cause for more than a decade, the extent to which lives would be lost, treasure spent, and burdens borne, was of course subject to interpretation, and political agenda and constraints.

Vietnam had emerged in the aftermath of the First Indochina (French) War as a country divided until nationwide elections could be held and the country reunited again peacefully under one duly elected leader, according to terms of the Geneva Accords. But with Ngo Dinh Diem having been installed with the backing of the United States in the south, the promise of Geneva had gone by the boards.

Following on the lead of the Eisenhower administration, the newly installed Kennedy administration pledged to shoulder a greater burden in support of Diem, and to counter a growing insurgency fueled by the promise of Geneva denied. This commitment translated into a nearly 25-fold increase in the number of American "advisors" in South Vietnam during Kennedy's brief three-year term in office, additional logistical support for growing South Vietnamese military force levels, and a corresponding increase and flow of war materiel. Transportation largely in ships crewed by American merchant seamen for as long as that logistical support was needed.[3]

"No other road to take"

On December 20, 1960, just a month before Kennedy's swearing into office, a coalition of southern-based political and religious organizations, some with communist leadership, and some not, came together at a secret location in the south under the banner of a new organization, the National Liberation Front (NLF) or Front for the Liberation of South Vietnam, with a common objective: to overthrow the Ngo Dinh Diem regime and rid the country once again of foreign—in this case

American—influence. It called for the overthrow "of the camouflaged colonial regime of the American imperialists and the dictatorial power of Ngo Dinh Diem, servant of the Americans" and for the implementation of "a government of national democratic union."[4]

Among those present for the secret gathering at which the NLF was officially launched was Mrs. Nguyen Thi Dinh, herself actively involved in resistance to the Diem regime since 1958, and now not only one of the founders of the new organization but regarded with the rank of general for her military leadership within the growing southern insurgency forces. Mrs. Dinh would later recall of that day:

> I looked at the large popular force and felt overjoyed. The armed units had expanded rapidly. Ben Tre Province now had close to a battalion of adequately armed troops. This was a real battalion, not a "fake" one. As for the strong and large "long-haired" force, I did not even know how many battalions of them there were. From now on, on the road of resisting the Americans and their lackeys, our people would stand firm on the two powerful legs of military and political strength to fight and achieve victory. There was no other road to take.[5]

National Liberation Front may have been the formal name of the fighting force, the name favored by the group's members, but the NLF's target, Ngo Dinh Diem, and those allied with him and his successors—including millions of Americans who would serve in-country in the decade following his demise—preferred to refer to those associated with the new organization as "Viet Cong" (Vietnamese communist).[6]

A Seaman's Recollections

Though shipping moving along the 40-mile channel to and from Saigon was certainly being monitored by military operatives of the National Liberation Front (NLF), the seamen manning the ships still generally considered the transit from the sea a relatively non-threatening and uneventful experience. What stood out in the memory of one seaman, Donald L. Merchant, first engineer in the Isthmian Lines cargo ship *Steel Admiral*, was the challenge of managing groups of enterprising "boarders" who, as the ship entered the port of Saigon, could suddenly appear scrambling over the side of their ship, looking to sell their wares.[7] Merchant, who arrived in Saigon with *Steel Admiral* in December 1960, and again in April 1961, recalled that upon arrival, and while the crew was still in the process of turning the ship to face downriver

> sampans came out from the right side of the river [across from the docking area] and a number of girls came up over the side on bamboo poles. They circulated through the quarters and even into the engine room before we had gotten the engine secured. Later on [at] about 2 a.m., I went down below because of some problem or other and found about six of them curled up on sheets of gasket material spread out under a ventilator on the machine shop floor. They were awaiting their transport home.

"One of them borrowed a flashlight," Merchant recalled, "and signaled into the darkness on the opposite side of the river. Soon a sampan appeared and put a pole with a hook over the side of the ship, and they slipped down it and off into the night. On later trips this practice was stopped as thieves came aboard too, and caused trouble."

While the cargo being delivered to Vietnam in *Steel Admiral* at that time is not known—presumably it was general cargo that included some quantity of military supplies—when Merchant returned to Vietnam again in October 1963, now as chief engineer in another Isthmian Lines ship, *Steel Traveler* (Captain Peter Walsh), it carried "six railroad boxcars on deck, and some drums also on deck for Saigon. The holds were topped off in Okinawa with military cargo for Saigon."

Kennedy never supported the sending of large-scale combat units to Vietnam, and stressed on a number of occasions that it was to the Vietnamese themselves that the burden must rest. "In the final analysis," he said in September 1963, "it is their war. They are the ones who have to win or lose it." Kennedy certainly did increase the amount of support extended to the Vietnamese, and that included a significant increase in the number of American advisory personnel sent to South Vietnam—a 25-fold increase—during his years in office.[8] Within only a few months following Kennedy's inauguration it was announced that military assistance for South Vietnam would be increased.

After General Maxwell Taylor's assessment visit to Vietnam in October 1961, a new effort code-named "Project Beef Up" was launched to further increase training, material, and logistical support for the fortunes of South Vietnam. This would include support for Vietnamese frogmen (Lien Doc Nguoi Nhia) who would be engaged not only in underwater demolition work but such things as merchant ship hull inspections.[9] In Kennedy's first year in office alone the number of American advisers in-country would increase from about 700 to some 11,000.[10]

Organizationally, the Military Assistance Command Vietnam (MACV) was established, replacing the Military Assistance Advisory Group (MAAG), in February 1962, and the Navy's Headquarters Support Activity, Saigon (HSAS) was commissioned in July 1962. Between early 1962 and the end of 1963 U.S. Navy personnel in-country, part of the overall number of American advisers, would rise from 292 to 742.[11] These advisers in particular would be involved with development of infrastructure and security arrangements that would have direct bearing on and potentially benefit merchant ship operations in-country by improving port management, river and port security, and offloading and warehousing of cargo. For seamen who had already been away from home for more than a month by the time they arrived in Saigon, some of those naval personnel would serve a particularly important function: delivering eagerly awaited mail to the ships.[12]

Operation Ranch Hand

As an indication of planned and newly implemented security measures for the shipping channels to Saigon, Operation Ranch Hand was initiated in January 1962 to reduce by chemical defoliant spraying vegetation that might provide close-in cover for VC fighters intent on slowing or sinking ships they knew would provide support for their American-backed adversary.[13] One U.S. naval officer who had served along the rivers during the war later described the eventual impact of defoliation upon mangrove areas thus: "The banks of rivers that were sprayed were often completely denuded of living vegetation. The Long Tau, Saigon's main shipping channel, was a scene of utter desolation. The land on either side stretching back many hundreds of yards, was blackened and bare, as if it had been swept by raging fire."[14]

The crucial importance of logistical support for the South Vietnamese was underscored by President Kennedy at various points during his term in office. At a news conference on February 14, 1962, for example, he provided an overview of the basic nature and rationale of support for South Vietnam, including the role played by logistical operations, the largest share of which was borne, by far, by ships operated by American merchant seamen. In answering one question at the news conference Kennedy noted:

> We have increased our assistance to the [South Vietnamese] government, its logistics, and we have not sent combat troops there, although the training missions ... have been instructed that if they are fired upon they are, of course, to fire back, to protect ourselves, but we have not sent combat troops, in the generally understood sense of the word. We have increased our training mission, and we have increased our logistics support, and we are attempting to prevent a Communist take-over of Vietnam, which is in accordance with a policy ... certainly since 1954, and even before then....[15]

While the number of American advisory personnel increased steadily and significantly during Kennedy's administration, the limits of that commitment seemed, at least to some key policy makers, to have been reached by early October 1963. Following the return of Secretary of Defense McNamara and General Maxwell Taylor, Chairman of the Joint Chiefs of Staff, from Vietnam, where they had gone on a fact-finding and assessment mission between September 25 and October 2, 1963, a recommendation was made in their classified report to actually begin a phased withdrawal of advisory personnel by the end of the year.[16] Providing a mixed review of the situation, the report underscored the belief that while the military campaign against the southern insurgency had "made great progress," that insurgency had strengthened and extended its reach. It also noted that the regime of Ngo Dinh Diem was "becoming increasingly unpopular."[17]

In the October 2, 1963, memorandum to the president, despite positive comments about military progress made against the southern insurgency, McNamara painted a frank and pessimistic picture of Diem and his brother and confidential advisor Nhu, showing little promise for their turn away from an increasingly repressive and authoritarian style of rule. "In essence," the McNamara Report stated, "discontent with the Diem/Nhu regime, which had been widespread just below the surface during recent years, has now become a seething problem. The Buddhist and student crises have precipitated these discontents and given them specific issues. But the problem goes deeply into the personalities, objective, and methods of operation of Diem and Nhu over a long period." The Diem regime had "turned increasingly," the report further noted, "to police methods, particularly secret arrests, that have almost all the bad effects of outright totalitarianism."[18]

The assessment of Viet Cong operations, rather than arguing it had been turned back to any great degree in size and effectiveness, painted a strikingly more alarming picture. It described an enemy that, if anything, was gaining in strength and weaponry; it cited evidence of greater activity not only in the southern delta areas but countrywide. "It should be noted," the report stated in concluding, "that this overall [military] progress is being achieved against a Viet Cong effort that has not yet been seriously reduced in the aggregate, and that is putting up a formidable fight notably in the Delta and key provinces near Saigon. The military indicators are mixed, reflecting greater and more effective GVN effort but also the continued toughness of the fight."[19]

As would soon be revealed in a subsequent classified report to President Kennedy, even the mixed "military indicators" referred to in the McNamara Report were based on false information that made them appear—even as mixed—more positive than they actually were.

Presumably reflecting and supporting the actual intentions of Kennedy at that point, not only for U.S. involvement in the war, but his own political plans for the future—though this remains a topic of some debate, despite the evidence, among historians of the Vietnam War—the McNamara Report made the following recommendations:

"As a start, we believe that a reduction of about 1,000 personnel for which plans have been in preparation since the spring can be carried out before the end of 1963. No further reductions should be made until the requirements of the 1964 campaign become firm."[20]

By the spring of 1963, if not earlier, Diem's attitude towards dissent of any kind, whether targeted at disgruntled veterans, students, or Buddhist monks—any who had taken to the streets or otherwise spoke out against him—was working against efforts by American officials to encourage a more democratic approach by Diem, which would be reflected in a variety of reform measures.[21] But those measures were not to come, and Diem found himself, by May 1963, having to deal with what came to be called the Buddhist Crisis. This continued not only with large demonstrations, but the first in a series of horrific self-immolations by Buddhist monks. That of Thich Quang Duc on June 11 was particularly notable, receiving wide coverage, and provided graphic images that contributed to a growing sense of discontent, both in Vietnam and in the United States, as to the wisdom of further support for Diem.[22]

The recommendation made by the McNamara-Taylor report subsequently became the order spelled out in NSAM 263, a classified action memorandum authorized by Kennedy on October 10, 1963. While approved and distributed to key officials within JFK's administration, the directive specified "that no formal announcement be made of the implementation of plans to withdraw 1,000 U.S. military personnel by the end of 1963." Indeed, while the withdrawal did occur as planned, it was described for public consumption as an "accounting exercise" presumably for political purposes. There seems little doubt that reservations, based on the actual situation on the ground in Vietnam, did exist among Kennedy's key advisers as to whether or not a phased withdrawal made sense at that point.[23]

The withdrawal, the first increment of which would number 1,000 advisors, was intended to correspond with an increased size and capability of the South Vietnamese military. That initial reduction in advisory personnel did take place before the end of the year, bringing the total number down from 16,752 in October to 15,894 by the end of December.[24]

The deaths of Diem and his brother Nhu on November 2, 1963—both assassinated inside an armored personnel carrier by their own military—forced an immediate reassessment of the situation. A major gathering of Kennedy administration officials and advisors in Honolulu, Hawaii, on November 10, 1963, generated additional optimistic statements as to the situation, but other backchannel reports during that period were not so rosy, and contributed to the drafting of another action memorandum that for all intents and purposes, if authorized for implementation, would effectively countermand the earlier action memorandum ordering a continued phased withdrawal.[25]

Kennedy's Vietnam burden ended for him on November 22, 1963, the day he was assassinated while riding in a motorcade in Dallas, Texas. The war then entered a new phase of uncertainty during which fateful decisions would have to be made regarding policy that either continued to support his intentions for withdrawal, or fed into escalation beyond where he had taken it with a significantly increased advisory presence in South Vietnam.

These decisions alone would have great bearing on the role of the American Merchant Marine in the conflict, and whether or not more, fewer, or somewhat the same number of ships crewed by merchant seamen would be making their way along the Vietnam Run, and to what extent seamen would find themselves increasingly in harm's way or not.

Answers to these questions were not long in coming. They would not only suggest in general terms the extent to which the United States would move more directly into the Vietnam "quagmire" and the changing nature of the war on the ground and in the air that might be encountered, but more importantly as far as merchant seamen were concerned what might lie ahead for them as they guided their ships along the winding river channels, and into port areas throughout South Vietnam.

Only four days after Kennedy's death, and but one day following his funeral, the question as to whether his and the country's burden would be picked up and expanded by others, or continue with the phased withdrawal that NSAM 263 had ordered, was answered. On November 26, Kennedy's successor, Lyndon Baines Johnson, signed off on another action memorandum—NSAM 273—that effectively reversed the apparent intentions of Kennedy as reflected in NSAM 263.[26]

While the new action memorandum stated that "the objectives of the United States with respect to the withdrawal of U.S. military personnel remain as stated in the White House statement of October 2, 1963," more pertinent now was the additional declaration that "programs of military and economic assistance should be maintained at such levels that their magnitude and effectiveness in the eyes of the Vietnamese Government do not fall below the levels sustained by the United States in the time of the Diem Government."[27]

McNamara's Memorandum

Soon after the assassination of Diem and Kennedy within a few short weeks of each other, the war entered a new phase of uncertainty during which fateful decisions would be made regarding policy that would either support JFK's apparent intentions for withdrawal, or feed into escalation beyond the point where he had taken it with a significantly increased presence of American advisory personnel during his three short years in office.

Defense Secretary McNamara's memorandum of early October, describing his and General Taylor's impressions of the situation in South Vietnam, and concluding with recommendations that would make their way into Kennedy's action memorandum initiating the first phase of advisory personnel withdrawals, was followed a month after Kennedy's assassination, now for the benefit of Johnson, with an even darker assessment of the situation. It underscored his deepening belief that the war could probably not be won by military means and updated reports on the strength and newly introduced armaments being used by the Viet Cong, weapons that would eventually be used with deadly effect against merchant ships making their way from the sea to Saigon.[28]

McNamara's report characterized the government that had replaced the Diem regime—the Military Revolutionary Committee—in sharply negative terms, concluding that, despite its existence, there was "no organized government in South Vietnam" and "strong leadership and administration procedures [were] lacking [and] Reports were received that province and district chiefs do not act because of the lack of direction and orders."[29]

Poor leadership, suggesting strong and effective replacements were urgently needed, was one thing. The fact that McNamara and others had been basing trend analysis and decision-making on woefully inaccurate and misleading information— reflected in his mission report to the president of early October—was another matter, one which would become a major issue in later years as senior American commanders became accused of putting forth inaccurate or misleading data and war trend information.

"It is abundantly clear," McNamara's December 21 memorandum "for the record" stated, "that statistics received over the past year or more from the GVN officials and reported by the US mission on which we gauged the trend of the war were grossly in error." He went on to say: "Conditions in the Delta and in the areas immediately north of Saigon are more serious now than expected and were probably never as good as reported. The Viet Cong control larger percentages of the population, greater amounts of territory."[30]

McNamara's memorandum provided more detailed information regarding the types of weapons that had begun to appear in the hands of NLF combatants in the south, weapons which increased their firepower against the ARVN and could be used effectively against combatant personnel and rolling stock in coming years, and against merchant shipping and naval craft operating in the southern delta areas.

"Large machine weapons," McNamara's memorandum noted, "such as recoilless rifles, mortars, and anti-aircraft guns, and men trained in their use, have appeared in the delta in recent months. It is not known whether they came through Laos and Cambodia and across the border, down the rivers, or by sea. Large weapons have not [yet] appeared in the northern sectors of South Vietnam."[31]

"Baby Flattops" Make Their Appearance

Along with increased quantities of small arms and ammunition, the basic gear to support a growing advisory presence in Vietnam, chemical defoliants, and such deadly killing concoctions as napalm, the brief years of the Kennedy presidency were also marked by the very visible arrival of what were known during World War II as escort aircraft carriers or "baby flattops"—commonly called "jeep carriers" in later years—bearing the first helicopters and fixed-wing and jet aircraft sent from the United States to South Vietnam.[32] These aircraft were typically accompanied by the units of military personnel who would in some cases fly them off those carriers, maintain them, engage in training Vietnamese in their use and maintenance, and use them otherwise—despite policy directives—in questionable operations in the field.

Crewed almost entirely by merchant seamen as part of the "nucleus fleet" of the Navy's Military Sea Transportation Service (MSTS), these escort carriers first began to appear making their way upriver to Saigon at the end of 1961, within months of Kennedy taking his oath of office. As part of the initial recommendation for additional "advisors" and military equipment for South Vietnam, two helicopter companies were ordered to be deployed to Vietnam. And that would involve the use of the first of the escort carriers. Loaded aboard USNS *Core* (T-AKV-41), the first of the aircraft carriers to be sent to Vietnam, under command of Captain R.C. Sandquist, these helicopter companies were soon on their way for Saigon.[33] The *Core* arrived with its priority cargo—32 Vertol H-21C "Shawnee" helicopters and 400 soldiers of the 57th Transport Company (Fort Lewis) and 8th and 9th Transport Company (Fort Bragg)—on December 11, 1961.[34] Some three months later a photograph of *Core's* arrival in Vietnam was run in a March 1962 issue of *Life* magazine.[35] By the time of the ship's arrival, American minesweepers had also been deployed in-country to make sure as much as possible that the sea approaches for those "jeep carriers" were clear of Viet Cong mines.[36]

Unfortunately, there were mines other than the floating type, namely "limpet" mines, often of local construction, that could be attached directly to a ship's hull. These could and would be used against American ships, and minesweepers could neither detect nor remove them for disposal before their deadly work could be done.

The "jeep carriers" were easy to spot, of course, as something formidable, and with aircraft removed from protective "cocoons" and deployed on deck as they were guided to position at the Saigon quay, represented the commitment that had been made by the young American president to the fortunes of Ngo Dinh Diem and the Republic of Vietnam.

Those ships became prime targets for Viet Cong operatives in the Saigon area, and if merchant ships calling on Saigon in those days might not have generated as much interest in the watchful eyes of the Viet Cong, the large profile and obvious military cargo on display on the ship's flight deck certainly did. It was not long after the arrival of *Core* in Saigon that plans began to be hatched for an attack on the ship or one of her sister ships that began to sail regularly on the Vietnam Run. Across the river from the Saigon quay, the NLF's 65th Special Operations Group kept close tabs on arrivals and departures of American ships, with special interest in the aircraft carriers. Eventually, they would put a plan of attack against one of those ships into action.[37]

Lam Son Nao had worked at the port facility in Saigon long enough to know his way around there quite well. What he knew, including the route through the sewer system to the deepwater quay along the Saigon waterfront, would help prepare the NLF's 65th Special Operations Group with which he had become involved for an attack which, if successful, would strike an important and highly visible blow for the southern insurrectionist cause. The initial target would be the USNS *Core*, returning on a subsequent voyage in part to load and carry out some of a growing number of aircraft that had been damaged during operations against the Viet Cong.[38]

On the evening of December 29, 1963, after planning that had no doubt extended back to the earlier arrival of *Core* to Vietnam, Lam Son Nao and his compatriot Nguyen Van Cay were set to make their way through the sewer system leading directly to the place where USNS *Core* and most of her unsuspecting crew lay quietly at rest. Each of the commandos carried approximately 40 kilograms (88 pounds) of explosive and a detonation device, which they moved, undetected, to the ship they were intent on sinking into the mud of the Saigon River.[39] After placing the "limpet" type mine against the hull of the ship, setting the detonation timer to shortly after 1:00 a.m., they moved back through the sewer system to a secure area from which they could await the explosion they hoped would send the *Core*, perhaps with many of her crew killed and wounded, to rest on the bottom of the river.[40]

They waited longer than they should have, until it was certain that something had gone wrong after all the planning and effort to sink the American ship. So, Lam Son Nao and Nguyen Van Cay retraced their steps to USNS *Core*, retrieved the explosives and detonation devices, and hauled it back to the jump-off point from which they had initially set out. Soon after it was determined that the batteries they had used on the device were defective. For want of properly charged batteries, the operation had failed in its mission.[41]

The *Core* and her crew, having unwittingly dodged much more than a bullet, soon got underway once again for the return voyage to the United States. Commando Nao had in the meantime reported back to his superiors with word of the failed mission; he was advised, apparently without reprimand, to plan a similar attack on another one of the American aircraft carriers as soon as the opportunity arose again, which it was sure to do.

Along with a similar quantity of explosives, and batteries fresh and fully charged this time, they would meet with success against a different but similar "jeep carrier" and a crew upon whom fate would not smile as favorably.

8

"Sealift's Future Termed Assured" (1964)

"I thought the ship was gonna go over because it tilted way over to one side, and then back to the other, then straightened up. And [then] it just settled on the bottom."
—Joseph Houston Forsyth, chief engineer, USNS *Card*

"I feel like a hitchhiker on a Texas highway in the middle of a hailstorm; I can't run, I can't hide, and I can't make it go away."[1]
—President Lyndon B. Johnson

By early 1964 President Lyndon Baines Johnson had come to realize, as he confided to a close advisor, that Vietnam had already become "the biggest damn mess I ever saw." "I don't think it's worth fighting for," he said, "and I don't think we can get out."[2]

If Johnson harbored misgivings about continued and deeper U.S. involvement in the Vietnam War, and the process of withdrawal from it, he nonetheless wasted little time ratcheting up that commitment within only a few days of the assassination of President Kennedy. On November 24, 1963, at his first Vietnam-related meeting with his advisors as president, he made it clear, as Secretary of Defense Robert McNamara would later recall, "that he wanted to win the war, and that, at least in the short run, he wanted priority given to military options."[3]

Two days later, on November 26, NSAM 273 was put into effect, countermanding Kennedy's authorization to initiate withdrawals of American advisors contained in NSAM 263.[4] Johnson had attended few meetings having to do with the situation in Vietnam while Kennedy was president. According to Secretary of Defense McNamara's account of his seven years as a close advisor to both Kennedy and Johnson, the latter "felt more certain than President Kennedy that the loss of South Vietnam [would have] a higher cost than would direct application of U.S. military force for the purpose of preventing that from occurring.... Win the war! That was his message."[5]

Despite whatever trepidation Johnson might have felt about maintaining and increasing militarily commitment to South Vietnam's fortunes, he seemed determined to do so, for all the reasons and rationales defining American Cold War policy following World War II. According to McNamara, he "feared the effect on our allies if the United States appeared unable or unwilling to meet our security obligations. But most of all [he] was convinced that the Soviet and Chinese" posed a serious threat to Southeast Asia. "He saw the takeover of South Vietnam as a step [by them] towards that objective—a break in our containment policy—and he was determined to prevent it."[6]

It has been posited that Johnson "inherited a god-awful mess [in Vietnam] eminently more dangerous than the one Kennedy had inherited from Eisenhower."[7] This suggests that despite the options laid out before him as to how he might proceed, to those of a similar mind—such as McNamara—there was only one viable option available: to proceed forward from a position of strength, providing whatever South Vietnam might need to survive in the face of a "red" tide already inundating areas they wished to defend along the East Asian containment line.

USNS *Card* upon arrival in Saigon in 1964 prior to her fateful encounter with Viet Cong commandos (U.S. Navy / Military Sea Transport Service).

Ultimately, however, what Johnson, insisting as he took over the bloodied reins of presidential leadership from Kennedy that he wanted to win the war, called "the biggest damn mess" he ever saw—and what others would soon be calling America's "quagmire" in Vietnam—was, to a large extent, of his own choosing and making.[8]

In a few short months following his accession to power and authorizing plans for moving forward, the "gloomy situation" in Vietnam, as Secretary of Defense McNamara described it after one of a series of fact-finding missions there in late 1963, would take yet a darker turn for the worse.[9]

Even though McNamara suggested to Johnson as late as March 16, 1964, that the policy "of reducing existing personnel where South Vietnamese are in a position to assume the functions" [to support such expectations[10] of Americans in-country] was "still sound," there was increasingly little at that point.

The assassinations of Diem and his brother Nhu had created a leadership vacuum within the South Vietnamese government, and there were serious repercussions from that which were soon apparent. There were reports of the strengthening—in both a military and political sense—of the southern insurgency.[11] The Viet Cong was extending its control, and appearing better equipped, with more high-powered weapons, many of Chinese origin, than ever before.[12]

McNamara noted in a March 16, 1964, memorandum to the president that "since July 1 [1963] the following items of equipment, not previously encountered in South Vietnam, have been captured from the Viet Cong:

Chicom [Chinese Communist] 75 mm. recoilless rifles.
Chicom heavy machine guns.
U.S. .50 caliber heavy machine guns on Chicom mounts."

"In addition," McNamara noted, "it is clear that the Viet Cong are using Chinese 90 mm rocket launchers and mortars."[13]

While these weapons had been captured during ground operations in southern delta areas, it was just a matter of time before many of them would make their way into the hands of NLF/Viet Cong operatives hoping to slow or more seriously interrupt American merchant and naval shipping along the river approaches to Saigon.

Security Along the Waterways

Security along the waterways in general—whether for deep-draft vessels or otherwise—was clearly viewed as problematic. "As to the waterways," McNamara noted in a memorandum to the president, "the military plans presented in Saigon were unsatisfactory, and a special naval team is being sent at once from Honolulu to determine what more can be done. The whole waterway system is so vast, however, that effective policing may be impossible."[14]

Adding to the alarm, and undercutting any optimism generated by reports of success against the Viet Cong in military engagements, were unsettling revelations that much of what had been presented by the South Vietnamese as factual and reliable in after-action reporting—and had served as the basis for earlier mission reports provided to both Presidents Kennedy and Johnson—had been misleading at best. On December 21, 1963, McNamara reported: "Viet Cong progress has been great during the period since the coup [against Diem] with my best guess being that the situation has in fact been deteriorating in the countryside since July [1963] to a far greater extent than we realized because of our undue dependence on distorted Vietnamese reporting. The Viet Cong now control very high proportions of the people in certain key provinces, particularly those directly south and west of Saigon."[15]

"The situation is very disturbing," McNamara concluded in stark terms. "Current trends, unless reversed in the next 2–3 months, will lead to neutralization at best and more likely to a Communist-controlled state."[16]

Ten days after his March 16 memorandum to the president described a worsening situation in Vietnam, McNamara shared some of his thoughts about Vietnam publicly in a speech delivered at an awards dinner in Washington, D.C. He pointed out that the situation in South Vietnam had "unquestionably worsened" and, reflecting what he had reported earlier to Johnson, he noted that, "given the kind of terrain and the kind of war, information is not always available or reliable."[17]

What he did not mention, however, is that information received from the South Vietnamese, upon which some memoranda to both Kennedy and Johnson had been based, was deliberately and grossly inaccurate. He summed up his speech, in a manner that spoke candidly to anticipated difficulties and length of time that would undoubtedly be involved in supporting South Vietnam against the Viet Cong and those providing them with logistical support, by saying: "The road ahead in Vietnam is going to be long, difficult and frustrating."[18]

Despite the initial withdrawal of advisers from Vietnam in late December, and projections that the number would be reduced further—but not until after the 1964 presidential election campaign was successfully concluded—President Johnson was encouraged to approve go-ahead planning for stepped-up overt and covert countermeasures to meet the growing threat posed by the southern insurgency now clearly receiving significant "external" support from North Vietnam and elsewhere.[19]

In a late January 1964 memorandum to the president, the Joint Chiefs of Staff expressed full support for the policy direction in which Johnson now clearly appeared to be taking the United States in contrast to his predecessor in the White House. "In keeping with the guidance in NSAM 273," their memorandum began, "the [U.S.] must make plain to the enemy our determination to see the Vietnam campaign through.... To do this, we must prepare for whatever level of activity may be required and ... then proceed to take actions as necessary to achieve our purposes surely and promptly."[20]

The Joint Chiefs made their pitch to the president at this time, as would McNamara and others, drawing upon perhaps the most central and widely used of the Cold War concepts relating to East and Southeast Asia, namely that of the "domino theory" that had been clearly articulated since the Eisenhower administration. Warning of the loss of one country after another to communist influence and control, as a line of tipped dominoes, should one country in the area be allowed to "fall" in such a manner, the focus was now clearly on South Vietnam.[21]

"In a broader sense," the Joint Chiefs argued, "the failure of our programs in South Vietnam would have heavy influence on ... Burma, India, Indonesia, Malaya, Japan, Taiwan, The Republic of Korea, and the republic of the Philippines with respect to US durability, resolution, and trustworthiness."[22]

Contained in the same memorandum to President Johnson was an additional warning related to the amount of time that might well be involved in successfully assisting South Vietnam in its fight against the "externally" backed southern insurgency. Their projected timeline could neither have made President Johnson feel any less anxious about the course he had embarked upon, nor made a still war-weary American public feel any more reassured as to where his Vietnam policies might be taking them.

"It would be unrealistic to believe," the Joint Chiefs noted, "that a complete suppression of the insurgency can take place in one or even two years. The British effort in Malaya is a recent example of a counterinsurgency effort which required approximately ten years before the bulk of the rural population was brought under control of the government, the police were able to maintain order, and the armed forces were able to eliminate the guerilla strongholds."[23]

The Joint Chiefs felt that the United States was then operating under "self-imposed restrictions with respect to impeding external aid to the Viet Cong" and argued it "must be prepared to put aside many of [those restrictions] which now limit our efforts, and to undertake bolder actions which may embody greater risks." Among the self-imposed restrictions to which they referred were "keeping the war within the boundaries of South Vietnam, avoiding direct use of US combat forces, and limiting US direction of the campaign to rendering advice to the Government of Vietnam."[24]

The use of tactical nuclear weapons as an option in Vietnam, as had been seriously proposed for helping the French as they were being ground down by the Viet Minh at Dien Bien Phu in 1954, was beginning to enter conversations once again between Johnson and his advisors now 10 years later in 1964. In a long memorandum to the president on March 2 of that year, for example, the Joint Chiefs actually suggested that rather than using conventional weapons as a deterrent against China, should it enter the war with ground forces in support of North Vietnam, "nuclear attacks would have a far greater probability" of success of turning back their incursion.[25]

While nuclear weapons would never be authorized for use in Vietnam, and Johnson continued to resist the lifting of the "self-imposed restrictions" at least in the short term, the use of covert intelligence gathering and sabotage operations moved forward. U.S. military advisory personnel, rather than being reduced in number, would be increased from the 16,000 or so to which Kennedy had taken it to some 23,000 by the end of Johnson's first full year in office.[26] While still modest compared to what was soon to come, logistical support for these advisors and development of the South Vietnamese military required a steady flow—a correspondingly increased flow—of all military supplies, equipment, replacement aircraft, and rolling stock needed to maintain operations against a steadily emboldened and strengthened enemy.

To that end, Secretary of Defense McNamara stated in a March 16, 1964, internal memorandum to the president that the United States was "now trying to help South Vietnam defeat the Viet Cong, supported from the north, by means short of the use of U.S. combat forces." As for operations directly conducted in the north itself, he emphasized that the U.S. "was not acting against North Vietnam except by a very modest covert program operated by South Vietnamese and a few Chinese nationalists."[27]

The "modest covert action" to which McNamara referred in March was actually part of something much larger than his statement suggested. A major "non-attributable" program of covert actions—code-named OPLAN 34-A—had been approved by the Joint Chiefs of Staff the previous September, and involved U.S.-backed sabotage and intelligence gathering operations conducted by South Vietnamese military largely in coastal areas of North Vietnam.

Unbeknownst to the American public until the release of the *Pentagon Papers* in 1971, those covert operations, in addition to the training and supply provided by the U.S., would also involve vessels of the U.S. Navy venturing into North Vietnamese waters—contrary to international agreement—to assist with putting ashore and retrieving teams involved with those operations.

Incidents occurring in the Tonkin Gulf later in the year, and leading to a deeper, large-scale commitment by the United States to the fortunes of South Vietnam, would relate directly to OPLAN 34A operations. But the context that provided for understanding those incidents, putting the onus many would come to believe more directly on U.S. Vietnam policy makers, would be revealed only years after the fact.

The USNS *Card*, a World War II–vintage "baby flattop" escort carrier, was secure at the stone quay in Saigon in the early morning of May 2, 1964, after transiting the Long Tau River without incident the day before. This veteran of Atlantic convoy service during World War II was one of the MSTS "nucleus" ships now calling regularly on Saigon and bringing in much-needed fixed-wing, propeller-driven aircraft and helicopters.[28] As such, she was crewed by civilian merchant seamen, who had signed on the ship through the Port of New Orleans.[29]

While the ship had arrived unscathed, she certainly had not gone unnoticed by the National Liberation Front (Viet Cong) 65th Special Operations Group, who understood the value of striking not only against the cargo these ships carried, but what they represented in general: a recommitment by the United States to the fortunes of South Vietnam.[30]

Though German U-boats had failed to stop the *Card* as her aircraft operated against them during World War II, the ship might still provide, as a stationary target now in Saigon, an opportunity for the Viet Cong to accomplish what German submarines had not.

Lam Son Nao, a member of the NLF 65th Special Operations Group who had previously worked on the docks in Saigon and knew them well, had been involved in a failed attempt to sink USNS *Core*, another escort carrier in Saigon late the previous year.[31] He now made his way again slowly with a small team of sappers through the sewer pipes leading to the deepwater stone pier in Saigon, tasked with placing explosive charges—what were commonly referred to as "limpet" mines—on the USNS *Card*, which had discharged its cargo of helicopters and fighter bombers and back-loaded older helicopters for return to the United States. The charge was placed successfully, with an automatic ignition set to go off some 10 minutes later, at three o'clock in the morning.[32]

Second Mate Raymond Arbon, 45, was on the ship's quarterdeck, making his normal rounds with less than an hour to go before he was scheduled to come off watch.[33] Down below, most of the crew who had not gone ashore were still asleep in their bunks, while a small group of engine department personnel stood their own watch below on the engine room platform.[34]

Suddenly, there was a "blinding flash and a jolting explosion" that threw Arbon to the deck, shaken but unharmed, sending water and debris in all directions. After listing sharply to starboard, then port, the *Card* righted herself quickly then sank to the bottom of the river—48 feet deep at that point—on an even keel.[35] With a draft of some 30 feet, not much more than the ship's flight deck and superstructure would remain visible above the waterline.

Chief engineer Joseph Houston Forsyth, 48, a Texan, had been asleep in his quarters forward and under the navigation bridge when the explosion occurred, throwing him out of his bed. "That's how much of an explosion it was," he later recalled, "and I thought the ship was really gonna go over because it tilted way over to one side, and then went way back over to the other side, and then straightened up. And it just settled on the bottom."[36] Forsyth quickly made his way towards the engine room area and realized that the explosion, whatever the cause, was largely below the waterline and "right away [had] flooded the engine room and damaged all the generators that were used for the light system and all; everything went off. The engine room was flooded." He recalled:

> We tried to go down there to see what damage it was, but they already had about 15 feet of water in there and we couldn't go down. The water was coming up over the boilers now.[37]
> The men in the engine room managed to get out of there right away. I understand that everybody was on the port side at the time, and the explosion happened on the starboard side. So they went right on up the ladder [and] got right out of the engine room right away. It was lucky nobody was in the lower part of the engine room; they were all on the operating Platform.

But there was still the matter of the boilers, and the possibility of an explosion. As Forsyth later explained it: "We were worried about that; that's why we wanted to try to get down into the engine room to see if we could get the fires out in the boilers. But evidently the water came in so fast that it put the fires out. The big danger was [that the] boilers being so hot that we thought maybe they would explode. So we cleared everybody from the danger point of the ship there, and later on we managed to look down there and the boilers were covered with water. So, I mean we were lucky there, that it cooled them off."[38]

If the attack on USNS *Card* reflected the potentially deadly nature of the Vietnam Run at this particular point in time, as well as continued commitment to affect the course of events there, those who called on Saigon and other port areas in-country still experienced the relatively peaceful and routine nature of most voyages, involving delivery of a typically wide variety of cargoes—some of a general nature, some specifically military—carried in by merchant ship.

Donald L. Merchant, an engine department officer who had made his first visit to Vietnam in 1956 in the SS *Steel Scientist* (Isthmian), had returned for the fifth time in February 1964, in the SS *Steel Traveler*, another Isthmian ship. Calling first at Da Nang—still commonly referred to by the French name, Tourane—the ship anchored out in the bay, offloading 2,800 tons of fertilizer into lighters. "On deck," Merchant later recalled, "were locomotives and trucks bound for Saigon. This caused a stability problem and necessitated ballasting fuel tanks with salt water."[39]

In contrast to what those aboard USNS *Card* would experience in Saigon a few months later, Merchant remembered that his stay there in February "was short and … peaceful enough but the only ships in port were American." He would return to Vietnam again later in the year, in October, and once more in *Steel Traveler* (Captain Daniel Spence), calling again initially on Tourane (Da Nang), with "several hundred tons of corn." Many of the crew hoped to go ashore there, but finding there was no launch service, they "launched a [motorized] lifeboat and ran it in to the river, passing an LST unloading cargo on a beach." The men "had a beer in a bar overhanging the river, and came back to the ship. It rained heavily at times and caused concern for the dryness of the corn."

The *Steel Traveler* sailed from Tourane (Da Nang) and proceeded to Cap St. Jacques—later reverting to the Vietnamese name of Vung Tau—at the mouth of the river channel leading to Saigon. At that point, Donald Merchant recalled, "a message was received to jettison 29 drums of nitro cellulose in the deck cargo. We got underway again and ran offshore a ways to get rid of the drums, and returned to the anchorage."[40]

After arrival in Saigon in late October 1964, in time to witness preparations for Vietnamese Independence Day, Merchant and other members of the ship's crew were on hand to see leaflets "dropped from a plane to tell all males of a certain age that they were being conscripted into the armed forces."

Cargo for Saigon included house trailers fitted out as contractors' offices. According to Merchant, "Isthmian often carried farm equipment and knocked-down trucks for International Harvester. There was a small shop near the dock gate set up by IH that could assemble about four trucks at a time."

Donald Merchant would return to Vietnam at least six more times, in *Steel Traveler* and other ships, before the war ended in 1975. As the situation in Vietnam intensified, not all would choose to return again along the Vietnam Run. Jackie Hall, a member of the Seafarers International Union (SIU) who normally shipped out of Detroit on Lakers, decided in early 1964 to go deep-sea. He caught the *Olga* (Sea Tramp) for various destinations in East Asia, including Saigon. On shore leave there he was enjoying a libation in a café when a "bomb"—perhaps a hand grenade—went off, according to a later account, "at a building next door, but it almost meant the end of the road for him."[41]

"Brother Hall isn't taking much comfort," his union newspaper reported, "that he almost ended up as the subject of a one paragraph news story in the papers back home."

Soon after returning with *Olga* to the states, Hall made his way once again to the hiring hall in Detroit to resume shipping out on the Great Lakes. It's not clear that he ever returned to Vietnam, though with the buildup that was to come, and the great need for seamen, he might well have done so.

One thing is clear, however: merchant seamen, thousands of whom would be returning along the Vietnam Run year after year, would increasingly be in harm's way as they and their ships came under direct hostile fire in a variety of deadly forms. As usual, too, they would be subject to the forces of nature, sometimes in an unforgiving way, as they made their way across the Pacific. It was just a matter of time before the first of them "ended up as the subject of a one paragraph news story in the papers back home."

The Tonkin Gulf Incidents

When the next turning point came in the Vietnam War it would be in the waters offshore, involving ships and smaller craft intent on their destruction. In the early afternoon of August 2, 1964, off the southern coast of North Vietnam, six North Vietnamese PT boats set out from the vicinity of the island of Hon Me and commenced torpedo attacks on an American destroyer, USS *Maddox. Maddox* had arrived on station from Keelung, Taiwan a few days before with a new electronic collection van welded on deck, and had begun patrolling off the coast of North Vietnam as part of DeSoto intelligence-gathering and broader covert OPLAN 34A operations. As fate and the long history of war in Vietnam would have it, *Maddox* would be in the crosshairs of some of those PT boats, resulting in an escalated phase of the war.[42]

With the approach of enemy PT boats detected, *Maddox* went to general quarters at 1530 hours, also notifying the carrier task group in the area that it was "being approached by high-speed craft with apparent intention of torpedo attack. Intend to open fire if necessary [for] self defense." Air support was requested, and four F-8E Crusaders were soon sent from USS *Ticonderoga.*[43]

Three of the North Vietnamese boats increased speed to between 30 and 50 knots, and closed quickly off the stern quarter of *Maddox*, which, in turn, fired "warning shots" at the attackers. The first of two torpedoes was fired at *Maddox* by one of the boats, identified as the T-336. One of the attackers was hit by five-inch fire from *Maddox*, and turned for home. As *Maddox* turned, two torpedoes passed harmlessly by. Two other boats then formed up to attack, and T-336 fired a second torpedo, which missed. While passing astern, the commander of T-336 was killed by fire from the destroyer.[44]

The F-8s from *Ticonderoga* engaged the PT boats, leaving one dead in the water, on fire, and sinking. Another, damaged, was taken under tow and removed from the scene. This surface action between *Maddox* and North Vietnamese PT boats lasted a reported 22 minutes. *Maddox* had been hit by one 14.5-millimeter round from T-336, resulting in slight damage—a hole in one gun turret—and no casualties.[45]

The second "incident" in the Tonkin Gulf took place two days after the first, on August 4. But unlike the earlier incident where fast North Vietnamese torpedo boats actually attacked USS *Maddox*, sending torpedoes on their way towards the ship while sustaining heavy damage to themselves and inflicting but one bullet hole to one of the American destroyer's gun directors, the attackers this time—many more of them seeming to appear on a screen before a Navy sonarman—were but phantoms, figments it would eventually be revealed of the sonarman's "overeagerness" combined with electrical weather disturbances.[46]

Maddox commander Captain John J. Herrick, after conducting an onboard investigation including several interviews of ship's crew, would conclude soon after in a report to CINCPAC that "review of action makes many reported contacts appear very doubtful ... freak weather effects and overeager sonarman may have accounted for many reports. No actual sighting by *Maddox*."[47]

Nonetheless, the "incident" as described by an "overeager" sonarman on a dark and stormy night in the Gulf of Tonkin would be used—presented as verified fact despite evidence to the contrary soon after the "incidents" and years later—by U.S. Vietnam policy makers, Secretary of Defense Robert McNamara leading the charge, to quickly push forward authorization for air strikes against North Vietnamese targets and a near-unanimous Congressional resolution to move the United States significantly more deeply into a new and costlier phase of commitment to the Vietnam War.[48]

A resolution "To Promote the Maintenance of International Peace and Security in Southeast Asia" was passed by both houses of Congress on August 7, 1964, just a few days after the second of the Tonkin Gulf incidents. It resolved: "Congress approves and supports the determination of the President as Commander in Chief, to take all necessary measures to repel any armed attack against the forces of the United States and to prevent further aggression."[49]

The sinking of an American escort carrier at dockside in Saigon earlier in the year had not been enough—it received little attention and did not outrage—to force home a Congressional resolution and determination for war-making if President Johnson saw fit to escalate in that direction. But the Tonkin Gulf incidents, resulting in little more damage on the U.S. side than a single bullet hole in a gun turret, and using reports of a second incident that would subsequently be revealed as groundless, would prove to be more than enough to create outrage and produce that resolution in quick order.

It would later be revealed publicly, as classified government communications were made available in *The Pentagon Papers*, that there had been covert provocations and violations of North Vietnam's territorial waters that contributed to attacks—called "unprovoked" at the Time—by their PT boats.[50]

James B. Stockdale, one of the Navy pilots from USS *Ticonderoga* who witnessed the incidents from the air, had this to say afterwards about the second of the two incidents: "No wakes or dark shapes other than those of the destroyers were ever visible to me. [I] had the best seat in the house to watch that event and our destroyers were just shooting at phantom targets—there were no [North Vietnamese] PT boats there ... there was nothing there but black water and American power."[51]

The president would, in turn, use that authority some months later to send in the Marines.

"A most nebulous situation"

The Tonkin Gulf incidents had resulted soon after in a near-unanimous congressional resolution that for all intents and purposes gave President Johnson *carte blanche*—without a formal declaration of war—to use whatever means he deemed necessary for dealing with the developing situation in Vietnam. Whether or not Vietnamese waters fell within the definition of "war zone" was a question now raised and which would need to be answered for purposes of insurance coverage and possible bonus compensation—as was done in previous war zones, most recently in Korea and the Suez Canal Zone—for seamen who would be entering Vietnamese territorial waters going forward.[52]

For those hoping to avoid raising rates charged by shipping companies for coverage of cargoes and assets, and those on the other side hoping to avoid paying those additional charges—which a war zone designation would require—this was a matter needing further discussion while at the same time keeping an eye day by day on the developing situation in Vietnam.

Seamen and officials of various maritime labor organizations were well aware that war zone bonuses had been paid out during World War II and more recently for service in Korea and during the Suez Crisis (1956). They too were monitoring closely developments and would soon enter into discussions as to the implications of Tonkin and further escalations of conflict between South Vietnam and its allies and their adversaries.

For the moment at least there was general agreement that the situation immediately following Tonkin and the resolution was unclear not only as to events on the ground and in Vietnamese waters, but as to future implications of it. One spokesman for the American Institute of Marine Underwriters referred to the crisis as a "most nebulous situation" requiring a wait-and-see attitude.[53] Maritime labor was generally quick to respond patriotically. "In such a time as this," Raymond McKay of the Marine Engineers Beneficial Association, District 2 declared, "the American Merchant Marine is as integral a part of the nation's armed forces as the Army, Navy, Air Force and Marines. The question of hazard pay should be the last thing to be brought up."[54]

Comet versus *American Charger*

Though the number of American military personnel in Vietnam by the middle of 1964 remained below 30,000, discussions regarding the readiness and capability of the Merchant Marine to support an enlarged commitment there had very much entered a new phase. And developments within the Navy's Military Sea Transportation Service (MSTS) suggested a growing reality of "gearing up" for this eventuality, with an eye quite possibly towards Vietnam and its logistical support needs.

By 1964 most of the American merchant ships built during World War II were then or would soon be 20 years old and approaching obsolescence. Some types, such as the Liberty ship (EC2), built in such great numbers during the war, were much slower than the later built Victory ships, and were therefore disappearing more quickly from the postwar commercial shipping routes. Many of these ships would continue in active service for another decade or more, or languish in reserve fleet storage beyond that waiting for breakout for the next national emergency. But a new generation of larger, faster merchant ship types, such as the Mariner (C4-s-1) and Challenger class ships, would in turn be proving to be more commercially viable and also attractive for military logistical support purposes. But even then, in the early and mid–1960s—and certainly by the later years of the decade (with the advent of revolutionary containership designs)—even the newer postwar generation of ships was perceived by some as having design flaws for future, long-term commercial and military service.[55]

Well before 1964, in fact, and while traditional break-bulk, lift-and-lower cargo ships would comprise the heart of American shipping fleets for years to come, design innovations and enhancements for cargo stowing and handling—some that had first appeared decades before—that offered obvious advantages for military and commercial operations were already being introduced. And these innovations, such as the roll-on/roll-off concept of design, were forcing comparisons with more traditional types, even if those were being made for faster runs than the standard World War II type cargo ships.

The emerging and anticipated requirements of a greatly expanded Vietnam sealift gave rise to test exercises that pitted older generation types against more modern designs, displayed the pros and cons, and provided valuable experience in combined naval and Merchant Marine logistical operations that seemed sure to come. These exercises, sometimes involving a few ships, and another more than 100 merchant and naval ship types, would not only provide valuable experience in large-scale convoy and ship-to-shore logistical support operations, the likes of which had not been seen since World War II, but also enable comparison of different ship types with an eye for the future, which was not too far off.

Steel Pike I, a simulated U.S. Marine Corps landing operation in southern Spain in October and November 1964, would provide, as Vice Admiral Glynn R. Donaho, commander of MSTS, would testify less than two years later, "a dress rehearsal for South Vietnam support in the sense that military power was projected into an area with no port facilities."[56]

And prior to Steel Pike I there were two other notable test operations conducted on a much smaller scale, one in 1963 involving two ships, SS *American Charger* and USNS *Comet*, in a trans-Atlantic comparison trial, and another in August 1964 involving just *Comet* in an exercise simulating wartime blackout conditions. These exercises would all provide valuable experience for actual application within a few short years in Vietnam.

Prior to Steel Pike a competitive exercise in 1963 involved two merchant ships of markedly different type, USNS *Comet*, a prototype roll-on/roll-off ship launched in 1957, and SS *American Charger*, a fast Challenger-class freighter launched into service in 1963 and, in comparison to *Comet*, of traditional—lift-on/lift-off—design when it came to loading and unloading cargo. Whereas USNS *Comet* became part of the MSTS nucleus fleet, SS *American Challenger* entered commercial service. As would become increasingly evident in the 1960s, and particularly in Vietnam, they represented differences that underscored the need for increased availability of the one type, and drawbacks of the other that ultimately doomed their continued use in the face of a more revolutionary and efficient ship design, the containership.

The exercise involving *Comet* and *American Charger* was proposed in 1963 by the United States Lines, and would take place in cooperation with the U.S. Army. Cargoes including tanks, ammunition trailers, and other vehicles would be loaded at Hampton Roads, Virginia, and transported to Bremerhaven, Germany for distribution to U.S. forces in the area. *Comet* and *American Charger* would race in two trans-Atlantic voyages and then offload, first at dockside, and then, on the second run, into lighters offshore.[57]

For the first voyage, roll-on/roll-off type *Comet* loaded 297 vehicles of 7,953 measurement tons, and subsequently unloaded that in Bremerhaven in just two hours and 23 minutes. *American Charger*, on the other hand, while making the run across in much less time—five days compared to seven—took seven hours and 11 minutes to unload her 6,773-measurement ton lift of 186 vehicles.[58]

On her second voyage *Comet* discharged 336 vehicles of 7,700 measurement tons into lighters, despite two delays involving lift-on/lift-off gear at two cargo hatches, in three hours and 26 minutes. *American Charger* offloaded 191 vehicles of 6,609 measurement tons in six hours and 41 minutes.[59]

The at-sea differential between the two ships was significant—*American Charger* crossed in five days at a record speed of 25 knots, while *Comet* clocked 19 knots (one knot over her design speed) in a seven-day crossing—but discharging was accomplished in considerably less time by the roll-on/roll-off vessel. The merits of each ship would be the subject of much discussion for some time to come. In assessing the USNS *Comet*'s performance Brigadier General William N. Redling, Commander, U.S. Army Transportation, Europe, said that there was "no question that we need this type of ship."[60] But he also pointed out the speed of both passage and cargo handling of the two types of ships.

Placing emphasis on the side of *Comet*, Admiral Gano argued: "The speed a ship travels in wartime is not as important as the speed with which it can unload its cargo at a beach. It would be protected by convoy in crossing the ocean and would be regulated by convoy speed."[61]

Captain John Le Cato, chief mate on USNS *Comet* during these exercises and later service as master of the ship for multiple runs to Vietnam, recalled his interactions with Captain Jones F. Devlin, then operations manager for U.S. Lines during these exercises. "Captain Devlin took a personal interest in the competition," said Le Cato, "which at times became somewhat warmer than just friendly rivalry, and I saw a good deal of him during cargo operations. [Later] I sent him a picture showing *Comet* 'rolling off' vehicles [in Cam Ranh Bay, South Vietnam] while a dozen or so conventional ships idled at anchor. I wrote across it 'Where's your goddam *Challenger* now?' Unfortunately, I never received an answer."[62]

Operation Blackout

USNS *Comet* was involved in another exercise, again between Hampton Roads and Bremerhaven, in August 1964, and only in competition with herself and arranged light conditions. Code-named Operation Blackout, the exercise was designed to evaluate how the ship would perform under simulated wartime blackout conditions while loading and offloading. Without normal illumination, *Comet* used only "small, shaded low intensity lights known as 'cats eyes,' luminous masking tape placed on the three decks of the ship used for vehicle storage, and battery-powered wands to guide drivers on the ship."[63]

Comet was loaded in Hampton Roads in three hours and three minutes, and unloading was accomplished in one hour and 21 minutes. Summing up the success of the operation afterwards, an Army officer noted: "[It] proves conclusively that the USNS *Comet* possesses a unique capability. She can enter a combat area port under complete blackout conditions, discharge cargo and clear port before daylight. This capability is vitally important because it reduces the vulnerability of the vessel and her cargo to enemy attack."[64]

While it's not clear whether or not *Comet* ever discharged under actual blackout conditions later in Vietnam, something could still be said for minimizing the amount of time ship and crew spent in a port that was subject to periodic rocket attacks. Some merchant seamen would come to understand that only too well.

Steel Pike I

The entire Second Marine Division—except for a few "ash and trash" units, as one Marine participant in the operation would put it—were moving out from Camp Lejeune, North Carolina, to board transports that would carry them, in convoy, to Europe. To some onlookers, the movement of Marines to Europe in such a way might have appeared unusual in late 1964. The Atlantic convoys—merchant ships with naval escorts—had ended with the defeat of Germany in 1945. And the last of the major amphibious landings—that of Southern France—had taken place the year before that. Now, in October and November 1964, Atlantic convoys—three of them, and with appropriate naval escorts—were in progress as a prelude to another amphibious landing operation, this time in the region of Huelva along the southern coast of Spain. But those convoys and invasion were to be of the "mock" variety, as some accounts described them, part of a 44-day peacetime exercise, the largest in history to that point: Operation Steel Pike I.[65]

Some 28,000 U.S. Marines and additional Spanish units—totaling some 30,000—would be moved into place and given logistical support by a combined naval and merchant fleet numbering some 130 ships and additional landing craft of various types and sizes. Some 17 of those ships—privately owned commercial cargo ships under contract to the Military Sea Transportation Service (MSTS), "nucleus" transport and cargo ships of the MSTS, and additional government-owned merchant types under General Agency Agreement (GAA)—would be crewed by American merchant seamen.[66]

Following by some two months the Gulf of Tonkin incidents and resultant congressional resolution, the seemingly unrelated amphibious landing exercise in Europe would, in fact, provide valuable experience and spotlight the use of a new postwar generation of merchant ship types that would, in fact, soon be inserted into the Vietnam logistical supply pipeline in less than a year. So too would World War II–vintage troop and cargo ships, designed for postwar use, receive valuable experience as integral components, along with naval warship types, in this exercise.

In testimony before the House Subcommittee on Merchant Marine in March

1966, Vice Admiral Glynn R. Donaho, MSTS commander, summed up Steel Pike relative to the Vietnam sealift, in this manner: "The success of the exercise was to some degree due to the high percentage of late merchant ship construction supporting the transit to and from the objective area. Exercise Steel Pike was, to some extent, a dress rehearsal for South Vietnam support in the sense that military power was projected into an area with no port facilities." Specifically, ships that would be identified later as fulfilling Steel Pike I requirements would be those "rated at 16 knots or better, and having at least one boom capable of making a 50-ton lift or better."[67]

"Experience in exercise Steel Pike proved conclusively," Donaho also pointed out, "that the improved cargo handling gear and greater capacity of the more modern U.S.-registered merchant ships made it possible to accomplish the movement of the Second Marine Division to Spain using only about two-thirds of the number of ships that would have been required using World War II shipping. This same advantage would apply to South Vietnam sealift support."[68]

When asked what specific improvements to ships would be particularly useful in future logistical support operations, Donaho replied: "Based upon the experience coming out of Steel Pike, heavier equipment, more generator capability, larger hatches, automatic hatch cover lifts and other sophisticated equipment, if I may say sophisticated, including automation, as in some of the newer ships."[69]

Among the more than 100 ships participating in Operation Steel Pike I were the following crewed by American merchant seamen:

Privately owned and operated: *Export Bay*, *Export Buyer* (American Export Isbrandtsen), *Del Sol* (Delta), *Christopher Lykes* (Lykes Bros.), *Mormacargo*, *Mormacscan* (Moore McCormack), *American Contender*, *Pioneer Moon* (US Lines), *Smith Victory* (E.J. Smith & Co.) (unsubsidized), *Couer d'Alene* (Victory Carriers) (unsubsidized).

Government-owned and operated by the MSTS: USNS *General Blatchford*, USNS *General Gordon*, USNS *General Geiger*, USNS *McGraw* (Victory type), USNS *Boyce* (Victory type), USNS *Crain* (Victory type), USNS *Greenville Victory*, USNS *Pioneer Valley* (T-2).[70]

Many of these ships, it turned out, would make their presence known in the coming years in Vietnam.

There was little optimism expressed in the closing months of 1964, except at times in public, about the situation in Vietnam and prospects for the future. Early in the year President Johnson had revealed, in private, his belief that the war there probably could not be won, yet he felt that there was no turning back. And various reports of a failing counterinsurgency campaign that had become "bogged down" along with growing Viet Cong strength and control of areas in the south only added to his pessimism as the year came to a close.[71]

Nonetheless, contingency planning for retaliatory air strikes and an increased American military presence to counter the Viet Cong—perceived now to be receiving greater support from the north—continued to be prepared and communicated to the president. One classified report, submitted by Maxwell Taylor after his return from Vietnam in November, read, in part: "If, as the evidence shows, we are playing a losing game in South Vietnam, it is high time we change and find a better way."[72]

"Without an effective central government with which to mesh the US effort," Taylor argued, pulling no punches, "the latter is a spinning wheel unable to transmit impulsion to the machinery of GVN." And his assessment of the Viet Cong itself, notably its "recuperative ability," would have been no less alarming: "Not only do the Viet Cong units have the recuperative powers of the phoenix," he wrote, "but they have an amazing ability to maintain morale."[73]

With the prospects of ultimate success in Vietnam not considered to be good by many analysts viewing the situation by the end of the year, some advisors to Johnson had prepared, just in case, a "fall-back objective" that could be used in the event of further setbacks. It would be important, a draft position paper of November 26 explained, "to make clear to the world, and to nations in Asia particularly, that failure in South Vietnam, if it comes, was due to special factors—such as a bad colonial heritage and a lack of will to defend itself—that do not apply to other nations."[74]

Nonetheless, planning and preparations continued for moving forward when and if word came down to more aggressively pursue military options. Any stepped-up posture would require matching sea logistical support. Steel Pike I had combined many ships—merchant and naval types—that would eventually be deployed to Vietnam. This had included two civilian-crewed troopships—USNS *General Blatchford* and USNS *Gordon*—that had both been withdrawn from reserve fleets not long after the Gulf of Tonkin incidents and resolution, and readied for renewed service. And while the need to tap into the NDRFs for government-owned merchant ships that would be chartered to private shipping companies under general agency agreement (GAA) had not yet come, two ships had actually been withdrawn from reserve fleets in December—without fanfare—for that purpose.[75]

It would take further developments on the ground, and a major decision to introduce large-scale combat units for the first time, before any corresponding decision was made to break out large numbers of cargo ships from reserve fleets to support such a major increase in ground forces.

A classified planning memorandum had been prepared and circulated by the Joint Chiefs of Staff in November that, if approved by the president and subsequently implemented, would raise the stakes in Vietnam beyond the "advisory" level commitment and, by so doing, drastically impact decision making regarding sea logistical support for American-led military operations in Vietnam.

In his November 14 memorandum, General Earl G. Wheeler, writing for the Joint Chiefs, argued: "Prior to air attacks on the DRV [North Vietnam], [we should] land the Marine special landing force at Da Nang and airlift Army or Marine units from Okinawa to the Saigon/Tan Son Nhut/Bien Hoa area, to provide increased security for US personnel and installations."[76]

Less than four months later, in March 1965, and very much following the letter and spirit of Wheeler's proposed plan, the Third Marine Expeditionary Force would go ashore in Da Nang "to provide security" for the main airport there. The first elements of the Army's First Cavalry Division would not be far behind, arriving at Saigon and other points in troopships operated by American merchant seamen.

The commander of MSTS had had high praise for the role of the Merchant Marine in the Steel Pike I operation and combined exercise between the U.S. Navy and Spanish units that ended in early November. But in comments before the Washington, D.C. Propeller Club on November 24 an issue was also raised that was then and continued to be argued in the coming year: the relative merits of sea versus air transport. Inflamed by comments by Secretary of Defense McNamara that air would supersede sea logistical support by a significant measure, Vice Admiral Glynn R. Donaho reassured those assembled that "the new emphasis on airlift for deploying forces in no way subtracts from the true importance of sealift—except for troops in certain specialized cases." Airlifting would serve to a lesser extent in combination with sea logistical support, Donaho remarked, but would not "preclude the requirement for sealifting over great distances the bulk of their heavier equipment and backup supplies."[77]

With reference to the attitude of Defense Secretary McNamara regarding airlift potential, a not untypical criticism was expressed by Congressman James R. Grover of New York at a later hearing into Vietnam shipping policies: "I think when we [speak of] future airlift we are in never-never-McNamara land of big dreams ... he is going to take hundreds of thousands of troops aboard these big airplanes which will never be built."[78]

This debate—which would sometimes result in heated exchanges between those arguing positions on either side—would rear its head in the coming year when, in the end, the vast majority of supplies required to support a rapidly growing American military presence in Vietnam—a figure usually put at or above 95 percent of the total—would make its way to theater by ship. And in the early years of that massive buildup, the majority of troops—a figure usually put in excess of 60 percent—would also be transported by ship.

In reporting Admiral Donaho's remarks before the Propeller Club, *The New York Times* headline read: "Sealift's Future Termed Assured."[79]

The years of dramatically increased logistical support to come for the war in Vietnam would prove that in no uncertain terms.

9

Breakout (1965)

"Defense Secretary McNamara's position that aircraft can replace ships in large scale military operations would seem to be knocked into a cocked hat."
—Morris Weisberger, president, Sailors' Union of the Pacific

"We sighted Cap St. Jacjues at the entrance to the Saigon River and radioed for a pilot. No answer. Proceeding further we saw why: the entrance was jammed with ships at anchor, there must have been at least 30 of them waiting to go upriver to Saigon. We selected a good spot clear of other ships, and reconciled ourselves to a good long wait."
—Paul J. Cogger, second mate, SS *Citadel Victory*

If Lyndon Johnson had held serious misgivings about the situation in Vietnam early in his presidency, events following the Gulf of Tonkin incidents in late 1964 would not have made him feel any more optimistic or less frustrated. As he and his advisors had moved Vietnam policy forward, authorizing retaliatory air strikes and stepped-up covert operations against North Vietnam, so had the southern insurgents—the National Liberation Front (NLF)—increasingly backed by North Vietnam, appeared stronger, more numerous, and better equipped—been striking back more boldly and successfully, both against South Vietnamese military targets as well as American military installations.[1] An American BOQ (Bachelor Officers Quarters) had been bombed in Saigon in late December 1964, killing two officers and wounding 58 others, and other attacks in early 1965—on an American advisors' barracks in Pleiku, helicopters at Camp Holloway near there in February, and the bombing of the U.S. embassy in Saigon in March—forced discussions of retaliatory strikes not only against targets in the south but the north as well.[2] The first of the Flaming Dart reprisal strikes began one day after the attacks on Pleiku, and Rolling Thunder—sustained bombing against the north—would begin in early March of that year.[3]

Johnson was extremely concerned about the instability of the South Vietnamese government, which, also in the early months of 1965, experienced a series of military coups d'etat. He vented his frustration at one point before a group of advisors, saying he was "sick and tired of this Goddam coup shit in Vietnam; it's got to stop."[4]

Adding to his and others' discontent were more images of Buddhist and student protests—notably in such places as Hue, Dalat, Da Nang, and Saigon—following announcement of new draft calls to replenish losses due to engagements of the ARVN (Army of the Republic of Vietnam) in the field, and desertions, which were on the rise.[5]

But, despite the misgivings, planning for an increased commitment to the fortunes of South Vietnam continued and, as noted, retaliatory airstrikes had begun in February and evolved into more sustained attacks of the north the following month. Since the primary airfield supporting these strikes was located in the northern port city of Da Nang, the need for increased security in and around the area was proposed, quickly authorized, and then followed in March by the landings of two Marine battalions— about 3,500 Marines—in Da Nang, the first of many more large-scale combat units to arrive in South Vietnam before the year was out.[6]

The shift from a more limited "advisory" presence to a major increase in force levels—amounting to just under 200,000 by the end of the year—required a corresponding increase in sea logistical support which the then operational fleet of the American Merchant Marine and the MSTS "nucleus" fleet of transports, tankers, and supply ships could not provide.[7]

The *Albion Victory*, one of scores of Victory ships withdrawn from National Defense Reserve Fleets in 1965 and 1966, is seen here getting work done at Pier 44, Brooklyn, New York, prior to moving to a loading berth to take on cargo for an initial voyage along the Vietnam Run (Maritime Administration).

By the early summer of 1965 something had to give, something more had to be done, to supplement the active fleet of merchant and naval ships being called upon to support a rapidly escalating war in Vietnam. Much had already been done in a relatively low-key manner—with little publicity and fanfare—within the atmosphere of "business as usual" that had initially been adopted in response to the emergency.

The civilian-crewed USNS *Comet*, a roll-on/roll-off type ship in service with MSTS, became one of the first ships ordered to support the buildup phase in Vietnam following the landing of Marines in Da Nang in March. John M. Le Cato, then first mate of the ship, recalled years later how and when that came about, and what was initially encountered upon arriving in-country some weeks later.

In May 1965 [the ship] … was undergoing a leisurely overhaul in Brooklyn. With very little warning, we had the repairs rushed to completion and loaded out for Vietnam. Cargo included the first LARCS (amphibious vehicles) shipped from the states. We carried twelve army men to service the vehicles and instruct the troops in their use. Our first port was Da Nang where we were met by a rather unconcerned naval representative who promised us several weeks at anchor before berth space would be available. While he was telling this to the Master, I had my deck crew opening the stern ramp and in about a half hour, the LARCs destined for Da Nang were heading for shore with the cargo for that post and we heaved up [the anchor] and headed for our next port, Qui Nhon.[8]

American shipping companies had responded to the call, providing additional ships from their respective fleets to assist the MSTS with full or partial ship loads of military cargoes.[9] Within the MSTS "nucleus" fleet itself, six USNS-designated troop transports regularly making the run between New York and Bremerhaven, Germany were shifted—somewhat quietly again—for use in the Pacific. These largely civilian-crewed transports, constructed during World War II in two basic types, were the 533'9" C4-type transport USNS *General Geiger,* capable of carrying about 2,500 troops, and the 608'11" P2 types USNS *General Darby,* USNS *General Maurice Rose,* USNS *General Alexander M. Patch,* USNS *General W.H. Gordon,* and USNS *General Simon B. Buckner,* which were designed to carry some 4,500 troops.[10]

Shifted to the East Coast ports of Charleston, South Carolina, Savannah, Georgia, and Mayport, Florida, troopships began embarking elements of the First Cavalry Division (Airmobile) within a few weeks of Johnson's July 28 announcement. While an Advanced Liaison Detachment and Advanced Party were flown out of Warner Robbins Air Force Base in Georgia in C-130s, arriving at Nha Trang on August 19 and 27, the Division's main body went aboard troop transports *Darby, Buckner, Rose, Patch, Geiger,* and *Upshur* in late August and did not arrive in Vietnam—at Qui Nhon—until mid- and late September 1965.[11]

These would be joined by other MSTS troopships, such as the C-4 types USNS *General Leroy Eltinge* and USNS *General R.M. Blatchford,* and together they would transport the bulk of the troops to Vietnam from late 1965 until early 1967, when

The USNS *General W.H. Gordon,* one of the World War II–vintage troopships crewed by merchant seamen that would be shifted from the Atlantic to the Pacific in 1965 for Vietnam service (U.S. Navy / Military Sea Transportion Service).

they were either returned to the Bremerhaven-Brooklyn Run or placed into "ready" reserve.[12]

One of the first to arrive in Vietnam as part of the crew of a troopship shifted off the European Run in late 1965 was Brian Hope, not long out of the Merchant Marine Academy, Kings Point, New York, who would spend months in-country, bringing ships into ports all along the coast of South Vietnam before his Vietnam service concluded in 1967. He initially completed two voyages to Vietnam in USNS *General W.H. Gordon* beginning in August 1965, and then later in November of that year went over with more troops aboard USNS *General Leroy Eltinge*. Hope would later recall:

> We took our first load of troops all the way up the Saigon River to the city of Saigon, which was rather surprising. Someone heard the North Vietnamese on their radio station boasting that they would sink the *Eltinge*, but the trip up and down the river was uneventful. We had a couple of GIs on the bow firing warning shots at any of the little sailboats or sampans that go too close to the ship.[13]

None of the five ships Brian Hope would ultimately ship out on to Vietnam during the war would come directly under fire, let alone be sunk as threatened while transiting the river channel to Saigon. But that dubious distinction was to come, inflicted—in a powerful command-detonated mining incident—against another American merchant ship making its way up the river to Saigon the following year, with significant loss of life.[14]

A number of ships that had previously been laid up in reserve fleet "boneyards"— including *Monticello Victory*, *Steel Admiral*, *Transorleans*, and *Transhartford*—had been reactivated, and other vessels—including the *Missouri* (C-4), *Fairwind* (C-2), and *Transwestern* (C-3)—had been added, without particular fanfare but at least prompting some maritime labor unions providing crews for them to report that "shipping had been particularly good in the month of May." *American Marine Engineer* of the Marine Engineers Beneficial Association (MEBA) reported to its members, for example, that, as for ships and jobs, there were "more to come in the months ahead."[15]

But few really knew what was coming, close on the shipping world horizon. Some, however, with a better idea as to anticipated logistical needs for a growing Vietnam logistical sealift, continued to suggest that nothing had really changed, that it remained "business as usual" rather than raise undue alarms or create premature political fallout, which an obvious scaled-up war footing might have created.

There was a growing concern, however, increasingly expressed, that despite the patriotic spirit of shipping companies to support the war effort, long established commercial commitments and relationships were in jeopardy, with potentially long-term consequences, if too many of their faster, more modern, post–World War II vessels were shifted from this trade to accommodate the military buildup in Vietnam. "The crisis also affects private operators," George Horne pointed out in the *New York Times* in February 1965, "since every vessel turned over to military use lessens a line's ability to meet its own commitments in regular commercial trade."[16]

Complicating matters, and generally adding to the crisis relating to shipping availability, was the decision on June 15, 1965, by three of the maritime officers unions—National Marine Engineers Beneficial Association (NMEBA), International Organization of Masters, Mates & Pilots (IOMM&P), and American Radio Association (ARA)—to go out on strike over the issue of manning scales for ships with partially automated engine rooms. This had caused some 103 ships belonging to eight subsidized shipping companies based along the Atlantic and Gulf Coasts to lay idle while calls were going out for ships for the Vietnam Run. While this dispute would last for some 78 days through the summer and into the fall, the unions agreed fairly early on to allow ships carrying only military cargoes destined for Vietnam to sail.[17]

Among strikebound ships released under this agreement were the *American Chieftain* and *American Contractor* (United States Lines), fast, newly built ships of 11,000 tons, cleared to unload in New York before sailing to destinations along the coast where military cargoes would be loaded for Vietnam. Other ships released and pledged to MSTS for hauling military cargo included *African Glade* and *Australian Reef* (Farrell Lines); *American Charger, American Commander,* and *American Champion* (U.S. Lines); *Jean Lykes, James Lykes, Doctor Lykes,* and *Gibbes Lykes* (Lykes Brothers Steamship Co.); *Santa Monica* (Grace Line); and *Neva West* (Bloomfield Steamship Co.).[18]

But more—something well beyond "business as usual"—still needed to be done, and quickly.

At a quarter to five o'clock in the afternoon of Friday, July 15, 1965, the phone rang in the office of Captain Thomas A. King, Eastern Region Director of the U.S. Maritime Administration (MarAd), in New York City. "We got the word to go," he recalled some years later. "No limits on money [and] overtime was no problem."[19]

Captain King later summed up the situation then facing those in charge of coordinating sea logistical support: "After exhausting the readily available supply of cargo-carrying tonnage in its own nucleus fleet, using space on cargo liner vessels in the South East Asia trade and having contracted for time-chartered tramp shipping, the Department of Defense's Military Sea Transportation Service requested the Maritime Administration to commence reactivating laid-up tonnage."[20]

That tonnage would soon begin being broken out from the various National Defense Reserve Fleets (NDRF) developed in the aftermath of World War II and scattered along the West, Gulf, and East Coasts of the United States.

Time was now of the essence. As Captain King was to explain, "on Saturday, 16 July 1965, the.... Reserve Fleets came alive with unaccustomed activity."[21]

Print media outlets, especially those centered in major port cities along the coasts, and with established maritime desks monitoring shipping news of the day, were quick to pick up on the order sent down by the government—something that had been anticipated—for the breakouts of ships from the reserve fleets to begin. Some reporters were clearly aware that the withdrawal of ships from reserve had actually already begun, and understood too that the government had, for various reasons, hesitated to go public with such a declaration.

Veteran maritime reporter Helen Delich Bentley of the *Baltimore Sun*, who would later report extensively from Vietnam, was among those breaking the news about the decision to begin major breakouts from the reserve fleets. "The government finally admitted today," she reported in the July 17, 1965, issue of the newspaper, "that it was taking merchant ships out of the reserve fleets to transport military cargoes to Vietnam."[22]

In San Francisco, word had also come to Pacific Coast District Ship Operations from MarAd, Ship Operations in Washington, D.C., to start breaking ships out from reserve fleets along the West Coast. But it wasn't exactly a "no limits" on expenses order, as Captain Tom King had put it on the East Coast, since it wasn't believed ships would be making more than one or a few voyages during the emergency. As Captain Tom Patterson, who as marine operations surveyor (later ship operations officer) would become very involved with breaking ships out of the National Defense Reserve Fleets on the West Coast later recalled, the instructions initially were to "do the voyage repairs and outfit them, but don't paint them; there'll probably be one trip, it'll be a short duration." This meant the ships would go out as they appeared in reserve fleet gray, with the preservative reserve fleet rating, which was pretty much "all oil, not made for salt water."[23]

They would come out in a series of 10 "flights"—four by the end of the year—of about 10 ships at a time, 14 in the first flight. Ships identified in the best condition were typically those selected first, for fewest expected voyage repairs that might be needed, and they were assigned initially to major shipping companies under General Agency Agreement (GAA), and transferred directly, and as soon as possible, to berths for repair and fitting out prior to taking on cargoes to support the rapidly growing war effort in Vietnam.[24]

Speed, within reason and safety and clearance protocols, was of the essence. Within 21 days, on average, each ship was towed from reserve, had necessary repairs completed, and was placed into service.[25]

While the 20-year-old Victory ships were by then no longer the preferred berth for a seaman who had already experienced a newer, postwar type, they certainly did provide an opportunity, and a quicker path to an upgrade, that might not have been available otherwise. As Tom Patterson put it, years later:

> You know, the Victorys weren't the choicest ship at that state of the art. When you come off a nice new Mariner, you don't want to go on that Victory. But at the same time, the Victorys were training ground. We got Chief Mates that had an opportunity to sail Master, you know. We had Ordinaries that went up to Boatswain. And I mean, everybody had a shot. It was like World War II on a smaller scale. It's an exciting time when you get into that. When you find ways to do things.[26]

Even before the decision was made to begin withdrawing "flights" of ships from the reserve fleets, the need for additional seamen to crew ships that had already been re-integrated into the active fleet in the early months of 1965, from other sources, had already begun to be felt. The word had gone out that shipping through various hiring halls was "good" and idle seamen on the beach were urged to make their way back to fill newly available berths in most ratings, licensed and unlicensed.

But the order in mid–August for the first "flight" of 14 ships, withdrawn from various reserve fleets, and anticipation of others to come before and after the turn of the year, immediately ratcheted up the need for crews to man them. The pressure was felt all along the line, from government agencies involved with ship activation, to the subsidized shipping companies tagged for operating reserve fleet vessels under General Agency Agreement (GAA), to the various maritime labor organizations charged with luring in members who, in many cases, had already "swallowed the anchor" in retirement some years before.[27]

This pressure to crew ships from rapidly dwindling rolls of active seamen called into question—brought into sharp critical focus once again—policies for recruiting, training, and retaining personnel then in deep-sea maritime trades. With replacement crews needed "yesterday" in growing numbers of cases, pressure was felt for creative thinking to some extent for supplementing these rolls, and this meant, among other things, the manner in which maritime academy and colleges would respond—would be allowed to respond—by either speeding up or delaying graduations while moving cadets more quickly and directly from sea training assignments prior to graduation to ships desperately in need of—indeed, unable to sail with already loaded vital cargoes—for want of entry-level licensed ratings, the third mates and assistant engineers required in their respective shipboard departments.[28]

SS *Linfield Victory*

Among the first "flight" of ships to be withdrawn from the NDRF for reactivation was the SS *Linfield Victory*, a VC2-S-AP3 type that subsequently compiled an outstanding record of service on the Vietnam Run. Built early in the final year of World War II and then placed into reserve soon after, *Linfield Victory* was later withdrawn for service in Korea, and was then placed into the Hudson River reserve fleet in 1957. She remained there until withdrawn again after more than seven years on the morning of July 19 and placed under the command of Captain C.L. Kinsey. *Linfield Victory* was reactivated in about three weeks' time at Bethlehem-Fairfield Shipyard in Hoboken, New Jersey, and commenced NSA Voyage #10-Alcoa #1 on August 13. She proceeded to Savannah, Georgia, loaded some cargo there until August 18, then proceeded to the Panama Canal, thence to San Francisco. At the Oakland Army Terminal she took on additional "special cargo," then loaded a deck cargo of trailers and vehicles, then steamed directly to Saigon, without mishap, arriving "at anchor, Siagon [*sic*] Pilot Station [probably Vung Tau] on 23 September." Her total elapsed time from reserve to "ready to discharge" was a respectable eight weeks, not requiring delay for major breakdown repair en route, as would be required by others. Though having a designed speed of 16.5 knots, *Linfield Victory* logged an average sea speed in excess of 17 knots.[29]

Linfield Victory discharged in Saigon, seemingly without delay—no doubt a reflection of a "priority" cargo—then proceeded to Cam Ranh Bay where, on September 25, she commenced discharging cargo into an Army barge alongside. A posted notice on board announced that, as per Colonel William F. Hart, Jr., shore leave privilege for the ship's crew had been denied. Cargo operations continued, on and off, and with rain—sometimes heavy—until October 19, when anchor was once again weighed, and *Linfield Victory* proceeded to Qui Nhon, arriving the next day. Cargo operations proceeded on and off until October 26, when the ship was underway again, for Manila. She arrived there on October 28, loaded cargo, departed for Poro Point, and began loading there on October 31. She departed Poro Point on November 1 and proceeded back to Qui Nhon, arriving there on November 3. *Linfield Victory* would remain there, discharging cargo that included "fire bombs," until November 22. Her chief mate, Richard Hicks, was reported to have received a serious head injury on the November 16 caused by a broken spreader cable while investigating heavy lift gear. He was removed on a stretcher to a hospital, and subsequently discharged from his duties on the ship.[30]

From Qui Nhon the *Linfield Victory* returned to Vung Tau Bay at the mouth of the Saigon River, arriving on the morning of November 23 and remaining at anchor there, idle, for the next six days. Finally, at 1336 hours on the afternoon of November 29, anchor aweigh, she proceeded up the Long Tau Channel to Saigon, letting go anchor again in Saigon after having arrived, without incident and in typical time, at 1735 hours. She remained in Saigon, discharging from holds #1 and #5, until December 1, when she proceeded downriver again without incident, took on salt water ballast, and set course for Yokohama, Japan. She received a course change for San Francisco, and then another for Pearl Harbor, Honolulu, Hawaii, where she finally arrived to end NSA Voyage #10-Alcoa #1 at 1200 hours on December 22, 1965.

The DeLong Pier

When American engineers first arrived in Cam Ranh Bay to survey what existed for the handling of deep-draft vessels, what they encountered was one long stone pier, built by the French in the early 1950s. There was work to be done, and quickly, to prepare for what was to come—a near armada of merchant cargo ships. One of

Taken in Cam Ranh Bay in late 1965, this photograph shows the troopship *Eltinge*, left, and the roll-on/roll-off cargo ship *Comet*, both part of the MSTS "nucleus" fleet crewed by merchant seamen. Additional port infrastructure beyond the one French-built pier in existence early in the American buildup period had been constructed by then. But there was more to come, including the introduction of DeLong piers (U.S. Navy).

the things that did quickly improve the situation, once they began to arrive, was the DeLong pier, called in retrospect "the greatest single aid in the rapid development of port sites in Vietnam."[31] Designed by an Army engineer during World War II, the DeLong was a prefabricated pier—some 90 feet by 300 feet long in its original configuration—supported by 18 tubular steel caissons, six feet in diameter and 50 feet long, placed in collars attached to the pier. The DeLong pier could be towed from a port close to its point of manufacture to, theoretically, any other port area in the world. The first real test came during the late summer of 1965, by which time the availability of berthing space to accommodate the rapidly growing fleet of merchant ships destined for Vietnam had reached crisis proportions, causing inordinately long delays and backlogs of ships in holding areas. So, a DeLong pier that had languished in storage for some time was ordered for delivery to Cam Ranh Bay, where additional pier space was, as elsewhere, desperately needed.[32]

The challenge was to tow this first DeLong the great distance from Charleston, South Carolina, by one route or another. It was decided to go via Suez rather than Panama, which would save a couple of days under tow. Nonetheless, after an August 11 departure, the tow would take some 81 days, log some 12,000 miles, and require fueling stops in the Azores, Gibraltar, Port Said, Aden, and Ceylon. Finally, on December 9, 1965, the first of four DeLong piers destined for Cam Ranh Bay was moved into place, then properly secured during the course of another week. By mid–December, Cam Ranh Bay was in business, with additional pier space ready for immediate use. Still, there were dozens of ships at anchor, waiting their turn for one of only four pier spaces, so the pace of turnaround did not yet quicken as significantly as needed. The additional DeLong piers, manufactured in Japan and, thus, requiring significantly less time to deliver, would be needed to quicken the pace of offloading. It was nonetheless a significant development, one of many that would be required at this point, in the right direction.

Eventually, with the installation of all DeLong piers and completion of service roads, causeways, connecting bridges, and an extensive complex of warehouses, Cam Ranh Bay became the largest logistical storage area in Vietnam, and one of the largest and most efficient ports in all of Southeast Asia.[33]

The SS *Citadel Victory*

Paul J. Cogger, 65, a master mariner who had first gone to sea at the end of World War I, had retired for the "last" time from a long seafaring career in early 1965. But when the phone rang one day in early September at his home in Panama City, Florida, and a voice on the other end asked if he would postpone retirement yet again to take a second mate job on one of the Victory ships that had recently been withdrawn from a "boneyard" fleet for the Vietnam Run—*Citadel Victory*—he gave in pretty quickly to the prospect of making "just one more" trip at sea, regardless of its destination. The *Citadel Victory* was at a shipyard in Tampa, Florida, for initial voyage repairs that would once again make the now 20-year-old ship fit, after years of idleness, for the long voyage to Vietnam.[34]

Cogger was soon winging his way to Tampa, where he joined Captain Hunt and Chief Mate Beasley for two additional weeks of "checking on the thousand and one items which are needed to reactivate a ship that had been laid up for eight years." By October 3 the *Citadel Victory* was pronounced fit to proceed to its first port—Mobile, Alabama. As Cogger later recalled, "We made it at half speed to test all the engine room machinery to see what further repairs might be necessary, here and there, since it was not possible to put a ship in first-class condition in the short time we had in Tampa."[35]

In Mobile, *Citadel Victory* loaded equipment for the 101st Airborne out of Fort Benning, Georgia, and then proceeded to Beaumont, Texas, to load additional equipment for the 82nd Airborne out of Fort Hood, Texas. She then proceeded to the Panama Canal, where boiler trouble forced the ship to be laid up for unscheduled repairs. From Balboa, C.Z., she proceeded to Los Angeles, finally arriving on November 4, one month after leaving the shipyard in Tampa.

Wilmington, California, the main port for Los Angeles, was intended as a brief stop for taking on fuel and water, but "so many electrical troubles had developed since the shipyard that it was decided to get them all repaired right there." It was an additional four days before, on November 8, the *Citadel Victory* finally got underway for her trans-Pacific voyage, which then involved a detour to Yokohama, Japan "to avoid a typhoon that was boiling northward" and to ensure that none of a deck load of trucks for the Army in Vietnam would not be lost. She arrived Yokohama on November 25, and finally departed two days later for Saigon, arriving at anchorage, Vung Tau (Cap St. Jacques) on December 4 to await the go-ahead for river transit to Saigon.

As Cogger later recalled: "Two months and a day after leaving the Tampa shipyard, we sighted Cap St. Jacques at the entrance to the Saigon River, and radioed for a pilot. No answer. Proceeding further, we saw why. The entrance was jammed with ships at anchor, there must have been at least 30 of them waiting to go upriver to Saigon. We selected a good spot clear of other ships, and reconciled ourselves to a good long wait."

With Saigon facilities not yet developed for the relatively quick turnarounds that would come within a few years, ships had to wait for weeks in many cases, based not necessarily on order of arrival but the priority nature of their cargo. Cogger and his shipmates had every reason to believe that they would have a long wait before even moving to an unloading berth. However, at about 1000 hours on the morning of December 7—a wait of less than three full days—a pilot came on board to take *Citadel Victory* up the Long Tau River some 40 miles to Saigon. The crew were told to remain off the open decks "so as not to be sniper-bait" and, as the ship finally approached its assigned dock in Saigon, it quickly became apparent why they had been given an early pass to leave the Vung Tau anchorage: about 150 soldiers were waiting for the precious deck cargo of trucks. "As fast as they were unloaded," Cogger recalled, "the GIs drove them off the docks until a large enough convoy was made up to strike out for Bien Hoa, their base."[36]

While trucks for the Army certainly qualified as priority cargo, as its reception and rapid removal suggested, a soldier looking to construct some proper "hooch" flooring in Bien Hoa had his own idea of prioritization, as it turned out. First Sergeant Flaherty, who had been involved in offloading operations, rounded up all the spare "dunnage" he could find and, with the good graces of the ship's crew, departed with a load of lumber that would do the trick for him and presumably his hooch mates. So, even "cargo" not on the manifest had its own value in those early days of getting set up.

Two days after her arrival in Saigon—on December 9, 1965—*Citadel Victory* was again on the move, heading downriver—"without regrets" as Cogger later put it—and proceeded north some 200 miles along the coast to Cam Ranh Bay, being developed as a major American base and boasting an impressive natural and protected anchorage area for ships but still requiring serious development to accommodate them. "Seabees"—the Navy's construction battalion—worked feverishly with a myriad of other outfits to bring the port up to par as quickly as possible. But in December 1965 it still had a long way to go.

"The trip up the coast was uneventful," remembered Cogger, "except for being challenged several times by our destroyers during the night. As soon as we blinked the proper code signal for that day, they acknowledged with a 'proceed' signal." Arriving at about noon on the day after its departure from Saigon, *Citadel Victory* was maneuvered among a good two-dozen other ships at anchor. "Figuring that we were in for a long stay," recalled Cogger, "we picked a good spot and dropped the hook to await our turn."

Citadel Victory and her crew were, indeed, in for a long wait in Cam Ranh Bay. The first of a group of new floating, prefabricated DeLong piers had only just arrived after an 81-day tow from Charleston, South Carolina. It was still not operational, and deep-draft ships could only be accommodated by an old stone pier that had been extended but could still only work a couple of ships at a time. So it was not surprising that *Citadel Victory* would remain at anchor for nearly three weeks, until December 29.

These were long, monotonous days at anchor, only interrupted by the arrival in the middle of the month by the northeast monsoon, which brought torrential rain and 40-mile-an-hour winds for a period of four days. Cogger remembered: "We kept the radar on continuously to make certain we weren't dragging anchor [and] rigged the upper decks with hoses leading to our fresh-water tanks and caught some rainwater."

The arrival of Christmas found the crew of *Citadel Victory* still at anchor, and under orders not to leave the ship. There were not yet any facilities to accommodate them ashore.

The "customary cheer" was broken out at noon, at least, and a celebration was afoot nearby. "We noticed an unusual brilliance to the north at the air base," Cogger recalled. "The next day we found out that Bob Hope had entertained the troops there."

Two days later, the *Citadel Victory* was finally moved to one of the two operational piers. Within two days, accompanied by the continuous cacophony of diesel-powered trucks entering and leaving the pier area, and fighter aircraft overhead, unloading operations were completed, and she was once again underway on a return to Yokohama, Japan. In addition to loading more supplies for Cam Ranh Bay, which would not be delivered for another two months, more boiler work—taking another eight days—was completed on the Victory ship. But the ship was underway again for a series of ports, starting at Kobe, Japan, where Japanese-made fire trucks were loaded for the Royal Thailand Air Force; Inchon, Korea, where surplus military equipment and 1,400 drums of asphalt were loaded; Naha, Okinawa, where bags of cement were loaded for construction of airfield runways in Vietnam; Bangkok, where the fire trucks were offloaded; and San Fernando, Philippines, where additional cargo and badly needed fresh water were taken on.

On March 5 the *Citadel Victory* was back in Cam Ranh Bay, where, while much still needed to be accomplished for handling the backlog of ships anchored out, visible progress had been made during the months she had been away, and the ship was taken immediately to an available docking area. This was a case again of cargo prioritization, which, they found, could work both ways: after the most urgently needed cargo was unloaded, the ship was shifted to an anchorage where, while a reefer ship was assigned the priority handling space which she had vacated, offloading would continue at a slower pace into barges that, when full, were moved ashore. To assist this cargo handling at night, cluster lights were rigged each night to illuminate the Army barges.

Once again, merchant seamen were not allowed ashore in Cam Ranh Bay, now in the early months of 1966, so they lived their lives entirely aboard ship, without shore leave during the weeks of not always continuous cargo handling. But important holidays were still commemorated, of course, with good cheer, as when, on March 17—St. Patrick's Day—Cogger took a large green cloth to the navigation bridge and "bent on" to a halyard, just below the South Vietnamese national flag!

Citadel Victory was finally free of the last of her cargo, but, with fresh water tanks nearly empty, could not get underway until they were at least partially replenished "from somewhere." Some water was secured from a small Army coastal tanker, enough to at least make it across the South China Sea to Manila. Anchor was weighed on March 23, Manila was reached two days later, and, after much more water was taken on from several water barges, she and her crew were finally homeward bound again, on March 25, across the Pacific. Her final destination, Portland, Oregon, was reached nearly three weeks later, on April 12, 1966.[37]

The *Citadel Victory*, one of the many vintage Victorys reactivated from reserve for the Vietnam sealift, had, and despite various delays along the way for additional repair, traveled some 29,471 miles during the course of 189 days. One hundred of those days had been spent in port, or waiting at anchor for dock space. The rest of the time—nearly three months—she was at sea. *Citadel Victory* and her crew had performed well.

The need for more ships began to be alleviated as one "flight" after another came out of the reserve fleets. The initial series of flights, totaling a reported 75 ships mostly of the "Victory" type, would be withdrawn from reserve by the end of the year, and more were to follow in the coming year. But, at the same time, this created a crisis in finding the requisite crew complements for those ships. There were various schemes proposed and implemented to meet the challenge, and many who had not thought of ever going to sea again were once again tempted to do so by the variety of appeals and ads that began to appear in print or were posted otherwise to lure them back. Many in their sixties—including Paul Cogger, who joined *Citadel Victory*—responded to the call, as did others in their seventies, and beyond. "We had a Third Mate on one ship," recalled Captain Tom Patterson of the Maritime Administration who had been intimately involved in the breakout process on the West Coast, "that was in his eighties—84 or something. Hell, I hope I look that good when I'm sixty!"[38]

McNamara: No Love Lost

Many advocates for maintaining a strong Merchant Marine capability were not happy at this time at what was considered a generally negative attitude on the part of Secretary of Defense Robert McNamara towards a supportive and constructive maritime policy. Statements made by McNamara had suggested—argued, in fact—that enhanced air transport capability would surely reduce the need for such a thing, only alienating an increasingly dissatisfied Merchant Marine lobby as to the appropriateness of having him as overlord of the DOD. Emerging problems relating to the role of the Merchant Marine and the maritime industry in general working with the Department of Defense in meeting the logistical challenge of another war many thousands of miles away only contributed to the ill will in dealing with a Secretary of Defense who never seemed fully appreciative or fully cognizant of maritime's needs in the run-up to Vietnam.

In the closing months of 1965 criticism towards McNamara's leadership of the DOD was increasingly apparent from various standpoints and quarters, both within and outside of government, and in the U.S. Congress this criticism of McNamara specifically regarding maritime matters appeared increasingly bipartisan, focused on issues relating to the Vietnam buildup, and pulled few punches when it came to McNamara and the DOD.[39]

A letter sent to McNamara in November 1965 by Representative Edward A. Garmatz (D–MD), chairman of the Merchant Marine and Fisheries Committee, and receiving wide coverage in the mainstream press, was a fair representation of feelings towards the Secretary of Defense at that time and touched on wide-ranging areas of concern. "I am astounded," Garmatz wrote, "that there is no evidence that your department has had in the past, nor even now possess, a concrete maritime logistics plan to support our armed forces in the Viet Nam area."[40]

"One can hardly read in the newspapers today," Garmatz noted, "without being made aware of poor logistic planning and wasteful utilization of available shipping space."[41] His letter underscored a number of issues that had come to light as a result of what he termed the "helter-skelter" method of shipping supplies to American troops in the Vietnam war zone. By failing to initiate removal of ships from reserve fleets more quickly, and not turning to other sources of shipping—such as American tramp ship operators—an undue burden had been placed on regular berth line operators that had threatened serious curtailment of commercial operations "with so much of their regular tonnage in military hands."[42]

Compensation rates offered to ship operators by the DOD, specifically the Navy's Maritime Sea Transportation Service (MSTS), had also become a major issue, "particularly at a time," Garmatz charged, "when the blood of American citizens is being shed in Vietnam." A spokesman for ship operators suggested that "the present Vietnam crisis offers ample evidence of MSTS's abuse of its chartering power."[43]

It was clear that discussions regarding sea logistical support for the war in Vietnam had, as had the war itself, entered a new phase by late 1965. Garmatz made it clear that a "full accounting" would be expected from McNamara and the DOD in Congressional hearings that were soon to come. Those hearings, which would begin before the 89th Congress, House Subcommittee on Merchant Marine, of the

Committee on Merchant Marine and Fisheries, were indeed close on the horizon and would run between February and June the following year.[44]

Also deeply involved in directing pointed remarks at McNamara in late 1965 regarding the Merchant Marine, as they would be in forthcoming Congressional hearings, were representatives of the major maritime unions. With scores of ships already having been withdrawn from reserve fleets by December, McNamara's earlier comments regarding the role air transport might play moving troops and supplies to far-flung areas of the world received particular attention from some labor leaders. "We do know," Joe Curran of the National Maritime Union (NMU) would declare in a telegram to McNamara, "that it has long been the policy of your department to downgrade the importance to our country of American ships and loyal American seamen."[45] Paul Hall of the Seafarers International Union (SIU) would point out at a convention of the AFL-CIO in late 1965 that "it was this same McNamara who just over a year ago made a great statement to the effect that the passenger ship was obsolete so far as military necessity was concerned. He was the man who led the parade for carrying out of the elimination of this industry."[46] And Morris Weisberger of the Sailors' Union of the Pacific (SUP) would declare to members of his organization that "Defense Secretary McNamara's position that aircraft can replace ships in large scale military operations would seem to be knocked into a cocked hat."[47]

While greater numbers of troops would actually be transported by air in wars in which the United States would later become involved, troopships—contrary to McNamara's assertions at the time—would transport the majority of troops deployed to Vietnam at least in the early buildup years.[48]

Foreign Flag and "Effective Control"

The Military Sea Transportation Service (MSTS) reserved the right to utilize foreign flag vessels, generally under charter to unsubsidized shipping companies, and did so on a fairly regular but limited basis when other sources for shipping were not readily available.[49] This became an issue of hot debate all over again when supposedly "allied" nations refused to clear their vessels for service to Vietnam, or crews of foreign flag vessels balked at the prospect of carrying military cargo into war zones in support of the United States. One of the notable examples of this problem occurred in late summer of 1965 when a ship of Mexican registry—*El Mexicano*, which had been chartered to an unsubsidized American shipping company—was placed on berth and "offered as a routine matter to MSTS" for a voyage that included Saigon.[50] The shipping company claimed there were "no restrictions" that might compromise carriage of military cargo, and loading proceeded. However, well into the loading process word was received that there had been a Mexican government ruling that its national law forbade dispatch of a Mexican ship to a combat zone. The cargo was removed, and booked to a Greek ship, *Stamatios S. Embiricos*, whose crew then refused to sail with a cargo destined for Vietnam. At this point the original charter was cancelled, and the cargo was taken aboard an American ship, *Bay State* (States Marine Lines); after a delay of several weeks, the cargo was finally scheduled for shipment to Vietnam on September 8, 1965.

Another incident involving a foreign flag ship, the Greek *Marilena P,* which had been chartered to the MSTS, occurred on August 27, 1965, when its crew also balked at sailing into the Vietnam war zone. That charter was cancelled on September 2, and the cargo in question was shifted to an American vessel that had become available.[51]

Turnaround

The influx of ships departing stateside with military cargoes for Vietnam, despite the delays caused by crew shortages, created their own problems on the other end, that is, in overcrowded ports, or approaches to them, where those desperately needed cargoes were either piling up shoreside, or sat for weeks on end awaiting the call to finally begin moving to berth.

While the experience of ships with "priority" cargoes was one thing—and might require a wait of a few days, if that, before receiving the go-ahead to start up the Long Tau Channel to Saigon—the experience of other ships, such as the *Steel Traveler*, which arrived, under command of Captain Jack Tate, at Vung Tau on November 1, 1965, was much different.[52]

Donald Merchant recalled the arrival of *Steel Traveler*, with 7,000 tons of "general (cargo), plywood, corn meal, beer, 10 flatbed trailers, structural steel beams, a road roller, drums of oil and tutuol [*sic*]." The ship expected a long wait before proceeding upriver, and had taken on extra fuel for the eventuality. With some 20 to 30 other ships waiting their turn, and a mixed cargo not deemed of a higher priority nature, the delay "was justified," Merchant later opined. "We waited 19 days before going up the river." What does a merchant seaman do for 19 days at anchor, without the liberty launch service that would only come later?

Much time was spent, of course, simply watching the comings and goings of other ships, as well as sights associated with the war. As Merchant remembered it,

> a loaded troop ship arrived every three or four days. A small escort aircraft carrier came in regularly transporting planes. The *Transglobe*, one of the first roll-on, roll-off ships, made numerous short trips to Okinawa for vehicles. Also mine sweepers, coasters, LSTs, and a large fleet of fishing junks were coming and going all the time.[53]
>
> We got fresh fish from the fishermen then occasionally, but later in the war, due to guerilla activities, any boat that approached a ship would have warning shots fired at them by the armed guard.

One saving grace for Merchant and others on the *Steel Traveler* was the use of the ship's powered lifeboat "for running errands between the ships carrying spare parts for repairs and taking the mail to up[river]bound ships, and picking mail and the current *Time* and *Newsweek* from outbound vessels."

By year's end, much had been accomplished in getting the Vietnam sealift underway. But seamen arriving there at that point still faced exceedingly long delays at anchor and holding areas, and prohibitions on shore leave in-country. And despite their "noncombatant" status, many came to understand only too well that the enemy did not discriminate when it came to target selection. While it could be said that most American merchant seamen whose ships did come under attack were extraordinarily lucky, escaping serious injury or death by mere happenstance and a matter of only a few yards, feet, or inches, not all were so lucky.

While several ships were attacked and damaged in Vietnam in the last half of

1965, seamen aboard those ships were fortunate for the most part to escape serious injury in those attacks. But for some on shore leave during this same period, Lady Luck had opted out of their company. On the evening of June 25, Able Seaman Charles W. Perry of the SS *Louise Lykes* was one of a dozen Americans—the majority military personnel—killed by a bomb blast at the My Canh "floating" restaurant along the Saigon waterfront. Long a popular shore leave destination, it was periodically a Viet Cong target as well.[54]

In another incident that September, George Bogdanovich, an SUP seaman from SS *Bengal Mail* (American Mail Line) was shot and killed in a Saigon bar, under somewhat mysterious circumstances.[55]

On Christmas Day, December 25, 1965, many American merchant seamen found themselves aboard ship in various locations in Vietnam. Not yet allowed in most areas to go ashore, and thus unable to enjoy entertainment provided military personnel in such areas as Cam Ranh Bay where Bob Hope and his troupe would perform on that day, steward departments did their best to provide meals that might at least be appropriate for the holiday, and be appreciated on that day.

Some Went Missing

In Qui Nhon, a shallow draft port where ocean-going cargo ships anchored out, two seamen from the SS *Express Baltimore*, Commodore Line—Third (or Second) Mate Stephen O'Laughlin and Able Seaman Ruben Bailon—were tasked that Christmas day with fetching the ship's master prior to the needed shifting of their ship. This would require a flight to Saigon, where the captain had gone for medical treatment. While O'Laughlin and Bailon were observed having a libation in a local hotel bar ashore, they never made it to the airport for the flight, and were never seen alive again.[56] Both went missing on Christmas Day. While the fate of Bailon has never been determined, that of O'Laughlin came to light in May 1968 when a Vietnamese being interrogated claimed he had seen him in a jungle camp near Da Nang where he and others were being held prisoner by the Viet Cong. O'Laughlin's family was not notified of this report until sometime in 1972. Then, in June 1973, his remains were recovered from a grave in Phu Yen Province; they were positively identified in 1976.[57]

Shore leave, always looked forward to by seamen after long voyages and delays at anchor, had proven fatal to some American merchant seamen in 1965. As the year came to a close, some things about the war—and the role merchant seamen would play in it—were becoming clearer. Force levels were being raised significantly as large unit deployments, accomplished primarily by civilian-crewed troopships, were ongoing to various points in-country. So too were the additional supply ships, dozens of which would be withdrawn from reserve fleets, that would also be crewed by merchant seamen—if they could be found.

While the increase in U.S. force levels was understood to be necessary for shouldering more of the burden for combat missions beyond the "enclaves"—that is, to engage in "search and destroy" missions against the enemy wherever they could be found—any optimism that this would soon turn the tide was short-lived, if it ever really existed.[58]

Late in November 1965 two battalions of the Army's First Cavalry Regiment, introduced to Vietnam two months before, ran headlong for the first time—after having been transported by helicopters—into a larger North Vietnamese Army (NVA) force that had made their own way south to the Ia Drang Valley.[59] The fighting became fierce and close, involving napalm strikes by fighter-bomber aircraft and even high level strikes by B-52 bombers (introduced to Guam for use over Vietnam earlier in the year). Casualties were heavy on both sides, and though COMUSMACV (Westmoreland) declared the fighting at Ia Drang to have been a "great victory," his take on the action was misleading at best.[60] The lessons learned by both sides in this first major clash between U.S. units and the NVA were instructive, and for the Americans involved and assessing stateside, sobering.

Though the North Vietnamese had suffered far greater losses, they also came away with the realization that the American "air cavalry" could be taken on effectively, and that they would ultimately prevail in their "peoples' war" against the foreign aggressor. And while General Westmoreland and mainstream news outlets pointed positively to what had occurred at Ia Drang, more realistic observers—including Secretary of Defense Robert McNamara—concluded that what the battle had revealed was that it was "going to be a long war."[61]

And whether or not it could still be won was another matter about which many were, still, not so confident.

It would indeed be a long war, and that meant American merchant seamen would be involved for as long as it took. Win or lose, it could not be undertaken without their involvement. That, as it would turn out, would be for more than another nine years.

And as the war turned more deadly for American soldiers, Marines, airmen, Navy, and Coast Guard personnel in the coming year, the same would be true for merchant seamen making their way there along the Vietnam Run.

10

Rung Sat

Through the Killer Jungle (1966)

"For a while we felt like a sitting duck in a shooting gallery, and everyone knows what a duck sitting around in a shooting gallery feels like."
—Alexander J. Leiter, able seaman, *Steel Architect*

"I went down to the engine room for the third time, but there still was
no sign of the men who had been [there] working with me."
—Herb Kenyon, chief engineer, *Baton Rouge Victory*

For a ship carrying a full load of 500-pound bombs it had the most incongruous
and ironic of names: *Our Lady of Peace*. But the Viet Cong knew what it was about,
and set out to destroy or at least disable it as it lay at anchor in Nha Be in the heart of
the Rung Sat ("Killer Jungle") Special Zone some seven or eight miles downriver from
Saigon.[1] The zone—so designated by the South Vietnamese military in 1962—was a
roughly 400-square-mile, pie- or brain-shaped area stretching from near Vung Tau
up-channel to Nha Be and beyond.

Extremely dense with mangrove swamp and jungle comprising most of it, the
area was deep in mud, had few passable roads, and the main, deep-draft shipping
channel, as chance would have it, ran roughly through its center.[2] It was therefore
both difficult to fully control militarily and a prime area for attacks against shipping by the Viet Cong, as it had been earlier by the Viet Minh during the French War
period.

Seamen on *Our Lady of Peace* and other ships at the Nha Be anchorage on May
26, 1966, were among those who had been targeted by VC special operations swimmers.[3] While in the process of weighing anchor, the boatswain on *Our Lady of Peace*
noticed something unusual secured with parachute cord to the anchor chain. Military explosive device specialists were called in and disarmed a mine containing 130
pounds of explosive material. According to one account, "there were two five-gallon
cans of *plastique* rigged so that when that part of the [anchor] chain hit the ship they
would explode." Because this was spotted in time, a major explosion involving the
ship's cargo of 500-pound bombs was averted.[4]

Not so fortunate, but still escaping serious damage, was the French merchant
ship *Milos Delmar*, which, while also weighing anchor there that day set off an explosive device of apparently similar design. But the damage seemed to have been minor
since it received little subsequent mention.[5] More notable was the damage caused by
a mine to the Panamanian-registered cargo ship *Eastern Mariner*, also at the Nha Be

SS *Baton Rouge Victory* after being sunk by command-detonated mine blast in the Long Tau River Channel below Saigon in 1966 (U.S. Navy).

anchorage that day. Damaged by a mine blast that reportedly blew a 10' by 20' hole in her starboard quarter, the ship and its cargo of bagged cement began sinking quickly by the stern into the mud of the river.[6]

Fortunately, the ship was able to be maneuvered to the side of the river, clear of the channel, before it settled there. "Lying on her starboard side, [the ship] remains as a grim reminder of how easy it is to attack ships in the area," *Baltimore Sun* reporter Helen Delich Bentley wrote some months later. "Still with her cargo of cement aboard, the Panamanian-flag freighter's superstructure peering from the river bottom tells the woeful story."[7]

The May 1966 mining incidents in the vicinity of Nha Be anchorage were by no means the first attacks—or attempted attacks—on merchant shipping in the Rung Sat Zone to that point in the year. The 661-foot British coastal tanker *New Guinea Trader* was attacked some 15 miles downriver from Saigon in mid–March, and one account noted that the ship had been "strafed … from a nearby swamp, wounding ten men." Set afire, *New Guinea Trader* "was towed to port after a U.S. Navy LST came to her aid with fire hoses." According to this account, the attack on *New Guinea Trader* had been "the third try by the [Viet] Cong to sink a ship to blockade shipping."[8]

Additional patrol craft, mine sweepers, air reconnaissance and response aircraft, and boots on the ground—those of counter operations groups of South Vietnamese Marines, U.S. Marines, and Seal Team One—were in the process of being introduced, and these would certainly add to the level of security provided to shipping along the navigation channel to and from Saigon.[9] But there was never a time, as seamen would learn all too well in succeeding years, when attack incidents of varying type could ever be fully prevented.

Another measure undertaken to improve security for shipping was to deprive the VC as much as possible of the mangrove and jungle cover that ordinarily extended to the river edges in the Rung Sat Zone, and from which attacks on shipping, minesweepers, and patrol craft could be conducted. Multiple applications were made in

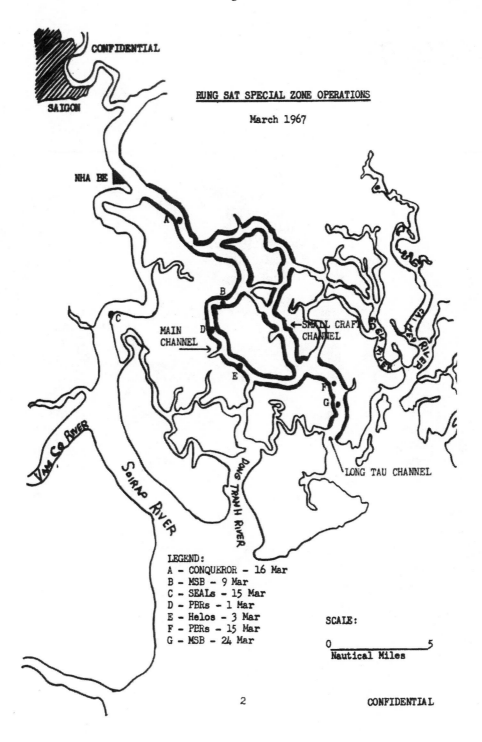

CONFIDENTIAL

SAIGON

RUNG SAT SPECIAL ZONE OPERATIONS

March 1967

NHA BE

A

B

C

MAIN CHANNEL →

D

SMALL CRAFT CHANNEL

SOI RAP RIVER

VAM SAT RIVER

E

F

G

LONG TAU CHANNEL

VAM CO RIVER

SOIRAP RIVER

DONG TRANH RIVER

LEGEND:
A - CONQUEROR - 16 Mar
B - MSB - 9 Mar
C - SEALs - 15 Mar
D - PBRs - 1 Mar
E - Helos - 3 Mar
F - PBRs - 15 Mar
G - MSB - 24 Mar

SCALE:

0 — 5
Nautical Miles

2

CONFIDENTIAL

Prepared by U.S. Navy intelligence for one of a series of classified monthly reports, this hand-drawn map of Rung Sat Special Zone, through which merchant ships passed to and from Saigon, indicates where ships and other vessels were attacked by the NLF/Viet Cong (USNFVMHS).

1966 of a chemical defoliant, much of which was transported on merchant ships to Vietnam, called "Agent Orange" for the orange-colored stripes running around the 55-gallon drums in which it was transported to and stored in-country.[10]

The applications of this defoliant—by fixed-wing aircraft and low-flying helicopters, often with specially rigged spraying arms—would have been observed by merchant seamen making the river transit from the South China Sea to Saigon. Certainly, as one seaman recalled some years later, the look of the landscape was much changed by this defoliant application. "The river had been sprayed with defoliants," seaman Donald Merchant recalled, "and the bushes along the banks were all brown and dead."[11]

While the use of defoliants was intended, of course, to deprive the enemy of cover, and therefore, it was argued, to save American lives, what was not known or revealed about the defoliants at the time were the short- or long-term health effects upon those it was intended to help. That was another matter altogether—one that would only be played out and litigated years later.[12]

Whether or not merchant seamen exposed to defoliants (later revealed to be carcinogenic) were harmed by this exposure may never be known. It could certainly be argued, however, that many were indeed not only exposed to carcinogenic defoliants but eventually developed serious medical conditions as a result. But, as civilians, American merchant seamen never came under the same monitoring and compensation that was eventually provided—and only after a difficult and drawn-out campaign to secure it—to those who served in military units and subsequently managed to file for it.[13]

Attacks of one form or another came with increasing frequency as the first year of the enlarged war gave way to the next. Sometimes attacks against merchant shipping, and ships of other nationalities, were viewed by American seamen from relative safety, as when, on February 27, 1966, the Panamanian-registered freighter *Lorinda* was, according to one account, "raked for an hour by VC fire with armor-piercing 57-mm shells and machinegun fire" that resulted in the wounding of six of her crew.[14] Another incident involved an attack on the tanker *Paloma*, some miles below Nha Be, on March 3. Word of this came over the radio to SS *Steel Architect* (Captain J. Kauserud), which was also heading downriver but closer to Nha Be at that point. "Alert, alert, a vessel is under attack at Point de L'est" came the warning, in time for commands and maneuvering to steer the ship out of harm's way.[15]

While 1966 dawned with some apparent improvement in reducing bottlenecks created by the introduction of scores of Victory ships from reserve fleets for service to Vietnam, this hoped-for relief was not to last very long. As troop levels rose, more "flights" of reactivated boneyard ships were added to the trans-Pacific pipeline, as crews could be found for them—increasingly also a challenge—creating yet more bottlenecks, long delays "on the hook" in many areas—both in-country and elsewhere where ships had to be held for weeks on end.

"The Longest Troop Lift"

The number of American military personnel in Vietnam by the end of 1965 had reached just under 200,000, nearly a nine-fold increase above the level of "advisers" in-country at the beginning of that year. That number would nearly double again by the end of 1966, with many more on the way. This was only made possible at that point with an increased number of troopships added to the Vietnam Run, steaming continuously between Vietnam and the East and West Coasts of the United States. And some of those ships would also be employed in transporting troops from allied nations, notably the Republic of Korea.[16]

The need for additional troopships, all of which would be crewed by merchant seamen, was anticipated at least as early as mid–1964, following the Gulf of Tonkin incidents and subsequent congressional resolution, when two of the many troopships built during World War II—USNS *General Gordon* and USNS *General Blatchford*— were withdrawn from reserve fleets and moved to shipyards for "de-mothballing" and to prepare them again for active service. They, along with a group of others shifted from service between New York and Bremerhaven, Germany, and others, would be available in time for moving some two-thirds of the hundreds of thousands of American military personnel lifted to Vietnam during the initial major buildup period from 1965 to 1966, and extending into early 1967.[17]

Two of the troopships involved in moving military units to Vietnam in 1966 were the "sisterships" USNS *Alexander M. Patch* and USNS *General William O. Darby*, both P-2-SE2-R1 hull types that had been launched a year apart at the Bethlehem-Alameda Shipyard in California in the last years of World War II.[18]

In July and August 1966 *Patch* and *Darby* participated in what MSTS publicists would call the "longest single point troop lift in the 17 year history" of that naval auxiliary service, steaming 12,358 miles from Boston to Vung Tau where some 3,124 troops of the 196th Light Infantry Brigade were disembarked. Departing Boston on the same day—July 15—the ships proceeded directly to and transited the Panama Canal on July 20. From there they headed to Long Beach, California, arriving on July 27 to take on fuel. The longest nonstop leg of the voyage would be the 7,219 miles from there to Vung Tau.[19]

Captain John M. LeCato, who took command of *Patch* after having been to Vietnam earlier as chief mate in USNS *Comet*, recalled this "longest" troop lift some years later in this way:

> There was a bit of friendly rivalry all the time, particularly since my friend and former skipper during the previous year on *Comet*, Captain Roy Christman, was in command of *Darby*, and this was the first time we had been working as equals. I learned a great deal during the years I sailed as [Chief] Mate and Second Mate under his command, and, I must say, I thoroughly enjoyed showing him how well I had learned my lessons.
>
> Also, First Engineer on *Darby* was Gene Spencer [and] we had some fine times when the two ships were in port together. We tried to turn the trans-Pacific trip into an old time steamboat race, but I don't believe either ship was ever completely out of sight of the other.
>
> *Patch* and *Darby* made two Korean [troop] lifts [to Vietnam] then returned to San Francisco for overhaul and drydocking, then resumed trans-Pacific troop lifts. Just before sailing I was transferred to a ship returning to New York. More and more troops were being airlifted and, by the time the war ended, the troopship was as much a thing of the past as the square-rigger.[20]

While most of the dozen or so troopships making their way to and from Vietnam in the early buildup period from mid–1965 into 1967 were of the P2 hull design types—the largest of the troopships constructed during World War II—a few of the somewhat smaller and slower C4 design types were also deployed for the Vietnam sealift. Those included USNS *General Leroy Eltinge* and USNS *General R.M. Blatchford*, the latter of which had been withdrawn from reserve in 1964, participated in Operation Steel Pike I that year, and was then assigned to the New York to Bremerhaven troop lift.[21]

Most of these ships—the P2s as well as C4s—would be withdrawn from the Vietnam Run—as troopships—generally by some point early in 1967 as replacement troops were increasingly airlifted, and those finishing in-country tours were returned, generally again, on commercial airline "freedom birds" that would deposit back in the United States—in a matter of hours instead of weeks—those who had completed tours of duty in Vietnam.[22]

A few of the P2 troop ships did remain on the Vietnam Run longer than most—and in perhaps one case as late as 1970—while both of the C4 troopships would be sold to the private sector—Waterman Steamship Company—for conversion into cargo ships, and, as such, would return to Vietnam in that capacity for the last years of the war.[23]

Returning to Vietnam for the third time in late 1965, Brian Hope was now a brand-new third mate on the C4 type troopship USNS *General Leroy Eltinge* after making his first two trips over on USNS *General Gordon* as junior deck officer fresh out of the U.S. Merchant Marine Academy. Whereas *General Gordon* had transported troops straight into Qui Nhon, Brian Hope would now experience for the first time, in *Eltinge*, the transit between Vung Tau and Saigon through the heart of the Rung Sat Special Zone.

"I made my trip on the *Eltinge* from 26 November 1965 to 6 February 1966," recalled Hope years later.

> We took our first load of troops all the way up the Saigon River to the city of Saigon, which was rather surprising. Someone heard the North Vietnamese on their radio station boasting that they would sink the *Eltinge*, but the trip up and down the river was uneventful. We had a couple of GIs on the bow firing warning shots at any of the little sailboats or sampans that got too near the ship. I remember that we had a Navy chaplain aboard, a Naval Academy graduate. He got *really* pissed off that these guys were scaring the local fishermen, or whatever they were, with gunfire, when, in his opinion, they were minding their own business.[24]
>
> The troops we had aboard were, as I recall, replacements for various units. The trip before I was aboard she had carried 2,500 Korean troops from the White Horse Division, a crack unit—really tough soldiers who earned a nasty reputation in Vietnam.[25]

The First Helicopter Repair Ship

Among the many types of ships crewed by American merchant seamen during the Vietnam War was the first of a new type: the helicopter repair ship. Considering the development and introduction of the "air mobility" tactic—the deployment of large numbers of helicopters for transporting troops to and from the field—it was no surprise that such a ship type would also be developed and deployed for the first time, in Vietnam, in early 1966.[26] It was the 538-foot USNS *Corpus Christi Bay* (T-ARVH-1), originally the Navy seaplane tender USS *Albemarle* (AV-5) and eventually incorporated into the MSTS "nucleus" fleet, that would be re-worked and designated as a helicopter maintenance and repair ship—the first of her kind—to then take up residence in Cam Ranh Bay in January 1966.[27]

Launched at the New York Shipbuilding Corporation yard in Camden, New Jersey, in 1940, the year before the United States entered World War II, *Albemarle* was in and out of service with the Navy until stricken from the Navy Register in 1962. She was then assigned to a reserve fleet before being loaned to the U.S. Army for conversion to a Floating Aircraft Maintenance Facility (FAMF). Then renamed *Corpus Christi Bay* on March 27, 1965, the ship was prepared for service with MSTS in early 1966 for support of the Army's aviation operations in Vietnam.

In addition to the ship's massive work and storage space—42,000 square feet of covered shop space, 12,400 feet of open work deck area, and another 10,000 square feet of storage space in addition to aviation and diesel fuel storage areas—the ship had what at the time was, for the Navy, a unique power plant design in that its boilers were partially automated, utilizing a console from which the number of boilers in use and fuel used by each boiler could be controlled with fewer personnel involved.

Skippered variously in Vietnam by Captains Harry Anderson, Jr., Sven Rydberg, and Knud T. Mortensen, *Corpus Christi Bay* was operated by an MSTS crew of some 130 civilian merchant seamen, and also provided berthing and living space for an additional 362 Army helicopter repair and maintenance technicians.[28]

As ships were added to the Vietnam Run during the early buildup period, so too were real targets of opportunity added for Viet Cong snipers and special operatives who desired nothing more than to impede the flow of ships carrying war supplies intended for use against them. Ships—and the merchant seamen who crewed them— would be fair game in all waterways and port areas, but if a ship could be sunk in the middle of a busy channel, thus blocking or slowing the flow to such a vital center of logistical support as the port of Saigon, then so much the better.

If any believed it was, under the circumstances, just a matter of time before such a thing or something close to it was to happen, and despite the precautions, they were right. The year was, in fact, to prove to be particularly deadly for the American Merchant Marine in Vietnam, which had thus far been luckier than might otherwise have been expected as far as losses due to enemy contact was concerned. But it was indeed just a matter of time, and for some the time was now far too short.

SS *Baton Rouge Victory*

The SS *Baton Rouge Victory* was one of the many veterans of World War II that had been withdrawn in early "flights" from National Defense Reserve Fleets, reactivated in shipyards, given minimal shakedown cruises, and added to the Vietnam Run.[29] By early 1966 she had performed well, requiring little outlay for repair, and not unduly delayed by breakdown, as others, following her initial period of shipyard reactivation. On July 28, 1966, *Baton Rouge Victory* sailed from San Francisco, with a crew of 45, and again set course for Vietnam, with a load of general cargo that included vehicles on deck.[30] She called first at Manila in the Philippines and then proceeded to Saigon, arriving off Vung Tau in the late morning hours of August 19. She lay at anchor and idle there for the next four days before getting underway again at 7:24 in the morning on August 23, heading for the deep-draft channel to Saigon, an apparent substitution for the SS *Creighton Victory* which, unlike *Baton Rouge Victory*, was loaded with ammunition. She moved without incident to a point some 20 miles—about half the distance up channel towards Saigon. What happened next was recalled a few months later by the ship's chief engineer, Herb Kenyon, who had been with the ship since her reactivation from reserve in December 1965[31]:

> "When we started up the Saigon River shortly after 0800 I went down to the Engine room and relieved First Assistant John A. Bishop at the throttle. [He] went up to breakfast and then returned to work in the fire room to assist maneuvering."

Kenyon saw Second Assistant Engineer Rummel in the engine room just before a massive explosion, which occurred "on or about 0910, August 23."

"I was at the throttle on the operating platform," Kenyon recalled. As a result of the explosion he was lifted up in the air, then fell back on the deck, momentarily stunned. "Immediately after [this]," he noted, "the two generators went out and a steam line carried away."

> The engine room was in total darkness, and I started to go up the ladder. Then realizing I had a flashlight in my pocket, I went back down and started circling the engine room. But I couldn't see any sign of life or hear any human sound. I met the two Third Assistant Engineers [M.E.J. Bredlau, who had been off-duty, and A.C. Benevedes] and a bedroom utility man who went below, and by that time the water had risen at least another 15 feet above the tank tops. We made further search, but it was futile.

"Death must have come instantly," said Kenyon, who also surmised that those killed had not suffered.

It was determined that the blast, presumably caused by explosives packed into a 55-gallon drum and detonated from shore, tore a 46-foot by 20-foot hole in the port side of the ship extending from the number three cargo hold past the engine room, flooding it quickly.[32]

"The engineers' response was excellent," recalled Herb Kenyon.

> As a matter of fact they were down there almost before I could get up. I then went to the bridge and informed the Master that I had left the engine turning over at 65 rpm and that the ship had sufficient power to be beached. I also asked the Master for help to get the men out of the engine room.[33]
>
> On the way down from the bridge I kicked on the emergency generator, but the circuits were damaged and out of order. I went down to the engine room for the third time, but still there was no sign of the men who had been in the engine room working with me. Naturally there was a lot of confusion during this period. However, everyone responded commendably.
>
> In the meantime the rescue craft had arrived to assist in providing protection and to help hold the ship on the bank. I asked some of the salvage people to send divers into the engine room to see if any bodies could be recovered, but I was told it was a precarious job right at that time, but they would pursue it later.[34]

In due course it was determined that the blast, probably caused by a pre-positioned, command-detonated charge, had quickly taken the lives of seven of the *Baton Rouge Victory*'s engine room crew, including First Assistant John A. Bishop, 41. The others were: Charles B. Rummel, 49, second assistant engineer; Chief Electrician Raymond Barrett, 62; Earl Erickson, 49, second electrician; James W. McBride, 38, oiler; Robert J. Rowe, 57, fireman-watertender; and Timothy M. Riordan, 26, wiper.

"It is with a feeling of deepest sorrow," Kenyon told a reporter afterwards, "that

I think of the loss of life of seven fine persons. They and only they were the heroes of the *Baton Rouge* incident."

While most of the ship's surviving crewmembers were quickly transferred off the stricken Victory ship, Kenyon himself remained on board for another five days before shifting to Saigon to await transportation back to the States.[35]

The *Baton Rouge Victory* had been moved to the bank of the channel, where recovery and temporary repair operations proceeded. The shipping channel was reopened the following day, and the ship was eventually removed to Singapore, where she was declared a constructive total loss, and sold for the scrap value of $90,850.[36]

The rapid escalation of war in Vietnam, reflected in rising troop levels, and accompanied by the breakout of scores of Victory ships from reserve fleets—such as the ill-fated *Baton Rouge Victory*—also meant that the often contentious and heated discussions related to maritime policy in general, and the myriad problems arising from conditions in Vietnam, would continue unabated from one year to the next. What, for example, was being done, and could be done, to speed up cargo handling and thus reduce delays of ships in-country? What about growing shortages of seamen in key ratings and related sailing delays of ships in the United States? What about providing improved medical, mail, and recreational services for seamen, not to mention shore leave—which was still being denied to seamen in some port areas—especially after those inordinately long holding delays—time "on the hook"—in-country? These were some of the many questions being asked and in urgent need of answers.

While government, industry, and maritime labor had long been engaged in often heated discussions as to the best way to maintain and develop a strong merchant marine, and in the spirit of compliance with the Merchant Marine Act of 1937, the order to break out ships from reserve fleets with the accompanying realizations as to crewing needs, training, shipboard conditions, compensation, and other matters took on new urgency.

Providing at least partial answers to the problems could sometimes come relatively easily, with few parties involved in the discussion and with little debate and argumentation. One example of that came in the early months of 1966 when, after a request on January 20 by Robert H.B. Baldwin, Under Secretary of the Navy, to the U.S. Coast Guard to "take appropriate action to alleviate the problem" of availability of licensed Merchant Marine officers. It was, after all, the Coast Guard that set sea service time standards and requirements for upgrading—both for licensed and unlicensed personnel—in the Merchant Marine. And if those requirements could be relaxed in the current emergency to speed up the process, then that would at least help to improve the situation. Thus it was that the U.S. Coast Guard announced, in mid–March, that sea service requirements for temporary third mate or temporary third engineer were reduced from three years to two years. A similar reduction in sea time was also announced for temporary upgrading in the higher licensed grades.[37]

Not surprisingly, and as soon revealed in a series of congressional hearings held from February to June 1966 and subsequently published under the title "Vietnam—Shipping Policy Review"—there was much often impassioned disagreement as to how to best characterize the state of affairs within maritime, specifically relating to Vietnam, with an eye towards the future as well, and how to proceed in implementation of a course of action. And there was always the possibility, which also needed to be considered and planned for—despite the challenge already presented by Vietnam—that another conflict requiring significant additional seaborne logistical support might break out somewhere else in the world.[38]

As noted, the addition of scores of ships broken out of reserve fleets in 1965 and 1966 ensured that greater tonnage of needed supplies would be sent to and arriving in support of American military personnel in Vietnam. But this also contributed once again to serious problems in a war zone that had not yet developed the port infrastructure sufficiently equipped to receive, unload, and send on their way again in a timely fashion those very same ships. By November 1965 it was reported that a total of 146 ships—mostly of the Victory type, but including such others as the smaller and slower C1 type, also of World War II vintage—had been broken out of "boneyard" reserve fleets, reactivated, and added to the Vietnam pipeline.[39] This had contributed once again to bottlenecks in-country, and extended delays for ships and crews being held in such places as the Philippines and Okinawa until word came to shift to Vung Tau or other in-country ports where additional delays of several days might be encountered before word came again, finally, to proceed up the river channel to Nha Be or Saigon. But delays were also often caused even before getting underway stateside, for want of an engineer, a mate, or key and Coast Guard-mandated members of the unlicensed crew. Thus, of those 146 ships withdrawn from reserve since the previous July, some 115 had been delayed at the docks for a total of 362 days waiting for crew members for which there was no substitution or authorization to sail short-handed without.[40]

Merchant Seamen and the Draft

Despite the crucial role played by merchant mariners in logistical support of the war in Vietnam—supplying what was generally put at around 95 percent of all forms of supplies, and transporting two-thirds of all troops to Vietnam through 1966—this role was still deemed, to the incredulity of many observers, as "non-essential" by the Interagency Advisory Committee on Essential Activities and Critical Occupations, which made recommendations regarding draft deferments.[41] And along with this attitude towards merchant seamen, local draft boards had been sending out notices to licensed merchant marine officers as well as those in the unlicensed ranks who generally had even less viable recourse in appeal.

While Captain Lloyd W. Sheldon, president of the International Organization of Masters, Mates & Pilots stated in February 1966 that he felt his organization was still meeting the demands for providing licensed navigation officers, he noted that if the draft boards "would stop taking trained mates off of their ships in the draft, it would be a lot easier."[42]

But in other areas, notably the ranks of shipboard engineers, demands were not in many cases being met, and ships were being held up in port as a result. Helen Delich Bentley of the *Baltimore Sun* reported in its March 8 issue that "at least seven ships now are unable to sail with cargoes for Vietnam because of a lack of licensed engineers." Four of these ships—mostly reactivated Victory ships—were being held up in San Francisco, and others along the Atlantic and Gulf Coasts.[43]

To help alleviate the manpower shortage, suggestions had been made late the previous year for enhanced training programs to move unlicensed seamen into the licensed ranks, and another proposal had been made subsequently to move up the graduation date for four-year cadets at the U.S. Merchant Marine Academy in Kings Point, New York.[44] Part of the problem, as identified by maritime labor as well as those in the media who reported on such things, had to do with resistance on the part of government maritime policy makers not only to get behind such recommendations, but to acknowledge in the first place that there were shortages of key shipboard personnel.

As Helen Delich Bentley put it in her article in the *Baltimore Sun on* March 9, 1966: "Although the Maritime Administration was urged last fall to set up a program to train young men as engineers, nothing has been done." She went on: "In fact, only recently Nicholas Johnson, Maritime Administrator, told a group in New York that he did not believe the reports about crew shortages and therefore did not intend to set up an intensive program to do anything about it."[45]

The Maritime Administration (MarAd) had requested at least as early as May 1966 that an "essential" status ruling for merchant marine personnel be made by the government, and in light of acute manning shortages in essential ratings that were clearly becoming a prime factor in the delays of many ships being held in port for want of an engineer, mate, radio operator, or skilled unlicensed seaman.

In his September 7 letter to Jesse M. Calhoun of the Marine Engineers Beneficial Association, Forrest D. Hockersmith, acting administrator of the Business and Defense Services Administration of the Commerce Department, explained that though he considered the ocean shipping industry and the Merchant Marine "essential to [the nation's] welfare and to the Allied fighting men in Vietnam," there were, to explain the decision to nonetheless deny draft deferments to merchant seamen, two criteria that "govern inclusion on the [draft deferment] list."[46] An industry had to be:

(1) necessary to the Defense Program, or basic health, safety, or interest, and (2) inadequate to meet defense and civilian requirements because of manpower shortages or for which the future manpower supply is not reasonably assured.

He further explained that the original petition submitted by the Maritime Administration was denied "because it did not meet both criteria at the time it was submitted."[47]

Thus it was that, using rationale that would be described by critics as both illogical and ambiguous, the decision denying deferments—either across the board, or for key ratings—was revealed in September, perhaps a month after the ruling had actually been made. It was greeted with derision by many within the maritime industry, labor organizations, supportive members of Congress, as well as those in the media who reported on such things.

"Since this decision has been made known," Helen Delich Bentley noted in the *Baltimore Sun* in mid–September, "many questions have been asked and many eyebrows have been raised as to how anyone could reach this conclusion at a time when cargoes of war material are pouring over the piers and across the high seas."[48]

Within maritime labor, for example, a telegram sent jointly by Captain Lloyd W. Sheldon, president of the International Organization of Masters, Mates, & Pilots (IOMM&P) and Jesse M. Calhoun, president of the Marine Engineers Beneficial Association (MEBA), was sent to John T. Connor, Commerce Secretary, criticizing his support for the decision to deny draft deferments to merchant seamen. They told

Connor: "[We] deeply regret you do not consider the logistic support of American and allied fighting men in Vietnam an essential activity."[49]

In a separate letter dated September 22 to Hockersmith, Calhoun said it was assumed "that in the event the present desperate shortages of skilled seamen and the obvious worsening of the situation cause, as has already occurred, increasing serious delays in sailings of vessels carrying military and other supplies to South Vietnam, your Administration will assume full responsibility for such [an] unfortunate result."[50]

In his role as chairman of the House Committee on Merchant Marine and Fisheries, Representative Edward A. Garmatz (D–MD) addressed a letter to Commerce Secretary Connor in which he said he found the ruling "extremely difficult to reconcile with evidence available" to him. "To refuse to exempt our experienced seamen from the draft is sheer folly," Garmatz, not mincing words, concluded in his letter.[51]

Fortunately, at least, local draft boards were authorized to consider and rule upon individual cases that came before them. With the requisite documentation for appeal, such as a letter from a maritime labor organization or shipping company as to the essential role an engineer, navigation, or radio officer would actually play on a ship heading for Vietnam, deferments were in most cases awarded. Nonetheless, there were cases of essential licensed officers being drafted right off the ships.

Those in the unlicensed ranks, however, whether skilled able seamen, oilers, and water tenders or not, were less fortunate at the hands of those local draft boards, if, given prevailing attitudes towards such a possibility, those seamen even bothered to seek that deferment. And as a consequence, many merchant seamen *even while serving on ammunition ships on the Vietnam Run* would be sent draft induction notices.[52]

As Helen Delich Bentley succinctly put it soon after the ruling on draft deferments for merchant seamen was made known, "all elements of the shipping industry are chafing at the demeaning term of 'non-essentiality' with which their industry has been tagged in the present Vietnam crisis."[53]

Crew Shortages, Delays, and Bottlenecks

The breakout of additional ships from reserve fleets throughout 1966, as much as they were needed, compounded problems that had first begun to appear late the previous year. And a problem in one area—such as the identified critical shortages of licensed engineers—often compounded a problem in some other area, such as creating departure delays for fully loaded ships, sometimes for additional weeks, in various stateside ports. Various proposals had been offered by the maritime unions that supplied the manpower to alleviate the problem of licensed crew shortages.[54]

Early in the year it was also suggested that the U.S. Merchant Marine Academy in Kings Point, New York, as well as other state maritime academies and colleges, should move up graduation dates for those nearing completion of their undergraduate education and entry-level training programs. When Nicholas Johnson of the Maritime Administration initially balked at the suggestion that he order such a plan for the federal academy, which was under his purview, he took some pointed flak, which only added to a growing sense of disappointment in his leadership of MarAd.

A cartoon in the March 1966 edition of MEBA's publication *American Marine Engineer* showed, as a reflection of this discontent, two helmeted soldiers in a fighting hole, one reading a letter to the other, presented in large, bold type: "...AND YOU HAVE TO WAIT A LITTLE WHILE LONGER FOR YOUR GUNS AND SUPPLIES, BECAUSE NICK JOHNSON SAYS HE'S AFRAID IF HE GRADUATES ANY MARINE ENGINEERS EARLY, THE COMMIES MIGHT THINK AMERICA IS GETTING TOO AGGRESSIVE...."[55]

While early graduation of engineers and navigation officers from academies and maritime colleges would eventually be implemented—but only starting early the following year—maritime labor unions set in motion their own plans for enhanced in-house training that would result both in upgrading of unlicensed seamen to the licensed ranks—from, say, able seaman to third officer, or FOWT to third assistant engineer—and the moving of lower-level licensed officers to higher levels, which would, in turn, create more opportunity for those seeking to utilize newly won entry-level licenses on deck and in engine rooms.[56]

As more and more ships were added to the Vietnam Run in 1966, delays of another sort began to reemerge in-country: ships being held "on the hook" in Vung Tau, Saigon, Qui Nhon, Cam Ranh Bay, and Da Nang, sometimes for weeks on end, or held in such places as Subic Bay in the Philippines or Okinawa until berths or anchorages became available in Vietnam. And it was not unusual either for a ship and crew to experience an inordinately long delay in one place, such as Vung Tau, to finally unload part of its cargo in Saigon, get underway again and shift to another port up the coast, such as Cam Ranh Bay, only to experience the same thing all over again before unloading the remainder of its cargo.[57]

The problem of those long delays "on the hook" in-country was compounded by the fact that seamen were told—ordered by shoreside military authority—to remain aboard ship because of a lack of facilities ashore, or launch service that could take them ashore even if facilities were available to them. While this was not so much the situation in Saigon—once a ship reached that point, at least, after a long delay elsewhere—it was still largely the case in Vung Tau, Qui Nhon, and Cam Ranh Bay. Reports from Da Nang in the north, where most ships were still anchored out in the bay, suggested the situation for shore leave had nonetheless improved by then.

There had been some improvement by the middle of 1966 in the lifting of restrictions that had prevented seamen from going ashore since the first reactivated ships arrived in Vietnam in the closing months of 1965.[58] There was still a gap, however, between the lifting of restrictions on paper and the reality. Contracts had been let for the implementation of launch services: Alaska Barge and Transport's fleet of utility vessels, which would eventually include some 10 LCM "Mike" boats for liberty launch service in in-country ports outside Saigon, had begun to arrive in South Vietnam in March 1966. Those 10 LCM "liberty launches" would eventually be assigned to Da Nang (4), Qui Nhon (4), Nha Trang (1), and Vung Tau.[59] But the service those LCMs would eventually provide, and which would finally make shore leave possible for many merchant seamen, was still not generally available. And civilian craft that might have been offered by locals for such service, and which might have been welcomed in previous years, were no longer authorized by the military authorities, for security reasons, to approach the ships.[60]

An Infrastructure for Shore Leave

The problems associated with restricted shore leave for American merchant seamen had been made all too clear early the previous year, and increasingly as more and more seamen arrived in reactivated reserve fleet ships. A series of meetings were held stateside in late 1965 and early 1966 by government, labor, and industry officials to assess, among a variety of topics, the situation regarding shore leave, and what that meant in terms of providing such things as improved access to medical, mail, and recreational services for seamen. In addition, visits were also made to Vietnam during this period by representatives from labor and industry to assess and make recommendations regarding port infrastructure improvements for receiving and off-loading merchant ships. At the same time, concerns needed to be addressed for providing services for merchant seamen after the Pacific crossing, and the additional time—often involving several weeks—"on the hook" in in-country anchorage areas—while waiting for offloading berths to become available or for barges to be brought out for the slow process of cargo transfer.[61]

Seamen would not have been authorized to go ashore in Cam Ranh Bay, for example, except in special cases of duty, finagling, or medical emergency, if it had not been for the construction of a United Seamen's Service (USS) center, and its opening there after some delay in October 1966.[62] Many could remember only too well how the area had been off limits to seamen since the previous year when reactivated reserve fleet ships had first made their appearance there. As noted, seamen had remained confined to ship for weeks, in a number of areas, until the prefab USS building was finally moved in on an LST, from Okinawa, and its doors opened to provide a place to relax and receive medical, mail, recreational, and other services ashore.[63]

Begun during World War II in 1942, the United Seamen's Service (USS) had grown over the years and, by 1965, when ships began to be broken out of reserve again for Vietnam, its centers were in some 15 ports around the world, but not, until 1966, in Vietnam. The foundation for the center in Cam Ranh Bay had actually been ready for a few months by the time the pre-fab structure was brought in. It had been preceded by a temporary tent structure in the port of Qui Nhon earlier that year, and other more permanent structures were to come in Vung Tau, Da Nang, and Nha Trang in the following year, and eventually in Qui Nhon as well.[64]

Containerization:
"I'd like to sink the son of a bitch"

The breakout of scores of mothballed World War II–vintage merchant ships from National Defense Reserve Fleets (NDRF) in late 1965 to provide logistical support for a massive military buildup in Vietnam had underscored the need for innovative thinking to address the growing problems of delays, logjams, and inordinately long turnaround times of ships in-country.[65]

Factors contributing to this were the traditional handling of break-bulk cargoes, still the manner in which most dry cargo ships, by design, were loaded and unloaded, by booms and slings, and by an inadequate port infrastructure that, while certainly improved somewhat by the end of 1966 with the addition of DeLong and other deep-water piers for unloading and increased barge and lighter inventory along with an enlarged harbor tug fleet to move them, still had a long way to go, and there was room for an innovation that would be greeted generally as a revolutionary concept for its immediate and long-term application.

Adding to the urgency for an innovative solution, despite temporary improvements in turnaround times, more ships were still to be broken out of reserve and added to the Vietnam Run, which would only add again to the problems that had been alleviated somewhat earlier in the year.[66]

What would prove to be revolutionary as far as cargo loading and unloading in Vietnam was concerned, and would eventually transform the ocean-borne shipping world in practical terms for added cargo handling speed, efficiency, security, and inventory control—and would change the very look of ships as well as the port facilities that served them—would be containerization.[67]

The concept of containerization—the use of wooden or metal boxes of varying size to significantly improve loading and unloading of ocean-borne commerce and military logistical support—had long been around. Indeed, use of hard boxes and crates was nothing new at all, but the concept of ocean-going vessels specifically designed to carry full or partial loads of large, standardized shipping containers that could be offloaded by self-contained vessels with heavy-lift capacity or by specialized shoreside "gantry" cranes, quickly placed onto flatbed trucks specifically designed and equipped to carry such things, and then whisked away off piers to shoreside storage yards or directly on their way to final destinations, was revolutionary. As was already being put into practice elsewhere—including Okinawa by the end of the year—this allowed a ship to completely unload in a matter of hours—less than a day, certainly—instead of in several days using the traditional method of ship booms that raised and swung and lowered slings filled with sacks and bales, and a myriad assortment of boxes and loose items.

While some shipping companies had experimented with forms of containerization prior to World War II, it was during the war that the U.S. Army, hoping to improve upon the time typically involved in the loading and unloading of break-bulk cargoes, began experiments involving containers. Then, in 1948, the "Transporter," a standardized container made out of rigid corrugated steel and with double doors on one end (typical of later containers), was developed by the U.S. Army Transportation Corps.[68] Measuring 8'6" in length, 6'3" in width, and 6'10" in height, it quickly proved useful during the Korean War, when, around 1952, another standardized shipping container, dubbed Container Express (CONEX) made its appearance.[69] The CONEX container, similar in size to the Transporter, would serve well in Vietnam years later, along with the larger 20- and 40-foot containers that would be introduced and brought to Vietnam in specially designed and older re-designed cargo ships. Those longer shipping containers continue in use today, filling vast storage yards in ports around the world.

Credit for pioneering the modern day containership revolution is usually bestowed upon Malcolm McClean, a trucking company founder who in 1956 purchased two World War II–vintage T-2 tankers and had them transformed into ships capable of loading 35-foot long shipping containers and the trailer chassis that would be used for moving them ashore. On April 26 of that year the first of these ships,

Ideal-X—known less formally as SS *Maxton* (for McLean's hometown in North Carolina)—loaded 58 containers at Port Elizabeth Marine Terminal, New Jersey, and set sail for Houston, Texas, where 58 semi-trucks were waiting to load and whisk them away. The first true commercially viable containership had ushered in the transformation of the ocean-borne shipping world.[70]

When asked at the time what he thought of the SS *Ideal-X* and what it represented, one representative of the International Longshoremen's Association (ILA), Freddy Fields, who no doubt understood as well as anyone what the long-term impact of containerization might be on his profession, reacted to the news of *Ideal-X* by saying: "I'd like to sink the son of a bitch."[71]

It's not surprising that early on, as planners were trying to figure out how to ship supplies to Vietnam in the quickest, most efficient way—and despite the necessary initial use of large numbers of World War II–era ships that were already approaching obsolescence and generally loaded and unloaded in the traditional more laborious and time-consuming manner—that the concept of containerization was reintroduced into the conversation.

Among the first to advocate the idea of containerization and use of containerships specifically for deployment in Vietnam was Jesse M. Calhoun, president of the International Longshoremen's Union, who had proposed this in October 1965 during the initial breakout period of ships from the reserve fleets. Calhoun participated in a series of meetings involving labor, government, and shipping organizations, and then traveled to Vietnam from December 1965 into January 1966 on a fact-finding mission to assess problems related to in-country cargo-handling, and to make recommendations for easing the delays and logjams that had developed there. He continued to press for containerization, and specifically recommended that containers be constructed out of plywood so they could be broken down after they were unloaded for construction needs in-country. During Congressional hearings in early and mid–1966 to discuss Vietnam shipping policy, Calhoun took issue with the decision by the MSTS to delay implementation of containership service directly to Vietnam in 1966, but, instead, to initially commence such service to Okinawa.[72]

"First of all," Calhoun pointed out, "you have double-handling. You have got to discharge them. You have to discharge the ship in Okinawa or Manila. Then you have to strip the containers down in [Okinawa] with Okinawan labor, whatever they get, and then you have to load it into the other ships, and how long this is going to take, I don't know, and then it has to be transported again to Saigon, anyhow."[73]

At that point, however, there were no containerships in service, and certainly none waiting to be reactivated from the NDRF.

Our "Leaky Pipeline" to Vietnam

In December 1966 an article in *Reader's Digest* titled "Our Leaky Pipeline to Vietnam" provided an analysis and status report of sorts of the role the Merchant Marine had been playing in logistical support of the war in Vietnam through September of that year. It served as a sharp critique as well of maritime policy, and attitudes towards the Merchant Marine that had resulted in a level of unpreparedness prior to the outbreak of the war, and concern for its future.[74]

With its large national distribution, and what was described as the "largest paid circulation" of any magazine in the world, the article by investigative journalist Lester Velie provided an important and widely circulated contemporary description of issues related to the Merchant Marine in the early buildup and reserve fleet breakout period between mid–1965 and late 1966. For those in the heartland of the country not having the almost daily exposure to the maritime industry reporting provided by major newspapers along the East, West, and Gulf Coasts, Velie's article in *Reader's Digest* would have been a major revelation if not an eye-opener into an aspect of the developing war in Vietnam and what was required to support it.[75]

Issues highlighted in Velie's article included most of those stemming from early discussions, debates, inquiries, and arguments as the maritime industry responded to and wrestled with problems associated with the rapid escalation of the war. Most important were the issues having to do with the relative merits of sea-borne versus air transportation, about which Secretary of Defense McNamara had and continued to receive much criticism; the problems revealed early on by the Vietnam experience, associated with reliance on "foreign flag" shipping in national emergencies; the retention of trained personnel, including Merchant Marine Academy and other maritime college graduates, in maritime-related professions; resultant crewing difficulties in the face of large-scale merchant ship breakouts from reserve fleets; in-country ship unloading delays; Selective Service issues pertaining to merchant seamen at a time when many ships were unable to sail due, in part, to the drafting of seamen in key ratings; and the crucial need for "surge power"—the ability to shift privately owned, subsidized merchant ships from commercially lucrative shipping routes—to fulfill the requirements of a national emergency involving cross-ocean logistical support of troops in the field.

Velie's article, devoting considerable space to the unfortunate initial breakout experience of one ship—*Malden Victory*—was a hard-hitting critique of U.S. national maritime policy, and the extent to which that had lived up to the promise, spirit, and requirements of the Merchant Marine Act of 1936 in the aftermath of World War II, and leading up to the war in Vietnam.[76]

"The Malden Victory is one of the 161 reserve fleet ships," Velie wrote, "on which we have been forced to rely to supply Vietnam—because we have been caught with our ships down." The United States had not kept up with modernization trends or maintained a robust and competitive shipbuilding program, Velie argued. "A babble of contending voices and interests has turned our ship industry, comparatively, into an orphan," he wrote.[77]

By the end of 1966 the United States had slogged yet deeper into the "quicksand war" in Vietnam. The number of American military personnel in-country had risen by then to some 385,000, and some 6,644 had been killed in action.[78] While it never was, and never would be the role of merchant mariners to slog into the "boonies" alongside soldiers and marines, for whom they otherwise provided the preponderance of logistical supply support from bullets to beer, and therefore would not ordinarily suffer such great losses, they too had lost some of their own that year, and would continue to do so.

As the year ended, some problems that had developed during the early buildup phase had been ameliorated somewhat with improvements to shoreside infrastructure, the DeLong piers, for example, and addition of harbor tugs, and lighterage for offloading into barges. But the addition of more de-mothballed merchant ships from reserve fleets onto the Vietnam Run—the number by the end of 1966 was generally put at 146—only added once again to in-country delays "on the hook" or while holding elsewhere until getting the word to proceed to anchorages in Vung Tau, Da Nang, Cam Ranh Bay, and elsewhere, where, depending on actual cargo priority, further delays might then be encountered.

There were other problems contributing to delays and turnaround times that were on the rise once again, and which would add significantly to voyage duration and costs. It was understandable, until port infrastructure was improved, how the addition of more ships to the Vietnam Run would make for larger groups of ships waiting at anchorage to proceed to their final in-country destinations. It was now being suggested in some reports that "feuding between the Army and the Agency for International Development (AID)" was contributing to the backlog of ships once again waiting to unload in Saigon.[79] Others placed blame, simply, on general mismanagement, still inadequate shoreside facilities, and shortages of—or poorly trained and equipped, or otherwise inept—stevedoring gangs.[80]

Whereas, as one New Orleans newspaper reported in October, the shipping backlog in and around Saigon had been "cut to near zero only a few months ago," the situation had "again become so serious that more than 60 freighters [were] waiting to be unloaded at this key port." This figure actually included some 50 ships waiting in Vung Tau to proceed up-channel to Saigon, and another dozen or so "anchored and waiting in the river near Saigon." The report went on to say that other ships were "being held as far away as Manila and Yokohama."[81]

According to government and shipping sources, the article reported, "the average waiting period for ships at that time was as long as 30 days."[82]

Something had to give, or be changed, since there was no sign of reduction in the numbers of ships making their way to Vietnam or the number of American and allied military personnel who would be arriving to begin their tours of duty in Vietnam. If anything, those numbers were expected to rise.

Protest at Newport

Ships were again being backed up, and turnaround times were seriously on the rise once again, due to sheer numbers of arrivals, and still inadequate port facilities. Adding to the problem by year's end, at least in Saigon, was a new development: some 2,600 Vietnamese dock workers went out on strike on December 26, for reasons relating to developments at the Army's new terminal, under construction, a few miles north of the city.[83] As a result, the unloading of perhaps 10 ships carrying military cargo had come to a halt. Some 300 American GIs were quickly detailed to take on stevedoring duties, but additional delays and bottlenecks were unavoidable in the short run despite their best efforts.[84]

The immediate reason for the Vietnamese work stoppage was the replacement of 600 workers by 71st Transportation Battalion personnel at the new terminal on the Saigon River, something they had been warned would happen as part of the construction plan, but to which the Vietnamese labor organizations nonetheless objected. Dubbed Newport, this new terminal, situated close to the highway used for transporting cargoes to the major bases at Bien Hoa and Long Binh, and which would reduce the movement of convoys through the streets of Saigon, had been under construction since the beginning of the year.[85] It would eventually add two piers, and four deep-draft berths, but they would not be available until early the next year. The terminal had in any case begun receiving shallow draft LSTs, which could be offloaded using ramps, and ships that could anchor out in the stream for the still slower process of offloading into barges.

According to one source at the time, a group of some 150 striking Vietnamese workers made their way to the Newport terminal where they quickly "set up a compound outside the gates. There, under improvised shelters, they sat, smoked and cooked over charcoal fires." One of their handmade signs on display read, in English: "We protest against the plot of the commander officer of the United States 4th Transportation Command, causing a hard life for the workers."[86]

The strike would continue, the shipping logjams would continue, the war would continue, but some relief would come in the early months of the new year, at least as far as the movement of ships and cargoes was concerned.

11

Turnaround (1967)

"We're not drawing ahead clearly ... or fast enough to optimize our confidence in achieving a 12–18 month turnaround."
—Robert Komer, director, CORDS, 1967

"In those days [1967] you could sit on the balcony of the Majestic Hotel bar in Saigon, hear a live band playing, and watch the war going on a few miles away across the river. It was a weird experience."
—Peter J. Bourgeois, second mate, SS *Elaine*

As the war moved into yet another year, there was a perceived mood of "cautious optimism" among at least some of President Johnson's inner circle of policy advisors.[1] Some even suggested that 1967 might well prove to be *the* decisive year—a "cross-over" or turnaround point—not only for preventing defeat but for turning what some feared might have been a *losing* cause into a *winning* one.[2]

Robert "Blowtorch Bob" Komer, a former CIA operative then serving on the National Security Council, and who would soon head up the Civil Operations and Revolutionary Development Support (CORDS) program in Vietnam, was a self-described "inveterate optimist" when it came to the war.[3] He had returned from Vietnam in early 1967 to report to LBJ that he was "more optimistic than ever before" and that the cumulative change since an earlier visit was "dramatic, if not yet visibly demonstrable in all respects." "Wastefully, expensively, but nonetheless indisputably," Komer argued in his report, "we are winning the war in the South.... We are grinding the enemy down by sheer weight and mass."[4]

The "sheer weight and mass" to which Komer referred was being delivered by air power and large-unit "search and destroy" operations, both of which, in turn, required huge amounts of logistical support reflected in the numbers of ships arriving and unloading in Vietnamese ports. That too relied on the continuing effort to improve and expand the port infrastructure.

Not all were as optimistic as Komer, however, including LBJ and Secretary of Defense Robert McNamara. Convinced it would be a long war, whatever the outcome, McNamara spoke more pessimistically than Komer of a "military standoff at a much higher level of conflict" that might result, at best, in achieving "a position where negotiations would be more likely to be productive." As for any kind of a time frame, McNamara had confided to President Johnson after his return from a visit to Vietnam in September that he saw "no reasonable way to bring the war to an end soon. Enemy morale has not been broken."[5] "The prognosis," McNamara concluded in his report to the president, "is bad that the war can be brought to a satisfactory conclusion within the next two years. The large-unit operations probably will not do it; negotiations probably will not do it. While we should continue to pursue both of these routes ... we should recognize that success from them is a mere possibility, not a probability."[6]

President Johnson's own misgivings about the war in Vietnam, articulated clearly years before in private conversations with his closest confidants—and which he seemed to share with McNamara—had been a source of torment for him. Now, in his State of the Union Address delivered before Congress on January 10, 1967, he suggested that waging war there was an "evil" preferable to the greater one of international Communism and the prospect it might continue to spread if not held along the Cold War containment line in Vietnam.

"We have chosen to fight a limited war in Vietnam," Johnson said, "in an attempt to prevent a larger one—a war almost certain to follow ... if the Communists succeed in overrunning and taking over South Viet-Nam by aggression and by force."[7]

Despite arguments made by Johnson and others to rally support for and motivate those who would be shipping out to serve in Vietnam, he could still describe the war, as he did in his State of the Union Address in such a way that reflected his own distaste for it. "No better words could describe our present course [in Vietnam]," he noted, "than those once spoken by the great Thomas Jefferson: 'It is the melancholy law of human societies to be compelled sometimes to choose a great evil in order to ward off a greater.'"[8]

Newport under construction at Saigon in 1966. Its completion would contribute significantly to reduced ship turnaround times during the war (U.S. Army).

DeLong piers, with the distinctive vertical supports, were towed to Vietnam over long distances from other countries where they were built and contributed to reduction of ship turnaround times during the war. The one shown here in Cam Ranh Bay at right would have become operational in 1966. At least two of the ships shown unloading are Victory ships (U.S. Navy).

Though opposition to the war continued to build at home, and as casualties in Vietnam continued to mount to an alarming degree, the long-established language of Cold War expressed in Johnson's speech, and now manifested in a "limited" hot war in Vietnam, maintained majority public and congressional support, at least for the time being, for the chosen course there.[9]

The tonnage of military supplies hauled to Vietnam in American merchant ships continued to rise in logistical support of the war in Vietnam, and those large-scale military operations to "search and destroy" Viet Cong and NVA continued to be planned and executed. Only a few days before Johnson's State of the Union speech, the largest such operation to that point—CEDAR FALLS—had been launched in the so-called Iron Triangle area of South Vietnam, and bases and ports that would provide support for that and other such operations continued to be developed.[10] Those extensive and costly construction undertakings by themselves suggested, as many more and less optimistic war policy makers wrestled with the implications of it all, that prosecution of the war was still a long-term matter.

"...despite all the protection"

Much had been done to improve security for merchant shipping in Vietnam in the two years following the landing of Marines in Da Nang in March 1965. River patrol vessels and quick-response aircraft had been introduced, herbicides had been sprayed in massive quantities to deprive the Viet Cong of cover along the river channels, armed guards were routinely placed aboard ships for the river transits, Operation Stable Door had been introduced to provide surveillance and security for harbor entrances and anchorages, and on-ground units—including SEAL teams—had been inserted into the Rung Sat Special Zone (RSSZ) and other areas through which ships would pass.[11] Nevertheless, as one U.S. Navy report noted in March 1967, "in the main channel to Saigon, the Viet Cong continued their attempts to harass and interdict patrols and merchant shipping."[12]

Those attempts, against naval vessels and merchant ships, were not only becoming more frequent, but also, with the introduction of more varied, powerful, and sophisticated weaponry—such as the Chicom 57-millimeter and 75-millimeter recoilless rifles—more deadly and destructive.[13] This was clearly demonstrated, for example, in attacks along the Long Tau River on February 26 against the Panamanian-registered coastal freighter *Lorinda*, and then again on March 18 against the American freighter US *Conqueror*.

The *Lorinda*, a 345-foot Panamanian-registered coastal freighter, was attacked by the Viet Cong some 18 miles south of Saigon while proceeding along the Long Tau River channel. She was hit by 11 rounds from a 57-millimeter recoilless rifle, seven striking her hull and four striking the ship's superstructure. The master and pilot were wounded, in addition to four others. After running aground, *Lorinda* was refloated and then moved to Saigon.[14]

Helen Delich Benley, maritime editor of the *Baltimore Sun* then reporting from Vietnam, filed an account the next month of an attack on US *Conqueror*. "The weekend shelling of the Liberty [*sic*] freighter *U.S. Conqueror* by the Viet Cong," she noted, "typifies the danger under which American-flag ships are flying the Long Tau River to Saigon."[15]

The US *Conqueror* was proceeding up channel to Saigon and had reached a point just a few miles below Nha Be when, on the afternoon of March 16, it was struck multiple times by what was described as recoilless rifle fire (another account reported there had also been mortar fire).

The monthly U.S. Naval Forces report for Vietnam included the following description of the incident:

> [A] merchant ship, [US] *Conqueror*, was struck by fire from Viet Cong positions on the east bank of the Long Tau, three miles downstream from Nha Be. A PBR patrol came to the ship's assistance and was taken under fire. The PBRs returned fire. Then a spotter aircraft joined the PBRs and helped suppress enemy fire with 2.75 inch rockets. [US] *Conqueror* sustained six hits during the engagement. One crew member and two U.S. Army military policemen were wounded. The extent of Viet Cong casualties was undetermined.[16]

While the Navy report was classified at the time, as well as brief, some additional details of the incident were made known publicly soon after by the American press and maritime labor publications. One member of the onboard armed guard detachment was mentioned—not by name—in most accounts as having been wounded, and his wounds were described as fatal. The ship's crewmember, Chief Cook Benjamin J. Vance, sustained a broken leg and shrapnel wounds, none of which were life threatening. Nonetheless, he was transferred to the Keshine military hospital in Yokohama, Japan, for further medical treatment.[17]

As for the US *Conqueror* itself, she was not holed below the waterline, nor was engine machinery damaged. However, lifeboats and the master's office were described as having been "demolished" by the recoilless rifle fire.[18]

"As safe a task as you could have over here"

At one point in the early buildup phase in Vietnam—through 1966—there were more than 20 dredges—both of the hopper and suction type—in operation in Vietnam, some Vietnamese, but most and the largest brought in from other countries, notably the United States, Japan, and Canada.[19] They became engaged in opening and improving navigation channels, creating ship turning basins, reclaiming hundreds of acres of land for base construction, providing sand for concrete production, and preparing the way for installation of deepwater piers. These vessels, generally crewed by civilian seamen—"dredgemen"—took up station in various areas from the northernmost reaches of "I" Corps area to its southernmost in the Mekong Delta, moving tons of sand, mud, and alluvial silt for distribution ashore or dumping at sea. They seemed to pose no particular threat, some would argue, and were of little interest otherwise to the enemy, since none had yet come under attack in more than a year.

But any belief that the dredges were somehow safer, more secure places to be—unlike other places in-country—was but an illusion that would soon be shattered by a new and deadly turn of events.

The dredges made it possible for military supplies to be moved more quickly and easily—and to some extent more securely—to areas otherwise blocked by accumulated sand and silt. And even if deep-draft ships would never be able to navigate to certain areas as a result of the dredges' work, such shallow-draft vessels as the various types of World War II–vintage landing craft that were being brought in—the LSTs, LSUs, and LCMs—would be able to do so, moving cargoes to final destinations that had first been offloaded from merchant ships and "nucleus" ships of the MSTS crewed by merchant seamen.[20] The dredges' role, therefore, was crucial, if not given the same attention as other types of vessels delivering the goods, enabling supplies to move by means other than along circuitous land routes that were anything but secure.

While dredging had been considered "as safe a task as anyone could have over here," as reporter Helen Delich Bentley of the *Baltimore Sun* reported hearing said in-country in early 1967, the reality of the dredges' important role in support of American, South Vietnamese, and allied operations in Vietnam was not lost on those determined to defeat, destroy, or at least slow them.[21] It was just a matter of time, some realistic observers no doubt concluded, before the dredges also came under direct attack, often with as deadly a result as was occurring with increasing frequency against other moving or stationary targets along the waterways, in the ports, and around other military base areas of South Vietnam.

The *Jamaica Bay*

The 170-foot cutterhead suction dredge *Jamaica Bay*, believed to be the largest dredge in Vietnam at least through 1966, had already worked to prepare the way for deep-draft shipping in Cam Ranh Bay, and for the installation of deepwater piers in Da Nang.[22] Shifted south to the Mekong Delta, and now just 150 yards east of the entrance channel to the new and still developing Dong Tam base—and some 150 yards again from the north bank of the Mekong River—the dredge was idle in the early morning hours of January 9, 1967, as most of her crew had gone ashore to enjoy a weekend leave in nearby My Tho, a few miles away, or possibly in Saigon, a longer distance to the north.[23] As fate and timing would have it, they would be the lucky ones in light of what was about to happen to the dredge in their absence.

At 0525 hours a massive explosion ripped a seven-foot by nine-foot hole in the *Jamaica Bay*'s starboard side. That was quickly followed by a second explosion, on the port side, resulting in a hole that measured seven feet by 15 feet and which sent the dredge to rest in the mud some 25 feet below. Three of the crew remaining on board were killed quickly by the blasts, while another was trapped in a flooded compartment with only a small pocket of air remaining; he would be rescued in time, and removed from the stricken dredge in a state of shock. A half-dozen other crew members were removed uninjured. In addition to the sinking of *Jamaica Bay*, with only portions of her superstructure still visible above the waterline, an LCM-6 secured alongside and typically used for transfer of supplies, and as a liberty launch, also sank as the much larger dredge went down.[24]

The explosions that sent *Jamaica Bay* to the bottom, presumably caused by command-detonated limpet mines attached to her hull, prevented the refloating of the dredge—and only after a difficult salvage operation—for another two months. In the meantime, another dredge—the *New Jersey*—would be shifted to the Dong Tam channel to continue the base construction project.[25] But *Jamaica Bay*'s bad luck would not end there: In early March, just four days after finally being refloated, the dredge sank in deeper water after encountering a storm while being towed to Vung Tau for further repairs. With the dredge now resting in some 35 feet of water, another salvage operation was deemed impracticable: *Jamaica Bay*, her days of service over, was allowed to remain where she had gone down.[26]

Dredge *Hyde*

There would be another, similar attack upon an American dredge in Vietnam—the *James F.C. Hyde*—before the year was out, far to the north in the northern I Corps area. Longer than the *Jamaica Bay* by more than 30 feet at 216 feet, *Hyde* was a hopper type dredge operated by the U.S. Army Corps of Engineers that had seen service during World War II and in Korea.

With a crew of 42 seamen, under command of Captain James Bartell, *Hyde* was deployed to Vietnam in 1966, becoming steadily engaged in dredging the Cua Viet bar—north of Quang Tri and just six miles south of the DMZ—to open and maintain access for LSTs providing support for the developing Cua Viet base.[27]

At four o'clock in the morning on May 9, 1967, the first of two command-detonated limpet-type mines attached to the dredge's starboard bow was detonated. Immediately following this initial blast the officer on watch ordered the dredge moved as quickly as possible to the south bank to minimize flooding. Two hours later a second mine, located on the dredge's port quarter, was detonated. Because of the earlier maneuver, the blast, which only produced a hole "the size of a grapefruit" in the ship's counter row, occurred above the waterline, resulting in minor damage to the after steering machinery room. But the initial blast was more serious: it opened a hole measuring some four by seven feet and resulted in flooding a ballast tank, boatswain locker, paint locker, carpenter shop, and sail locker. Fortunately, however, in contrast to the attack on *Jamaica Bay*, no casualties were reported. Repairs proved so successful that *Hyde* was back in operation within 36 hours.[28]

The attacks on dredges *Jamaica Bay* and *Hyde*, the first since such operations had begun in Vietnam in late 1965 in conjunction with improvement of navigation channels and port and base development, would by no means be the last. As Richard Tregaskis, author of *Guadalcanal Diary* during World War II, would note in a later work having to do with military base construction in Vietnam, the deadly attack on *Jamaica Bay* was "only the first of a series of violent attacks levelled on the dredges as they came in succession" to Vietnam in 1967 and succeeding years.[29]

In with the New, Out with the Old

Though many ships built during World War II—now all more than 20 years old—would continue moving along the pipeline to Vietnam more or less in their original configurations, many of those broken out of reserve fleets in 1965 and 1966 would begin to either be returned there in 1967, or sold for scrapping as no longer viable for commercial or future military service. It was reported in August, for example, that 16 of the 172 government-owned ships broken out of reserve fleets and assigned to private shipping under General Agency Agreement (GAA) were being "shunted from active service to semiretirement" into standby status in the ports of San Francisco and Seattle until either called back into service, placed back into reserve for long-term storage, or disposed of otherwise.[30]

As total MSTS shipments of military supplies continued to rise to Vietnam and elsewhere in Southeast Asia during the year and through the next: 1967 would mark the peak year for shipments carried in government-owned merchant ships operated under General Agency Agreement (GAA) by private shipping companies.[31] This was clearly a reflection of the reduced size of the GAA fleet of merchant ships as one year gave way to the next.

Increased efficiency of operations in-country, and the composition of the fleet itself—the addition of containerships, for example—would actually contribute to an overall reduction of ships involved in the Vietnam sealift from a reported 294 earlier in the year to some 252, of which 129 were privately owned and 123 government-owned and under General Agency

Agreement, reported on the Vietnam Run as of October.[32] That figure did not include, apparently, MSTS "nucleus" ships crewed by merchant seamen.

The removal of the first group of government-owned Victory ships from active service was made possible in part, published reports noted, by "a sharp reduction in vessel turnaround time" in Vietnam and elsewhere in Southeast Asia, and would have the expected benefit of freeing up some 600 seamen, as *The New York Times* reported, "for duty on faster and more modern ships, which have frequently been delayed because of the shortage of experienced ratings."[33]

The impact of containerization on ship turnaround times was also cited as a factor in the decision to pull Victory ships off the Vietnam Run. So too was the increased availability of deepwater berths. During the course of the year, for example, all four such berths under construction at Newport, just up-river from Saigon, would be completed and made available for ocean-going ships.[34]

While this development painted an improved picture, at least so far as conditions in Vietnam were concerned, and suggested that there would be fewer delayed or short sailings due to manpower requirements, it also meant that availability of seagoing jobs in stateside hiring halls where such jobs were assigned became somewhat tighter to come by in the later months of 1967.

By October 1967, MSTS had announced that additional Victory ships—bringing the total for the year to 33 when combined with earlier withdrawals—had been taken off the Vietnam Run and either placed into permanent or temporary lay-up or were awaiting another, final disposition at the hands of breakers.[35]

The year would usher in significant changes in the complexion of the fleet of merchant ships setting out on the Vietnam Run. New, modernized, drastically altered conversions were being introduced, and Victory ships in their original configurations were being withdrawn in increasing numbers. This trend would continue, even as the war continued to expand and intensify. The introduction of government-owned ships formerly in reserve to the Vietnam Run had created concerns by private shipping companies relating to the Wilson-Weeks Agreement of 1954, wherein U.S.-flag carriers would be given priority over government-owned or chartered vessels. It set "general instructions for the use, transfer and allocation of merchant ships in peace and in war."[36]

Most of the World War II–era troopships would also be taken out of service during the year, thus having their own impact on availability of seafaring jobs, and were being sent off to languish for the most part in reserve fleets until facing their own ultimate fates in due course before the breakers.[37]

Six of the reconfigured ships would be C-2s owned and operated by Sea-Land Services, which, under a $70-million contract worked out with the Department of Defense, would provide direct containerships service commencing in mid-year between San Francisco or Seattle and either Da Nang or Cam Ranh Bay.[38] A seventh Sea-Land ship, also a converted C-2 and with a capacity for hauling 274 containers, was expected to shuttle between Cam Ranh, Qui Nhon, and Saigon. Four of the Sea-Land ships were expected to be self-sustaining, with heavy lift capacity and capable of loading and unloading containers of 35-foot length.[39] Three other ships of the larger C-4 hull type, capable of carrying 609 of the 35-foot containers, would not be self-sustaining but loaded and unloaded by specially developed gantry cranes already in use in the United States and which Sea-Land agreed by contract to install in Da Nang.[40]

Sea-Land had entered into a contract in 1966 to provide containership service from the West Coast to Okinawa. Some had argued then that it would have been better to run their ships directly into Vietnam, rather than having to offload in Okinawa only to have to load containers onto another ship again for delivery to Vietnam. The 1967 contract, another development to improve in-country turnaround times, would soon rectify what some had argued had been a mistake.

Another shipping company that had previously signed a contract with the

Department of Defense to provide modernized ships for service to Vietnam was Seatrain.[41] Part of the movement in 1967 to reconfigure ships and make them more suitable for carrying cargo to Vietnam and elsewhere in Southeast Asia, and resulting in quicker turnarounds, was the announcement by Seatrain Lines that it was in process of converting nine ships for that purpose. According to a Seatrain press release at the time, the ships were "specially configured 560-foot former tankers whose holds and decks have been completely cleared to enable them to carry tanks, trucks, self-propelled guns, construction equipment, helicopters and airplanes, in addition to ammunition and other military cargo."[42] The ships would also be designed for carrying containers and rail cars.

One contemporaneous account noted that each of the Seatrain ships was "being equipped with two 45-ton cranes, which will be capable of discharging 35 tons of cargo a minute." Howard M. Pack, Seatrain's president, said of *Seatrain Puerto Rico* that "the ship's greatest value is its ability to carry an almost unlimited mix of vehicles and weaponry, enabling it to carry unit-loads of combat-ready equipment."[43]

As the first of the nine ship conversions to be completed, *Seatrain Puerto Rico* entered service in its new incarnation in early January 1967. Three other similar ships would follow *Seatrain Puerto Rico* after their own conversions at the Maryland Shipbuilding and Drydock Co., in Baltimore. Three additional tankers were converted for Seatrain at the Newport News yard, and two others at the Savannah Machinery Foundry Corp. in Georgia. Following *Seatrain Puerto Rico*, the eight remaining ships were scheduled for delivery at monthly intervals, with one of the Maryland conversions scheduled for delivery in February.[44]

Seatrain Florida Runs the Gauntlet

Most if not all of the ships converted for Seatrain in 1967 would see service in Vietnam in that and subsequent years. At least one—*Seatrain Florida*—would be attacked while transiting the Long Tau River channel to Saigon within a few months of its emergence from the Newport News, Virginia, shipyard in its new guise.[45] But *Seatrain Florida* would earn the dubious distinction of being attacked not once but *twice* during the same 40-mile river transit to Saigon in August 1967. Most of what we know about those attacks is contained in the monthly U.S. Naval summary for Vietnam, relevant portions of which are as follows:

> On the morning of 1 August, 12 miles southeast of Nha Be [the ship] was attacked from the river bank by Viet Cong riflemen and machine-gunners. The outburst was quickly suppressed by PBRs and an Army helicopter fire team during a brief following action in which three Viet Cong were killed and one helicopter was damaged.[46]
>
> Forty-five minutes later, five miles farther upstream, SEATRAIN FLORIDA came under heavy automatic-weapons and recoilless rifle fire from the east bank of the Long Tau River. Once again the PBRs and helicopters launched an immediate counter attack, with the patrol boats delivering 60-mm mortar fire against the enemy positions while the helicopters struck members of the enemy contingent fleeing inland. At least four Viet Cong were killed during the two attacks. There were no U.S. casualties.

In addition to the brief information provided in this (then classified) report—which says nothing about any damage done to *Seatrain Florida*—the *Seafarers*

Log, a publication of the Seafarers International Union (SIU) representing all unlicensed crew personnel of the Seatrain fleet, provided a few additional details of what it reported (erroneously) as a single attack on the ship: "Saigon—The U.S. military command in Saigon has confirmed that heavily fortified Communist gun positions camouflaged along the banks of the Long Tau River ... fired upon the SIU-manned Seatrain Florida (Seatrain Lines) using a variety of automatic weapons and heavy recoilless rifle fire."[47]

The *Seafarers Log* noted that there had been "damage to one vehicle on deck" but no loss of life to crew. Discrepancies between the naval report and the *Seafarers Log* included the latter's reference to the attack having occurred 15 miles southeast of Saigon, and there having been "fighter-bombers" involved in the counter-attack as well as helicopters.

What additional damage might have been done by the several "heavy" recoilless rifle rounds reported to have hit the ship has not been determined. Most importantly, in any case, was the fact that, once again, all members of the ship's crew had escaped injury as *Seatrain Florida* ran the gauntlet that August day on the way up to Saigon.

The new year was to usher in a major turnaround of sorts on the Vietnam Run. In nautical application, the term was all about the time involved from a ship's arrival in port to the point of weighing anchor or casting off mooring lines to get underway again following discharge of cargo.

For others, the word could of course also represent a larger reality—or hope, at least, by those involved—for progress in the war and longer-term prospects forward. Both ways of defining or otherwise considering the term "turnaround" would very much be on the minds, perhaps in the guts as well, of those operating and manning merchant ships to the Vietnam war zones, and those prosecuting a war fraught with uncertainty, and which for some had already gone on too long, cost too much treasure, and taken too many lives.

Turnaround times for merchant ships in Vietnam were a reflection in part of how well development of port facilities was progressing and stevedoring operations were going in the first year of the sealift following the series of breakouts or withdrawals of "flights" of ships from National Defense Reserve Fleets (NDRF). Turnaround time, once—before the buildup—involved perhaps a week on average, but had turned into multi-week, even multi-month-long waiting games in some cases that would seem to improve only to regress as another group of ships was withdrawn from reserve and placed into the logistical support fleet, or other factors interceded and worked against efficient and timely unloading operations.

By early 1967 the average turnaround time for a ship involved in the Vietnam sealift had been reduced somewhat but was still averaging about 19 days, a considerable reduction from the previous year but still not good enough.[48] By June, the average number of days had been reduced to just under two weeks.[49] Contributing to this improvement in turnaround time was the addition of piers—including the DeLongs—and unloading berths that did not require the slower process of offloading into barges and lighters while anchored out.

While manpower shortages continued to be a problem in early 1967, a turnaround of sorts would also take place in this regard as the year wore on. A number of factors in particular would contribute to the improvement of available shipboard personnel, and, therefore, a reduction in sailing delays caused by crew shortages.

These included the enhanced upgrading programs undertaken by maritime labor unions representing both licensed and unlicensed seamen, and moved up graduations at the U.S. Maritime Academy in Kings Point, New York—there were 200 graduated at Kings Point in February, four months early, 124 engineers and 76 deck—and early graduations at state maritime colleges and academies. This included the graduation of 107 at the New York Maritime College, Fort Schuyler, in April, 35 of whom were scheduled to depart for San Francisco, for Vietnam service, the day after graduation.[50] Another development would contribute to a reduction in manpower shortages in 1967: the first withdrawal of groups of reactivated Victory ships from active service on the Vietnam Run. As this took place, their crews were then available to other ships that might otherwise have been short-handed and delayed.

Newport

A major improvement of the in-country port infrastructure was realized in July 1967 with the opening of a new U.S. Army–operated port facility—considered part of the Saigon port complex—with the imaginatively named tag of Newport. This, in the form of a "T"-pier, added more berths as well as buoys from which cargo ships as large as the C-3 type could be accommodated—offloaded, turned, and sent off downriver again. Conceived the previous year for development in an area just upstream from Saigon, the first of its eventual four berths were formally dedicated at the end of January.[51] Ships had been offloaded there from buoys since late the previous year, and others would continue to be unloaded in that manner even as berths were made available there.[52]

With the use of Vietnamese stevedores not always to the liking of those in charge of MSTS in-country operations, one of the planned advantages of Newport was also to transfer unloading responsibilities within the new facility to Army stevedores.[53] Anticipating this, Vietnamese stevedores were let go with two-week pay severances in late December 1966, resulting in a five-day longshoremen's strike in Saigon, which in itself only contributed at that point to continued delays and bottlenecks in the area.[54] Nonetheless, that, and gradual introduction of Republic of Korea (ROK) stevedores elsewhere, paved the way for the speed and efficiency that was to come in Newport, and overall, in the new year.[55]

There was certainly no let-up in the pace of commitment to the war in Vietnam, and the peak of American force levels would not actually come for more than another two years, during the summer months of 1969. Military operations throughout South Vietnam required that sealift levels keep pace, which by and large they did. Though shortages of certain supplies were at times reported for one reason or another, the ships kept coming, port development continued in earnest, and, despite continued delays "on the hook," seamen were beginning to experience the kind of relief that only shore leave, local establishments, and the facilities and services of the United Seamen's Service clubs could provide.

The introduction of launch service, expedited by a contract agreement between MSTS and Alaska Barge and Transport, would help do the trick.[56] Seamen in various areas had found themselves confined for too long to their ships—weeks longer, in many cases, than a trans-Pacific voyage might have taken, anchored out within sight of land, deprived of the basic opportunity and ritual of shore leave, after those long weeks at sea. Now, and after a year's delay in some cases following the initial buildup, proper "liberty" launch service was being introduced by some 10 of the smaller LCM landing craft—otherwise known as "Mike" boats—which were soon making their way around anchorages in Da Nang, Cam Ranh Bay, Vung Tau, and elsewhere, taking on seamen for shore leave destinations, and later depositing them back to their ships.

The opening of the USS center in Cam Ranh Bay, in October 1966, had finally changed things for the better there for many seamen, and in time centers would be added in other port areas.[57]

SS *Green Wave*

Among the many privately owned cargo ships under charter to the MSTS in 1967 for Vietnam service was the SS *Green Wave*, Central Gulf Lines, under command of Captain Swen Johannson. Launched in 1944 as a Squier-class troop transport for the U.S. Navy as USS *General C.G. Morton*, then transferred to the Army in 1946, and again to the MSTS for use as the troop transport USNS *Gen. C.G. Morton* in 1950, the 522-foot ship was acquired by Central Gulf from MSTS in April 1967 as part of its Ship Exchange Program, and converted in Tampa, Florida, for carrying dry cargo. She departed Tampa in September, proceeded to Vietnam via Panama and Yokosuka, Japan before arriving at Vung Tau anchorage on November 11, 1967. According to Larry Fosgate, who had signed on in Tampa as her deck cadet out of the Merchant Marine Academy, *Green Wave* carried a load of general cargo that included vehicles, telephone wire, traffic counters—which he speculated might have been for monitoring movements along the Ho Chi Minh Trail—beer, and, of all things, snow plows (for clearing brush).[58]

"We swung at an outer anchorage at Vung Tau," Fosgate later recalled, "for about a week. Alaska Tug and Barge was the contractor providing launch services with a 'Mike 8' (LCM 8). One night while returning to the ship (last anchorage out) we had to stop short of and gingerly go around a mine floating very low on the surface. We carried no lights so only by luck or providence did we see it at all in the wee morning hours."

"Our scheduled trip up river was delayed one day by the rocket attack on the SS *President Buchanan* (recoilless rifle round in her fresh water tank—no casualties). We then went up a day later as screen for an MSC [*sic*] Victory ship loaded w/ ammo for Cat Lai." Once at Saigon, he continued, "we worked cargo to barges while moored to buoys in the river off the end of Tu Do Street and had to ride the small water taxis operated by sub-teen girls to and from the pier."

"A strict curfew in the port went down at 2100, I believe. No water traffic after that time until dawn under the penalty of being shot on sight by any of the army guards (one at each end of the ships), in the river 24 hours/day in the channel and during dark in port."

Rheingold Beer: Looking for a Home

While the delivery of beer was always much appreciated—and many tons of it were brought into Vietnam on merchant ships—some of it, for some reason, couldn't be given away. Fosgate of *Green Wave* recalled: "We were to have delivered 660 tons of Reingold Beer from Bayonne [New Jersey] in Saigon. The soldiers there didn't want it [and] neither did the [ship's] crew—we delivered every can. The soldiers in Cam Ranh, our last stop, didn't want the beer either so they back-loaded us with several 100 tons of 'retrograde' for the USMC in Da Nang and we went there. The Marines took the beer, and didn't complain."[59]

Arrival of the First "Box" Ships

The introduction of containership service to Vietnam, first suggested by ILA president Teddy Gleason after his visits to Vietnam in 1965 to assess the cargo-handling situation there, then put out for bids but then postponed again by MSTS in late 1966, finally came to pass on August 1, 1967, with the arrival of Sea-Land Service's converted C-2 SS *Bienville* in Da Nang.[60] The port of Da Nang had undergone major transformation in the intervening period, with piers constructed, berths added, and special gantry cranes installed that would soon handle unloading of the 40-foot containers that Sea-Land, the winner of a two-year contract negotiated with MSTS, soon began hauling to Vietnam from its containership terminal in Oakland, California.

Having arrived at an Observation Point pier in Da Nang at 10:30 in the morning, SS *Bienville* began discharging her containers at 2:00 in the afternoon after unloading top-stowed equipment, and by 5:00 the next morning—after but 15 hours—had completed unloading more than 220 35-foot containers representing some 7,221 measurement tons of cargo, a task that would normally have taken some five days otherwise.[61] It was clear from the get-go the difference that containerization—and the proper port infrastructure to handle it—could make in speed, efficiency, and turnaround time, as well as the added benefit of security and reduced pilferage.

Bienville would be followed by two other converted, self-sustaining C-2s, each with a capacity for carrying 226 of the 35-foot containers, establishing this container service to Da Nang from the ports of Oakland and Seattle. In addition, three larger, non-self-sustaining C-4s, each converted to have a capacity for more than 600 containers, would provide direct containership service to Cam Ranh Bay, which was also being equipped with gantry cranes to handle the Sea-Land containers.[62] Due to the fact that C-4s could not be accommodated in other ports, including the newly completed Newport near Saigon, an additional seventh containership—also a converted C-2—was to be added, her arrival timed to coincide with that of the C-4s, to provide shuttle service out of Cam Ranh Bay.[63]

If the year represented a positive turnaround in other respects, and even a reduction at its mid-point in the ships required for the Vietnam sealift, there was no reduction in enemy attacks on merchant ships, and other civilian-crewed support vessels such as dredges and tugs.

Mines and explosive devices of various types were employed by the Viet Cong, and despite best efforts to detect and defuse before serious harm was done to ships, or casualties inflicted upon seamen, hits were too often scored nonetheless. Ships often came under small arms, automatic weapons, mortar, and rocket-propelled grenade attack, and, increasingly, recoilless rifles were deployed against them along the rivers and elsewhere.

The *President Buchanan* found out only too well in November 1967 that attacks often involved the simultaneous use of a variety of weaponry. The 564-foot Mariner Class *President Buchanan*, a 20-knot cargo ship built at Sun Ship in Chester, Pennsylvania, in 1952, had been chartered to the MSTS by American Presidents Line (APL) in October 1967. With a crew of 58, under command of Captain Eugene A. Olsen, *Buchanan* proceeded to Vietnam soon after from the West Coast, and arrived at Vung Tau in the third week of November 1967.[64] Then, on November 18, the ship proceeded up the Long Tau channel towards Saigon to the vicinity of mile marker two, still some 30 miles below Saigon, when at about 12:45 in the afternoon she came under heavy attack by a force of Viet Cong later estimated at between 20 and 30 fighters. In the space of about 10 minutes, some early published reports stated, the ship was struck some 19 times by recoilless rifle and small arms fire. In addition it was reported, possibly erroneously, that mortars had also been involved and scored hits, punching holes in the ship's steel hull—all above the waterline—and superstructure that ranged from six inches to two- and one-half feet in diameter.[65]

There was a quick response by U.S. Navy helicopter gunships and four PBR patrol boats, the attackers were engaged, and weapons recovered included what was described as a Chicom 75-millimeter recoilless rifle.

Despite damage to cargo handling and hatch machinery, the electrical and radar system, major damage to the third mate's quarters, and the holing of a freshwater tank, there were no fires, and most importantly—somewhat miraculously—no casualties were reported.

In a cable to company representatives in San Francisco soon after the attack, Captain Olsen reported: "Pilot and watch crew were admirable under fire [and] all hands performed admirably." Captain Olsen was later presented the Merchant Marine Meritorious Service Award for his own role in the action.[66]

There are numerous examples of American merchant ships being attacked while underway during the Vietnam War, and that on *President Buchanan* is but one showing the type and effectiveness of weaponry used against them. An incident underscoring another typical and oft-repeated method against ships either at anchor or secured at a shoreside berth occurred on December 22, 1967, when the SS *Seatrain Texas*, a roll-on/roll-off type vessel under command of Captain C. LaCroix, was holed before dawn by an explosive device while it lay at anchor in Nha Be some nine miles below Saigon. Tearing a hole extending some five feet above the waterline to about two feet below, the flooding was quickly contained by the ship's crew, which fortunately suffered no reported casualties. From there, the ship eventually made its way to Osaka, Japan, where it was repaired in drydock.[67]

There was good reason for constant vigilance against Viet Cong swimmers and sappers intent on targeting merchant shipping throughout the war. The author remembers well, for example, how a Navy patrol boat circled his ammunition-laden ship all night while it was anchored out in Da Nang in 1969, tossing concussion grenades in a circuit around the ship. The threat was very real, as the crews of *Seatrain Texas* and several other ships came to understand only too well.

For the fleet of ships broken out of "boneyards" for the Vietnam Run, 1967, marked a turning point, for their actual numbers—generally put at a maximum of 172—and represented a peak in terms of their contribution—measured by measurement tonnage carried—to the Vietnam war zone. A significant improvement in port facilities and unloading operations by mid-year, coupled with inauguration of containership service, first to Da Nang and Qui Nhon, in early August, fed into the decision by the Defense Department later that month to reduce the number of reactivated Victory ships that had been placed into service. So it was then that government-owned ships operated under General Agency Agreement by various American shipping companies had, by the end of 1967, carried some 3,809,917 measurement tons of cargo to Vietnam—more than 28 percent of the total carried by all MSTS-controlled ships that year—the largest number in any given year of the Vietnam War before, or in those remaining years of war still to come.[68]

A Keelung to Saigon Shuttle

From early 1966 and well into 1967 Peter J. Bourgeois served as second mate, out of New Orleans, in the jumboized Liberty ship *Elaine* (Captain Thomas B. Smith) for a long voyage initially from Norfolk to Mombasa with a load of corn.[69] After discharging in Mombasa and headed back to the Red Sea, *Elaine* was diverted to Keelung, Taiwan to begin a chartered shuttle between there and Saigon, which extended the voyage, as it turned out, well over a year. Some 10 years later, Beauregard recalled those shuttling days, and his time in Vietnam, on a ship that in its new configuration was not always quite up to the task:

> The *Elaine* made about 8 knots on her good days, and 3 or 4 against adverse weather conditions. The addition of the big, new no. 4 [cargo] hold right in front of the house made her a good carrier of cargo, but she still had the same rudder and the same 2,000 horsepower up-and-down steam reciprocating engine, so when trying to steer a course into any kind of wind when the ship was light, once the bow fell off to one side or the other you might spend the whole night or day with the rudder hard aport or hard astarboard and still never get back to within 15° of your desired heading. There was simply too little power and too little rudder for the size ship [511'] she had become.[70]
>
> Eventually we made it to Keelung and spent about a month loading agricultural-type cargo from farm tools and implements, bagged fertilizer, etc. Then, after a four-day trip across the South China Sea, we anchored off Cape St. Jacques [Vung Tau] at the mouth of the Saigon River. A week at anchorage, then up the river to tie up at the buoys in midstream at Saigon. It took about six weeks to discharge all the cargo into sampans—then back to Keelung, fighting the northeast monsoon all the way in an empty ship. The return voyage to Keelung took 8 or 9 days.
>
> This pattern was repeated over and over. I think I made 4 or 5 shuttle runs between Keelung and Saigon, and our 12-month articles expired in Saigon. There were no crew replacements being sent there, because of the war, so we all stayed on and took her back to Keelung. From there, the company flew us home.
>
> No one ever shot at us, and yet we used to sit on deck with a drink in the evening and watch the planes strafing and dropping napalm and explosives not far away, calculating the distance to the battle by the time it took the sounds of the explosions to reach us. In those days, 1966 and 1967, you could sit on the 4th-floor balcony of the Majestic Hotel bar in Saigon, hear a live band playing, and watch the war going on a few miles away, across the river. It was a weird experience.[71]

The vast improvements in port facilities, cargo-handling capability, and turnaround times in-country—not including the much longer turnaround generally experienced by some like Peter Bourgeois and the crew of *Elaine*—might well have contributed, without close attention given to other realities, to a sense of optimism relating to the war. General William Westmoreland, the commander of U.S. forces in Vietnam at that time, spoke optimistically in late 1967 as to the war's progress—as had other foreign military commanders in Vietnam at other times—as prospects for the war were about, in fact, to take a turn southward.

Some Americans spoke optimistically of a turn, and others of perceiving a "light at the end of the tunnel" as the year drew to a close. Those monitoring frequency of attacks on merchant ships, on the other hand, and realizing there was no let-up in that regard, might not have felt inclined at that moment in time to agree. The next year would only contribute, and as such attacks increased, to grim prognostications by many. And that "light at the end of the tunnel," some would point out, "is sometimes the headlight of another on-rushing train."

Perhaps a better analogy, in nautical terms, might have been to say two ships were heading towards each other at night on a collision course, without benefit of radar, collision-avoidance systems, or visual aids.

Given what was to come in the new year, the less optimistic analogies would appear in hindsight to have been much more apt.

12

The Fireworks of Tet (1968)

"It was like any quiet little port you might visit [in 1959] on a routine voyage.... There was little difference in 1963 when I returned to Saigon on the SS *Kyska*. But this last trip was like sailing into a battlefield."
—Harold Hess, OS, *Cape Junction*, 1968

"We waited for the next blast, which would mean the end of everything."
—James Cochran, AB, *Cuba Victory*, 1968

The SS *Cape Junction* had finally arrived in Saigon on January 28, 1968, after the long voyage around from Sunny Point, North Carolina, where she had taken on a full load of ammunition.[1] The start of the major "Tet" lunar new year holiday in Vietnam was but a few days away, and at least some members of the ship's crew understood that, despite the war, it might be a particularly good time and place for a long-anticipated shore leave.[2]

It was also generally understood that the likelihood of major military action on such a holiday as "Tet" was unlikely. That was, in fact, the word from some Vietnamese workers encountered along the waterfront as the start of the solemn yet joyous and often fun-filled time of year drew closer and closer. "Nobody fights on Tet," some were reported to have said.[3]

But that was not, or had not always been, true, as even a casual investigation of Vietnam's history might have revealed. There was, in fact, at least one major precedent for it, demonstrated by the Vietnamese nationalist Nguyen Hue, who, on the eve of another Tet lunar new year commemoration in 1789, infiltrated his troops into the capital city, and began an attack the next morning against unwary Chinese troops, many of whom at that point were no doubt sleeping off the effects of imbibing too much rice wine for a holiday that, for them as well, was preeminent.[4] Despite Chinese expectations to the contrary, this incident leading to their expulsion from the country underscored the fact that things did not always turn out as hoped, especially for foreigners who had, regardless of whatever rationale had been used, entered Vietnam by force of arms.

General William Westmoreland, commander of American forces in Vietnam some 180 years later, might have had a clue on another Tet New Year's Eve when handed a small statue of Nguyen Hue by a Vietnamese acquaintance.[5] But he, as so many others not properly instructed or otherwise receptive to the lessons of Vietnamese history, did not have a clue, until the proverbial dung began to hit the fan on the last day of January 1968.[6] And, as the historical record also reveals, Westmoreland was deceived by erroneous numbers—and by himself—into thinking that enemy forces arrayed against him had been reduced in what had become, well before then, a war of attrition.

Bruce Nusbaum, an engine department rating in the *Cape Junction*, had caught the last liberty launch ashore on January 31, just in time for the anticipated fireworks that would signal the start of the Tet holiday. It soon became clear, however, and throughout Vietnam, that superimposed upon the widespread sounds of traditional celebratory fireworks, was gunfire, also signaling the start of a concerted and coordinated major offensive by Viet Cong and North Vietnamese Army regulars against American, South Vietnamese, and allied targets throughout the country.[7]

"That is not fireworks," Rick Daly was told while ashore from the C-2 *Wild Ranger*, which had come into Newport, "those are rockets!"[8]

Those on *Cape Junction*, Nusbaum recalled later, "were able to witness some of the attack first hand": "At one time, gunfire from across the Saigon River struck a barge immediately behind the point [where another ship] the *Seatrain Washington* was docked." "Gunfire was going on from all sides of us," he noted; he would later learn that a reported "167 VC were killed in a field just a few yards off the bow of our anchorage."[9]

Close to the action itself, as Nusbaum noted, the SS *Seatrain Washington*, one of a group of World War II–vintage T-2 tankers that had been transformed into multipurpose cargo carriers, suddenly found itself becoming a safe haven for various merchant mariners, Army and Navy personnel, and others who were close at hand and suddenly unable because of the emergency to return otherwise to wherever they

The SS *Del Rio*, shown here unloading at Saigon, was one of a number of merchant ships attacked by Viet Cong during 1968, the year of the Tet Offensive (U.S. Navy / Military Sea Transport Service).

needed to go.[10] So, for a period of time, they remained on *Seatrain Washington*, which provided shelter and hospitality for days until the tide of the Tet Offensive began to subside in the nearby streets of Saigon.[11]

In light of the hospitality provided during the Tet Offensive, Admiral Ramage, commander of MSTS, would later note publicly that he was "proud to be in some manner connected with the officers and men of the good ship *Seatrain Washington*."[12]

The impact of Tet on shipping patterns in Vietnam was dramatic. After having made considerable progress in the previous year to shorten turnaround times of ships unloading in-country—including the official opening of Newport just upstream from Saigon—the immediate institution of curfews and the shortening of hours worked each day by longshoreman resulted in much longer unloading times once again for a period of weeks. Bruce Nusbaum recalled that "a normal visit to the port of six or seven days was turned into a three-week stay."[13] And ships were otherwise backed up as a result, and held for longer periods while waiting for the go-ahead from such places as Manila, Subic Bay, and Okinawa to move into Vietnamese ports from those and other holding areas, or to weigh anchor from such places as Vung Tau to begin the river transit upstream to Nha Be, Cat Lai, or Saigon and Newport berths.

Twenty-one-year-old Don Moir flew into Saigon on the eve of Tet to report to the MV *Chevron*, a T-1 tanker, as third mate.[14] But the agent did not know quite where the ship was or when it would arrive. Tucked into what he would later describe as a "truly third rate hotel" near the Saigon market, and without much money, Moir "survived on '33' Beer and Chinese soup for eight days" until finally notified the ship was due in Phan Rang, up the coast, within the week. He was soon winging his way to Phan Rang on an Air Vietnam aircraft he'd later describe as a "French built tail dragger" that had "belched smoke and fire during repeated attempts to start it" but which eventually started and took off.

Fortunately, Moir spotted the *Chevron* from the air during final approach across Phan Rang Bay "because no one at the Phan Rang air base had any idea that there were ships out there, and obviously no idea where all their fuel magically appeared from to sustain their many flight operations."[15]

The air base in question, a few miles from the port, had been built initially by the Japanese during World War II, and then used by the French until their defeat in 1954. To accommodate American aircraft the runway had been extended to some three times its original length during the early buildup period. Fuel was indeed supplied by ships, but only shallow draft types such as the T-1 type *Chevron* could be used for Phan Rang.[16]

MV *Chevron* would shuttle down from Cam Ranh Bay, taking on cargoes of highly flammable aviation gas—AVGAS—and then pumping off through a single 4' pipe that supplied the airfield from the Phan Rang anchorage. That, coupled with daylight-only offloading due to tapping and pilferage by locals at night otherwise, tended to make the rate of unloading leisurely. Moir spent five months involved with this assignment.[17]

While Phan Rang might have seemed relatively secure during his time there— the greatest threat was, perhaps, the highly poisonous sea snakes that convinced him, after a seaman from another ship was bitten and hospitalized, to remain out of the otherwise pristine waters of the bay there—Cam Ranh Bay was another story, and one that might well have ended Don Moir's life in early 1968.

"We had been lightering aviation fuels from a Norwegian supertanker named the *Vesta*," he recalled.

> The *Vesta* was riding to her port anchor, the *Chevron* made up alongside her port side. The VC divers had attached a mine to the port anchor chain of the *Vesta*. We were the last lighter alongside, so she spent considerable time stripping her tanks. The *Chevron* got underway after completion of loading at about 1600. I left my undocking station aft and walked to the bridge when a huge blast shook us all, breaking a few of the heavy port glasses aboard. Fortunately, the mine did not detonate during transfer operations, nor while we were alongside. The *Vesta* was even luckier. Very little is more volatile than an empty gas tanker, yet for some reason she did not explode. A very large hole was blown in the port side of the focsle, but watertight integrity was maintained and she was able to proceed to a shipyard under her own power.[18]

As is all too well known, not all casualties and near-casualties in-country were inflicted by the VC or NVA. As Moir recalled about yet another incident that might have turned rapidly south: "Everyone who spent any time in Vietnam surely remembers the constant [use of] flares at night. One night one of those magnesium delights landed on the deck of our little gas-laden tanker. Many anguished minutes were spent trying to extinguish this lethal light."

"That seemed to be the irony of Vietnam," Don Moir reflected some 14 years after he had been there with the *Chevron*. "No one ever knew the enemy. The danger was just simply under the surface, all around."[19]

"Friendly Fire"

And then there were incidents of so-called "friendly" fire when Americans were fired upon inadvertently by their own or other allied troops. Merchant seamen in Phan Rang and elsewhere in-country were by no means exempt from exposure to this potentially lethal occurrence. "One sleepy Sunday afternoon," Moir recalled about an incident in Phan Rang, "the Captain was ashore for mass [when] incoming artillery [rounds began] splashing all around the bay."

> The Chief Mate charged into action. Running around chopping mooring lines with a fire axe, yelling at sailors to disconnect the cargo hose. I was directed to the portable radio the Navy provided us to communicate with the air base and the "swifty" patrol boats that were supposed to support us in case of attack. The Navy acknowledged my call and dispatched a "swifty." The heat had evidently gotten to the Chief Mate though, for all his great efforts to get underway he failed to notify the engine room to get the main engine ready! So now we were drifting helplessly with the rounds falling arbitrarily around us. After 10 or 15 minutes of abject fear, the shelling stopped. Later information showed the source of this shelling as South Korean troops newly moved into a fire base on the back side of a surrounding hill. Finding nothing on his chart to indicate any port or activity in Phan Rang Bay, the Korean commander decided to lob some target rounds out into the bay for practice. The Navy denied our attack bonus claim on the grounds that it was "friendly fire." Personally, I never saw anything quite as unfriendly.[20]

In the succeeding days and weeks of this early phase of the Tet Offensive, ships came under fire or were threatened by other means in various locations stretching from the Long Tau shipping channel to Saigon in the south to the port of Da Nang in the north. In the early morning hours of February 1, 1968, the first day of the first full month of Tet, SS *Stella Lykes* was anchored out in Da Nang Bay with a load of ammunition and narrowly escaped serious damage from a limpet-type mine placed on its hull. Able Seaman Joe Douvierre was on gangway watch and had spotted a sampan, presumably with Viet Cong aboard, "lurking" close by, and alerted those on duty on the ship's bridge. They in turn radioed Navy security. In the meantime, Douvierre threatened several times to throw his coffee cup at those in the sampan, as if it were a grenade, forcing them to stay down as the vessel drifted away. Soon after, the sampan, presumably armed with automatic weapons, was engaged in a firefight by a patrol boat and destroyed. The threat seemed to have been eliminated, but it was not entirely.[21]

Upon close inspection of the ship, a mine—presumably attached by a swimmer from the sampan—was discovered attached to the starboard side of *Stella Lykes'* hull. It was removed by an EOD team, but an attempt to deactivate it was unsuccessful. While being towed away, the mine, equipped with a timing device, exploded harmlessly. Thus, on that particular occasion, additional planned Tet "fireworks" by a Viet Cong team were limited, and a catastrophe to *Stella Lykes* and crew was prevented.[22]

The headline in *The NMU Pilot* later read, "Routs Viet Cong with Coffee Cup."

However, at Cat Lai, an unloading area principally for ammunition that had been developed the previous year some six miles downriver from Saigon, and up from Nha Be, other ships were not so lucky.[23] In two attacks soon after midnight on February 14, the *U.S. Tourist* (Clipper Marine), at anchor and in the process of unloading 3,000 tons of ammunition, came under multiple combined rocket, mortar, and small arms fire attacks from the port side—first, commencing at 12:05, and then again at 1:30 p.m.—resulting in damage to superstructure, lifeboats, and stern.[24] One round passed through the ship's smoke stack, leaving "a large, irregular hole, larger than a man's body," but, except for shrapnel wounds to the chest and back of the ship's first mate, Chester A. Briscoe, there were no other casualties. After completing temporary repairs, the ship proceeded to Manila, and then to a shipyard in Jacksonville, Florida, for additional repair work.[25]

Then, four days later, a sister ship, *U.S. Explorer*, was also attacked at Cat Lai. She took five direct hits—including one to the engine room and another through the stack—but was able to proceed soon after to Subic Bay in the Philippines for repairs. No casualties were reported. After "quick repairs" were completed at Subic the ship returned to Cat Lai to complete unloading.[26]

Later that month, on February 25, SS *Arizona State*, then a modern, Mariner-class freighter, was attacked on the port side while en route to Saigon some six miles northeast of Nha Be. According to one published report soon after: "The Reds scored a number of hits on the funnel and deck house area. However, crew members were inside areas that were not hit. [The ship] was scheduled to go to San Francisco for repairs."[27]

Rudolph Patzert was third officer in SS *Tulane Victory* when the ship was attacked on April 25 in the Saigon River, close to where *Arizona State* had been attacked, while northbound from Vung Tau. The attack began at 10:03 in the morning, eased at 10:07, continued at 10:17 and was over by 10:20.[28]

"There was no casualties from the attack," Patzert later recalled, "though an A.B., Edward Richard was nearly torn to pieces when a rocket penetrated into the steering engine space. Richard had just gone to the next deck above for a breathing spell."

"The rockets made 9 direct hits on the vessel: #1 hold, #2 hold, #3 bulkhead, #3 lifeboat (penetrated the lifeboat and through into the Officers' Mess room), directly below the lifeboat another rocket went into the Stewards Cold Room, through several hanging turkeys and into the coils of the freezing system, another hit into #4 jumbo boom, #4 hold, #5 hold, and the last hit right through the steering engine space, knocking out the starboard switchboard panel."

There was later corroboration and additional detail provided, as well as some discrepancy indicated by the monthly U.S. Naval summary report, which stated that the merchant ship "received at least two RPG-7 rocket hits, plus heavy automatic weapons fire, along the starboard side. Penetration damage was sustained in five positions and the starboard life boat was heavily damaged. There were no personnel casualties."

"There was no panic and the ship proceed[ed] up the river to Saigon. News of the attack preceeded us and we were cheered by the sailors on the ships docked as we proceeded up to Newport Docks in Saigon."[29]

There were multiple attacks on merchant ships and MSTS nucleus fleet ships crewed by merchant seamen in the month of May. The SS *Del Sol*, Delta Lines, came under rocket and 50-caliber automatic weapons fire on May 2 some 10 miles below Saigon as she was making her way northbound towards the city. She was hit by rockets three times: the first striking amidships, the second under the navigation bridge, and the third next to the galley.[30]

At about the same time that *Del Sol* was being attacked, USNS *Fentress* came under attack while offloading at Newport just up from Saigon. While the World War II era Victory ship was "holed in six places," there were no casualties reported.[31]

A Mortar Attack at Cat Lai

During the same point in early May when *Cape Junction* and USNS *Fentress* came under attack a few miles upstream, SS *Transnorthern*, a Victory-type freighter owned and operated by Hudson Waterway, completed the long run around from Sunny Point, North Carolina, and arrived at Cat Lai with a full load of ammunition.[32] She was secured to buoys fore and aft, booms swung out, with barges in place alongside for offloading when, shortly before midnight, mortars rounds—the number would be put at 60—began raining down on the nearby military installation.

As Fred Hicks of the ship's deck department later recalled, "mortar shells exploding in close proximity to an ammo ship with open barges of ammo alongside presented a very great hazard to the entire crew aboard."[33]

With mortars passing overhead from the opposite bank, the ship was quickly darkened as cargo operations were brought to a halt. It was subsequently noted in the ship's log: "Stop cargo operations and darken ship due to heavy mortar fire in close vicinity of ship."

A little less than two hours later, with all-clear sounded, cargo operations were resumed. However, that would not be the last time the crew of *Transnorthern* would find themselves in the line of fire during that visit to Cat Lai. Late the next day another mortar barrage took place. The ship's deck log would later note:

2150—Stop cargo operations and darken ship due to heavy mortar fire in close vicinity of ship.

2325—Resume cargo operations.[34]

As Fred Hicks later noted in a report to the Seafarers International Union (SIU) soon after his return to the States, the response from Cat Lai to the second mortar attack carried its own threat to those aboard the (three) ships offloading from buoys just offshore in the stream. "The friendly mortar and machinegun fire to silence the second attack," he wrote, "also presented a hazard as this ship situated between the two banks was in the line of fire."

Fortunately, Hicks could also report that after all was said and done—and despite some frayed nerves—there "was no damage done to the SS *Transnorthern*."[35] However, as the ship was returning to Vietnam some three months later with another full load of ammunition for Cat Lai, it would not be as fortunate.

That ships making their way along the river approaches to Saigon, and calling on such places as Nha Be and Cat Lai downstream from Saigon, were regularly subjected to attack, and especially in this year of the Tet Offensive, there was no doubt. But the ongoing Tet Offensive of 1968 would directly threaten ships that had also made their way safely to Saigon. For it too was well within reach of the 122-millimeter rockets sent on their way with deadly effect from bamboo and wood launchers easily constructed and transported by NLF fighters in the area.

SS *Cuba Victory* Gets a "Good Thumping"

Doug Hoerle, a 1962 graduate of the Merchant Marine Academy, signed on as *Linfield Victory*'s second assistant engineer after the ship was withdrawn from the National Defense Reserve Fleet (NDRF) with the first breakout "flight" during the summer of 1965.[36] Operated by Alcoa Steamship Company and making multiple runs to Vietnam, *Linfield Victory* became MarAd East Coast's "poster" ship of a World War II–vintage Victory that, after years in mothballs, could and would do well, compiling a record in the first year of the Vietnam sealift that, unlike many others, did not include serious breakdown delays.

As second assistant, Hoerle no doubt had something to do with the *Linfield Victory*'s respectable record, and repairs completed while underway and without benefit of—and delays caused by—visits to shipyards along the way. After a period of leave, and now upgraded to chief engineer, he shipped out again in August 1967 in *Cuba Victory*, another early breakout from the reserve and assigned to Alcoa, making three four-month trips on that ship with loads of ammunition from Port Chicago, California, to Vung Ro; Sunny Point, North Carolina, to Da Nang; and finally, in April and May 1968, from Sunny Point again to Cat Lai a half-dozen miles downstream from Saigon.[37]

Ray Guild, another seamen in *Cuba Victory* on that voyage to Cat Lai, recalled a few months afterwards that despite the sounds and sights of war seemingly on "all points of the horizon, the imminent danger of war seemed remote because of a young lady who ran the liberty launch. Her seamanship became obvious when she let go her lines, goosed the engine and kicked the wheel into a general heading for Saigon. She then became hostess and barmaid, opening cans of beer with a 'church key' which she proudly wore on a lanyard around her neck. Upon inquiry, she coyly insisted that VC meant 'very clean.'"[38]

Despite the distraction provided by shore leave and launch operator, the war was indeed close by, as the crew of *Cuba Victory* soon found out in no uncertain terms at about an hour after midnight on May 25. "We were unloading ammo into barges," Doug Hoerle recalled nearly 40 years later, "when we got nailed by a floating mine that had gotten trapped between our hull on the port side of #5 hatch and a tug that was repositioning the ammo barge from #1 hatch to #5. It was about 0100 hours and we got a pretty good thumping."[39]

"We were awakened by an explosion that could have put us all in another world," Ray Guild recounted. "A mine had drifted down the river with the current and had gone off on our port quarter. The ship, a barge of ammo, and a tug boat alongside shared the force of the blast."[40]

Ralph Rumley, an oiler, and James Cochran, fireman-watertender, were on duty in the engine room when the blast occurred. Cochran later recalled: "Ralph and I were at the sand box at the time. The explosion knocked Ralph off his feet. A flying coffee cup caught me in the side and I fell on top of Ralph. The blast caused a complete power failure and, in total darkness, we waited for the next blast which would mean the end of everything. We were relieved, of course, when it did not come."[41]

"The true miracle of the whole ordeal," Ray Guild reflected after his return to New York later that year, "was that no ammunition exploded."[42]

But despite another case in which the crew of an American merchant ship loaded to the gills with ammunition had been extremely lucky—almost inexplicably so—others working the cargo on the barge, and aboard the Army tug, were not so fortunate.

Night cook and baker "Big Red" Blackwell later described what he experienced and saw that day on *Cuba Victory*: "It was quite a sensation trying to grab a life jacket, find seaman's papers and that one pant leg in the dark. I went out on deck to investigate [and] saw a tug sinking, and a body lying on a barge. I went below again. The galley was a mess: eggs were on the overhead, pots on deck, the plates had blown off the range, the electric grill had become loose from its brackets and so had the galley blower."[43]

But the damage to ship, tug, and barge was far more serious than eggs splattered on the overhead. As many as seven Vietnamese longshoremen working the barge were killed, and an American GI on the tug was seriously injured. Chief Engineer Doug Hoerle later summed up the damage to the *Cuba Victory* in this way: "No hull puncture but we took a lot of mechanical damage in the engine room and shaft alley. The propeller shaft had flexed 9 inches at its middle, [and] line shaft bearings were toast."[44]

James Cochrane had also summed up the damage, soon after the fact: "We wouldn't be going anywhere under our own power for a long time. Floor plates had been thrown in all directions, all the main bearing heads and bases were cracked except for the forward one. One had blown completely off." And, giving credit where it was due, he praised the ship's engineers and specifically the chief engineer, Doug Hoerle. "They came immediately to the engine room to give assistance wherever it was needed," he said. "The first assistant restored our power and when we checked the hull for possible leaks, none were found."[45]

The *Cuba Victory* was towed first to Nha Be, and then to Vung Tau, where it discharged the remainder of its cargo. "During the river transit," Ray Guild recalled, "the ship was thoroughly invaded by crickets. They promptly dug in for what proved to be a two-week siege of hopping, singing and chirping. One group homesteaded a winch bed forward of the mid-ship house and formed a glee club which serenaded us all night—every night."[46]

"Ultimately," Doug Hoerle remembered years later, "we were towed to a Yokohama shipyard for repairs. After two weeks in the yard we sailed back to the East Coast."[47]

Soon after returning to New York from Japan, *Cuba Victory* was placed into dry-dock for further evaluation and repair work. In an article written in late June 1968 about the fateful voyage to Cat Lai, Ray Guild wrote: "The ultimate fate of the *Cuba Victory*, now a veteran of three wars, is unknown but with all due respect to a ship that refused to blow up, no one on board will be disappointed if the trip terminates in drydock. For the time being, we are 'finished with engines.'"[48]

"Confirming active service in the area"

Certainly at this point in the Tet Offensive, and to varying degrees in the three prior years following the introduction of large-scale units to Vietnam, American merchant seamen and their ships had been taking their share of hits while making their way along the Vietnam Run. A number of those seamen had been killed in the process, and some of their ships had been sunk.

And while nothing could ever make up for the loss of life, it seemed appropriate to many by then that a form of official recognition—a service ribbon "confirming active service with the United States Merchant Marine in that area"—was nonetheless authorized on May 20, 1968, for seamen who had served in-country at any time from July 1965.[49]

On June 3 the SS *Steel Apprentice*, a C3-type cargo ship operated by Isthmian Steamship, in Saigon for 12 days, had largely completed unloading at Pier 5 in the port, and was planning to get underway downriver again later that morning.[50] Ordinary Seaman Harold Hess, a transplanted West Virginian from New York, had come off watch and hit the rack sometime shortly after 1:30 in the morning when, as he described it some weeks later, "the shell hit and shook the entire ship." He recalled: "Then I heard the second shell smack the Victory [ship], and right after that, a third round splashed into the bay." Determined to have been 122-millimeter rockets that struck both *Steel Apprentice* and the *Gretna Victory* nearby, damage was done to both ships, but, while no casualties were sustained by seamen on either ship, two Vietnamese longshoremen were killed on the Victory ship, and four others wounded, when a rocket hit the hatch being worked.[51]

The hull of *Steel Apprentice* had been holed by the 122-millimeter rocket in the vicinity of cargo hold number one, which was empty. There was no fire, and after a temporary patch was welded in place the ship was able to get underway for the return trip to the States. They arrived at Long Beach, California, on June 24.[52]

A Birthday "Gift" from the Viet Cong

Twenty-two-year-old Bill Stephenson signed on the USNS *Lt. Robert Craig* as third assistant engineer on June 10, 1968, for what would be his fourth voyage to

Vietnam—all on MSTS "nucleus" ships—since the early months of 1966.[53] Launched the same year and month that Stephenson was born, USNS *Craig* was taking on a full load of ammunition at the Army's Military Ocean Terminal in Sunny Point, North Carolina, for what he expected, as he wrote reassuringly to his parents in Ohio, would be another voyage without major incident, as the others had been, on the Vietnam Run.[54]

Stephenson would later write to his parents again from the Philippines that on this particular voyage "instead of spending Christmas in Viet Nam" he would most likely spend his 23rd birthday there. "The VC didn't give me anything for Christmas," he wrote, "and I hope they don't give me anything for my birthday."[55]

Unfortunately for him, by the time his birthday rolled around again in late August the VC would have already delivered—about a week before the fact—a birthday "present" to him and the crew of the USNS *Craig* that he and they would not soon, if ever, forget.

After taking on fuel in Panama and transiting the canal, the trans-Pacific crossing, though hardly producing much more than a five-degree roll, was anything but routine for the crew of the World War II–vintage ship. Generator and steering gear problems forced an unscheduled stop in Hawaii, and an ailing rudder, though not repaired until later, was cause for more concern.[56]

"As for the ship," Stephenson would write home, "breakdowns are good experience and break up the monotony. I have had more breakdown experience on this ship than most people going to sea get in their whole lives."[57]

After arriving in Subic Bay in the Philippines, the *Craig* was held there for nearly three weeks—a reflection of the changed situation in Vietnam. Stephenson took advantage of his time there to purchase carved mahogany gifts, fish from the deck of the ship—successfully—and write lengthy and detailed letters to his parents in which he continually urged them not to worry about him. And he received mail while there, from home, and from his draft board that "scared hell" out of him before he realized it contained a "permission to leave the U.S.A." document and certification of his 2-A status—"deferred because of civilian occupation (non-agricultural)"—that would be good until July 1968.[58]

The call finally came after some three weeks on the hook at Subic to proceed across the South China Sea to Vung Tau, where the *Craig* arrived and anchored out on August 10, two months after Stephenson signed on in North Carolina. From there, after a short delay, USNS *Craig* proceeded up channel a day or so later to Cat Lai, an oil and ammo terminal about seven miles below Saigon where large quantities of ammunition had been offloaded since the previous year.

Secured to two buoys, fore and aft, unloading operations into barges got underway and continued around the clock, with work done by Vietnamese stevedores, a Korean foreman, and American GIs keeping score and a watchful eye. Three ammunition ships seemed to be constantly present, with arrival of a replacement soon after one had weighed anchor and departed. The *Craig* carried mostly 155-millimeter artillery shells, and it seems that much of this ammo was used in the very near vicinity of Cat Lai.

"One place over here is as dangerous as another," Stephenson wrote home from Cat Lai during his two-week stay there.

> Being on the ship is probably the worst place. The artillery batteries at Da Bay is constantly shelling the whole area around here to keep the V.C. away from the ships.... About 3 days ago they were shelling about a mile away and you could feel the blasts if standing on deck,

and the noise was considerable. We are anchored in the middle of the river and offloading on barges. One shell landed right at the edge of the river about a [half] mile away. Over water ½ mile looks like 100 feet.

They shell day and night, and there is always between 3 and 20 [heli]copters in the air around here. There are all sorts of boats, swamp boats with big air propellers, PBRs, LCMs, LCUs, LCIs, all sorts of [Vietnamese] boats, barges, tugs, and a hundred others.[59]

Cat Lai was a busy place, and the artillery cover, circling helicopters, and presence of patrol craft that could respond quickly to any threats to its priority cargo, suggested tight security that might have falsely reassured the unwary. But this was still an area basically surrounded by "killer jungle" from which, under cover of night especially, well-planned attacks of various types could and would still be made.[60]

If Cat Lai itself did not have much to offer a merchant seaman perhaps accustomed to much larger port areas in urban settings, Saigon itself was only an hour away upriver by liberty launch. After going ashore in Cat Lai a couple of times—launch service was, at least, available and regular for shore leave there—Bill Stephenson decided he'd not go ashore there again in the week or more remaining to unload the ship into barges.

After some 11 days at anchor in Cat Lai, discharge of the *Craig*'s cargo of ammunition was nearly complete with the exception of additional 155-millimeter artillery rounds remaining in cargo hold #3. At 5:00 in the morning Bill Stephenson continued writing a letter home that he had begun in Vung Tau several days before but had not been able to mail from there. Sitting on a wooden crate in the ship's machine shop he described his two visits to Saigon, his stay in the Hotel Victoria where he had dined and enjoyed a few vodka Collinses while watching illumination flares drift over the city, and hearing the occasional sounds of 250-pound bombs exploding in the distance. He had watched episodes of *Bonanza* on Armed Forces Television—a taste of home—and during the day had purchased a smoking jacket, and books about lineal mathematics, calculus, and Hoyle's rules, so he could settle arguments aboard ship during card games once and for all.

Stephenson shared his thoughts about the future and his plans to return to school, and expressed uncertainty about whether or not he would continue shipping out on ships of the MSTS nucleus fleet. About a half hour into his letter he left the machine shop, intending to return.

Five minutes later—at a time later logged into reports as 0542 hours—the *Craig* was hit about two feet above the waterline, just above the ship's boilers and aft of the #3 cargo hold, by a Soviet-made 122-millimeter rocket. It punched a hole four feet in diameter in the general vicinity of the machine shop, and turned the crate on which Stephenson had been sitting into splinters.

The *Craig* remained afloat, was secured well enough by her damage control personnel to get underway not long afterwards for the transit back down channel to Vung Tau where a steel plate was welded in place over the hole made by the one rocket that had hit its mark (others had been seen going over the ship).[61] It was from there, on August 23, that Bill Stephenson finished his letter home to his parents and brothers. He casually mentioned, after finishing a description of his visits to Saigon, that they had arrived in Vung Tau where their remaining cargo would be unloaded. He said he had received a letter from his mother and that he didn't expect, after hearing from her, that the old home place would be recognizable when he returned home again, which he hoped would be at the end of September. His 23rd birthday was but four days away, and he expected to commemorate that in Olongapo City once the *Craig* returned across the South China Sea again to the Philippines.

Stephenson made no mention of repairs being made to the ship in Vung Tau, or of the attack on it at Cat Lai, that birthday present from the VC that he had hoped never to receive. And, as it turned out, that fourth trip to Vietnam was to be his last.[62]

On August 25, 1968, two days following Bill Stephenson's arrival in Vung Tau from Cat Lai, the SS *Transnorthern* began making its own way up-channel from Vung Tau after having returned with another full load of ammunition for Cat Lai.[63] "We were coming up the river to Cat Lai," ship's delegate James Bush recalled not long afterwards, "when the Viet Cong attacked."

> Shells pierced the hull and caused damage to five cases of heavy [artillery] shells which were part of the cargo. All that saved the ship was the fact that the shells were not fused. Two days later, after the *Transnorthern* had reached Cat Lai, we were moored to a buoy in the river [as the ship had been three months earlier] and unloading cargo. The VC let loose with shell fire directed toward the Army compound across the river, but they were firing over our vessel and we had to black out the lights and electrical system for safety. Again, we were lucky. There were no injuries and the ship was not damaged.[64]

Casualties

The *Transglobe* (Hudson Waterways), a C-4 that had been converted into a roll-on/roll-off vessel with a stern ramp and mechanized roadway, had been withdrawn from the regular New York to Bremerhaven Run in 1966 for the Vietnam sealift.[65] She departed New York for Southeast Asia on February 12, 1966, and entered regular shuttle service between Vietnam and Naha, Okinawa, compiling a record 151 days in the Vietnam war zone in 1967, and something near that again in 1968. *Transglobe* typically carried up to 130 semitrailers, numbers of military vehicles, in addition to general cargo, and in so doing had delivered more military cargo to Saigon and Da Nang, it was reported at the time, than any other ship. On return trips she had hauled out large amounts of damaged military vehicles for repair or trans-shipment at Naha.[66]

Fired at on a number of occasions during her channel transits to Saigon, and holed by Viet Cong fire for the first time in May 1968, none of *Transglobe*'s crew had been listed as casualties during nearly two years of service within the Vietnam war zone.[67]

But all that changed in August 1968.

Under the command of Captain Leon Jean, and while still on its regular shuttle run in the area, it was attacked while northbound on the Long Tau River, and some 14 miles downstream from Saigon, on August 30, 1968. Two projectiles described as the newly introduced "trash can" type rockets—which had reportedly been designed for penetrating the hulls of merchant ships—hit the ship in the general area of its crew quarters, and one entered the fo'c'sle of unlicensed deck department seaman Ernest Goo, 39, a native of Hawaii.[68]

"He was in his room washing for breakfast when a rocket came through the hull and exploded in his room," recalled Captain Jean some years later. "It scared the hell out of me. I ran aft and found his room loaded with blood. I remember calling the Navy and saying we were under attack."

"We wrapped him up and tried to get the ramp down for the helicopter to land. It only took a couple of minutes [for it to arrive] but it seemed like hours. He was DOA when they got him to Saigon."[69]

The body of Ernest Goo, a merchant seaman and member of the Seafarers International Union (SIU) since the mid–1950s, was returned to Hawaii and buried in a military cemetery.[70]

The port of Da Nang in the northern "I Corps" military sector of South Vietnam had been developed rapidly after the initial buildup commenced in mid–1965 and, though most ships carrying ammunition and AVGAS were still anchored out in its bay for security reasons, additional deepwater berths—including DeLong piers—had been added to accommodate an increased number of cargo ships.

For reasons having to do with its particular geography—mountains looming to the north provided good cover for VC rocketeers targeting both the anchorages and piers that were well within range—it was not long before American merchant seamen and military personnel soon began referring Da Nang as "rocket city" and would continue to do so for as long as the war continued.

Jack Bernard Self, 58, from Mobile, Alabama, joined the SS *US Defender*, under the command of Captain John Hamby, in Long Beach, California, as its third mate on October 8, 1968.[71] Born in Mississippi, and a resident of Mobile, Alabama, Self had long been a licensed Merchant Marine officer affiliated with the Masters, Mates & Pilots. Two of his brothers had also served in the Merchant Marine. One, George R. Self, had been a master mariner during World War II, and a younger brother, Berry H. Self, boatswain in the SS *Lasalle* (Waterman) had been lost in 1942 with all 52 of his ship mates when the ship was torpedoed 350 miles southwest of the Cape of Good Hope. Carrying a full load of ammunition, it was reported that the explosion that obliterated the ship and crew could be heard 300 miles away.[72]

After completion of loading operations, the ship sailed for Da Nang, and arrived there late in the day on November 12. Five days later, at about 1:15 in the morning—typical for this sort of thing—a group of rockets rained down on the deepwater pier area of Da Nang, striking the *US Defender*, holing it in at least three places.[73]

Jack Self sustained shrapnel wounds, and died in a military ambulance on the way to a hospital.[74]

Vung Ro: "We just got the hell out"

At 12:30 in the morning of November 30, 1968, while in the process of unloading some 2,000 tons of explosives—including 750- and 500-pound bombs, and napalm—in Vung Ro Bay, the SS *Battlecreek Victory* (Grace Line) suddenly came under rocket attack "from up in the hills just off shore, just a few thousand yards from the beach." "Suddenly," Captain Harold W. Files later recalled, "Second Mate Chester Danksevich ran in to tell me this was the real thing."

Rockets "started coming right over the bow." "I went full astern on my first bell," Files said. "We left the pier with the booms out and there was a tanker loaded with jet fuel about 100 yards outside. It was a close thing but it didn't involve any heroics. We just got the hell out. We were told later that we were the target. If we hadn't gotten away when we did, it would have been 'adios.'"[75]

Attacks on merchant shipping in December, though not occurring with the frequency of some previous months in the year, would continue nonetheless, taking different form and at different points as the year of unprecedented attacks ground to its conclusion. Highlighting incidents in the Rung Sat Special Zone and approaches to Saigon, the monthly report generated by U.S. Naval Forces, Vietnam summed up these attacks as follows:

> There were four attacks against merchant ships on the Long Tau during the reporting period. On 3 December, a mine detonation about 10 meters astern of the SS *Gopher State* and 500 meters ahead of the SS *Cartagna* with no friendly casualties. On 4 December, a detonation occurred midships, outboard side, of the SS *Kara* which was moored alongside the Shell Pier at the Nha Be Fuel Farm. The vessel suffered minor damage but there were no friendly casualties.
>
> On 17 December, the MSTS ship *Cape San Martin* came under attack while proceeding north on the Long Tau. All rockets missed the ship. On 20 December, the SS *Pioneer King* [*sic*] was attacked by rockets about 18 miles south-southwest of Saigon with no friendly casualties.[76]

This year of the Tet Offensive was to be a costly turning point in the war, and many more Americans, shocked by rising numbers killed and images graphically depicting the course as well as nature of the war, turned in sufficiently large numbers against it to make the ending of it, come what may, a position that, frankly, had to be supported by all major presidential candidates. And counted among the casualties, in a political sense, was President Lyndon Baines Johnson himself, who declared early on in the year, and as a surprise to even his closest advisors, that he would not run for re-election. But despite the platform of Richard M. Nixon, the winning candidate in the November election, and his own oft-repeated declarations during months of campaigning that he had a "secret" plan to end the war, the war would actually continue for the United States—for Americans—until a truce was finally agreed upon, for another four full years. And even from the point of that agreed-upon truce that ended participation by American ground forces, the war itself would actually continue for more than another two years beyond that point.

For those civilian seamen manning the cargo ships, however, the war would continue to the bitter end—the very last days of the war itself—placing them, as they had been in the very beginning of it all, very much in harm's way—and as witness—on the front lines of history in Vietnam.

This story, for American merchant mariners at least, would continue for another six years, and beyond.

13

Peak (1969)

"The boat drifted farther aft, and when it drew abeam of the No. 5
[cargo] hold, a 2,000-pound bomb came out through the hole in the
ship, falling into the midship section of the life-boat. Several men
jumped or fell out of the boat as it capsized."
—Excerpt from Marine Board of Investigation
Report on the sinking of SS *Badger State*

The hellacious Tet Offensive and subsequent course of events in Vietnam in 1968 had changed the trajectory of and expectations about the war there, and America's role in it.

Merchant seamen had played their part, and took more than their share of hits than in previous years. But for all the strikes by enemy rockets, RPGs, mortars, recoilless rifles, and automatic weapons, as well as by the various types of mines deployed against merchant ships in 1968, the new year would prove to be comparatively worse for the U.S. Merchant Marine in that regard, and for the numbers of seamen lost while serving on the Vietnam Run.

In the first four months of 1969 alone there were at least 25 direct attacks and mining incidents involving ships crewed by merchant seamen in South Vietnam.[1] From that perspective at least—the view from ships making their way along the Long Tau shipping channel to Saigon, riding at anchor or secured fast to piers in rocket-attack prone ports along the coast of South Vietnam—there was no let-up in the targeting of ships involved in continuing logistical support for military operations in-country as the year of the Tet Offensive now gave way to the next.

The Viet Cong and NVA still understood the importance of—and the threat posed to them by—those merchant ships and what they carried. That reality had not changed, and would not until the very end of hostilities came more than six years later.

It was noted in the U.S. Naval Forces Vietnam monthly report for March 1969, for example, that there had been nine attacks, some resulting in casualties to merchant seamen, as "the enemy continued to exhibit his ability to attack merchantmen in the Long Tau River, Saigon's vital lifeline to the sea."[2]

Among the American merchant ships taking fire in the early months of 1969 were *Bacyrus Victory, Lafayette, Lawrence Victory, Louise Lykes, Linfield Victory, Ocala Victory, Overseas Rose,* and *President Pierce.*[3] Many others—American and those flying foreign flags—would be added to the list of ships attacked in later months, including one that would be sunk by mine in the harbor of Nha Trang.

This new year, the fourth full year of large-scale American involvement in the war, would see U.S. troop levels rise to a peak number of some 549,500, and the requisite supplies to support those troops would also rise to a peak—15,844,200 measurement tons—before those figures began to be reduced in each of the remaining years of the war.[4] As before, at least 94 percent of those supplies would be carried in ships crewed by merchant seamen: privately owned ships under contract to the Navy's Military Sea Transportation Service (MSTS), the "nucleus" ships of the MSTS fleet, and government-owned ships—mostly World War II–vintage Victory ships that had been withdrawn from National Defense Reserve Fleets, brought back to life, and were subsequently operated under General Agency Agreement (GAA) for as long as needed.[5]

The peak for tonnage hauled by those ships brought out from reserve would actually come not in 1969, but in 1967, as many of them were withdrawn from active service in 1967 and 1968, and more again in the current year, as newer, faster, more efficient, modernized, and increasingly containerized ships were introduced to the Vietnam Run, along with improved port infrastructure and cargo handling operations in-country.[6]

Some 172 ships had been withdrawn from reserve fleets and placed on the Vietnam Run under General Agency Agreement (GAA) with private shipping companies. By August of 1969 that number had been reduced, according to one report, to 75, and

Shown here unloading at Saigon in 1969 is a Victory ship, in the background, and USNS *Pvt. Frank J. Petrarca*, one of the "nucleus" ships of the MSTS. *Petrarca* was one of the smaller C1-M-AV1 types intended for coastal and inter-island work in the Pacific during World War II (U.S. Navy / Military Sea Transportation Service).

by October the number had been reduced further to 60.[7] Despite reduction in the active GAA fleet, considerable concern remained among American shipping companies and those advocates of a strong and viable Merchant Marine as to the continuing negative financial impact of the government-owned ships on the privately owned fleets.[8]

That 1969 would represent the peak year of U.S. involvement in the Vietnam War for both the greatest number of troops deployed and amount of cargo delivered in support of that force was directly attributable to the impact casualty figures and images that came out of Vietnam the previous year—the year of the Tet Offensive—and the massive numbers of Americans who had taken to the streets to protest continuing involvement in the war or found ways otherwise to insist on an end to that involvement.[9] The presidential election campaign of 1968 responded to constituent pressure and anger not only toward American casualty figures, but the broader destructive nature of the war and civilian casualty figures estimated in the hundreds of thousands and beyond, and reflected a turning wherein presidential candidates of both major political parties ultimately put forward platforms that pledged an end to U.S. involvement in the war.[10]

But exactly how those political candidates might further define, honor, and implement that position if elected remained to be seen, though it would soon be revealed as the new year unfolded.

By January 1969 Richard Nixon—who had campaigned as others to end U.S. involvement in the war—had been elected and inaugurated as the next president of the United States. "We are caught in war, wanting peace," he remarked, and he had said he had a plan, which would only be revealed if and when he were elected, to achieve that end. How he planned to deliver on his promise to end American involvement in the Vietnam War would begin to emerge some months after he took office in foreign policy declarations, with broad application as specifically for Vietnam, that would come to be known as the Nixon Doctrine.[11] This as it turned out, much to the anger of his detractors, would have less to do with actually ending the war than it did with continuing it by other means. This would involve reducing American ground forces in-country in phases—beginning with 25,000 in July—while looking "to the nation directly threatened," as expressed in the Nixon Doctrine, "to assume the primary responsibility of providing the manpower for its defense."

The French had used a racially explicit reference—"yellowing"—for their own attempt to significantly increase the number of Vietnamese within their military forces in Indochina, while a similar process ordered by Nixon, known as "Vietnamization" and commencing with an initial withdrawal in July 1969 and continuing in phases through 1972, would increase the size of the South Vietnamese military forces to more than one million.

Nixon's plan to achieve not only peace but "peace with honor" would take another four years to accomplish, in the form of a truce, and left the South Vietnamese fending largely for themselves—without American ground forces at least—for more than another two years beyond that point. As it applied to Vietnam during his term in office, three components would be implemented simultaneously, and with some urgency: replacement of American ground, air, and naval forces in Vietnam with Vietnamese—the essence of what came to be called "Vietnamization"; the training and equipping of those forces; and the stepped-up, largely covert operations to reduce the so-called Viet Cong Infrastructure (VCI) in South Vietnam of the CIA-directed Phoenix Program.[12]

With the force levels capped at some 549,500 by the midpoint of the year, this would represent the peak number of American military personnel in-country during the war, and the point from which there would be a reduction in increments, with an initial removal of 25,000 in July and larger increments thereafter. Some 60,000 military personnel were expected to be removed by December 15, 1969.[13]

The reduction of military personnel did not necessarily translate into a simultaneous and corresponding reduction in the civilian personnel who crewed the dry cargo ships and tankers, and which would that year haul the greatest monthly tonnage to Vietnam—also a peak figure—of all years since the big buildup began in 1965, and as the war ground on into the next decade.

The continued conveyance of ammunition and military supplies to Vietnam in support of a diminishing American military force, and a growing South Vietnamese one—as long as that might be needed—was crucial. And it would be the hundreds of merchant ships, and thousands of American seamen required to operate them, that would remain in service on the Vietnam Run well beyond the removal of the last American combat units, and to the "bitter end" of the war for the South Vietnamese in 1975 as well.[14]

Most attacks on American merchant ships in 1969, as in previous years, occurred along the winding, 44-mile deep-draft shipping channel between Vung Tau and Saigon. Typical of these incidents, among others, were those on SS *Louise Lykes*, on February 8, and another on SS *Lafayette* the following month. *Louise Lykes*, one of 12 highly automated, 20-knot C4-S-66a hull type Gulf Clipper cargo ships, and, at 540 feet and with six cargo holds among the larger ships then on the Vietnam Run, took a direct hit to the wheelhouse by what was described as an 80-millimeter rocket. Captain W.E. Alley and the Vietnamese pilot on duty, T.T. Khyon, were both wounded—Alley to the leg and shoulder, and Khyon more seriously to the neck and chest, and requiring an immediate evacuation by helicopter.[15]

While the generally reliable U.S. Naval Forces Vietnam monthly report for February would subsequently declare that "there were seven enemy attacks on commercial shipping during the month" and that "all of these occurred during the period 23–27 February," it had failed to mention the attack on SS *Louise Lykes* that had taken place on February 8.[16]

Then, on the morning of March 18 while also making her way up-channel to Saigon, the SS *Lafayette* (Waterman) was attacked suddenly by what one contemporaneous account reported as artillery but which was more probably recoilless rifle fire. *Lafayette* was hit multiple times by shells that pierced her hull midships, about 15 feet below the main deck just above the waterline. Damage was confined to the fuel oil settlers, and no casualties were reported. Then, after proceeding further up-channel, the ship came under attack again by what was described as artillery (or mortar) fire. According to one account published two months later in a maritime union newspaper, "the shells raised geysers of water just off the *Lafayette*'s bow, but this time there was no damage at all except to the crew's already-frayed nerves."[17]

After arriving in Saigon, and while unloading operations were underway, steel patches were welded over the holes in the *Lafayette*'s hull. She later returned down-channel afterwards without further incident, but with stories to tell.

Anthony Notturno, one of the *Lafayette*'s able seamen, recounted to a reporter after returning to the States: "I used to read about things like this in the newspapers, and I would think they only happen to other ships. I don't feel that way anymore."[18]

"Rocket City"

Da Nang, the port city well to the north in the "I Corps" military sector, was notorious for rocket attacks, and for that reason was long referred to as "rocket city" by those stationed or calling there during the war in merchant and naval ships. One description of a rocket attack in February 1969 was provided in the U.S. Naval Forces Vietnam monthly historical summary for that month:

> Hardest hit among U.S. Navy activities were I Corps Danang Naval Support Activity and vicinity on 23 February, as estimated 20–30 enemy 122-mm rockets, fired in three volleys, impacted in the NAVSUPPORT, Danang deepwater piers. The initial casualty report revealed no U.S. Navy personnel casualties, however, material and property damages were extensive. The adjacent ARVN ammunition dump received several rocket hits which set off secondary explosions which spread shrapnel fragments over a wide area, causing fires and destroying and damaging U.S. Navy structures and materials.[19]

One witness to the rocket attack in Da Nang on February 23, 1969, was merchant seaman Francis E. Davis, who had seen the Vietnam War through various phases and from the decks of different ships. He had first been to Vietnam on the Liberty ship *Jose Marti* in late 1954, after it had been diverted to the northern port of Haiphong out of Japan, in support of refugee evacuations following the French defeat.[20] Now, in February 1969, and as he had been for part of the previous year, Davis was in Da Nang as cargo pumpman on USNS *Saugatuck*, an MSTS nucleus fleet tanker that had seen service in World War II, Korea, and during the early buildup of American ground forces in Vietnam in the latter half of 1965.[21]

"If you visited Da Nang then," Davis recalled years later, "you could see these storage ships anchored in the middle of the harbor, usually with a cluster of smaller vessels moored alongside. We handled JP4, motor fuel, diesel fuel, and Av Gas—a total of millions of barrels. About twice a week a big British or Dutch Shell job would moor alongside and top off our tanks."

Da Nang had been called "rocket city" by American seamen and military personnel since well before Davis arrived in *Saugatuck*, and for reasons having to do with the particular geography of the area: mountains and extensive jungle terrain just to the north and within range of Da Nang's harbor provided good cover for VC rocketeers.

"There was a 122mm rocket attack on the base several times a week," Davis remembered, "[and] Charley also lobbed one occasionally at the ammo dock where there were usually a couple of American ships, but they always fell short. One night, though, they hit the ARVN ammo dump, which blew for 22 hours, with thousands of ear-splitting explosions; and they also hit a 150,000-barrel tank of jet fuel that I had that day topped off—totaled it, of course."

Unfortunately, the historical record and this writer's memory provide ample evidence that those VC rockets did not always fall short of the deepwater piers in Da Nang in those years. At least one American merchant seaman at the deepwater pier in Da Nang had been killed the previous year by rocket fire (see Chapter 12). And the writer vividly recalls that while his ammunition-laden cargo ship lay at anchor for replenishment of an ammunition dump he was told had been blown by VC sappers— or possibly rockets—some weeks before, the quiet and darkness of night was suddenly shattered as he stood deck watch, and a group of rockets hit their mark a few miles away—by chance or design—at those deepwater piers. Another merchant ship, which he only learned much later was a Vietnamese butane tanker, had been hit and burned through the night, sending a huge plume of dark smoke seaward well into the day. From a passing liberty launch a day or two later what had once been seen as an upright, living ship was now capsized, with only its bottom visible.[22]

Possible attack by VC swimmers against those ships anchored out in the harbor—most with highly explosive cargoes of ammunition and aviation gas—continued to be taken very seriously by those charged, the U.S. Navy in those days, with providing security. "A Navy launch circled the ship," Davis recalled, "and detonated under water a vial of nitro at 15-minute intervals. This was also continuous—night and day—protection against scuba divers with limpet mines."[23]

On the Dredges: One "Tour" Too Many

A small fleet of civilian-operated dredges—at one point there were more than a dozen—were put to work in Vietnam beginning with and following the major buildup in Vietnam in the second half of 1965. These dredges were of differing types, most of the suction variety but a few of the larger, ocean-going hopper types as well. Altogether, they were charged with deepening and widening channels for deep-draft ships, shallower-draft ships, and various types of landing craft, and were involved with a myriad number of projects to improve the logistical infrastructure in-country. Hopper dredges—the largest being those few operated by the Army Corps of Engineers—used long tubes—the largest being 30' in diameter—to vacuum up silt, sand, and harbor muck, store it on board in an internal hopper, and transport it away to another area, including off-shore, where bottom "doors" would be opened to jettison what had been taken on for removal. Suction-type dredges using flexible piping to remove both sand and other material and then deposit it wherever it might be needed were employed for various essential projects that included pier and bulkhead construction, landfill and reclamation, road access and causeway construction—sometimes using coral deposits that had been blasted out—and providing many hundreds of tons of sand for production of concrete that was used for base, port, and airfield construction.[24]

Some might have thought at one time that dredges were relatively safe places to work, even within a war zone. However, some of them were quite substantial—the size of small ships—and as such made for potentially attractive targets, even if they did not carry priority cargoes used for prosecuting the war. Their work was nonetheless vital, allowing for increased numbers of vessels transporting those priority war materiel and related cargoes to navigate inland waters, to approach areas that had earlier been inaccessible, and to tie up at piers, bulkheads, and ramps that had been constructed in areas that had previously been little more than mud flats or the outer edges of mangrove swamp. They also constructed turn basins in waterways that hitherto had been too narrow for that maneuver.

As too many who worked the dredges, often for one-year "tours" were to learn soon enough, they would indeed become targets of—and sometimes be wounded or killed by—mines floated or attached, and rockets fired by the Viet Cong. Three dredgemen had lost their lives, and others had been wounded, when the Dredge *Jamaica Bay* was holed in the Mekong Delta by a command-detonated mine on January 9, 1967.[25] By the time it had been sunk, *Jamaica Bay* had removed some 2.3 million cubic yards of silt from the river it had been assigned to clear. Three other dredgemen were wounded when two limpet mines holed the 216-foot dredge *Hyde* at Cua Viet near the DMZ in May of that year.[26]

Willie J. Williams, a resident of Jacksonville, Florida, and a member of the *Hyde's* steward's department, was one of those wounded on the dredge *Hyde* in 1967. Though a civilian, he was awarded the Purple Heart medal, normally reserved for military personnel, for his injuries. The two other civilian seamen wounded on *Hyde* were also presented with the medal. But things would be different for Williams when he returned to Vietnam again for a second one-year tour, this time on the Corp of Engineers' hopper dredge *Davison*. On January 17, 1969, his luck finally ran out when he was killed in yet another attack by the Viet Cong on an American dredge operating in Vietnam.[27]

It had become clear long before then that, in Vietnam, and certainly on the dredges, which the enemy understood quite well were playing a crucial part in the war against them, there were few if any truly "safe" places to be.

Using 122-millimeter and 102-millimeter rockets, RPGs—including the improved RPG-7—limpet and floating mines, recoilless rifles, machine guns, and small arms fire, the Viet Cong continued to inflict casualties throughout the year upon those who manned the cargo and tanker ships, dredges, and other vessels operated by American civilians and military personnel along the waterways and in the harbors of South Vietnam.

There were fewer attacks, however, on merchant ships in the last three months of 1969, as indicated in the U.S. Naval Forces monthly report for October, November, and December, perhaps indicating a shift in focus by Viet Cong operatives in the Rung Sat Special Zone (RSSZ) and elsewhere in-country.[28] However, the use of limpet and either command-detonated or anchor-chain rigged floating mines against shipping—one resulting in the sinking of a ship in Nha Trang Harbor in October—did make a notable if brief appearance in these reports. According to the report for October: "On 16 October, the cargo vessel *Kin Wah*, under Panamanian registry, was mined and sunk in the Nha Trang harbor."[29] There was no indication as to casualties in this report, nor whether the sinking of *Kin Wah* had been accomplished by the use of a limpet or other floating-type mine. While an American ship had not been the target of this particular mining attempt, it would not be long again before another would be targeted for mining in another area.

At the Nha Be anchorage in the Rung Sat Special Zone (RSSZ), which despite the best efforts of Stable Door monitors and countermeasures seemed continually subject to mining incidents, whether successful or not, another was detected and dealt with within a few weeks of the Nha Trang Harbor incident. The monthly U.S. Naval Forces Vietnam report for November contained the following somewhat lengthy and detailed description of that incident involving the SS *Seatrain Maine*:

> The RSSZ Explosive Ordnance Disposal Team removed a mine from the SS *Seatrain Maine* on the night of 5 November. The ship was anchored approximately 1000 meters

north of Nha Be, 400 meters off the Shell Tank Farm Pier. The Vietnamese EOD team observed a line attached to the ship's anchor chain. The team cut the line and towed the mine clear of the ship to the east of the river where they determined that the mine was a four feet by 20 inches and contained six sections with a pointed buoyancy tank in front. The mine was held together by metal rods and contained approximately 150–200 pounds of explosives. The RSSZ EOD team stated that the mine failed to detonate due to a faulty firing mechanism (water soluble washer type). The EOD team destroyed the mine at 1040 on 6 November.[30]

This description of the incident concluded with the following short list of "vessels in the immediate area":

Vessel	Location	Distance from SS *Seatrain Maine*
SS *Transnorthern*	Cat Lai Anchorage	8,000 meters
SS *Antinous*	Cat Lai Anchorage	8,000 meters

A floating mine of similar dimensions (six feet by 18 inches) had been found by a PBR patrol not far from the Nha Be anchorage on January 17. It was towed to Nha Be for EOD inspection and disposal. At 8:45 p.m. while work on the mine was in progress, it exploded, killing three U.S. Navy personnel, seriously wounding six others, and 12 others less seriously.[31]

The U.S. Naval Forces, Vietnam monthly report for the last month of 1969 made reference to only one incident involving merchant shipping or ships otherwise crewed by civilian merchant seamen. This was an attack on USNS *Provo*, an MSTS nucleus fleet stores ship, in the Long Tau shipping channel at 8:41 in the morning on December 28.[32] According to the report, "USNS Provo reported what appeared to be two B-40 rocket rounds fired from the east bank of the Long Tau shipping channel in the vicinity of check point five. The USNS Provo reported that the first round impacted 1000 yards to the port side and that the second was 100 yards to the port side. The ship received no hits, and no casualties were reported."[33]

Thus, the year, at least so far as merchant shipping and American merchant seamen were concerned, seemed to end on a relatively benign and incident-free note. However, tragically, there was more to come in the final days of December. And as it would turn out, the greatest single-incident loss of U.S. Merchant Marine personnel on the Vietnam Run during the war, though occurring far from the shores of Vietnam itself, would be inflicted not by the Viet Cong or NVA, but by the forces of nature.

The Ordeal of SS *Badger State*

Thirty-seven-year-old Richard Hughes had shipped out from San Francisco for many years, and had also worked ashore there as a patrolman for the National Maritime Union for a period of time. The war in Vietnam found him once again making his way to the ships, sea bag slung over shoulder, to play his own part on the Vietnam Run. In early December 1969 he went aboard the *Badger State* (States Marine Lines) at the U.S. Naval Weapons Depot near Bangor, Washington, as its boatswain

SS *Badger State* departed U.S. Navy Ammunition Depot, Bangor, Washington, in December 1969 with a full load of bombs. But after encountering major storms that it was not able to outmaneuver and having cargo shift in its holds, its crew fought a losing battle to save it. They abandoned ship and many were lost in the process (U.S. Air Force).

to ready the World War II–vintage, C2-type cargo ship for yet another trans-Pacific voyage.[34]

In five years the *Badger State* had already made a dozen trips to Southeast Asia in logistical support of the war in Vietnam. This was to be her un–Lucky Thirteenth.[35]

The loading of ammunition—palletized, unfused, 500-pound bombs and additional 2,000-pound bombs in metal crates, two to a crate—commenced on December 9. The crates containing those one-ton bombs would be stowed in a single layer in the #5 hold's upper 'tween deck.[36]

Despite concern voiced by the ship's master, Captain Charles T. Wilson, regarding the amount of cargo slated for the ship and how it would be distributed in the ship's hold during loading operations, issues were resolved, and loading was completed on December 14. And anticipating that additional wooden dunnage might be needed for shoring while underway, it was also placed on board prior to departure. As boatswain, Richard Hughes would probably have had input into the decision to do that.

With her master and a crew of 39, and a reported 5,336 long tons of cargo, *Badger State* was soon making her way through the Strait of Juan De Fuca and out into the Pacific, which she reached on the morning of December 14, bound westward for Da Nang.

Traveling at a speed of just under 15 knots, *Badger State* immediately began encountering heavy weather, and west-to-southwest seas, as a result of which she was not riding comfortably at the outset. Trim adjustments were made, speed was reduced slightly, and orders were received for a change of course to a more southerly route with the expectation of improved weather and sea conditions.

But the improvements never came. The next day, December 16, *Badger State* reported that though they had complied with the diversion order, the ship was encountering following winds and seas, confused swells, and was rolling to as much as 40 degrees. Some shifting of cargo had by then taken place, and repairs to its stowage were made by the crew. In charge of the deck crew, Richard Hughes would have been at the forefront of that work.

On December 17 the situation worsened. Several more rolls of 40 degrees were experienced, and a second course diversion order with a new heading almost due south could not be complied with completely due to even increased rolls in the range of 45 degrees. That evening some of the palletized 500-pound bombs in the #3 lower 'tween deck shifted, some dunnage splintered, and one bomb was "steel on steel" with the ship. A casualty report was submitted to CTF 31. The crew constructed a special pallet for the loose bomb and, using some of the extra dunnage that had been brought on board, re-secured the cargo.

Later in the day it was determined that cargo had shifted in four of the other holds.

On December 18, with *Badger State* continuing in what was described as confused swells to 20 feet, cargo was "adrift" in four hold areas—#1 upper 'tween deck, #4 upper and lower 'tween deck, and #5 upper 'tween deck—but was re-secured by mid-morning after extraordinary effort by the crew. Unable to fully come to its most recent course diversion heading, another was requested. A new order directed *Badger State* to assume a westerly heading. This was achieved and maintained until mid-afternoon on December 19 when moderate leakage was discovered in worn hull shell plating in the portside shaft alley area about five feet below the propeller shaft.

To help deal with this latest situation the ship was slowed to about 13 knots while a cement patch was placed over the problem area in question. This remedy did the trick, and leakage in that area was contained and no longer an issue. But sea conditions, continuing rough weather, and almost continually shifting cargo—despite the crew's best efforts—required almost constant attention elsewhere. Broken dunnage was being replaced from a dwindling supply, and a new series of additional course changes was requested and made in attempts to alleviate serious cargo stowage problems and strain on an overworked crew.

At one point on December 22 it was reported that *Badger State* had been hove-to—virtually stopped in position—for some six hours because of extreme rolling to 35 degrees.

The dunnage normally used for shoring cargo was by this time nearly depleted.

The situation was so bad now that off watch personnel from all departments were being turned-to to assist with cargo reshoring and re-securing. Some 315 miles south of Alaska's Adak Island, in the far southwestern Aleutians, *Badger State* reported that she could not hold on the recommended course because of continuing 35-degree rolls.

At about this time "heavy banging noises" were heard coming from the #3 lower hold. But that was an area that had been loaded without providing proper access for inspection and reshoring, if needed. So there was nothing that could be done in that area regardless. And by then, too, all cargo holds required additional reshoring and re-securing.

Captain Wilson radioed an urgent request to Fleet Weather Central that they get him "south to good weather as soon as possible." Unfortunately, while the weather would moderate for those struggling to bring *Badger State* safely through, that proved to be only a brief respite in their ordeal. On Christmas Day, Wilson would later report, the ship went through "one of the worst storms" he had "ever seen in the Pacific Ocean outside of a typhoon."[37]

Another course diversion order had been received on December 24 to proceed to Pearl Harbor in Hawaii, which at that point was some 1,600 miles distant. Late that same day *Badger State* acknowledged the order, and also reported that they had been forced to heave-to several more times to counter rolls of 20 degrees or more, which were only contributing to the ongoing problem of shifting cargo.

Christmas Day brought no gifts from the weather gods. To the contrary: an unpredicted storm with hurricane-force winds and "large, confused seas" was encountered early in the day. On at least one occasion the ship rolled to as much as 50 degrees; other rolls were in the neighborhood of 45 degrees, and the ship was not even able to heave-to because of the confused nature of the seas. By this time Captain Wilson had been on the ship's bridge continuously since December 22, and the crew had been working "nearly around the clock" in their attempt to secure the cargo that was loose in all holds.

The crew was using "anything [they] could get [their] hands on," Captain Wilson would later testify. "This was all we could do. We had no [dunnage] material left for shoring of any kind." Instead, such things as mattresses, life vests, furniture—even frozen meats from the meat locker—were thrown in desperation into areas where it was hoped they might do the most good to shore and prevent contact between the cargo of aerial bombs and the ship.

Late in the day *Badger State* requested an escort, and additional shoring materials.

But the time for sending out an SOS distress call soon arrived, and was made for the first time at 4:05 on the morning of December 26. Shortly thereafter a course diversion order was received that directed *Badger State* towards the nearest port, which happened to be some 500 miles away at Midway Island. Another cargo ship, *Flying Dragon*, en route between Japan and Long Beach, California, had been asked to rendezvous with the stricken *Badger State*. But it was still also some 500 miles away.

Fortunately, the *Badger State*'s SOS signal had in turn tripped an auto alarm on the MV *Khian Star*, a Greek cargo ship that was much closer to *Badger State* than *Flying Dragon*—some 40 miles west of *Badger State*'s position of 36 degrees 48 minutes North, 172 degrees 40 minutes West. The Greek ship immediately "put about" and radioed she should make it to *Badger State* within about three hours.

According to a report later filed by personnel from *Khian Star*, the wind force in the general area was nine on the Beaufort wind scale—strong, gale force—and seas were running to 40 feet.

At about one o'clock in the afternoon on December 26 *Badger State* was hit by another severe blast of weather. The ship was running before a westerly gale, and it was felt that a more westerly diversion towards Midway would only contribute further to the dire situation. A decision to heave-to was made again after seas caused a roll of 50 degrees to starboard and then 52 degrees to port. This extreme rolling caused damage to the #2 lifeboat that rendered it useless.

It was now determined that some of the 2,000-pound bombs in the #5 upper 'tween deck had separated from their metal pallets. Off-watch personnel were turned-to again to assist with attempts to re-secure this cargo, the uncontrolled movement of which was producing visible sparks in the darkened hold. Boatswain Richard Hughes, who had already worked continuously through Christmas Day, was in charge of this work. It was later reported that he had "worked virtually without rest for a 30-hour period" and that, while "attempting single-handedly to wrestle one of the loose 2,000-pound bombs back into its cradle, Hughes sustained a serious back injury."

All hands were advised at around this time to either put on life jackets or keep them close by for use should it come to that; it was looking more and more like that might be the case.

The ship's master had ordered the starboard—No. 1—lifeboat prepared for launching. He attempted to keep the ship hove-to on an optimum heading while using 50 to 60 RPMs forward from the ship's plant. But the seas—huge swells from both the west-northwest and west-southwest—worked against these efforts as heavy rolling of the ship continued.

Shortly after daylight on December 26 the rolling of *Badger State* caused some of the 2,000-pound bombs to come in hard contact with the starboard side of the ship; several holes were punched in the hull plating. With increased daylight Captain Wilson was able to direct the ship more favorably in the confused swells. Nonetheless, she continued to roll to 20 degrees as cargo continued to move around dangerously in the holds.

As *Khian Star* became visible in the daylight, a fateful decision was made to bring the *Badger State* about for a heading more directly towards Midway Island. According to one account, "personnel were ordered off the weather decks and full speed ahead was ordered" to effect the maneuver. But the ship continued to roll heavily, and it soon became obvious that this new course, with the largest swells now on the ship's starboard beam, could not be held.

A further adjustment was made to lessen the rolling when, at about 8:00 a.m., an explosion occurred in the No. 5 upper 'tween deck area. Despite everything from reefer stores and mattresses and linens having been tossed into the hold in hopes of providing cushioning to reduce bomb-on-bomb and bomb-on-hull impact, the effort had been in vain as hatch covers were blown off, hatch booms were set askew, and burning mattress and linen material was shot aloft into the early morning sky.

"This is when I made the decision to abandon ship completely," Captain Wilson later testified; he feared a more general explosion within the ship. At that point he immediately sounded the abandon ship signal using the ship's whistle and on the general alarm. Engineers, after checking with the navigation bridge, closed the throttle and secured all fires in the ship's boilers.

Some four to five miles away, seamen on *Khian Star* had seen the telltale flash coming from *Badger State*. The ship's master, Captain Evagellos Iros, later said that they had observed "a light or flash and then black smoke from the after end of the ship. The *Badger State* was too far away from us for one to see them get into the starboard lifeboat."

As engine room personnel secured that area as per abandon-ship protocol, the starboard lifeboat was readied for launching and began taking on members of *Badger State*'s crew. With the ship's stern to the sea, and losing forward momentum, Captain Wilson ordered the lifeboat with 35 aboard to move away from the ship as quickly as possible.

"How we managed to lower a lifeboat," one of the seamen recalled later, "I don't know."[38]

But once launched large swells forced the lifeboat back and up to the boat deck again, before, and despite every effort to move away, it was forced aft along the ship's hull. A large, jagged hole—estimated at 12 feet long and eight feet high—was clearly visible on the ship's starboard side and in the vicinity of #5 hold's upper 'tween deck.

As the lifeboat drew abeam of #5 hold one of the 2,000-pound bombs fell through the hole in the ship's side and landed square in its middle section. The boat capsized, and men either jumped or fell into the sea. Able Seaman George Henderson, who would become one of only 11 of the 35 in the boat to survive, recalled afterwards that the 40-foot seas were "full of bodies." He managed to climb onto an inflatable raft that had been dropped by an Air Force rescue aircraft recently arrived out of Hickham, and he assisted four or five others to enter the raft. "But," he said, "there were some we just couldn't do anything for."[39]

Those in the sea now had to contend as well with gooney birds—large birds of the albatross family that often followed ships to feed on their galley slops. "The birds hit us as soon as we were in the water, 40 or 50 of them," one seaman later recalled. "They went after the men who were too weak to defend themselves, and after we were rescued we saw them attacking the bodies."

The *Khian Star* was now on the scene and began to circle and rescue as many survivors from *Badger State* as possible in extremely difficult sea conditions. "The waves were throwing us really high," said AB George Henderson. "We finally saw the masts of *Khian Star*. After that we felt much better. At least we knew somebody was in the area and coming to help us."

Khian Star had rigged Jacob's ladders for boarding survivors, and many of her crew complement of 19 seamen were standing by to assist with life rings, life lines, life preservers, and a helping hand if they could just get close enough. The Greek ship's freeboard was about 11 feet, and as one account put it, "she was rolling 30 to 50 degrees as large swells swept over her main deck."

These were not exactly optimum conditions for sea rescue, and a number of those who had survived in the water to this point would perish as exhaustion and the forces working against them proved to be too much, and despite the selfless and heroic efforts of those on *Khian Star*.

While those in *Khian Star* did what they could to pick up any who were already in the water, some of whom were still clinging to the lifeboat that was drifting away, five remaining seamen aboard *Badger State*—including Captain Wilson—gathered on the port side of the main deck. With their life preservers secured, and with additional life rings for buoyancy, they all went over the side into the frigid waters still swept by gale-force winds. Only three of these five—Captain Wilson, Third Mate Willie Burnett, and Fireman-Watertender Samuel Kaneao ultimately survived.

Boatswain Richard Hughes, who had worked tirelessly to the point of exhaustion aboard *Badger State* and had sustained a serious back injury in an effort to re-secure one of the larger bombs, had somehow made it most of the way up one of the Jacob's ladders, as seamen reached out to grab him. But a huge wave knocked him back into the sea and he was unable to return. He was not recovered, and became one of the 26 lost in the incident.[40]

Fourteen survivors were picked up by *Khian Star* by noon on December 26. But the search continued into the night and next day, and was joined by the SS *Flying Dragon* and U.S. Air Force and Coast Guard aircraft, which had arrived at different points during the rescue and recovery operation. *Flying Dragon*, which had first been contacted when still some 500 miles away, located the overturned lifeboat and several bodies, but only one could be recovered. Two inflatable life rafts from *Badger State*, and others that had been dropped from aircraft, were located but were all empty.

Survivors were eventually brought by *Khian Star* to Yokohama, Japan, where they were debarked on January 10.

As for the *Badger State*, she remained afloat for several more days, and consideration was given to scuttling the vessel to remove it from the sea lanes. But weather and sea conditions, and the continued possibility of explosion on the ship, prevented that. A Navy salvage tug with an ordnance team aboard did arrive to relieve the *Flying Dragon* on December 30, and to continue with the fruitless recovery search. She remained in the area until January 5, and as *Badger State* appeared to be settling slowly by the stern as seas continued to enter the hole that had been blown in her hull nearly two weeks before.

Finally, in a position recorded at 39 degrees 6.5 minutes North, and 168 degrees and 12 minutes West, radar contact with the ship was lost as she sank into the deep depths of the Pacific Ocean.

For his actions during the December 1969 ordeal of the SS *Badger State*, her boatswain, Richard Hughes, was posthumously awarded the American Merchant Marine Seamanship Trophy, with the following citation: "Richard Hughes' heroic actions aboard *Badger State* manifested the skill, intelligence, devotion to duty and bravery that represent the highest traditions of the United States Merchant Marine. His gallant struggle to save his ship and his shipmates beyond doubt cost him his life."[41]

Not long after survivors of *Badger State* were brought by *Khian Star* to Yokohama, a U.S. Coast Guard Marine Board of Investigation convened to take testimony and evaluate circumstances that contributed to *Badger State*'s ordeal, loss of 26 members of her crew, and the ultimate demise of the ship itself.

In its summary remarks the Marine Board expressed high praise for the captain and crew of *Badger State*. "Throughout this ordeal," it was noted, "the actions of the Master and crewmembers of the *Badger State* were in the best traditions of the sea. Although their untiring efforts failed to save the vessel, the calmness and devotion to duty which they exhibited undoubtedly prevented even more extensive loss of life."[42]

Many causal factors and recommendations were suggested by the Marine Board of Investigation, which were largely concurred with by the commandant of the U.S. Coast Guard after review of the findings, and by the National Transportation Safety Board.

During the course of hearings in Yokohama praise was rightfully bestowed by Captain Wilson upon his crew and that of *Khian Star*, which had reversed course, raced to *Badger State*, and, with a display of outstanding seamanship in the face of extremely severe weather and sea conditions, rescued 14 survivors of the ill-fated, mortally wounded ship.

It would seem that when all was said and done the most telling summary of what had contributed perhaps most to the ordeal and ultimate fate of *Badger State* and her crew—in addition to weather and sea conditions, inadequate weather forecasting, lack of a full load of cargo, less than ideal metacentric height distribution of cargo, and the resultant extreme shifting of cargo—was what had not been done and provided even before the ship left the United States.

In his initial summary report sent by radiogram to States Marine in New York while still en route to Yokohama in *Khian Star*, Captain Wilson concluded: "14 men survived. Lack of enough spare shoring material [dunnage] ... to great extent caused the loss of *Badger State*."[43]

So, it could be said that for want of sufficient dunnage, a ship and many lives were lost.[44]

While the war would grind on for Americans, in fact, for another four full years, and take the lives of more than another 20,000 Americans—including merchant seamen—the look of it, its composition and configuration, and, indeed, manner in which it was fought to some extent, was changing.

The Look of the Fleet

Merchant seamen, as civilians, were not, of course, factored into drawdown figures of American military personnel being announced and beginning to be withdrawn from Vietnam in the second half of 1969. While the process of Vietnamization had begun with replacement of Americans by Vietnamese and transfer of military equipment and facilities assets, and would ultimately result in the ranks of the South Vietnamese military swelling to over one million—making it one of the largest such forces in the world—other factors would determine for the most part the number of ships and merchant seamen continuing to make their way along the Vietnam Run in the remaining years of the war.[45]

The number of government-owned ships taken out of reserve and placed under General Agency Agreement (GAA) with private shipping companies had been drastically reduced between 1967 and 1969. This had been a function of improved in-country port and cargo-handling infrastructure and the introduction of modernized, more efficient, and to some extent increasingly automated ships. Larger ships, some having been converted and jumboized from standard length T2 tankers, and others from obsolescent troopships, were making their presence known, and particularly visible as a different kind of ship type that had begun to arrive in-country, beginning in late 1967, piled high with shipping containers.

These first-generation containerships, and the requisite shoreside infrastructure, not only made it much quicker to load and unload, but initiated the process of replacement for many cargo ships, constructed decades earlier, that used booms and slings, and required many additional days to load and unload. With the increased efficiency and reduced time involved with containerships, fewer ships ultimately would be required to get the same job done. That in turn contributed to a reduction in the numbers of seamen engaged in the Vietnam sealift. Vietnamization was less a factor in the reduction of seafaring jobs, therefore, than the actual types of ships being produced, and now making their way into the Vietnam-bound shipping lanes. American seamen were not, after all, being replaced by Vietnamese on the ships, as were Americans in ground units, aboard U.S. Navy riverine and port-based vessels, and on the various types of aircraft of the military services.

While the introduction of containerships, heavy-lift, and additional roll-on/roll-off types of ships were taking the place to some extent of those government-owned, General Agency Agreement (GAA), mostly Victory-type ships in their original break-bulk configurations, the overall number of ships moving along the Vietnam pipeline was declining, as were the numbers of seafaring jobs required to operate the fleet. Some 380 ships manned by American seamen—those privately owned ships under charter to the MSTS, the nucleus (USNS-designated) ships of the MSTS fleet, and some 144 of the GAA ships (mostly Victory ships)—were reported to have been involved in the Vietnam sealift as of October 1968. That number of ships would have represented some 15,000 merchant seamen, not including replacement crews on the beach, actively manning the fleet of Vietnam-bound ships at that time.[46]

That number of Vietnam-bound dry cargo and tanker ships would have been reduced significantly more by the end of 1969, as yet more of the Victory ships broken out of reserve fleet "boneyards" under General Agency Agreements beginning in 1965 were either returned to reserve or, in many cases, made one final voyage to a shipbreaker in Taiwan or elsewhere. While some of the GAA ships would continue making their way along the Vietnam Run through the next year, all would be removed from active service to Vietnam by the end of FY 1971.

But even as the size of the Vietnam-bound fleet was shrinking, its increased efficiency, coupled with improved shoreside facilities and cargo-handling, still resulted in the delivery in 1969 of more supplies to the in-country drop-off points than ever before.[47]

To be sure, and though their numbers had been reduced, there were still many of those 24- and 25-year-old, World War II–vintage Victory ships making their way to Vietnam as 1969 came to a close. Still mainstays of the privately owned fleets, the government-owned nucleus fleet of the MSTS, and the fast-dwindling fleet of ships that had come out of reserve fleets along the Atlantic, Pacific, and Gulf Coasts for Vietnam service not too long before, their reputation as the "workhorse" ships of the Vietnam Run, it can be argued, was still and would remain secure.

But the look of the Vietnam-bound fleet of ships crewed by American merchant seamen was indeed changing, and would continue to do so in the year ahead.

The first full year of the Nixon presidency had represented a peak for U.S. involvement in the Vietnam War, both for the point to which military force levels would reach as well as for the correspondingly high level of logistical support—indicated in measurement tonnage—that arrived overwhelmingly by ship to sustain that. A grimmer indicator of involvement, the deaths of American service personnel associated with prosecution of the war, had actually reached its peak the previous year, the year of the Tet Offensive, though more than another 21,000 Americans would die in Vietnam under Nixon's watch before truce accords were signed in early 1973.

Nixon's "secret" plan to end the war, not revealed until after he was elected to the presidency, was not really a plan to end the war at all, but to have it continue with

South Vietnamese having taken over the burden of the fight on the ground, along the coast, the inland waterways, and—with the exception of high-level bombing with American air crews delivering the B-52 payloads that was to come following the truce—in the air.

For the U.S. Merchant Marine the peak number of ships engaged in providing logistical support appeared to have come at the end of 1968, with the number put at 380 ships by the Maritime Administration in October. That number would drop off markedly as the remainder of the ships that had been taken out of reserve under General Agency Agreement continued to be withdrawn from Vietnam service until, by the end of 1971, there were none to be seen.

The number of American merchant seamen actively engaged in crewing the ships making their way along the Vietnam Run had also peaked by late 1968 and early 1969. While those numbers are difficult to determine precisely, as crew complements varied significantly depending on ship type, time of construction, later conversions, and whether dry cargo or tanker ships were involved, a rough crew complement average, times the number of ships still believed to have been loading for Vietnam by the beginning of 1969, would have put the number of seamen at between 16,000 and 17,000, not including seamen "on the beach" hoping to catch a Vietnam-bound ship needing a replacement crew. As the number of ships actively engaged continued to be reduced in the final years of the war, the time involved in waiting to catch an available ship, depending on such variables as key rating availability and seniority, would also have begun to lengthen significantly compared to the early buildup and reserve fleet breakout years.

14

Vietnamization (1970)

"An air of unreality pervaded everything having to do with the turnover."
—R.L. Schreadley, *From the Rivers to the Sea*

"What we had was an odd assortment of radio repairmen, clerk typists, truck drivers, riflemen, and others who were, as they said at the time, 'so short they could walk under the door,' when they were rounded up and trucked to the Newport Docks to discharge the good ship Albany."
—Brett Witaker, second mate, SS *Albany*, 1970

A solemn memorial service was held at the National Cathedral in Washington, D.C., on Thursday, May 28, 1970.[1] But this time it was not for the likes of a recently departed president or some other statesman of note, but for American merchant seamen who had lost their lives while serving in Vietnam, Korea, and World War II.[2] For the few if any times merchant seamen had been so honored in this iconic place, it was, for its rarity, unusual.

The cathedral had previously been the site for memorial or funereal services for two American presidents who had supported policies that had moved the United States—and therefore merchant seamen—down the slippery slope, or along the long course, to war in Vietnam: Harry S. Truman and Dwight D. Eisenhower. And similar services would be held there for two other presidents—Richard M. Nixon and Gerald Ford—who would continue to perpetuate American involvement in the war or oversee the final painful months leading to the fall of Saigon in 1975.

While fewer merchant seamen by far had been lost on the Vietnam Run than in World War II—the numbers who had perished by 1970 would be counted by the score, not the thousands—it nonetheless was fitting, and the timing seemed appropriate as Americans took stock of, or loudly spoke out against, the current war in which they were engaged, and from which the United States had begun to extricate itself ever so slowly late the previous year.

"These men selflessly laid down their lives in the defense of their country," remarked Maritime Administrator Andrew Gibson at the National Cathedral that day in 1970, "[while] carrying troops and vital supplies to the battlefields overseas."[3]

By late May 1970, when the ceremony honoring American merchant seamen was held at the National Cathedral, several merchant ships had already been attacked in the early months of the year, in port and while making their way along the Long Tau shipping channel to Saigon.[4] The attacks on the Long Tau, often referred to as "harassment" attacks in the monthly reports filed by U.S. Naval Forces Vietnam, caused their share of casualties, but they were seldom fatal. While merchant

SS *Beauregard*, one of several World War II–vintage merchant ships that were converted into a new type—the containership—appears here entering Cam Ranh Bay in 1972.

ships were holed and damaged otherwise, they were rarely if ever stopped in their tracks due to attack-caused mechanical failure, and none were ever sunk by the RPG, recoilless rifle, or mortar rounds fired at them by the Viet Cong on the river channel approach to or from Saigon.[5]

Floating and attached limpet-type mines, on the other hand, were another matter, as those manning USNS *Card*, SS *Baton Rouge Victory*, SS *Eastern Mariner*, and other vessels crewed by merchant seamen in-country had found out all too well.[6]

One example of an attack by "shaped charge" that did serious damage to a merchant ship in early 1970—but did not result in casualties—occurred at 4:55 in the pre-dawn hours of March 12 in Qui Nhon as SS *Amercloud* was in the process of discharging cargo at North 2, a DeLong pier there. What happened was later described in a confidential report prepared and distributed by the U.S. Army's Headquarters, 5th Transportation Command:

> The explosion was external, believed to be a directional charge which entered the vessel 120 feet aft of the bow on the port side at an 80 degree angle. The charge blew an 18 by 6 foot hole in hold #2, and continued on, resulting in a 9 by 10 inch hole in the starboard side of the hull. The charge entered directly below the waterline, rupturing one fuel tank. No cargo damage was sustained as the hold was empty at the time of the explosion. Three of the four compartments in hold #2 flooded, resulting in a 10 degree list of the ship. The *Americloud* was moved to an inner harbor anchorage, discharged of all cargo and sailed under its own power on March 14 for shipyard repairs.[7]

As for attacks along the Long Tau Shipping Channel transits in early 1970, in all cases—including three Victory ships still remaining under General Agency Agreement (GAA) for service to Vietnam—the weapon of choice of the Viet Cong had been the B-40 (RPG-2) rocket launcher, and at least 30 incoming B-40 (and other unspecified) rounds would be counted during what the U.S. Naval Forces Vietnam monthly summary reports generally referred to as "harassment" attacks on merchant shipping. One merchant seaman located in the port side galley area of SS *Windsor Victory* in the morning hours of May 18 was wounded—but not fatally—when four rockets were directed at his ship near the intersection of the Nha Be and Dong Tranh Rivers.[8]

He would no doubt remember that particular harassment levied upon his ship for the rest of his life.

Fortunately, and while the previous year had seen the loss of too many American merchant seamen while serving on the Vietnam Run, no additional names had been added—at least not in those early months of 1970—to the list of those honored on May 28 at the National Cathedral in Washington, D.C.

But many in those days of large-scale antiwar demonstrations at home—and just a few weeks following the killing of students by National Guardsmen at Kent State in Ohio, and others at Jackson State in Mississippi—might have questioned Gibson's statement that any losses at that point in time had much if anything to do with the defense of the country.[9] Nonetheless, the gesture of remembrance would have been appreciated by those who attended the memorial service in the iconic National Cathedral, and no doubt by those who heard otherwise that American merchant seamen had been honored in this way, and at that place.

While the timing of the memorial service in the National Cathedral did coincide with a transition that was taking place in the Vietnam War and continuance of the planned drawdown of American military services represented therein, it would have little impact on continuing logistical support requirements or the fleet of merchant ships that continued making the run to Vietnam during this period of "Vietnamization" and beyond. That fleet, still numbering perhaps 300 ships, would have a noticeably changed look due to the removal of scores of World War II–vintage ships that had been withdrawn from service by mid–1970, and by those, such as containerships, that had been added in their stead.

Dating back to early 1968, by which time it had become accepted to one degree and in one way or another as part of a presidential campaign platform for Democrats and Republicans alike, it was understood that the United States would have to begin reducing its military footprint in—its commitment to—Vietnam. That reduction in size and commitment had begun to be called different things, from "de-Americanization" by Secretary of Defense Melvin Laird, to "Vietnamization" by then President-elect Richard Nixon in December 1968.[10] That would in turn become part and parcel of what would become known as the Nixon Doctrine.[11]

Early on, the actual implementation of policy associated with Vietnamization became known by a variety of acronyms. The U.S. Navy, which through Operations Market Time and Open Door had been heavily involved with river channel mine sweeping, port entry and anchorage security, and development of in-country infrastructure for handling cargo brought along the Vietnam Run, began to use the acronym ACTOV—for "Accelerated Turnover to the Vietnamese" for their own plan for scheduling transfer of in-country "assets" while still providing a training and advisory function to the South Vietnamese.[12] As U.S. naval forces were reduced and returned to the United States, this would require an expansion of the VNN—the Vietnamese Navy—to operate these assets and to provide leadership for operations, such as river channel security and assault, once largely their own responsibility.

Among the very last of the GAA ships to come off the Vietnam Run were the SS *Lane Victory* and SS *Occidental Victory*, which had both come into San Francisco in April to await final disposition.[13] At about the same time on the East Coast, SS *Santa Clara Victory* was also taken out of service and placed back into a national reserve fleet, this time in the James River Reserve in Virginia.[14]

Other Victory ships had already been placed back into various reserve fleets—those that had escaped closure—but several other ships, such as SS *Bucyrus Victory*, were destined for one-way trips to scrapyards (in her case in Taiwan), where they would be stripped of reusable parts and equipment and then finally cut up as their lengthy careers in logistical support of multiple wars came to a final ignominious end.[15]

The completion of the five-year program involving those 172 GAA ships did not go unnoticed and without appropriate ceremony and presentation of kudos upon those who had been involved with breakouts, shipyard reactivation, taking operational charge of the ships, and manning them from a dwindling labor pool, and those thousands of seamen who took the ships out, repaired them underway, and brought them safely in most cases into the various ports in South Vietnam. In various locations where government officials made speeches and awarded certificates of appreciation, the base statistics were the same: 172 GAA ships, of which 161 had been broken out of reserve; some 1,800 individual voyages completed to Vietnam; and some 8.9 measurement tons of cargo delivered.[16]

Andrew Gibson, the Commerce Department's maritime administrator, and once a Merchant Marine ship master himself, was front and center, in March 1970, bestowing kudos in 1970 upon the imminent completion of the GAA ship program for the Vietnam sealift. He praised the 40 shipping companies involved "for seeing that the ships are run efficiently and effectively." He praised the 50 or so shipyards on all coasts of the United States "that reactivated these ships for the [Vietnam] sealift."[17]

Many privately owned Victory ships did remain in service, however, and continued to make their way to Southeast Asia, as other World War II types that had undergone major conversions in postwar years—some for container and roll-on/roll-off service—thus having their careers extended in that way. The Navy still operated Victory ships, crewed by merchant seamen—and almost exclusively as ammunition carriers—as part of the MSTS "nucleus" fleet, soon to be renamed Military Sealift Command (MSC) to more accurately reflect, as it was explained, its mission.[18]

For those manning the ships, however, and with all those GAA vessels having been removed from service, the boom days accompanying the early buildup years were coming to an end. There were fewer berths available, hiring hall activity had slowed, and waits to ship out were once again being extended.[19]

But as the war in Vietnam continued, and despite the ongoing drawdown of American force levels in-country, there remained an urgency during this time of Vietnamization to shore up South Vietnam, to build up, equip, and further train its armed forces, with the hope and expectation, as dwindling a commodity that it seemed to many, they could carry on the fight largely without the help of the United States.

The pipeline of cargo ships would certainly remain open—and remain crucial to success—and would be maintained as efforts continued to leave South Vietnam as a viable, independent entity. Whether or not South Vietnam would have the will and the required leadership to see it through remained to be determined. And the tests of that would not be long in coming.

The SS *Albany* was one of those World War II types—a C-4 cargo ship and therefore significantly longer at 523 feet than the Victory—that continued to make her presence known in the harbors and along the rivers of South Vietnam in 1970 and beyond.[20] In July, after having delivered a load of bombs for the American air base at Vayama, Thailand, she had made her way to the deepwater anchorage at Vung Tau, near the entrance to the upriver channel to Saigon.[21] During the night and early morning before it was scheduled to begin the 40-mile transit upriver with its remaining cargo of steel and cement, concussion grenades had been set off in the waters around the ship, a routine to which its crew had become more or less accustomed.

"An unusually close grenade rang the hull," recalled Second Mate Brett Whitaker, who had been asleep after having enjoyed a good—perhaps too good—shore leave in Saigon the night before with the ship's radio operator, "Mad" Albert Reinhart. "At that time I realized something was amiss; the sun was shining and the ship's vibrations told me we were underway."[22]

"A quick check of the porthole revealed a fireball as another rocket exploded. Had the *Albany* been a house amidship vessel, this gin mill commando would have been hamburger." Realizing that he was in extremis, and "having no place to dig a hole, manfully," Whitaker did what he felt was the best thing to do under the circumstances: he took refuge in the head "and slammed the door." Eventually, the action ceased, but only briefly. As Whitaker described it, "Charley had just stopped to re-load or whatever you do with rockets" because by the time he reached the radio room, "the fun had started again."

By this time, the *Albany*'s radio operator could not even get word out as to his ship's name and position because "there was so much traffic on the air [as] every ship in the convoy was ... telling river security—or 'moon River'—that the *Albany* was under attack."

Helicopters did arrive to bring a halt to the attack at that point, but the *Albany*'s gauntlet of fire on the river had not yet ended, as it turned out.[23]

"We were attacked again that day at Checkpoint 7," Whitaker recalled. "However, by then I was a seasoned veteran and did not turn into a spineless jellyfish. Besides, I was in the Chief Mate's office [by then] and shielded by a deck cargo of steel pipe."

Upon arrival at Newport in Saigon an inspection of the *Albany* revealed only slight damage to the ship's hull where "an apparent dud had hit." Nonetheless, as Whitaker recalled, "it was a bitch of a way to cure a hangover."

Second Mate Brett Whitaker encountered a problem that he had not seen before after the arrival of SS *Albany* to the Newport docks during that summer of 1970:

After a rather thrilling convoy up the Saigon River ... we began discharging our cargo of bagged cement and steel beams. Things went reasonably well for a day or so, until the Vietnamese longshoremen went on strike. I never learned how their grievance was resolved, but when they were finally ready to go back to work the Army countered by locking them out and sending G.I.s to do the longshore work.[24]

This development might not have been too bad if the soldiers had been even semi-skilled. Additionally, we were burdened with the problem of their attitude. What we had was an odd assortment of radio repairmen, clerk-typists, truck drivers, riflemen, and others who were, as they said at the time, "so short they could walk under the door." These troops were in Saigon for final processing before their flights back to "The World." A few were literally packing for their flight when they were rounded up and trucked to the Newport Docks to discharge the good ship *Albany*. I immediately deduced that I might have a motivational problem to overcome.[25]

I was standing the 1600–2400 watch. During the first few evenings I had managed to detect developing disasters in time to defuse them and avoid vessel damage or bodily injury. The Mates on the other watches were not as fortunate, and on a few occasions had shut off all power until order could be restored. Naturally, NCOs and officers were impossible to find when needed. We were pretty much on our own with unskilled, pissed-off soldiers. Some of them were amazed when they discovered that the ship was "hollow on the inside."

As a result of the level of aptitude and enthusiasm of the conscripted "longshoremen" the cargo was not outturning in the best of condition. I think more spilled concrete was bulldozed into the Saigon River than ever reached its intended destination in bags. The steel fared somewhat better due to it sturdier composition.

From the beginning of this unfortunate situation the Chief Mate and Captain had been protesting our mistreatment with radio messages, letters, and telephone calls to Military Sealift Command. The [ship's] log contained numerous entries in red describing interesting behavior during cargo operations.

As I recall, we were either ignored or instructed to stop whining and get the discharge completed.

We thought we had finally reached the proper authority when one afternoon a jeep covered with whip antennas and flashing lights parked on the dock. A Lt. Colonel, a Captain, and a Sergeant came on board. Assuming them to be our saviors from MSC, I ushered them into the saloon [mess] where the Captain and other officers were having coffee.

After the introductions were made and cups filled, our Captain stated that he was glad somebody had been sent to alleviate our problem, and started describing the situation in some detail.

The Lt. Colonel looked a little perplexed, then cleared his throat and said that he had come on board in hopes of obtaining some frozen lobster tails for the Officer's Club; although he was with MSC, he had no interest other than his lobster tails.

After an awkward silence, we suggested that the Colonel and his party try the *Flying Dragon* which was a reefer ship docked ahead of us.

The Chief Mate then retired to his office to compose yet another letter.[26]

Newport was not the only place where problems relating to cargo handling were encountered during the Vietnamization transition process. As a result, with the general exception of container and roll-on/roll-off type operations, which had quickly proven to be more efficient and far less prone to damage and pilferage, additional unexpected delays continued to be experienced by crews of traditional break-bulk ammunition and general cargo ships—still the predominant type—as Vietnamization continued to be implemented.

A lengthy report prepared by Colonel C.C. Reynolds, in command of the 5th Transportation Command, Qui Nhon, in May 1970 and describing cargo-handling operations for the period ending on April 30 is revealing. The following excerpt underscores both the problems being encountered with break-bulk cargo during that period and, by contrast, the speed and efficiency of more innovative methods of shipment:

(a) On 27 February the SS Overseas Eva arrived with ammunition consigned to the ARVN and it was given to the ARVN to work with their stevedores unit and a civilian contractor. In three days the ARVN stevedores discharged only 118 S/T. On 1 March the operations were stopped by the Coast Guard inspectors for repeated violations of safety practices.

(b) The Sea-Land Ammunition Movement (SLAM) program as started on 3 April with the arrival of the LST 399 from Cam Ranh Bay with 21 loaded Ro/Ro [roll-on/roll-off] trailers. Discharge time was three hours. The program initially calls for one LST every three days, eventually phasing to a daily operation.

(c) On 2, 3, and 4 April the ARVN again attempted to work an ammunition vessel, the SS *Rappahanock*. Operations were extremely slow and were stopped on many occasions due to hazardous handling, especially on the part of unqualified winchmen. On 4 April the operations were assumed by Han Jin Transportation Company to expedite the discharge of the vessel.[27]

The transition involving reduction in American military forces in-country, accompanied by hopefully matching increases in South Vietnamese military personnel, would have consequences for merchant seamen calling on Vietnam in 1970 and subsequent years. The transition for the U.S. Navy in 1970 was, for example, significant. By February of that year approximately half of the "afloat assets" in the ever-dangerous Rung Sat Special Zone (RSSZ) area, through which merchant ships passed on the way to and retuning from Saigon, were under operational control of the South Vietnamese navy, and that included all of the minesweeping vessels. A Vietnamese officer was by then in command of patrols on the Long Tau River.[28]

By the end of the year, all of the remaining U.S. Navy river combatant craft, including 293 PBRs and 224 riverine assault craft, had been transferred to the South Vietnamese. From a peak of 38,083 U.S. Navy personnel in-country at one time, it would be reduced to a reported 16,757 by the end of the year.[29] What ramifications any of this might have for merchant ships moving along the river approaches to Saigon or elsewhere in-country at this time might not have been immediately clear.

Designed as a traditional break-bulk cargo ship and converted much later for carrying containers as part of Sea-Land's innovative and quick-turnaround service to Vietnam, SS *Beauregard*, smaller than other containerships that did not have access to some areas, provided coastwise shuttle service from one in-country port to another for a number of years.[30] In calling on Cam Ranh Bay, Da Nang, Qui Nhon, or Newport—all equipped now to handle the large containers—she would typically arrive and depart either on the same or the following day.

In her new incarnation, and with containers piled high on deck, the *Beauregard* also now made for an especially good target.

Bertil Hager, who had been going to sea since 1937, served as deck maintenance able seaman, and ship's chairman, for much of the *Beauregard*'s time in-country. He later provided details of one attack that occurred as the ship was in river transit to Saigon on September 22, 1970.[31] At least four rockets were seen coming at the ship by various members of her crew. Fortunately, the VC rocketeer's aim was poor, and the ship continued on her way with no harm done. River patrol craft responded and fired towards the general area from which the rockets had been launched.[32]

The *Beauregard*'s master, Captain A. Stewart, later argued in a report to the U.S. Navy authority in Saigon authorized to assess such attacks for possible purposes of crew compensation that it would have been "plainly unusual [for the Viet Cong] to attack PBRs with [a] large target like [our] ship available."[33] Nonetheless, the suggestion by Captain Stewart that the rocket fire was directed at his ship—and not nearby patrol craft—was subsequently disallowed.

Whether or not *Beauregard* had actually been targeted on September 22, 1970, will remain the subject of controversy by those who were involved and choose to remember the incident. Nonetheless, that there had been a reduction of such incidents in the closing months of 1970—for whatever reasons—there can be no doubt. November and December would prove remarkable in that regard as well, with one notable and officially acknowledged exception: that involving the SS *President Coolidge* as she made her way along the Long Tau Channel on the afternoon of November 1.[34]

Anyone involved for any amount of time as a seaman on the Vietnam Run, or in logistical support of other battlefronts at other times, knows that in wartime the role of the

Merchant Marine takes on meaning that transforms and transcends its peacetime role of carrying ocean-borne commerce from one point of the world to others. Those operating ammunition-laden cargo ships, crewing vessels upon which are parked military aircraft and vehicles, tankers hauling gasoline to fuel them, and construction materials used for airfields and roadways from and upon which they will operate against enemy positions, are not just there "minding their own business" as they might be in purely commercial enterprise, and as war rages around them. And as some of their own—ships and those who operate them—are lost in the process to rocket fire, mining, and various other types of weapons of war that are intended, not for commercial exchange purposes, but to destroy them.

And so it seemed fitting to many when, on August 1, 1970, the very name of the U.S. Navy arm charged with chartering and coordinating the movements of merchant ships to and within the Vietnam war zone—the Military Sea Transportation Service (MSTS)—was changed after more than two decades, to more accurately reflect, it was argued, its mission. From that point on, to the present, the name would be Military Sealift Command (MSC).

As Vice Admiral Arthur R. Gralla, the newly appointed MSTS commander put it, "Sealift has a more forceful connotation. It means planning; it means being prepared to operate in a wartime contingency environment which 'sea transportation' just did not connote."[35]

Death of a Swimmer

Thousands of concussion grenades, intended to keep enemy swimmers away from merchant ships anchored out in harbors with cargoes of ammunition and highly volatile aviation gasoline, were detonated in circuits made by Stable Door personnel around those ships throughout the war. Whether or not any swimmers got too close to any of those grenades is something few if any seamen ever learned, but their use was nonetheless reassuring for those on the ships, and few—including this writer—lost much sleep through the night as those grenades were tossed in the water around their ships by U.S. Navy personnel assigned to Stable Door duty.

On occasion, however, references to enemy swimmers and their demise—either by capture, or worse—were entered into the U.S. Naval Forces Vietnam's monthly historical summaries. These reports, declassified years later, highlight Stable Door activities, including encounters with swimmers. One such example of that is the following description of the successful mining of SS *Amerigo*, and the attempted mining of SS *Overseas Rose* in Cam Ranh Bay, which appeared in the monthly summary for September 1970:

Unit Two [Stable Door] personnel had their hands full at Cam Ranh Bay on 22–23 September. At approximately 2144 H on 22 September, LCPL 66 reported small arms fire in the vicinity of Pier Five (ammo pier) and investigated. The pier sentry had fired upon a swimmer alongside the pier. EOD divers were called to the scene and discovered a charge consisting of 120 pounds of C-4 explosive, blasting caps, detonating chord, and a pull-friction release type detonator attached to the hull of the Overseas Rose at Pier Five. The charge was towed out of the area and disarmed by the cool EOD team members. All other ships in the area were checked for charges with negative results.

The following morning at 1036 H[ours] the SS Amerigo, also moored at Pier Five suffered a detonation which was located on the starboard side, aft of the starboard boiler in the engine room. The ship lost all power and began flooding in the engine room. She was towed to the opposite side of the turning basin and allowed to settle in 18 feet of water on the sandy bottom. The ship was later dewatered, temporarily patched, and returned to Pier Five where more permanent repairs were effected.

In a footnote to this action, the body of a swimmer was found in the harbor on 24 September. The body had a bullet hole through the right wrist and damaged facial bones thought to be caused by close proximity to an underwater concussion grenade. It was believed that this was the swimmer sighted by the sentry two nights before. Evidently, two or more swimmers were involved in the attack which damaged the Amerigo and unsuccessfully attempted to mine the *Overseas Rose*.[36]

Closing Stable Door

Harbor and anchorage monitoring and security for merchant ships was provided as part of the U.S. Navy's Operation Stable Door, an outgrowth in November 1966 of Operation Market Time, the Navy's offshore watercraft interdiction operation. There is no telling how many merchant seamen would have been killed, injured, or had their ships sunk under them into the mud and sand of such places as Da Nang, Nha Trang, Cam Ranh Bay, Vung Tau, Nha Be, and Saigon had it not been for the work of Stable Door patrol boat crews and EOD teams that spotted, removed, defused, and destroyed the water mines laid, attached to, or placed close by their ships.

The number of lives saved, though incalculable, might well have been many, and most seamen would not have been aware of the work these teams had performed.

As part of the drawdown of U.S. military forces taking place in Vietnam, Stable Door's responsibilities for harbor and anchorage security and mine detection, deactivation, and disposal were fully transferred over to the Vietnamese navy by year's end. Stable Door Unit Three, Qui Nhon, was the first to be turned over, on June 15, and that was followed by Unit Four, Nha Trang, on July 1. Unit One, Vung Tau, came next, on September 1, and that was followed by the last of the units to be turned over— Unit Two, Cam Ranh Bay—on November 25, 1970.[37] American personnel for all Stable Door units had peaked at about 500, a relatively small portion of the more than 20,000 U.S. Navy personnel who would be withdrawn by the end of the year. The total drawdown from all services for the year would number some 177,800.[38]

Summarizing the accomplishments of the various units of the Inshore Undersea Warfare Group, it would be noted that they had "protected approximately 17,000 ships per year of which over 10,000 were checked by Stable Door EOD teams. Harbor Defense Units inspected an average of 1,400 junks per month and confiscated tons of contraband."[39]

Along with the accomplishments were the losses. "During the four years of harbor defense operation," one report also noted, "13 U.S. sailors were killed and another 14 wounded in action."[40] These numbers certainly would have included those killed and wounded in an earlier incident while attempting to disarm a floating mine brought by a patrol boat to Nha Be, which might otherwise have found its mark on a merchant ship in transit in the Long Tau shipping channel.

Fittingly, at the end of November 1970, and in tribute to those in the "Brown Water Navy"—including Stable Door personnel, who had kept an eye on merchant ships while patrolling the shipping channels and anchorages in their "swifties" and "skimmers" and no doubt saved the lives of merchant seamen in those areas while performing their duties—Commander Naval Forces Vietnam would note: "I am sure that the countless merchant seamen who depended on you to clear the way join me in thanking you for an outstanding job."[41]

President Coolidge: ## "The lull ... was suddenly broken"

Another ship with the name *President Coolidge*, a passenger-ship-turned-trooper, had been lost during World War II while transporting thousands of American troops when it inadvertently wandered into a "friendly" minefield in the South Pacific in late 1942, was run onto a coral reef, and sank in shallow water.[42] Now, 28 years later, and in Vietnam's Long Tau shipping channel, Viet Cong rocketeers were taking aim on another incarnation of an APL ship by that name, a C4 hull type, Mariner Class cargo ship representing a new generation of merchant ship design and construction.[43] If not actually expecting to sink this 523-foot ship using their B-41 rocket launchers, they might at least do her and whatever cargo she carried serious harm, perhaps even kill some of those seamen who moved her now northward along the Long Tau Channel to Saigon.

"The lull that persisted in the past two months," the monthly U.S. Naval Forces Vietnam summary would recount for November 1970, "was suddenly broken when on 1 November at 1415 H[ours], the SS *President Coolidge*, transiting north on the Long Tau Channel, came under fire from the east bank, three miles southeast of the Nha Be Navy Base. An estimated three B-41 rockets were fired at the ship, but there were no hits. An aftermath investigation revealed that some debris from the air blast settled on the fantail of the vessel."[44]

So, while the string of consecutive months without merchant ship attack incidents had been broken, the record of poor marksmanship exhibited by Viet Cong rocketeers—all merchant seamen transiting the Long Tau in those days would have gratefully agreed—had not improved.

With the process of Vietnamization moving significantly forward in 1970, and the complete turnover of river patrol, minesweeping, and Stable Door harbor and anchorage security responsibilities having been effected by year's end, the question remained: would the South Vietnamese navy, and by extension American merchant seamen, fare as well in the coming year?

Commander R.L. Schreadley, USN (Ret.), who served as director of a special history project while on the staff of Commander Naval Forces Vietnam and would later chronicle the role of the U.S. Navy in Vietnam in his seminal work *From the Rivers to the Sea*, would provide at least a partial answer to the question: "The [Long Tau] river would never be closed to navigation, but it would never again be as secure as it was then."[45]

Despite evident changes that were taking place as a result of the drawdown of American military forces in Vietnam by the end of 1970, it was clear that, going forward—and it would still be for more than another four years—American merchant seamen would clearly be operating within a "wartime contingency environment" while continuing to man their ships along the Vietnam Run.

15

Empty Ship and Last Ship Sunk (1971–1972)

"The blast was so violent that some cargo was thrown through the skin of the ship on the opposite side [of the pier]."
—U.S. Naval Forces Vietnam summary, August 1971

"More shiploads of supplies and equipment arrived to overload the Vietnamese logistics system ... the whole thing bordered on insanity."
—R.L. Schreadley, *From the Rivers to the Sea*

Something quite remarkable occurred along the winding Long Tau Shipping Channel to Saigon between January and August 1971: there were no attacks on merchant ships reported during that eight-month period.[1] Some statistician keeping track would note in the monthly U.S. Naval Forces Vietnam summary for August that 2,865 ships had "transitted [sic] the Long Tau safely" during those months without an incoming B-40 or B-41 rocket, recoilless rifle, mortar, or any other type of round directed at a merchant ship seen or heard by merchant seamen aboard any of those ships. In the five previous years of keeping score along the Long Tau that was unprecedented.[2]

Certainly the ongoing process of Vietnamization, begun in late 1969 and which had transferred much of the equipment and burden otherwise already from the Americans to the South Vietnamese would not have explained this, since Viet Cong and NVA attackers made no distinction as to whether or not cargoes moving along the Long Tau were intended for use by American, South Vietnamese, or their other allied military units.

"The enemy has been hard pressed"

There were, in fact, a variety of reasons posited as to why there had been a prolonged lull in the usual attack pattern along the Long Tau, which had for years averaged multiple attack incidents—sometimes a dozen or more each month—against merchant ships moving through the Rung Sat Special Zone (RSSZ), through the heart of which flowed the Long Tau. As good an explanation as any was provided in the U.S. Naval Forces Vietnam monthly summary for August 1971:

Prime factors for the quiet ten months on the channel have been complete defoliation on both sides of the channel, USN Seawolf, and PBR escort of each ship transitting, constant minesweeping, and RF [Reaction Force] units daily patrolling the entire length of the channel for two kilometers on either side. Clearly the enemy has been hard pressed to take any action, though a sapper battalion has been reported in the area.[3]

The Making of a Watermine Sapper

As if to point out that, despite the downturn of attacks on merchant shipping in 1971, there still remained the prospect of attack operating from below the surface of the muddy Long Tau and in other areas, the monthly U.S. Naval Forces historical summary for August 1971 included a lengthy and detailed description of the training, equipping, and deployment of watermine sappers, otherwise known as watersappers or, simply, swimmers. While making specific reference to one unit—the North Vietnamese 471st Naval Sapper Battalion, which operated in Quang Nam Province—the report noted that it "provided a good picture of the watersapper and his activities throughout the First Coastal Zone." This description, citing in turn the First Coastal Zone intelligence officer, is provided here largely in its entirety:

> All personnel received three months infantry training and six months watersapping training in North Vietnam. They can assemble and place: land mines against fortifications, command detonated mines, and water magnetic acoustic mines. All company and battalion level cadre have had previous combat experience in the south....[4]
>
> Each man has his own snorkel, some grenades, a dagger signal flare, and five meters of nylon line. Each sapper cell is equipped with one AK-47 with a folding stock. Each company has one B-40 and one B-41 rocket launcher with three rounds for each. The battalion has a total of approximately 30 water pressure mines, and a 15 watt radio.
>
> Although seemingly poorly equipped, he is trained to be patient, and calculative, and to use his ingenuity. He has been known to use mild, fear inhibiting drugs when attacking. Each sapper is trained to reconnoiter a target thoroughly before launching an attack. A healthy swimmer with good endurance can stay in the water many hours. Research has shown that about six hours in the water is the maximum time a swimmer will need and is able to stay in the water. He will conserve his weapons, even to the extreme of making practice runs using dummy charges. It is not uncommon for a team leader to observe a target for 30 days or more until he discovers a weakness in defenses. In many cases an attack will not be launched unless an exploitable flaw can be identified to the satisfaction of the team leader. The professional sapper is not suicidal.
>
> The hours of 2300 to 0400 are often mentioned by PWs and Hoi Chanhs; but the team leader will choose an attack time when he feels the target is most vulnerable. The sapper will favor the path of least resistance to the target, and will use distance and currents to his advantage. His approach will be on the surface up to about 200 yards of the target even if he has scuba [self-contained underwater breathing apparatus] gear. Frequently, swimmers will use debris to cover their approach to a target ship or bridge and as flotation. Where there is heavy sampan traffic in the vicinity of an anchorage, mines may be transported to the target by boat. This is accomplished by slinging the mine under the keel of the sampan and proceeding as close to the target as possible before cutting the mine free. This method can also be used to lay a mine in a channel.
>
> A swimmer's maneuverability is one of his greatest assets. Not only can he vary his course to attack, but also he can dive, tread water, hide behind anchor chains, rest on a ship's rudder, etc. In addition, he can move through water with virtually no propulsion noise.
>
> However, low water temperature can limit his endurance. Nighttime underwater navigation is exceptionally difficult. A swimmer is often hampered with the ordnance and

miscellaneous gear he must bring with him. Water currents and anti-swimmer defenses can be a critical element in the execution of an attack.

This, then, is the enemy.

While there was unusual quiet, and no incidents involving attack by rocket, recoilless rifle, mortar, or even small arms fire on merchant shipping along the Long Tau Channel during the first several months of 1971, there were telltale and even more blatant signs of ongoing activity in the area by watermine sappers. Not having much to report otherwise in those monthly U.S. Naval Forces summaries relative to so-called "harassment" attacks on shipping, things more directly related to mining activity were noted, ranging from the discovery in January of another 500-pound bomb in the RSSZ that was "believed to be intended for use in the Long Tau" to the recovery by MID 91 boats of two sections of conductor wire—one 24 feet long, and another half that length—also in the month of January.[5]

While such things indicated that not much was really happening even with respect to watermines in the early months of 1971, one notable attack in the making, but which would ultimately not succeed, occurred at the Nha Be anchorage a few months later. On April 23, 1971, just before midnight, as noted in the monthly U.S. Naval Forces summary for that month, "an 80 kilo [176-pound] mine was detected by a ship's crewmember being placed alongside the shell tanker ACTEON by two swimmers at the Shell Tank Farm two kilometers northwest of LSB Nha Be. The security force was alerted and the two swimmers were probably killed, but no bodies were recovered. The mine drifted approximately 500 meters upriver and was detonated by fire from the security force."[6]

The *Acteon* and her crew had been very lucky that day in April when targeted by watermine sappers, but the American dry cargo ship *Green Bay*, in process of unloading at a DeLong pier in Qui Nhon some months later, would not be so fortunate.

A merchant seaman stands before SS *Green Bay* after it was sunk by a limpet mine placed on its hull by a Viet Cong "swimmer" in 1971 (Courtesy National Maritime Union).

SS *Green Bay*: The Last Ship Sunk

While the Viet Cong did not appear to have had anywhere near the "field day" against merchant ships it had displayed along the Long Tau channel in previous years, successful attacks of various type were still recorded in 1971, most notably the mining attack on the 26-year-old former troopship *Green Bay*, a 523-foot, 11,000-ton cargo ship, in Qui Nhon harbor on August 17 of that year.[7] An explosive device later estimated to have contained between 400 and 600 pounds of explosives was placed against the ship's hull below the waterline, and detonated as she was moored at a DeLong pier. The explosion ripped a massive hole in the hull, and the ship settled quickly at a 45-degree angle in 40 feet of water. Fortunately, there were no casualties reported by Central Gulf Steamship Company, which owned and operated the ship under contract to the Military Sealift Command (MSC). The crew of officers and 28 unlicensed seamen were transferred ashore, and eventually paid off and repatriated.[8]

The U.S. Naval Forces Vietnam monthly historical summary for August 1971 provides additional details of the successful mining attack on SS *Green Bay*:

> Harbor security against the water sapper threat continued to be of prime concern as enemy sappers succeeded in mining yet another large ship in Quin Nhon Harbor on 17 August.
>
> Sometime between the hours of 2100 H—2300 H on 16 August, a swimmer silently floated a 400 pound charge on the incoming tide from the south end of the De Long Pier. He secured the charge to the underside of the pier support structure and caisson approximately 300 feet from the north end of berth N-Z. Two USA and two ARVN sentries failed to notice anything unusual. So did the PADD (Portable Acoustic Doppler Detector) watch personnel, who had been permanently positioned on a barge attached to the north end of the De Long Pier for approximately two weeks prior to that night. The swimmer also slipped past VNN waterborne assets on patrol in the vicinity of the De Long Pier.[9]
>
> At 0100 H of the following morning, a tremendous explosion ripped the stillness at the De Long Pier, and the SS *Green Bay* went down by the stern with a hole 15 feet high and 45 feet wide torn in her starboard side. The blast was so violent that some cargo was thrown through the skin of the ship on the opposite side.
>
> The mine detonation slightly injured three personnel: two Korean stevedores and a crewmember. The Seventh Fleet salvage vessel, USS *Current* (ARS-22) arrived in Qui Nhon at 2200 H on 17 August to commence salvage operations.

The mining of *Green Bay* spelled the end for the 26-year-old cargo ship. After plates were welded in place, water pumped out, and the ship was refloated, she was towed to Hong Kong, never to return to Vietnam or to reenter commercial service. Sold to breakers, *Green Bay* was scrapped the following year.[10]

In the aftermath of the successful mining attack against SS *Green Bay*—what the monthly U.S. Naval Forces summary for August 1971 would describe as "the fourth involving major ships in Qui Nhon Harbor in the past 17 months"—there was a major review of existing harbor security conditions and procedures, and what could and should be done not only for Qui Nhon but "to tighten harbor security measures throughout the coastal areas of Vietnam."[11] The following recommendations were made, and, to varying degrees, implemented:

"All MSC interest vessels were directed to steam at night near Qui Nhon; port security should be intensified by bring[ing] the number of security guards up to full strength, and by increasing their training; waterline lighting should be installed at the De Long piers; and physical barriers to block underwater entry into the pier were to be constructed."[12]

"Additionally, there should be increased surveillance of all craft in the harbor; [wooden or other forms of separator] camels used at berths N-1 and N-2 [in Qui Nhon] should be improved to permit better visibility of water area between ships and pier; and unauthorized craft should be barred from approaching pier within one kilometer."

It was noted that, in light of recommendations made for all areas, those involved with harbor security in Cam Ranh Bay requested—contrary to the dictates of Vietnamization requirements—that U.S. Navy EOD Team 36 be allowed to remain in place at Cam Ranh Bay for as long as needed, and that there be "expedited delivery of four PADD sonar devices for anti-swimmer detection."[13]

As if to underscore the fact that water mines of all types would continue to be a threat in various areas of South Vietnam regardless of improved measures taken to counter them, the SS *Seatrain Ohio* experienced a bone-rattling close call when, while in the process of anchoring on August 30, 1971, in Vung Tau Harbor, it experienced a submerged mine explosion.[14]

Fortunately, the mine was not attached but lay on the bottom of the harbor below the ship in some nine fathoms (54 feet) of water when it detonated. There was no damage to the ship.

At least one more attack incident against an American merchant ship—in the Long Tau Channel to Saigon—would be reported before the end of the year. According to the Navy's monthly report for November 1971:

> At 1530 H[ours] on 8 November, the merchant ship *Raphael Semmes*, transiting north on the Long Tau shipping channel, reported being hit by rockets fired from the south bank in the vicinity of [designated map position] XS 996 750. Subsequent investigations revealed that she may have been hit by shrapnel.... At the time of the incident, two PBRs of RPD 51 were escorting the ship and an RF company was providing a ground sweep on each bank in the immediate vicinity....[15]

Raphael Semmes proceeded to Saigon without further incident, and no casualties were subsequently reported.

The number of American military personnel in Vietnam had been significantly reduced by early 1971 from the peak level of 1969, and Vietnamization, the plan to increase the South Vietnamese military forces as Americans were being withdrawn, was much more evident by then. And while more than 150,000 American troops remained in Vietnam by the end of the year, the South Vietnamese military would soon be tested much more directly as a standalone entity.[16]

The Merchant Marine, not directly subject to or affected by Vietnamization downsizing policy, continued to do its part, hauling in another 10,841,291 million more measurement tons of military equipment and ammunition in 1971 (down from 13,578,428 MT in 1970), while engaging in "retrograde" movement of military vehicles and aircraft that would be removed either for repair and return or disposal of otherwise.[17]

The reduction of American military units, locked into a timetable, was one thing, but the role of civilian merchant seamen, never counted in the withdrawal schedule and numbers, remained crucial during this period to both assist with the withdrawal and provide for continued logistical support for units that remained in-country for the time being, and for the expanding presence and role of the South Vietnamese military forces which, it was hoped, would ultimately be able to stand on its own.

As the year dawned there was an urgency to it all that, for some perhaps reading the tea leaves or viewing the "writing on the wall" better than others, carried a sense of pending, inevitable doom. If South Vietnam's own military forces could be brought up to the hoped-for level as American forces were withdrawn, and up to speed with training, then perhaps there was still a chance to successfully stem off the storm that loomed from the north and operated from within.

The so-called Nixon Doctrine and its plan for Vietnamization would increasingly test South Vietnamese capabilities in combat. And the Cooper–Church Amendment, legislation passed by the U.S. Congress in December 1970, made certain that if incursions were to be made by ground troops outside the borders of Vietnam, they could not include American units. Thus, when Operation Lamson 719 was launched into Laos on February 8, 1971, to cut the flow of enemy troops and materiel along the Ho Chi Minh Trail in that area, the South Vietnamese military was put to a major test, though supported by American aircraft.[18]

As one historian would later note, "the operation not only failed to destroy … the Ho Chi Minh Trail, but exposed the South Vietnamese army's deficiencies."[19] "Conceived in doubt and assailed by skepticism," the effort, Henry Kissinger said, "proceeded in confusion."[20]

Huge quantities of military equipment were in the process of being turned over in-country, but it needed to be both maintained and operated adequately for effective deployment in the field. There was growing concern, however, if not publicly admitted, as to whether that could and would be done, given time constraints imposed for turnover of assets to and training of the Vietnamese, and their ability to take charge of those assets and the mission.

In an independent inspection report prepared early in 1971 for Vice Admiral Robert S. Salzer, the new commander of remaining U.S. naval forces in Vietnam, it was noted that the coastal and river forces that had by then gone over to South Vietnamese control were virtually in a state of "operational ineffectiveness."[21] While this did not exactly bode well for those, such as merchant seamen, who depended on those very forces for their own river transit and port security, Admiral Salzer would later suggest, "God knows, if the Viet Cong had not become so disorganized they'd have had a field day there [on the rivers] the way the Vietnamese let their river boats deteriorate."[22]

Merchant ships continued to bring in large amounts of cargo along the rivers and into the coastal ports, as in-country logistical operations underwent their own changes as a result of Vietnamization. It did not appear that there was a want for the required supplies, thanks to the role played by merchant seamen, but the question arose as to whether or not those goods were becoming too much for the Vietnamese who had replaced American military logistical support personnel to handle. Some observers on the ground at that time thought that might actually be the case.

"More shiploads of supplies and equipment arrived to overload the Vietnamese logistics system," naval historian Richard L. Schreadley reflected years after the war, "and now there were simply not enough Americans left to manage the situation.

Many millions of dollars went swirling down the Vietnamese drain in a final orgy of 'accelerated' turnover. To many, the whole thing bordered on insanity."[23]

One of the many ships arriving in Vietnam at this time was *SeaTrain Puerto Rico*, which had started out during World War II as a T-2 tanker and, much later, in 1966, was lengthened and converted into a heavy-lift, multipurpose cargo ship, and then placed in service on the Vietnam Run.[24] As such, she carried a typical variety of military vehicles and aircraft—and general, palletized cargo—that, despite what appeared as "overload" to some observers, was no doubt well received by others for whom it was intended. Seaman Thomas A. Galka, arriving for the first time in Vietnam on a merchant ship late in 1971—he had served there previously with the Marines—described ship and cargo many years later in the following way:

> The old *Puerto Rico* was an odd ship. A sort of bastardized vessel [with] a T-2 stern, and the deck looked exactly like a small escort aircraft carrier. This impression was reinforced by the fact that we were carrying small spotter scout planes, larger aircraft, and helicopter gunships and transports. They were all brand new, unpainted yet and situated on top of the deck—just like a carrier. Below decks in the massive cargo storage areas and holds were tanks, trucks, jeeps, ammo, and every conceivable form of military supplies. The sides of the deck area and fore and aft didn't escape either. We had containers of P.X. supplies everywhere, gas tanks, generators, etc. all crated up.[25]
>
> The favorite cargo, however, was the pallets of beer, probably destined for some Army club. I recall quite well that it was Falstaffs. We might have had 7 or 8 such huge pallets up forward. No one was naïve, in the slightest. It was explained to me that no one expected that entire shipment to reach its final destination, unscathed. No, not at all. An excessive amount was placed aboard to provide for "losses at sea, due to heavy seas," etc. In other words, pilferage.

On this voyage, at least as far as a significant part of the cargo of Falstaff beer was involved, there was indeed a significant loss of it "at sea" when all was said and done.

Vietnamization was going forward apace, and change was quite evident, but much of it—the experience ashore—still, for the time being anyway, had a familiar look to seamen in the closing months of 1971. "No recollection of 'sin city' [Saigon] would be complete," recalled Thomas Galka years later, "without the mention of two words—TUDO Street! There it was: pimps, whores, b-girls, G.I.s, seamen, shops, restaurants, bars, gambling, dope, black market, you name it—it was there in abundance!"

> It was there I learned how in all probability [some] Merchant Marine officers were responsible for upsetting the *status quo*. The prices for things were long established by soldiers who didn't have much money and didn't allow prices to escalate. This suited the vast majority of seamen—officers and unlicensed—just fine. But I observed on more than one occasion some lonely old Second Mate, for example, shelling out a bundle to an amazed bar girl. This was frowned upon, but ... they proceeded to grossly overpay for services—real and implied—and this only resulted in future monetary hassles for all.
>
> Everyone thought that we were millionaires, and compared to the average Vietnamese we were indeed rather well off, if not actually rich, even a lowly messman. I always took it as a game, actually. The locals, no matter where, were against you, matching wits with your valuables as the prize. And indeed that is exactly what it was, a match.
>
> The Vietnamese were perhaps the best I've ever seen at a con, or theft, but again I say this as a compliment, not an indictment. Since they received precious little aid, funds,

food from their own government—all that U.S. aid went on the black market to the highest bidder (and he sure wasn't some little old peasant farmer)—then they were forced to supplement their incomes, any way they could. It is also a known fact that we were viewed as interlopers, intruders, although I would say that any real hatred was reserved for the U.S. armed forces, not seamen, really.

Thomas Galka would not return to Vietnam again until his arrival on SS *Iberville* (Waterman) in 1974, by which time the look and feel of Saigon for seamen who had been there before would seem quite different.

By early January 1972 the American force level in Vietnam had dropped to a reported 157,000, which represented a decrease of some 386,000 from the peak of 1969. The remaining numbers of the various forces still in-country at this point are revealing as to how far Vietnamization had proceeded, and what the implications might be for the coming year. The U.S. Army—combat units and a much larger number of support personnel—stood at 119,700.[26] Navy personnel were now down to 7,800 in-country, with another 13,000 on ships offshore.[27] The Marines, who had removed the bulk of their force by the middle of 1970, was now down, suggesting its continued importance as Vietnamization played out.[28] The Coast Guard, which had transferred most of its in-country assets to the South Vietnamese under a program aptly code-named SCATTOR, for Small Craft Assets, Training and Turnover of Resources—was down to only 100 by the first week of January 1971.[29]

While those on the merchant ships had not seen a comparable percentage decrease in their own numbers, they increasingly bore witness to the changed look of the in-country areas along and to which their ships took them.

Whether or not the pace of Vietnamization was considered too rapid, as Schreadley suggests, merchant mariners played a central role in a series of code-named operations in 1972 in response to developments on the ground and, it seems clear, at the once-secret negotiation table in Paris where Henry Kissinger and the North Vietnamese Le Duc Tho continued to hammer out details for an eventual ceasefire agreement. Early in the year Operation Empty Ship undertook to remove quantities of surplus military equipment, utilizing space on ships made available after initial deliveries of cargo.[30] It was praised by Admiral John McCain, Jr., commander of U.S. Naval Forces, Pacific, who commented that, "for the first time, an American fighting force is returning home with its equipment without leaving the battlefields and depots filled with military supplies."[31]

While the operation no doubt was perceived at the time as successful by some, McCain's assessment would appear premature and overly positive in light of developments not much later that year, and certainly as viewed eventually in the war's immediate aftermath. Any hope that this removal of equipment might have represented at that time was soon shattered by unexpected new developments at the hands of the North Vietnamese.

A major new offensive named in honor of one of Vietnam's most revered heroes, Nguyen Hue, was launched by the North Vietnamese using some 600 tanks and on three fronts in early April 1972.[32] Three divisions—some 30,000 PAVN troops—poured directly southward, supported by tanks, across the DMZ, and another 20,000 moved from Cambodia into Binh Dinh Province north of Saigon, while another three divisions moved finally from eastern Laos into Kon Tum Province in the Central Highlands.[33] Dubbed the Spring or Easter Offensive by those caught off-guard by and on the receiving end of the offensive, it would soon require a reversal in the retrograde flow of American military equipment as represented by Empty Ship. Secretary of Defense Melvin Laird had said some weeks before that such a nationwide offensive was "not a serious possibility," and General Westmoreland had suggested that the enemy, if it undertook such a campaign, would not be able to last more than "a few days" because of a lack of "staying power."[34]

The scope and duration of the Nguyen Hue Offensive underscored once again the woeful dangers of the optimistic spin represented by American military policy makers and commanders during the Vietnam War.

With fewer than 10,000 American combat troops remaining in Vietnam by this time, and their use restricted, the onus on the ground had very much shifted to the South Vietnamese, whose military forces had come to number over one million by the end of 1971. But American aircraft based in Thailand, or operating off aircraft carriers in the Gulf of Tonkin, responded in support of the South Vietnamese, who had been surprised and sent headlong into retreat in the north. Operation Linebacker, a combined U.S. Airforce and Navy operation, would commence on May 9, 1972, and last into October; it would be the first continuous bombing campaign against North Vietnam since Rolling Thunder had ended towards the end of 1968.[35]

Operation Enhance

Misplaced optimism as to the progress of peace talks seems to have contributed to the premature birth of Operation Empty Ship and the removal of shiploads of U.S. military equipment from South Vietnam. The hindsight of only few months would reveal this clearly, and the need to ship large quantities of military cargo to South Vietnam once again, and quickly.

In what would be dubbed Operation Enhance, Nixon ordered on May 19 a resupply of war materiel to South Vietnam, most transported in ships crewed by merchant seamen, some in C-130 transport aircraft for earliest arrival, and all for delivery by the first of August 1972.[36]

While dozens of additional helicopters, scores of jet fighters and other aircraft, more patrol boats, artillery and anti-tank weapons, along with two air defense artillery battalions, three artillery battalions, and two M48A3 tank battalions would seem significant at the time, it would pale in comparison to another massive infusion of military hardware that would follow later in the year, as the war and on-again, off-again peace negotiations continued to the end of the year.[37]

In the period between Operation Empty Ship and the start of Operation Enhance, most American merchant ships arriving in-country came and went largely without incident, while seamen noted changes that reflected this phase of the war. Donald Merchant, returning to Vietnam in early May 1972 as navigation officer on SS *Steel Traveler* (Captain Spence), later described his arrival in Saigon, just before the start of Operation Enhance, at that time:

There was no delay [at Vung Tau] and we proceeded right up the river. The defoliants used on the river bank were scaringly effective, with nothing but mud and a few stubs back a mile on each side of the river.[38]

Saigon was relatively quiet. The berths were full of ships but [there was] little military in evidence. [We] arranged for a contractor, Dien-Co, to do some welding jobs on deck, and another, Quack Tuu, to clean the bilges and the distilled water tanks.

The general cargo [unloading] was finished by May 9, so we shifted to the buoys to discharge about 7,000 tons of grain in the lower holds. The ship was immediately surrounded by barges and boats of all kinds. Women made up the long shore labor force as most of the men were off fighting the war. They also brought aboard a restaurant service and laundry for their own use.

Going ashore was by a sampan fitted with a single cylinder engine with a long shaft over the side of the stern in place of the oar of former days. You were taken to a ferry landing opposite the My Canh floating restaurant and took a larger sampan across the river. Curfew on the river was at dark.

Contractors worked on lifeboat and winch repairs. One of the Dien-Co's men got severely burned while working on a winch.

The cargo was finished on May 15, [and we] sailed in the afternoon for Sattahip, Thailand.

On May 2, a few days after *Steel Voyager*'s own safe arrival in Saigon, Nixon went public with his decision to not only increase bombing raids in North Vietnam but, for the first time, and despite repeated requests to do so, to cut off the arrival of merchant shipping to Haiphong and other northern ports. With Soviet and Chinese ships making regular calls to these ports, this decision to lay mines, effectively closing Haiphong and the other northern ports, had not been done before at any point in the war, for fear of inadvertently widening the conflict.[39]

"These actions are not directed at any other nation," Nixon explained to the American people. "Countries with ships presently in North Vietnamese ports have already been notified," he explained, "that their ships will have three daylight periods to leave in safety. After that time, the mines will become active and any ships attempting to leave or enter these ports will do so at their own risk."[40]

Various types of mines had, of course, been deployed by the Viet Cong and NVA in the south against American, South Vietnamese, and allied shipping—sometimes quite effectively—but the estimated 11,000 mines dropped by air in the north all but shut off access to Haiphong for the better part of a year, until after they were swept or self-deactivated.[41] For one reason or another, some 26 merchant ships, including several of Soviet registry, were unable to leave Haiphong during the three-day "safe" period prior to the mine activation, and as a result remained stranded there until well into the next year.[42]

Despite the American bombing campaign—some would argue because of it—the once secret talks between Kissinger and Le Duc Tho, only made known publicly in early 1972, were resumed in August and continued into October.[43] It had become increasingly clear that some sort of ceasefire agreement would eventually be achieved. Kissinger had gone back to Paris with an ultimatum from Nixon to "settle or else," and that was soon followed by stepped-up bombing of North Vietnam and mining of its ports. Nonetheless, a turning point in negotiations seemed to come in early October, prompting Kissinger to encourage South Vietnam's president Thieu to "seize as much territory as possible" in advance of a final settlement.[44]

Enhance Plus

The word also went out from the Department of Defense to step up deliveries of military equipment to South Vietnam once again in a limited time frame, that is, in advance of any final ceasefire agreement. This would again involve American merchant ships, and Military Sealift Command (MSC) "nucleus" ships crewed by American merchant seamen, in what became known, building upon an earlier Operation Enhance to replenish during the Spring Offensive, as Operation Enhance Plus.[45] Commencing in mid–October and expected to continue into early November, aircraft would also be employed to fly in military supplies from various allied countries, but the tonnage ultimately carried by aircraft, while significant, was once again far exceeded by that transported by ship.[46]

Along with a transfer of rolling stock, ammunition, and assorted military supplies, aircraft were delivered to the South Vietnamese air force in large numbers, making it what was reported to have become the fourth largest air force in the world at that time. And, keeping in mind requirements known to be coming in an eventual agreement, the ownership of several military bases, developed over the years by the U.S. military to support their operations in-country, were secretly transferred in a short amount of time to the South Vietnamese military forces.[47] Operation Enhance Plus was reportedly completed within six weeks.[48]

"Peace is at hand"

On October 21, 1972, four days after Le Duc Tho's meeting with Kissinger in Paris, North Vietnam officially approved the proposed ceasefire accord that had been hammered out between Le Duc Tho and Kissinger.[49] While the draft treaty was denounced by Thieu, Kissinger declared publicly on October 26: "We believe that peace is at hand … we believe that an agreement is within sight."[50] Kissinger was sent to Saigon to speak with Thieu, who countered with 69 amendments that included withdrawal of NVA from the south and proposed that the DMZ be maintained in perpetuity. Kissinger suggested to Nixon upon his return that Thieu's amendments "verge[d] on insanity."[51]

The peace talks were stalled by the insertion of Thieu's monkey wrench into the works. They continued once again, into December, and were suspended on the 13th by Le Duc Tho.

American merchant seamen bore witness to a war that would still not quit as 1972 came to a close, despite the drafting of a ceasefire agreement that had for all intents and purposes been agreed to by the United States and North Vietnam by late October. But Kissinger's declaration that peace was "at hand" at that point was premature, as Thieu's intransigence and list of 69 additional amendments to the ceasefire agreement prompted an order by Nixon for both more bombing and mining of North Vietnam's ports, prolonging at great cost to both sides the inevitable.

The quantities of measurement tonnage of cargo delivered in 1972, while down from previous years, were still significant, making prosecution of the war possible, for better or for worse.

16

The "Leopard Spot" Ceasefire (1973–1974)

"Free movement of merchant ships is guaranteed by Article 3 (a) [of the Paris Peace Agreement]."
—George Aldrich, DOD legal briefing paper, 1973

"Even Saigon was vastly different now that it was in its last days of glory ... and Tu Do Street was a shadow of its former self."
—Thomas A. Galka, SS *Iberville*, 1974

A ceasefire, unveiled formally as the "Agreement on Ending the War and Restoring Peace in Vietnam," was finally agreed to and signed on January 28, 1973, by representatives from the United States, South Vietnam (RVN), North Vietnam (DRV), and the Provisional Revolutionary Government (PRG) of the southern-based National Liberation Front (NLF), formally ending involvement by the United States in the Vietnam War.[1]

It took cajoling, threats to cut off further military assistance to South Vietnam, a late bombing campaign—what would be known for its timing as the "Christmas bombing"—directed at Hanoi and Haiphong, and the mining of North Vietnamese ports and waterways to convince South Vietnam's president, Nguyen Van Thieu, to reluctantly sign the agreement. And what was agreed to now in the first month of the new year was what had essentially been agreed to by all involved parties—except the South Vietnamese president—months before that final bombing campaign.[2] The bombing—considered superfluous by many and resulting in the destruction and loss of life typical of B-52 bombing strikes—had also been ordered in part to reassure President Thieu that the United States still had his back.[3]

For Vietnamese nationalists introductory wording that had been placed in the Geneva Accords ending the First Indochina or "French War" in Vietnam in 1954 was repeated up front in the opening lines of the ceasefire agreement that now ended the "American War" in Vietnam more than 18 years later.[4]

"The United States and all other countries respect the independence, sovereignty, unity, and territorial integrity of Viet-Nam," the ceasefire agreement began, "as recognized by the 1954 Geneva Agreements on Viet-Nam."[5]

This time around, however, there would be no reference, as there had been in 1954, to a "temporary" division of Vietnam with a demilitarized zone—what would become known as the DMZ—and national elections that would be held two years later to once again reunify the country. Fearing that the popular nationalist Ho Chi Minh

211

would have been elected if held, those elections were prevented from taking place. The driving force behind that would be the United States, and dominant architects of Cold War and Vietnam foreign policy determined to prevent the "loss" of Vietnam to communism, and adjoining countries as a row of dominoes might fall one after the other.

But the failure of Geneva, as those representing North Vietnam and nationalists in the south viewed it, would not be repeated: this time in the ceasefire agreed to there would be no reference to an arbitrary DMZ dividing the country, no reference to nationwide elections that would be held some years hence. And whereas in 1954 it was agreed that opposing combatants and their supporters would move either above or below a "temporary" division of the country until those elections took place, there would be no such forced movement this time of opposing combatants.

That had been a fundamental flaw of the Geneva Accords in 1954, negotiators representing the DRV and PRG had argued vehemently. And South Vietnam's President Thieu had ultimately been forced to accept that. Instead, combatants would be allowed to remain "in place" in the south rather than "temporarily."

Except for the familiar opening, neither the wording of the Geneva Accords nearly two decades before nor the manner in which key provisions would be ignored and circumvented on behalf of a newly created state in the south would be repeated. That had been one of the major sticking points in ceasefire negotiations on which North Vietnam and the PRG would not budge, and which President Trieu had to be convinced—virtually threatened by the withholding of further American support— to very reluctantly agree to remove from his list of demands.

Merchant seamen in Vietnam react to news of the ceasefire agreement in 1973 (Courtesy National Maritime Union).

Viewed on position maps, these approximate areas of control by combatants had the appearance, some said, of leopard spots. It would be from these areas that subsequent military operations, with opposing combatant forces having been heavily resupplied earlier on the one hand by American merchant ships and aircraft during Operation Enhance Plus, and by Soviet and Chinese ships on the other hand (prior to the mining of northern ports and waterways), would inevitably come.

Also among the agreed-upon terms: "Within sixty days of the signing of this agreement, there will be a total withdrawal from South Viet-Nam of all troops, military advisers, and military personnel, including technical military personnel and military personnel associated with the pacification program, armaments, munitions, and war materiel of the United States and those of the other foreign countries."[6]

The agreement would also require that, "from the enforcement of the cease-fire to the formation of the government provided for, the two South Vietnamese parties ... not accept the introduction of troops, military advisers, and military personnel including technical military personnel, armaments, munitions, and war materiel into South Viet-Nam."[7]

However, the ceasefire agreement also stated, including wording that would directly impact the future role of American merchant mariners in Vietnam, that "the two South Vietnamese parties" would "be permitted to make periodic replacements of armaments, munitions and war materiel which have been destroyed, damaged, worn out or used up after the cease-fire, on the basis of piece-for-piece of the same characteristics and properties, under the supervision of the Joint Military Commission of the two South Vietnamese parties and of the International Commission of Control and Supervision."[8]

With a requirement for removal, and restrictions for re-entry about to be placed on foreign warships, that burden and responsibility would naturally be transferred exclusively to merchant shipping. Despite clearly stated prohibitions against armed patrols or combat operations on the ground, along the rivers, offshore, and in the air, it was also made clear in the protocol to the ceasefire agreement that those restrictions would not otherwise hamper or restrict the following:

"Civilian supply, freedom of movement, freedom to work, and freedom of the people to engage in trade, and civilian communication and transportation between and among all areas in South Viet-Nam."[9]

This meant, as was stated in a further clarification contained in a Department of Defense briefing paper at the time, that "free movement of merchant ships is guaranteed" by the ceasefire agreement.[10]

In North Vietnam's ports and approaches, however, "free movement" of merchant ships was another matter.

Mines that had been sown in North Vietnamese ports and waterways the previous year were also expected to be removed or deactivated by the end of the requisite 60-day time period, and that would be undertaken in Operation End Sweep through the end of March 1973.[11] Whether due to a lack of confidence that it had been done completely, the Soviet Union and People's Republic of China made it clear that their sea logistical support of North Vietnam would not be continued. Thus, the NVA and, by extension, the PRG/NLF would have to make do with existing stocks which, while severely diminished in the wake of the Spring Offensive of 1972, would be sufficiently built up again prior to the final offensive that was to come.

The United States, on the other hand, was now virtually unhindered by floating or attached limpet mines as it had been before, and did not feel compelled for other reasons to discontinue shipments via the sea logistical line. Supplies and the ships that carried them, though reduced, continued to serve an important logistical support role. Expenditures for future shipments of aid were, however, being reduced by Congressional mandate.[12]

Despite accusations by South Vietnamese leadership that there were major shortages of available military equipment and supplies, it was also made clear by independent audit that the reality suggested otherwise. As historian Marilyn Young has put it: "Although Thieu and the American Embassy complained bitterly of a lack of supplies, a General Accounting Office audit reported large quantities of unused military equipment and some $200 million worth of items gone missing, including 143 small warships, a couple of million dollars' worth of ammunition, and $10 million in small arms."[13]

Much equipment transported to the South Vietnamese military either remained unused in storage, was unaccounted for in large number, or, in the case of small arms ammunition, and in comparison to estimates of usage by the NVA and NLF, was being grossly and needlessly over-expended in the field despite advice to the contrary to reduce such expenditures.[14]

Operation Roll-Up

Between January 29 and March 29, 1973—the 60-day period specified by the ceasefire agreement—an operation, dubbed Roll-Up and involving some 20 merchant ships, was undertaken to either remove military equipment and supplies from the country or reposition it in-country for use by South Vietnamese military forces. By the time of its completion, some 144,876 tons of U.S. and an additional 82,833 tons of allied military cargo had been moved by this fleet of ships.[15]

At the end of the 60-day period following the signing of the ceasefire agreement, what was described as "the last plane load of American troops" departed Vietnam from Tan Son Nhut airport in Saigon on March 29, 1973. Consisting of "68 Army, Navy and Air Force personnel who had been responsible for processing the day's withdrawal" activities, these Americans were not, in fact, the last to leave but served more of a "symbolic" function.[16] Other American military personnel connected with the Joint Military Commission would depart with less fanfare some days later, while about 50 military attachés and the 159-man embassy Marine guard, and a smaller group of 14 on a graves commission would remain in-country for as long as circumstances required.[17]

Speaking briefly at Tan Son Nhut prior to the departure of the last symbolic contingent of Americans, Colonel Bui Tin of the North Vietnamese delegation was heard to remark, "This is an historic day. It is the first time in 100 years that there are no foreign troops on the soil of Vietnam."[18]

Hundreds of American civilians who had worked in various government functions remained in-country. As the ceasefire agreement made clear as well, hundreds of American merchant seamen would continue to arrive and roam familiar shoreside haunts as their ships loaded with general cargo and approved military aid continued to flow into Vietnam from the United States and elsewhere.

The Last Voyage of SS *Steel Voyager*

One of the merchant ships calling on South Vietnam in the early ceasefire period was *Steel Voyager* (Isthmian), a veteran of long service stretching back to soon after her launching at Pascagoula Shipbuilding in Mississippi in 1944.[19] Following initial service as the Navy attack transport *Hamblen* (APA 114) during World War II, *Steel Voyager*'s long postwar service with Isthmian Lines commenced in 1947, continued for the next 26 years, and included several voyages in logistical support of the war in Vietnam.[20]

What turned out to be *Steel Voyager*'s last voyage—to the surprise, it seems, of most of her crew—to various ports in Southeast Asia in 1973, including Saigon, was described years later by Russell R. Rowley, who had been an ordinary seaman in the crew. Having served previously in Vietnam with the U.S. Army, Rowley returned a few years after his discharge as a merchant seaman. His description is revealing not only of the types of cargoes typically being carried to

Vietnam during those years, but also of changes visible to him and other merchant seamen as their ships called on Vietnam in the time period immediately leading up to and following the ceasefire.[21]

"I made the last trip on board the SIU-contracted *Steel Voyager*," Rowley recalled, "during May to August of 1973.

> The jobs on the *Steel Voyager* came up in the Seattle union hall, and the ship was located in the Swan Island Shipyards.[22] A full crew was needed and a charter bus drove us down to join the ship. When we left the yards we went to Rainier, Oregon, and loaded lumber. We went through the Panama Canal Zone and discharged part of our load of lumber in Camden, New Jersey and the other part in Port Elizabeth, New York [sic]. After discharging the lumber we started loading general cargo for the Far East. Most of the cargo was military stuff, and "giveaway" things to under developed Asian countries. We had on board asphalt machines, water trucks, cars for military dependents, truck tires, and a large amount of steel wire for Saigon. We loaded this, where it was produced, in Georgetown, South Carolina.
>
> We transited the Panama Canal and our first port was Yokohama, then Pusan, Korea, then Singapore, Bangkok, Sattahip, and finally Saigon. We were in Saigon for about a week. I was in the Army in [19]69-to 70 in Viet Nam and had been to Saigon once before. It was entirely different this time though.
>
> When I was a GI the girls on Tu Du [sic] Street were sarcastic foul-mouthed wenches and Saigon was alive with American soldiers and soldiers of other nations. In August of 1973 this had changed drastically. The city of Saigon was very quiet. The prostitutes were very engaging and friendly and there were few occidentals to be seen.
>
> We stayed our entire time in Saigon, tied up by the Seamen's Club (or Port Club) unloading wire, tank tracks, and truck tires. We didn't "night steam" at all. One afternoon a patrol boat of ARVNs (Army of the Republic of Vietnam) tied up alongside and began off-loading truck tires into their boat. The Chief Mate saw what was happening and started yelling at them. They immediately fled up river. One of the Alaska Tug and Barge Company's tugs chased them and was able to apprehend them. I don't know what happened after that. We all agreed they should have made a run for the open sea.
>
> When we first arrived in Saigon an American seaman came aboard. He had lost his seaman's papers for a year and had decided to spend the time on the beach with his Vietnamese wife in Saigon. He knew a few of the guys on the *Steel Voyager*, so we "spread the tarpaulin" and gave him cigarettes, soap, money, and other odds and ends to make life more comfortable for him while he was confined to the beach. One of the ABs I stood

watch with was also married to a Vietnamese woman. She was in her ninth month of pregnancy when we were in Saigon. He had bought a Honda motorcycle for her in Yokohama, but customs would not allow him to bring it into the country without paying an outlandish sum. (100% duty) They couldn't be bribed, and we sailed with the motorcycle on board. The poor guy didn't even know if his wife had their child OK. We all thought he might jump ship but he stuck with us.

When we left Saigon we were supposed to load cargo in Hong Kong. In the middle of the night we changed course for Taiwan. We arrived at a little harbor where we thought we would load cement. It soon became evident though that the ship was sold to the breakers.

When we pulled into the harbor we started throwing stuff over the side to people following the ship with junks. One of the breaker's agents saw what was happening and tried to stop us. When he was unable to, he yelled something in Mandarin at the people in the junks and over the side to a waiting tug which took us ashore to customs and a waiting bus to Chi-Lung (Kee-Lung). We could see part of the bow and the backbone of the *Steel Rover* lying on the beach. We were all sad to leave the *Steel Voyager* to such an ignoble death as that of her sister ship. Although she was old and rusty she was still very sound and was a happy ship.[23]

By the end of 1973, and despite the ceasefire that had at least temporarily brought an end to fighting and had resulted in the pull-out of the last American military personnel in Vietnam, there were still some 26,500 ARVN and 39,000 North Vietnamese and Viet Cong reported to have been killed by the end of that year.[24]

Merchant ships making their way along the Long Tau shipping channel between Vung Tau and Saigon reported few attack incidents of any kind in 1973 and 1974. The ceasefire had specifically allowed for free movement of civilian shipping, and the DRV, in issuing its "Five Forbids" directive to its forces in the field, had taken a position that would reduce the chances for violations, presumably including attacks on American merchant ships, that might cancel out the ceasefire agreement.[25]

But attacks on other targets of opportunity, such as installations along the shores of the Long Tau that might otherwise benefit the South Vietnamese military in operations against them, were still fair game. This reality was demonstrated in dramatic fashion on May 20, 1974, when the Caltex fuel tanks at Nha Be—near where hundreds of American merchant ships had offloaded ammunition for many years—was attacked during the night by Viet Cong sappers. Dynamite charges were secured to two fuel tanks, one of which was successfully detonated. The result was described later that day in a *New York Times* report filed from Saigon:

> Military sources said that three Vietcong infiltrators dynamited a 250,000-gallon fuel tank at Nha Be early today, sending huge balls of fire into the sky above South Vietnam's largest fuel depot.
> The sources at Nha Be, 10 miles southeast of here [Saigon] said that two of the infiltrators escaped and a third was shot.[26]

In addition to the Nha Be sapper attack description, contact between North and South Vietnamese forces not far from Saigon, reflective of the point to which the "ceasefire war" had evolved by then, was also reported.

> North and South Vietnamese forces exchanged intense fire in the fourth day of fighting around Ben Cat, 25 miles north of Saigon, in a Cambodia-Saigon corridor that has long been a route for Communist infiltration toward the capital.
> South Vietnamese officers there reported a particularly heavy North Vietnamese barrage before dawn to cover an infantry attack on a bridge between Ben Cat and nearby An Dien, a village that fell to the North Vietnamese on Friday.[27]

Whether the loss of one 250,000-gallon fuel tank at Nha Be in May 1974 was a significant factor or not, by the time of the sapper attack there the available fuel supply situation had become increasingly dire for the RVNAF. One report stated that, due to fuel shortages by that time, only 55 percent of RVNAF field and air equipment assets would actually be authorized to operate, and even then at reduced levels. This was reflected, for example, in the reduced number of aircraft sorties allotted between early 1973, when some 200 sorties were allowed, the end of that year, when only 80 were allowed, and the first half of 1974 when sorties against enemy positions had been reduced to between 30 and 60.[28]

By the time of the May 1974 sapper attack on Nha Be and other actions recounted at that time, the territory grabbed by the ARVN in the Mekong Delta region the year before had been largely recaptured by the NVA and PAVN.[29] The artillery barrage, taking of a bridge, and capture of the village of An Dien were relatively small incidents in a series of actions that nonetheless seemed to signal a shift in the fortunes of the opposing combatants. In addition to losing territory gained during 1973, South Vietnam's military was losing soldiers at an alarming rate—some 200,000 desertions would be reported in 1974. And though the NVA had lost many, its reported strength in the south, despite its losses in 1973 and 1974, appeared to have risen from some 150,000 to as many as 200,000 by the end of 1974, moved into place largely as a result of improvements made in the north-to-south corridor.[30]

The ARVN had depleted ammunition and other resources in its misguided campaigns of 1973, as if believing that they—and funds to sustain them—still came from a bottomless pit, as the encouragement of Nixon leading up to and following the ceasefire might have suggested. But the waters feeding that well were beginning to dry up, despite whatever promises might have been made.

General Pham Quoc Thuan, the ARVN III Corps commander, would later recall that fuel and ammunition for his forces in the field had been cut by 30 percent between the first quarter of 1973 to the last quarter, and this represented a 60 percent reduction from the previous year. Moving into 1974, there would be a further reduction of 30 percent in the first quarter, and an additional 20 percent reduction in the second quarter.[31]

That was reflected in the refusal by Congress in April 1974 to increase military aid to South Vietnam, and then in a reduction of military appropriations by Congress in August 1974 from a requested $1 billion to $700 million.[32]

Thomas A. Galka returned to Vietnam for the second time as a merchant seamen in late 1974. While changes were already evident in-country during his first visit on SS *Seatrain Puerto Rico* in 1971, he noted a difference as he arrived in Saigon as a fireman/watertender on the SS *Iberville*, a Mariner-type cargo ship then operated by Waterman Steamship Company.[33]

"Even Saigon was vastly different," Galka recalled, "now that it was in its last days of glory."

The once haughty women forgot all about escalation of prices. Indeed, their money had further devalued, and TuDo Street was now a shadow of its former self. Many bars and shops were closed up or operating on a shoestring budget. It wasn't gaudy or flagrantly wicked anymore. Personally, I found this to be an improvement. One could almost go about life and various pursuits of pleasure in an almost normal way. The carnival atmosphere was a thing of the past. Now I had much more time to explore and sight-see in town. Places like the famous "Imperial Hotel" were still operating; now I was able to lounge around in leisure, the pace had slowed considerably. There were still many fine French-type restaurants to be sampled, too. It was a carefree time for the Americans, if not for the South Viets. I no longer felt, as I did [on my] first seafaring trip to Vietnam; I was leery and a bit uneasy then, as I had been [while in the Army earlier] used to walking around the countryside fully armed and prepared during my war days. I distinctly recall feeling almost "naked" [in 1971], strolling around without my trusty M-16 rifle. The era of Viet Nam was rapidly closing, and you could sense the difference in the country and the people.[34]

The Last Thanksgiving

American merchant seamen bring their holidays with them to wherever in the world they happen to be for the occasion. And a good chief steward, anticipating that in advance, will prepare for it in such a way that appropriate menus—replete with "all the fixin's"—will be prepared for crew and, if in port, for a possible guest or two, or 50.

Such was the case in Saigon in late November 1974 aboard SS *Seatrain Louisiana* and SS *Seatrain Washington*, as would be described in a story some months later by Chief Steward Roy R. Thomas and published in the *Seafarers Log*[35]:

Thanksgiving Day 1974 found the SS *Seatrain Louisiana* and SS *Seatrain Washington* moored one ahead of the other and working cargo in Saigon, the Republic of Vietnam.

Captain Gene Laski of the SS *Seatrain Louisiana* decided we needed a "family dinner" on this particular holiday. A "family dinner" to Capt. Laski, being a family man, is with children, and he decided to contact the American Embassy to see if he could arrange to "borrow" some children for this occasion.

The embassy put Capt. Laski in touch with the Holt Children's Service in Saigon, and the result was 50 abandoned and orphaned children from their organization as guests for dinner.

But Capt. Laski is not just a "family man," he is also a "practical family man" and so he appealed to Capt. George Walker of the SS *Seatrain Washington* to help him entertain his guests. Also a family man, Capt. Walker gladly invited 25 of the children to dinner on his ship, and the party was on!

The 50 children, aged 6 to 10 years, had a great time on the ships. Even though their knowledge of English was limited, affection and compassion know no language barriers.

First, the children were hosted to Cokes and 7-Ups on the bridge where they used the ship's whistle and binoculars. Then they were given a tour of the ship which ended in the Crew's and Saloon Messrooms where the steward department gave their all-out effort, and a good time (and dinner) was had by all. After dinner, each child was given a small bag of candy, nuts and fresh fruit.

So Capt. Laski had his dinner and the children found men who indeed "spoke their language" in the crews of these two ships.

And, yes, turkey was on the menu for this—what was to turn out to be the *last*— Thanksgiving celebrated by American merchant seamen in Vietnam.

The "leopard spot" ceasefire seemed destined for failure, and did not hold much beyond the initial 60-day phase articulated in the Paris agreement. That was, it seems clear, what the opposing Vietnamese combatants wanted: Thieu's Republic of Vietnam still hoped to secure itself permanently and separately in the south, while the Democratic Republic of Vietnam—North Vietnam—and its southern allies, the Provisional Revolutionary Government—the Viet Cong—would settle for nothing less than to fulfill the promise of the earlier Geneva Accords— reunification free from foreign interference—at long last.

Though it had been a failure in creating the conditions for permanently stopping the war—perhaps never a realistic nor needed expectation—and achieving the "peace with honor" Nixon had publicly sought, and at one point proclaimed had been achieved, it nonetheless had provided the path for the large-scale—if not ultimately final—withdrawal in all respects of the United States from the war in Vietnam after so many years.[36]

The ceasefire war, launched for all intents and purposes within only weeks of the signing of the ceasefire agreement, had claimed the lives of more than 90,000 ARVN, NVA, and VC in 1974 alone.[37]

In December 1974 the Politburo of North Vietnam agreed upon a two-year, two-phase plan to achieve victory against the ARVN, and to once and for all reunify the country, thus fulfilling the failed promise of the Geneva Accords that had ended the French War some 20 years before. Commencing first in the Central Highlands in the south, it envisioned major operations through 1975, continuing into 1976, and even into 1977 if necessary.[38] Attacks involving some 8,000 NVA troops began, initially in Phuoc Long Province, in mid–December. Overwhelmed, ARVN forces in the area pulled back within a few weeks, leaving Phuoc Binh, the provincial capital, as well as the entire province, under control of the NVA by the first week of January 1975.[39]

Thus began an offensive that, to the surprise of even General Van Tien Dung and the NVA and PRG military forces under his command, would require not two years but less than five months to complete. Within that same time period, since warships of the U.S. Navy had been prohibited by ceasefire statute from entering onshore waters (waters that begin at the coastline), American merchant seamen would play a major role, making last-minute deliveries of general cargo and military supplies, and providing transport for Vietnamese civilian refugees and the panicked ARVN fleeing the onslaught southward along the coast of South Vietnam.

The tally of American dead and wounded had come at last to an end. But certainly not for the Vietnamese themselves. The war would continue for some months into the new year as the rapid pace towards its conclusion surprised not only the defeated and onlookers, but the eventual winners of the conflict as well.[40] Those of the Merchant Marine continued, for all intents and purposes, as they had many times and in many places before, as both witness to and participants in the final act of the unfolding tragedy.

In addition to the final cargo-laden voyages along the Vietnam Run, merchant mariners would once again play a primary role in the humanitarian crisis soon to unfold in the ports and along the coast of Vietnam. They had been through that before at such places as Hungnam during the Korean War, and later in the immediate aftermath of the so-called French War in Vietnam. However, the scale of the crisis to come, and the central role of the American Merchant Marine in it, would in some ways be unprecedented.

Unlike the situation in Vietnam almost two decades earlier, when merchant ships would play their final role there moving refugees in relatively orderly fashion and within a given timeframe specifically proscribed by international agreement, American merchant mariners would be called upon again to move Vietnamese refugees—now fleeing before a war—with far less notice and time to prepare, and under the guns of those propelled by the looming victory within their grasp.

17

Evacuation Under Fire (1975)

"I've been in the evacuations of Dunkerque and Korea, but I have never seen anything like this."
—John Lambert, chief officer, SS *Transcolorado*

"There were three other merchant ships in the [Da Nang] area now and all were taking rocket fire from ashore."
—Joseph Delehant, SS *Pioneer Contender*

"Custer, dog-tired, slumped at his elbow. Only several minutes later did he muster the strength to speak. 'We've got a 240 LZ waiting to pick us up,' he shouted over the whine of the [boat's] motors. Soon, as if on cue, a red, white, and blue smokestack and the dark shape of an American cargo vessel loomed up out of the fog, The nameplate read: *Pioneer Contender*."
—Frank Snepp, *Decent Interval*

It all came crashing down, sooner and faster than many—even those realistic as to the prospects of it happening—feared to imagine. Now, in early March 1975, nearly 20 years after the American-conjured and supported experiment in nation-building had begun in Vietnam, the Republic of Vietnam—South Vietnam—was on the verge of collapse.[1] And so too were the dreams of many Americans who had hoped, after all the lives lost and treasure squandered, that a way might still be found and the country established once and for all as a bulwark against communism along the East Asian containment line.[2]

But that, it was all too clear now, was not to be.

"The sea is our only hope"

There were many reasons why: some would blame it on a premature withdrawal of active involvement by the United States or subsequent cutbacks of authorized funding and material support for the South Vietnamese military. Others would point to serious corruption within and a general failure of leadership in South Vietnam. Still others, taking a long look back into Vietnamese history, argued it never had much of a chance in the face of an age-old spirit of independence ("doc lap"), tested time and time again during various periods of foreign intervention—Western and Asian—in their homeland, no matter how that might have been justified or rationalized, whether within or without, by those who supported it.[3]

Nonetheless, the South Vietnamese Army (ARVN) and Marines were now, in early March of 1975, in a retreat to southward, not helped by South Vietnam President Thieu's surprising order to abandon northern provinces and the Central Highlands. Ban Me Thuot, the important city and provincial capital in the Central Highlands, in a development that would be considered a crucial turning point in South Vietnam's fortunes, would be captured by PAVN forces on March 11. The strategy of drawing a defensive line across South Vietnam between Ban Me Thuot and the port city of Nha Trang on the coast soon went by the boards.[4] Even as an attempt was made, unsuccessfully, to retake the city, its capture by a determined, well-equipped and fueled North Vietnamese Army set in motion, amidst a house-to-house search of the city by soldiers of the PAVN, an evacuation of tens of thousands of civilians and ARVN along the primary route—Route 21—that ended some 70 miles away on the central coast of South Vietnam.[5]

One woman swept up with her family in the mass exodus down to the coast, Tran Thi Minh Canh, would later describe the fear-driven panic she and thousands of others felt, when she wrote:

Vietnamese evacuees were towed out to the merchant ship *Pioneer Contender* by the barge-full in Da Nang in April 1975. That ship would be involved in transporting more evacuees at one time—some 16,600—than any ship before or since (MSC).

> Tonight we are running in agonizing terror that supersedes all other needs, all other considerations. Others run alongside us but we hardly notice them in our feverish race to the sea. Friends become foes; neighbors become enemies as we rush to reach our salvation. The sea is our only hope.... We left with nothing except a few satchels of clothing and as many pieces of jewelry as we could hide on our bodies to trade for food or shelter, or our lives.[6]

While the experience described by Tran Thi Minh Canh was horrific enough, and would be shared by others moving towards and along the coast of South Vietnam in the coming days and weeks, descriptions of refugee movements and attempts to board American merchant ships and other watercraft for points further south would turn

This photograph gives a good idea of the extent to which unprecedented numbers of Vietnamese refugees were crammed aboard *Pioneer Contender* during evacuations ahead of the North Vietnamese Army in April 1975 (Military Sealift Command).

much worse. Artillery, rocket, and mortar fire would rain down upon some of their columns—especially when their route coincided with that of retreating convoys of ARVN and Vietnamese Marines—and, as would be witnessed by many American merchant seamen, some ARVN soldiers forced their way through civilian crowds, actually using their weapons upon hapless civilians they had once sworn to defend and who now blocked their access to space on ships they also desperately hoped to board.[7]

It would be President Thieu's decision on March 15 to pull back from Kontum and Pleiku—"that fateful day in the history of the Republic of Vietnam," as Defense Attaché H.D. Smith would call it in a report soon after the fact—that would further open the floodgates of refugee and ARVN evacuations from the Central Highlands towards the coastal port cities of Tuy Hoa and Nha Trang.[8]

With a more direct route between Kontum and the coast at Qui Nhon—Route 19—closed off to them by PAVN forces, the movement of retreating ARVN units and civilian refugees was more directly southward initially to Pleiku, and from there down along a little-used, poorly maintained former logging road—designated 7A—that would lead from there southeastward to the coast at Tuy Hoa, and from there along Route One to Nha Trang.[9]

"The Road of Blood and Tears"

A large convoy of ARVN soldiers and military vehicles began moving out of Pleiku, under the cover of night (but with headlights turned on) along Route 7A towards the coast on March 16, 1975, hoping to reach Tuy Hoa—more than a hundred miles away—with their assets intact. The PAVN leadership had not expected that this route might be taken by the retreating ARVN, which in turn had counted on moving well out of Pleiku before their movements were detected. But the addition of a large contingent of civilian evacuees—numbering an estimated 160,000 at one point—had also not been planned for, and that mass of humanity with its own assortment of vehicles contributed to turning a largely undetected operation into something else.[10]

PAVN forces would soon be sent in pursuit of the ARVN convoy and, with ARVN Ranger units acting as a rear guard, incoming artillery, rocket, and mortar fire soon began to take a tremendous toll, not only on retreating ARVN and their equipment, but on civilian evacuees as well. Other factors, including the need to strengthen and construct bridges along the route, and even serious incidents of "friendly fire" from misdirected RVNAF airstrikes, would not only contribute to delays of the convoy's movement but also cause thousands of casualties along the way. The images that would come from what the one journalist accompanying the convoy and stream of desperate refugees would dub the "Road of Blood and Tears" would be horrific and heartbreaking.[11]

In the end, after more than a week of nearly constant attacks, making their way along on foot and with little food and water—and some swept away by swollen streams and rivers they had attempted to swim or walk across—only an estimated 60,000 civilian evacuees from the original 160,000 or so coming out of Pleiku would arrive safely to the coast, on March 25, where their evacuation by ship and other watercraft even then was not certain.[12]

In less than a week, on April 1, Nha Trang would also come under the control of PAVN forces.[13]

While some units stood their ground well, making strong defensive stands at different points then pulling back in relatively good order while engaging in some cases in determined and effective rearguard action while holding their units together even in retreat, others—succumbing in part to what some analysts would refer to as the "family syndrome"—began a disorderly, headlong, panicked retreat.[14] Soldiers, fearing capture and worse at the hands of the North Vietnamese Army working with main-force units of the NLF, cast off not only weapons but uniforms as well, hoping to blend in among the mass of civilians also trying to stay ahead of the battle lines, to increase their own chances of survival.

But many of the ARVN, as would soon be revealed, retained their weapons as they made their way to coastal evacuation points and forced their way on to rescue vessels, using them in many cases upon civilians who happened to stand in their way.

On the same day that the civilian and ARVN evacuees out of Pleiku, those who survived the ordeal along the "road of tears," finally reached the coast at Tuy Hoa—March 25—the city of Hue to the north was attacked and captured by PAVN forces. That in turn triggered yet another desperate evacuation out and over to the nearest point along the coast which was at the mouth of the Perfume River and within 12 kilometers of the ancient cultural center of Vietnam. The base known as Tan My had been developed near there in 1967, and while the shallow draft of the approach to it could not accommodate ocean-going cargo ships, dredging and construction of ramps provided access for various shallow draft craft including the larger LSTs that would participate in evacuation operations in the short time—late that same day—before Tan My itself fell to the oncoming PAVN offensive.[15]

While thousands of civilian and ARVN evacuees would be taken out aboard landing craft operated by the South Vietnamese navy, others would be turned away, and at least one military unit that had arrived intact would opt to continue moving southward on the ground, towards and over the Hai Van Pass, hoping to reach the major evacuation point at Da Nang where they too could be accommodated.[16] Most of them, however, would not make it to their intended destination.

The major northern port of Da Nang, more able to evacuate by deep-draft ships, would in turn become overrun in due course as refugees poured in not only from the north, but from the south. Included in that northward flow of refugees converging on Da Nang, in addition to those making their way on the ground, would be those evacuated out of the large American base with its shallow draft harbor at Chu Lai.[17] Before it too was captured by PAVN and local VC/NLF forces, a number of shallow draft landing craft of the South Vietnamese Navy were ordered to proceed from Qui Nhon to Chu Lai to assist with evacuation operations. These included two LSTs, an LSM, and six smaller landing craft, presumably LCM "Mike" Boats. Most of the 6,000 civilians and military personnel reported to have been successfully evacuated were transported to Re Island, where they were disembarked on March 27, two days following the fall of Chu Lai; the remainder were taken to Da Nang and disembarked not long before it too would be overrun by PAVN and local nationalist forces.[18]

Within a few days of the fall of Hue, and the evacuations out of Tan My to the north and Chu Lai to the south, Da Nang's population would more than double to over a million, and continue to increase in succeeding days to come.[19] And with the threat of PAVN and main force VC units very real there as well, those fleeing would now be looking for the route and means of escape that, as for others who had already evacuated out of the Central Highlands, seemed the only option available: seaward.

The developments on the ground, and movement of refugees ahead of the rapidly moving NVA offensive, prompted the Department of State to request on March 24 through the Defense Attaché Office (DAO), American Embassy, Saigon, that assets be made available and moved into place as quickly as possible to assist the evacuation of refugees by sea.[20] The main airport in Da Nang was soon to send off its last over-loaded commercial flight, with some Vietnamese hanging on to wing flaps and others about to be crushed in wheel compartments. The sea escape route would then be the only viable option.

Many of those now former ARVN, pushing aside Vietnamese civilians who blocked or slowed their way, also fled towards Da Nang, over and through the Hai Van Pass, where a vessel—any kind of vessel—might be boarded to continue the flight southward by water.[21]

On March 25, the day after the initial request went out for assets to be moved to Da Nang to assist with evacuation, the first two merchant ships—*Pioneer Contender* (Captain Edward C. Flink) and *Transcolorado* (Captain Tyler B. Castle)—were ordered to move to Da Nang as quickly as possible. *Pioneer Contender*, in the process of unloading ammunition up the Saigon River at Newport when the call was received, would be the first to arrive, early on March 28, by which time the situation was already well out of hand.[22]

Loading of refugees from barges had been well underway, if chaotic, when the last of the American officials to escape, by three outboard motorboats held for that purpose, moved out to rendezvous with *Pioneer Contender*, the first of seven ships crewed by American merchant seamen to participate in the Da Nang evacuations. As Frank Snepp, a CIA operative in-country during the evacuations, later described it, what greeted one of the American officials as he scrambled up onto the deck of the ship, was horrific: "The scene that greeted him as he swung up over the railing of the *Contender* was every bit as nightmarish as anything he might have found in Da Nang. Over 1,500 South Vietnamese troops were sprawled, lounging, fighting among themselves on the main decks and the bridge, and practicing their aim at the hapless Vietnamese civilians in their midst."[23]

A Vietnamese woman was being raped on deck by an ARVN soldier as others pointed their weapons at the woman's husband to keep him at bay. With angry and armed ARVN on board, the ship was on the verge of being commandeered and sailed at gunpoint directly to the Philippines.[24]

As Frank Snepp would later describe an exchange in *Decent Interval*:

"They want to sail to the Philippines," one of [the American civilians] bellowed at Howard [alias for CIA logistics officer, Da Nang], pointing at a group of armed Vietnamese troopers on the deck just above. "They've locked the captain on the bridge."

Howard scarcely paused to think what he was doing. He motioned to several of the U.S. Marine guards who had come out of Da Nang with him and quickly outlined a plan. After checking their weapons they began the climb to the bridge. The four Vietnamese troops at the forward rail were too busy talking among themselves to notice, and before they could do so much as lock and load, Howard and the marines rushed them and pinned them to the deck. Moments later one of the marines broke the lock on the hatchway, and a flustered captain [Flink] and several crew members emerged from the recesses of the cabin. "You know," the captain grumbled as he tried to compose himself, "they told me in Saigon we were coming here to pick up surplus American vehicles. I had no idea we'd be facing this."[25]

Joseph Delehant, the *Pioneer Contender*'s Third Mate, described some years later his impression of the ship's first encounter with refugees in Da Nang:

The people on the barges had been there 2–3 days and were hungry and thirsty. Some were already dead. Approximately one third of them were armed ARVN—deserters of the South Vietnamese military—who had boarded the barges at the expense of women and children. We boarded them from the starboard gangway, and the 40 crewmen (full complement from the *Contender*) and 30 other Americans and Europeans (from first tug) attempted to disarm and load the people, Newborns, old, crippled, wounded, scared, naked, hungry, thirsty, crazed people with all their worldly possessions in small sacks. There were hundreds of orphans who couldn't remember ever having parents and others who had lost their parents only hours before. Mothers wailing for their lost children.[26]

We had had no time to anticipate the problems which would arise and the people became very restless with thirst. There were only 2 fresh water outlets on the maindeck to get fresh water from. We rigged garden hoses and got all of our garbage cans and put them down in the hatches to hold water. We used our ship's cargo gear to lower people into the hatches and off the crowded decks. It took a lot of time to do these things because the people were everywhere, thirsty, lost, scared and in some cases small riots would start over the small supply of water. We loaded approximately 9,000 people in 10 hours and proceeded to Cam Ranh Bay with no food or sanitation facilities. Ships work had to go on. We worked every waking minute to try to ease the strain. There were many sick and infirm people. Babies born, crying babies, and human excrement everywhere.

We got to Cam Ranh the following afternoon [March 29] and received a warm welcome from a well-organized group of dignitaries, boy scouts, and military personnel. We discharged the people in a few hours and thought our job was done. Far from it.

The following morning we headed back to Da Nang. You can imagine the condition the ship was in. The crew worked round the clock trying to clean the ship and anticipate some of the problems we would be confronted with. When we got there, there was chaos. Da Nang was completely overrun by now. No help was available. Just thousands and thousands of people outside the harbor on fishing boats and barges in a 4-foot swell. Some of the people had been on the barges for 5 days.

There were three other merchant ships in the area now and all were taking rocket fire from ashore. The port control was [now] based on a tug and we had communications problems. So we just started loading. We were better prepared this time but the people were much weaker than before. Also about one half were ARVN. They were coming aboard on both sides of the ship this time—lines were thrown over the side to pull up belongings and people were climbing up the ropes. They had enough automatic weapons, pistols, knives, and grenades aboard to take Fort Knox, and the crew had nothing. Many small children fell between the ship and the barge and were crushed. Mothers wailed.

We finally finished loading [at] about 11 that night—about 9,000 people. We had this group aboard for 2 ½ days and when we got to Cam Ranh there was no one there to meet us. There had been riots at the pier that day and it was considered unsafe for any of our allies to be there. We discharged the load ourselves. Hundreds were carried off on the backs of the crewmen. All night we ran water into a barrel ashore because there was no water for them to drink there. We were exhausted and the piles of human excrement could be measured in feet. We discharged a full pallet load of dead babies (heart-breaking, but necessary).

From there we went down to Vung Tau for bunkers. The crew rested one night and then got on deck again to clean up—an impossible job. We spent about 18 hours in Vung Tau and went back to a now-besieged Cam Ranh. Same scene all over again but this time we picked up 16,600 people. There was a good amount of rocket fire but this time I don't think they were trying to hit us. We were sitting ducks.

With superhuman effort we picked up the hook and headed for Vung Tau. On the way down we stopped at Phan Rang and picked up 45 Marines from the U.S.S. *Fredricks* [sic]. They were a big help for an exhausted crew and 16,600 people. It was impossible to move about. There were people everywhere—packed like sardines. Still no sanitation or food or medicine. Crew members gave up their rooms for the sick, and women having babies. Some babies were born on the stinking steel decks.

We got to Vung Tau and they sent us to Phu Quoc Island on the west coast of Vietnam just south of Cambodia.[27] A day's run. We got there, dropped the hook and sat there through the blazing sun for 4 days. The 45 Marines left and we got another contingent of 65 men and just tried to keep the people alive with water. The Navy got some food to us, but the people rioted when it came and we couldn't distribute it. The ARVN deserters would steal the food from the women and children and sell it to them.... The stronger men were jumping over the side to try to swim the 1½ miles to shore. People used signs that they were hungry and thirsty and wanted to go ashore. We could do nothing. 80% of the people, refugees, crew and Marines had pinkeye and disentary [sic] and some unbelievable infections.

After 6 days of having the people aboard we finally discharged the first 4,000 of them into a barge. We were desperate. On the 7th day they were gone.

We went from there to Saigon for cleaning and rest. We needed both. We stayed there for 10 days and watched Viet Nam fall. Saigon's fall was more imminent every day.[28]

Pioneer Commander (Captain Peter J. Strachota), another of three U.S. Lines ships involved in first phase of refugee evacuation, would be one of the last to board refugees directly offshore, and in that case off the beaches of what had once been an important R&R area for American soldiers and Marines: China Beach.[29,30] One account later described the deadly interaction between Vietnamese civilians and Vietnamese marines as they vied for access to two ships then off the beach:

Down to the beach, looking for ships they went. The sands where GIs and Vietnamese once lay between refreshing dips in the South China Sea was now itself a sea—of humanity. Everyone who was able to do so stayed clear of the bitter Marines. Not everyone was able to."

By chance, the Marines wound up on two ships—a Vietnamese naval vessel with no name and the *Pioneer Commander*, back from dropping off refugees at Cam Ranh Bay to pick up another load. About 1,000 Marines jammed the Vietnamese ship. Another 2,000 or so made it to the *Pioneer Commander*.

Others swam, some came out in sampans and lifeboats, motorboats and fishing boats. On nets and stairs [accommodation ladders] they scrambled aboard the big American ship. Perhaps 50 persons died when they made the mistake of trying to clamber on the ship in front of armed Marines. Marines opened up with their M16s and fought with their hands to kill. The toll of those who drowned or were crushed between the *Commander* and smaller boats is unknown. But it was high.[31]

USNS *Sgt. Andrew Miller*

Another of the seven MSC-controlled ships crewed by American merchant seamen that evacuated refugees out of Da Nang was the USNS *Sgt. Andrew Miller*

(Captain Kurt Ostmeyer). One of the "nucleus" ships of the Military Sealift Command (MSC), and a "Victory" type built in the last year of World War II, *Miller* had been involved in the movement of Vietnamese refugees 10 years earlier as part of Operation Passage to Freedom following the French defeat in 1954.[32] Now, initially in three trips along Vietnam's coast between Da Nang and Vung Tau, the first of which went to Da Nang and involved the loading of some 7,500 refugees, *Miller* would eventually evacuate about 15,300 refugees. Some 300 were transported from Tuy Hoa to Phu Quoc Island during the second trip, and during the third of these runs the ship returned to Cam Ranh to load another 7,500 refugees, which were also brought to Phu Quoc.[33] During that last trip to Phu Quoc refugees attempted to divert the ship to Vung Tau, but were not successful due to the presence of U.S. Marines on board.[34] In final evacuation operations during and immediately following the fall of Saigon, USNS *Miller* would transport another 10,000 refugees, for a combined refugee lift of some 23,000, the third most of the 15 ships crewed by civilian seamen and listed by the MSC as having been involved in evacuations.[35]

SS *Transcolorado*

Called upon initially on March 29 while unloading ammunition in Saigon (Newport) to race to Da Nang to assist with evacuations there, *Transcolorado* never, in fact, quite made it. According to a report written a few weeks after the fact by the ship's third assistant engineer, Charles A. Welch, the C-4 type freighter was perhaps a half-hour out on March 31 when it received new orders to turn around and proceed south. Soon after, Welch recalled, "We met a tug towing two barges stacked with soldiers and people who had fled Da Nang two days earlier."[36]

After getting the barges alongside, soldiers with weapons were disarmed before being allowed aboard. "This turned out to be a wise move," wrote Welch, "as soldiers took over two other ships at sea."

"We got 3,000 of them on board—what a sight! After the people were aboard, the barges looked like regular garbage scows. There were quite a number of dead on the barges. These people had been at sea for 48 hours without water or food."

The providing of drinking water for the refugees until *Transcolorado* could deposit them in Cam Ranh Bay on April 1 was described by Welch: "We had ballast fresh water, and the Chief [Engineer] hooked up the standing feed pump and pumped it through the deck fire line to give them water for ten minutes every hour."

The rapidity with which events were unfolding along Vietnam's coast became all too apparent to the crew of *Transcolorado* soon after their arrival in Cam Ranh Bay. After discharging all civilian refugees and soldiers at a pier, word came within four hours that all disembarked refugees would have to be reboarded along with about 5,000 more and transported further down the coast to Vung Tau. They arrived there the following day and all were then discharged into landing craft on April 3.

Transcolorado proceeded that same day to rendezvous with the U.S. Navy off Phan Rang, where another 3,000 refugees were embarked from USS *Durham*.[37] These refugees were then brought to Phu Quoc Island, where *Transcolorado* anchored out along with other ships until ship-to-shore transportation—towed barges—was finally provided. (According to Welch these refugees were brought to Vung Tau where the ship arrived on April 5.)

Before clearing out of Vietnam for the last time, the *Transcolorado* made a stop in Saigon, Welch reported: "We unloaded the cargo we had brought for Saigon and Cambodia. Now we are loading damaged tanks, trucks, jeeps and other equipment and are supposed to take them to the Philippines. Meanwhile, they are fighting 25 miles from here."

Interviewed afterwards, *Transcolorado*'s chief officer, John Lambert of Winlock, Washington, had this to say about what he had experienced during the refugee evacuations: "I've been in the evacuations of Dunkerque and Korea, but I have never seen anything like this."[38]

USNS *Greenville Victory*

Some 7,000 refugees boarded USNS *Greenville Victory* as part of the evacuation out of Cam Ranh Bay. As the ship's master, Captain Raymond Iacobacci, set course for Phu Quoc Island, the ship's chief steward, Carl Moore, and his department crew had to do what they could to provide meals not only for the ship's complement of 47 seamen but a refugee contingent numbering in the thousands, which, hardly a week before, neither Moore nor the ship's entire crew could have dreamed might suddenly become their charge.[39]

"I knew they liked rice," Moore recalled, "so I cooked all we had. Every bit of it. Every grain. I even used all the spaghetti and macaroni. I used everything."

To cook as much rice as possible, as quickly as possible, the ship's 30-gallon steam kettles were put to use, in addition to all available pots and pans, and even the galley sink: drain plugged, it was rigged with a steam hose to boil the water. Together, and with the element of practical creativity typical of a seaman when required, that did the trick. Rice was cooked with any available fish and meats, then delivered in 30-gallon cans to points on deck and into cargo holds via wooden stairs that had been installed beforehand to accommodate access for refugees. As a means of providing an important staple and also for helping encourage movement and distribution of refugees on the ship, five-pound sacks of salt were placed in strategic locations on deck and below.

"We tried to feed the children first," Moore recalled. "I had eight or nine cases of condensed milk and mixed it with water. The children loved it. I gave them what candy I could dig up, and they seemed to be very happy."

As it turned out, *Greenville Victory* was one of the ships that disgruntled refugees, presumably not long separated from the ARVN or Vietnamese Marines and still armed, attempted to divert by force to locations more to their liking, such as Vung Tau or the Philippines. While most ships, such as *Pioneer Contender*, had successfully resisted this, *Greenville Victory*, having arrived off Phu Quoc Island on April 4 and awaiting debarkation of refugees into barges, decided it could not. Captain Iacobacci, out of concern for crew, passengers, and ship, agreed to this demand, and directed the ship to Vung Tau where it arrived that afternoon. All refugees were put ashore there by 6:30 that evening.[40]

After this ordeal, the crew of *Greenville Victory* made its way up-channel to

Newport above Saigon, where some three weeks were spent putting the ship back into order, cleaning out holds, resupplying, getting medical attention for some of the crew, and waiting for further orders. Those orders would soon come.

On May 2, after having returned to Vung Tau (where another two tons of rice were delivered) and with the final evacuation of Saigon underway, *Greenville Victory* boarded 3,000 more refugees. The ship then proceeded without incident to Subic Bay, Philippines, where all refugees were offloaded. Altogether, they had transported some 10,000 refugees within and from Vietnam.

As the experiences of *Greenville Victory, Pioneer Contender*, and other ships involved in the refugee evacuation made clear early on, something had to be done quickly to provide additional assistance and security on board. A ship's crew of 50 or so, without weapons of their own, found it extremely challenging and exhausting to handle the numbers of refugees that were coming aboard, many with weapons, without any backup. *Greenville Victory* had been forced at gunpoint to divert to Vung Tau; the master of *Pioneer Contender* had been briefly locked up by still-armed ARVN soldiers on his own ship and almost had it commandeered and forced to sail directly to the Philippines. In various other cases armed ARVN and Vietnamese Marines had indiscriminately fired at and killed many civilians approaching or on board ships to clear a way and make room for themselves.[41]

On April 1, by which time Da Nang had already fallen to the NVA and evacuation operations had ceased there, and Cam Ranh Bay was on the verge of falling, President Gerald Ford authorized deployment of some 700 U.S. Marines to assist directly with continuing operations further down the coast of Vietnam. While it would take additional days for Marines to begin boarding ships, groups of from 50 to 60 of them would commence boarding in the first week of April at various points to either load or unload refugees. Marines were pictured on page one of *The New York Times*, for example, boarding *Transcolorado* off Phan Rang on April 9. *Pioneer Contender*, after having been to Da Nang twice, and then loading 16,600 refugees in Cam Ranh Bay—an unprecedented number, before or since, anywhere—finally received help when teams of Marines were boarded to assist with their refugee evacuation operation.[42]

The NVA's push southward towards Saigon continued, but for seamen who had participated in the work and challenges of the initial phase of refugee evacuations along much of the coast of South Vietnam, it was a lull of sorts before the final storm that most felt—and could often hear—was coming. In the two weeks following the initial refugee embarkations in Da Nang on March 28, some 113,000 refugees had been moved southward, sometimes put ashore only to be taken back aboard within a few hours as word of the approaching NVA was received. But, by the second week in April, ships and crew could now turn to other matters, generally on standby status and until new orders came down.

During this period in mid–April there was still much work to be done, however, hopefully along with a good and well-deserved shore leave at some point for some. Ships needed serious cleaning after having carried thousands of refugees, generally without the most basic facilities having been rigged beforehand; there had been no time for that. Fresh stores and provisions for probable future evacuation operations needed to be brought aboard. Seamen in need of medical attention would need time for that. And a little R&R would be in order if and when port was reached where that could be had, and before orders came for the next round, whatever that might be.

With most of the ports of South Vietnam having fallen by then, Saigon was about it for any shore leave.

Pioneer Contender had, by April 11, made its way back to Saigon (Newport). There, Chief Officer Joe Delehant would note in his personal log a few days later that "everyone in the crew [except watch-standing Mates] is out living it up."[43]

As for what might come next, Delehant noted, "We still don't know what we're going to do. There are a bunch of ships standing by waiting for orders. In a week's time we'll know what's up."

At least one other ship involved in evacuation operations—*Transcolorado*—had also returned to Saigon, in its case to complete offloading remaining cargo that had been brought from the States but held partially on board so the ship could get underway as quickly as possible to join the initial evacuation operation in Da Nang. Once that was done, according to the ship's third assistant engineer, Charles Welch, writing from Saigon on April 17, the crew loaded damaged tanks, trucks, and jeeps and other equipment bound for the Philippines. He added: "Meanwhile, they are fighting 25 miles from here." Welch also noted that another American merchant ship, *Green Wave* (Central Gulf Lines), had "just come in empty to get cleaned and pick up junk."[44]

Before signing off, Welch would add: "We'll be glad to get out of here before the Viet Cong seal off the river." That would happen less than two weeks later.

Four days after Welch wrote from Saigon, South Vietnam's president, Nguyen Thieu, having watched his armed forces steadily retreat southward in the face of the NVA offensive, following his own questionable orders to abandon the northernmost provinces and retreat from the Central Highlands, resigned. Four days later, on April 25, he flew to Taiwan with 30 tons of personal baggage.[45]

By the time of President Thieu's resignation American merchant seamen had already done extraordinary duty during the first phase of refugee evacuations out of Da Nang, Cam Ranh Bay, and elsewhere along the coast of South Vietnam. Now, as they flushed out human excrement and debris from cargo holds, and brought supplies and foodstuffs on board to feed additional thousands beyond their crew complements, they prepared their ships and themselves for what was still to come.

They at least had these few weeks now to prepare, had some idea what was to come, which was much more than they had had when, while engaged in earlier and routine offloading of cargo, they had suddenly received orders to quickly get underway for northern ports surging with refugees desperately looking for escape seaward.

As events continued to unfold in rapid succession on the ground, options for additional expected evacuation operations would diminish until, from southern areas as well, the only way out would be by sea. The use of fixed-wing aircraft—including for the "baby lift" out of Saigon's Ton Son Nhut airport—had been ongoing since early the previous month.[46] But that option was soon to close: it would shift to a brief, 18-hour period of evacuation by helicopter, and finally to watercraft of various types to convey evacuees down-channel to the coast and, hopefully there, to rescue by the few merchant ships that happened to be close in-shore, and the naval ships of Task Force 76 farther out.

The Interagency Task Force (IATF) to receive, process, and resettle Vietnamese refugees had been ordered formed by President Gerald Ford on April 16, 1975.[47] Then, on April 23, Operation New Life was formally launched to transport refugees—the number would eventually be put at around 130,000—to temporary tent camps, mostly on Guam, for processing and eventual relocation again, mostly to the United States.[48]

On April 24, to coordinate communications between Washington, D.C., and the nine civilian-crewed ships under the control of the Military Sealift Command, Donald Birney, chief of the MSC office in Saigon, was flown out to the USS *Blue Ridge*, command ship for TF 76.[49] As so many others who would evacuate out in the last week of April 1975, Birney would not set foot in Vietnam again.

The Last Ships Out of Saigon

After having a brief and badly needed refitting and resupply respite during the middle two weeks of April, the last ships crewed by American merchant seamen to leave the interior of South Vietnam—whether with Vietnamese evacuees on board, or otherwise having taken on military equipment and related cargo—began to do so on April 25, the day after Birney moved the MSC command center to USS *Blue Ridge*.

One month to the day following the evacuations out of Tan My and Chu Lai to the north and south of Da Nang, the SS *Green Wave*, tasked with loading and evacuating refugees out of the Saigon area, arrived in Newport.[50] With some 625 refugees taken on board, the ship headed downriver, out to sea, and thence to Subic Bay in the Philippines. Once there, it would take on additional refugees before departing for the temporary refugee processing and housing center on Guam.[51]

On April 26 another merchant ship, the *American Challenger* (U.S. Lines), already a veteran of earlier evacuation operations farther up the coast, docked at Long Hai near Vung Tau, loaded some 8,600 refugees, and then proceeded with them to Phu Quoc Island. It too would sail for Subic Bay, on April 30, with 2,500 refugees from Phu Quoc and another 2,500 taken aboard at Vung Tau.[52]

The next day, anticipating the imminent arrival of PAVN forces, remaining cargo ships still at Newport were ordered out.[53] Since PAVN sappers would attack facilities at the Newport Bridge the next day, April 28, that order had come none too soon. According to Frank Snepp, those ships "at nearby [Newport] docks sailed for Vung Tau, all of them empty." Which ships those might have been were not specified and have not been identified.[54]

The Last Voyage to Vung Tau

In March 1975 the SS *Pioneer Contractor*, U.S. Lines, a 530-foot cargo ship under the command of Captain Paul Gregwate, took on a full load of ammunition at Sunny Point, North Carolina, then proceeded for the long voyage around for the intended delivery in Thailand.[55] But as timing and destiny would have it, it was diverted en route to Vung Tau, down the river channel from Saigon, to assist with refugee evacuation operations.

As the arrival of North Vietnamese troops in Saigon was imminent, and the last viable means of evacuation from Saigon—by helicopter from a few rooftop locations—was soon to commence, *Pioneer Contractor* would be one of only a handful of

American merchant ships remaining in Vietnam in the final few days of the war. The ship might well have been, in fact, the last one to arrive at Vung Tau with a full load of military cargo destined for an army on the verge of ceasing to exist.

As Eugene Kauder, *Pioneer Contractor*'s radio operator, would describe it not long after:

> We arrived amidst a vast armada of Naval and Merchant vessels standing by outside the 12 mile limit [as required under terms of ceasefire agreement for ships of the U.S. Navy]. We went into Vung Tau harbor to anchor and discharge cargo into barges while several vessels were leaving for international waters, fleeing the approaching Viet Cong and North Vietnamese army. We discharged some 1,200 tons in 36 hours.[56]
>
> At night, fires and explosions could be seen and heard along the nearby shore. A boatload of Arvin [sic] soldiers came out to notify the stevedores that the city had all but fallen. [They] quit work and left for shore.
>
> When we left for the 12 mile limit to night steam, we took aboard 87 Vietnamese refugees. They were missionaries representing World Christian Youth Group [and arrived in] a large boat with tons of supplies, rice, canned milk, diapers, sleeping mats, utensils, etc. The ship's crew ... labored all night taking aboard the cargo and stowing it. Outhouses were prepared freshwater hoses rigged and food preparations were made for an additional 6,000 refugees allotted to us by the Military Sealift Command.
>
> The following day we once again went into Vung Tau harbor, anchored for further discharge, but MSC ordered us back to sea as the city was already in Communist hands.[57]
>
> We were still awaiting orders to take aboard the 6,000 refugees [when] dozens of fishing vessels appeared alongside with signs in English—SOS, Out of Water, Help Us, etc. Several fleeing Arvin helicopters tried to land on our hatches, and [cargo] booms had to be laid out to prevent them from landing as a crash and fire might have [had] disastrous consequences due to our cargo of ammunition.
>
> About two dozen large fishing vessels with at least 5,000 people, with suitcases, motorcycles and other worldly goods, came alongside and tied up. They were out of food and water, but thanks to good preparation aboard the [ship] ... we were able to feed and resupply the helpless refugees.
>
> We were finally turned down by the military in [taking] aboard refugees due to our [remaining] cargo of ammunition and no room in the holds. April 29th and 30th, the sky was filled with hundreds of helicopters ... as they came and went upriver to Saigon, evacuating the remaining Americans, including Ambassador [Graham] Martin.[58]

After *Pioneer Contractor* transferred the refugees that had initially come aboard to a U.S. Navy ship, it got underway for Sasebo, Japan. With that, *Pioneer Contractor*'s time assisting Vietnamese evacuees, and involvement otherwise in the Vietnam War, had come to an end.

As PAVN rockets had begun to fall on Ton Son Nhut airport and other areas in downtown Saigon soon after dawn on April 28, 1975, for the first time since 1971, the evacuations by fixed-wing aircraft from there came to an end. Soon after, with Ambassador Graham Martin finally having ordered a full-scale evacuation, the planned and appropriately named operation code-named "Frequent Wind," utilizing helicopters and multiple rooftop and ground landing and take-off zones in Saigon, got underway.[59]

"Frequent Wind" would last but 18 hours, during which time nearly 7,000 American and Vietnamese evacuees would be lifted out to aircraft carriers waiting offshore.[60] Most of those transported by helicopter during those hours between April 29 and 30 would then be transferred to merchant ships for the two-day voyage to

Guam, in some cases directly or via the Philippines. While the images of "Frequent Wind" seared into the collective memory are those associated with helicopters atop the American Embassy (and Defense Attaché Office) rooftop in Saigon—and of many helicopters that could not be accommodated being summarily pushed off the decks of carriers into the sea—it would largely be to American merchant seamen that the baton of responsibility would be passed to complete the passage of tens of thousands of Vietnamese evacuees to refugee processing camps in Guam and at Wake Island before their eventual resettlement in the United States.[61]

Helicopters would not, however, be the only way that Vietnamese, and many Americans still remaining in Saigon and nearby areas, would make their way out to the coast and finally onto merchant and naval ships waiting and searching for them off and closer in-shore. A variety of tugs, barges, and small watercraft—some reserved by design for anticipated evacuations, and others commandeered, would be made available for the fortunate few able to make their way to and find room in them.

In the days immediately preceding the final evacuation by "Frequent Wind" helicopters, the possibility of evacuation by barge had been proposed, but fell largely on deaf ears within the American Embassy and Defense Attaché Office.[62] Fortunately, planning for it had proceeded, and would in the end provide transportation downriver for many. During the chaos, confusion, and panic that would characterize April 29, one embassy official would recall that the use of barges had been suggested at one point, and he proposed some should make their way to the Newport docks to secure barges there and begin loading refugees onto them.

"Jesus," someone more in the know would shout back, "that place has been out of bounds since yesterday. The VC are all over the place!"[63]

The Last Convoys Out

On April 29, with "Frequent Wind" underway, remaining personnel of the Military Sealift Command (MSC) office in Saigon loaded communications equipment onto the tug *Chitose Maru* in Saigon and joined a convoy shaping up there for transit down-channel to the coast.[64] In addition to that tug there were other assets of Alaska Barge and Transport, the private contractor that had been assisting with port development and logistics for years: two additional tugs, two barges, and the chartered LST *Boo Heung Pioneer*.[65] With American and Vietnamese office personnel aboard tugs, and thousands of refugees loaded onto barges, the convoy set out for the winding, 40-mile journey down to Vung Tau and beyond. Some small arms fire was taken along the way, without casualties taken, and first Vung Tau, then open waters of the South China Sea were finally reached. The tug and barge convoy eventually spotted and approached USS *Bay Ridge*.

On the afternoon of April 28 the last of the American vessels remaining at Newport were ordered out, and either directly down to Vung Tau or, as Frank Snepp would later recall, "to withdraw to the more secure Khanh Hoi navy yard near the center of town." Snepp would recount in *Decent Interval*:

> Not long afterward, as the first of three American tugs swung into the Khanh Hoi loading area, pandemonium erupted on the wharf as hundreds of anxious Vietnamese pushed and jostled each other to be first in line. The skipper pulled back into midstream to wait

for the turmoil to subside. In the meantime another tug arrived with two more barges. As it turned out, the extra passenger space they provided far exceeded what was needed. During the remainder of the afternoon only about 6,000 people, well below the combined capacity of the barges, were taken aboard. In repeated calls to the Embassy, [Naval Attaché Captain Cornelius] Carmody urged that additional evacuees be rounded up and sent down to the docks. But with the streets of downtown Saigon now a bog of humanity, his plans were in vain. As Carter, Polgar and so many others in the Embassy searched desperately for passenger space, the barges sat idle and half empty.[66]

Later in the afternoon of April 29, related Snepp, "the last of the American tugs and barges at Khanh Hoi pulled away from the docks and sailed south toward Vung Tau, most of them still only half full. Among those on board was one of the Embassy [USAID] officers who had made the voyage possible in the first place, Bob Lanigan. Except for a scattering of sniper fire near the mouth of the river, his trip downriver to the sea was as leisurely as a Sunday excursion."[67]

Evacuation out of Can Tho

There would be another tug and barge convoy making its way to the sea on April 29, but out of Can Tho to the south. With time running out, and the rapidly deteriorating and increasingly chaotic situation of dealing with thousands of Vietnamese still desperately wanting to get out of Saigon, the American Embassy had neglected to provide adequate advice for American Consulate staff in Can Tho, the largest city in the Delta area to the south of Saigon. "Get out," was the cryptic word that had come down.[68]

The CIA radio man brought along five portable radios that might have been very useful for the Can Tho consulate evacuation party, but Saigon had neglected to provide classified frequencies. As they set out downriver for the coast in two LCM "Mike" boats, an old rice barge (soon rejected for leaking), and a small boat on which a machinegun had been set up, and not knowing what to expect or what they might encounter there, those radios were of no help.[69]

"The rest of the Delta had been abandoned," consulate political officer David Schiaccitano was to recall a few years later.[70]

> We didn't know where the hell we were going. We just floated down the river [Song Hau] … all the Vietnamese were seasick. We didn't have any food. We had water, but it wasn't adequate for very long. We got to the mouth of the river near dark, still not knowing what to do. So we decided to head out to sea and hoped somebody would find us.
>
> In the darkness and rain, our two [flat-bottomed] boats had a hell of a time seeing each other. The lights didn't work on one of the LCMs. In the middle of the storm we decided to strap the boats together. We were all inexperienced sailors.… It was wet, dark, and slippery. No starlight, no moonlight. We only had lights on one LCM.
>
> Around eleven o'clock that night we saw a glow in the distance. We tried to hold a straight course in the rough water to reach the horizon. And around 2:00 a.m. we reached a freighter. It was an old Liberty ship [sic], the *Pioneer Contender*.
>
> Leaning over one of its rails was one of the CIA men who had fled Cam Tho by helicopter. He got out on the stern and was looking down at us and laughing. He was making a joke about it, "Hey, too bad you had to get wet."[71]

In Saigon on that evening of April 29, forward columns of the NVA entered the outskirts of the city.[72] By the next morning an armored column, "coming in from the north, rumbled down Hong Thap Tu Street and turned left onto Thong Nhut Boulevard to face the presidential palace. As the tanks rolled through the gates into the spacious courtyard, one of the crew rushed up the stairs to unfurl the red and yellow Vietcong flag from a balcony." Shortly thereafter, Colonel Bui Tin, the ranking NVA officer on the scene, was approached by General Minh representing the South Vietnamese government. They had the following exchange:

"I have been waiting since early morning to transfer power to you," Minh told Bui Tin.

"There is no question of your transferring power," said Bui Tin. "Your power has crumbled."[73]

With the arrival of PAVN tanks on the grounds of the presidential palace in Saigon, the long Vietnam War had, for all intents and purposes, ended. With that, reunification of Vietnam, a country arbitrarily and temporarily divided at Geneva in 1954, had once again at long last and such tremendous cost, become a reality.

While "Frequent Wind" began and ended within a matter of only 18 hours between April 29 and 30, 1975, American merchant seamen would continue to board Vietnamese refugees—who, arriving to the coast and continuing beyond in boats not designed for offshore seas—could be considered the first of the "boat people" who would leave Vietnam in subsequent years. The fortuitous appearance of the *Pioneer Contender* to the Can Tho evacuees off the mouth of the Bassac River on April 30 was an example of that. And for a few more days going forward, until TF 76 finally withdrew from the area, more merchant ships—and MSC nucleus ships crewed by merchant seamen—would come upon, and otherwise take aboard from temporary holding areas, refugees for final runs to refugee camps before they too departed the area for home.

Pioneer Contender would dock at Vung Tau on May 2, load 6,000 for Subic in the Philippines, and arrive there the next day. Some 2,000 of the 6,000 taken aboard at Vung Tau would be disembarked at Subic (for later transfer to Guam) before *Pioneer Contender*, which had been the very first to arrive in Da Nang more than a month earlier at the start of evacuations along the coast, continued on to Guam to disembark there the last of the refugees it would transport during the evacuation operations.[74]

Other merchant and MSC "nucleus ships" making their final runs out of the area to Guam would include *American Challenger*, which would bypass Subic and head directly to Guam with 5,000 refugees; *Green Wave*, which would move between ships of the U.S. Seventh Fleet, taking on some 4,000 refugees from them before sailing for Guam; *Pioneer Commander*, which would depart with 5,000; *Green Forest*, which would load 3,000 at Con Son Island, for Subic; USNS *Miller*, with 4,500; *Greenville Victory*, with 3,000; and USNS *Kimbro*, with 4,500, including some who had arrived there in "an old, barely seaworthy Saigon ferryboat," and also including 30 Americans, three Swiss, one Belgian, 11 French, six Chinese, 47 Koreans, and 10 Filipino nationals. *Kimbro* would arrive at Subic on May 4, unload refugees there, and prepare to finally head to Guam. The day before arriving at Subic, Captain Taylor of *Kimbro* would radio to MSC Far East in Yokohama that one refugee, Nguyen Thi Hieu, had given birth to a six-pound, four-ounce boy. He was given the name Kun Kimbro.[75]

When all was said and done, some 130,000 Vietnamese would be evacuated out by fixed-wing aircraft, helicopter, and by ship between March and early May 1975.

Some 50,493 (including 2,678 orphans) were taken out by fixed-wing aircraft before Ton Son Nhut was shut down; nearly 7,000 were evacuated by helicopter during "Frequent Wind"; 58,000, according to an MSC estimate, were evacuated by ship from Vietnamese coastal waters. Nearly 112,000 of the overall 130,000 would be taken to Guam before most of them would again be transported to the United States.[76]

Operation New Life, begun on April 23 and involving many of the American merchant ships involved in initial evacuations along the coast of South Vietnam, would extend to the end of October (formally concluding on November 1)—well after the "liberation" of Saigon by the PAVN, as these evacuees were transported mostly to a tent city set up on Guam to receive, process, and temporarily house them. But, anticipating the destructive typhoon winds and rain typical for the area late in the year, these refugees would be relocated, mostly to the United States, by the end of the year.[77]

The American Merchant Marine had once again played a major role in refugee evacuation, now at the conclusion of a war that, it can be argued, stretched back nearly 30 years. But even as the last of the refugee-laden cargo ships departed for the temporary refugee holding and processing centers at Guam and elsewhere, the work of merchant seamen providing assistance to other Vietnamese choosing to flee their country was, as it would develop, far from over.

As other Americans returned from Vietnam to pick up their own lives once again in the United States, thousands of merchant mariners—most of whom had also served in Vietnam, in logistical support of the war there—were engaged now in typical peacetime commerce on their ships. In returning once again in succeeding years to and through the South China Sea on their way to other port destinations in South and Southeast Asia, they would often come upon, and go out of their way to rescue (when ships of some other countries were explicitly ordered to avoid such voyage-extending delays), those who would forever be known as the "boat people" of Vietnam.

So, for this continued humanitarian work, there was yet another chapter to be written about the role of the U.S. Merchant Marine in the Indochina Wars and their aftermath.

Refugees Evacuated by MSC-Controlled Ships March 28 through May 15, 1975*

Ship	Total no. Refugees
American Challenger	23,500
American Racer	3,900
Boo Heung Pioneer	7,200
Green Forest	8,000
Green Port	15,000
Green Wave	5,200
Pioneer Commander	22,000
Pioneer Contender	34,200
Pioneer Contractor	100

Ship	Total no. Refugees
Seapac tugs and barges	6,800
Transcolorado	11,800
USNS *Greenville Victory*	10,000
USNS *Sgt. Truman Kimbro*	8,200
USNS *Sgt. Andrew Miller*	23,000
Vera B	150
Total	179,050

*Sealift, June 1975, 24.

18

Captain Flink's Story
The 16,600

"You take a New York subway train during rush hour, lock all the doors for seven days, and you'll see what it was like."
—Captain Edward C. Flink

Author's note: The son and grandson of sea captains, Edward Constantin Flink was born in Jersey City, New Jersey in 1922 and first went to sea as a teenager in four-masted lumber schooners under his father's command.[1] He entered the Merchant Marine Academy in 1940 and served as a ship's officer during World War II and for many years thereafter. During the Vietnam War, as master of SS *Pioneer Contender*, he was involved in the evacuation out of Cam Ranh Bay of the greatest number of refugees—16,600—ever transported at one time by a merchant ship, a feat unparalleled in the annals of maritime and naval history.[2] Flink was interviewed at his home by the author in Massapequa, New York in 1990. Following are excerpts from the interview transcript.

* * *

I was master on the *Pioneer Contender*, and on our first run to Vietnam and most of the time we carried ammunition, going into Saigon.[3] We'd carry ammunition, and a couple of times we'd carry general cargo, depending on the need. Port Chicago [California] was mainly where we went [to load] but we'd also go up to Bangor [Washington]. Remember when they had that ship [*Badger State*] that the bombs were rolling around in, and they lost it?[4] After that incident we were the second ship to load up there. And needless to say everything was well shored [with wood dunnage]; we had more shoring than we had ammunition. We were also taking ammunition out of Sunny Point [North Carolina]. At one point I even went up to Leonardo, up here in New Jersey, to load ammunition. That's down there right off Sandy Hook, you know, near where the race track is.

Cat Lai

I was most of the time on the ammunition run, a lot of the time to Cat Lai [near Saigon].[5] They worked ammunition there all the time and unloaded it pretty quick most of the time. You had quite a few frogmen scares [there]. In fact, on three different occasions I had frogmen reported alongside the ship. Of course the panic button was pushed, and procedure was followed. They used these concussion grenades, and they dropped them in the water—it was supposed to be at random times. At first it was off the ship; they had a regular armed guard that used to come around and drop them right off the ship. Later on they had a gunboat that went around the ship to do that.

[The up-channel transit to Saigon] well, just a rough estimation, for a while we were shuttling about three times a year [so] I'd say about 15 or 20 times. It was all flat [and] they had defoliated the whole river all the way up by the time I went up there.[6] I've had ships ahead of me that were fired on, and ships behind me that were fired on, and we were fired on too. We had one pilot one time who said every time he went down the river he got into hot water; he's always had a ship where they sent a rocket over or put a couple bullets into the side of the ship.

Captain Edward Flink at his home in Massapequa, New York (Author photo).

We've had of course quite a few bomb scares with frogmen. [We never got hit] but they were coming pretty close. You could see the rockets—the smoke—another ten feet and it would've hit the [ship's navigation] bridge.

In Vung Tau at the mouth of the river we had to change anchorage every, well, [not at] a set time. Say for instance we'd anchor in one spot for maybe six hours and then move to a different anchorage and stay there for 12 hours, and the next time it'd be four hours, just to confuse any watchers.

[In March 1975] we left the States with a full load of general cargo, and we went into Saigon up at what they call Newport, an Army terminal for all the military goods. I finished discharging there, and we received orders to go to Da Nang to pick up some heavy lifts [rolling stock] on the way up to bring down to Saigon.[7] Well, we were preparing for heavy lifts on the way up, and when we got to Da Nang, the MSC [Military Sealift Command] told us not to enter the harbor, just to hang on outside the harbor and not to let anybody on board.

Da Nang

We got up to Da Nang on the 28th of March and they told me not to anchor, and not to let anybody on board. And if we did anchor just to drop one hook so we could get going in a hurry. Later on in the morning the MSC rep came out and said not to let anybody on board. He cancelled the [previously scheduled] cargo and said we were going to take refugees instead.

On the boat deck of the ship I [then] had the American Consul with his family, [and] five other various consuls: Japanese, Philippine, with their families and the office personnel. And they took up the whole boat deck. I also had the head doctor for the UN ... Dodd. And they figured out that with the space, which was the deck of the ship, half a hatch ... on deck, and in the upper 'tween decks—the reason for that is that they had to keep half a hatch open so that the people in the 'tween deck would be able to get fresh air ... air circulation. They figured out the cubic feet [and that] I could only carry a total of 5,000 refugees.

Well we started loading the consul people at around 11:00, and then they put me out into the outer harbor and they said to start loading the regular refugees. They were going to send a barge [of evacuees] out to load on the ship. They had the Marines out there that were attached to the American Consul; they were the security guard for the ... well, hush-hush equipment and whatever they had that they brought on with them. And they counted heads, and when they got to 5,000, why, that was it. I picked up [the anchor] and left. And the ship that was behind me was supposed to pick up the rest of them. These people from the American Consul, and the refugees, I took right to Saigon.

Da Nang Again

In Saigon I had the crew clean up the ship a little bit, and then they sent me on up ... back to Da Nang again. And this time it was on March 30. They told me to get up there as soon as I could, but to stay outside, a couple miles off the port, until noontime. The [Pioneer] Commander was in there at that time loading refugees. They were afraid that if they brought in two ships, why, they'd have a panic. They had a panic anyway for the simple reason that they had a mix-up in orders: first they were going to evacuate the town, and then they were going to hold the town.[8] Consequently with the refugees, why, they wanted to get out. These were the civilians who didn't care where they went as long as they got away from the fighting. They overran the pier area. They overran the barge. And it was regular chaos. In the meantime there was fighting going on in the perimeter of the city. So, it was really something.

Well, after the [Pioneer] Commander got loaded up they told me I could come in, and she was still loading refugees on the way out. She dropped the barge off when she left. In the meantime I went in there and started loading, [at] around 2:00 in the afternoon. This was in the outer harbor; the inner harbor was regular turmoil.

They had a barge on either side [of the ship]. And they would come up, as you see, with the cargo nets and gear. And then they had Jacobs pilot ladders, any way at all that they could come up there. What I tried to do with the crew was ... anybody that had any visible arms [weapons], why, we'd throw them over the side, to keep any problems under control. But, there again, the fellas broke down their rifles and stuck them in their knapsacks and ... whatever you have like that where you hid these things.

We were supposed to leave at sunset, but it was 10:00 before I got the barges unloaded. And this was floating around in the outer harbor. In the meantime I was notified that the North Vietnamese were coming down, the frogmen were coming down and were gonna try and put a bomb against the hull of the ship. So this is one reason why we were steaming around all the time. And I finally decided [to] start heading out towards sea. So when the barges were empty, why, we just cut them loose; they just floated away [and] a towboat was supposed to come up and pick up the barges. Well, they eventually did, but the only trouble was that every time we got close to land, why we'd receive small arms fire.

Towards the end there, just before we left [on] the final run, they had bigger stuff, like howitzers—our own [captured] Army stuff being fired back at us. That started, so we took off after that.

The second trip up, that was when Da Nang fell. I took out the American consul and the last of the Americans, and all the personnel that was connected with the American government at the time. And there was supposed to be 5,000 refugees, but who counts after ... after it gets dark. This time I took these to Cam Ranh Bay, where I dumped them off.

There again, I went in there and went alongside the pier, discharged the refugees, and the American consul and his family, and the last of the Americans—officials— [and] they were flown directly to Saigon with the remaining consul executives.

And then from Cam Ranh.... I was running low on fuel. I was getting down to where I had five days of fuel on board. So, running around the coast like that, where you don't know what's going to happen, why you want a little 'gasoline.' So they sent me down to Vung Tau at the mouth of the Saigon River, and they sent down two barge loads of fuel—about 5,000 barrels. It was enough to hold me for a while.

Then from there they were supposed to send the barges down, oh, by around 1:00 in the afternoon, but they didn't show up until 8:00 the next morning. In the meantime, the crew was cleaning up the ship, and we took on fuel, and from there they sent us back up to Cam Ranh. This was April 3.

Cam Ranh Bay

Now in Cam Ranh the [*Trans*]*Colorado* was in there; she was anchored and was loading refugees. They had two tow boats in there. You had an LST—*Enzo Pioneer*— which was a Philippine LST that was bringing out refugees. We were supposed to go alongside the pier but we didn't do it because the barge was in there with this Philippine tow boat. They were loading refugees.

They were fighting just over the top of the hill from where the pier was. What it is, going into Cam Ranh Bay itself, you enter from the ocean and pass through a couple of islands. And going into Cam Ranh Bay, it's only about a quarter mile wide, and then the bay itself is quite big. And we were afraid that we would get stuck in there, in case they did lose control of the port. As it was, the [*Trans*]*Colorado* finished loading around noontime, and he took off. He said he had enough refugees on board, and he was afraid that the boats that were coming up there were going to get in to his propeller. So he took off.

16,600: A Record Number

In the meantime they sent this barge load that was being loaded at the pier. The Philippine towboats towed it out alongside the ship. So there again we were loading refugees from the barge. They told us that we had to be out before sunset. In the meantime the Philippine LST loaded up at the pier and come out and discharged her refugees at the same time that we were discharging from the barge. And this took place, and the barge got empty and they towed it back in again. And they were loading some more refugees onto the barge. In the meantime I took up the rest of the refugees off this LST that was in there. This was the time that I picked up the 16,000.[9] I was supposed to take them from Cam Ranh Bay to Saigon.[10]

So the barge had 5,000 refugees on it, and the LST had another 5,000 on it. But while the barge was alongside the ship, why you had all these fishermen coming out in their fishing boats, loaded down, and as fast as the people were getting off the barge more people were getting onto the barge from the fishing boats. That's how I ended up with the 16,000—because they just kept coming and coming.[11]

And what they did was ... the fishing boat would come out and put his bow up to the barge, or to the gangway—whichever he could get to—and the refugees would get off. And the last one would put the engine full astern. And of course the boat backs away and another comes in. In the meantime this boat that has nobody on board—the refugees are off and the fisherman is off—is going around in circles, until the fuel runs out or it burns up or bangs into another boat, gets a hole in it and sinks. So all this added to the confusion, all these fishing boats just running around in circles [as] these boats just kept on going astern. The rudder would flip one way and the boat would go in a right-hand circle. It'd flop over to the left and would go in a left-hand circle. And after a while, after you've got 20 or 30 boats going like that [and] there's bound to be a few collisions. And the engines would get overheated, because most of them weren't built for going astern, nobody's tending the engine, a little gasoline or fuel slops around ... and of course some of those Vietnamese boats they leak like sieves to begin with, so, there again, they sunk. I didn't actually see any sinking, but I saw some burning—the smoke attracts your attention. Probably the owners that wanted to get out ... some of them set their boats on fire, sort of a "scorched earth" policy in some respects.

Under Fire

It was getting towards dark, pretty close to six o'clock, when I left Cam Ranh Bay. Leaving Cam Ranh Bay, why there again, we had some rockets fired at us just before we left on the way out. We were steaming around in the bay. We had one rocket fired at us while we were loading refugees, and we had several fired at us as we went out through the pass. [The rockets] hit the water and you could see the geyser of water where they hit. You could hear the detonation of the charges; it was close.

The Last Ship Out

After we got out through the pass, Cam Ranh Bay fell. Of course the [Vietnamese] Navy detachment that was holding the pass were overrun by the North Vietnamese. And we got just on the other side of the island going out—it's a zig-zag course going out—and just as we got on the other side of the island there was a big cloud of black smoke, where the Navy base was there was a large explosion. So we just made it out.

We were the last ship out. And some of the refugees I took out the last time were some of the refugees I brought in the first time [from Da Nang]. So, you figure that one out. They couldn't get out and they wanted to get out, and we were the last ones there.

And in Cam Ranh Bay you could see the fighting. When we left you could see the fighting right down on the pier, and on the road that went up to the airport. You could see a man running down the road, and all of a sudden he flops down and doesn't get up any more. Or he makes a cartwheel and lands in an awkward position, and that was it. They were actually … you could see people being … the soldiers being annihilated.

Then after we left Cam Ranh Bay we had orders to proceed to Saigon. And about two hours out the Navy got a hold of us—the Fifth Fleet [*sic*]—and, well, I've got on my notes here [that] they put on 48 Marines the first time.[12] They couldn't put any Marines on board while we were in the harbor; we had to be out in international waters. So after we left, why, they called me back in again; I was outside the territorial waters, the three-mile limit. Marines weren't supposed to be on a civilian ship, but because of the special circumstances they did put Marines on board because they did have trouble with, we [could] say, the disgruntled Vietnamese troops on the other ships. They've had incidents where they had regular gunfights on the ships. You've probably heard too where there were, what was it, 35 men killed on one ship.[13] So as a precautionary measure they put these Marines on board. And I used them as a security guard to keep all of the Vietnamese out of the midship house. The reason for this is simply that the crew has to operate the ship; they're working and they have to have some sleep and rest.

So, as I said, the refugees … the only place we didn't have them was on the bridge and on the flying bridge, and inside the stack! They were in all five cargo holds and on deck, and also, well, boat deck, bridge deck—even in the lifeboats.

Phu Quoc

The first day after we got to Phu Quoc on the west coast of Vietnam, about 300 miles north of the southernmost point of Vietnam—it's an island, the French had it as a penal colony, the reason being that it could be pretty well patrolled with the prisoners having some freedom on there—well, they figured this was the safest place for the Vietnamese refugees.[14]

They sent me around the [*Pioneer*] *Commander*, the [*American*] *Challenger*, well, the other U.S. Lines ships that were in there with us. And the [*Pioneer*] *Contractor*, the [*Trans*]*Colorado*. Also the *Greenville* [*Victory*] and [USNS] *Sergeant Miller*. The *Sergeant Miller* was the one that was having trouble; I think that they were threatening to take over the whole ship.[15] And the [*Trans*]*Colorado* was another one they threatened to take over, and beach so that they could get off. They were getting impatient to get off.

The [16,600] refugees were on board [*Pioneer Contender*] for approximately seven days.[16] They were only supposed to be on board for eight hours, which was the time it would have taken to go from Cam Ranh Bay to Vung Tau at the entrance of the Saigon River. But as we were approaching Vung Tau I received orders to proceed to Phu Quoc. And that's the reason why I had them on board for seven days. This was the total crowd; it took them two days to discharge all the refugees, so some of them were on there for a longer period of time.

As I said, you take a New York subway train during the rush hour, and lock all the doors for seven days, and you'll see what happens. You ate and slept where you stood. Sleeping, why, you'd sleep one on top of the other. It looked like a bunch of spaghetti all wrapped together. Well, you sleep on my shoulder, and I'll sleep on somebody else's shoulder ... and things like that. Most of them usually, the Vietnamese have a habit of squatting. And they can sit on their haunches for hours without any ill effects because this is one of their natural ways of sitting. But *you* sit on your haunches for a while and you get up stiff as a board. They've got a knack for it; they do it day in, and day out. So there's no problem with them, they can do it [sleep] on their haunches.

Food and Water

As far as food was concerned, the Tenth Fleet [*sic*] sent over "Mike" boats every day with food.[17] And the first time they sent it over I figured if I put it back, everything on #3 hatch, I could distribute it from three hatch to both ends. Well, with the crowd and the near panic that was going on, that didn't work out too well. So it got to a point where I had the "Mike" boats discharge at each hatch: several sling loads of food at each hatch, and distribute it hatch by hatch. And even so, every time the food came aboard, why, it was a near riot; there was a mad scramble for it.

Water: the ship was able to make enough water for, shall we say, general consumption. They have their own evaporators where we can distill sea water, make it pure distilled water, no salt or anything. In fact you can use it in your battery if you want to. So the water detail started at six o'clock in the morning when people started waking up, and it lasted until 10 o'clock at night when they started going back to sleep again.

We took empty barrels and cut out the tops, scoured them out so we could use that as a reservoir. And also the garbage cans that we had: we dumped the garbage and scrubbed them good. And these green plastic bags you have for leaves and God knows what—we used that as a liner in the garbage cans. So we had enough to where we put two containers, or two barrels, down each hatch, and a couple on deck. We had enough garden hose to where we started from the midship house: one hose went aft and the other hose went forward. The crew, with a Marine assistant, used to go around ... they'd start from one hatch and fill up two barrels of water, and then they'd go to the next hatch and fill up the other two barrels, and so on until they got all the way up forward. And then they'd start from midships again and go through the same process all over again. And the same thing back aft. So by the time you got the two drums full at the extreme end, why, the ones closest to the house were empty again. So this was just a continual process—they just kept filling up the barrels.

And the Vietnamese ... my biggest kick was when they first come aboard the ship, since their religion is very closely associated with water, why, they'd come on board the ship and they'd wash their feet first before they'd take a drink of water.

And of course they were used to having gallons and gallons of water, and here we only had a limited supply. And we'd see these people washing their feet in distilled water, instead of washing their feet, you know, when it's necessary. It was kind of a rugged thing on that.

Going Overboard

Well when we were finally anchored in Phu Quoc some of the younger members we had on board the ship—they had been military personnel—they were getting anxious, and it was crowded conditions. It was hot and there was little air circulation. And about two or three days after I was there—two days—why some of these fellas were getting a little unhappy about the situation. So, we were sheathed for ammunition with two by twelves and regular sheathing that was put on top of the regular sweat battens in the hatches. So what they would do, they were taking these two by twelves off the bulkheads, knocking the nails out and throwing them over the side and swimming to shore. The first time they tried, there was about 20 of them that jumped over the side with these boards, with their personal possessions strapped on their backs. But the thing is, well, they started out on the slack water, and the tide changed so to get to shore they … it took a long time.

Now the regular Vietnamese patrol boats that they had out there, from the Vietnamese army, that were connected with Phu Quoc, they were patrolling the waters. And of course the ones that were fairly close to the ship, why, they picked them up. But then the later ones, when it got towards dark, you could see them head towards land. And out in the dark, when there were no lights, all of a sudden you'd hear a burst of machine gun fire. So you assumed that the patrol boats took them as enemy and fired on them and killed them all. They were supposed to protect the waters, so they just opened up on them.

Well, that was the first day. The second day…[we] had another 150 swimming ashore. And it averaged out to … well, I had over 200 swimmers jumping off the ship—every day a couple or five or ten or a group of them. They wanted some sort of flotation because it was, there again, a good mile to the beach. One of them, took out one of these flotation tanks out of the lifeboat. Well, there again, a tank is two by three by four foot long, and of course it's filled with Styrofoam, a new type Styrofoam with plastic covering on the outside of it. And they throw it in the water, and of course the guy who wanted to use it he couldn't get up on it because it was too big for him. Those tanks are supposed to hold six people. Well, needless to say, I had to get a new tank when I got back to the States.

When the refugees found out we had supplies—emergency supplies—in the lifeboats, why, it took them only five minutes to clean out the water and all the rations out of the lockers that are in the lifeboats, completely. Once I saw them start rummaging around in the lockers, why, I quickly sent one of the Marines down there to pick up the flares, the pistol, and the compass for the lifeboat. There again, if you shoot off one of those flares it can do quite a bit of damage in the right place.

Now when we finally did start discharging the refugees into the barges, they sent out five "Mike" boats to take off the ones that were sick, and the girls that were pregnant, that were close to their time.

Deaths and Births

There [had been] births and deaths [on board]. I had about 80 elderly people pass away on me, the exact number I can't say because what happened was they'd pass away and their families would drop them over the side at night when nobody was watching. And unofficially there was 130 births that I know of. This was due to the tension, conditions, and God knows what. The births and deaths were all unofficial because there were no records kept, and the babies were born on the hatch or on deck, with a midwife or somebody that knew something about it. We did lose several babies because of malnutrition, improper care, and superstition—that had something to do with it too. You take a mother that's been living up in the hills or out in the boondocks someplace where she isn't close to modern conveniences, the baby gets sick [and] she goes to the local witch doctor or "medicine man" or whatever you call him. They still exist. And if he can't cure the baby, why, she just sits there and rocks the baby until it dies. And that's what happened here: the baby could've been saved but there again the mother … she didn't know what to do.

Roughnecks

Then too, when we started discharging the refugees, of course there were quite a few military personnel that had on civilian clothes. Putting them on the shore at Phu Quoc the port authorities went through a regular routine of asking each person where they'd been, what they did, where they come from and everything else, and this took quite a bit of time. So these soldiers wanted to get out of there and get back—see if they could infiltrate—get behind the lines so that they could help out with the war situation. And they were very unhappy about this holdup. So the commander from the island trickled word through the grapevine out to the Tenth Fleet, and they trickled it back to me with the suggestion that … don't send the roughnecks ashore because they're having a hard time screening them. So keep them aboard the ship and send them out last. Well, how the heck do I know who's the military and who isn't if they're walking around in civilian clothes? So as long as they got off the ship I'm not worrying about it. As I said, it took two and a half days to get them unloaded, so I let them worry about it. But I mean it was kind of surprising because here were their own people and they said keep the roughnecks.

Well, while we were there the first group of Marines—what did I say, 36?—were relieved by a second group. This time it was, the second group was 67. They come off one of the aircraft carriers. Let me see, there was the *Blue Ridge*, which was the command ship, a helicopter attack ship. And the *Fredericks* [sic] and the *Dubuque*. Well the *Fredericks* [sic] and the *Dubuque* were more or less assigned to my ship to keep Marine personnel on board the ship and also to supply the ship with food every day. And the *Blue Ridge*, she was command.

And one day you'd see her, and the next day you wouldn't.[18]

The first group of Marines I had, the captain and the sergeant were the only ones that had any experience; the rest were fresh out of boot camp. Well, after being on board the ship for about three days, why they had their baptismal of fire, of sorts, on the ship. And the same thing with the second group. Well the second group was a bigger group, and there you had your medics, and a couple of sergeants, and others who had combat experience. And they were used to this, so things went a little smoother. And of course with a bigger group they're better organized to take care of things, whereas [with] a small handful, why, you do the best job with what you have.

And that first group [of refugees], after they left the ship [and] because of the crowded conditions, you had, well I call it "red eye"; it's an inflammation of the eye that after a while, why, the whites of your eye turn beet red. And your eye lids come down to where they're slits. You have to bathe your eyes about every four hours with good wash, and wear dark glasses to cut down the glare of the sun. It's an infection. With 16,000 people on board the ship, I mean there's a certain amount of, shall we say, dust particles in the air, sanitary conditions were next to nothing, and of course once you start getting a case of dysentery with one group, why it spreads through the whole ship. The same thing with this eye infection. Of course if you're living in excretions—like they tell me in Guam, "just plain shit"—it's something. So they ... left the ship pretty well tired, and they [had] started getting dysentery, and quite a few of them were getting this red eye infection.

Well two or three days later some of the Marines in that first group came back by the ship in one of the "Mike" boats that had food on board for the ship, and they were saying hello to everybody on the ship, and every one of them had a bald haircut. They claimed that they wouldn't even let them into their quarters before they stripped all their clothing off, and were disinfected and examined, before they were allowed to mix with the rest of the crew.

After the Phu Quoc incident, then they had this ... the code name was "Big Wind" [*sic*].[19] This was after May 1. All the refugee ships with their escorts assembled on the northeast point of Vietnam to regroup, to pick up the remaining refugees and to transport them to the Philippines and to Guam. Now after I was—this is jumping a little ahead of time—after I got finished at Phu Quoc we went back up to Saigon. We were ordered there but never got there because Saigon had fallen at that time.[20] And we were just about off Vung Tau when we got this order to regroup in the southeast quadrant to pick up refugees.

Well, in the meantime, they sent me south, on the south end of the Saigon estuary with a ... well, I call them one of these floating drydocks. It's an attack ... repair ship. They can sink it down into the water, and they have four "Mike" boats inside the hull. Originally they were designed to pick up a small destroyer or a destroyer escort to repair them. But lately they've built helicopter decks on top of them and they have the "Mike" boats inside.[21] One of these ships was supposed to stay with us south of the Saigon estuary. They were supposed to evacuate the rest of the Americans from—not Saigon, but the city just south of it.[22] They were supposed to bring them out with a chopper, and the chopper lands on the deck of the repair ship or the floating drydock, as I call it. And then they were supposed to bring the refugees over to the ship. In other words, they were just a landing platform for the choppers, and I was the evacuee ship.

We stayed there and that kind of fell through. We had ... there was no choppers but there were two "Mike" boats loaded with refugees that had come out of Saigon through the back way, you may say. There was another channel coming down from Saigon but it was for shallower draft vessels. We picked them up instead.

And after that then they sent us up from there. They sent us up to Vung Tau itself with the *Sergeant Miller*. She was up there laying off Vung Tau with the same orders as I had to pick up—there was supposed to be three barges of refugees coming down the river—to pick them up and bring them down to the staging point, the southeast staging point. Well she was in there, and the escort that was with me said, "We'll go on in fairly close to the *Miller* and wait for your barges."[23]

At the time the *Miller* had one barge alongside. So I come in, steamed in, and I had all these fishing boats trying to get on board the ship. Well I didn't let them on until we got up fairly close to Vung Tau itself. And I just dropped one shot [of anchor chain]—which is 15 fathoms—in the water, just enough to hold the ship so she wouldn't swing around too much.

Under Attack

And all of a sudden, why we didn't have the barges alongside, and of course the crew is looking around, looking at the *Miller* and seeing what the problem is over there, and all these fishing boats and the barge of refugees coming at us. There's a lighthouse on the point that was still further in. In other words we were still within a mile and a half [or] two miles from the lighthouse. And all of a sudden while we were anchored there, just about ... the [Chief] Mate came back up, and we started getting geysers of water popping up around the ship. And all of a sudden there's a little whistling to go along with the geyser. So our escort he took off—he was about on our starboard side, laying on our starboard quarter—we were more or less headed in towards Vung Tau. So he started huffing and puffing [and] he come by and he said, "We advise you to move out a little further."

Well, needless to say, after the fourth geyser came shooting up fairly close to the ship, why we turned around and headed out to sea. The Mate was still in the process of heaving the anchor up when I turned the ship around to head out.

We went out further and steamed at slow speed. The Philippine tow boat come alongside and brought the barge-load of refugees. There again, we had only one barge—one of those big, deep-sea-going barges—and we took those people on board. And there again, the little fishing boats, they had in fact a little fleet of them floating around trying to get on board the ship. But they told me: "Just one barge load and that's it. Get out of there."

In the meantime they had a couple of these choppers—American choppers—fly out. There were refugees again. They landed on the barge next to the *Miller*. In fact, they landed on the barge and they killed a couple of people in the barge that was tied up alongside the *Miller*. Well, we were lucky enough where we didn't have anything like that.

"Time to Fly"

These refugees I picked up from Vung Tau. Vung Tau had already fallen and the barge of refugees just about made it by before the Vietnamese that were in Vung Tau turned their guns on the barges that the people coming down from Saigon were on. Well they told me to go back down into the staging area that was down there in the southeast corner of Vung Tau. So I started in and they had a group of fishing boats [that had been] commandeered by the South Vietnamese Army. They were very unhappy and of course they were all armed with M-14s and side arms. And as they come close to the ship they started firing their guns off. Well needless to say, when they started firing their guns off and they were behind me, well I hooked up and told them [engine room] to give me 21 nozzles as soon as they could. And I got out of there.

In the meantime I got a hold of the *Blue Ridge*, which was in command of the whole operation, and told them I was being harassed by these fishing boats, [that] they wanted to get on board the ship. They wanted to get out of there. Part of it was trying to attract my attention, but when those little "bumble bees" are flying through the rigging, I don't think that's trying to attract my attention. I mean they might've thought so, but when the "bumble bees" start flying, it's time for me to fly.

Well I got a hold of the *Blue Ridge* and they told me to steam out to sea until I was over the horizon and then come on back down to the staging area. Well I got back down to the staging area and, as I say, you had the whole evacuation fleet down there, plus the Tenth Fleet [*sic*] as escort service. We had the doctors from the fleet come over to inspect the conditions on the ship to make sure that we could ... be able to carry the refugees to the Philippines and/or to Guam.

Well we ended up—the three U.S. Lines ships—while we were in the staging area, these fishing boats that had the soldiers on showed up.[24] And they were going around from ship to ship trying to get on board the ship. Well we couldn't do anything until we got word from the *Blue Ridge* how many we could take; they told us only 5,000. Well I had my 5,000—my quota—already, and these soldiers, why, they were extra. So it was finally decided that the three U.S. Lines ships would split the soldiers up and take them on to the destination. Well, I said all right. For a while I was kind of unhappy about it because they were armed. Well it finally ended up where, all right, I'll take them but they come on board the ship without arms. They can bring their personal possessions, but no arms. So I finally ended up with another 600 soldiers. Of course, the high rank boys didn't show their rank; as far as anyone knew they were common, ordinary, run-of-the-mill soldiers.

So my Marine guard we had on board, they went down, they had a sort of a stage—or float—between the gangway, or underneath the gangway, so the Vietnamese soldiers as they come off the [fishing] boat onto the float they were searched for arms. Any arms were dumped right there, right in the water. And then they come back up on board and put them up on, well, pushed the civilians off from on top of the mast houses and put the soldiers up there, with the idea that if we had any trouble, why, it's a raised platform and we could control them a little better. And of course the Marines I had up on the wing of the bridge and the flying bridge, why they had a good view of them so that if anything happened they could, shall we say, stop it before it got started. But as it worked out they were very ... after floating around for three hours going from ship to ship, why they were happy to be on board.

After that incident, why we took off. It was the *Commander, Contender, Challenger,* the *Contractor,* we were—the three [?] of us—the first to leave the staging area, with escort destroyer and, well I call them floating dry docks, supply ship. The idea was that if we had any dire medical problems ... of course, the Marines had put on a medical detachment: a doctor with three assistants, to take care of problems on the ship. And if there was anything outstanding, why this escort ship—the floating dry dock—since it had a chopper on its flight deck, why it could transfer any patients back and forth. But as it was, I had two soldiers that had shrapnel [wounds], and the medical corps that was on the ship couldn't handle it. So they sent in a doctor, flew him in with a chopper with his male nurse as assistant. And they operated on these two Vietnamese soldiers and removed the shrapnel that was imbedded in their bodies. But there again, I had quite a bit of what they call "third class Americans." Well, "third class Americans" were classified as the Vietnamese that worked in the American Consul or associate organizations connected with the American Consul.

So they, with the three ships, we were headed for Subic Bay [Philippines]. And then from there to Guam. Well the idea was that once we got close to Guam they'd spread the ships out and come in six hours apart. Since my spot was the last ship to come in, they told me to come into Subic, because I had the majority of the [Vietnamese] soldiers in this flotilla, plus the "third class citizens," it was advisable that I come in first.

So I went into Subic Bay, and right behind when you go into Subic Bay, Grand Island, when you come in, there's a sort of an "R and R" resort for Navy personnel at Subic. This is where I dropped them off. In Subic I got rid of the "third class citizens" and the soldiers. There again, I was over my 5,000 limit—it was actually over 6,000. So when the soldiers and "third class citizens" go off it dropped me back down to 4,000 [still on board] when I left Subic Bay. But when they got off in Subic Bay, why everybody got the DDT treatment: they got sprayed with the white powder as they come off. And then they were more or less…. I don't know, I think they probably ended up in Guam too, some place. But they were airlifted then.[25]

In the meantime the other ships left for Guam and of course they were ahead of me. They still had about 5,000 aboard. And the destroyer escort. We saw them in Guam and they wanted to know how long we could keep up that 21 knots. Well, we could go for 30 days like that. He said, "Well, another day and you guys would've had to tow me into Guam!" He didn't have that much fuel. What he was doing … the three of us were sailing at 21 knots keeping in convoy, and he had to go more or less about 12 miles ahead of us. Because once he blew [boiler] tubes, why, he had to slow down blowing tubes; he had to do this twice a day. So he'd disappear over the horizon twice a day, once during the daylight hours, and once at night. He stayed with us at 21 knots, but every time he had to blow tubes he'd have to speed up to get at least eight or 10 miles ahead of us. Then he'd drop back down again while blowing tubes.

Going into Guam, as I say, we were the last ones going into Guam. All the excretions—shall we say manure that they had on board ship—they shoveled it off first. And that was all put in a truck and put out in a special dump where they could keep it contained and get it disinfected. In the hatches all the liquid—water that they didn't use, and all the piss—well, I had anywhere from, depending on the configuration of the hatch—you take number two and number six [hatches], they were very sharp. Well, I had six feet of water in those: piss and water. In the flatter hatches—three, four, and number five—well, I had three feet of water. Now to pump that out they couldn't do it because of the solids that blocked up the pipe. So we had to get a barge alongside that had one of these deep-well pumps. They put the pump down in the hatch and pumped all this stuff out into the barge. Now when the barge got full, they took it out to sea and dumped it out there in the ocean.

* * *

Author's note: The *Pioneer Contender* set sail from Guam after nine days, finally homeward bound, on May 16, 1975. She stopped briefly at Pearl Harbor, Hawaii, on May 23, departing the same day on the final leg of the voyage for Oakland, California. Thus ended her 58th voyage with United States Lines, and the 19th voyage under Military Sealift Command control, after some 128 days. Well before the return of *Pioneer Contender* and her crew to the United States, their extraordinary accomplishments in support of final evacuations out of South Vietnam had received not only page-one publicity in various publications, but recognition in the U.S. House of Representatives as remarks by the Honorable Leonor K. Sullivan of the Merchant Marine and Fisheries Committee, along with documentation describing the role of *Pioneer Contender* and other ships of the United States Lines fleet in refugee evacuations, was entered into the *Congressional Record* for April 17, 1975.[26]

In her remarks Sullivan emphasized the need for maintaining a "U.S.-flag [shipping] capability" and opined: "No greater support could ever eventuate for our position than that which has just occurred off the coasts of South Vietnam so far away from the United States." The documentation accompanying her remarks, a U.S. Lines press release, highlighted the *Pioneer Contender*'s unprecedented role in support of evacuations out of Cam Ranh Bay, to wit:

> When it became apparent that Cam Ranh Bay would fall the *Pioneer Contender* was ordered to resume rescue operations. An incredible mass of humanity crowded onto the ship—built to carry cargo, not passengers—filling every inch of hold and deck space. The official count for the number of refugees from Cam Ranh Bay to Phu Quoc Island ... was 16,600.
>
> A spokesman for the Military Sealift Command said that this was the largest number of refugees ever carried on a ship of any kind. The previous high occurred during the Korean War when a ship [*Meredith Victory*] carried 14,000 refugees.[27]

19

Mayaguez
The Last Battle

"They turned their guns on me screaming 'Out! Out!'"
—Frank Conway, FOWT, SS *Mayaguez*

What some now call the last battle of the Vietnam War began, not at some crucial point in the Central Highlands of Vietnam, or as North Vietnamese tanks rumbled towards the gates of Saigon in the south, but nearly two weeks after Saigon was captured by the PAVN, as Cambodian gunboats approached an American containership—the *Mayaguez*—some 60 miles off the Cambodian coast, fired machine gun and RPG warning shots across its bow, forcing it to stop, then boarded and took control of it.[1]

"We are about to be boarded by hostile gunboats," the ship's captain, Charles T. Miller, was able to radio out before all communications were cut with the outside world.[2]

The Cambodians, speaking little English and appearing quite young to the crew of *Mayaguez*, were nonetheless well-armed and meant business. What few words of English they spoke, along with body language, were nonetheless clearly understood.

"They turned their guns on me screaming 'Get out! Get Out!' I was afraid to move," Frank Conway, a fireman-watertender on *Mayaguez*, would later recall. "I wanted to turn off the ship's [boiler] fire when we left the ship [but] there was no communication."[3]

Despite the initial impression and uncertainty of the situation, the crew of *Mayaguez* would come to speak of the kindness and good treatment provided by their captors, even if the meals—sometimes given to them from the Cambodians' own meager rations—largely consisted of fish heads and rice. When their cigarettes ran out, the Cambodians provided the *Mayaguez* crew with a homegrown alternative. As one account would later describe it: "The Cambodians gave them about a pound of their tobacco which was farmed from trees. The crew rolled it in some newspaper and found it a good, but strong, substitute."[4]

Journalist Sydney H. Schanberg, who would later shock the world with his accounts of the Khmer Rouge "killing fields," reported afterwards that "Captain Miller and his men all said they were never abused by their Cambodian captors. There were even accounts of kind treatment—of Cambodian soldiers feeding them first and eating what the Americans left, of the soldiers giving the seamen the mattresses off their beds."[5]

252

Fully armed U.S. Marines with gas masks move quickly on May 15, 1975, to retake SS *Mayaguez* **from Cambodian Khmer Rouge and rescue its captive Merchant Marine crew. The ship was found to be empty.**

The SS *Mayaguez*, a C-2 type merchant ship built during World War II, had been converted into a containership—one of the first—by Grace Line in the early 1960s, and then, as part of Sea-Land's growing containership fleet, completed a number of voyages to Vietnam during the war.[6] Its departure from Hong Kong on May 7, 1975, came only a week after the frantic final departure of American evacuation helicopters and merchant ships out of Saigon as the People's Army of Vietnam (PAVN) were actually entering the city. Anticipating the defeat of South Vietnam, *Mayaguez* was one of the American ships that had been directed to Saigon—in its case to load several containers with cargo removed from the American Embassy to prevent its capture, destruction, or use.[7]

Mayaguez had returned after the final evacuations to one of Sea-Land's regular commercial routes between Hong Kong, Sattahip, Thailand, and Singapore. It departed Hong Kong with 267 containers on board—107 of them containing general cargo, 90 others described as military/government in nature, and an additional 70 that were empty.[8]

It was while en route five days later, an estimated 60 miles off the coast of Cambodia and some six miles from Poulo Wai Island in what Captain Miller would later describe as a regularly used commercial navigation route, that the ship was stopped by Cambodian gunboats. The Cambodians would claim that the ship was moving through Cambodian not international waters, was carrying military supplies, and was a "spy ship" on a mission for the CIA.[9]

Bill Bellinger, a messman on *Mayaguez*, began keeping a log of events following the ship's capture by the Cambodian Khmer Rouge:

"Hard telling at this stage," Bellinger noted, "what is going to happen. Sparks [radio operator Wilbert N. Bock] got off a message that he was sure was received as they were boarding. So I imagine someone is now issuing a strong protest."[10]

The uncertainty as to whether word had gotten out about the ship's capture would lessen somewhat early on Tuesday, May 8, as the first search aircraft began appearing overnight and continued from that point on. "Until the planes appeared overhead," Bellinger would later recall, "we weren't sure they even knew where we were."[11]

At 6:00 that morning, with the crew of *Mayaguez* still on the ship, Bill Bellinger would write in his log that there hadn't been "any pushing around or rough treatment of any kind so far. They seem satisfied to let us go about our normal routine."

But they would not be long for their location near Poulo Wai Island where they had been stopped and boarded, nor for the *Mayaguez* itself. A few hours later Bellinger would note in his log:

"We are underway with one of the gunboats leading us down the coast to a port undisclosed. Voice of America broadcast states that President Ford had demanded the release of this ship and crew or gave the consequences. I haven't noticed any worried looks on the faces of any of our captors, however."[12]

At 4:30 that afternoon Bellinger experienced a setback of sorts, and wrote of the crew's separation from the ship: "Well they have taken my glasses and pen but I still

A Cambodian Khmer Rouge gunboat alongside *Mayaguez* as photographed by one of the ship's crew who was about to become captive of the Cambodians for three days (Military Sealift Command).

have a couple of pencil stubs. They have taken us off the ship and we are in two groups in small fishing boats heading to one of the islands."

This was Koh Tang Island, some 30 miles closer to the mainland, and where *Mayaguez* would remain until its recapture. But its crew remained there for only a short time. As Bellinger would note in his log at 5:15 late that afternoon: "They have now transferred us onto the larger boat and we are all together again. They are keeping us on the open deck and the sun is fierce. There are no docks on the island here and they are not putting us ashore and seem undecided just what to do with us. We are all scared as men can get now. At least I am and I don't think I am any less a man than anyone else."[13]

The sun's heat would soon be the least of their worries in the face of what was to come on May 14, the next and third day of their captivity at the hands of the Khmer Rouge.

"We are underway again," Bellinger noted in his log, "and they have given indication they are going to return us to the ship. U.S. jets and prop driven aircraft overhead all night. They have some heavier weapons on the island and they have been firing on the planes all night. Oh shit we are veering off and passing the ship. God knows where we are going now. They have two of their gunboats out ahead of us, leading us."[14]

The crew of *Mayaguez* was largely unaware what was going on elsewhere, both on the diplomatic front, as well as in action, which at that point was limited to engagement of American aircraft with Cambodian gunboats and in bombing raids conducted against the Cambodian mainland in an attempt to influence negotiations that were underway and release of *Mayaguez* and its crew. This would not end well for the gunboats, three of which were reportedly sunk, four others disabled in the water, leaving but one to limp back to the Cambodian port of Kampong Som (Sihanoukville).[15]

Some aircraft would soon turn their attention to the one gunboat on which the crew of *Mayaguez* were being held, and which had turned towards the mainland.

As journalist Sydney Schanberg was to report some days later, "the whole crew [had been] put on one of the fishing boats, which set off for Sihanoukville. This was the hair-raising journey during which they were harassed by American airplanes."[16]

That four-hour journey, something hair-raising and then some, was described in the following way by Bill Bellinger in his log:

> The jets have returned to us now and are firing bursts across our bow. Bob Philips and I are just about the only ones not stretched out flat on the deck.[17] He is an ex-Marine and both of us have been in close air ground support situations before. We know they are not trying to hit but to force us to turn back to the ship. Bob and I are just sitting here watching them come on.
>
> Those jet jockeys are really good. They are laying heavy caliber rounds and rockets to within 20 yards of our bow and starboard side. Most of the crew is completely terror stricken now. One man is cryin. Holy Mother of God! They did attack the boat about ten minutes ago. They came straight in and dumped gas only. I feel like I am on fire and my eyes are watering so bad I can hardly see. We are all terror stricken and crying now.[18]

Captain Miller would say later:

> If we were strafed or bombed once, we were bombed a hundred times by our jets. Ten foot forward of our bow light. Rockets and machine gun fire. When they saw that was not going

to work, two jets overflew the boat from bow to stern approximately 70 feet above us and they tear-gassed us.[19]

The first gassing wasn't too bad. I don't blame the pilots. They were only trying to keep us out of Sihanoukville. They wanted us returned [to *Mayaguez*]. After a half hour passed and we were still going, we were gassed a second time. Everybody on the boat vomited. Skin was burning; a couple of men were struck by shrapnel.

The third engineer, who had a bad heart, passed out for about 20 minutes. We thought he was dead. We didn't actually realize the condition he was in ... because we were all pretty sick ourselves.

After we got in close to Sihanoukville the jets left us alone and they put the reconaissance plane on top of us again.

On Wednesday, May 14, while the crew of *Mayaguez* was being moved to Sihanoukville—and strafed, rocketed, and gassed in the process—planning for an operation to recapture the *Mayaguez* where it was anchored out at Koh Tang Island was underway. Those who planned the operation, which would involve assault and boarding by Marines, were not aware at that point of the actual location of the ship's crew, but hoped they were aboard the ship. In addition to Marines, the operation would involve Navy and Air Force personnel as well as a volunteer team of merchant seamen who would do what they could to get the ship reactivated and underway once recaptured.[20]

The Merchant Marine would come from USNS *Greenville Victory* under the

Chief Officer Clinton J. Harriman, left, and 2nd Assistant Engineer Michael A. Saltwick, of USNS *Greenville Victory*, discuss the planned assault to retake *Mayaguez* with Commander Robert A. Peterson aboard USS *Holt*.

command of Captain Raymond Iacobacci, one of the "nucleus" ships of the Military Sealift Command fleet crewed by merchant seamen. Not too long before, *Greenville Victory* had been involved in refugee evacuations out of South Vietnam as Saigon was on the verge of being captured by the People's Army of Vietnam (PAVN).[21]

The seamen from *Greenville Victory*, its Chief Officer Clinton J. Harriman, Assistant Engineer Karl P. Lonsdale, and four additional unlicensed seamen—Saltnick, Griffin, Rodriguez, and Rivera—were flown to Utapao Air Base in Thailand where they joined 20 Marines—part of a larger force of 200 that was to assault Koh Tang Island itself—who would retake the *Mayaguez*, free its crew, if there, and then move the ship away.[22]

Unfortunately and tragically, as events were soon to reveal, there would be a crucial delay in communications—attributed to a variety of reasons—between those who planned the operation, the Marine assault force itself, those involved in negotiations with the Cambodians, and the Cambodians holding the crew of *Mayaguez*. So the assault would go forward, and additional casualties—including those with names among the last to be sand-blasted later onto the Vietnam Veterans Memorial "wall" in Washington, D.C.—would be added to the long list of American casualties compiled for more than a quarter century.[23]

After the four-hour hair-raising and gut-wrenching ordeal of the crew being transferred by fishing boat as American planes unsuccessfully attempted to force it to reverse course to Koh Tang Island, the crew of *Mayaguez* arrived with their captors at Sihanoukville. They were then transferred again to Rong Samlen, another island farther to the west.[24]

On Thursday, May 15, 1975, all would finally come to a head. But while there would be success, it would not turn out quite as expected or hoped.

Captain Miller later recounted: "It was finally agreed they would take the crew back to the ship, get power back on the radio telephone and I would call Bangkok [American embassy] and order overflights and bombing of Sihanoukville, Koh Tang, Pulao Wai be halted."

"I promised them faithfully that I could do this to get our release. Around 7:30 we were all put in this Thai fishing boat with five Thai fishermen who had also been captured by the Cambodians."[25]

Bill Bellinger, now without pen and glasses, would nonetheless still manage to note in his personal log at noon that day that they were in the coastal port of Kampong Saom. "My eyes are still burning but I can see better again," he wrote, adding that he and his fellow captives were "still cursing those jet jockies," whose skill they couldn't help but admire as they came "straight in from bow to stern and blanketed the boat [with tear gas]."[26]

Bellinger noted: "The people here are massed along the sea wall and in the shacks beyond. The air of hostility and hatred is thick enough to cut with a knife. Even their women are armed. The jets have been circling high and are now coming in on low passes and we have been ordered out of the port. There are two Red Chinese cargo ships at the dock."

At about 5:00 that afternoon Bellinger noted again:

We are now in an abandoned fishing village on one of the islands. They seem to have taken it over as an operations base for the gunboats. They have at least a dozen and maybe more. They have a man here that speaks English. Maybe now we can find out what they want and what they intend to do with us. Beginning to come dusk now and I need the sunlight to write without my glasses.[27]

Bellinger and the entire 39-man crew of *Mayaguez* would not have to wait much longer to finally get answers to the questions as to their fate at the hands of the Khmer Rouge. Unbeknownst to them events involving the Marine assault force on Koh Tang Island would be playing out that day as well, and with surprisingly costly results.[28]

The chain of events involving the crew of *Mayaguez* that day at least would begin to move in quick order, in some ways surprisingly for them, and ending as they had been hoping, and perhaps some praying fervently, for going on three full days.

One contemporaneous account would describe it this way:

> The crew was herded back aboard the fishing vessel, guarded by the Cambodian soldiers. They cast off and headed off and headed out to sea escorted by one of the gunboats. About a mile out, the gunboat pulled alongside and the guards jumped from the fishing vessel to the gunboat. With the real fear that the Cambodians might still turn on them and shoot, the crew watched closely as the gunboat pulled out of sight. All were now free, both the 29-man crew of the Mayaguez and the Thai fishermen who had spent five months in captivity.[29]
>
> The boat headed out toward the Mayaguez which was still several hours away. The happy Thais cooked a delicious fish breakfast for everyone. For the first time in three days the crew ate heartily and happily.

At 6:00 early on that evening Bill Bellinger, writing once again from the *Mayaguez*, described his return from captivity, first in the Thai fishing boat to the destroyer *Miller*, as follows: "I am now back aboard the Mayaguez, safe, unharmed and emotionally drained. We were released this morning and as we got within sight of the ship, a destroyer [*Wilson*] moved out to meet us. They kept their guns trained on us until we were positively identified. Then they swung them off and a loudspeaker boomed out the words 'Crew of the Mayaguez welcome aboard.' And I almost blubbered like a baby."[30]

Captain Miller's recollection of the arrival at the destroyer *Wilson* was later reported by Sydney Schanberg from Singapore:"Finally, as they were approaching the destroyer Wilson ... about 10:30, Captain Miller said, 'I hollered out and asked permission to come alongside; the skipper used his Bull horn, asked if we were the [*Mayaguez*] crew and they all shouted with joy.'"[31]

Any joy Captain Miller might have felt upon his and his crew's release by the Cambodians, and their return to *Mayaguez*, would be tempered by reports of the Marine assault on Koh Tang Island, which began just before their release but which they would only begin to learn about afterwards. Meeting surprisingly fierce resistance by the well-armed Khmer Rouge fighters there, it had not gone well. Tragically, the cost—what might have been avoided had word of diplomatic negotiations come sooner—would be high, both in action on the ground and due to an accidents involving a helicopter intended to support but never reaching the Koh Tang Island assault.[32]

Many would lament the lag time involved in getting word to the Marine assault force about to suffer casualties—needlessly, if only communications had moved more quickly to inform them that the *Mayaguez* crew had already been released a few hours before—during its time on Tang Island. The overall number of American military personnel killed in the incident, generally put at 41—two more than the number of Merchant Marine crewmen of *Mayaguez*— would include 23 killed in the crash of a helicopter transporting them to U-Tapao Airport in Thailand, where they were to link up with the Marine force that would be sent into Koh Tang.[33]

However, more recent research into the *Mayaguez* Incident suggests—with hard evidence—that the communication *had* gone through to Washington, D.C., in advance of the assault, that it *could* have been called off shortly before it was set into motion using a number of helicopters tasked to transport some 200 Marines, most of whom had not seen combat before. This research suggests further that for (geo) political reasons, and having to do with showing the world that, and despite its recent defeat in Vietnam, the United States was still powerful and could and would still "kick ass" if called upon to do so.[34]

As Senator Barry Goldwater would express it at the time: "It was wonderful, it shows we've still got balls in this country."[35]

There was celebration in the White House in Washington, D.C., when word was received that *Mayaguez* had been recaptured, with no resistance aboard the ship, and where its crew had not been found. Peter Maguire describes reaction in the Ford administration to news of the ship's recapture and release of its crew: "Minutes before the first helicopters landed [at Soh Tang Island].... 'The President and his chief of staff exchanged whoops of joy,' wrote *Newsweek* at the time, 'Henry Kissinger beaming ear to ear, the lot of them celebrating what seemed in that taut midnight to be a famous victory.'"[36]

Members of the crew of *Mayaguez* after their release by Cambodian Khmer Rouge and arrival in Singapore: (left to right). Francis Pastrano, messman; Carlos Guerrero, fireman-watertender; Raymond Friedler, QMED; Frank Conway, fireman-watertender.

But much had gone wrong with the assault to retake *Mayaguez* and free its crew, who were elsewhere. Forty-one Americans had been killed, three of whom were Marines—a machine gun team—who had actually been inadvertently left behind on Koh Tang island. They were subsequently killed there or captured and executed back on the Cambodian mainland.[37]

On May 17, soon after arriving in Singapore with *Mayaguez*, Captain Miller spoke to press reporters anxious for his comments about what he and his crew had experienced as captives of the Cambodian Khmer Rouge.

Sydney Schanberg, in attendance, would observe that "Captain Miller and his 38 crewmen looked reasonably well but some, including the captain, showed signs of sleeplessness and deep emotional strain."[38]

By then, having learned what had transpired during the assault on Koh Tang Island, intended—but mistakenly—to effect the release of the crew of *Mayaguez*, Miller appeared overwhelmed with emotion, with gratitude towards those who had fought there on their behalf.

A veteran of Merchant Marine service in the Pacific during World War II who had witnessed attacks by Japanese "kamikaze" suicide aircraft, Miller considered the strafing and gassing by American aircraft in the attempt to force the fishing boat in which he and his crew were being taken to Sihanoukville to turn back to *Mayaguez* the "worst experience" of his 42-year career as a merchant seaman. But he had nothing but praise for the pilots involved.[39]

"You have to give our pilots credit," Miller said. "They can put thread through the eye of a needle [from] a mile away. They did everything that was possible without blowing us out of the water to try to get this boat to turn around and take us back to the ship."

"Twice during his account," reporter Schanberg would observe during Miller's comments before the press, "the captain choked up, tears filing his eyes—once when he spoke of being finally picked up by the destroyer Wilson about 10:30 a.m. on Thursday and again when he spoke of meeting a wounded marine major in the ship's hospital."[40]

"I talked to the marine major," Miller said, "that took in the first chopper to Koh Tang Island [that] was shot down. He had about a quarter of his back torn off from shrapnel. I cried. People were being killed to save us." And Miller would also say of the Marine: "He took it like a soldier. 'Captain, all I wanted to see was your men released. Don't worry about me.'"

"Let me tell you one thing," Miller would tell the press in Singapore. "If it wasn't for our Air Force, Navy and our Marines, I don't think this crew would be standing before you now."[41]

At that point Captain Miller would not have known that his ship, the *Mayaguez*, played a central part in what is rightfully referred to as the "last battle of the Vietnam War." He would not have known what led up to it as options were being weighed by the Ford administration, and eventually acted upon in ways history has come to question and even condemn. And he would not have known what actually occurred in the assault on Koh Tang Island, and the circumstances that contributed to the last three names—those of Joseph Hargrove, Gary Hall, and Danny Marshall, U.S. Marines—being sand-blasted forever into the Vietnam Veterans Memorial wall.

Mayaguez would continue "plying the Gulf of Siam" (Thailand) for a few more years, as one reporter would put it in 1976, but only a year after its capture by the Khmer Rouge and the events leading up to its recapture and immediately beyond, even its master, Captain Charles T. Miller, would admit it had begun to look "worse than an old Greek tramp." In fact, and not just for its looks but especially for its long years in service, its years were numbered to about another three.[42]

The owner of *Mayaguez*, Sea-Land, would announce in February 1979 that the ship, built in 1945, and then some 34 years old—easily beyond the average lifespan for a merchant ship—was "too old to be efficient" and would be scrapped.

"It's always sad when a good hard working ship is laid to rest," one maritime reporter would observe appropriately after Sea-Land's announcement. "But it's especially sad when a ship like the *Mayaguez*, which has truly left her mark on history, is relegated to the boneyard."[43]

PART THREE

Aftermath

20

Boat People

"Hell, though, displayed our fears: fear of pirates, fear of starvation, fear of poisoning by biscuits soaked in motor oil, fear of running out of water, fear of being unable to stand up, fear of having to urinate in the red pot ... passed around from hand to hand, fear that the scabies on the baby's head was contagious, fear of never setting foot on solid ground, fear of never seeing the faces of our parents, who were sitting [on the boat] in the darkness surrounded by two hundred people."[1]
—Kim Thuy, *Ru*

"We had to just lay them on deck like sticks of wood, because they had been sitting so long they couldn't move."
—Captain Harlan Jackson, USNS *Sealift Arctic*

Hernell Edwards was standing out on the deck of the containership *President Roosevelt* on October 22, 1978, taking a break from his duties as the ship's chief steward, when he spotted a small vessel of some sort far off in the distance.[2] He detected movement—what looked like a flag being waved—and went quickly to report what he had seen to an officer on duty. Upon closer inspection the small vessel turned out to be a fishing boat loaded to the gills with people, and obviously in need of assistance.[3]

Under the command of Captain Leonidas S. Jordan, the *President Roosevelt* was en route to Singapore with a full load of containers when the "boat people" were spotted in the South China Sea. As per standard operating procedures and orders for American merchant and naval ships at that time—and in contrast to directives being followed by ships of many other countries—preparations were immediately made for approaching and then bringing the refugees on board.[4]

"We found 217 Vietnamese refugees packed into a fishing boat which was lying low in the water," Edwards recalled. "They had been adrift for 14 days. They were out of water and their food was very low."[5]

With the refugees all transferred safely over to *President Roosevelt*, the boat that had stayed afloat long enough to carry them to this point was summarily put to the torch by members of the ship's crew, thus ensuring that, its job done, the boat would not be a hazard to any other vessel moving through the area.

Chief Steward Edwards and his department personnel would now have their hands full well beyond normal as they worked to provide meals and otherwise accommodate these Vietnamese refugees for as long as they remained on board their ship. Including one full day in Singapore as they were processed and given inoculations

Among the lucky ones who were rescued, Vietnamese boat people in a typically overloaded vessel are about to be taken aboard an American merchant ship in the South China Sea.

prior to debarkation, the refugees would be on the American containership for nearly three days.[6]

These Vietnamese boat people were among the lucky ones; tens of thousands of others would perish in their own attempts to reach welcoming shores elsewhere. Other ships—at least three—had passed these particular boat people by, though one German ship had stopped to at least replenish their water at one point; but that had also been depleted apparently well before the *President Roosevelt* came to their rescue.[7]

The rescue of Vietnamese boat people at this point in 1978 was part of a new "wave" of at-sea rescues as well as a change in immigration policy that, in 1976 and 1977, had restricted Vietnamese refugee arrivals to cases involving "family reunification" only. As such they proved to be relatively slack years for such arrivals.[8] Nonetheless, following the initial massive evacuation of refugees from South Vietnam in early 1975, which, in addition to use of fixed-wing aircraft, helicopters, and ships was marked by the presence of escaping Vietnamese in small boats—the first "boat people"—rescues continued to be made by ships crewed by American merchant seamen in those and succeeding years.

Because of the immigration policy restrictions imposed at that time, however, limiting them initially to cases involving family reunification, refugees taken on board ship, then safely debarked in such places as Singapore, were then moved to temporary refugee camps before then being flown out, in most cases to countries other than the United States.

Representative of rescues made by ships crewed by American merchant seamen in the slack years for refugee arrivals in the U.S. were the following: on August 22, 1976, USNS *Hudson* rescued 47 refugees off a 50-foot-long boat in the South China Sea; on January 29, 1977, USNS *Sealift Arabian Sea* rescued 23 Vietnamese boat people in the South Indian Ocean; in summer 1977, SS *Ponce* rescued 13 Vietnamese in the South China Sea; and in May 1978, SS *American Trader* rescued 35 boat people some 400 miles southwest of Subic Bay, Philippines.

For the crews on some of these ships, as time and events would tell, these rescues of Vietnamese boat people would not be their last.

The complexion and magnitude of what would be called the "second" wave of Vietnamese boat people would become evident by mid–1978 as tensions rose between Vietnam and China, which had supported North Vietnam during the "American" War. These neighboring countries shared a history often marked by tension, warfare, and long periods of occupation—of Vietnam by China—that extended back in time for millennia. Now, within a few short years of the end of the war in which they had cooperated against the American-"puppet" regime in the south, a new geopolitical alignment marked by Chinese support of the genocidal Pol Pot regime in Cambodia and support of Vietnam by the Soviet Union had begun to cause major backlash against ethnic Chinese (Hoa), which would compel tens of thousands more to flee Vietnam overland, to China, and by boat, many to Hong Kong—if they could make it.

As historian Marilyn B. Young would later put it, "a million and a half ethnic Chinese (Hoa) became hostage to these tensions."[9]

Barry Wain, a journalist who reported frequently from Hong Kong on the growing refugee crisis in Southeast Asia, would later observe: "The human deluge hit Southeast Asia in the second half of 1978 along with a freakish series of tropical storms. Both caused havoc. Indochinese refugees, in the numbers that had been feared ... inundated countries of the region, while floodwaters swirled across much of the same territory. Behind the departure of tens of thousands of Vietnamese was an unannounced but officially sponsored program to facilitate the exit of ethnic Chinese and others considered undesirable."[10]

Two events in late 1978 and early 1979 would escalate tensions to the breaking point, and cause the exodus of boat people from Vietnam to reach unprecedented levels: the invasion of Cambodia by Vietnam on December 25, 1978, and the resultant Chinese "punitive" attack against Vietnam across their shared border on February 17, 1979.[11]

It was in this context that many more sightings and rescues of Vietnamese boat people in the South China Sea and elsewhere—what would characterize a "second wave" of boat people—would occur.

"God heard our plea, for the big ship came closer"

The USNS *Sealift Arabian Sea* had been there before—involved in a rescue of Vietnamese boat people—when it plucked 23 refugees from the South Indian Ocean back on January 29, 1977. Now, some 250 miles northeast of Singapore late on the morning of September 8, 1979, and under the command of Captain Robert Ruse, *Sealift Arabian Sea* received a distress signal from another ship. *Sealift Arabian Sea* was in position now to respond again, and did so immediately, changing to a new course and proceeding until a small boat came into view.[12] Overloaded with what turned out to be 46 Vietnamese men, women, and children—including five under the age of three—the boat, its engine disabled, was drifting and had perhaps a foot of free-board. After maneuvering around the boat, it was secured with lines to *Sealift Arabian Sea*, and, at about 7:30 in the evening, the refugees it carried were brought on board the ship using a variety of means depending on the gender, age, and ability of the boat people.

Males deemed fit and old enough to do so came up from the boat using the vertical pilot (Jacob's) ladder. Women and older children were transferred by bo'sun chair, and small children and infants were placed in large cooking kettles and hoisted aboard. Safely aboard *Sealift Arabian Sea*, all 46 of the boat people were taken to the stern of the ship where they were given oranges and bananas, led to bathing areas, and then given new clothing by members of the ship's crew.

The story of this group of Vietnamese boat people was described by one of them in a statement later presented to Captain Ruse of *Sealift Arabian Sea*.[13] Representative of the experiences of many Vietnamese refugees during this period, it appears here largely as written by its anonymous author(s):

We started our trek in search of freedom in the capitalist world at 4 p.m. on August 27, 1979. The plans were to gather the rest of our families at 8 p.m. on August 27, 1979 but we were forced to leave them behind because our boat was spotted by communist troops who opened fire on us. For fear of being imprisoned if we came back to shore, we and the other people headed for the high seas although our fuel and food supplies were very low.

After 43 hours at sea, our engine began to develop mechanical failure, and we had to head back about 30 miles into the Vietnamese waters. We stayed there for four days to repair the engine and ask for fuel and food from other boats.

At 7 p.m. on September 3, 1979 we started again on our journey going into the direction of 180 degrees, and four days later we met a Malaysian fishing boat which refused to rescue us but they did give us 70 liters of fuel and some rice, and showed us the way to get to Malaysia. After 48 hours of constant running we met with several other boats but none of them made any attempt to rescue us.

In the morning of Saturday September 8, 1979 we spotted a ship heading toward us and we left our food to signal the ship. I guessed God heard our plea, for the ship came closer and circled us three times then stopped and by 7:25 p.m. we were allowed aboard.

The crew took us to the rear of the ship and we were given oranges and bananas to eat. Then we took a bath and were given new clothes, the old ones, well we threw them away, giving back to Vietnam what belonged to Vietnam, except our hearts which dearly love the Motherland.

The ship's captain and crew took extremely good care of us and we were served meals like we never ate before in Vietnam and each meal was sufficient to feed an entire family. We were given packs of cigarettes such as 'Salem' and 'Pall Mall,' the kinds that, while back home, we could only dream of but were never able to get one, much less a pack.

We would like to express our deep gratitude to the captain and crew of the ship that rescued us and made us feel like we were born again, and to our parents whose souls protected us through the whole ordeal. We do not know when we would be able to repay them but we would like to wish the captain, the crew and all their families all the best and may God be with them always.

We do not know when we would be able to return to Vietnam, a land that saw us born and is now seeing our parents and friends suffering, but we will always carry the hope of seeing our beloved Vietnam again someday.[14]

While rescue could be performed entirely by pulling directly alongside boats, and then utilizing ladders and hoisting gear to transfer all refugees in that way, other ships launched lifeboats to approach "boat people" and then transfer the young and infirm. One good example is that of USNS *Sealift Antarctic*, en route to load oil in the Persian Gulf, which responded to a distress call received from a U.S. Navy patrol aircraft in the South China Sea in April 1980. "Upon reaching the scene about 25 minutes later," Captain John Holster would later report, "we found a fishing boat about 35 feet long, which was crammed with people." It was determined that the "boat people" were from Nha Trang and had been at sea for two weeks. Because the ship was in ballast and "riding high" it was decided to lower a lifeboat for approaching the fishing boat. Twenty-eight women and children—nine under the age of five—entered the lifeboat, which was then lifted back on board the ship. Thirty-two men and boys, after being searched for weapons on their boat, were then able to reach the deck of the ship using its Jacob's ladder. In typical fashion the refugees were well cared for, fed, given medical attention, and given clothing by members of the ship's crew, before being transferred ashore in Singapore.

"The officers and crew of the *Sealift Antarctic*," the ship's master, Captain Holster, would report, "displayed a high degree of seamanship in the rescue operation, and even higher degree of human kindness in caring for these unfortunate people once they were aboard."[15]

Various factors compelled many thousands of Vietnamese to risk their lives—and to leave family and graves of ancestors behind—as they set out into the South China Sea in small, overloaded, under-powered, and under-stocked vessels not intended for that purpose and the sea and weather conditions many would encounter.[16] There were the immediate results of a war suddenly ended, in a reunified but devastated country, with victors now imposing policies of an obviously punitive nature upon the vanquished.

While there were immediate and understandable reasons why thousands of people decided at different points to leave their homeland behind by taking to small, overcrowded unseaworthy boats for unknown destinations, a greater understanding of the situation that faced them, and beyond a purely ideological one, requires a longer view and consideration of more fundamental causes and historical context.

As one writer who has looked at the plight of Indochina refugees in depth has put it, "almost a century of colonization followed by decades of war had turned South Vietnam into an artificial zone, first a piece of France in the East, then a little America. The injection of billions of dollars of foreign aid had created an economy that was just as false. It has spawned a Western-style consumer society with all its attendant—and for Vietnam, irrelevant—gadgetry."[17]

Furthermore, and in addition to whatever internal policies had been imposed in an attempt to regain order and stability out of the economic void created by the collapse of such conditions, Barry Wain has observed: "Vietnam was never allowed to participate in the community of nations. After its humiliating defeat, the United States seemed psychologically incapable of reconciliation with its former adversary—despite language of reconciliation that had been introduced into cease-fire negotiations. Apart from maintaining its trade embargo against Hanoi [until 1994], Washington led a successful campaign to block non-communist assistance to Vietnam."[18]

The end of the Vietnam War, as a consequence of the war itself, had ushered in a prolonged period of hardship for the Vietnamese throughout the reunified country. Economic conditions caused by the war and its abrupt end, policies imposed from within on the south by the winning party in the conflict, and an embargo imposed from without (despite a promise by the United States to assist the Vietnamese) fell most heavily upon the south, driving an impulse to flee by whatever means possible. For most choosing to do so, small boats otherwise used for fishing or local transportation on internal waterways and along the coast were the only options. Thus came about what has been called the first "wave" of Vietnamese boat people to leave the country in the years between 1975 and 1977.[19]

In time other factors, such as a vicious border conflict between China and Vietnam in late 1978, contributed to a second "wave" of Vietnamese boat people, who tended in that case to be of Chinese ancestry. Ethnic Chinese in Vietnam had long dominated certain aspects of the Vietnamese economy—such as rice distribution—and as a backlash response in especially difficult economic times had come under attack by other Vietnamese. The military conflict with China, brief as it was, and fears of a Chinese "fifth column" in support of the mammoth neighbor to the north, only exacerbated this attitude and backlash.[20]

Then again, the desire for family reunification would play an ever-increasing role in compelling many to take to the sea in boats to take their chances against natural elements, as well as other humans who might pray upon them as largely defenseless and potentially holding possessions of value intended to sustain them once—and if—they landed on a friendly shore.

Hoarding supplies, and gasoline intended to fuel aging and overworked engines that, hopefully, would carry them to safe harbor elsewhere, they too set out under the cover of night and in craft that were generally and grossly overloaded, as part of this second wave of boat people that would extend into the early 1980s. Other "waves" would follow, well into a second decade beyond the end of the "American" war.[21]

Boat people who were discovered after days, even weeks, by passing ships with humanitarian inclinations, and perhaps clearance from ship owners to stop and offer assistance, were indeed the lucky ones. Many thousands of others—some estimates suggest a number as high as a quarter million—perished, after having encountered weather and sea conditions not easily imagined before setting out, or were set upon, robbed, abused, raped, and killed by pirates out of Thailand and Malaysia who left them behind dead or dying in their wakes.[22]

Diverting to rescue Vietnamese boat people presented various challenges for mariners depending on weather, sea conditions, and of course the number of refugees who would need to be boarded and then accommodated for as long as it might take until they could either be transferred to another vessel or disembarked at a port along the way. One ship that was tested in this regard was the 587-foot tanker USNS *Sealift Arctic* (Captain Harlan E. Jackson), which happened upon a drifting and heavily overloaded boat in the South China Sea while en route from the Persian Gulf to Okinawa on October 27, 1980. Spotted by Chief Mate Frank Neuman, the boat in distress turned out to be some 60 feet long and carrying 313 refugees.

The situation was, as Captain Jackson later described it, "the most pathetic thing you've ever seen."[23]

With the boat dead in the water, and in heavy seas, *Sealift Arctic* was maneuvered close enough for lines to be secured to it. Because of sea conditions it was decided that lifeboats from the tanker would not be launched for the rescue operation. Captain Jackson later reported:

> We [encountered] a little difficulty because the rope kept breaking. But we put Second Officer M. Star Wells on board and he passed up those who were too weak to get on the ladder. We had to just lay them on deck like sticks of wood because they had been sitting so long they couldn't move.[24]
>
> We had them lying on deck from my office right on down the passageways. The crew [also] took them into their rooms just so they'd have a place out of the rain or sun. When the children were first brought aboard, they were dazed, weak, and frightened because they did not know what was happening. But when they realized they were safe, they smiled and laughed.

Temporary replacement clothing was fashioned by the ship's crew from mattress covers and pillowcases. "You just cut a hole in the top and sides for them," Captain Jackson explained.

Second Mate Wells was in charge of medical treatment for the refugees, and later described how many of the refugees appeared upon initial examination after their rescue: "Whenever we removed their clothes their skin just peeled off from [exposure to] the oil, urine, and sea water they had to sit in."

With medical supplies and food running low, U.S. Navy helicopters were sent out to resupply the *Sealift Arctic*. Chief Cook George B. Carosine and his galley crew were involved for three days providing meals for the refugees until they were finally disembarked in Okinawa. And seamen did what they could otherwise to assist the refugees in their temporary home aboard the ship. Captain Jackson recalled that members of the crew "held babies in their arms, cooing to them until they fell asleep. They shared their quarters with them. They wrapped them in bed sheets and table cloths after carefully cleaning their wounds."[25]

These 313 Vietnamese boat people were also among the lucky ones for having an American merchant ship not only spot them but immediately go to their rescue when, as Assistant Secretary of Commerce for Maritime Affairs Samuel B. Nemirow later noted in commendation of the crew of *Sealift Arctic*, it was "apparent that several ships in the vicinity were reluctant to pick up the refugees due to the large number of people involved."[26]

It seems too that many ships simply had orders not to divert and stop for boat people regardless of the number of people who might have been on board their vessels.

Some American ships, especially those making the regular run between Indonesia, Singapore, and Japan that required transit through the South China Sea, made multiple rescues, sometimes within days of each other, on the same day, or over the course of years. The LNG *Aires*, a liquid natural gas carrier built two years after the war in Vietnam ended, is a good example.[27] It seems the ship, which actually had been involved in a sea rescue—of 21 seamen from a lifeboat launched from a sinking ship of Panamanian registry—on her maiden voyage to Osaka, Japan in 1977, was destined for this type of thing right from the start. Then, in late 1980 while underway in the South China Sea between Tobata, Japan and Arun, Indonesia, LNG *Aires* rescued 21 Vietnamese boat people, the first of three such rescues, after their distress signal was spotted by a vigilant seaman aboard the ship.[28]

The rescue operation, the first of the three rescues by LNG *Aires* of Vietnamese boat people over the years, was later described by Ordinary Seaman David Hecht for what they all would be: well-coordinated, interdepartmental efforts. "While the deck department was lowering the gangway and preparing to tie the fishing boat to the ship," he would write, "the engine department was slowing engines down. As this was going on, Chief Steward Joseph Kundrat was busy setting up an emergency station on deck while Chief Cook George Taylor, Jr. was preparing sandwiches for the travel weary guests."[29]

"Things were just returning to normal," Hecht continued, "when AB Bob Smith notified the bridge that Nguyen Thi Bich Phung was beginning labor. She was immediately taken up to the ship's hospital where preparations were made to deliver the first child born on an SIU [contracted] LNG carrier." The child—a healthy baby girl—was delivered by the ship's chief mate, William Gatchel, and Cargo Engineer Skip Doty, who were assisted by Second Mate Jon Anderson.

While Gatchel later remarked that "the feeling was indescribable," Doty said that he had "been involved in many deliveries on the *Aires*, but none quite like this one."[30]

The crew of LNG *Aires* was involved in its second rescue of Vietnamese boat people when, at about 3:00 on the afternoon of June 24, 1982, and again en route to Arun, Indonesia, 40 refugees were rescued in the South China Sea. With winds estimated at 35 knots and seas between 12 and 15 feet, conditions for a sea rescue were far from optimum. According to Captain David Spence, the ship's master: "The transfer of refugees was difficult and very hazardous. The transfer of the smallest children was done with danger to Amin Rajab, AB, and Randy Doty, Cargo Engineer. These two seamen hung onto the bottom gangway platform and pulled four small children up onto the gangway."[31]

These refugees had been at sea in their small boat for seven days, and were without food and water at the time of their rescue by LNG *Aires*. They were not in good shape when they were brought onto the ship's deck. Able Seaman Bill Mullins later reported that "it seemed like they were half dead. Some could not even walk." And one woman was described as unconscious and running a dangerously high fever. Nonetheless, and with Chief Mate Bill Gatchel once again in charge of the ship's medical team, all of the refugees were well on their way to recovery by the time they were put ashore in Singapore.

In a letter sent to the Seafarers Union soon after the rescue, Mullins said in a familiar refrain that it had "truly [been] a team effort all around. The crew worked into the night treating the sick, bathing the children, and feeding the babies."[32]

"It was really gratifying," Captain Spence later remarked, "to see all of the crew pitch in on various jobs of arranging for places to put the refugees, donating clothing, and, of course, the first aid teams working on those that needed immediate aid. I am proud of these people."[33]

A third rescue of Vietnamese boat people was made by *Aires* years later, on the morning of July 2, 1989, more than 14 years following the end of the Vietnam War. This time a total of 133 men, women, and children were transferred from what was described as a two-masted junk. That number was more than twice the number rescued by *Aires* on two previous occasions. Once again under the command of Captain Daniel Spence and en route from Arun, Indonesia with another load of liquid natural gas destined for Japan, *Aires* was maneuvered alongside the engineless junk so that the ship's starboard side gangway could be utilized for the rescue. These refugees had been on their badly overcrowded vessel for 10 days, had very little food, and but five gallons of water remaining when they were rescued by the crew of LNG *Aires*.[34] Also among the lucky ones, the refugees were well cared for—given medical attention, fed, provided with access to showers and clothes washing machines, and given clothing by members of the ship's crew—before being put ashore in Japan to await processing by representatives of the United Nations.

With that, and in three separate incidents, LNG *Aires* had rescued a total of 194 boat people, including these 133, over the course of more than 14 years after the end of the Vietnam War.

Thiem Vuong had served as an officer with the ARVN—the South Vietnamese Army—and soon after the war ended was seized and imprisoned for four years until released and then placed under house arrest.[35] Life was hard for Vuong and his family, and he decided at one point that he, his wife Mai Tran, and their three young children would attempt to flee Vietnam under the cover of darkness in a small boat. "If we stayed in Vietnam, we'd die separately," Vuong would later recall. "So I made a decision. If we died [on the boat, at least] we'd die together."[36]

The Vuong family joined 57 others, and, on June 19, 1980, they boarded a 35-foot fishing boat, the *Thang Loi* ("Victory"), and headed out into the South China Sea.

Hoping to attract the attention of a passing ship, some of the group stayed awake all night burning torches made from clothing. Many ships passed them by, either because the *Thang Loi* had not been spotted or because strict orders from ship owners and operators had been issued not to stop or divert to approach any small boat they did happen to spot.[37]

In 10 days conditions on a small, dangerously overcrowded, poorly equipped and under supplied boat subject to threatening sea and weather conditions can become intolerable. But the Vuong family and the others on that boat had little choice but to tolerate as best they could the previously unimaginable situation they were in.

Then, at sunrise on June 29, 1980, a ship came into view and, instead of turning away and disappearing over the horizon as others had, it kept coming closer and closer until it began to dawn on the boat people that help was about to arrive. One of the Vuong children would recall many years later: "My mom was crying and laughing at the same time. She said, 'We're going to live.'"[38]

The ship turned out to be the 935-foot tanker LNG *Virgo* (Captain Hartmann Schonn), another one of the eight Energy Transportation fleet that ran regularly through the area. The *Thang Loi* had been spotted by a seaman on morning watch, Don Walsh, and there was no question but that they would divert, approach, and do whatever the situation required.

After pulling alongside the *Thang Loi*, two seamen from the ship's engine department—Ken Nelson and Dan Hansen—were lowered down to take a look at the situation and to evaluate the condition of the boat. They soon radioed back to the *Virgo*: "This ship is unseaworthy—we got to take them aboard." But there was more to it than that. As Hansen later put it, "You'd have to be inhuman to look at all those faces and just move on."[39]

With that, the boat people, ably assisted by the seamen, made their way onto the big ship, while the boat that had carried them so far and, for all intents and purposes, close to the brink of death for many, was holed and set adrift, soon to sink purposely below the waves so as not to be a hazard to navigation for any other passing vessels.

All 62 Vietnamese who had gone aboard the *Thang Loi* in Vietnam some 10 days earlier had survived their ordeal and would, indeed, live. After climbing or being hoisted on board LNG *Virgo*, reflecting an act that would be repeated on other ships, some of the grateful boat people knelt down and kissed the ship's deck.

LNG *Virgo* was headed "outbound" and was able to arrange for a rendezvous by radio with another American ship—the USNS *Antarctic*—in the area and bound for Singapore. The Vuong family and the other boat people rescued by LNG *Virgo* that day were later transferred to *Sealift Antarctic*, one of the civilian-crewed ships of Military Sealift Command (MSC) that was operating in the area.[40] They were taken to Singapore, and would spend several months in refugee camps there and in Indonesia before going to the United States, where they would eventually settle in San Jose, California.[41]

As the crew of LNG *Virgo* waved good-bye to the boat people they had rescued that day in 1980 none could have imagined then that some of them—members of the Vuong family and some of the crewmembers from LNG *Virgo*—would actually meet again many years later.

How many Vietnamese boat people were rescued by ships crewed by American merchant seamen would be difficult to say for certain, but it must be a figure well into the thousands. The number was easily approaching 2,000 or more by 1982, based solely on articles and brief reports printed in maritime labor and related publications during that period.[42] And as many more such rescues certainly did take place throughout the 1980s and even into the early 1990s—by which time conditions and policies in Vietnam had reduced the impulse to take to the seas in small boats—the actual total number of rescues must have been well beyond those that came to light in sources mentioned here.[43]

By the 1990s, in fact, many of the "boat people" who had been among those fortunate enough to have survived their perilous journeys—often due to the sharp lookouts on American merchant ships—were actually beginning to make their way back, at least for visits, to their "beloved motherland" of Vietnam.

Sometimes soon or long after having been involved in rescues of Vietnamese at sea, word would come to some seamen of the importance of their actions on the lives of those who had been rescued. Eventually, some of those who had been "boat people" would write and publish their own accounts of their experiences, and therein would often be found words of gratitude for those who had not only rescued them, but quite possibly saved their lives.

Each rescue required not only the skills of trained and experienced seamen, but the compassionate hearts to change course, put commercial priorities aside for the moment, and even go above and beyond at some personal risk at times to save the lives of others who were obviously not far from death's door. This reality and the meaning of such humanitarian acts when others had passed them by were not lost on many of the rescued refugees who had been the beneficiaries of such life-saving acts.

Glen Hutton, an able seaman on the SS *Beaver State* who had spotted a small boat filled with Vietnamese refugees in the South China Sea in June 1981, did hear directly nearly a year later from one of the 34 refugees who been aboard that overloaded boat. His ship was making its way from Indonesia to Japan when Hutton saw the boat in distress. Soon after, the boat people were brought aboard his ship, cared for, fed, and clothed, before being put ashore in Singapore. *Beaver State* then continued on its way. Hutton eventually returned to the United States and the following year received a letter, postmarked from Wichita Falls, Texas, from one Tam Thanh Luong.

It seems that Luong, a young man who had been rescued along with his family—his pregnant wife, three children, a brother, and a nephew—by *Beaver State* that day in June 1981, had made his way to the United States after having spent some five months in a refugee camp in Singapore, and then another five months in another camp in Indonesia before being processed out and allowed to emigrate to the United States. In his letter, which contained a photograph of Luong and his family—now including a new baby boy—Luong said that his children had "to grow up fast" in the refugee camps and were glad to be in the United States, along with most of the refugees that had been rescued by *Beaver State*.[44]

"Are you surprised, Mr. Glen Hutton?" Luong had begun his letter. "I am Tan Thanh Luong, one of the 34 Vietnamese people rescued by your ship. We still remember that you are the one to first discover our boat. We never forget your favor."

"It was like a beautiful June day in New York," recalled Able Seaman Howard Bethell of a rescue of Vietnamese boat people that took place in the South China Sea on Sunday, May 17, 1981, as the SS *President Jackson* (American President Lines) steamed from Singapore to Keelung, Taiwan.[45] Under the command of Captain Scott Robeson and with a crew of 45 plus an additional 12 paying passengers on board, the former Navy troop transport—now a commercial break-bulk and containership—had just completed the change of the morning watch when a small boat was spotted in the distance. The *Jackson* was slowed and maneuvered so that a rescue using one of the ship's lifeboats could be effected. The following entries were later made in the ship's log:

Boat crew[:] Capt. Scott Robeson, David Larsen, AB, Micky Crowley, Bill Hedrick, AB, Chuck Hartwig, AB, Midshipman Randle Brown, King's Point 1/C Engine Cadet, Chief Eng[ineer] John Sharf, 1/Asst Engineer Mark Embrey

Sunday, May 17, 1981 at 0800 sighted boat with people moving flags Boat apparently not in distress [and] under own power. Called Master.

0847	Vessel dead in water.
0855	Boat made fast + given food and water. Crew passed down cig[arettes] and clothing. Master contacted Navy + Singapore.
1200	Position L[atitude] 6°41' N Lo[ngitude] 108°13' E
	Man overboard from boat [and] swimming toward vessel.
1242	[41] Boat people aboard.[46]

With all refugees on board and being tended to, the *President Jackson* continued on her way until the next morning when a distress signal from another boat was sighted. The following entries were subsequently made in the ship's logbook:

1035	Sighted orange distress signal on port bow.
	Position La[titude] 12° N Lo[ngitude] 111° 55' E
1126	[28] Boat people aboard. Chief Engineer + First Assistant [Engineer] chopped hole in boat with fire axe. Will rendezvous with Pres[ident] Wilson, Capt. Norman Johnson.

May 19. 1227 Stopped vessel to disembark boat people to [President Wilson]
1548 Boat secured + [resumed] full ahead.

Mr. Gerald Carbiener, Purser + Mrs. Richard Marshall RN of Santa Cruz, California [had] attended to sick boat people.

Deck Gang held a tarpaulin muster [and] collected	$250.00
Carpenter, Homer Mershon gave $100.00 Stewards Dept. $150.00	
Black Gang	140.00
Total	540.00

After arranging for the transfer of all 69 refugees to her southbound sister ship *President Wilson*, which subsequently delivered them at Singapore, the *President Jackson* continued on to Keelung, Taiwan. They were then homeward bound across the Pacific to Tacoma, Washington, arriving during the first week of June 1981. In an interview with the *Seattle-Post Intelligencer* afterwards, Able Seaman Howard Bethell described the rescue of Vietnamese boat people by the crew of the *President Jackson*. Expressing some anger that many ships had passed the boat people without stopping, he reported that "one Japanese ship had stopped and gave them some water and soda pop and flares." And then, he said, "they kept right on going."[47]

Howard Bethell, a merchant seaman since the late 1930s who had had two ships torpedoed out from under him during World War II, planned to "swallow the anchor" and retire in 1982. While preparing to come out on deck that year on what would have been his last ship before his retirement—APL's *President Wilson*—he returned to his quarters not feeling well. He was found dead in his bunk soon afterwards, victim of a fatal heart attack at the age of 67. Bethell was buried at sea as he might have expected.[48]

As many—no doubt most—of those who survived the experience of leaving Vietnam in a small boat would later attest, time could not diminish the significance, the impact, or the trauma of that experience. Having come so close to death as the bare necessities of life dwindled, and ran out, and as the typically well-worn small craft upon which they had pinned their hopes set out into the unpredictable South China Sea, only to have it lose power at some point, they faced the ever-threatening prospect of being swallowed up by the dark waves.

As Lauren Vuong, a boat person at the age of seven, would later recall, "death was certainly imminent" before the big ship, LNG *Virgo*, came along to rescue those who were so close to death's door.[49]

The memory of it, regardless of time involved, would remain with boat people for the rest of their lives. It is understandable, too, that having been rescued so close to death by a passing ship crewed by American merchant seamen, that the gratitude they felt for having been rescued, for the care received, and for the delivery once again to *terra firma* where a life could be claimed again might last for a lifetime. As another former boat person would express it many years later, "Every time I have a good meal, I think of them."[50]

For some, that memory and gratitude would turn into a need to find their rescuers at a later stage in their life, to express that gratitude—and the significance of what had been done for them—to those whose own fates had brought them together on a day that would long have meaning for them as well. Letters would be written—sometimes anonymously, sometimes not—and sent or otherwise delivered to a ship captain or other representative of a ship's crew that had been involved in a rescue. Still others, grown up to adulthood, would need in time to express their gratitude, if only they could find a way, to reconnect—even decades after the fact—in person, to a seaman who had been involved in saving their lives, in making as they would come to understand it if they did not fully in their youth, everything that was to become possible.

Lauren Vuong, who at the impressionable age of seven had been rescued off a 35-foot fishing boat in the South China Sea along with four other members of her family and 57 other boat people after 10 days in 1980, is a very good case in point.

After spending months in refugee camps in Singapore and Malaysia, Lauren, her parents, and her two siblings would finally settle in San Jose, California. There, where she would become known as Lauren, she would excel in school, and eventually earn a degree in the law.[51]

But Lauren Vuong, understanding the significance of what her rescuers at sea had done—had given to her and her family while other ships passed them by—developed in time a great desire to find some of those seamen who had saved her life that day in 1980 in the South China Sea. They had, after all, made everything else that was to come possible for her and her family. So, in time, Lauren began a search for her rescuers. After nearly 10 years of internet searching, contacting maritime labor and government organizations, Lauren finally did make contact that would lead to an emotional and tearful reunion.[52]

That reunion would come in 2017, some 37 years after waving good-bye to the LNG *Virgo*, by which time that little girl had become a 44-year-old woman. Traveling cross-country with her mother, Lauren Vuong made her way to the State University of New York Maritime College at Fort Schuyler in the Bronx for an industry conference at which she knew that some of the former crew of LNG *Virgo* would be in attendance—and anticipating as well the reunion with the boat people they had rescued.

Ken Nelson and Dan Hanson, the ones who had first been lowered down from LNG *Virgo* to get a good close look at the boat people aboard the *Thang Loi*, were there waiting for them at the conference. The greetings and outpouring of emotion would take a while, but they would eventually have a chance to share their recollections with those at the conference. Questions would be asked too, and when the subject came around to the decision to approach and then take aboard the boat people that fateful day in 1980, Hanson replied, "You'd have to be inhuman to look at all those faces and just move on [as other ships did do]."[53]

There would be many comments made by American merchant seamen involved in rescues of Vietnamese boat people as to why, beyond articulated government or company policy, they willingly participated in these rescue operations. It was clearly for humanitarian reasons, a matter of the heart, which would also impact their lives and stand out as particularly meaningful in their lives in decades to come. But the reasons given, and impact that might have had, was also reflected in comments made from ashore by those directing the operations of ships that would become involved in boat people rescues. Bruce Cuneo, retired president of Energy Transport Corporation, is a case in point. Interviewed in 2017 for an article about the reunion of Vuong family members and some of the crew from LNG *Virgo* that had rescued them, he would address the factors that weighed in the decision-making process: "It cost $100,000 a day to run these [LNG] ships, so to divert one for a day is expensive, but we did it, time and time again. We delivered valuable cargo, but rescuing people and giving them a new life, you can't match that."[54]

Perhaps, in light of everything that had come before—all the years of transporting troops (including French ones as early as late 1945) to Vietnam, delivering the vast majority of tools and supplies of war that would equip and sustain "grunts" in the field and pilots in the air for better or for worse in a war that would increasingly be questioned and opposed ultimately by a majority of the American people—there might perhaps have been a degree, some measure of a redeeming quality to it, in the end, in the saving of lives in the South China Sea and elsewhere in those years—decades, in fact—following the end of the Vietnam War.

Some seamen might indeed say that it was the case for them, the saving of lives rather than contributing to the taking of lives for a questionable cause. But for most, perhaps, whether they had served in ships making their way along the Vietnam Run or not, it was simply the right and humane thing to do.

According to a study of the Vietnamese immigrant population in the United States published a few years after the 2000 census was taken, that population was relatively small prior to the major evacuations by sea and air that took place between March and May 1975; by the end of the year it had grown to more than 120,000. After that it "roughly doubled" in each decade between 1980 and 2000 as refugees left Vietnam by small boat and otherwise. From that point on the Vietnamese immigrant population continued to increase at the rate of some 26 percent in the first decade of the new millennium. By 2014, when there were some 1.3 million Vietnamese immigrants in the United States, they represented the sixth largest immigrant group in the country behind only those who had arrived from Mexico, India, China, the Philippines, and El Salvador. At the time, this represented three percent of the 42.4 million immigrants known to be living in the United States.[55]

21

When the Ships Returned (and the Search for MIAs)

"The return to a port symbolic of the Vietnam conflict proves that our two countries have come a long way in building relations over recent years."

—Captain Lee Apsley, USNS *Richard E. Byrd*

It was something those Vietnamese old enough to remember had neither seen nor heard of in three decades.

Now, in November 2003, an American warship—the guided missile frigate USS *Vandegrift*—was making its way up the winding 40 miles of the Long Tau shipping channel between Vung Tau and Ho Chi Minh City, formerly Saigon.[1] As one account described it: "Escorted by a Vietnamese patrol boat, the frigate made its way into Saigon Port with U.S. and Vietnamese flags flying. A chain of white-uniformed sailors stood along the ship's railings as it came in."[2]

"The American group, led by ship Commander Richard Rogers," the account continued, "disembarked down a red-carpeted walkway to be greeted by a Vietnamese delegation headed by Vice Minister for Foreign Affairs Nguyen Duc Hung."[3]

Ceremonies that followed took place in front of City Hall before a monument honoring Ho Chi Minh, the Vietnamese revolutionary who had led resistance against France and the United States until his death in 1969, and after whom Saigon was renamed at the conclusion of the war.

American warships had been prohibited from entering Vietnamese waters since the signing of the Paris Peace Accords in 1973. And while the possibility of American warships returning to Vietnam for voyage repairs or other purposes was raised during the first visit of an American Secretary of Defense—William Cohen—to Vietnam following the war, in 2000, he reported afterwards that he believed port calls by such ships were likely at some point, but "not in the immediate future."[4]

The arrival of *Vandegrift* three years hence announced to those present that the future had arrived.

It can be argued that the presence of American warships such as *Vandegrift*, and those that would soon follow the visit of Secretary of Defense Cohen to Vietnam in 2000, as much as they spoke to an ever if slowly improving relationship between Vietnam and the United States—and the introduction of increased military-to-military relations between the two countries—had at its core growing concerns for maintenance of commercial sea lanes—the freedom of navigation—for ships crewed by

USNS *Richard E. Byrd*, one of the newer "nucleus" ships of the Military Sealift Command crewed by merchant seamen, and one of the first to enter Vietnam following the war (Military Sealift Command).

merchant seamen destined for Vietnamese ports and moving through Vietnam's offshore waters, namely the South China Sea to other destinations.[5]

From the standpoint of the major maritime and naval powers—particularly China and the United States—operating in the South China Sea and other areas of East Asia, the priority was about maintaining access to, if not control of, sea lanes for the sake of ocean-borne commerce. It was upon those sea lanes, and the dry cargo and tanker ships that traversed them each and every day, that their economies heavily depended.[6]

One important Vietnamese port that had been developed and played a major logistical role for South Vietnam and the United States during the war, and would figure significantly into the postwar future of Vietnam and its relations with the United States, was Cam Ranh Bay. As one observer would put it early in the second decade of the twenty-first century:

> Cam Ranh Bay plays perfectly into the Pentagon's places not bases strategy, whereby American ships and lines can regularly visit foreign military outposts for repairs and resupply without the need for formal, politically sensitive basing arrangements. U.S. naval platforms—aircraft carriers, destroyers, resupply and hospital ships—are already visiting Vietnamese ports on a periodic basis. Ngo Quan Xuan, the Foreign Affairs Committee vice president, was blunt: "U.S. presence is needed for a free maritime climate in the South China Sea."[7]

Circumstances had changed over time, diplomacy had resulted in a series of new agreements between the countries, and heightened geopolitical tensions involving

China and the sovereignty claims of other countries in the South China Sea had much to do with American merchant and naval ships being welcomed back to Vietnamese ports at long last.[8]

It was noted at the time of the four-day visit by *Vandegrift* and her crew that it had been "a landmark meeting" a week earlier in Washington, D.C., between Vietnamese Defense Minister Pham Van Tra and U.S. Secretary of Defense Donald H. Rumsfeld that had been "the first time a senior Vietnamese military official has visited Washington."[9] After receiving an invitation in turn from Pham Van Tra to visit Vietnam, Rumsfeld would do so in 2006, further contributing to the process of normalization resulting in yet more visits to Vietnam by ships of the U.S. Navy and Merchant Marine. Also reflective of a growing military-to-military relationship would be the signing in 2005 of an International Military Education Training agreement between the two countries.[10]

There were of course other ports developed during the war as major logistical support areas that would join Ho Chi Minh City and Cam Ranh Bay soon enough in having long-prohibited American warships—including those of the Military Sealift Command crewed by merchant seamen—coming to call once again.

Following *Vandegrift*'s historic visit to Ho Chi Minh City in November 2003, the port of Da Nang, located in present-day central Vietnam, and in what had been the northern reaches of South Vietnam before the war's end resulted in reunification, would be next to receive an American warship. The arrival of the guided missile frigate USS *Curtis Wilbur* (DDG-54) there on July 28, 2004, "for a scheduled port visit" was recorded as being the second U.S. warship to visit Vietnam, and the first to make an appearance in Da Nang since 1973. As USS *Vandegrift* had done, and others that would soon follow, here was yet another ship which by its very presence represented a new phase of not only bilateral national relations but geopolitical realities as well.[11]

The Return of Vietnamese "Boat People"

For only the third arrival by a U.S. Navy warship in Vietnam since the end of the war, another guided missile frigate, USS *Gary* (FFG-51), was selected, reaching Ho Chi Minh City for a five-day visit on March 30, 2005.[12] Particularly noteworthy was the fact that in command of the ship was Lieutenant-Commander Quoc Bao Tran, who had left Vietnam as a seven-year-old some 30 years earlier, as one of the first of the Vietnamese "boat people" shortly before the North Vietnamese Army entered Saigon at the end of the war.[13] Here, personified by Tran, was one clear indication not only how much time had passed since the end of the war, but that some "boat people" had reached a point in their lives where returning to their homeland for the first time was welcomed.

"I'm overwhelmed, overjoyed and of course excited," Tran remarked in ceremonies soon after his return, "[and] I'm looking forward to seeing the place where I was born."[14]

Noting that USS *Gary*'s arrival in Vietnam coincided with the 10th anniversary of the start of normalization between the two countries, U.S. Ambassador to Vietnam Michael Marine emphasized: "The most important thing for both of our nations and peoples to do is to continue to look forward, not backward."[15]

Quoc Bao Tran's return to Vietnam in command of a U.S. Navy vessel would not be the last time a "boat person" would return for the first time in such a capacity. Arriving at Da Nang four years later in command of USS *Lassen*, a guided missile destroyer, was Captain H.B. Le, a native of the city of Hue in central Vietnam. Le's father had been commander of the South Vietnamese Naval Support Base at Nha Be, a short ways downriver from Saigon. He had fled Vietnam with his family in a fishing trawler with 400 others in the final days of the war and was rescued on May 2, 1975, in the South China Sea by the crew of USS *Barbour County*, a LST.[16] Le's family would make their way eventually to Northern Virginia, and he would go on to attend the U.S. Naval Academy in Annapolis, graduating with merit in 1992. Le rose steadily through the ranks, and in 2009 assumed command of the *Lassen*.[17]

"My crew and I are proud to be able to represent our country to the people of Vietnam," remarked Le upon his return. "This visit is a symbol of the friendship between our two nations, and we are deeply honored to be a part of it." Captain Le went on to say that he felt "very humbled by the amazing opportunity" to come to Vietnam after more than 34 years. "I feel so fortunate to bring *Lassen* and my crew to Vietnam."[18]

Two other ships, USS *Patriot* (Lieutenant-Commander Colby Howard in command) and USS *Salvor* (Lieutenant-Commander Richard D. Brawley), represented the fourth visit to Vietnamese ports by ships of the U.S. Navy, and the third such visit to Ho Chi Minh City itself.[19] The ships—one of the mine countermeasures type and the other for search and rescue operations—made their way up the Long Tau shipping channel to Ho Chi Minh City in July 2006. Not having quite the imposing look and historical significance of those ships that had been the first to arrive in Vietnam as relations between the countries had improved sufficiently to allow for that, and thus not receiving the same coverage in the major news outlets, their visits nonetheless also represented the nature of an evolving relationship between Vietnam and the United States beyond whatever scheduled voyage repairs and routine maintenance was accomplished otherwise.

As Lieutenant-Commander Richard D. Brawley of *Patriot* would put it during welcoming ceremonies in Ho Chi Minh City: "We are now doing something that very few Navy ships have had the opportunity to do before us. We are confident this visit will lead the way for a stronger bilateral relationship between our two countries."[20]

Words of welcome were delivered by Major Le Thanh Hai, reportedly of the Vietnamese "Coast Guard," who said: "We are glad to welcome them to our country. We feel connected between militaries, between nations.... They are friends we want to show them Vietnam to experience our country."[21]

While Major Le's reference to a military-to-military connection was not always mentioned let alone stressed in the early goings of normalization, the importance and reality of such a thing would increasingly be expressed as geopolitical tensions relating to developments in the South China Sea continued to be felt by those redefining strategic and economic needs to counter Chinese moves in the area.[22]

While a merchant ship—even piled high with shipping containers—might not have drawn as much attention as the first returning American warships, it is no doubt the case that USS *Vandergrift*, USS *Curtis Wilbur*, USS *Lassen*, USS *Patriot*, and USS *Salvor* had already been preceded to Vietnam—to both Ho Chi Minh City and Da Nang, and without much if any fanfare—by American merchant ships. Trade relations between the two countries had begun to resume not long after the establishment of diplomatic relations and the lifting of a trade embargo in 1995. Some accounts of the *Vandergrift's* arrival had provided some historical context, noting for example that the United States and Vietnam had successfully negotiated a trade agreement in 2001 that led to the U.S. becoming "[by 2003] the top importer of Vietnamese products with bilateral trade totaling about $3 billion a year."[23]

Between 2001 and 2003, in fact, exports from the U.S. to Vietnam more than doubled, and imports from Vietnam more than quadrupled. And from the end of 2003 through 2008 exports to Vietnam would more than double again, while imports from Vietnam would nearly triple again. With the top five types of exports to Vietnam in one annual report being machinery, automobiles, cotton, animal feed and materials, and plastic materials, merchant ships by most reckonings would have been engaged in transporting the vast majority of those imported—and exported—goods between the two countries.[24]

Of significance for its impact not only on trade relations between Vietnam and the U.S. but also specifically for the encouragement given to privately owned shipping companies, was the approval by the U.S. Congress in January of 2007 of Permanent Normal Trade Relations (PNTR) with Vietnam, and the conclusion of a bilateral Maritime Agreement between the two countries in March that more fully opened the maritime transport and services industry of Vietnam to U.S. shipping companies.[25]

The year 2007 was marked by the arrival in Vietnam of five ships of the U.S. Navy, including that of USS *Pelielu*, an amphibious assault ship, in Da Nang in July, and USNS *Bruce C. Heezen*, the first of the civilian merchant mariner-crewed ships of the Military Sealift Command (MSC) that would be arriving in Vietnam from that point on.

Pelielu had embarked an international contingent of medical and engineering personnel in Australia for providing assistance in those areas to Vietnam. This would be part of a multi-national naval exercise known as Cooperation Afloat Readiness and Training (CARAT), which for the first time would have Vietnamese observers and medical personnel taking part.[26]

Another of the Military Sealift Command's ships arriving in Vietnam in 2007—only the second to do so as the two countries continued with the process of normalization, was the USNS *Bruce C. Heezen* (Captain Bruce LaChance), an oceanographic survey vessel that called on Da Nang from October 17 to 20 of that year. It was the first Pathfinder-class ship of that type to ever call on Vietnam, and with a crew of 26 merchant mariners and a Naval Oceanographic Office detachment aboard, it took aboard eight Vietnamese hydrographers for a hands-on demonstration involving the charting of an obstructed waterway some three miles outside the harbor of Da Nang.[27]

Dr. Le Cong Thanh, deputy director of Vietnam's Center for Hydrography and Meteorology who was aboard *Heezen* for the ship's port call, would later remark: "We hope *Heezen's* visit is the first step towards increased cooperation in the future."[28]

Heezen would in fact return to Vietnam two years later as part of a month-long Joint POW/MIA Accounting Command (JPAC) mission searching for American aircraft downed during the war in Vietnam's offshore waters. Their work would prove to be one good example of the little-known role also played by merchant seamen in the search for missing military service personnel.

While merchant seamen are generally and understandably associated with privately owned and operated dry cargo ships—such as the containerships that began to make their appearance in Vietnam in the late 1960s—they also made up the crew complements, as civilians, of ships of the U.S. Navy's Military Sealift Command (MSC), during the course of the Vietnam War, long before, and going forward to the present day. In fact, the first American ship mined and sunk by the Viet Cong during the war, the World War II–vintage "baby flattop" escort aircraft carrier USNS *Card*, as one of the "nucleus" fleet ships of the MSTS (later renamed MSC), was crewed by civilian merchant seamen.

Under terms of the Paris Peace Accords of 1973 those ships of the MSC fleet had been prohibited, as well as military vessels of other foreign nations, from entering Vietnamese waters.[29] But with changing times, MSC ships also began returning to Vietnam, which meant that the merchant seamen who crewed them also began arriving in that way, in addition to their arrivals on merchant ships engaged in commerce beforehand.[30]

In Search of the Missing

The long ongoing search for the Missing in Action (MIA) in Vietnam is something not generally associated with merchant seamen. In June 2009, however, soon after the return of USNS *Bruce C. Heezen*, ships began to be involved in the search for aircrews who had disappeared into the offshore waters of Vietnam after being shot down during the war.[31] One of the oceanographic survey ships of the MSC fleet, *Heezen* had actually first arrived in Vietnam two years earlier to conduct a brief training mission that involved surveying an underwater obstruction in the vicinity of Da Nang. Returning in 2009, *Heezen* was now part of the Joint POW/MIA Accounting Command (JPAC), which, for the first time, would involve an American naval vessel for a month-long search of sites in deep and shallow waters believed to contain downed aircraft with the remains of American MIAs. Boarding the *Heezen* for this survey work were members of the Vietnam Office of Missing Persons (VNOMP).[32]

Joint JPAC and VNOMP Teams had previously searched for MIAs in underwater sites offshore, but using only Vietnamese vessels. The deployment now of *Heezen* for this purpose represented the first time an American naval ship would take part in such an operation.[33]

"The use of a U.S. Navy oceanographic survey ship on JPAC's search operations in Vietnam could significantly expedite the discovery of underwater crash sites," remarked Lieutenant Colonel Todd Emoto, commander of JPAC's detachment in Hanoi. "Vietnam's cooperation in allowing the ship to operate in her waters is a big step forward and greatly appreciated by the U.S. government and the families of those Americans still missing."[34]

USNS *Heezen* would be followed to Vietnam in 2011 by another civilian-crewed survey vessel of the Military Sealift Command—USNS *Bowditch*—for further underwater searches for American MIAs.[35] Under the command of Captain Mike Farrell, the ship's crew of 24 merchant mariners and an embarked team of oceanographers and hydrographers arrived in late May for a month-long underwater crash site survey operation. Three additional personnel from the Hanoi JPAC detachment and five

Vietnamese from the Office for Seeking Missing Persons were also embarked, and together they would complete a total of 15 missions off Da Nang, Quang Nam, Thua Thien-Hue, and Quang Tri Provinces.[36]

After successful completion of the crash site survey operation *Bowditch*'s master, Captain Farrell, remarked, "For the crew of *Bowditch*, it has been a rewarding experience working with the JPAC and Vietnamese liaisons to complete a mission that has so much meaning for the American people."[37]

While this work was clearly meaningful, it was but the beginning of a multi-year process involving returns by Underwater Recovery Teams to identified sites, positive identification of aircraft involved, further dives to recover human remains, and lengthy periods of forensic analysis to conclusively identify the recovered remains before family could be notified and public announcements of successful identification of once missing service personnel could be made.[38]

Success, when it came, was the result of efforts and the expertise of many, including those merchant seamen who had operated and navigated the ships involved in survey and recovery operations.

Another of the first merchant mariner-crewed ships of the Military Sealift Command (MSC) to call on Vietnam was USNS *Safeguard*, which arrived at Ho Chi Minh City on September 27, 2009, for voyage repairs and maintenance.[39] Under the command of Captain Peter Long, the gray, 255-foot ship with the distinctive blue, gray, and gold stripes of the MSC on its stack began moving out of Vung Tau up the winding, 40-mile Long Tau Channel to Ho Chi Minh City.[40]

Scheduled to complete routine voyage repairs and maintenance in Ho Chi Minh City (HCMC), this was not the sort of thing that under normal circumstances would be considered particularly newsworthy. But the appearance of this ship at this particular point in time was something more than routine: it was historic, representing—as the presence of ships have often done through time, and certainly during the course of Vietnam's modern history—an historical or geopolitical turning point of some sort.[41]

The arrival of *Safeguard* actually represented the culmination of a series of diplomatic developments and agreements between Vietnam and the United States in the first decade of the new millennium. These included a Bi-lateral Air Transport Agreement that had been completed in December 2003 and that resulted in the first direct flights between the United States (San Francisco) and Vietnam (Ho Chi Minh City) in December 2004.[42] As for the impact it would have on the restoration of movement of ocean-borne shipping between the two countries, the signing of a Bi-Lateral Maritime Agreement in March 2007 would make that possible.[43] This agreement would not only be an encouragement for trade purposes but once again make services available that would benefit private shipping companies as well as the U.S. Navy.

As Lieutenant-Commander Mike Little, who had been involved in making arrangements for *Safeguard*'s arrival in Vietnam, would later put it: "Ship repair normally doesn't get too exciting, [but] it was great being there when *Safeguard* came up the river and into the shipyard, and I was even more proud when it left on time [on September 12] with all the work complete."[44]

With repairs completed to *Safeguard*'s lifeboat davits, transformers, ladder walls, and piping—work that certainly might not make the evening news—the ship's arrival and presence in HCMC spoke to changing geopolitical realities involving not only Vietnam and the United States, but China as well.

These particular ships, as their outward appearances might have suggested, were not intended for frontline naval fleet actions. There were no sharply menacing bows, weapons, or military launch apparatus visible on these ships. Rather, important as their roles were for providing logistical support—and, in the case of *Safeguard*, a search and rescue capability—their arrival in such ports as Ho Chi Minh City, Da Nang, and Cam Ranh Bay might not have had quite the same impact, raised as many eyebrows, as ships clearly designed for war. Those ships, with officers and enlisted personnel lined along decks in "Class A" white uniforms—not typically part of a merchant seaman's wardrobe—beginning early in the first decade of the new millennium, represented as clearly as any ship might, that things—geopolitical configurations—had changed.

With decades having passed since American ships of any kind had called on Vietnamese ports, those that began to return there in the early years of the new millennium represented not only the new look of U.S.-Vietnam relations, but the very new look of the fleet of ships that would make their way to Vietnam in increasing numbers as a result of improved diplomatic and trade relations between the two countries, and even cooperative military-to-military relations between the two countries that reflected broader changing geopolitical circumstances of countries washed by—or regularly enjoying freedom of navigation through—waters of the South China Sea.

USNS *Richard E. Byrd*

Joining the MSC Western Pacific fleet in 2009 was another ship of more recent construction, USNS *Richard E. Byrd* (T-AKE-4), a replenishment cargo type ship.[45] Launched less than two years before from National Steel and Shipbuilding Co. shipyard in San Diego, California, *Byrd* sailed with a crew of 123 merchant mariners, supplemented by a small contingent of U.S. Navy special mission personnel, and would serve as a command ship for the Military Sealift Command in the Western Pacific.[46]

Having entered service for the first time more than three decades after the end of the Vietnam War, *Byrd* represented a new generation of ships sporting the distinctive multicolored stack stripes of the Military Sealift Command. With Vietnam making its shipyards available in various locations for voyage repairs, replenishment, and routine maintenance, *Byrd* would take advantage of these services for the first time in Van Phong Bay between February and March 2010. A deepwater port in an isolated area that had not figured prominently in the war, Van Phong Bay was being developed by Vietnam as a new tourist destination that would provide access and services for ocean-going ships.[47]

Then, in August of the following year, presumably with significantly more fanfare than had been the case in Van Phong, *Byrd* and her crew of merchant seamen returned yet again to Vietnam, this time to Cam Ranh Bay, the magnificent natural harbor that had figured so prominently as a major logistical support area during the war.[48] The arrival of *Byrd* was historic: though it was certainly not the first return visit of a ship of the U.S. Navy to Vietnam, it nonetheless represented the first time in some 38 years that an American naval vessel had entered Cam Ranh Bay.[49]

While the *Byrd* had been scheduled during the course of its three-day visit to Cam Ranh Bay to have various forms of maintenance and repairs completed there, including repair to piping, an overhaul to its salt water cooling system, the cleaning of her hull, and polishing of the ship's propeller, the significance otherwise of the ship's visit there was not lost on either members of her crew or local officials who came to participate in welcoming ceremonies.

"The U.S. Navy's return to a port symbolic of the Vietnam conflict," ship's master Captain Lee Apsley would note, "proves that our two countries have come a long way in building relations over recent years."[50]

Then in June 2012 *Byrd* returned yet again to Vietnam for additional voyage repairs in Cam Ranh Bay. It was during that visit that the USNS *Richard E. Byrd* and her crew of merchant seamen also welcomed the arrival of an American Secretary of Defense, Leon Panetta.[51] While not the first head of the Department of Defense to actually visit Vietnam following the war—William Cohen in 2000 and Donald Rumsfeld in 2007 would precede him—he would be the first to make an appearance in what had been one of the most important logistical bases of support, continually receiving merchant dry cargo, ammunition, and tanker ships, during the war.

Cam Ranh Bay was the place where Russia's Baltic fleet had put in prior to setting out for its rendezvous with disaster at the hands of the Japanese in the Straits of Tsushima in 1905; which had been developed by the U.S. as a major logistical support base area during the Vietnam War; and to which tens of thousands of desperate refugees and ARVN soldiers had fled in 1975 to then be evacuated out on ships manned by American merchant seamen.

Panetta's visit to Cam Ranh Bay, as much as it represented the continually evolving postwar relationship between Vietnam and the U.S.—while at the same time conjuring up memories of an earlier time of war—was also intended to convey an unmistakable message to other nations, particularly those with competing vested interests in the South China Sea, and with clear implications for the future.[52]

As they had been many times in the past, stretching back at least to the months immediately following the end of World War II, American merchant seamen had once again returned to Vietnam, on this occasion to Cam Ranh Bay, during Secretary of Defense Panetta's visit, both as witness to yet another historical moment in time, in Vietnam, and participants in making that history.

It was not just to the same general area that Panetta had come that day, but to the deck of the ship operated by those seamen—USNS *Richard E. Byrd*—that he would actually make his way.

"Access for United States naval [and other] ships into this facility," remarked Panetta, "is a key component of this relationship, and we see a tremendous potential for the future."

He emphasized that it would "be particularly important to be able to work with partners like Vietnam, to be able to use harbors like this as we move our ships from our ports on the West Coast, ports or stations here in the Pacific."[53]

That American merchant ships would continue moving cargoes along the important sea lanes of the South China Sea, and ships of the U.S. Navy would continue calling on Vietnam's ports while also maintaining a presence in contested areas within the "first island chain" of the South China Sea, there could be no doubt.

After his own visit to Cam Ranh Bay, and with merchant mariners aboard USNS *Richard Byrd*, Secretary of Defense Panetta would remark: "The United States has long been deeply involved in the Asia-Pacific. Through times of war, and peace, under Democratic and Republican leaders and administrations, through rancor and through comity in Washington, through surplus and through debt. We were there then, we are here now, and we will be here for the future."[54]

Vietnam and the United States had developed each in their own way to the point when, in the late 1990s and in the early decades of the twenty-first century, they moved from diplomacy to signing off on a series of mutually beneficial agreements involving among other things deepwater ports and services that might be provided therein, and the arrival of American ships once again—merchant and naval ships— that would benefit their economies on the one hand, and also provide security and strategic advantage on the other. This was in keeping with both Vietnam's "Three No's" policy and the "places not ports" policy of the United States.[55]

The visit to Cam Ranh Bay by Secretary of Defense Panetta, and the arrival of USNS *Richard E. Byrd* with its crew of American merchant mariners aboard, reflected those national policies. The United States had formally ended its role in the Vietnam War nearly 40 years before Panetta's visit aboard a ship crewed by American merchant seamen in Cam Ranh Bay. That represented both how far relations between Vietnam and the United States had progressed in the intervening years, yet reflected how in other ways the process of reconciliation in the war's aftermath continued. Once again, merchant seamen had witnessed and been part of the developing history of Vietnam and the relations between the two countries. More directly related to the war, and the process of healing and reconciliation that would continue into the indefinite future, was the role some merchant seamen had played in the search for and recovery of the remains of the missing in action.

American merchant mariners had been making their way along the Vietnam Run, in times of war and peace, for many decades; and no doubt their presence will continue to be felt for many decades to come.

Epilogue

Return to Tam Bao

In October rain
Tam Bao's doors locked shut so
Use memory gate.
—M.G.

The Vietnam Airlines jet began its descent through heavy overcast on its final approach to Tan Son Nhut Airport in Ho Chi Minh City, formerly Saigon. This was in October 1993, and it had been more than 20 years—24 in my case—since any of our group of seven had last been there, and under quite different circumstances.[1]

As we waited quietly for our first glimpse after so many years, each was lost in his or her own thoughts as to what this return meant, and what our hearts and guts were saying as memories of our individual experiences there suddenly washed over us.

Decades have passed again since that first of two return visits for me—there would be another in 1998—and what I remember most of that first glimpse as we came down through the clouds was not the city itself, but the winding, brown, snake-like river that led to, around, and beyond it, and is so much a part of memories of that place. That river—the Long Tau—became for many American merchant seamen who made the 40-plus-mile transit along it, a place where death, they knew, might come quickly around any bend, or at any point in between. Too many seamen had, in fact, been lost to enemy attack while making their way from the sea to Saigon through an area that came to be known as the "Rung Sat" or killer jungle.[2]

My opportunity to return to Vietnam came after I learned about and became involved with Project Hearts and Minds (PHAM), an organization created by and for veterans to assist with the process of reconciliation—both with themselves, and the former enemy.[3] It was hoped that PHAM would generally contribute in its own way as well to an improvement in relations between Vietnam and the United States. While the name itself seemed somewhat unfortunate to me, conjuring up earlier failed attempts to win over a hostile or at best apathetic populace long exploited by colonial powers and often exposed to a brutal foreign military presence, the organization nonetheless did what it set out to do. We carried cartons of medical supplies, mostly, and an occasional soccer ball, which would then be delivered to hospitals, clinics, orphanages, and schools throughout the country.[4]

Our PHAM medical missions of reconciliation would begin some 18 years after the end of the Vietnam War. Despite the communicated intent of the United States during peace treaty negotiations in 1972, and even earlier, to assist Vietnam with economic and other forms of reconstruction assistance in the war's aftermath—something that President Richard Nixon would declare was "in a sense considered an American tradition"—geopolitical realities and priorities of the day, and intense efforts by some U.S. policy makers at the time, blocked such a "tradition" from being implemented in any form for nearly two decades.[5] President Jimmy Carter had actually approved the State Department's policy of "simultaneous normalization" with Vietnam in September 1977, but that was not to be for many years to come. As his National Security advisor Zbigniew Brzezinski, no fan of the Vietnamese, would admit about the process of normalization with Vietnam at that time, "I shot that down."[6]

And then came Vietnam's invasion of Cambodia in late 1978, which while effectively putting an end to Pol Pot's genocidal "killing fields" in Cambodia, made blocking the policy of normalization with Vietnam much easier to justify. Fortunately, the humanitarian support provided to Vietnam by American NGO organizations such as PHAM would not be blocked, thus making medical supply missions, such as ours in 1993, possible. It would not be until the following year, however, that the punitive trade embargo against Vietnam would be lifted, and "normalization" of relations formalized with an exchange of ambassadors in 1995. Thus it was in this context that the first of several medical missions to Vietnam would take place during the 10 years PHAM remained in existence.

Many members of PHAM also came to embrace an interest, as author and "old Vietnam hand" Lady Borton had emphasized to us during a later visit to Hanoi, in

A section of the Long Tau River Channel along which ships moved between Saigon and the sea during the Vietnam War (Author photo).

establishing and maintaining longer-term relationships with people and organizations we came to know along the way.[7] This personal maintenance of relations with the Vietnamese continues for some of us to the present day, and as we have also worked to come to terms with our individual experiences in Vietnam during the war.

As a former merchant seaman whose ship sailed to South Vietnam loaded with some 8,000 tons of 250- and 500-pound bombs that would be used in support of Marine Corps air operations out of Da Nang, mine had not been the experience of friends and fellow PHAM delegation members who had served tours in-country and in some cases been wounded in combat. Two members of our 1993 group—Frank Corcoran, who had served with the Marines, and Dayl Wise, who had been a recon sergeant with the Army's First Cav—had had that experience, and been evacuated out and back to the United States. The two of them would eventually do me the honor of standing by me as best men—yes, I needed two to make sure that I made it to the altar on time—as I entered into marriage for a second time nearly 20 years later.

While I make no comparisons with the experiences of those of my PHAM brothers and sisters, I can say that as far as my own experience in Vietnam was concerned, it was also a defining personal experience for me, and has shaped my life in ways that I never could have imagined back in 1969.[8]

I have long believed—despite the specific differences of our wartime experiences—that those of us who were there in any capacity and for any length of time during the war—were all cogs in the same wheel of a war machine that was inserted, most of us involved with PHAM would come to believe, in a place and at a time where none of us belonged.

For me—and I could only speak for myself—returning to Vietnam could be a valuable experience on different levels, and certainly benefit my work in academia, which included the teaching of Vietnamese history and the Vietnam War. I would be returning to places where I had been, and travel to others not only for the important work of reconciliation that was at the heart of the PHAM mission, but also to learn and bring back knowledge I would share with students and colleagues upon my return. And if in the process I might revisit some places where I had been during the war, and see places I knew otherwise were associated with the American Merchant Marine experience in Vietnam, then so much the better. That would also become an objective of my first return to Vietnam.

What I did not know before this first return, but would find out in no uncertain terms soon after our arrival, was the extent to which some combination of my own brief Vietnam service, coupled with what I would come to learn in intervening years following the war, would impact my experience during that first return. Never considering before that I had much if any of my own personal "baggage" to deal with, I would be in for a surprise in that regard not long after my first return to Vietnam in October 1993.

Vung Tau

When all our neatly packed cartons were impounded by Vietnamese customs in Ho Chi Minh City, and later gone through one by one, item by item (with us present, at least), our in-country itinerary had to be changed. We ended up with free time on our hands on the front end as we waited for our medical supplies to be released. To put this time to good use a road trip to the coast at Vung Tau, planned for our last full day in-country, was moved up in the itinerary.

Known as Cap St. Jacques during the French colonial and war period, Vung Tau had been an in-country R&R area during the American War—both for Americans *and* Viet Cong, we came to understand. For merchant seamen it could be a place to go for enjoyment too, but it also served as an offloading for troops and cargo, and was where merchant ships anchored, often for long waits "on the hook"—depending on the priority designation of cargo—before getting clearance to commence the 40-mile river channel transit to Saigon.

In the last days of the war, as forces of the Peoples' Army of Vietnam (PAVN) approached, attacked, and then captured Saigon, Vung Tau also became one of the last places from which thousands of South Vietnamese military personnel and civilians would be evacuated by ship. Though I had not actually been there before, going to Vung Tau was certainly something that I wanted to do, for both the planned visit to a medical clinic there and its association with this history and the involvement of the Merchant Marine.

While in Vung Tau we also had the opportunity to visit a Buddhist temple complex, and a Cao Dai temple (where my poor French actually proved useful for communicating with the chief priestess). We also enjoyed a seafood lunch at a restaurant overlooking the bay where American merchant ships had once been anchored. That visit, despite some initial annoyance due to the delay in getting started for points north, turned out to be well worth it.

Before eventually getting underway for those points north, I convinced my group to visit the Saigon waterfront and the rooftop garden lounge of the Majestic Hotel.[9] Graham Greene had written the Majestic into *The Quiet American* as a place to which the journalist Thomas Fowler had walked one evening and "stood awhile watching the unloading of the American bombers" in what would have been one of the last years of the French War period. I knew also that many merchant seamen and others had enjoyed some shore leave time there while in the hustling and bustling capital city of South Vietnam during the later American War. And along with visiting other places such as the iconic cathedral, a Buddhist pagoda, and the history museum, the visit to the Majestic Hotel provided our group a moment to relax together, to discuss the start of our return visit to Vietnam, and the days that lay ahead for us there.

Newport

One of the areas we had passed as we left from HCMC for the coast at Vung Tau, and later as we returned, was an important port complex that had been developed during the war to provide additional logistical support infrastructure in-country for American and South Vietnamese military forces. Given the imaginative name of Newport, it helped to significantly reduce delays—"turnaround" time of cargo ships—once it became fully operational by 1967, for merchant ships waiting "on the hook" at Vung Tau and elsewhere for berths to become available for offloading. One of our group, Robert "Tack" Trostle, had been stationed there with the Army during his yearlong tour in-country, and was involved as cargoes were unloaded, moved to on-site storage or onto trucks for immediate shipment of priority cargoes to nearby bases, such as Long Binh. One great advantage of Newport was that such operations, essentially into and out of Saigon, did not involve moving cargoes through the central downtown streets of the city.

Tack Trostle would have liked to have returned to Newport, by whatever name it was then called, for a look-see, but that was not in the cards as it turned out, either with the group or by himself; he could only wave as we went by in our minivan. Some of us would have that chance—to return specifically where we had been during the war—but some, even if given the chance, would no doubt have passed on the opportunity if presented with it. There would in any case be other places of interest to visit—some seen during the war, but many experienced for the first time—before our group set out to finally make our first deliveries of medical and other supplies. We visited the history museum, pagodas, the iconic Notre Dame Cathedral on Tu Do Street, and the University of Ho Chi Minh City, where I met with faculty and presented a hard-bound copy of my doctoral dissertation to the university rector. Having to do with public reaction to the policy of supporting the French—including the transportation by ship to Vietnam of initial contingents of French troops in late 1945—the discussion turned at one point to the later sinking in Saigon of the USNS *Card*, one of the ships of the then Military Sea Transportation Service (MSTS) crewed by American merchant seamen.

At least one member of the university faculty said that he knew of that incident, though I suspect others certainly did as well.

Hopefully, the dissertation remains there still, accessible to all somewhere on a shelf at the University of Ho Chi Minh City, as a lesser-known part of the story of American involvement in the "French War" that some of them at least might appreciate.

While we did encounter members of the former South Vietnamese military—ARVN or otherwise—those encounters were spontaneous ones, on the street as it were, and not planned as other arranged meetings were with groups of veterans who had fought with the former enemy—the National Liberation Front (NLF) or North Vietnamese Army (NVA). And while those planned meetings with former NLF or NVA, sometimes accompanied by tea and sweet cakes, or a veritable feast that included Vietnamese beer, were extraordinarily genuine, heart-felt experiences of reconciliation in their own right, they nonetheless left some of us with an unsettling realization. Veterans of our former enemy struggled in their own ways, something to which members of our group, as veterans, could readily relate, to secure proper medical assistance and benefits in the wake of their own military service. But they appeared to have one thing, we discovered, that veterans of the South Vietnamese military forces did not, namely, their own veterans organizations, not to mention adequate medical care and benefits that should normally be made available to veterans elsewhere.

Increasingly, as we traveled elsewhere in Vietnam, we would pose a question to groups of veterans with whom we met and by whom we were fêted: what consideration is given to other veterans, who do not have their own veteran organizations? The standard reply, that they too were "welcome but choose not to participate" just did not wash with most of us.

Genuine "Cognac Brandy"

With periodic rain, and temperatures cooler than expected, I decided one day in Ho Chi Minh City to purchase and share with my travel companions a bottle of what its label described in large gold letters as "Cognac Brandy" and with accompanying numbers that suggested it might be potent. This would do the trick for a bit of warming and perhaps ceremony at the end of such a day as this, I thought. Back in our hotel room, Dayl Wise and I thought we'd sample it, to make sure it would be suitable for sharing. I removed the cork, poured some of the light brown liquid into a glass, searched (in vain) for the aroma of a fine, or even lesser, cognac, and allowed a small amount to play with the taste buds. The words that quickly came back from them was: "Colored sugar water, fool, not a trace of alcohol in it!"

This was certainly a disappointment, and good for a laugh too after the initial shock wore off. "No wonder it was so cheap," my friend offered. And from that day on—for decades now—I have not been able to live that one down since Wise and I remain good friends, and he does take the opportunity on occasion to remind me, and tell the tale to others.

Return to Da Nang

On approach now to the airport in Da Nang, in reunified central Vietnam—what was once referred to as being located in the northern "I Corps" military area of South Vietnam, I was feeling closer now to where I had been briefly as a merchant seaman in 1969. There was the magnificent bay where our ammunition-laden ship, the *Fairport*, had lain at anchor and eventually offloaded some 8,000 tons of cargo into barges alongside. There were the mountains off to the north, and one we knew as Monkey Mountain off to its southern side and overlooking the sea approaches. And there was the Han River—known as the Tourane during the French period—that emptied into the bay, and where, near its mouth, we would go and hang out for a period of time with a cooling libation while on shore leave.

I had not been to the Da Nang airport before, however, so as we taxied along after landing I was seeing for the first time the rows of half-pipe-shaped revetments where military aircraft had been stored and serviced. Back in the day these concrete and rebar constructions protected aircraft from rocket and mortar attack, but such cover did not extend, unfortunately, to other things—such as merchant ships—that were periodically subjected to rocket attack.

Our ship had brought in bombs of varying size that I understood would be flown out on Marine F4U "Phantom" fighter-bombers that were stored and serviced in those revetment shelters. We had learned that the ammunition dump had been hit either by rocket fire or sappers not long before, and we were among the ships sent in to replenish it.

Da Nang had been referred to as "rocket city" for good reason. The Viet Cong would fairly regularly set up their wooden and bamboo launchers in the hills north of the city and send in groups of a half-dozen or so rockets at a time, then fade quickly back into the thick cover available to them. I came to understand the appropriateness of the name one night—early morning at about 1:00—as I stood at deck security watch on our ship. The darkness of the night sky was suddenly lit up in the vicinity of the deepwater piers, and that was followed a few seconds later by the sound of detonating rockets and resultant explosions. A merchant ship had been hit, and continued to burn well into the day, sending a huge plume of dark smoke seaward towards Monkey Mountain.

A day or so later I went ashore, and our liberty launch—an old LCM "Mike" boat landing craft—went right by the spot where that ship had once been a living and upright entity. All that could then be seen as we moved slowly along was the ship's bottom, the rest having gone under at some point after it capsized. Some of our ship's crew had been in a nearby hotel that had been damaged in the attack, but none had been injured. I did not learn the identity of the ship and what it was carrying (butane gas) until many years later.[10]

By chance, we ended up in a fine hotel—the Bach Dang—overlooking the Han River near where I had gone ashore back in 1969. Its name would have had no meaning for me, nor most other Americans, during the war. However, as I delved more deeply into Vietnam's history afterwards, its significance became clear: it represented and honored the memory of a place and events that occurred in Northern Vietnam, a bay or tributary near Haiphong where the Vietnamese had staged successful and decisive surprise attacks against foreign invasions centuries before—a Chinese invasion fleet in the late tenth century, and again against a Mongol fleet in the thirteenth century. Knowing that the Chinese and later Mongol fleet were making their way down to that area to launch an invasion, the Vietnamese drove large, sharpened, possibly iron-tipped, poles—sharp end up—into the mud at low tide. The invading fleets came in, anchored at high tide, and when it went out again, the wooden troop and supply transports were impaled, and either sank or were held like sitting ducks, on the spikes. The Vietnamese then attacked, and those actions proved decisive and ultimately led to wresting independence back from the Chinese after hundreds of years, and to the retreat of the Mongols northward again, never to return.

While sharpened wooden—and bamboo—spikes would indeed continue to be used against other foreign invaders even well into the twentieth century, other more modern and sophisticated weapons would be deployed against the iron and steel ships arriving with troops and military supplies from afar. The objective—to expel those forces from the country—would, of course, still be the same, and ultimately successful as well. This time, in 1993, the irony of that, and this hotel named for that place in this location, was not lost on me.

Return to Tam Bao

One thing I had hoped to do at some point when I went ashore in Vietnam in 1969 was visit a Buddhist pagoda. Sitting at Mama Li's refreshment stand by the river in Da Nang one day, I asked her for a suggestion in that regard, and the next thing I knew I was in a pedicab (cyclo) heading out into the city for parts unknown. The driver peddled away and brought me to a structure not too many blocks from the waterfront, and gestured that this would be the place. I dismounted and walked over to it, unsure of the protocol since—at 21, and a stranger in a strange land—what did I know? Determined nonetheless I forged ahead, and something, perhaps other pairs of shoes parked outside the entrance, prompted me to remove mine, which I did, and then entered the pagoda.[11]

This certainly was another world from what lay outside, and it was empty, at least of humans besides myself. At the far end on a raised platform was an assortment of large representations of the Buddha, some lying prone and others in a sitting position. I moved forward a little more and stopped, taking it in. If I had known better, or been more comfortable with the situation, I might have sat down on the floor—there didn't seem, as I recall, to be any chairs in the room—and contemplated my situation, or, as I learned to do much later, meditate for a while. But, as I said, beyond a rudimentary interest and probably less knowledge on the subject, I didn't know much better so just stood there.

Suddenly, a man in a monk's or layperson's basic gray and nondescript garb entered through a side door to my right. He moved across the room in front of me, as if walking on air, and sat down against the room's wall to my left. I'm not sure how

Tam Bao Pagoda, Da Nang, South Vietnam, visited by the author in 1969 (Author photo).

long I remained there that way, but when I turned to leave he was still sitting there, looking straight ahead across the room, perhaps inwardly in meditation, or with his peripheral vision keeping track of me.

I did have my camera with me—a vintage Leica from the 1930s that had been my father's—and took one picture of the inside of that room, which shows that monk sitting there as he was. I might not have done that if I had known better, but am glad I did, allowing the photographer's—perhaps the Ugly American's—instincts to take precedence, because I treasure that image.

Flash forward 24 years later now to October 1993. I have returned to Da Nang with my PHAM group, and we have some time on our hands before hitting the road to deliver medical supplies. We have been to the Cham Museum, another of my bright ideas, and it has seemed to work well for the group, especially considering we have had our knowledgeable guide and translator Anh-dung "JoJo" Tran along with us. There we have learned, by viewing perhaps the most extensive collection of its remaining sculpture, about the other—Indianized—civilization to inhabit the area that is now Vietnam, and which has long since disappeared.[12] I propose now that we go to the pagoda that I had visited during the war, which I know more about now from having done some homework in preparation for this trip: the Tam Bao Pagoda, built in the early 1950s during the late French War period.

In a steady rain we make our way to the Tam Bao, find it not too far away, and dutifully—all eight of us, including JoJo—pile out to hopefully enter it as I had done back in 1969. But it is closed—locked tight—and there does not seem to be a soul around. I can only provide a few details of the interior from memory and, after taking a few more photographs there, we pile back into the minivan and are soon on our way again to the next stop that day.

The briefest experience, such as I had at Tam Bao in 1969 while on shore leave, can remain imprinted for life, while much else from the memory bank falls by the wayside. Given the opportunity, I was only too glad to make my way there again, with the concurrence and company of my PHAM travel companions. Even though its doors were shut to us, it didn't really matter so much to me; I had returned to that place—something I never really thought I would do—and to this day continue to use the memory gate on occasion to reenter that peaceful sanctuary where a lone monk sat.

Mama Li's Place

Having returned to Da Nang I was certainly thinking about another place—Mama Li's place along the river—where many of us congregated for a short or longer while when on shore leave. It was basically an open-air beer and refreshment stand, and Mama Li, assisted by her two young daughters said to have been born from a relationship with a French soldier, was very possessive about her customers. It was perhaps on my second time ashore in Da Nang when I made the mistake of sitting down at another beer stand within sight of Mama Li's. As I was sitting there with an opened can of beer in my hand, she suddenly appeared directly in front of me, grabbed my arm, pulled me to my feet, and, heading back over to her place in a huff, said, "You buy beer from Mama Li!" So, of course, from then on that's what I did. She was quite a character, always moving around, and her reputation had preceded her all the way back to the States, where a shipmate who had been to Da Nang had first told me about her. When I pressed him for details he said to me, "Don't worry, don't worry, you'll find out, you'll find out after we get over there." And he was right: in no uncertain terms, I did.

It was from there, Mama Li's place, where I watched somewhat entranced the small ferries, propelled by one person—usually a woman, it seemed—standing with two crossed sweep oars in the center, crossing the river with a few passengers and their cargo.

Fast forward to 1993: those small traditional river ferries were still there, and once again I was drawn to them with camera in hand. And looking upriver now there is also a large, modern ferry carrying perhaps hundreds of people, and vehicles as well, making its way back and forth across the river. That, I had not remembered from 1969. Times in some real ways had certainly changed. I suspect, though, that those small ferries will always remain in business, and the graceful movements of a woman propelling them in traditional *ao dai* garb is still to be seen.

Da Nang would serve as a point of departure for PHAM's road trips north to Hue, Loc Hai at the coast, and elsewhere, and southward to Chu Lai, Quang Nhai, and My Lai on the Batangan Peninsula. Medical supplies were delivered to the Clinic in My Lai, and we walked through the hallowed ground, now an historical park, where the massacre of hundreds of Vietnamese civilians had taken place in 1969, and with markers showing the names of members of families, from very young to old, who had been killed there. These markers were placed in front of raised earth platforms where homes had once stood before their destruction. One by one we approached an outdoor altar, burned incense, and prayed or reflected each in our own way. This was a powerfully emotional and important stop along the way for us, and one that would be repeated by other PHAM mission groups in support of the medical clinic there, before the organization called it quits in 2001 after a decade's operation.

The road down to My Lai from Da Nang went right by an entrance to Chu Lai, developed as a major American base during the war. One of our group members, Bob Hennel, had served with an Army helicopter maintenance company there working on, maintaining, washing out, and scrounging parts for helicopters that operated out of that base located along the South China Sea. Here was another one of the few times during this return visit to Vietnam when our itinerary allowed for at least brief stops where someone had been during the war. And once again, while literally making it to the front door—or gate in this case—entrance for a closer look-see was denied.

The base at Chu Lai was still in operation, by the Vietnamese military, so there would be no access, and little time was had to work with in any case. After more photos were taken at the gate—its wartime letters still clearly visible—it was time to board the minivan once again and head back up to Da Nang to prepare for yet another departure.

Heading north towards the Hai Van Pass—what in French days had been identified on maps as the Col de Nuage, or Pass of Clouds—we climbed ever higher above but continually in view of Da Nang Bay, which, as we wound slowly up, and back and forth on switchbacks, revealed itself fully and colorfully before the sea itself as we continued to ascend this mountain spur. In my mind's eye I could still see the dozens of merchant ships anchored out, a Navy escort aircraft carrier that had come in while we were there—helicopters lifting off its deck—and all the various liberty launches, harbor tugs, barges, and craft making their way to and from during that busy time of providing logistical support for the American and South Vietnamese military operations around Da Nang and elsewhere in the I Corps area.

Arriving eventually at the highpoint we stopped for refreshment and souvenirs, and there was incense for sale near a roadside altar where you could pray, if you felt inclined, before beginning the long descent back down the mountain. Some of us walked over to an old French fort that had guarded the pass. Now deserted, I imagined a few ghosts from the failed French campaign still keeping an eye on the place.

Our days from there, and until our eventual departure back to the States a week or so later, were spent traveling to clinics at Loc Hai, just over and beyond the Hai Van Pass near the South China Sea; a general hospital and the old moat-surrounded Citadel where Vietnam's emperors had kept their thrones in Hue, and which had been heavily fought over and damaged during the Tet Offensive of 1968; the tomb complex of the Emperor Tu Duc and the Orphan Care Institute not far from Hue, to which our organization would return repeatedly. We enjoyed a sublime boat ride with traditional musicians on the Perfume River in Hue, to which we had been treated by the general hospital there, and another meeting with veterans who had fought with the National Liberation Front (Viet Cong). I also made a solo visit to the rector of the University of Hue, to whom I presented another copy of my doctoral dissertation.

Dr. The, Director of Hue General Hospital, with the author, left, and Dayl Wise, right, after boxes of medical supplies—some visible here—were delivered to the hospital by PHAM in 1993 (Courtesy Frank Corcoran).

Any one of those stops north of the Hai Van Pass would be deserving of several more pages here, but since they relate directly to neither my personal experience during the war nor that of most other merchant seamen making their way along the Vietnam Run, I have decided not to linger more with them here due to space constraints. However, suffice to say, they added up to one extraordinary experience for us all that, to varying degrees, was probably life-changing, and to which we would long refer as marking turning points in the transformative and healing process of reconciliation.

1998: Going "Up Country"

I did return to Vietnam for a second time on a PHAM medical supply mission, this time with a group of three others, during the summer of 1998.[13] That took us first into Hanoi, the capital of North Vietnam during the war and now of a reunified country, where we visited the tomb of the nationalist Ho Chi Minh in Ba Dinh Square, where he had delivered the Vietnamese Declaration of Independence from the French in September 1945. We spent time around the Lake of the Restored Sword to view an early morning session of tai chi, and later sat out enjoying refreshments and a meal while watching young and old—a Vietnam now very much at peace— enjoying life strolling, playing ball, sharing a meal, and just enjoying time together as we might back home.

The small lake here got its name from the mythical story of Le Loi, perhaps Vietnam's most revered hero, who, the oft-repeated story goes, was given a golden sword by a magical turtle that emerged from the lake, and with which Le Loi went off to defeat an army of the Ming Dynasty Chinese in the fifteenth century. I was not surprised when, after we had made our way into the old French opera house to watch a production of Vietnam's unique water puppets, the story that was first depicted, using puppets controlled by long wooden sticks that would, among other things, actually emerge from the shallow water spewing sparks from their mouths, was that of none other than the incident of Le Loi and the magic turtle at Kiem Lake.[14]

It was there too, sitting near the lake one afternoon that I purchased pirated and poorly printed paperback copies of Bao Ninh's controversial, and for a time banned, novel *The Sorrow of War*, and also Graham Greene's *The Quiet American*. Greene had written in that book about an encounter that took place in Hanoi at the famous Metropole Hotel, and that became another place I convinced my PHAM mission group—reduced that year to just four of us: Corcoran, with whom I had been on the 1993 PHAM mission; Gail Moroso, who had worked as a civilian nurse in Vietnam for about two years during the war; and Marcia Engelhardt, also a civilian nurse who had worked in Thailand during the war—to visit. We each had a cooling drink, and paused there for a while to discuss that era depicted in Greene's book, reflect on the day's events, and where the days ahead would soon take us.

Those days took us down the length of Highway One—portions of which had been referred to as the "street without Joy" during the French War—all the way from Hanoi to Da Nang. Stops included more orphanages and clinics—some in the north, near Vinh for example, which we had not visited before, and others we had visited before in 1993, near Hue and Loc Hai.

When we arrived at the river that roughly bisects the former demilitarized zone (DMZ), we stopped briefly, before crossing the bridge, to view an old French block-house, and a war memorial there. We then proceeded westerly off Highway One towards the Laotian border to visit a national military cemetery. While there we were met by more veterans of the NVA, and I, as the only one in our party not wearing shorts, was invited to walk amongst the graves and burn incense wherever I chose to do so. I accepted that offer, ventured in, and viewed many graves, all with Vietnamese names and dates from either the French or American war periods. I burned incense, bowing three times at each grave where I left it, and then slowly returned to my group. That was one of many solemn and awesome experiences for me during my two return visits to Vietnam.

Though it would not be our last stop, I will end this now at the beach near Xa Loc Hai Clinic, which we visited again just to the north of the Hai Van Pass. Once again I opted to stay back while my friends eagerly made their way to the warm waters of the South China Sea. And as the poet Robert Frost might have expressed it, it would make all the difference for me in terms of takeaway experience.

At a restaurant with an open-air seating area overlooking the beach and the sea beyond, I sat with Van, our guide and interpreter—the son of a former NVA artilleryman—and Colonel Tran, a veteran of long service with both the Viet Minh and the National Liberation Front, a man who would have been older than myself. He was missing an arm. We chatted for a while about the war, and at one point I gestured towards the sea and the direction from which my ship had arrived in 1969. "I first came to your country by sea from that direction," I said.

Colonel Tran, a veteran of long service with both the Viet Minh and National Liberation Front (aka Viet Cong), with the author in Loc Hai, Vietnam, 1998 (Courtesy Frank Corcoran).

Colonel Tran was polite, perhaps showed the trace of a smile, but his facial expression betrayed little interest otherwise. Why, indeed, should it have? It was clear that he did not, in any case, want to talk any more about the war—not with me, anyway—and he did not reply directly to my comment. Instead, he began a new thread in the conversation, asking about my family and if I had any children.

"Yes," I replied, "I have a son and a daughter. My son was born in the year the war ended here. And do you have children?"[15]

Yes, he also had children, of which he was proud, and from that point on for the little time we had left, that's mostly what we talked about.

We could hear the sound of the surf, and people laughing—perhaps including my friends who had known Vietnam in a time of war, perhaps others too young to conjure that up. Though thoughts of the war would always return for Mr. Tran and me, now was the right—a good time—to let it go. Sitting there then, talking about our children in the peace of the moment, was all that mattered.

Returning to Vietnam after "doing time" there during the war, in any capacity and for any amount of time, is certainly not for everyone, and for understandable reasons. For others, including those of us who had the opportunity to do so as part of PHAM medical supply missions of reconciliation, it was welcomed if with some trepidation for some—notably combat veterans, whose time there had been particularly traumatic. When it came to the war, how we understood and considered it in retrospect, those of us about to join a PHAM mission had come to the point where making a first return to "The Nam" made sense. Doing so, however, was another matter depending on the nature of our individual experiences during the war, and the extent to which we had each come to terms with that in the intervening years and decades.

For me, the one former merchant seaman in the group—for extra good measure—I appreciated that central to the PHAM mission was to promote reconciliation, both as it might occur between us and the Vietnamese, and in the kind of reconciliation that can and was intended to take place within ourselves as we came to terms with our individual war-related experiences.

My one-on-one lunchtime conversation with Colonel Tran, who had long fought with the National Liberation Front, against foreign military intervention, and in the cause of his country's long-delayed reunification, stood out among many other encounters with the former enemy as good examples of what PHAM was begun to foster. It represented something having to do with memory and a process that, by returning to a place at a later time, and during a time of peace, can superimpose another experience—a more positive one—upon it.

No, it does not wipe away memory—and perhaps a deeply traumatic one at that—of war. It doesn't quite work that way. But showing that with a former enemy who had once attempted to end your life in pursuit of his cause, it was still possible—had become possible—to break bread together with them, to stand and toast them across a table, to experience peace together, even acknowledging a form of universal brotherhood, in fact, at long last.

No, it is not for everyone. But even for a merchant seaman, once riding shotgun on a ship loaded to the gills with ammunition—the kind that would be dropped from planes to cause unimaginable destruction to life and property—returned to Vietnam for the first time in 24 years, and then again five years later, did represent reconciliation in the forms it was intended to do.

Returned from First Return: PHAM 1993 Medical Supply mission group, just returned from Vietnam, to Newark, NJ, October 1993. Five of the group had served in Vietnam during the war, and it was the first return to Vietnam for all of them. Pictured, back row, left to right: Corcoran, Conlin, Hennel, Gillen; center wearing traditional Vietnamese mandarin's clothing: Alvarez; front row, left to right: Wise, Trostle.

Vietnam represents much more to me now than a country at war with my own. There are memories now, for example, of being given a helping hand and helped at times to make my way around when that has not always been so easy for me. To those to whom I refer, including the sons and daughters of some of those who fought against our country, long, long ago, I will be forever grateful.

Chapter Notes

Preface

1. The SS *Fairport* was a Waterman Steamship Corp., flush-deck, C2 hull type cargo ship launched into commercial service in 1946.

2. "NSA Fire Crews Quick To Subdue Ship Blaze," *The White Elephant News*, Vol. 3, No. 12, July 11, 1969. See also n. 22, chapter 13.

3. The author did not learn the identity of this ship until many years later, after receiving a packet of information related to the incident from the Navy Historical Center, Washington, D.C. It was actually a Vietnamese butane tanker, the *Phong Chau*, and the U.S. Navy Support Activity, Da Nang newsletter made much of the fire-fighting efforts of a Navy fire-suppression team called upon to fight the fire. But there was no mention of either the ship's crew or any casualties that might have resulted from the rocket attack upon the ship and nearby facilities.

4. William Stephenson interview with author.

5. The percentage figure for cargoes transported by ship varies depending on source but is usually in this range.

6. For details of the American troopship movement to Vietnam in late 1945, and the reaction of many American merchant seamen to their involvement in it, see chapter two, above, and my doctoral dissertation, "Roots of Opposition: The Critical Response to U.S. Indo-China Policy, 1945 to 1954" (New York University, 1991).

7. "Other Voices: American Civilians 'In Country' During the Vietnam War" was held at the Vietnam Era Educational Center in Holmdel, NJ on October 20, 2000.

8. Admiral U.S.G. Sharp and General W.C. Westmoreland, *Report on the War in Vietnam* (Washington, DC: USGPO, 1968), 116, 172.

Chapter 1

1. What is commonly referred to as French Indochina came together initially as the *Union Indochinoise* (Indo-Chinese Union) in 1887. This included the three regions of Vietnam absorbed in stages by France commencing with the southernmost, which was given the name Cochin-China, the long central portion named Annam (a name used long before by China for Vietnam), and the northernmost area, named Tonkin. Cambodia was also part of this initial configuration. Laos was added in 1893.

2. Japan occupied the northernmost area of Tonkin in 1940, and the remainder of French Indochina the following year.

3. Cochin-China in the south, Annam in the center, and Tonkin in the north became incorporated into the French empire, each with a somewhat different official status. Cochin-China became a French colony, ruled by a French governor; Annam and Tonkin were incorporated as "protectorates" ruled by French residents ostensibly working through the Vietnamese court at Hue, and with the traditional Vietnamese elite. See Ngo Vinh Long's description of French rule in Vietnam in Douglas Allen and Ngo Vinh Long, eds., *Coming to Terms: Indochina, the United States, and the War* (Boulder, CO: Westview Press, 1991); Marvin E. Gettleman, Jane Franklin, Marilyn B. Young, and H. Bruce Franklin, eds., *Vietnam and America* (New York: Grove Press, 1995), 4–18.

4. The present-day configuration of Vietnam did not become finalized until after it had completed its "march south" against the Indianized civilization of Champa in the fifteenth century. For more regarding Champa and its long, often antagonistic relationship with Vietnam, see, for example, George Coedes, *The Making of Southeast Asia*, trans. H.M. Wright (London: Routledge and Kegan Paul, 1966).

5. For an account of the earliest role of French missionaries in Vietnam, see, for example, Helen B. Lamb, *Vietnam's Will to Live: Resistance to Foreign Aggression from Early Times through the Nineteenth Century* (New York: Monthly Review Press, 1972), 37–41; Stanley Karnow, *Vietnam: A History* (New York: Viking Press, 1983), 59–61.

6. This appeared in a 1778 report made by Commander Chevalier, then at Chandernagor, India, to his superiors in France. See Lamb, 61.

7. From Taboulet, 448, as quoted in Lamb, 84.

8. A French force with Senegalese and Algerian colonial troops first attacked Saigon on February 16, 1859.

9. For an excellent account of the economic importance of Vietnam for France, and the

nature of French rule during that period, see Ngo Vinh Long, *Before the Revolution: The Vietnamese Peasants Under the French* (Cambridge, MA: MIT Press, 1973).

10. Vietnam had lost its independence to China for nearly 1,000 years, until the early tenth century, CE. For many of those years it had been named "An-Nam" by China, a name generally translated as "pacified south" and which, for obvious reasons, was quickly shed by the Vietnamese once they regained independence in 939 CE. The name was reapplied by the French to the central region of the country, and Vietnamese were often referred to by Westerners as "Annamites" during the French occupation period. The name, always conjuring periods of foreign occupation and control, was shed quickly once again by the Vietnamese following the French defeat in 1954.

11. For the best account of the American shipbuilding program during World War II see Frederic C. Lane, et al., *Ships for Victory: A History of Shipbuilding Under the U.S. Maritime Commission in World War II* (Baltimore: The Johns Hopkins Press, 1951).

12. U.S. Department of Defense. *United States-Vietnam Relations, 1945–1967* (Washington, DC: Government Printing Office, 1971), Book 7, V.B. 1, 30.

13. "Charles Bohlen's Minutes of the Roosevelt-Stalin Meeting at Livadia Palace, February 8, 1945," U.S. Department of State, *Foreign Relations of the United States*, Diplomatic Papers, The Conferences at Malta and Yalta, 1945 (Washington: Government Printing Office, 1955), 770.

14. Though we can only speculate as to how Roosevelt might have shaped the course of events in the aftermath of World War II, and what role if any France would have had in Vietnam, his position regarding the future status of colonial peoples, though evolving and not entirely clear, stood in contrast to that of Truman. See, for example, *Papers of Franklin D. Roosevelt*, Vol. 19, 004 as referenced in James MacGregor Burns, *Roosevelt: The Soldier of Freedom* (New York: Harcourt Brace Jovanovich, 1970).

15. Philippe Devillers, *Histoire du Viet-Nam de 1940 a 1952* (Paris: Editions du Seuil, 1952), 149–150, as quoted in Edward R. Drachman, *United States Policy Toward Vietnam, 1940–1945* (Rutherford, NJ: Fairleigh Dickinson University Press, 1970), 129, n. 35.

16. Charles de Gaulle, *The War Memoirs of Charles de Gaulle: Salvation, 1944–1946*, trans. Richard Howard (New York: Simon and Schuster, 1960), 242.

17. Department of State, Telegram No. 17 (sent via U.S. Army Signal Corps), September 22, 1945, "French and Indo-China," from Caffery (Paris) to AMEMBASSY (Chungking), 2–3, as quoted in Archimedes Patti, *Why Viet Nam? Prelude to America's Albatross* (Berkeley: University of California Press, 1980), 380.

18. In later years few histories would make reference to the 1945 troopship movement to Vietnam involving American troopships and merchant seamen. A notable exception appeared in *The Indochina Story*, but this was little more than passing reference, with few details provided as to the extent of the operation or specific ships involved. My own research would expand upon that and appear in early chapters of my doctoral dissertation completed at New York University in 1991. See Michael Gillen, "Roots of Opposition: The Critical Response to U.S. Indo-China Policy, 1945–1954."

19. The beginning of the Vietnam War continues to be debated, depending largely on whether or not the date of the formal declaration of independence by Vietnamese nationalists from French rule—September 2, 1945—is accepted for that, as I and other historians maintain, or as has more generally been the case, the French naval bombardment of Da Nang in December 1946, resulting in the evacuation of Viet Minh nationalist forces, under Ho Chi Minh, from Hanoi to a new base of operations farther to the north.

Chapter 2

1. The words "Official—Truman Announces Japanese Surrender" were first displayed on the Times Square Tower at 7:03 in the evening of Tuesday, August 14, 1945. In a lead story the next day *The New York Times* described how the city "Let Go" in Times Square as "hundreds of thousands Roar Joy" after the "Victory Flash" was received. *The New York Times*, August 15, 1945.

2. David R. Boylan telephone interview with the author, August 27, 1983.

3. Some two dozen Americans had arrived in Hanoi by the end of August 1945. These included operatives of the OSS and Air Ground Aid Section, which had arrived first—on August 22—under the command of Major Archimedes Patti. They were soon joined by a small U.S. Civil Affairs and Military Government group (CAMG) under the command of Colonel Stephen Nordlinger. See Ronald H. Spector, *Advice and Support: The Early Years of the U.S. Army in Vietnam, 1941–1960* (New York: The Free Press, 1985), 56.

4. Major Patti and other members of the OSS were present when Ho Chi Minh delivered his speech in Ba Dinh Square. In his important memoir describing that and other events in Vietnam immediately following the end of World War I, Patti records Ho's words with a slightly different variant in translation: "Do you hear me distinctly, fellow countrymen?" Archimedes L.A. Patti, *Why Vietnam? Prelude to America's Albatross*, 250. For another description of Ho Chi Minh's speech see William J. Duiker, *Ho Chi Minh: A Life* (New York: Hyperion, 2000), 322–324.

5. *Boston Herald*, October 8, 1945.

6. David R. Boylan, letter to the author, March 29, 1980.

7. Troops returning on ships and disembarking along the Eastern Seaboard were brought into three primary ports: Boston, New York, and Hampton Roads, Virginia. According to data supplied by the U.S. Army, and provided by the American Merchant Marine Institute, 597 troopships, including many Victory and Liberty type cargo ships converted for that purpose, delivered 616,542 returning service personnel during an 84-day period between V-E Day in early May to early August 1945, the month before *Stamford Victory* arrived with additional returning troops. During this period some seven ships a day arrived on average in the three primary ports along the East Coast. The comparative number of ships arriving in these ports is as follows: New York (344), Hampton Roads (174), Boston (79). The average number of troops arriving in Boston on each ship during this 84-day period was 1,738. See "GI's Coming Home on American Ships," *Marine Engineering and Shipping Review*, October 1945, 158.

8. David R. Boylan letter to the author, March 29, 1980.

9. Francis Dooley, telephone interview with the author, January 21, 1982. Dooley was the Deck Maintenance/Able Seaman in SS *Georgetown Victory* for the voyage to Vietnam in late 1945.

10. David R. Boylan, letter to the author, March 29, 1980. His list of estimated dates for voyage departures and arrivals for *Stamford Victory* were contained in a subsequent letter written on March 24, 1981.

11. For the full text of Truman's speech with commentary soon after the fact, see *The New York Times*, October 27, 1945, 33.

12. As one example of assistance provided by the United States to France, and which would be applied directly to its needs in Vietnam and throughout French Indochina, some 75 ships, including 31 of the EC2-S-C- (Liberty) type cargo vessels, were sold to the French under provisions of the Merchant Ship Sales Act of 1946. That purchase was made easier by the U.S. government, which deposited a credit of more than $17 million with the U.S. Maritime Commission for this purpose. See *Marine Engineering and Shipping Review*, "Vessels Sold Under Provisions of Merchant Ships Sales Act of 1946," February 1947, 58–62.

13. David R. Boylan, letter to the author, March 29, 1980.

14. Boylan letter to author.

15. In an official report submitted to the Combined Chiefs of Staff by the Supreme Allied Commander, South East Asia, Vice Admiral Mountbatten, it was noted that "Minesweeping and surveying of the sea approaches, the anchorage at Cap St. Jacques, and the river to Saigon, had been completed, and sea communications

opened, by the 28th September." Quoted in Allan W. Cameron, ed., *Viet-Nam Crisis, A Documentary History*, Vol. 1 (Ithaca, NY: Cornell University Press, 1971), 59.

16. The estimate of American ships involved and French troops moved in this operation is my own, and was first presented in an unpublished research paper—"Sailing Into War: The U.S. Troopship Movement to Vietnam in 1945"—as partial fulfillment of doctoral degree requirements at New York University, in 1984. Much of this information subsequently appeared in a chapter of my doctoral dissertation, completed at NYU in 1991. See Michael Gillen, "Roots of Opposition: The Critical Response to U.S. Indochina Policy, 1945–1954," 99–128.

17. David R. Boylan, letter to the author, March 29, 1980. He later estimated that *Stamford Victory* arrived in Saigon on November 17, 1945, and departed on November 20, 1945, for Borneo and Brisbane, Australia, and eventually completed the voyage—his last as a merchant seaman—in New York in May 1946. David R. Boylan, letter to the author, March 24, 1981.

18. According to agreements arrived at during the Conference at Berlin (Potsdam) in July 1945, the British were given responsibility for disarming and repatriating the Japanese in Vietnam below the 16th parallel, while the Chinese were given the same task in the northern sector. For one description of the British role in Vietnam at this time, see George Rosie, *The British in Vietnam* (London: Panther, 1970).

19. Rosie, *The British in Vietnam.*

20. U.S. Department of State, *Bulletin*, XIII (October 21, 1945), 646, as quoted in *Vietnam Crisis*, 64–65.

21. This is my own estimate. The number of French troops carried to Vietnam in American Victory ships at this time varied between 1,000 and 2,000, and would have been in the range of 1,500 on average. Given that at least eight ships, and as many as 12, were involved in the operation, the total number of French troops involved would therefore have ranged from 12,000 to 18,000, or between about 24 and 36 percent of the total French force of 50,000 estimated to be in Vietnam at the start of 1946.

22. On American interest in establishing France as a "bulwark" against Soviet influence in the immediate aftermath of World War II see, for example, Daniel Yergin, *Shattered Peace: The Origins of the Cold War and the National Security State* (Boston: Houghton Mifflin Co., 1977), 88–89.

23. Patti, *Why Vietnam?*, 325.

24. Patti, *Why Vietnam?*, 278. Patti had also written to Wedemeyer that "Viet Minh [was] strong and belligerent and definitely anti–French." He advised: "Suggest no more French be permitted to enter French Indo-China and especially not armed." Spector, *Advice and Support*, 57.

25. Henry Dooley, letter to the author, December 10, 1981.

26. Memorandum, "The 88 Personnal [sic] of the Troopship S.S. Pachaug Victory" to the National Maritime Union, November 2, 1945, U.S. Maritime Commission, Mail and Files Section, File No. 901–14892, "Pachaug Victory."

27. *NMU Pilot*, February 15, 1946.

28. *NMU Pilot*, February 15, 1946.

29. *NMU Pilot*, February 15, 1946.

30. *NMU Pilot*, February 15, 1946.

31. *Stars and Stripes* (West Europe Edition), November 22, 1945, as quoted in *The Militant*, December 8, 1945, 3.

32. *PM Daily*, November 12, 1945, 20.

33. *The Militant*, December 15, 1945. The Atlantic Charter was the product of meetings held in secret in Placentia Bay, Newfoundland between President Roosevelt and British Prime Minister Winston Churchill aboard the heavy cruiser *Augusta* and battleship *Prince of Wales* in August 1941. War goals and principles were agreed upon, and in the third of its eight points it was emphasized that these leaders respected "the right of all peoples to choose the form of government under which they will live; and they wish to see sovereign rights and self-government restored to those who have been forcibly deprived of them." Though subject to varying interpretations and debate subsequently, the Charter was considered a "beacon" of hope for many people ruled by colonial powers, and the nationalist Ho Chi Minh would say in 1945 that it "was looked upon as the foundation of future Vietnam." For one of the most complete accounts of the Atlantic Conference, see Theodore A. Wilson, *The First Summit: Roosevelt and Churchill at Placentia Bay 1941* (Boston: Houghton Mifflin, 1969).

34. Patti, *Why Vietnam?*, 364–365.

35. Arthur Hale to Mr. Holland, December 1945, Philip E. Gallagher Papers, U.S. Army, Department of Military History, Washington, D.C., 20.

36. Hale to Holland.

37. *The Pentagon Papers: The Defense Department History of United States Decisionmaking on Vietnam*: The Senator Gravel Edition, 4 Vols. (Boston: Beacon Press, 1971) (hereinafter cited as *PP* [Gravel], I:1,I, A., PA-24; Patti, *Why Vietnam?*, 380.

38. For a description and analysis of early opposition to U.S. support of the French in Vietnam during this period and in the decade following, see Gillen, "Roots of Opposition: The Critical Response to U.S. Indochina Policy, 1954–1954" (PhD diss., New York University, 1991).

Chapter 3

1. U.S. Department of State *Bulletin*, XIII (October 21, 1945), 646.

2. *PP* (Gravel), I: 17–18.

3. Another good source for background and details relating to the Atlantic Conference is James MacGregor Burns, *Roosevelt: The Soldier of Freedom* (New York: Harcourt Brace Jovanovich, 1970), 125–131; *FRUS*, 1941, Vol. I (Washington: USGPO, 1958).

4. Samuel P. Hayes, ed., *The Beginning of American Aid to Southeast Asia: The Griffin Mission of 1950* (Lexington, MA: Heath Lexington Books, 1971), 3.

5. In addition to some 1,300 French military personnel released from incarceration in Saigon, the French moved quickly otherwise to reestablish a military presence in Vietnam following the Japanese surrender. While this would be prevented in the north due to Chinese control there until after the accords agreed to in March 1946, portions of the French Fifth *Regiment d'Infanterie Coloniale* (RIC) began to arrive in the south at least as early as September 12, when one company of the 5th RIC was flown into Tan Son Nhut airport from Rangoon. According to Archimedes Patti, formerly with the OSS in Vietnam, these French military personnel were moved "directly to the ammunition depots, the port facilities, and military warehouses" in Saigon. A few weeks later some 1,000 French military personnel debarked in Saigon from the French cruiser *Triomphant*, and they were soon followed in the final months of the year by the arrival of several thousands more troops of the 5th RIC aboard American troopships. See Patti, *Why Vietnam?* 298, 562; David G. Marr, *Vietnam 1945: The Quest for Power* (Berkeley: University of California Press, 1995), 542, 545; Gillen, "Roots of Opposition," 99–150.

6. George McT. Kahin, *Intervention: How America Became Involved in Vietnam* (New York: Alfred A. Knopf, 1986), 435, n. 13; *New York Herald Tribune*, March 10, 1947;

7. Kahin, *Intervention*, 7.

8. Department of Defense, *United States-Vietnam Relations, 1945–1967*, Book 1, Part 1, A, A-24.

9. Harold Isaacs, *No Peace for Asia* (New York: Macmillan, 1947), 161.

10. Under provisions of the Merchant Marine Ship Sales Act of 1946, passed in February 1946, some 75 ships including 31 of the EC2-S-C1 (Liberty) type cargo vessels were sold to the French. The purchase was expedited by the U.S. government, which deposited a credit of more than $17 million with the U.S. Maritime Commission for that purpose. See *Marine Engineering and Shipping Review*, "Vessels Sold Under Provisions of Merchant Marine Ship Sales Act of 1946," February 1947, 58–62; L.A. Sawyer and W.H. Mitchell, *The Liberty Ships: The History of the 'Emergency' Type Cargo Ships Constructed in the United States During the Second World War*, 2nd Edition (New York: Lloyd's of London Press, Ltd., 1985), 15; Noel Clinton Eggleston, "The Roots of Commitment: United States

Policy Towards Vietnam, 1945–1950," (PhD dissertation, University of Georgia, 1977), 55, 90, 201; U.S. Department of State, *Treaties and Other International Agreements of the United States of America, 1776–1949*, Charles I. Bevans, ed., 12 vols. (Washington: USGPO, 1968–1974), 7, 1146; Department of Commerce, Report on Indochina, August 2, 1946, 9.

11. This was the assessment of former OSS operative Archimedes Patti. See his *Why Vietnam?*, 380.

12. See Yergin, *Shattered Peace*, 88–89.

13. Department of Defense, "Policy Statement on Indochina," September 27, 1948, *FRUS*, 1948 (Washington, DC: USGPO, 1974), VI, 48, as quoted in Herring, 7.

14. Yergin, *Shattered Peace*, 88–89.

15. The American policy of political neutrality towards Indochina and Vietnam specifically seemed to have changed at least as early as September 1945 when General Gallagher was directed to intercede on behalf of the French in negotiations with Lu Han, commander of Chinese occupation forces in the northern sector of Vietnam as had been designated and agreed to at the Potsdam Conference for postwar handling of disarmament and repatriation of the Japanese. After receiving new orders from his superiors in Washington, Gallagher, as historian George McT. Kahin explains, "undertook to influence Lu Han to help the French regain control over the northern half of Vietnam, but the Chinese were in no hurry to comply." See Kahin, *Intervention*, 19–20. See also Edward R. Drachman, *United States Policy Toward Vietnam, 1940–1945*, 135–137.

16. The articulation of the threat posed by the Soviet Union, and by extension attitudes towards Ho Chi Minh and any identified as within the Soviet ideological orbit, was notably evident in a "long telegram" sent to the U.S. State Department by George F. Kennan in February 1946. This surfaced again publicly in an article published in *Foreign Affairs* in July 1947 by "Mister X," which was a pseudonym used by Kennan, still working for State. This established the concept of "containment" toward the Soviet Union as the foundation for Cold War policy that would play a major role in the evolution of U.S. Vietnam policy and eventual large-scale intervention in the Vietnam conflict.

17. Ho Chi Minh was too readily dismissed in the Cold War context and beyond as a communist and "tool" of the Soviet Union, despite the fact that his credentials as a Vietnamese nationalist—an attitude long established by his family and pre-dating the existence of the Soviet Union—was well known.

18. See for example Robert Shaplen, *The Lost Revolution* (New York: Harper & Row, 1965), 27–35.

19. The reference to Cam Ranh Bay, which would become a major logistical supply port and base for the United States starting in 1965, is in Moffat's December 1946 letter from Vietnam to the State Department. *United States and Vietnam: 1944–1947*, Staff Study, Senate Committee on Foreign Relations (Washington: USGPO, 1972), Appendix II, 41–42; Porter, I, 129–130.

20. For references to attacks on Japanese merchant shipping in Cam Ranh Bay and surrounding areas during World War II see, for example, Samuel E. Morison, *History of United States Naval Operations in World War II*, Vol. XIII, *The Liberation of the Philippines: Luzon, Mindanao, the Visayas, 1944–1945* (Boston: Little, Brown and Co., 1959), 166–169; Mark P. Parillo, *The Japanese Merchant Marine in World War II* (Annapolis, MD: Naval Institute Press, 1993), 143; John Prados, *Combined Fleet Decoded: The Secret History of American Intelligence and the Japanese Navy in World War II* (Annapolis, MD: U.S. Naval Institute Press, 2001).

21. Porter, *Vietnam*, I, 130.

22. Porter, *Vietnam*.

23. Porter, *Vietnam*.

24. In later testimony before the U.S. Senate, Abbot Low Moffat, chief of the State Department's Southeast Asia desk in the mid-1940s, who had interacted with Ho Chi Minh in-country on a number of occasions, commented that he "never met an American, be he military, O.S.S., diplomat, or journalist, who did not reach the same belief: that Ho Chi Minh was first and foremost a Vietnamese nationalist." Senate, Causes, Origins, and Lessons, 169; see also Kahin, *Intervention*, 7.

25. For the full text of the March 6 accord, including the timeline for French withdrawal from Vietnam, see Gettleman, et al., *Vietnam and America*, 41–48; Porter, *Vietnam*, I, 95–97.

26. For the relationship between the European and Southeast Asia "desks" of the State Department, specifically regarding Southeast Asia and "matters relating to the European colonies" in the area—wherein the views of the European desk would prove dominant—see Kahin, *Intervention*, 434, n. 8, and Kahin's seminal *Nationalism and Revolution in Indonesia* (Cornell University Press, 1952). For Abbot Low Moffat's views and his "discerning assessment of the weaknesses in the majority position," as George Kahin has put it, see Moffat's testimony in Senate, *Causes, Origins, and Lessons*, 161–174.

27. Patti, *Why Vietnam?*, 382.

28. Harold Isaacs, *The New Republic*, February 3, 1947, 18.

29. Factors that contributed to Ho's entering into negotiations with the French during this period are discussed in various sources, including Bernard B. Fall, *The Two Viet-Nams*, 72; Ellen J. Hammer, *The Struggle for Indochina*, 145–152; Joseph Buttinger, *Vietnam: A Dragon Embattled*, Vol. I, 362–366; Kahin, *Intervention*, 20; Patti, 382.

30. George McT. Kahin and others have

referred to the March 6 accord, which "on paper" appeared to offer much towards Vietnamese autonomy, as a "sham." See Kahin, *Intervention*, 22. See also Buttinger, *Vietnam*, 373–387; Hammer, *Vietnam's Will to Live*, 150–177; Fall, *The Two Vietnams*, 73–74.

31. Duicker, *Ho Chi Minh*, 373–377.

32. Duicker, *Ho Chi Minh*.

33. Patti, *Why Vietnam?*, 383. For a brief biographical sketch of d'Argenlieu, see Patti, *Why Vietnam?*, 475–476.

34. Regarding the French bombardment of Haiphong, and civilian casualties stemming from that, see Kahin, *Intervention*, 22–23, 442, n. 56; Hammer, *Vietnam's Will to Live*, 193, n. 9. Not surprisingly, Hammer suggests that the casualty figure provided by the French was a conservative estimate.

35. For Ho Chi Minh's and the DRV's initial reaction to the outcome of the Chinese civil war, and early contact with the newly formed People's Republic of China (PRC), see Duicker, *Ho Chi Minh*, 416–18.

36. The language of NSC 48, approved on December 30, 1949, is a case in point. See *PP* (Gravel), I: 39.

37. Having been removed from the State Department's Southeast Asian desk in 1947, Moffat served in various far-flung diplomatic posts until his retirement from the diplomatic service in 1961. He remained opposed to growing U.S. involvement in the Vietnam War, and regarding policy decisions that had been made in the crucial years of the late 1940s, he later said: "I was bitterly disappointed, but the die was cast. We were going to follow a hard line on Communism wherever it put up its ugly head. I thought we were right back in the wars of religion." See *The New York Times*, April 23, 1996, B, 9.

38. For contemporaneous references to the use of Marshall Plan funds for the re-imposition of colonial rule in Southeast Asia, see for example, *The New York Times*, December 22, 1948, 1; *Far East Spotlight* (Committee for a Democratic Far Eastern Policy), November 1948, 10–11. For a later recollection of the diversion of funds for this purpose see Dean Rusk, *As I Saw It* (New York: W.W. Norton, 1990), 424.

39. Harold R. Isaacs, "Indo-China: A Fight for Freedom," *The New Republic*, February 3, 1947, 16–18. As a war correspondent for *Newsweek*, Isaacs was sent to Vietnam in late 1945 to witness and report on events following the Japanese surrender. His recollections, including one of the few eyewitness accounts of American troopships arriving with French troops, were the basis for *No Peace for Asia* (New York: Macmillan, 1947).

40. Regarding the use of Marshall Plan funds for the French war in Indochina, see, for example, Owen Lattimore, *The Situation in Asia* (Boston: Little, Brown and Co., 1949), 194; Eggleston, *Roots of Commitment*, 86–87; See also *PP* (Gravel), I: 184.

41. Fred Killingback interview with author, October 23, 1982. The *African Dawn* was a 479-foot, 6,577 gross ton, C2-S-B1 type cargo ship built for Farrell Line at Federal Shipbuilding and Drydock Co., Kearny, New Jersey in 1942. After being sold to the Maritime Administration in 1960, and having its name changed to *African Lake* in 1965, the ship was finally laid up in 1969 and then scrapped in 1972.

42. Killingback interview with author.

43. *Public Laws*, Chapter 626, 714.

44. French casualties (undefined) in Indochina have been put at about 8,000 for 1948, and a total of about 30,000 (undefined) between 1946 and early 1949. Total French Union casualties (all categories) for the entire First Indochina (French) War range from 55,000 upwards to 110,000 or more depending on which forces are included in the count, and who is doing the counting and analysis. In coverage relating to the 1997 dedication of a memorial to French war dead in Indochina, total losses were put at 55,000, though the number of names actually placed on the memorial was limited to 34,798. French historian Michel Bodin of the *Faculte des Sciences humaines Guerre d'Indochine* would put the total number of casualties sustained by all forces fighting for the French Union—French soldiers "from the metropole," North African colonials, French Foreign Legionnaires, indigenous (Indochinese) regulars, and auxiliaries in the Associated States of Indochina—at 112,032. See Anne Swordson, "France's Lonely Vietnam Memorial," *The Washington Post*, February 24, 1997; "France Pays Late Homage To Its Dead In Indochina," *The New York Times*, December 20, 1996, Section A, 6; www.indochine.uquam.ca.

45. Passed by a vote of 238–122 in the House of Representatives and 55–24 in the Senate, the Mutual Defense Assistance Act was signed into law by President Truman on October 6, 1949.

46. SFRC, Hist. Series, "Military Assistance Program, 1949," 35–36 as quoted in U.S. Government and the Vietnam War, I, 55. Lippmann's critical views regarding the Truman Doctrine and containment policy are discussed at length in his book *The Cold War: A Study in U.S. Foreign Policy* (New York: Harper & Row, 1947). See also Gillen, "Roots of Opposition," 216.

47. Kahin, *Intervention*, 27; *FRUS*, 1948, 6:48.

48. Kahin, *Intervention*, 25; *PP* (Gravel), I: 40.

49. Early reference to the Bao Dai Solution and the U.S. pledge to support this was reported in *The New York Times*, January 25, 1949.

50. *PP* (Gravel), I: 39.

51. Memorandum, Raymond B. Fosdick to Philip Jessup, November 4, 1949. See Porter, I, 214–215. For another related reference to Fosdick, from whose pen criticism of U.S. Indochina policy at this time seemed to "flow freely," see Eggleston, *Roots of Commitment*, 119.

52. Kahin, *Intervention*, 26.

53. Kahin, *Intervention*.

54. For critical reaction to evolving U.S. Vietnam policy between 1946 and 1949 see Gillen, "Roots of Opposition," 151–222.

55. Fosdick memorandum to Jessup, November 4, 1949.

56. Hayes, *The Beginnings of American Aid to Southeast Asia* (D.C. Heath and Company, 1971), 5.

57. Hayes, *The Beginning of American Aid to Southeast Asia*, xi.

58. See note 16, above.

59. *PP* (Gravel), I: 195.

60. For an early iteration of what would become known as the "domino theory" regarding potential loss of areas of Southeast Asia to communist influence and control, see for example NSC 64, "Report of the National Security Council on the Position of the United States with Respect to Indochina, February 27, 1950, *PP* (Gravel), I: 76–77, 361–362]. Regarding the Griffin Mission, see also *PP* (Gravel), I: 367–370.

61. Hayes, *The Beginnings of American Aid to Southeast Asia*, 1–2.

62. *PP* (Gravel), I: 195.

63. For a good description and analysis of Chinese and Soviet attitudes leading up to their formal recognition of the Democratic Republic of Vietnam (DRV), the reactions of Viet Minh leadership towards the newly formed People's Republic of China (PRC), and immediate impact of formal recognition on Viet Minh military operations, see, for example, William J. Duicker, *Ho Chi Minh: A Life* (New York: Hyperion, 2000), 416–423, 425–430.

64. Kahin, *Intervention*, 35. U.S. concern about support of the PRC for Viet Minh military operations against the French in northern Vietnam, and acknowledgement of movement of weapons and equipment from China to the border area with Vietnam for that purpose, begins to appear soon after formal recognition between the PRC and DRV became a reality. See, for example, *PP* (Gravel), I: 362.

Chapter 4

1. Based on crew description. According to a later note about *Steel Rover* in an Isthmian Lines website, the voyage origination was Baltimore and destination—with California, Manila, Hong Kong, and Vietnam in between—was Port Swettenham (later Port Klang) in Malaysia. See www.isthmianlines.com/ships.

2. *Seafarers Log*, October 13, 1950, 6.

3. Some 465 ships of this standard hull type were built in the United States between 1939 and 1945, including many—such as Bogue-class escort carriers—completed for service with the U.S. Navy. Others, such as would join the fleet of American President Line ships—were completed as combination cargo and passenger ships. The C-3 had a designed service speed of 16.5 knots, was 492 feet in length—much faster and some

50 feet longer than the "Liberty" ships, and 37 feet longer than and with equivalent speed to the faster "Victory" type cargo ships—built during World War II. The service of many would be extended after conversion to containerships in the late 1960s and early 1970s. See Lane, *Ships for Victory*, 28.

4. Truman announced publicly on May 8 that the United States, "convinced that neither national independence nor democratic evolution exists in any area dominated by Soviet Imperialism, considers the situation such as to warrant its according economic and military equipment to the Associated States [of Indochina] and France." Department of State, *American Foreign Policy 1950–1955: Basic Documents*, Vol. 2 (Washington, DC: USGPO, 1957), 2365–2366.

5. *Seafarers Log*, October 13, 1950, 6.

6. Fred E. Huntley, letter to the author, April 14, 1980.

7. Huntley letter to author.

8. *Seafarers Log*, October 13, 1950, 6.

9. *Seafarers Log*.

10. Huntley letter to the author, April 14, 1980.

11. *Seafarers Log*, October 13, 1950, 6. According to a later note in the Isthmian Steamship Co. website, shelling of the SS *Steel Rover* commenced at 11:30 a.m. local time, and was attributed to "2 unidentified motor junks. The attackers fired 5 shells causing superficial damage and no casualties" www.isthmianlines.com/ships.

12. Huntley letter to the author, April 14, 1980.

13. Specific recommendations for the dispatch of an American military advisory group, initially to monitor the distribution and use of military equipment, and expenditures of funds, were made by the Melby-Erskine mission after its visit to Vietnam in July 1950. The first members of the new Military Assistance Advisory Group (MAAG) arrived in Saigon in September 1950. The MAAG in Vietnam would number 65 officers and enlisted personnel by October 1950, and more than three times that number within a year. On the Melby-Erskine mission and the creation of the MAAG, see Spector, *Advice and Support*, 111–121.

14. *Seafarers Log*, October 13, 1950, 6.

15. *Seafarers Log*.

16. *Seafarers Log*.

17. Lucien Bodard, *The Quicksand War* (New York: Little Brown and Co., 1967), 220.

18. Bodard, *The Quicksand War*.

19. Bodard, *The Quicksand War*.

20. Bodard, *The Quicksand War*.

21. Kahin, *Intervention*, 83.

22. *PP* (Gravel), I: 373.

23. Spector, *Advice and Support*, 115.

24. For the early history and increase in MAAG personnel in Vietnam during the First Indochina (French) and Second Indochina

(American) War periods, see *Ibid.*, 115–21, 146–47, 259–62, 291–95, 378–79.

25. Fall, *Street Without Joy*, 33–34.

26. For more on the defeat of French forces in late 1950 in the far northern areas of Vietnam, including Lang-son, see *Ibid.*, 32–33; Spector, *Advice and Support*, 125.

27. Fall, *Street Without Joy*, 32–33.

28. Fall, *Street Without Joy*.

29. For what he calls the "the de Lattre Interlude" period in Vietnam from 1950 to 1951, see Spector, *Advice and Support*, 135–148.

30. Spector, *Advice and Support*, 143.

31. While there are, no doubt, earlier references to the concept of what would become known as the "domino theory"—the expected "falling" of countries in Southeast Asia in succession should a key country in the area be taken over by a communist regime—it appears in an important classified policy memorandum, NSC 64—"The Position of the United States with Respect to Indochina"—on February 27, 1950. PP (Gravel), I: 76–77, 361. See also "Statement of Policy by the National Security Council on United States Objectives and Course of Action With Respect to Southeast Asia," June 25, 1952, in PP (Gravel), I, 385–386.

32. Spector, *Advice and Support*, 14; Fall, *Street Without Joy*, 6.

33. Fall, *Street Without Joy*.

34. Fall, *Street Without Joy*, 47.

35. Spector, *Advice and Support*, 119.

36. Spector, *Advice and Support*, 120.

37. Fall, *Street Without Joy*, 39.

38. General de Lattre was one of nine commanders-in-chief of the *Expeditionnaire Francais en Extreme-Orient* (CEFEO)—the French Far East Expeditionary Corps—in Vietnam between 1945 and 1956.

39. Regarding the withdrawal of cargo ships from the various reserve fleets during the Korean War, see, for example, Louis Francis Harlow, "An Analysis of the National Defense Reserve Fleet, The Ready Force Component and Their Capacity To Meet National Emergency," Thesis for the Master of Arts Degree, Naval Postgrad School, Monterey, CA, 1979, 18. https://apps.dtic.mil/dtic/tr/fulltext/uz/a075418.pdf. A full breakdown of the types of ships removed during this period has not been determined, but as of early 1952, with nearly a year remaining to the Korean War, the National Shipping Authority provided the following list of ship types broken out of reserve during the first two years of the war: 442 Liberty ships, 29 Victory ships, 13 C1s, 11 C1-M-AV1s, 2 passenger ships (probably of the C3 hull type). See *The Master, Mate & Pilot*, February 1952, 11. In their published history of the Victory ship construction program during World War II, authors L.A. Sawyer and W.H. Mitchell state that 196 Victory ships were ultimately broken out of reserve for service during the Korean War. See Sawyer and Mitchell, *Victory Ships and Tankers*, 29.

40. James Brady has used this common reference to the Korean War as the title for his published memoir about service in Korea as an infantry platoon leader. See James Brady, *The Coldest War: A Memoir of Korea* (New York: Orion Books, 1990).

41. This would have been one of 98 Liberty ships purchased by Greece from the United States between 1946 and 1947. The identity of this particular ship has not been determined, but another Greek Liberty, the *Ioannis K*, become a fixture—and photographed later by many American GIs while on R&R leave in Vung Tau—after running aground in the same general area in 1968.

42. *Seafarers Log*, July 1950.

43. *Southwestern Victory*, a VC2-S-AP2 type cargo ship built in 1945 by California Shipbuilding Corp., was one of some 778 ships withdrawn from the National Defense Reserve Fleets (NDRF) for service during the Korean War. These NDRFs had been created to provide storage and upkeep for many of the unprecedented numbers of merchant ships constructed in the United States during World War II. While many of the ships withdrawn from reserve for Korea—including the other "Victory"-type cargo ships mentioned in this chapter—were among this number, fewer than 500 of the "Victorys" were actually built during World War II. Because of their speed they were considered particularly well suited for postwar trans-Pacific service, but most of the ships withdrawn for this first "national emergency" for which the NDRFs were developed if needed, were actually of the slower EC2- "Liberty ship" type. When the reserve fleets were later used beginning in 1965 for the Vietnam sealift (a smaller number had also been withdrawn in 1956 for the Suez emergency)—some 170 ships—mostly of the Victory type—would be withdrawn from reserve for service in many cases extending into the early 1970s, before either being returned to reserve fleets or sold for scrap. For background on the NDRF program, with specific reference to numbers of ships withdrawn for the Korean War, see Harlow, "An Analysis of The National Defense Reserve Fleet."

44. Francis J. Dooley, letter to the author, June 7, 1982.

45. Dooley letter to author.

46. Dooley letter to author.

47. Dooley letter to author.

48. Dooley letter to author.

49. Dooley letter to author.

50. Deliveries made to Saigon by these 150 ships in the early months of 1952 were a significant part of an overall total of 539,847 tons (valued at $334.7 million) made to both Saigon and Haiphong between June 1950 and December 1952. See *FRUS*, 1952–54, 13:156–57 as cited in Kahin, *Intervention*, 37, n. 11.

51. "More Help For Vietnam," *The New York Times*, June 1, 1952, 8.

52. "More Help For Vietnam."

53. Department of State Press Release No. 473, June 18, 1952, *U.S.-Vietnam Relations*, Book 8, 518–519; Porter, *Vietnam*, I, 410.

54. *Greeley Victory* was a VC2-S-AP2 type Victory ship launched at Permanent Metals Corp., Yard No. 2, Richmond, California in August 1945, too late for service during World War II. The ship was placed in a National Defense Reserve Fleet (NDRF), then withdrawn for Korean War service. As Eugene Kauder's recollections reveal, this also included service to Indochina, as was the case for other ships "broken out" for Korea. The ship was later placed in the James River, Virginia NDRF.

55. Letter from Eugene Kauder to author, October 16, 1979.

56. Kauder letter to author.

57. Kauder letter to author.

58. The approval of additional funds for the French in Indochina in late 1953 and early 1954 increased the overall underwriting of the French War to a reported 78 percent in 1954, an amount representing approximately one third of the total foreign aid commitment of the United States in 1954. See George McT. Kahin, *Intervention*, 42, 446, n. 26; *PP* (Gravel), I: 77, 408.

59. *West Coast Sailors*, July 27, 1951, 1.

60. *The Master, Mate and Pilot*, August 1951, 4.

61. *The Master, Mate and Pilot*.

62. *Lynn Victory* was a VC2-S-AP2 type Victory ship launched at Bethlehem-Fairfield Shipyard, Baltimore, Maryland in 1944, placed in service during World War II, then placed in a reserve fleet after the war. It was withdrawn from reserve for service in Korea, and again for Vietnam, before being returned to the NDRF, James River, Virginia.

63. *Seafarers Log*, March 7, 1952.

64. Robert Shaplen, *The Lost Revolution* (New York: Harper & Row, 1965), 82.

65. Bernard Fall, *Street Without Joy* (Mechanicsburg, PA: Stackpole Books, 1994), 55. Fall notes here that in addition to equipment manufactured in China, American-made equipment captured during the war in Korea was also supplied to the Viet Minh. See also Porter, *Vietnam*, I, 447; Spector, *Advice and Support*, 24–25, n. 8.

66. Kahin, *Intervention*, 38.

67. Gillen, "Roots of Opposition: The Critical Response to U.S. Indo-China Policy."

68. Nesa F. DuBuyne, Congressional Record Service, "American War and Military Operations Casualties Lists and Statistics," 2018. The overall figure here is broken down as follows: Direct battle-related deaths: 33,739; other causes: 2,825. The number of wounded in action not resulting in death is given as 103,284. These figures represent a downward revision from earlier sources.

69. Bernard B. Fall, *Hell In A Very Small Place: The Siege of Dien Bien Phu* (Philadelphia: J.B. Lippincott Co., 1967), 293–294; Kahin, *Intervention*, 40.

70. Porter, *Vietnam*, I, 421; Spector, *Advice and Support*, 168, n. 7.

71. Porter, *Vietnam*.

72. Porter, *Vietnam*, 421.

73. *PP* (Gravel), I, 383; Porter, *Vietnam*, I, 410.

74. Porter, *Vietnam*, 439; Spector, *Advice and Support*, 172.

75. Spector, *Advice and Support*, 167.

76. *U.S.-Vietnam Relations*, Bk. 9, 11–14, as cited in Porter, *Vietnam*, 426–28.

77. Porter, *Vietnam*.

78. Porter, *Vietnam*.

79. While the United States continued to support the French in Indochina following World War II, pressure was placed on them to grant a greater degree of autonomy to the Vietnamese. NSC 48 (February 1950) stated: "The United States has, since the Japanese surrendered, pointed out to the French Government that the legitimate nationalist aspirations of the people of Indochina must be satisfied, and that a return to the prewar colonial rule is not possible." Unfortunately, France was only willing to go so far, to allow incremental steps towards greater autonomy but only within the French Union. That remained the insurmountable crux of the problem, to the bitter end. For this quotation and the full text of NSC 48, see *PP*, I: 361.

80. Shaplen, *The Lost Revolution*, 94.

81. Peter Macdonald, *Giap: The Victor in Vietnam* (New York: W.W. Norton and Co., 1993), 117. For additional information on the background, appointment, and reputation of Navarre, see MacDonald, *Giap*, 109–111; Spector, *Advice and Support*, 173–175.

82. Fall, *Street Without Joy*, 105; Spector, *Advice and Support*, 175.

83. NIE-91, June 4, 1953, "Probable Developments In Indochina Through Mid-1954," *PP* (Gravel), I: 391–404. This would also appear in U.S.-Vietnam Relations, Bk 9, 45–55, and Porter, *Vietnam*, I, 440–448.

84. Porter, *Vietnam*.

85. Porter, *Vietnam*.

86. Spector, *Advice and Support*, 172–173.

87. "Report by Lt. General John W. O'Daniel to Joint Chiefs of Staff on U.S. Joint Military Mission to Indochina," July 14, 1953, as appears in Porter, *Vietnam*, I, 452–453; *U.S.-Vietnam Relations*, Bk. 9, 69–79, 85–86.

88. *U.S.-Vietnam Relations*, 175; Porter, *Vietnam*, I, 452–453; Spector, *Advice and Support*, 175.

89. Fall, *Street Without Joy*, 105.

90. Fall, *Street Without Joy*, 178, n. 51, 176, n. 46.

91. Fall, *Street Without Joy*.

92. *U.S. Government and the Vietnam War*, I, 130, as quoted in Gillen, "Roots of Opposition," 327.

93. Gillen, "Roots of Opposition," 327, n. 33.

94. *U.S. Government and the Vietnam War*, I, 130.

95. *U.S. Government and the Vietnam War*, 131–132; Gillen, "Roots of Opposition," 328, n. 35.

96. *CR*, 99, 7789; Gillen, "Roots of Opposition," 326–329.

97. Department of State Documents, "U.S.-French Supplementary Aid Agreement on Indochina: Letters Exchanged By Dillon and Foreign Minister Bidault, September 29, 1953" in Porter, *Vietnam*, I, 474–477.

98. Porter, *Vietnam*, 474.

99. Porter, *Vietnam*, 475–477.

100. Fall, *Street Without Joy*, 105.

101. Macdonald, *Giap*, 124–125.

102. Fall, *Street Without Joy*, 105–106.

Chapter 5

1. Francis E. Davis letter to author, February 5, 1979. *Jose Marti* was one of more than 2,700 "Liberty"-type cargo ships built during World War II. The ship was sold for commercial use in 1951, underwent a series of name changes as such until, as *Nata*, she was scrapped at Hirao, Japan in 1966.

2. France began its movement of troops and equipment southward from northern Vietnam on August 5, 1954. Two days later the United States Navy began movement of assets as part of Task Force 90's evacuation support operation, code-named Passage to Freedom. See Schreadley, *From the Rivers to the Sea*, 29–31. See also Edwin Bickford Hooper, et al., *The United States Navy and the Vietnam Conflict*, Vol. 1, *The Setting of the Stage to 1959*. Washington, DC: Department of the Navy, Navy Historical Division, 1976.

3. Heath to State Department, February 9, 1954, 751G.00/2–954, Records of State Dept., as quoted in Spector, *Advice and Support*, 189.

4. Fall, *Hell in a Very Small Place*, 432.

5. In one history of Task Force 90 (Operation Passage to Freedom), the combined number of U.S. Navy and American civilian-crewed, privately owned ships involved in the operation is put at 107. This included 47 naval ships with USS prefix, 14 civilian-crewed ships of the Navy's Military Sea Transportation Service (MSTS), 11 privately owned merchant ships under contract to the MSTS, 26 LSTs, and nine LCUs. See Ronald Bruce Frankum, *Operation Passage to Freedom: The United States Navy in Vietnam, 1954–1955* (Lubbock: Texas Tech University Press, 2007). Richard Schreadley describes the initial group of Task Force 90 ships as consisting of five APA attack transports, two AKA attack cargo ships, two LSDs (Landing Ship Dock), two APD high speed transports, and four LSTs (Landing Ship Tank). Ships of the MSTS fleet and privately owned under contract began joining the operation after the first few weeks. He stated that within three months there were more than 100 U.S. Navy and MSTS ships involved in the

operation. See Schreadley, *From the Rivers to the Sea*, 29–31.

6. See note 5.

7. Francis E. Davis letter to author, October 20, 1979.

8. For details regarding the Provisional Military Demarcation Line as described in the Geneva Accords, see Porter, *Vietnam*, I: 642–643. For background and analysis relating to the Geneva Accords see, for example, *PP* (Gravel), I: 108–178.

9. For particulars relating to the Demilitarized Zone (DMZ) as detailed in the Geneva Agreement, see PP (Gravel), I: 108–178.

10. Davis letter to author.

11. Davis letter to author, February 5, 1979.

12. The number of Viet Minh troops, administrative cadres, and members of their families moving north varies but is generally estimated at between 130,000 and 150,000. The "best current estimate" arrived at by the compilers of the *Pentagon Papers*, George McT. Kahin has noted, was 134,269. See *PP* (GPO Edition), 2 [IV, A.5 Tab 1]:17.). The 150,000 figure is that of R.B. Stebbins and the Research Staff of the Council on Foreign Relations, which noted that this number of Viet Minh troops and their families were transported north in Polish and Russian ships during the period allowed for relocation. See Kahin, *Intervention*, 75–76, and notes 16 and 17 for those pages. R.L. Schreadley on the other hand, in his study of the U.S. Navy in Vietnam states that "fewer than" 100,000 went north during this period; however, he does not provide a source for that assertion. See his *From the Rivers to the Sea*, 30.

13. Kahin, *Intervention*, 76, n. 17. Kahin notes that Catholics leaving northern Vietnam for the south represented approximately one half of the total Catholic population in that area, and their arrival to Saigon and the vicinity would nearly double the size of the Catholic population in that area.

14. The USNS *General A.W. Brewster* was a 523-foot-long Attack Transport (AP-155) built for the U.S. Navy during World War II. It had a capacity for carrying 3,823 troops. *General Brewster* was transferred to the Army Transport Service after the war, and later to the Navy's Military Sea Transportation Service (MSTS). As such she had a crew of civilian merchant seamen with the exception at times of a small number of U.S. Navy communications and other specialists.

15. In *Deliver Us From Evil* Tom Dooley devotes a chapter to describing the over-the-beach evacuations—with references to *Jules Verne* and *General Brewster*—from the province of Bui Chu. See Thomas A. Dooley, *Deliver Us from Evil* (New York: Signet Books, 1961), 95–100.

16. Dooley, *Deliver Us from Evil*. Dooley was medical officer on USS *Montague*, the first ship of Task Force 90 to arrive for refugee evacuation operations from Haiphong in August 1954.

He assisted with boarding an initial 2,061 Vietnamese refugees, and remained on the ship for two round-trip runs between Haiphong and Saigon. He was then attached to the newly created Preventive Medicine and Sanitation (PMS) Unit tasked with developing temporary camps around Haiphong and providing medical care for refugees there before they were cleared for embarkation for transportation to Saigon and other destinations in the area. Dooley remained in Haiphong until the very end of the 300-day period provided by the Geneva Accords for regrouping movements to the south, and north, of the 17th parallel.

17. Dooley, *Deliver Us from Evil*.

18. Fall, *The Two Viet-Nams*, 153–154; Kahin, *Intervention*, 76–77.

19. Kahin, *Intervention*, 77; *Pentagon Papers* (NY Times Edition), 16–17; *PP* (Gravel), I: 579.

20. Kahin, *Intervention*, 76, n. 18.

21. Chester Cooper, *The Lost Crusade: America in Vietnam* (Dodd, Mead & Company, 1970), 130 as quoted in Kahin, *Intervention*, 76.

22. See "Lansdale Team's Report on Covert Saigon Mission in 1954 and 1955" in *PP*, Gravel), i: 573–583; See also "Cold War Tactics After Geneva in Gettleman et al., *Vietnam and America*, 81–96.

23. The first American ships to arrive in Haiphong as part of Task Force 90, Operation Passage to Freedom were the U.S. Navy Attack Transports *Menard* and *Montrose*, both of which departed with the first loads of refugees for the south—*Menard* with 1,924 refugees on board and *Montrose* with 2,100—on August 17 and 18, 1954, respectively.

24. *Seafarers Log*, August 20, 1954, 14; March 4, 1955.

25. Charles A. Welch interview with author, September 27, 1982. For a contemporaneous account of the meeting of ships' crews held in Saigon that Welch was unable to attend, see "Future Grim, Saigon on Feverish Bender," *Seafarers Log*, March 4, 1954.

26. Welch interview with author.

27. Welch interview with author. See also Hooper, *The United States Navy and the Vietnam Conflict*, 288.

28. Welch interview with author.

29. M.C. Cooper letter to author.

30. Cooper letter to author.

31. Welch interview with author.

32. Cooper letter to author.

33. Welch letter to author.

34. For the most complete book-length account of Operation Passage to Freedom to date, including the names of all American merchant ships, and civilian-crewed ships of the U.S. Navy's Military Sea Transportation Service (MSTS), see Ronald B. Frankum Jr., *Operation Passage to Freedom: The United States Navy in Vietnam, 1954–1955* (Lubbock: Texas Tech University Press, 2007).

35. Frankum Jr., *Operation Passage to Freedom*, 193–195, 202–203.

36. Of the more than 800,000 persons known to have moved south during the 300-day relocation period by either sea, air, or overland, some 310,848 were transported in American ships involved with Task Force 90, Operation Passage to Freedom. The vast majority of this number—a reported 293,002—were Vietnamese civilians. Another 14,868 of the overall number were Vietnamese military personnel, while an additional 2,978 French military personnel were also transported in American ships. While most by far—more than 587,000— moved by sea transportation, some 213,635 were airlifted by the French. The remainder of the overall number— some 41,328 Vietnamese civilians—found their own way south, presumably overland or by small watercraft of various types. See Frankum, *Operation Passage to Freedom*, 205; *MSTS Magazine*, July 1955.

37. Francis Davis letter to author.

38. On the production of the C1-M-AV1 types specifically for deployment to the Southern Pacific during World War II, see Lane, *Ships for Victory*, 628, 640.

39. The *Hennepin* was launched in 1944 as a C1-M-AV1 type Attack Cargo Ship (AK-187) for service with the U.S. Navy in the Pacific. She was transferred to the Army Transportation Service after the war, and then to the Navy's MSTS when she departed Yokohama on August 30, 1954, to join Task Force 90, Operation Passage to Freedom. She arrived in Haiphong on September 7, 1954, and was involved for more than three months—until December—carrying cargo to Saigon and Cap St. Jacques in support of the evacuation operation.

40. *Ibid.*

41. Regarding USNS *Herkimer*, see Frankum Jr., *Operation Passage to Freedom*, 191.

42. *Sealift Magazine*, August 1962, 23.

43. NSC 5492/2 "Review of U.S. Policy in the Far East," August 20, 1954, U.S. Vietnam Relations, Book 10, 731–733, 726–737. See also Porter, *Vietnam*, I: 666–668.

44. Porter, Vietnam, I, 667.

45. See "Lansdale Team's Report on Covert Saigon Mission in 1954 and 1955" in *PP*, I: 573–583.

46. Porter, Vietnam, I, 64–65.

47. Frankum, *Operation Passage to Freedom*, 204. In *Deliver Us From Evil* Dr. Thomas A. Dooley, who had remained in Haiphong to the bitter end of the 300-day regrouping period, only makes reference to one ship being on hand as the refugee camps, and such things as the Catholic Mission in Haiphong, were being closed out, the civilian-crewed troopship USNS *General Brewster*.

48. Fall, *The Two Viet-Nams*, 129. While the precise numbers are elusive, *Esperance* was one of several French warships and troop transports

known to have been operating in areas of Indochina between 1945 and 1955. Others included *Richelieu* and *Triomphant*, which delivered troops to Saigon in October 1945, as well as the cruisers *Suffren* and *Gloire*. Troopships included the *Cephec* and *Barfluer*. See, for example, Ellen Hammer, *Vietnam's Will to Live*, 119; *Le Guerre D'Indochine, 1945–1954*.

Chapter 6

1. For descriptions of Diem's return to Vietnam, see for example Robert Shaplen, *The Lost Revolution*, 101–104; Karnow, *Vietnam*, 218.

2. Karnow, 218.

3. Karnow, 213.

4. Shaplen, *The Lost Revolution*, 105–106.

5. For Lansdale's own description of his and the Saigon Military Mission's arrival and early days in Vietnam, see "Lansdale Team's Report on Covert Saigon Mission in 1954 and 1955," in *The Pentagon Papers* (Gravel), I:573–583. See also Marvin E. Gettleman, et al., eds., *Vietnam and America*, 81–92.

6. Regarding the Military Assistance Advisory Group (MAAG) providing cover for CIA SMM personnel, see Gettleman, 85.

7. "Lansdale Team's Report," *PP* (Gravel), I: 573–583.

8. Regarding the use of "black propaganda" to influence movement of Vietnamese refugees from the northern to the southern sector, see for example, Fall, *The Two Vietnams*, 153–154; Kahin, *Intervention*, 76–77.

9. Bernhard Fall has written that of approximately 860,000 Vietnamese refugees who left the north for the southern sector, some 600,000 of them were from Vietnam's Catholic minority. This represented some 65 percent of the total Catholic population of North Vietnam, while more than 99.5 percent of the non-Catholics were reported to have remained in place. See Fall, *The Two Viet-Nams*, 154.

10. Regarding the numerical impact of Catholic refugee movement from north to south on the overall Catholic population in the southern sector see, for example, Kahin, *Intervention*, 76, n. 17.

11. Regarding Diem's resignation as Minister of the Interior under Bao Dai in protest against French influence on the court, see, for example, Fall, *The Two Viet-Nams*, 239; Shaplen, *The Lost Revolution*, 108.

12. For the circumstances of Diem's arrest and subsequent release by the Viet Minh following the Japanese surrender in 1945, see, for example, Fall, *The Two Viet-Nams*, 240–241; Shaplen, *The Lost Revolution*, 109–110.

13. Fall, *The Two Vietnams*, 235, 240; Kahin, *Intervention*, 79.

14. Fall, *The Two Viet-Nams*, 236.

15. Regarding Ho Chi Minh's cooperation with the United States during World War II, see, for example, Young, *The Vietnam Wars*, 1–19; Kahin, *Intervention*, 11–13; Patti, *Why Vietnam?*, 45–58; Duiker, *Ho Chi Minh*, 292–294.

16. For comparison of Diem's and Ho Chi Minh's somewhat similar early nationalist influences and education, and decisions that led to their eventually taking widely divergent paths, see, for example, Fall, *The Two Viet-Nams*, 235–240.

17. While Ho Chi Minh had organized the Viet Nam Doc Lap Dong Minh—commonly known in its abbreviated form as Viet Minh—in 1941 specifically to resist the Japanese occupation, and would cooperate with U.S. military forces in doing so, the nature of Diem's relationship with the Japanese was quite different, and still subject to differing characterizations. George McT. Kahin's particular assessment, for example, has been to state that "in the eyes of a significant number [Diem's] nationalist credentials had been tarnished by his willingness to work with Japanese occupation authorities." See Kahin, *Intervention*, 79.

18. Seth Jacobs, *America's Miracle Man in Vietnam: Ngo Dinh Diem, Religion, Race and the U.S.* (Durham, NC: Duke University Press, 2004).

19. Jacobs, *America's Miracle Man in Vietnam*.

20. For Cardinal Spellman's visit with refugees aboard USNS *General Howze* in Saigon in January 1955, see *MSTS Magazine*, "Passage to Freedom," March 1955, 5.

21. See Morgan, *The Vietnam Lobby*. Regarding expectations that Ho Chi Minh would probably have won the national elections if they had been allowed to be held in July 1956 as per the Geneva Accords, see, for example Shaplen, *The Lost Revolution*, 120.

22. Fall, *The Two Vietnams*, 242–243.

23. Ralph Braibanti, "The Southeast Asia Collective Defense Treaty," *Pacific Affairs*, Vol. 30, No. 4 (December 1957), 321–341.

24. For an excellent description and analysis of SEATO and the role it played in the formulation of U.S. Vietnam policy, see Kahin, *Intervention*, 71–76.

25. Young, *The Vietnam Wars*, 46.

26. Young, *The Vietnam Wars*, 47.

27. Regarding the immediate need for revitalizing Diem's military and police forces, and the Seven Point Program conceived to affect that end, see Spector, *Advice and Support*, 237–238.

28. Spector, *Advice and Support*, 231–232.

29. Spector, *Advice and Support*.

30. Spector, *Advice and Support*, 256, 259.

31. Spector, *Advice and Support*, 247–249.

32. Kahin, *Intervention*, 61, 63–64; Young, *The Vietnam Wars*, 38–42, 52–54.

33. Young, *The Vietnam Wars*, 47.

34. Burchett, *Inside Story of the Guerilla War*, 120.

35. Shaplen, *The Lost Revolution*, 119–120.

36. Joseph G. Morgan, *The Vietnam Lobby: The American Friends of Vietnam, 1955–1975* (Chapel Hill: University of North Carolina Press, 1997).

37. Kahin, *Intervention*, 80.

38. Young, *The Vietnam Wars*, 58.

39. Young, *The Vietnam Wars*, 53–54.

40. *PP* (Gravel), I: 611.

41. This quote, while appearing at different times, using different language, and spoken in reference to a variety of foreign leaders who U.S. presidents believed were worth supporting in different areas, despite their serious flaws, is often attributed to Harry S. Truman in reference to the Nicaraguan dictator Somoza.

42. For a contemporaneous back-channel U.S. Government communication revealing both the overt and covert characteristics of TERM, and manner in which additional personnel were surreptitiously added to MAAG contrary to ceiling authorized by the Geneva Accords, see, for example, Telegram from Ambassador in Vietnam (Durbrow) to Department of State, January 24, 1958, Office of the Historian, "The Role of the TERM; The Question of the MAAG [personnel] Ceiling" at history.state.gov. See also Spector, *Advice and Support*, and Vietnam War Timeline: 1956–1957 at: VietnamGear.com.

43. Spector, *Advice and Support*, 256.

44. Spector, *Advice and Support*, 257.

45. Spector, *Advice and Support*, 261.

46. Robert D. Murphy letter to Secretary of Defense, May 1, 1956, U.S.-Vietnam Relations, 10: 1058; Spector, *Advice and Support*, 262.

47. Regarding the absorption of "temporary" TERM personnel permanently into the ranks of the MAAG—contrary to international agreement limitations that had been placed on MAAG—see *PP* (Gravel), II: 416, 438. For the "continuing problem posed by overt and covert status of TERM in Vietnam" and personnel limits reflected in the Geneva Accords, monitored by the International Control Commission (ICC), and how MAAG might figure in alleviating the problem, see Telegram from the Ambassador in Vietnam (Durbrow) to DOS, January 14, 1958. DOS, Central Files, 751G.5-MSP/1–2458.

48. Donald J. Merchant letter to author, April 12, 1982.

49. Launched in 1943 as a C3-S-A2 hull type, converted and entered service in 1944 as U.S. Army Troopship *Sea Owl*, then returned to U.S. Maritime Administration in 1946, the ship entered private commercial service with Isthmian Lines as *Steel Scientist* in 1947. It was sold for scrapping in 1971.

50. Launched as *Sea Porpoise*, a C3-S-A2 hull-type Army troopship at Ingalls Shipbuilding Corp. in 1943, this ship was returned to the U.S. Maritime Administration after the war, and then sold to Isthmian for commercial service in 1947. She was operated by Isthmian, as *Steel Flyer*, until sold for scrapping in 1971.

51. For an analysis of Diem's attitude and the rationale of the United States for not honoring the mandate for holding nationwide elections in Vietnam as mandated by the Geneva Accords, see for example, Kahin, *Intervention*, 88–90.

52. Pham Van Dong letter to Diem, March 7, 1958, Vietnam News Agency, in Porter, *Vietnam*, 2: 34–36.

53. The MAAG attachment at Bien Hoa at that time consisted of 13 Americans who were tasked with providing advisory support to the South Vietnamese 7th Infantry Division. See Spector, *Advice and Support*, 329.

54. The attack at Bien Hoa resulting in what are considered the first American military personnel killed in the Vietnam War is described in Spector, *Advice and Support*, 329; Karnow, *Vietnam*, 10–11; Young, *The Vietnam Wars*, 69.

55. Spector, *Advice and Support*, 329.

56. Spector, *Advice and Support*.

57. Young, *The Vietnam Wars*, 53.

58. John F. Kennedy inaugural address, January 20, 1961.

59. USNS *Core* arrived at Saigon on December 11, 1961, with the first delivery of helicopters and their air and ground crews.

Chapter 7

1. With the start of Operation Ranch Hand in January 1962 the spraying of chemical defoliants from aircraft, largely for the purpose of depriving the enemy of cover that might be used for attacks, including against shipping, began in earnest. These defoliants were also used to a lesser degree to deprive the enemy combatants of food sources. These defoliants not only changed the look of the land, as noted by those who had moved through those areas over time, but would eventually be found to have contributed to cancer and birth defects.

2. Jfklibrary.gov.

3. Regarding the increase of U.S. military advisors in South Vietnam beyond the numbers authorized by the 1954 Geneva Accords, and through 1962, see, for example, Kahin, *Intervention*, 139. See also *The Pentagon Papers* (Gravel), II:454.

4. For a personal account of the creation of the National Liberation Front by one of its founders, see Mrs. Nguyen Thi Dinh, "No Other Road to Take," in Gettleman, et al., *Vietnam and America*, 165–188. For the guiding principles of the NLF see "Manifesto of the South Viet Nam National Front for Liberation, December 1960" in Porter, *Vietnam*, 86–89. See also Gettleman et al., *Vietnam and America*, 188–192. For an account of early post-Geneva organizational work in South Vietnam considered the "embryo" for the future NLF, see Wilfred G. Burchett, *Vietnam: The Inside Story of the Guerilla War* (New York: International Publishers, 1965), 119–126.

5. Gettleman, et al., *Vietnam and America*, 187.

6. Spector, *Advice and Support*, 316.

7. Donald L. Merchant letter to author, April 12, 1982.

8. OASD (Comptroller) SEA statistical summary, Table 103, 26 September 1973; Table 860B, February 18, 1976; Table 322, April 19, 1972; Table 350A, October 5, 1973. See also *America in Vietnam*, 24.

9. Schreadley, *From the Rivers to the Sea*, 38.

10. Gettleman, et al., *America in Vietnam*, 24.

11. Schreadley, *From the Rivers to the Sea*, 37, 43.

12. Schreadley, 43.

13. Operation Ranch Hand was begun on January 11, 1962, and by the end of its nine years in operation some 18 million gallons of chemical defoliants had been sprayed in Vietnam and Laos. See Schreadley, *From the Rivers to the Sea*, 39–41.

14. Schreadley, *From the Rivers to the Sea*, 41.

15. *PP* (Gravel), II: 809.

16. *PP* (Gravel), II: 769–770.

17. *PP* (Gravel), II: 751.

18. *PP* (Gravel), II: 758–759.

19. *PP* (Gravel), II: 755.

20. *PP* (Gravel), II: 756.

21. See Gettleman, et al., *Vietnam and America*, 216–225. For an eyewitness account of the self-immolation of Thich Quang Duc written by an American journalist based in Saigon, see *Reporting Vietnam*, I, 79–85.

22. Regarding the Buddhist Crisis that resulted in the downfall of Diem, see *PP* (Gravel), II: 225–228, 232–236; Gettleman, et al., *Vietnam and America*, 216–224.

23. Whether or not Kennedy seriously intended to continue drawdown of U.S. advisory personnel in South Vietnam remains a subject of debate. However, in addition to the National Security Action Memorandum (NSAM) ordering the drawdown, there is much evidence otherwise to support the argument, not the least of which was the initial withdrawal of 1,000 advisors taking place before the end of 1963. Roger Hilsman, JFK's Assistant Secretary of State for Far Eastern Affairs, has argued that Kennedy had not only ordered Secretary of Defense McNamara to begin planning for a phased withdrawal as early as July 1962 but "had laid the groundwork for doing so" that resulted in the initial withdrawal of 1,000. See Hilsman's letter to the editor, *The New York Times*, January 20, 1992. See Also Theodore C. Sorensen and Arthur Schlesinger, Jr., "What Would JFK Have Done?" *The New York Times*, December 4, 2005, 13. See also *The Pentagon Papers* (Gravel), II: 160–200, 769–770.

24. Gettleman, et al., *America in Vietnam*, 24.

25. *PP* (Gravel), III: 11, 171–178.

26. Porter, *Vietnam*, II: 221–223.

27. Porter, *Vietnam*, II: 222.

28. Porter, *Vietnam*, II: 222.

29. "Memorandum for the Record by McNamara," December 21, 1963, in Porter, *Vietnam*, II: 232.

30. Porter, *Vietnam*, II: 233.

31. Porter, *Vietnam*.

32. The Escort carriers, which would commonly come to be called "baby flattops" and "Jeep carriers," evolved out of a C3-S-A2 merchant ship hull type, and were used as convoy escorts involved with considerable success in anti-submarine warfare. For a description of how they figured in the American shipbuilding program during World War II see Frederic C. Lane, *Ships for Victory: A History of Shipbuilding Under the U.S. Maritime Commission in World War II*, 612–614.

33. Launched as a Bogue-Class "Escort Carrier" (CVE-13) in May 1942, *Core* saw active service in the Atlantic in convoy escort and anti-submarine warfare during World War II. She was reclassified following the war as "Escort Helicopter Aircraft" (CVHE-13) in 1955, then as "Utility Aircraft Carrier" (T-)(CVU-13) with MSTS and a civilian crew in 1958. As such *Core* was deployed to South Vietnam for the first of multiple times in 1961. See *The New York Times*, December 12, 1961, 21.

34. *The New York Times*, December 12, 1961, 21.

35. *Life*, March 16, 1962.

36. Still in the advisory period before the introduction of large-scale American combat units, some 12 MLMS "minesweeping launches" were provided by the United States for "river forces" usage by the South Vietnamese Navy, with support from U.S. Navy advisory personnel then being introduced into the country. Additional larger minesweepers were also being introduced for offshore "sea force" use. It would not be until May 1966 that the U.S. Navy deployed Mine Squadron 11, equipped with between 12 and 13 57-foot fiberglass hulled MSBs at Nha Be on the Long Tau Channel below Saigon. See *Schreadley, From the Rivers to the Sea*, 38; Sherwood, *War in the Shallows*, 17–19.

37. Regarding the NLF 65th Special Operations Group and the failed attack on USNS *Core*, see Ho Si Thanh, *The Commandos of Saigon: Untold Stories* (Hanoi: People's Army Publishing House, 2007), 11–13.

38. Ho Si Thanh, *The Commandos of Saigon*.

39. Ho Si Thanh, *The Commandos of Saigon*.

40. Ho Si Thanh, *The Commandos of Saigon*.

41. Ho Si Thanh, The Commandos of Saigon.

Chapter 8

1. This was spoken in confidence to LBJ's press aide Bill Moyers, and later broadcast in 1983 in the PBS/WGBH (Boston) documentary program "LBJ Goes to War (1964–1965)."

2. *The New York Times*, February 15, 1997.

3. Robert S. McNamara, *In Retrospect: The*

Tragedy and Lessons of Vietnam (New York: Times Books, 1995), 102.

4. *PP* (Gravel), II: 769–770.

5. McNamara, *In Retrospect*, 102.

6. McNamara, *In Retrospect*.

7. McNamara, *In Retrospect*, 101.

8. French and American writers, each writing about different phases of the Vietnam War, would find similar references to use in describing the nature of the war in which their countries had become inextricably involved. One of Lucien Bodard's books about the First Indochina (French) period, for example, would be published under the title *The Quicksand War: Prelude to Vietnam* (1967), while one of David Halberstam's books about the Second Indochina (American) war would be published under the title *The Making of a Quagmire: America and Vietnam During the Kennedy Era* (1965).

9. Secretary of Defense, Memorandum for the President, December 21, 1963, *PP* (Gravel), III: 495.

10. Secretary of Defense, Memorandum for the President, March 16, 1964, *PP* (Gravel), III: 500.

11. Secretary of Defense, Memorandum for the President, December 21, 1963, *PP* (Gravel), III: 494–496.

12. Secretary of Defense, Memorandum for the President, 502.

13. Secretary of Defense, Memorandum for the President.

14. Secretary of Defense, Memorandum for the President, 495.

15. Secretary of Defense, Memorandum for the President, 494.

16. Secretary of Defense, Memorandum for the President.

17. McNamara, *In Retrospect*, 116.

18. McNamara, *In Retrospect*.

19. Kahin, *Intervention*, 147.

20. The Joint Chiefs of Staff, Memorandum for the Secretary of Defense, January 22, 1964, *PP* (Gravel), III: 497.

21. Public Papers of the President of the United States: Dwight D. Eisenhower, 1954, 381–390.

22. The Joint Chiefs of Staff, Memorandum for the Secretary of Defense, January 22, 1964, *PP* (Gravel), III: 497.

23. The Joint Chiefs of Staff, Memorandum for the Secretary of Defense.

24. The Joint Chiefs of Staff, Memorandum for the President.

25. McNamara, *In Retrospect*, 111.

26. The figure given for American advisory personnel in Vietnam by the end of 1964 is generally put at just under 23,000, an increase of some 45% from the level at the end of 1963. See *PP* (Gravel), III:90.

27. Secretary of Defense, Memorandum for the President, March 16, 1964, *PP* (Gravel), III: 500. The expression of non-attribution appears at various points in official communications later published in *The Pentagon Papers*. Emphasizing the

need to publicly deny covert operations, this contributed to misinformation provided in the immediate aftermath of the Tonkin Gulf incidents. See, for example, *PP* (Gravel), III: 117–118, 141.

28. Commissioned in November 1942 as USS *Card* (CVE-11) with a U.S. Navy crew, the ship was decommissioned in May 1946 after service in World War II, then recommissioned in May 1958 as USNS *Card* with the Navy's Military Sea Transportation Service (MSTS) and operated with a civilian crew of merchant seamen. Additional medical, communications, or special mission specialists would be added as needed, as would be done for other ships of the MSTS fleet. At the time of the mining attack in Saigon in May 1964 *Card* was still operated as an MSTS "nucleus" ship with a civilian crew. After repairs and resuming service with MSTS, *Card* was finally decommissioned in March 1970, struck from the register later that year, and then scrapped in Clatskanie, Oregon in 1971.

29. Joseph Houston Forsyth interview with the author, August 22, 1982.

30. The role of the 65th Operations Group is described in Ho Si Thanh, *The Commandos of Saigon: Untold Stories* (Hanoi: People's Army Publishing House, 2007).

31. See description of the failed attack on *Core* in 1963, chapter 7, above.

32. There is a discrepancy in accounts of the timing of explosive detonations on USNS *Card*. Those who placed the charges have recorded that as happening at 3:00 that morning. See Ho Si Thanh, *Commandos of Saigon*.

33. Raymond Arbon's recollections appear in *Sealift Magazine*, July 1964, 3, 6; [State of] *Washington Post*, May 2, 1964, A1, A9.

34. *Washington Post*.

35. Forsyth interview with author.

36. Forsyth interview with author.

37. Forsyth interview with author.

38. Forsyth interview with author.

39. Donald L. Merchant letter to the author.

40. Merchant letter to the author.

41. *Seafarers Log*, February 21, 1964.

42. For a brief description and analysis of the Tonkin Gulf incidents, including related Defense Department Press Releases of August 2–3, 1964, see Marvin E. Gettleman, et al., *Vietnam and America*, 250–252. See also Marilyn B. Young, *The Vietnam Wars*, 119–121, and Stanley Karnow, *Vietnam: A History*, 366–373.

43. Steve Edwards, "Stalking The Enemy's Coast," USNI *Proceedings*, February 1992, 60.

44. "The Phantom Battle That Led to War," *U.S. News and World Report*, July 23, 1984, 3–36; Robert J. Hanyuk, "Skunks, Bogies, Silent Hounds, and Flying Fish: The Gulf of Tonkin Mystery, 2–4 August 1964," *Cryptologic Quarterly*, Winter 2000/Spring 2001, Vol. 19, No. 4/Vol. 20, No. 1. See also Kahin, *Intervention*, 219–227.

45. Kahin, *Intervention*.

46. For references to conditions that

contributed to the sonar malfunction or mis-reading, see, for example, Captain Herrick's report to CINCPAC soon after the investigation aboard *Maddox* following the incident.

47. Captain Herrick's report to CINCPAC was not made public for another 10 years. See Kahin, *Intervention*, 221.

48. Kahin, *Intervention*, 220–221.

49. For the full wording of the Tonkin Gulf Resolution see Gettleman, et al., *Vietnam and America*, 252.

50. For the connection made soon after the first Tonkin Gulf incident between it and U.S.–sponsored covert operations conducted against North Vietnam as part of Oplan 34A, see, for example, "Telegram from [Secretary of State] Rusk to [General] Taylor," August 3, 1964, in Porter, *Vietnam*, Vol. II, 301–302.

51. Stockdale's eyewitness account of the second Tonkin Gulf incident was first made public in *The Washington Post* on October 7, 1984. For a more complete account see James Stockdale and Sybil Stockdale, *In Love and War* (New York: Harper & Row, 1984), 3–36. See also, Stockdale, *A Vietnam Experience: Ten Years of Reflection* (Stanford: Hoover Institution, 1984).

52. For one early news account of "war risk pay" soon after the Tonkin Gulf incidents see Don Bevona, "May Demand War Risk Pay," *New York Herald Tribune*, August 10, 1964.

53. Bevona, "May Demand War Risk Pay."

54. Bevona, "May Demand War Risk Pay."

55. While new, more modern merchant ship types were designed and constructed in the decade following World War II, none of these ships anticipated the revolution in modifications and new ship design construction that were to follow, in part because of issues that came to light—such as inordinately long turn-around times and port security—soon after the major logistical buildup began in Vietnam in the mid-1960s. The new ship type that would emerge, begin appearing along the Vietnam Run in the late 1960s, and contribute to the disappearance of traditional break-bulk, boom-loaded and unloaded merchant ship types, was the containership. The appearance of containerships—initially from existing traditional freighters that had been modified to meet the new demand, will be discussed in a later chapter here.

56. Vietnam—Shipping Policy Review, Part 2, 308.

57. "USNS 'Comet' and U.S. Lines 'American Charger' Wind Up Transatlantic Cargo-Handling Tests," *Sealift Magazine*, November 1963, 3–5, 16–17.

58. "USNS 'Comet' and U.S. Lines 'American Charger' Wind Up Transatlantic Cargo-Handling Tests," 3.

59. "USNS 'Comet' and U.S. Lines 'American Charger' Wind Up Transatlantic Cargo-Handling Tests," 4–5.

60. "USNS 'Comet' and U.S. Lines 'American Charger' Wind Up Transatlantic Cargo-Handling Tests," 16.

61. "USNS 'Comet' and U.S. Lines 'American Charger' Wind Up Transatlantic Cargo-Handling Tests."

62. Le Cato letter to author, June 4, 1979. The ship involved with USNS *Comet* in this exercise was actually the *American Charger*. It was, however, of the post-World War II Challenger class of merchant ships, which might explain Captain Le Cato's incorrect reference to the ship's name.

63. "Comet Stars in Operation Blackout," MSTSLANT *Mariner*, Vol. 13, No. 9, September 1964, 1, 7.

64. "Comet Stars in Operation Blackout."

65. On Steel Pike I see, for example, Lieutenant Colonel James B. Soper, USMC, "Observations: Steel Pike and Silver Lance," USNI *Proceedings Magazine*, November 1965, Vol. 91/11/753; Robert S. Burns, "Big War Game for Merchant Fleet," *New York Herald Tribune*, October 11, 1964; "NMU Crews Shine in Defense Test," *NMU Pilot*, November 12, 1964, 20; "Defense Test Proved Value of U.S. Fleet," *NMU Pilot*, December 10, 1964.

66. For the number of American ships involved in Steel Pike I crewed by merchant seamen, privately owned and part of the U.S. Navy's MSTS fleet, and figures relating to troops and cargoes carried, see Lieutenant Colonel James B. Soper, USMC, "Observations: Steel Pike and Silver Lance," *Proceedings Magazine*, November 1965, Vol. 91/11/753, 50–54. See also Burns, "Big War Game," *The New York Herald Tribune*, October 11, 1964.

67. Vietnam—Shipping Policy Review, Part 2, 308.

68. Vietnam—Shipping Policy Review, Part 2, 310.

69. Vietnam—Shipping Policy Review, Part 2, 316.

70. Burns, "Big War Game," *The New York Herald*, October 11, 1964; "Crews Shine in Defense Test," *The NMU Pilot*, November 12, 1964.

71. *PP* (Gravel), III: 666–667.

72. *PP* (Gravel), III: 668.

73. *PP* (Gravel), III: 667–668.

74. *PP* (Gravel), III: 657.

75. "MSTS Troopships to Recrew," *NMU Pilot*, August 6, 1964, 4.

76. *PP* (Gravel), III, 629.

77. PP (Gravel), III: 406.

78. Vietnam—Shipping Policy Review, Part 2, 406.

79. "Sealift's Future Termed Assured," *The New York Times*, November 25, 1965, 73.

Chapter 9

1. Regarding the continued strengthening of the southern insurgency (NLF/VC) in late 1964

and early 1965, see for example, "NSC Working Group in Vietnam, 24 November 1964," *PP* (Gravel), III: 651–652; See also General Maxwell Taylor Briefing, November 27, 1964, *PP* (Gravel), III: 667–673; JTM to MCN, "Proposed Course of Action in Vietnam" and "Annex—Plan of Action for South Vietnam," 3/24/65 (first draft), *PP* (Gravel), III: 694–695.

2. JTM to MCN, "Proposed Course of Action in Vietnam."

3. For an early reference to use of reprisal strikes against North Vietnam following the attack on the U.S. BOQ, Saigon in late December 1964, see, for example, *Pentagon Papers*, Gravel Edition, Vol. III, p. 138.

4. "American Experience: LBJ Goes to War" (1964–1965), PBS/WHYY. This was the recollection of Jack Valenti, Special Assistant to President Johnson and later longtime president of the Motion Picture Association of America.

5. For coverage of Vietnamese student demonstrations, see for example, *The New York Times*, August 22–24, 1964. For context and analysis of Buddhist and Vietnamese student demonstrations between 1964 and 1966, see for example, Kahin, *Intervention*, 227–29, 268–69, 309, 414–32; Young, *The Vietnam Wars*, 167–68.

6. Planning for and decision to make initial landing of U.S. Marines at Da Nang in March 1965 are referenced in *PP*, III: 629.

7. U.S. military strength by the end of 1965 was put at 184,314. See *PP* (Gravel), II: 417.

8. Captain John M. Le Cato letter to author, May 22, 1979.

9. The Military Sea Transportation Service (MSTS), which had the responsibility for moving the majority of troops to Vietnam in the initial buildup years, was notified by the Department of Defense in mid-April 1965 to provide troopships for this purpose. Most would be shifted from the European Run. See Lane C. Kendall, "U.S. Merchant Shipping and Vietnam," 131. Due to the lack of publicity given to the initial buildup of logistical support capability, some media outlets would eventually suggest it had been done in secrecy. See, for example, Edward A. Morrow, "Secret Build-Up Laid to Pentagon," *The New York Times*, August 20, 1965.

10. The large troopships used in the early years of the Vietnam War, all constructed during World War II, were basically of two types: the larger P2s and the C4s. At 610 feet long overall, the P2s were the largest ships built by the U.S. Maritime Commission during World War II. Origins of the troopship construction program, designs produced, contracts awarded, and final numbers constructed are described in Frederic C. Lane's *Ships For Victory: A History of Shipbuilding Under The U.S. Maritime Commission in World War II* (Baltimore: The Johns Hopkins Press, 1951), 617–626.

11. Lane C. Kendall, "U.S. Merchant Shipping and Vietnam," *Naval Review* (1968), 130,

139. For one account of shipboard routine aboard Vietnam-bound transports in the early buildup period, see, for example, "Life Aboard Vietnam-bound Transport Described as 'Varied' For Troops," *Sealift Magazine*, June 1966, 16–18.

12. The percentage of troops carried to Vietnam in American civilian-crewed transports in the early buildup years is generally put at around 60 percent.

13. Captain Brian Hope letters to author, February 7, 2015, February 25, 2015; January 24, 2018.

14. The *Baton Rouge Victory*, one of the ships withdrawn from reserve for the Vietnam sealift, was sunk by a command-detonated mine while transiting the Long Tau River to Saigon on August 23, 1966. Seven members of its engine department were killed in the blast.

15. *American Marine Engineer* reported to members of MEBA, District 2 in its June 1965 issue, for example, that "shipping has been so good lately" due in part to the reactivation of a number of ships from reserve, including *Monticello Victory, Olga Achilles, Steel Admiral, Transorleans,* and *Transhartford.* These withdrawals from reserve fleets, clearly intended to provide support for the Vietnam buildup, were not given much publicity otherwise.

16. George Horne, "Military Sea-lift Getting Started," *The New York Times*, July 17, 1965.

17. For contemporary accounts of the 1965 maritime strike see, for example, George Horne, "Shipping Strike Rivals Resume Parley," *The New York Times*, August 7, 1965.

18. Horne, "Military Sealift Getting Started," *The New York Times*, July 17, 1965.

19. Captain Thomas A. King interview with author, January 19, 1979, New York, NY.

20. Captain Thomas A. King, "Ships of the National Defense Reserve Fleet Sail Again," USNI *Proceedings*, August 1968, 139.

21. King, "Ships of the National Defense Reserve Fleet Sail Again."

22. Helen D. Bentley, *The Baltimore Sun*, July 17, 1965.

23. Interview with Captain Thomas Patterson, 5 June 1981, Baltimore, MD.

24. See, for example, Helen D. Bentley, "U.S. Takes 15 Ships Out of Reserve Unit," *The Baltimore Sun*, July 18, 1965; "Ships for Vietnam Being Rushed," *The Baltimore Sun*, July 25, 1965; Walter Hemshar, "Reactivating Ships for War Duty," New York *Herald Tribune*, August 1, 1965.

25. "Merchant Shipping Support in the Viet Nam Crisis," U.S. Department of Commerce, Maritime Administration, March 22, 1966 (unpublished for internal distribution); King, "Ships of the National Defense Reserve Fleet Sail Again," USNI *Proceedings*, August 1968, 139.

26. Captain Thomas Patterson interview with author.

27. Regarding crew shortages and return of retirees to active service, see, for example, "Extra

Vietnam Ships Hard to Man from Fading Rolls," *The New York Times*, July 21, 1965; John P. Callahan, "Officer Shortage at Sea is Feared," *The New York Times*, December 11, 1965.

28. Regarding maritime academy and college responses to manpower shortages, and decisions to adjust requirements and graduation dates, see for example, George Horne, "U.S. Calls Parley on Sealift Crews: Engineers Needed in Ships with Vietnam Supplies," *The New York Times*, December 21, 1965; John P. Callahan, "Officer Shortage at Sea is Feared," *The New York Times*, December 11, 1965; John P. Callahan, "U.S. Urged to Act on Engineer Need," *The New York Times*, December 30, 1965.

29. Based on material drawn from *Linfield Victory* deck log for NSA voyage #10, U.S. Maritime Administration, Eastern Region Archives, New York.

30. *Linfield Victory*, deck log.

31. See, for example, Lieutenant General Carroll H. Dunn, *Vietnam Studies: Base Development in South Vietnam, 1965–1970*, Washington, DC: USGPO, 1991.

32. Richard Tregaskis, *Southeast Asia: Building the Bases: The History of Construction in Southeast Asia* (Washington, DC: USGPO, 1975), 238, 353.

33. For early development of Cam Ranh Bay from having only one (French-built stone) pier capable of accommodating a few deep-draft ships, see, for example, Vice Admiral Edwin Bickford Hooper, USN (Ret), *Mobility, Support, Endurance: A Story of Naval Operational Logistics in the Vietnam War 1965–1968* (Washington, DC: Department of the Navy, 1972), 157–159. See also Robert S. Mansfield and William L. Worden, *Towboats to the Orient: A History of Alaska Barge and Transport In the South China Sea* (Seattle: PAC, 1970).

34. Paul J. Cogger, *Finished with Engine* (New York: Vantage Press, 1972).

35. *Citadel Victory* was among the ships—all of the "Victory" type—removed from various reserve fleets in the third "flight" to be withdrawn for Vietnam Service. See "SIU Companies Receive Twelve More Victorys," *Seafarers Log*, September 3, 1965.

36. Cogger, *Finished with Engine*.

37. Cogger, *Finished with Engine*.

38. Captain Thomas J. Patterson interview with author.

39. "N.M.U. Warns McNamara," *The New York Times*, September 2, 1965.

40. Robert S. Burns, "'No Logical Plan' For Viet Shipping," *New York Herald Tribune*, November 19, 1965, 38.

41. Helen Delich Bentley, "Viet Shipping Practices Hit By Garmatz: McNamara Asked To Give Full Accounting of Needs," *The Baltimore Sun*, November 19, 1965, A2.

42. "McNamara Chided Over Logistics," *The New York Times*, November 19, 1965.

43. Bentley, "Viet Shipping Practices Hit," *The Baltimore Sun*, November 19, 1965, A2.

44. Burns, "'No Logical Plan For Viet Shipping," *New York Herald Tribune*, November 19, 1965, 38; "U.S. Ships' Cargo Plight," *New York Herald Tribune*, December 6, 1965.

45. For Curran's remarks about McNamara, see, for example, George Horne, "U.S. Ships Urged for War Effort," *The New York Times*, October 15, 1965.

46. For Paul Hall's comments regarding McNamara see "American Merchant Marine and Maritime Policy" in *Proceedings of the Sixth Constitutional Convention of the AFL-CIO*, San Francisco, California, December 9–15, 1965, 7.

47. For Weisberger's comments see *West Coast Sailors*, September 10, 1965.

48. The number of troops carried by ship to Vietnam compared to air transport in the early buildup years, that is, between 1965 and 1967, is generally put at around 60 percent.

49. "Navy Denounced on Hiring in Asia: N.M.U. Urges Halt in use of Japanese Seamen," *The New York Times*, April 22, 1965.

50. Lane C. Kendall, "U.S. Merchant Shipping and Vietnam," 136–137, 140; Helen Delich Bentley, "U.S. Ship Gets Viet Cargo Foreign Vessels Rejected," *The Baltimore Sun*, September 1, 1965; "Union Wants War Cargoes on U.S. Ships: Suit Threatened For Viet Shipments on Foreign Vessels," *The Baltimore Sun*, September 2, 1965; Robert S. Burns, "N.M.U. Threatens to Sue U.S.: Wants U.S. Ships for Military Cargo," *New York Herald Tribune*, September 2, 1965; Robert S. Burns, "Crew Balks at Trip to Viet Nam," *New York Herald Tribune*. See also, "More and More Foreign Ships Refuse U.S. Viet Cargoes," *Seafarers Log*, October 1, 1965, 5. Robert S. Burns, "Indians Desert Vessel Taking U.S. Arms to Viet," *New York Herald Tribune*, October 15, 1965; "Japanese Ship Lines Quit Viet Nam Run," *Marine Digest*, October 9, 1965, 16; Helen Delich Bentley, "Foreign Ship Use Allowed," *The Baltimore Sun*, October 19, 1965; "3 More Crews Refuse To Move Vietnam Supplies," *The Baltimore Sun*, October 26, 1965, A1, 2; Robert S. Burns, "MSTS Open to Use of Foreign Shipping," *New York Herald Tribune*, November 6, 1965; Helen Delich Bentley, "First Foreign-flag Ship Chartered After New Plea," *The Baltimore Sun*, December 30, 1965.

51. Regarding the *Marilena P*, the *El Mexicano*, and the "foreign flag" issue as it pertains to the Vietnam War, see Kendall, "U.S. Merchant Shipping and Vietnam," 136–137. Kendall notes that foreign-flag ships carried three percent of U.S. military cargo in 1965, the first year of large-scale U.S. involvement in the war. That figure increased to five percent the following year.

52. Donald L. Merchant letter to author, April 12, 1982.

53. Merchant letter to author.

54. Regarding bombing incidents at the My Canh "floating restaurant" in Saigon on June 25, 1965, see *The St. Louis Post Dispatch*, June 25, 1965. In this particular incident two separate explosions took place, resulting in 29 killed and 100 wounded. Among eight Americans killed in the blast five were military personnel and three were civilians.

55. *West Coast Sailors*, December 24, 1965.

56. "2 Merchant Seamen Missing in Vietnam," *West Coast Sailors*, January 21, 1966; The Moonduster Chronicles (www.djc/NL/dec01/fpow.htm) reported the recovery of O'Laughlin's remains some years later. What became of Bailon has never been determined.

57. The Moonduster Chronicles.

58. The pros and cons of the "enclave" strategy manifested in deployment of U.S. Marines to Da Nang in March 1965 were described in a March 18, 1965, telegram from General Maxwell Taylor to Secretary of State Dean Rusk. In that Taylor essentially provides the rationale for moving beyond the defensive attitude it reflected—and initiating offensive "search and destroy" missions—as would be approved by President Johnson a few months later. See *PP* (Gravel), III: 445–447. See also Porter, Vietnam, Vol. 2, 364–366.

59. For the most complete eyewitness account of the battle at Ia Drang see Lieutenant General Harold G. Moore and Joseph L. Galloway's *We Were Soldiers Once...and Young: Ia Drang—The Battle that Changed the War in Vietnam* (New York: Random House, 1992).

60. Having embraced the belief that Vietnam War was a "war of attrition" and could be measured and assessed by the number of enemy combatants killed in comparison to American and South Vietnamese losses, General Westmoreland could and did conclude—and spin for public consumption—that the battle at Ia Drang had been a success. But the battle, fought late in the first year of large-scale unit commitment by the U.S. was a major eye-opener to many, including Secretary of Defense Robert McNamara, who began to question not only the validity of the attrition argument in the context of Vietnam, but the expected length of the war itself and its ultimate outcome. For analysis of the Ia Drang battle at it relates to the "war of attrition" concept, see, for example, Young, *The Vietnam Wars*, 161–162; Karnow, *Vietnam*, 479–480.

61. Galloway, the only reporter who covered the battle, overheard McNamara make this comment while on the return from Vietnam. For that, and lessons derived by both sides, see Moore and Galloway, *We Were Soldiers Once*, 339. "The implications of the buildup were made abundantly clear," one government analyst was to note at the time, "by the bloody fighting in the Ia Drang Valley in mid-November." See *PP* (Gravel), IV, 303.

Chapter 10

1. Schreadley, *From the Rivers to the Sea*, 33, 76–78, 279–89; Carl A. Nelson, "Controlling the Rung Sat Special Zone," *Vietnam Magazine*, October 1996, 22–28, 54. The distance from Saigon downriver to Nha Be is usually put at between seven and eight miles. The overland route, via a "narrow, heavily traveled, potholed highway" was about 12 miles. See, for example, Helen Delich Bentley, "Ammunition Ships Face Danger," *The Baltimore Sun*, January 30, 1967.

2. Bentley, "Ammunition Ships Face Danger."

3. Schreadley, *From the Rivers to the Sea*, 282.

4. Donald Merchant letter to author, April 12, 1982.

5. Schreadley, *From the Rivers to the Sea*, 282.

6. Schreadley, *From the Rivers to the Sea*.

7. Bentley, "Ammunition Ships Face Danger," *The Baltimore Sun*, January 30, 1967.

8. *West Coast Sailors*, March 25, 1966.

9. As mine sweeping and patrol craft of the U.S. Navy were introduced to the river approaches to Saigon they would also certainly come under attack, with deadly consequences. For multiple incidents involving one such vessel—the minesweeper MSB 54—see Schreadley, *From the Rivers to the Sea*, 282–283.

10. Fred A. Wilcox, *Waiting for an Army to Die: The Tragedy of Agent Orange* (New York: Random House, 1986).

11. Donald Merchant letter to author, April 12, 1982.

12. For one account of a swift boat officer—Lieutenant Elmo Zumwalt, III—who was exposed to Agent Orange along the rivers of South Vietnam and probably died as a result of that exposure—and the man who ordered the use of such chemical agents in-country—his father, Admiral Elmo Zumwalt Jr.—see their book, written with assistance from John Pekkanen, *My Father, My Son* (New York: Macmillan Publishing Co., 1986). See also Wilcox, *Waiting for an Army to Die*.

13. A process was established, after a long and difficult campaign by veterans groups and others to establish the carcinogenic and therefore medically harmful nature of Agent Orange, to file to the Veterans Administration for compensation for exposure to Agent Orange and other so-called "tactical herbicides" used in Vietnam. According to the VA benefits website, the "VA presumes that veterans were exposed to Agent Orange or other herbicides if they served: In Vietnam anytime between January 9, 1962, and May 7, 1975, including brief visits ashore or service aboard a ship that operated on the inland waterways of Vietnam." www.benefits.va.gov. As civilians, though serving on ships of the U.S. Navy MSTS "nucleus" fleet, and ships otherwise under MSTS (MSC) General Agency Agreement contract to private shipping companies, merchant seamen were not, of course, considered for nor otherwise entitled to this compensation.

14. "SIU Escapes Vietnam Ambush," *Seafarers Log*, April 22, 1966.

15. Alexander J. Leiter, "SIU Vessel Outflanks Viet Cong to Escape Saigon River Ambush," *Seafarers Log*, April 1, 1966, 11.

16. The Republic of Korea (ROK) sent more than 300,000 troops to Vietnam—second only to the United States—among foreign nations supporting the South Vietnamese cause. American troopships were very involved moving these troops. ROK casualties are given as more than 5,000 killed, and nearly 11,000 wounded during the years of their involvement. www.en.asaninst. org; www.imhe.mil.kr/imhcroot/data/vietnam. list.jsp. See also *PP* (Gravel), IV: 470.

17. The transports USNS *General R.M. Blatchford* and USNS *General W.H. Gordon* represent two different types of troopships built during World War II: *Blatchford* with a C4-S-A1 type hull and, as such, 522'10" in length, and with a service speed of some 16.5 knots, and *Gordon* a larger P2-type troopship, 622'7" in length and with a service speed of some 20–21 knots. After service during World War II and the Korean War, both ships, having become part of the MSTS "nucleus" fleet, were eventually laid up in reserve when, in 1964, they were withdrawn in the aftermath of the Tonkin Gulf incidents and then added to the New York to Bremerhaven Run. *Blatchford* had also participated in Operation Steel Pike I in late 1964. Then, soon after the major buildup began in Vietnam in mid-1965, they were shifted from the Atlantic to the Pacific to transport some of the first units to Vietnam late that year (see chapter 9, above). Following multiple voyages to Vietnam in 1966, both ships were taken out of service and laid up in reserve, *Gordon* in the James River, Virginia, and *Blatchford* at Suisun Bay, California. While *Gordon* would languish in reserve until struck from the Naval Register in 1986, then sold for scrap the following year, *Blatchford* would return to service in Vietnam after conversion for Waterman Steamship as a containership. Her active service extended in Vietnam as *Stonewall Jackson* as a result, then after the war as *Alexander Stephens*, the ship nonetheless met her ultimate fate, well before the *Gordon*, in 1980, at the hands of ship breakers in Taiwan.

18. Both USNS *General Alexander M. Patch* and USNS *General William O. Darby*, after service during World War II, and then as U.S. Army transports in the early postwar years, became part of the Navy's Military Sea Transportation Service (MSTS) in 1950, then served during the Korean War. Both were involved later transporting troops between New York and Bremerhaven, before being shifted in support of the Vietnam buildup in August 1965. *Darby* was taken out of service in 1967, was eventually placed into the NDRF, James River, Virginia, before being shifted to the Norfolk Naval Shipyard to serve as a temporary berthing and messing facility there. Taken out of service in 1991, returned again to the NDRF, James River, *General William O. Darby* was struck from the Navy Register in 1993. Sold for scrapping in 2004, she was removed from the NDRF in 2005 to Brownsville, Texas where she faced the breakers; scrapping was completed in September 2006. After completing two voyages to Vietnam in late 1965, *Darby*'s sister ship, *Patch*, was returned to New York to resume service to Bremerhaven in early 1966, sailed again to Vietnam, in company with *Darby* for the "longest troop lift" from Boston, then transported Korean troops to Vietnam during two voyages. Then, in 1967, she was taken out of service, placed first in reserve in New York before being shifted to the NDRF, James River, in 1970. Struck from the Naval Register in 1990, *General W.O. Darby* was sold for scrapping, also at Brownsville, Texas, in 2001. These two sister troopships had begun their days at the same place—Bethlehem-Alameda Shipbuilding Corp., Alameda, California—and ended at the same place, the breakers in Brownsville, Texas—if five years apart—after long careers that included service in three wars.

19. Captain John Le Cato letter to author, June 4, 1979; *Sealift Magazine*, September 1966.

20. Le Cato letter to author, June 4, 1979.

21. One of some 65 ships built during World War II with the U.S. Maritime Commission C4 hull type—most of which were troopships—*Eltinge* had been in reserve from 1962 until May 1965 when she was withdrawn for Vietnam service. *Eltinge* transported initial elements of the 101st Airborne Division to Vietnam, and, despite a serious breakdown that required towing to Midway for repairs, completed a number of additional troop lifts to Vietnam before being withdrawn from service in early 1967—as other troopships—and placed into "Ready Reserve."

22. For a discussion of military air transport in Southeast Asia during this period, see Ray L. Bowers, "The United States Air Force in Southeast Asia: Tactical Airlift," Department of Air Force History Office, 1983.

23. While most of the larger P-2 troopships were taken out of service or otherwise off the Vietnam Run by 1967, some of the smaller C4-S-A1 hull type troopers were converted to containerships and returned to the Vietnam Run in that capacity, thus extending their service in the war by some additional years. One example of this conversion was that of the USNS *General R.M. Blatchford*. The troopship was taken out of service in January 1967, laid up in the Suisun Bay NDRF in California before being leased and later sold to Waterman Steamship Corp. and withdrawn from reserve in March 1969 for conversion. The work was completed at Portland, Oregon, and the ship emerged as the containership *Stonewall Jackson*, reentering service to Vietnam in 1970. Following the war, and after having been renamed *Alexander Stephens* in 1978—after yet another southern Confederate

leader—the ship was finally sold for scrapping to a Taiwanese breaker in 1980.

24. Captain Brian Hope letter to author, February 25, 2015.

25. Captain Brian Hope letter to author, January 27, 2018. On this occasion the *General Eltinge* transported the U.S. Army's 1st Infantry Division, the first time an entire division had been moved to Vietnam at one time in one transport ship.

26. The concept of "air mobility"—the extensive use of helicopters for moving troops, cargo, medevac operations, and aerial rocket artillery assaults to the field—came into full fruition with the creation of the 1st Cavalry Division (Airmobile) in 1965. For a history of the concept and how it evolved from its earliest roots, see, for example, E.M. Flanagan, Jr., *Airborne—A Combat History of American Airborne Forces* (Random House, 2002).

27. "World's First Helicopter Repair Ship is Frequent Host to Military Leaders," *Sealift Magazine*, October 1967; "Meet the MSTS Fleet (72): USNS Corpus Christi Bay," *Sealift Magazine*, June 1968.

28. Harold C. Hutchison, "This WWII–era ship got new life fixing helicopters in Vietnam," www.wearethemighty.com.

29. After being withdrawn from a reserve fleet in one of the first "flights" in 1965, *Baton Rouge Victory* was among those ships that performed well, and with minimal expenditures for and no delays caused by repairs in the early goings. This was revealed in documentation provided in congressional hearings in early 1966. See Vietnam—Shipping Policy Review, Part 3, 745.

30. "MEBA men feared dead," *American Marine Engineer*, September 1966, 2, 14; "Red Mine Sinks U.S. Ship; Seven in Crew Are Killed," *Stewards News*, September 2, 1966, 13; "7 Killed in Black Gang; SUP Ship Sunk by Viet Cong Mine," *West Coast Sailors*, September 9, 1966, 1.

31. *American Marine Engineer*, "MEBA men feared dead," September 1966, 2.

32. *American Marine Engineer*, "MEBA men feared dead."

33. *American Marine Engineer*, "MEBA men feared dead."

34. *American Marine Engineer*, "MEBA men feared dead."

35. *American Marine Engineer*, November 1966, 9.

36. After *Baton Rouge Victory* was refloated, towed to Vung Tau, and then to Singapore, she was sold to ship breakers in Hong Kong for $90,850. A later history of the Victory ship indicates that the ship ended up instead in Taiwan, where she was scrapped. "Ship Sunk in War Put Up For Sale; Bids Asked for Dismantling Baton Rouge Victory," *The Baltimore Sun*, March 25, 1967; "Mine-Sunk Ship Sold for Scrap," *The Baltimore Sun*, May 4, 1967; L.A. Sawyer and W.H. Mitchell, *Victory Ships and Tankers*, 44.

37. George Horne, "Ship Crew Rules Relaxed in Crisis; U.S. Acts to Offset Growing Shortages Caused by War," *The New York Times*, February 17, 1966; "Ship Manpower Rules Relaxed; Coast Guard Acts to Relieve Shortage," *The Baltimore Sun*, March 21, 1966.

38. "Viet Shipping Due Hearing; Garmatz Gives Preview of Committee Interests," *The Baltimore Sun*, June 17, 1966.

39. Of the 172 government-owned ships contracted out to private shipping companies for the Vietnam Run by the end of 1966, under General Agency Agreement (GAA), 161 had been taken out of National Defense Reserve Fleets (NDRF) commencing in August the previous year. Nearly 100 of those ships—mostly Victory AP-2 and, to a lesser degree, AP-1 types—were withdrawn from reserve in 1966, thus contributing significantly to manning-related issues during the course of the year. See Lane Kendall, "U.S. Merchant Shipping and Vietnam," USNI Proceedings, 135.

40. Helen Delich Bentley, "172 U.S. Ships Are Delayed; Arms Tieups of 454 Days Laid to Crew Shortages," *The Baltimore Sun*, November 27, 1966, D31, D35.

41. "Seafaring Deferments Are Nixed," *American Marine Engineer*, September 1966, 3.

42. "Unions Score Draft Move; Criticize Connor For Going Along With Decision," *The Baltimore Sun*, September 8, 1966.

43. Bentley, "172 U.S. Ships with Arms are Delayed," *The Baltimore Sun*, November 27, 1966, D31, D35.

44. "U.S. and 5 State Maritime Academies Will Graduate Classes Early in 1967 to Meet Vietnam Demand," *American Marine Engineer*, November 1966.

45. Bentley, "Vietnam Ship Needs Head Into Problems of Manning," *The Baltimore Sun*, March 7, 1966.

46. "Draft Policy's Lack of Logic Hit by Calhoun," *American Marine Engineer*, October 1966, 3, 12.

47. "Draft Policy's Lack of Logic Hit by Calhoun."

48. Bentley, "Shipping Industry Questions Non-Essentiality of Sailors," *The Baltimore Sun*, September 19, 1966; "Seafaring Deferments are Nixed," *American Marine Engineer*, September 1966.

49. "Unions Score Draft Move; Criticize Connor For Going Along With Decision," *The Baltimore Sun*, September 8, 1966; John P. Callahan, "Officer Shortage At Sea Is Feared," *The New York Times*, December 11, 1965; "U.S. Urged To Act on Engineer Need," *The New York Times*, December 30, 1965.

50. "Draft Policy Lack of Logic Hit by Calhoun," *American Marine Engineer*, October 1966, 2.

51. "Seafaring Deferments Are Nixed," *American Marine Engineer*, September 1966, 3.

52. The author recalls how, after a three-

month voyage to Da Nang, Vietnam in 1969 on an MSTS-chartered Waterman C-2 cargo ship carrying ammunition, a draft reclassification notice—to "1-A" (eligible to be called)—was waiting for him from the Selective Service. He did ship out again that year, but decided, not in position to obtain an "essential" rating waiver, to return to university studies. In December of that year, receiving a high number in the newly introduced draft lottery system, he was no longer subject to the draft.

53. See n. 49, above.

54. "Apprenticeship School Bows in Baltimore," *American Marine Engineer*, September 1966, 3, 8.

55. *American Marine Engineer*, March 1966.

56. Regarding maritime labor's enhanced and newly developed upgrading training programs to meet increased demands for licensed and unlicensed merchant seamen in 1966, see, for example, "NMU Upgrading Program: Best Equipped, Most Thorough In Maritime Industry," "BMO Graduates First Class," *The NMU Pilot*, February 1966, 5; "D-1 Members Overwhelmingly For Apprentice Training Program," *American Marine Engineer*, March 1966, 7; "LEAP [Licensed Marine Engineers Apprenticeship Program] Applications Flood District No. 1 Branches," *American Marine Engineer*, July 1966, 3; "Apprenticeship School Bows in Baltimore," *American Marine Engineer*, September 1966.

57. For contemporaneous accounts of Vietnam-bound ship delays, see, for example, Bentley, "MEBA Head Says 7 Ships On Viet Run Lack Officers," *The Baltimore Sun*, March 9, 1966; "Vietnam Only Accents Need Of Ship Officers, Group Told," *The Baltimore Sun*, April 7, 1966; "Freighters Are Delayed By Crew Shortages," *Marine Digest*, September 17, 1966; Bentley, "172 Ships With Arms Are Delayed: Weapons Cargo Tieups of 454 Days Laid To Crew Shortages," *The Baltimore Sun*, November 27, 1966, D31; "Crew Shortages Hinder War Effort," *Hear This* (U.S. Merchant Marine Academy), Vol. XXI, No. 11, December 1966.

58. Letter from Robert A. Lewis, American Consul, Saigon, to National Maritime Union Vice President Mel Barisic, regarding improved shore leave in Qui Nhon, *NMU Pilot*, June 1966, 16.

59. "Conditions for Seamen improve in So. Vietnam," *NMU Pilot*, August 1966, 6.

60. "OK Shore Leave in Vung Tau—But It Isn't Easy," *NMU Pilot*, October 1966.

61. "Union Acts to Ease Problems of Seamen in Viet War Area," *NMU Pilot*, March 1966, 9, 24; "Vietnam—Shipping Policy Review," Part 2, 305.

62. "USS Club in Cam Ranh Bay," *NMU Pilot*, June 1966; "Conditions Improve for Seamen in South Vietnam," *NMU Pilot*, August 1966, 6; *Sealift Magazine*, November 1967, 8.

63. "'Pearl Harbor to Cam Ranh Bay': United Seamen's Service Celebrates Twenty-fifth Anniversary," *Sealift Magazine*, November 1967, 8.

64. "USS to Open Center in Cam Ranh Bay," *NMU Pilot*, August 1966, 6.

65. As meetings and hearings were held early and later in 1966 involving representatives from government, industry, and maritime labor organizations, the suggestions for containerization, both in the form of standardized containers into which cargo would be placed, and the specialized ships (conversions or designed as such prior to initial construction and launching) took on increasing urgency to ease offloading and ship turnaround times in-country. See for example, "'Package' Plan For Moving Arms To Vietnam Studied," *The Baltimore Sun*, February 18, 1966; Bentley, "Cargo Plan To Counter Viet Jam," October 28, 1966.

66. By January 1, 1967, a total of 172 ships, including 161 that had been broken out of reserve fleets following the start of the major buildup in mid-1965, had come under General Agency Agreement (GAA) for Vietnam service. See Kendall, "The Merchant Marine and the Vietnam War," *Proceedings*, 1971.

67. "Vietnam—Shipping Policy Review," Part 2, 296–297; Part 3, 610–611.

68. "History and Development of the Container—The 'Transporter,' Predecessor to the CONEX," www.transportation.army.mil.

69. Marc Levinson, *The Box: How the Shipping Container Made the World Smaller and the World Economy Bigger* (Princeton, NJ: Princeton University Press, 2006).

70. Levinson, *The Box: How the Shipping Container Made the World Smaller*; Brian J. Cudahy, *Box Boats: How Container Ships Changed the World* (New York: Fordham University Press, 2008); www.maritimeprofessional.com/ideal-x.

71. Not surprisingly, this colorful comment by ILA official Freddy Fields in reaction to the containership prototype can be found in various sources having to do with the history of containerization. See, for example, Wesley Jew, "How a Box Changed History: The Shipping Container Story," www.universalcargo.com; "Who Made America—Innovators—Malcolm McLean," PBS.org.

72. "'Package' Plans for Moving Arms to Vietnam Studied," *The Baltimore Sun*, February 18, 1966; "Vietnam—Shipping Policy Review," Parts 2 and 3.

73. "'Package' Plans for Moving Arms to Vietnam Studied."

74. Lester Velie, "Our Leaky Pipeline to Vietnam," *Readers Digest*, December 1966, as reprinted in *West Coast Sailors*, December 9, 1966, 4.

75. Born in Kiev in 1907, Velie became a journalist and editor for such publications as *Readers Digest*, *Colliers*, and the New York *Journal of Commerce*. He became known for investigative reports into such things as organized crime, city politics, lobbying, and labor. He died in Norman, Oklahoma in 2003.

76. Velie, "Our Leaky Pipeline."

77. Velie, "Our Leaky Pipeline."

78. According to the Defense Casualty Analysis System (DCAS), National Archives, there were 6,350 deaths—mostly killed in action, or subsequently as a result of wounds—recorded for American military personnel serving in Vietnam in 1966, more than three times the number for the previous year. www.nationalarchives.gov/militaryrecords/vietnam

79. Bentley, "MSTS to Ship Civilian Aid to Vietnam," *The Baltimore Sun*, October 14, 1966.

80. "Danang Port Conditions Incredible," *American Marine Engineer*, August 1966, 6.

81. *New Orleans States-Item*, October 3, 1966, in "Vietnam—Shipping Policy Review," Part 3, Hearings Before the Subcommittee on Merchant Marine of the Committee on Merchant Marine and Fisheries, House, 89th Congress, 2nd session, May-June 1966, USGPO, Washington, 1966, 760.

82. "Vietnam—Shipping Policy Review," Part 3, 760.

83. Tom Buckley, "G.I.s Move to Unload War Cargo as a Strike Ties Up Port of Saigon," *The New York Times*, December 27, 1966, 1, 5.

84. Buckley, "G.I.s Move to Unload War Cargo."

85. The early phase of Newport and other port construction in Vietnam was discussed in testimony before the House Committee on Merchant Marine and Fisheries, Merchant Marine Subcommittee in Washington, DC on March 16, 1966. See "Vietnam—Shipping Policy Review, Part 2, USGPO, Washington: 1966, 281. See also Richard Tregaskis, *Southeast Asia: Building the Bases: The History of Construction in Southeast Asia*, USGPO: 1975.

86. Buckley, "G.I.s Move to Unload War Cargo."

Chapter 11

1. *PP* (Gravel), IV: 387.

2. Some of the most optimistic assessments regarding the status of military operations in Vietnam by late 1967 were those of COMUSMAC (General Westmoreland), who suggested that a "cross-over" point, when the infiltration of North Vietnamese forces into South Vietnam was no longer keeping up with their losses, had possibly been achieved earlier in the year. In what was considered a war of attrition, that was presented as an indication of success—a "light at the end of the tunnel"—that might well in time result in victory. For comments made in reports by Westmoreland in late 1967 that reflect this optimistic thinking, see, for example, *PP* (Gravel), IV: 518, 538–539.

3. *PP* (Gravel), IV: 420.

4. *PP* (Gravel), IV: 420.

5. *PP* (Gravel), IV: 348.

6. *PP* (Gravel), IV: 353.

7. DOS *Bulletin*, January 30, 1967, 158; *PP* (Gravel), IV: 661–62.

8. *PP* (Gravel), IV: 661–62.

9. According to the Vietnam Conflict Extract Data File of the Defense Casualty Analysis System (DCAS), National Archives, some 11,363 war-related deaths of U.S. military personnel were recorded for 1967. Combined with 6,350 for the previous year, 1,928 for 1965—the year when large-scale units were first introduced in Vietnam—and 416 recorded for prior years, a total of more than 20,000 had been recorded by the conclusion of 1967. See Archives. Com. Regarding the increase of domestic opposition to the war, one study looking at both Korea and Vietnam noted a similar percentage decrease (15 percent) in public support for the wars each time the killed-in-action figure increased in each case by a factor of 10. See John E. Mueller, *War, Presidents and Public Opinion* (New York: John Wiley & Sons, Inc., 1973), p. 60.

10. *PP* (Gravel), IV: 401.

11. Helen Delich Bentley, "Way To Saigon Diligently Guarded," *The Baltimore Sun*, March 20, 1967, C9; "Navy Crew In Viet Ports Guard Defenseless Vessels," *The Baltimore Sun*, March 20, 1967, C10.

12. "U.S. Naval Forces Vietnam Monthly Historical Summary, March 1967."

13. The American-made 57-millimeter and heavier 75-millimeter recoilless rifles were introduced as anti-tank weapons during World War II. Generally mounted on a tripod, or vehicle, the lighter version could also be shoulder-fired. Chinese manufactured versions—commonly referred to as "Chicom" (Chinese Communist)—were deployed against merchant shipping, and otherwise, during the Vietnam War by the Viet Cong and NVA. The 75-millimeter version could penetrate 4" of steel or armor-plating, and thus were effective in holing the hulls and bulkheads of ships.

14. Sherwood, *War in the Shallows*, 98.

15. Bentley, "Way To Saigon Diligently Guarded," *The Baltimore Sun*, March 20, 1967, C9.

16. "U.S. Naval Forces Vietnam Monthly Historical Summary," March 1967, 1–3.

17. "Conqueror Shows Battle Scars," *NMU Pilot*, May 1967.

18. Bentley, "Way To Saigon Diligently Guarded," *The Baltimore Sun*, March 20, 1967, C9.

19. Sherwood, *War in the Shallows*, 189.

20. "MSTS Relies Heavily On Its LST's For Shallow Draft Vietnam Ports," *Sealift Magazine*, October 1967, 5, 22.

21. Bentley, "Salvage of Dredge Frustrating," *The Baltimore Sun*, March 17, 1967.

22. Bentley, "Salvage of Dredge Frustrating."

23. Built in an area of abandoned rice paddies, dredging for the Dung Tam Base Camp near My

Tho was begun in August 1966. By the time the area was ready for actual facility construction in early 1967—including construction of housing for some 5,000 military personnel and dependents, a surgical unit, and an asphalt runway for fixed-wing aircraft—some 600 acres, nearly a square mile, and rising to a height of some five feet or more, had been reclaimed from the river by the dredging process. Sherwood, 188.

24. Sherwood, *War in the Shallows*, pp. 145–46.

25. Bentley, "Salvage of Dredge Frustrating," *The Baltimore Sun*, March 17, 1967.

26. Sherwood, *War in the Shallows*, 145–46.

27. Commander Frank C. Collins, Jr., "Maritime Support of the Campaign in I Corps," USNI *Proceedings, Naval Review 1971*, 9, 172; Hooper, *Mobility, Support, Endurance*, 123.

28. Hooper, *Mobility, Support, Endurance*.

29. Richard and Moana Tregaskis, *Southeast Asia: Building the Bases: The History of Construction in Southeast Asia*, U.S. Navy Seabee Museum (1975).

30. Bentley, "Viet Sealift Cutting Back; Increased Efficiency Will Ease Ship Shortage," *The Baltimore Sun*, August 14, 1967; "16 Vessels Taken Off Vietnam Run; Ships From Reserve Fleet Given Standby Status," *The New York Times*, August 16, 1967.

31. Press release, "Cargo Movements Within Southeast Asia, Fiscal Years 1965–1970," U.S. Military Sealift Command, October 27, 1968.

32. Warner Bamberger, "Vietnam Sealift Reported Eased: M.S.T.S. Able To Return 35 Cargo Ships To Lay-up," *The New York Times*, October 29, 1967. Bamberger reports here that the total number of ships under M.S.T.S. control for Vietnam had reached a peak of 294 earlier in the year, but was reduced to 252 by October with the withdrawal of these 35 ships.

33. The total number of seamen made available by removal of these ships from the Vietnam Run was estimated by one source to be about 600, for an average of 38 per ship. However, since most if not all of these ships would have been of the "Victory" type—which typically had a crew complement closer to 45—that figure seems to be lower than the actual number. See "16 Vessels Taken Off Vietnam Run," *The New York Times*, August 16, 1967.

34. Helen Delich Bentley, "The U.S.-Built Ports of South Vietnam: End of the Life-line for Allied Forces," *Navy Magazine*, May 1967, 40.

35. "Removal of Sealift Ships Urged," *The Baltimore Sun*, October 30, 1967.

36. "Removal of Sealift Ships Urged," *The Baltimore Sun*. Regarding the Wilson-Weeks Agreement, name after Secretary of Defense Charles E. Wilson and Secretary of Commerce Charles Sinclair Weeks, who negotiated and signed the agreement in 1954, see, for example, Maritime Transportation Research Board, *The Sealift Readiness Program: The Commercial Implications of a*

Military Contingency Call-Up (Washington, DC: National Academy of Sciences, 1975), 4–5. See also Vice Admiral A.J. Herberger, USN (Ret.), Kenneth C. Gauden, and Commander Rolf Marshall, USN (Ret.), *Global Reach: Revolutionizing Systems for Military Sealift, 1990–2012* (Annapolis, MD: U.S. Naval Institute Press, 2015), 7.

37. Among the government-owned troopships of the MSTS "nucleus" fleet that were removed from service to Vietnam in late 1966 or at some point in 1967, and either placed in "ready reserve" or returned to National Defense Reserve Fleets were: USNS *Darby*, USNS *Mann*, USNS *Patch*, and USNS *Patrick*. USNS *Weigel* completed her final voyage on the Vietnam Run in December 1967. USNS *Pope* and USNS *Gordon* were not taken out of commission and placed back into reserve until 1970, but whether or not they continued in service to Vietnam, or were shifted back to the New York to Bremerhaven Run until removed from service has not been determined by the author.

38. "Seven Sealand Ships to Join MSTS U.S.-Vietnam Sealift," *Seafarers Log*, April 14, 1967. See also "Million Tons of Cargo Per Month Now Average For MSTS in Vietnam," *Sealift Magazine*, June 1968, 14–15.

39. Bentley, "Navy Using Containerships For Vietnam," *The Baltimore Sun*, July 16, 1967.

40. Bentley, "Navy Using Containerships for Vietnam."

41. Werner Bamberger, "Navy Augments Vietnam Shipping; Charters 7 Cargo Vessels in $70-million Contract," *The New York Times*, March 30, 1967.

42. John B. O'Donnell, Jr., "Arms-Cargo Ship Ready For Service; Seatrain Puerto Rico is First of Nine to be Converted," *The Sun*, January 8, 1967.

43. O'Donnell, Jr. "Arms-Cargo Ship Ready For Service."

44. The *Seatrain Puerto Rico* conversion was followed, in order, by *Seatrain Carolina*, *Seatrain Florida*, *Seatrain Maryland*, *Seatrain Maine*, and *Seatrain Delaware*. For a good description of the use of World War II–era T2 tankers for these conversions, see L.A. Sawyer and W.H. Mitchell, *Victory Ships and Tankers* (Cambridge, MD: Cornell Maritime Press, 1974), p. 150, 165, 175–76.

45. "U.S. Naval Forces Monthly Historical Supplement," August 1967, IV, 21–23.

46. "U.S. Naval Forces Monthly Historical Supplement."

47. "Seatrain Florida Attacked by VC; No One Injured," *Seafarers Log*, August 18, 1967, 67.

48. Charts, "Time in Vietnam For Deep Draft Cargo Ships Departing the RVN Area," *Sealift Magazine*, June 1968; Bentley, "Defense Shipments Reach 1,700,000 tons in Month," *The Baltimore Sun*, May 19, 1967, C1, 15.

49. Bentley reported from Vietnam on August 13 that all four of the Newport deepwater berths were in operation by then. See "Viet Sealift

Cutting Back," *The Baltimore Sun*, August 14, 1967.

50. George Horne, "200 Get Degrees From Kings Point: Graduation 4 Months Early to Fill Vietnam Needs," *The New York Times*, February 11, 1967; "200 Kings Pointers Graduate Early: Administrator Gulick Key Speaker Praises Class for Accelerated Study," *The Kings Pointer*, Vol. II, No. 3, March 1967; "Merchant Marine Graduates Wasting No Time in Shipping Out for Vietnam," *The New York Times*, February 8, 1967; "'Cram Schools' Called Necessary To Cut Deck-Officer Shortage," *The New York Times*, March 5, 1967.

51. Bentley, "Logistics Is Vast Vietnam Task," *The Baltimore Sun*, March 13, 1967.

52. "U.S. Opens Port on Saigon River," *The Baltimore Sun*, July 10, 1967; Bentley, "U.S. To Give Vietnamese Saigon Berth; Move Follows Reports of Port Betterment in Recent Weeks," *The Baltimore Sun*, April 30, 1967, D25, D29; "Vietnam Ship 'Logjam' Aided By New Port of 'Newport,'" *Seafarers Log*, September 15, 1967; Bentley, "Saigon Piers To Test Rule; Dockers May All Quit With GI's Only At Newport," *The Baltimore Sun*, January 18, 1967, C7, C11.

53. Bentley, "Saigon Piers To Test Rule; Dockers May All Quit With GI's Only At Newport," *The Baltimore Sun*, January 18, 1967, C7, C11.

54. Soldiers from the Republic of Korea (ROK)—more than 300,000 served in Vietnam, second only to the United States for countries allied to South Vietnam—had a reputation not only for being well-trained and accomplished fighters, but also for their skill as longshoremen where in such places as Cam Ranh Bay and Da Nang they supplemented or largely took the place of Vietnamese stevedores. The author recalls that during the weeks his ship was anchored out in Da Nang harbor in 1969, ROK stevedores unloaded a cargo of ammunition in no-nonsense fashion once barges were brought out to receive it. For background on ROK military forces in Vietnam see, for example, ea.asaninst.org.

55. Though commonly referred to in contemporaneous accounts as Alaska Tug and Barge, the actual name for this private contracting company, which made a major contribution to port improvement and management during the war, was Alaska Barge and Transport (AB&T). See Richard S. Mansfield and William L. Worden, *Towboats to the Orient: A History of Alaska Barge and Transport in the South China Sea* (Seattle: PAC, 1970). As a reflection of and appreciation for the role of AB&T in one port area, see, for example, JO2 Ray Tills, USN, "MSTS Unit At Nha Trang, Vietnam, Is Smallest, But One Of Busiest," *Sealift Magazine*, December 1967, 14–15. See also "MSTS Relies Heavily On Its LST's For Shallow-Draft Vietnam Ports," *Sealift Magazine*, October 1967, 5, 22.

56. "U.S.S. Club Sweetens Cam Ranh Bay Blues," *The NMU Pilot*, August 1967, 12; "U.S.S. Center Opens in Qui Nhon," *The NMU Pilot*, May 1969, 25.

57. Larry K. Fosgate letter to the author, July 1987. In its original incarnation, *Green Wave* was one of nearly 60 troop transports constructed during World War II utilizing the Maritime Commission C-4 hull type. See Lane, *Ships for Victory*, 619–620.

58. Lane, *Ships for Victory*.

59. "First Containership To Reach Vietnam Discharges in Record 15 Hours," *Sealift Magazine*, October 1967, p. 20. Helen Delich Bentley, reporting from Vietnam in July 1967 made reference to the anticipated arrival of *Bienville*. See "Navy Using Containers For Vietnam," *The Baltimore Sun*, July 16, 1967. See also "U.S. Naval Forces Vietnam Monthly Historical Supplement August 1967," iv, 48.

60. "U.S. Naval Forces Vietnam Monthly Historical Supplement."

61. In reference to the hoped-for introduction of converted C-4s to the Vietnam Run, Helen Delich Bentley, maritime editor of *The Baltimore Sun*, noted somewhat critically in January 1967 that "both the Navy and the Maritime Administration have been responding somewhat slower than appears necessary in releasing the 25 decent C-4 ships from the reserve fleets for conversion to specialized vessels for the Vietnam sealift and other uses. Fourteen have been released, but they are still holding back on ten while studying the offers longer. Meanwhile, of course, time is wasting." And Bentley noted: "The irony of the entire situation is that the bottoms which are nearly a quarter of a century old will modernize the struggling American merchant marine because it is in such sad condition." See Bentley, "Around the Waterfront: Containerships Urged For War," *The Baltimore Sun*, January 27, 1967. "Million Tons of Cargo Per Month Now Average For MSTS in Vietnam," *Sealift Magazine*, June 1968, 14.

62. "Viet Cong Heavily Bombard U.S. Freighter Near Saigon," *The New York Times*, December 16, 1967.

63. "U.S. Naval Forces, Vietnam Monthly Historical Supplement, November 1967" [Declassified]. It was reported herein that a 75-millimeter recoilless rifle had been recovered in the aftermath of the attack.

64. "VC Bombard APL's President McKinley [sic] on Saigon R.," *The Master, Mate & Pilot*, January 1968, p. 10.

65. "Viet Cong Blast Seatrain Texas, No Casualties Are Reported," *The Master, Mate & Pilot*, January 1968, 10.

66. *Sealift Magazine*, June 1968, 15; Military Sealift Command Press Release No. 10–10, "Military Sealift Command Cargo Movements to and Within Southeast Asia, Fiscal Years 1965–1970," October 27, 1970.

67. Captain Peter J. Beauregard letter to author, June 18, 1987.

68. Captain Beauregard letter to author.

69. Though more EC2- S-C1 type "Liberty" ships were constructed in American shipyards during World War II than any other merchant ship type, very few of the more than 2,000 that survived war service were actually lengthened— or jumboized—as *Elaine*. This description of how one such ship fared against adverse weather and sea conditions suggest why that might have been the case. Nonetheless, *Elaine* continued in service for nearly 10 years following conversion, until taken into Taiwan, where she met her ultimate fate before the breakers in 1968. For more about jumboized and other postwar Liberty ship conversions, see John Gorley Bunker, *Liberty Ships: The Ugly Ducklings of World War II*, Annapolis, MD: U.S. Naval Institute Press, 1972, 197–198, and L.A. Sawyer and W.H. Mitchell, *The Liberty Ships: The History of the 'Emergency' Type Cargo Ships Constructed in the United States During World War II* (Devon: David & Charles, 1973), 23–24.

70. Captain Beauregard letter to the author, June 18, 1987.

71. For what would be revealed as Westmoreland's overly optimistic assessment of the situation in Vietnam in late 1967 see, for example, *PP* (Gravel), IV:518; Karnow, *Vietnam: A History*, 514.

Chapter 12

1. "Veteran Seafarers of Vietnam Run Witness Full Measure of Action," *Seafarers Log*, October 25, 1968, 23.

2. "Veteran Seafarers of Vietnam Run Witness Full Measure of Action."

3. "USS Director Ed Sette comes out unhurt after Vietcong Tet attack," *The NMU Pilot*, April 1968, 36.

4. Helen B. Lamb, *Vietnam's Will to Live*, 58.

5. Young, *The Vietnam Wars*, 216.

6. For analysis of Vietnam as a war of attrition, the preoccupation with "body counts" as a reflection of military success in the war, and Westmoreland's use of those numbers to assess the war's progress, see, for example, Ronald H. Spector, *After Tet: The Bloodiest Year in Vietnam* (New York: The Free Press, 1993), 220–221; Young, *The Vietnam Wars*, 163–165, 187–187, 220–222. In 1982 CBS aired "The Uncounted Enemy: A Vietnam Deception," which argued that estimated numbers of Viet Cong casualties and effective numbers, and Westmoreland's presentation and explanation of them to the public, had been misleading and contributed to over-confidence and poor preparation for and response to the Tet Offensive. Westmoreland sued CBS for libel and, after more than two years of litigation, the suit was settled out of court in 1985.

7. "Veteran Seafarers of Vietnam Run Witness Full Measure of Action," *Seafarers Log*, October 25, 1968, 23.

8. Rick Daly interview with author, ND.

9. "Veteran Seafarers of Vietnam Run Witness Full Measure of Action," *Seafarers Log*, October 25, 1968, 23.

10. "MSTS Saigon 'Troops' During Tet Offensive—Armed To Repel Vietcong Boarders," *Sealift Magazine*, June 1968, 12–13.

11. "MSTS Saigon 'Troops' During Tet Offensive," 12–13.

12. *Sealift Magazine*, June 1968, 19.

13. Merchant seaman Bruce Nusbaum reported that his ship, *Cape Junction*, which had arrived in Saigon from Sunny Point, North Carolina with a full load of ammunition on January 28, 1968, did not finally depart until February 17, some three weeks later, a reflection of the impact of the Tet Offensive on turnaround time. See "Veteran Seafarers of Vietnam Run Witness Full Measure of Action," *Seafarers Log*, August 25, 1968, 13.

14. Captain Don Moir, letter to author, October 1982. The *Chevron* was one of 20 T1-M-BT2 type tankers built during and shortly after World War II. Launched as *Taverton* at Todd-Houston Shipyard in 1945, *Chevron*—so re-named in 1946—had an overall length of 325' (309' BP), beam of 48' and maximum draught of 12'10" which made her suitable for use in such shallow-draught ports as Pham Rang. See Sawyer and Mitchell, *Victory Ships and Tankers*, 190, 200.

15. Captain Moir letter to author, October 1982.

16. For references to early port infrastructure development operations in Pham Rang, and description of a July 4, 1968, Viet Cong ground assault on the Alaska Tug and Barge Co.'s temporary camp setup, see, for example, Mansfield and Worden, *Towboats to the Orient*, 36, 38, 75, 77–80.

17. Captain Moir letter to author, October 1982.

18. Captain Moir letter to author.

19. Captain Moir letter to author.

20. Captain Moir letter to author.

21. "Routs Viet Cong with Coffee Cup," *The NMU Pilot*, April 1968.

22. "Routs Viet Cong with Coffee Cup."

23. "Ammo Unloading in Saigon Slow Again," *The Steward News*, September 20, 1968.

24. "Cargo Ship Unloads Ammo Despite VC Attack," *The Master, Mate & Pilot*, February 1968, 3; "NMU crew and ship wounded from North Vietnamese attack," *The NMU Pilot* [ND], 35.

25. "Cargo Ship Unloads Ammo Despite VC Attack."

26. "Close Shave," *The NMU Pilot*, May 1968, 44.

27. "SS Arizona [State] Hit By Cong Shells," *The Stewards News*, March 15, 1968, April 12, 1968. According to the U.S. Naval Forces,

Vietnam Monthly Historical Summary for March 1968, *Arizona State* had been hit by three rounds from a recoilless rifle; it made no mention of casualties or damage to the ship.

28. Rudolph Patzert letter, July 16, 1968.

29. Rudolph Patzert letter.

30. "Viet Cong Attacks Del Sol; No Casualties, Damage Slight," *Seafarers Log*, May 24, 1968.

31. *Sealift Magazine*, July 1968, 20.

32. *Transnorthern* was launched as *China Victory*, a VC2-S-AP3 type Victory ship, at the California Shipbuilding Corp. in Los Angeles in January 1944. She was sold private after the war, and renamed *Smith Leader* (1962) before being acquired by Hudson Waterways in 1965 and given the name *Transnorthern*. Sold to Buckeye Steamship Co. in 1969, and renamed *Buckeye Victory*, the ship was finally scrapped in Kaohsiung, Taiwan in 1972.

33. Fred Hicks letter to author, September 7, 1982.

34. Excerpts from *Transnorthern* deck log provided by Fred Hicks.

35. Fred Hicks's report to SIU provided to author by Fred Hicks.

36. Doug R. Hoerle, "Merchant Marine in Vietnam," email to author, December 29, 2007.

37. Doug R. Hoerle email to author.

38. "Seafarers Encounter Floating Mine During 'Routine' Vietnam Voyage," *Seafarers Log*, July 5, 1968, 13.

39. Hoerle email to author, December 29, 2007.

40. "Seafarers Encounter Floating Mine During 'Routine' Vietnam Voyage," *Seafarers Log*, July 5, 1968, 13.

41. "Seafarers Encounter Floating Mine."

42. "Seafarers Encounter Floating Mine."

43. "Seafarers Encounter Floating Mine."

44. Hoerle email to author, December 29, 2007.

45. Hoerle email to author, December 29, 2007.

46. "Seafarers Encounter Floating Mine During 'Routine' Vietnam Voyage," *Seafarers Log*, July 5, 1968, 13.

47. Hoerle email to author, December 29, 2007.

48. "Seafarers Encounter Floating Mine During 'Routine' Vietnam Voyage," *Seafarers Log*, July 5, 1968, 13.

49. Medals and service ribbons (bars) had been authorized for merchant seamen by the U.S. War Shipping Administration for service during World War II. In addition to medals for distinguished and meritorious service, a Combat Bar (with silver star if appropriate) was made available, as well as theater service medals (and ribbons) for service in the Atlantic, Mediterranean and Middle East, and Pacific War Zones. Merchant Seamen also qualified for a World War II Victory Medal, and for those captured and imprisoned, a Prisoner of War Medal, issued by the Department of Defense, was also made available. Medals and service ribbons were later authorized by the U.S. Maritime Administration for service during the Korean and Vietnam Wars. A Merchant Marine Expeditionary Medal—not war or campaign specific—has more recently been made available for merchant seamen serving on ships in support of Operations Desert Shield, Storm, Enduring Freedom, and Iraqi Freedom. For a complete list and descriptions of U.S. Merchant Marine Medals and Decorations, see www.marad.dot.gov.

50. "Steel Apprentice Has Close Call When VC Rocket Tears Into Hull," *Seafarers Log*, July 19, 1968, 13.

51. "Steel Apprentice Has Close Call When VC Rocket Tears Into Hull."

52. "Steel Apprentice Has Close Call When VC Rocket Tears Into Hull."

53. William H. Stephenson interview with author, March 1, 1979. The USNS *Lt. Robert Craig* was launched in August 1945 as SS *Bowling Green Victory*, a VC2–2s-AP2 type Victory ship. Acquired by the U.S. Navy's Military Sea Transportation Service (MSTS) in 1950, she continued in service as USNS *Lt. Robert Craig* (T-AK-252) from then until 1973. In addition to service in the Pacific and Atlantic, and later service in Vietnam, *Craig* had been deployed in support of the French in Indochina from March through May 1954.

54. William H. Stephenson letter to parents, June 12, 1968, provided to author by William Stephenson.

55. William H. Stephenson letter to parents, August 1, 1968.

56. William H. Stephenson letter to parents.

57. William H. Stephenson letter to parents.

58. William H. Stephenson letter to parents.

59. William H. Stephenson letter to parents, August 11, 1968.

60. As described in one contemporaneous account, "Cat Lai was developed in the summer of 1967 on the premise that it was somewhat safer and more protected from the Viet Cong. Too, barges can discharge directly onto the shore on the right side of the river, making it easier for trucks to pick up the ammunition and transport it to Long Binh and Bien Hoa without moving through the streets of Saigon. Most of the petroleum for Saigon also is discharged at Nha Be, making it doubly dangerous to have ammunition ships in the area." *The Steward News*, September 20, 1968.

61. Stephenson interview with author, March 1, 1979.

62. Stephenson letter to parents, August 22, 1968.

63. Fred R. Hicks letter to author, September 7, 1982; "Crew Unharmed in VC Shellings of Transnorthern," *Seafarers Log*, September 27, 1968.

64. "Crew Unharmed in VC Shellings."

65. "Ro-Ro Transglobe Is Top on VC's 'Most Wanted,'" *The Master, Mate & Pilot*, January 1969.

66. "Ro-Ro Transglobe Is Top on VC's Most Wanted."

67. "Ro-Ro Transglobe Is Top on VC's Most Wanted."

68. "Shipmates Recall SIU Member Killed Aboard Transglobe in 'Nam," *Seafarers Log*, February 1992.

69. "Seafarers Recall SIU Member Killed."

70. "Seafarers Recall SIU Member Killed."

71. "War Claims First Offshore Member," *Master, Mate & Pilot*, January 1969. Vung Ro Bay, while much smaller than other ports, would eventually—once the area was deemed secured in mid-1966—provide deepwater berths in support of Army operations, and relieving pressure on Tuy Hoa. As periodic rocket attacks from surrounding mountains would clearly demonstrate, however, Vung Ro Bay, as other areas, was never entirely "secure."

72. "War Claims First Offshore Member."

73. "War Claims First Offshore Member."

74. "War Claims First Offshore Member."

75. "Skipper Recalls Harrowing Attack," *Local 88 Bulletin*, International Organization of Masters, Mates & Pilots, January-February 1969; *The NMU Pilot*, February 1969.

76. USNFVMHS, December 1968. This was actually SS *Pioneer Ming*, not *Pioneer King* as the monthly naval report indicated. Launched as a C4-S-1A hull type freighter by New York Ship in 1954, it was later lengthened by 100 feet at Todd Shipyard, Brooklyn, transformed into a C6-S-1W type as the containership *American Legacy*. She was scrapped in 1983. See also "Under Viet Cong Attack," *Local 88 Bulletin*, International Organization of Masters, Mates & Pilots, January-February 1969; "The VC Can't Stop NMU," *The NMU Pilot*, March 1969.

Chapter 13

1. U.S. Naval Forces Vietnam Monthly Historical Summaries, January–April 1969. While these summaries have been extremely useful, and generally make reference to most incidents involving merchant vessels in a given month, these references vary considerably in length and details provided. Other incident reports, and eyewitness accounts found contemporaneously in other published sources, do not always find their way into these summaries.

2. USNFVMHS, March 1969.

3. *USNFVMHS*, January-April 1969. In addition to merchant ships attacked between January and April 1969, the USNS *Perseus*, another World War II–era Victory ship that had been acquired by the MSTS in 1961 for its "nucleus fleet," and thus also crewed by merchant seamen, was also attacked, on April 27, sustaining what was described as "minor damage." See USNFVMHS, April 1969.

4. According to figures released by the Military Sealift Command (formerly named MSTS) in 1970, 1969, was indeed the "peak" year for total military sealift cargo movements to and within Southeast Asia. It also proved to be the "peak" year for tonnage transported to and within the area by ships of the MSC "nucleus" fleet. Whereas a total of 15,844,200 measurement tons (MT) of cargo were moved to and within the area by government-owned ships and privately owned ships in 1969, surpassing the 15,126,737 MT moved in the previous year, that figure would drop off to 13,578,428 in FY 1970, and continue to drop in each year that the United States remained involved in providing logistical support for the war in Vietnam. Press release, U.S. Navy Military Sealift Command, October 27, 1970. Release No. 10–10.

5. The percentage figure for logistical support transported by ship during the Vietnam War, compared to air transport, generally ranged from 94 to 98 percent depending on the source. One variable would have been the number of troops transported, which, as troopships were taken out of service, was increasingly accomplished by air transport. For the use of the 94 percent figure by a government source see, for example, "MARAD Head Praises U.S. Fleet's Major Role in Korean, Vietnam Wars," *District 2 Marine Engineer*, July 1969, 6.

6. The peak year for tonnage carried to Vietnam in ships withdrawn from National Defense Reserve Fleets (NDRF) and operated under General Agency Agreement (GAA), was 1967, when 3,809, 917 MT were lifted to and within Southeast Asia. This would compare to 3,798,812 MT transported to area in FY 1970, and then, reflecting the drastic reduction of ships operated under GAA agreement then taking place, 2,966,423 MT in 1969, 756,725 MT in 1970, and only 4,510 MT—representing one light shipload—in FY 1971. There is no tonnage indicated for FY 1972, the last full year of U.S. involvement in providing logistical support in Vietnam prior to the negotiated truce reached at the beginning of 1973. See Press release, U.S. Navy Military Sealift Command, October 27, 1970, Release No. 10–10.

7. "U.S. Fleet Gets Less Viet Tonnage," *The Baltimore Sun*, August 25, 1969; House Merchant Marine Panel Sets Hearing on Reserve Ships," *The New York Times*, October 11, 1969.

8. "U.S. Fleet Gets Less Viet Tonnage."

9. For context and analysis relating to the Vietnam antiwar movement, see, for example, Charles DeBenedetti and Charles Chatfield, *An American Ordeal: The Antiwar Movement of the Vietnam Era* (Syracuse, NY: Syracuse University Press, 1990). See also, Gettleman, et al., *Vietnam and America*, 295–338; Young, *The Vietnam Wars*, 192–209.

10. DeBenedetti and Chatfield, *An American*

Ordeal; Gettleman, et al., *Vietnam and America*, 295–335; Young, *The Vietnam Wars*, 210–231. For an interesting comparison of American public opposition to the wars in Korea and Vietnam, and the similar way in which that opposition grew as casualty rates increased in each case by a factor of one, see John E. Mueller, *War, Presidents and Public Opinion* (New York: John Wiley & Sons, 1973).

11. What came to be known as the Nixon Doctrine was first enunciated in remarks Nixon made in Guam on July 25, 1969, during a tour of East Asia. Initially referred to as the Guam Doctrine, it was formalized, and generally known as the Nixon Doctrine going forward, in a speech made before Congress on November 3, 1969. As he described it, this defining foreign policy statement consisted of three general areas: "First, the United States will keep all treaty commitments. Second, we shall provide a shield if a nuclear power threatens the freedom of a nation allied with us or of a nation whose survival we consider vital to our security. Third, in cases involving other types of aggression, we shall furnish military and economic assistance when requested in accordance with our treaty commitments. But we shall look to the nation directly threatened to assume the primary responsibility of providing the manpower for its defenses."

12. Vietnamization"—at least Nixon's understanding of it—would be spelled out in his November 3, 1969, speech to the nation. For the text of the entire speech, and a brief introduction, see Gettleman, et al., *Vietnam and America*, 434–445.

13. Nixon himself put the number of American military personnel in Vietnam on the day he took office in January 1969 at 540,000. The peak figure eventually reported by the U.S. Government is put at 549,500. See U.S. Government, "Statistical information" (2010). The number reported to be in the initial withdrawal group is generally placed at 25,000, and Nixon pledged in his November 3 speech to the nation that the total figure of troops withdrawn by year's end would be 60,000. The total number remaining in-country by the end of the following year would be put at 335,790 by the U.S. Government.

14. While U.S. military forces were required to be withdrawn within a few months of the signing of the 1973 truce ending hostilities, civilian merchant seamen, while no longer making their way to Vietnam in "nucleus" fleet ships of U.S. Navy's Military Sealift Command, would continue to arrive in privately owned and operated merchant ships for various authorized purposes, and then in evacuation operations as the war was ending with the South Vietnamese defeat in early 1975.

15. "Lykes Ship Damaged By Viet Cong Gunners; Master And Pilot Injured," *Lykes Lines Bulletin*, 1969, 6.

16. USNFVMHS, February 1969, 1.

17. "Enemy Salvo Hits Lafayette In Estuary of Saigon River," *Seafarers Log*, May 1969.

18. "Enemy Salvo Hits Lafayette In Estuary of Saigon River."

19. USNFVMHS, February 1969, 1.

20. Francis E. Davis letter to author. See chapter five for Davis's role in Vietnamese relocation movements following the French defeat.

21. USNS *Saugatuck* was initially laid down at the Sun Shipbuilding and Drydock Co., Chester, Pennsylvania as SS *Newton*, a standard T2-SE-A1 tanker type. Renamed *Saugatuck* and delivered to the U.S. Navy for service during World War II, the ship later became part of the MSTS nucleus fleet, saw service during the Korean War, and later in Vietnam. *Saugatuck* was shifted to lay-up in the James Rivers NDRF in 1974 before being removed for final disposal in 2006.

22. This rocket attack was witnessed by the author, who was standing deck security watch on SS *Fairport*, an ammunition ship that was anchored out in the harbor. According to *The White Elephant News* of the U.S. Naval Support Activity, Da Nang, the ship (unnamed in that account) was a Vietnamese coastal tanker carrying a "highly volatile" cargo of petroleum. "At the height of the spectacular blaze," the report stated, "the listing ship capsized. Fuel cans on the pier exploded and the blaze spread to two barges, two tugs, and numerous fishing boats in the area." The report praised "the quick action of the men on board the fire boats and those from the fire station [who] in the face of danger may have averted a fire of major proportions." There was no mention of the ship's Vietnamese crew or whether or not there had been any casualties. "NSA Fire Crews Quick To Subdue Ship Blaze," *The White Elephant News*, Vol. 3, No. 12, July 11, 1969. In the later U.S. Naval Support Activity, Da Nang Command History for 1969, declassified, the ship in question was identified specifically as the Vietnamese butane tanker MV *Phong Chau*, but as before there was no information provided regarding casualties.

23. The author also recalls the use of explosive charges being set off in a circuit around his ship during the night. While vials of nitro might well have been used at some time, in some locations, as Davis asserted, the author's own understanding was that concussion grenades—not "vials of nitro"—were used for this purpose during the month—June 1969—that he was in Da Nang. Also, unlike the recollection of Francis Davis, the gunboat crew in charge of this duty did not continue this throughout the day, but broke off at 0600 and moved away towards their base at the foot of Monkey Mountain.

24. See chapter 11, 184–186, n. 19–20, above.

25. For description of the 1967 mining incident and subsequent attempt to salvage the dredge *Jamaica Bay*, see chapter 11, 186–187, n. 22–26, above.

26. For description of the 1967 mining and

subsequent salvage operation involving the dredge *Hyde*, see chapter 11, 187–188, n. 27–28, above.

27. "Willie J. Williams Killed by Viet Cong," *The NMU Pilot*, 1969.

28. USNFVMHS, October-December 1969.

29. USNFVMHS.

30. USNFVMHS, November 1969, 88. *Seatrain Maine* was one of nine T2-SE2-A2-type tankers acquired from the U.S. Maritime Administration as part of the Ship Exchange Program and subsequently jumboized for Hudson Waterways Corp. in 1966 and 1967 "to carry shipping containers, railway wagons and vehicles." Many of these conversions later carried war materiel to Vietnam. See Sawyer and Mitchell, *Victory Ships and Tankers*, 175–176, and chapter 11, above.

31. USNFVMHS, January 1969.

32. USNFVMHS, December 1969. The USNS *Provo* (T-AG-173) was launched as SS *Drew Victory* at Oregon Shipbuilding Corporation, Portland, Oregon, in June 1945 and underwent a series of name changes in the immediate postwar period before being transferred to the U.S. Navy's MSTS for its nucleus fleet in 1962 as USNS *Provo*. As such she eventually became an auxiliary or "Forward Floating Depot" for delivery of parts and supplies between Subic Bay, the Philippines, and port areas in Vietnam.

33. USNFVMHS, December 1969, 99–100.

34. Unless otherwise indicated, the day by day summary of developments on *Badger State* is from the U.S. Coast Guard Board of Investigation Marine Casualty Report, released on December 7, 1971.

35. "Badger State Sinks: Three MEBA Men Among 25 Dead in Ammo Ship Explosion Tragedy; 14 Saved Incudes 3 Engineers," *The American Marine Engineer*, January 1970, 1, 6.

36. "Badger State Sinks: Three MEBA Men Among 25 Dead."

37. "MM&P Honors Greek Ship For Heroic Rescue in 'Badger State' Disaster," *The Master, Mate and Pilot*, March 1970, 2–3.

38. "Twenty-six seamen are lost as SS Badger State Explodes," *The NMU Pilot*, February 1970, 26.

39. "Twenty-six seamen are lost as SS Badger State Explodes," 27.

40. "Seamanship Trophy awarded posthumously to R.D. Hughes," *The NMU Pilot*, July 1970, 6.

41. "Seamanship Trophy awarded posthumously to R.D. Hughes." See also "President honors NMU hero at White House," *The NMU Pilot*, September 1970, 4–5.

42. In summary the Marine Casualty Report concluded that "the casualty was caused by a combination of factors. After a shift of cargo the 2,000-pound bombs came adrift from their palletized stowage. A low order detonation of one of the bombs occurred as a result of impact of heat generated as the bomb slid and rolled in number

five [cargo hold] upper 'tween deck. The detonation resulted in a hole in the starboard shell plating and possibly additional damage to one forward bulkhead of number five hold."

43. For much of Captain Wilson's subsequent testimony before a Coast Guard investigation into the circumstances involving *Badger State*, see, for example, "MM&P honors Greek Ship For Heroic Rescue in 'Badger State' Disaster," *The Master, Mate and Pilot*, March 1970, 2–3.

44. In an interview with the author in the early 1980s, Joseph Stackpole (Maine Maritime, 1964), who had served as Second Mate on *Badger State* during its initial voyage to Vietnam in 1965, suggested that there might have been an additional factor contributing to the ship's final demise. *Badger State* had been involved in the "cement shuttle" between Taiwan and Vietnam during his time on the ship and in later voyages, and that had contributed to accumulation of "residual cement" that, when attempts were later made to pump it out with water had "clogged bilge suction lines" and had "probably not [been fully] cleared of cement." When Stackpole eventually left the ship, he did so suspecting, in part because of the cement situation, that "the *Badger State* was doomed." The suspicion might well have been a premonition.

45. "380 Ships Manned by U.S. Seamen Involved in Vietnam Sealift; But MSTS Head Doubts Aging U.S. Fleet Can Do It Again," District 2 Marine Engineer, September 1969, 8.

46. "MARAD Head Praises U.S. Fleet's Major Role in Korean, Vietnam Wars," District 2 Marine Engineer, July 1969, 6. Statistics provided in this article support the long-standing argument that between 1965 and 1969 some 94 percent of logistical-support cargo shipped to Vietnam was carried in ships crewed by American merchant seamen. Sixty-seven percent of that total, 20,711,400 metric tons, was carried in privately owned U.S.-flag ships, while the remaining 27 percent of the total percentage, 8,170,000 metric tons, was carried in government-owned ships withdrawn from reserve fleets for the Vietnam Run.

47. The MSTS would report that 15,844,200 measurement tons of cargo were hauled to Vietnam in 1969, following 15,126,737 MT delivered in 1968, and preceding 13,578,428 MT in 1970. The amounts would continue to drop off in succeeding years.

Chapter 14

1. "Memorial Held For Seamen Lost In Vietnam Sealift," *District 2 Marine Engineer*, June 1970.

2. "Memorial Held For Seamen Lost In Vietnam."

3. "Capt. Andrew Gibson M.A. Administrator," *The Master, Mate & Pilot*, February 1969, 3.

4. Based on the monthly U.S. Naval Forces Vietnam Monthly Historical Summaries, there

were eight merchant ships attacked in the Long Tau shipping channel to Saigon between January and May 1970. There were an additional six attacks in the month of June.

5. In addition to the sinking of USNS *Card* by limpet mine while the ship was at pier-side in Saigon in 1964, the most notable sinkings of merchant ships by floating mine in the Long Tau shipping channel during the war were those involving SS *Eastern Mariner*, in 1966, and SS *Baton Rouge Victory*—when seven of her crew were killed—in 1966. There were other ships sunk by mine in at least two other ports along the coast of South Vietnam during the war.

6. Few attempted or successful mining attacks against merchant shipping or MSTS/MSC "nucleus" fleet vessels crewed by merchant seamen appear in the monthly U.S. Naval Forces Vietnam Historical Summaries for 1970. Notable exceptions—both incidents taking place in Cam Ranh Bay—appear in the summaries for May and September.

7. U.S. Army, "Operational Report—Lessons Learned," 5th Transportation Command for Period Ending April 30, 1970, 3.

8. USNFVMHS, May 1970.

9. For descriptions and analysis of reaction on college campuses to the Cambodian incursion, and the related killing of students at both Kent State in Ohio and Jackson State in Mississippi, see, for example, Myra MacPherson, *Long Time Passing: Vietnam and the Haunted Generation* (New York: Doubleday and Co., 1984), 88–89, 514, 571; Young, *The Vietnam Wars*, 248–249.

10. Young, *The Vietnam Wars*, 230, 240–41.

11. Young, *The Vietnam Wars*, 240–41; Karnow, *Vietnam*, 593–96.

12. Schreadley, *From the Rivers to the Sea*, 163–65, 329–47, 362–63.

13. Ernest Rapley, "5000 'On Beach' In U.S. Cutback Of Viet Shipping," *San Francisco Sunday Examiner & Chronicle*, 26 April 1970, A16.

14. "Last Viet Ship Back in Lay-up," *District 2 Marine Engineer*, June 1970.

15. "Bucyrus Victory To Scrap Heap," *West Coast Sailors*, 8 May 1970.

16. "Last Ship Back in Lay-up," *D-2 Marine Engineer*, June 1970.

17. "Gibson Commends Vietnam Sealift Shippers' Contribution," *D2 Marine Engineer*, April 1970; District 2 MARAD Award Honors Role in Viet Sealift," *D2 Marine Engineer*, December 1970, 1, 4.

18. *Seafarers Log*, September 1970, 4.

19. Ernest Rapley, "5000 'On Beach,'" *San Francisco Sunday Examiner & Chronicle*, April 26, 1970, A16.

20. Launched as the *General M.B. Stewart* (AP-140) on October 15, 1944, at Kaiser in Richmond, California, the 522'10" ship saw service as a trooper with the U.S. Navy until decommissioned in May 1946. Later serving as an Army transport, used for carrying refugees from Europe and troops from Korea, the ship was transferred to the Maritime Administration in 1958 and placed in the NDRF, Hudson River, until sold to Albany River Transport in 1967, rebuilt as a cargo ship, and renamed *Albany*. Entering commercial service in 1958, *Albany* saw service in Vietnam before later conversion as the drill ship *Mission Viking*, and finally facing the scrapper's torch in 1987.

21. Brett Whitaker, letters to author, September 13, 1982; November 30, 1982.

22. Whitaker, letter to author.

23. USNFVMHS, June 1970. 52; Whitaker, letter to author.

24. Whitaker, letter to author.

25. Whitaker, letter to author.

26. Whitaker, letter to author.

27. U.S. Army, "Operational Report—Lessons Learned, 5th Transportation Command for Period Ending 30 April 1970," 3.

28. Schreadley, *From the Rivers to the Sea*, 289.

29. Schreadley, *From the Rivers to the Sea*, 165, 240, 321, 346.

30. Constructed as a C-2 type merchant ship during World War II, *Beauregard* was later involved in Vietnamese refugee evacuations out of Haiphong after the French defeat in 1954. The ship was among other C-2s converted from a traditional boom-and-sling freighter to a containership in the mid-1960s and, as such, was involved in providing container feeder service between Cam Ranh Bay and other ports in South Vietnam until the war ended in 1975.

31. Bertil Hager, letter to E. Sheppard, SIU, October 14, 1970.

32. Captain A. Stewart statement, September 22, 1970.

33. Captain Stewart statement.

34. Captain Stewart statement.

35. "Vice Admiral Gralla takes command of Military Sea Transportation Service," *The NMU Pilot*, May 1970, 12.

36. USNFVMHS, May 1970.

37. USNFVMHS, June, July, September, November 1970.

38. For an excellent description, and personal impressions of the author, of U.S. Navy force drawdowns in 1970, see R.L. Schreadley, *From the Rivers to the Sea: The U.S. Navy in Vietnam*, 345–46, 362, 369.

39. USNFVMHS, November 1970, 62.

40. USNFVHS.

41. USNFVHS, 45.

42. The loss of the troopship *President Coolidge* in a mine field while entering Luganville Bay, Espiritu Santo Island, New Hebrides, on October 26, 1942, is described in Captain Arthur R. Moore, *A Careless Word...A Needless Sinking* (Kings Point, NY: American Merchant Marine Museum, 1985), 226.

43. Launched as *Cracker State Mariner* in 1954, the 9,271-ton ship was acquired by APL in 1956 and renamed *President Coolidge*. After

Vietnam service *President Coolidge* was sold in 1974 to American Export Lines and renamed *Export Defender*.

44. USNFVMHS, November 1970.

45. Schreadley, From the Rivers to the Sea, 289.

Chapter 15

1. Based on USNFVMHS reports relating to Long Tau shipping channel incidents, January to July 1971.

2. USNFVMHS, August 1971. Viet Cong sapper units had operated in the Rung Sat Special Zone area between Vung Tau and Saigon for many years. When the USNFVMHS for August 1971 noted that a "sapper battalion [was] reported in the area" there may actually have been such a unit there at least since the USNS *Card* had been sunk at a Saigon pier by water mine sappers of the NLF 65th Special Operations Group in 1964, if not before.

3. USNFVMHS, August 1971.

4. USNFVMHS.

5. USNFVMHS, January 1971, 56. Following the turnover of U.S. Mine Division minesweepers to the South Vietnamese navy's Mine Interdiction Divisions (MID) in 1970, the boats operated by them—largely 57-foot fiberglass-hulled minesweepers—were then generally referred to in reports as MID boats. See Schreadley, *From the Rivers to the Sea*, 289; www.minedivision113vietnam.com; www.navy.togetherweserved.com.

6. USNFVMHS, April 1971, 66,

7. USNFVMHS, August 1971.

8. *The NMU Pilot*, September-October 1971, 6.

9. USNFVMHS, August 1971, 69.

10. The mining of *Green Bay* put an end to her active service life after more than 25 years. She was refloated on September 1, 1971, towed to Hong Kong, and finally scrapped in 1972.

11. USNFVMHS, August 1971, 72.

12. USNFVMHS.

13. USNFVMHS, August 1971, 73.

14. USNFVMHS, 81.

15. USNFVMHS, November 1971, 28.

16. Department of Defense, Manpower Data Center; www.gilderlehrman.org.

17. While figures for retrograde tonnage movements from Vietnam for 1971 are elusive, figures provided by the Military Sealift Command (formerly MSTS) for cargo movements to and within Southeast Asia (Thailand and Vietnam only) for fiscal year 1971 show a grand total for the year, combining government-owned ships and commercial ships, of 10,841,291 measurement tons (MT), a reduction from the 13,578,428 recorded for FY 1970. A total of 7,555,144 MT, suggesting further reduction in war-related shipments, would be reported for FY 1972. U.S. Navy, Military Sealift Command, Washington, DC, Release No. 10–10 (and later).

18. Karnow, *Vietnam*, 629–630.

19. Karnow, *Vietnam*, 629.

20. Karnow, *Vietnam*, 629.

21. Schreadley, *From the Rivers to the Sea*, 365.

22. Schreadley, *From the Rivers to the Sea*, 370.

23. Schreadley, *From the Rivers to the Sea*, 372.

24. "Seatrain Puerto Rico Negotiates Saigon River," *Seafarers Log*, November 1971, 22.

25. Galka letter to the author, April 28, 1982.

26. The number of U.S. Army personnel in-country at the beginning of 1972 was put at 119,700. By the end of August the number was reported to be 39,000. See *The New York Times*, January 4, 1972.

27. The number of U.S. Navy personnel in-country at the beginning of 1972—not including some 13,000 offshore with the Seventh Fleet—was reported to be 7,800. *The New York Times*, January 4, 1972.

28. The number of U.S. Marines reported to be in-country at the beginning of 1972 was put at just 500. *The New York Times*, January 4, 1972.

29. Regarding SCATTOR, see Schreadley, *From the Rivers to the Sea, 342–343*.

30. *West Coast Sailors*, September 7, 1973.

31. *West Coast Sailors*.

32. The North Vietnamese referred to this as the Nguyen Hue Offensive, after one of Vietnam's greatest military heroes. It was commonly known by Western observers as the "Easter Offensive" for its timing with the Christian holiday schedule. See Schreadley, *From the Rivers to the Sea*, 372.

33. Schreadley, *From the Rivers to the Sea*, 372.

34. For General Westmoreland's comment regarding the "staying power" of the North Vietnamese Army (NVA), see, for example, Karnow, *Vietnam*, 640.

35. For a description of Operation Linebacker, which countered the "Easter Offensive" using tactical jet-fighter aircraft from May 9 until October 23, 1972, see, for example, Schreadley, *From the Rivers to the Sea*, 373.

36. William J. Webb and Walter S. Poole, *The Joint Chiefs of Staff and the War in Vietnam, 1971–1973* (Washington, DC: Office of the Chairman of the Joint Chiefs of Staff), 213–215.

37. Arnold S. Isaacs, *Without Honor: Defeat in Vietnam and Cambodia* (Baltimore, MD: Johns Hopkins University Press, 1983), 511.

38. Donald Merchant letter to author, April 12, 1982.

39. For an account of the ordering and implementation of aerial mining of North Vietnamese waters, including approaches to the Port of Haiphong, that bottled up many merchant ships until mines were subsequently swept or deactivated by programmed timers, see Schreadley, 373–374, 377–378.

40. "Background Information Relating to Southeast Asia and Vietnam," in Gareth Porter, *Vietnam*, Vol. 2, 566.

41. W.L. Greer, "The Mining of Haiphong Harbor: A Case Study in Naval Mining and Diplomacy" (Institute For Defense, 1997).

42. Schreadley, *From the Rivers to the Sea*, 374.

43. For one of Defense Secretary Kissinger's takes on negotiations with Le Duc Tho, see "Press Conference Statement by Kissinger, December 16, 1972 (Extract)," in Porter, *Vietnam*, Vol. 2, 587–590.

44. Karnow, *Vietnam*, 648.

45. "Memorandum for the President from the Assistant Secretary of Defense Installations and Logistics," Department of State, in Porter, *Vietnam*, Vol. 2, 583–84. See also Webb and Poole, *The Joint Chiefs of Staff and the War in Vietnam*, 213–215; Elizabeth Hartsook and Stuart Slade, *Air War in Vietnam Plans and Operations, 1969–1975* (Newtown, CT: Defense Lions Publications, 2003), 220–222; Isaacs, *Without Honor: Defeat in Vietnam and Cambodia* (Baltimore, MD: Johns Hopkins Press, 1983), 48–49, 511. It was noted that last deliveries of military supplies under Operation Enhance Plus would be made by or were in route in international waters by November 10. In actuality, one report would note, the last shipment of supplies would not arrive, presumably by ship, until December 20, 1972.

46. Based on material obtained from the MACV Official History, comparison of shipments made by air and sea during Operation Enhance Plus reveals that some 5,000 short tons arrived by air while some 100,000 short tons arrived by sea. www.riciok.com/cease_fire/organization_for_the_cease_fire.htm.

47. Karnow, *Vietnam*, 648–649.

48. Webb and Poole, *The Joint Chiefs of Staff and the War in Vietnam*, 213–215; Hartsook and Slade, *Air War Vietnam Plans and Operations, 1969–1975*, 220–222.

49. Karnow, *Vietnam*, 650.

50. Karnow, *Vietnam*, 651.

51. Karnow, *Vietnam*, 650.

Chapter 16

1. "Agreement on Ending the War and Restoring Peace in Vietnam," U.S. Department of State, Bureau of Public Affairs, News Release, January 24, 1973, 32–79. See also Gettleman, et al., *America and Vietnam*, 471–486; *The New York Times*, January 25, 1973, 15–25.

2. Gettleman, et al., *America and Vietnam*, 471–472. In introductory remarks to the text of the ceasefire agreement, the fundamental similarity between the October and January ceasefire agreements is noted, as the nearly identical wording of introductory statements in both the 1954 Geneva Accords and the 1973 ceasefire. See also Karnow, *Vietnam*, 654; Young, *The Vietnam Wars*, 278–279.

3. Young, *The Vietnam Wars*, 278–279.

4. Agreement on Ending the War, Chapter 1, Article 1.

5. Agreement on Ending the War.

6. Agreement on Ending the War, Chapter 2, Articles 5 and 6.

7. Agreement on Ending the War, Article 7.

8. Agreement on Ending the War.

9. Protocol to the Cease-Fire Agreement, Article 2 (b); Article 3 (a) (1).

10. George Aldrich, DOD legal briefing paper, 1973, in Porter, *Vietnam*, II, 602.

11. Schreadley, *From the Rivers to the Sea*, 377–379. See also, Edward J. Marolda, ed., *Operation End Sweep: A History of Minesweeping Operations in North Vietnam* (Washington, DC: Naval Historical Center, 1993).

12. Karnow, *Vietnam*, 660.

13. Samuel Lipsman, Stephen Weiss, et al., *The Vietnam Experience: The False Peace* (Boston: Boston Publishing Company, 1985), 150; Karnow, *Vietnam*, 654.

14. Young, *The Vietnam Wars*, 291; Arnold R. Isaacs, *Without Honor: Defeat in Vietnam and Cambodia* (Baltimore, MD: The Johns Hopkins Press, 1998).

15. Lipsman, Weiss, et al., *The Vietnam Experience: The False Peace*, 150; Isaacs, *Without Honor*, 126; Young, *The Vietnam Wars*, 290.

16. The code name Operation Roll-Up had first been used in the late 1940s and into the early Korean War period to recover and refurbish military equipment that had been "left behind" in the Pacific at the end of World War II for the Far East Command (FEC). These recovered tanks, armored cars, artillery, and other surplus equipment—in excess of 200,000 tons—were transported to Japan for refurbishment and subsequently deployed to Korea, in American-flag merchant ships. For more information regarding Operation Roll-Up, see www.history.army.mil/books/PD-C-03, 58–59. See also Salvatore R. Mercogliano, *Fourth Arm of Defense: Sealift and Maritime Logistics in the Vietnam War* (Washington, DC: Department of the Navy, 2017).

17. For a good contemporaneous description of the ceremonial and symbolic departure of the "last" American military personnel to leave Vietnam—including those actually left behind for approved finishing up duties (a 14-man graves commission, for example), and the American Embassy guard detail, see H.D.S. Greenway's article "Last GIs Leave South Vietnam," *The Washington Post*, March 30, 1973, in *Reporting Vietnam*, Part Two, *American Journalism 1969–1975*, 464–469.

18. *Reporting Vietnam*, Part Two, *American Journalism*.

19. *Reporting Vietnam*, Part Two, *American Journalism*, 464.

20. www.isthmianlines.com.

21. www.isthmianlines.com.

22. Russell R. Rowley letter to the author, August 17, 1980.

23. Located some eight miles from the mouth of the Willamette River, Swan Island was the site of Portland, Oregon's first airport from 1927 to 1940. During World War II one of the Kaiser Shipyards was located there, constructing some 455 ships, including 147 T-2 tankers and additional Liberty- and Victory-type cargo ships. Following the war Swan Island remained an important industrial and manufacturing center, and for ship dry-docking and repair.

24. Rowley letter to author, August 17, 1980.

25. Young, *The Vietnam Wars*, 290.

26. Young, *The Vietnam Wars*, 289. The "Five Forbids" promulgated by North Vietnamese leadership in the immediate ceasefire period were: attacking the enemy, attacking the enemy carrying out land grabs, surrounding enemy outposts, shelling outposts, and building combat villages.

27. "Vietnam Fuel Depot Reported Attacked," *The New York Times*, May 20, 1974, 12; www.nyti.ms/1GX1u17.

28. www.nyti.ms/1GX1u17.

29. Lipsman, Weiss, et al., *The Vietnam Experience: The False Peace*, 146.

30. Karnow, *Vietnam*, 658.

31. Karnow, *Vietnam*.

32. Lipsman, Weiss, et al., *The Vietnam Experience: The False Peace*, 146.

33. Lipsman, Weiss, et al., *The Vietnam Experience: The False Peace*, 150.

34. Thomas A. Galka letter to the author, April 28, 1982.

35. Galka letter to the author.

36. "Orphans, Seatrain Crews Enjoy a 'Family Dinner,'" *Seafarers Log*, March 1975.

37. DOS, Office of Media Services, "Address of the President as delivered on live Radio and Television," January 23, 1973.

38. Lipsman, Weiss, et al., *The Vietnam Experience: The False Peace*, 148.

39. Peter Macdonald, *Giap: The Victor in Vietnam* (New York: W.W. Norton & Co., 1993), 333–335; Lipsman, Weiss, et al., *The Vietnam Experience: The False Peace*, 158–160; Young, *The Vietnam Wars*, 292.

40. Young, *The Vietnam Wars*, 292.

41. Karnow, *Vietnam*, 663.

Chapter 17

1. For a contemporaneous military analysis of the pull-back of South Vietnam's military forces from the northern I Corps provinces and the Central Highlands, and the subsequent impact of leadership decisions contributing to those movements, see "Final Report by the Defense Attaché, Saigon, Maj. General H.D. Smith, May 1975," in Porter, *Vietnam*, Vol. 2, 659–663.

2. While Vietnam was generally considered a key area in the East Asian Cold War containment line, and one of the "dominoes" that needed to be prevented from falling, the man most regarded for his advocacy of containment policy, the diplomat and historian George F. Kennan, was principally concerned about Soviet expansionism, and actually less so about Vietnam. In fact, he was opposed to the United States becoming more involved in the Vietnam War. Regarding Kennan and Vietnam, see, for example, Walter L. Hixson, "Containment on the Perimeter: George F. Kennan and Vietnam," *Diplomatic History*, Vol. 12, No. 2 (Spring 1982), 149–163.

3. Frank Snepp, the CIA's chief strategy analyst in South Vietnam at the time of the final evacuations, would later sum up his own feelings about the remarkable and rapid collapse of the country's military forces in the face of the PAVN final offensive when he wrote: "Although the Ford Administration would blame Congressional aid cut-backs for the disaster, the root cause was shoddy leadership, particularly in Saigon. Having promised [Gen. Ngo Quang] Truong not to withdraw the Airborne Division precipitously, [President] Thieu had reversed himself overnight, without giving his MR [Military Region] 1 commander adequate time to adjust his defenses, and he had changed his mind at least twice about the defense of Hue. To add to the chaos, he had refused to keep his own commanders—or his allies—informed of his plans." Frank Snepp, *Decent Interval* (New York: Random House, 1977), 261. For arguments to the contrary, see, for example, Smith, "Final Report," in Porter, *Vietnam*, Vol. 2, 659–663, and Veith, *Black April*, 497–499.

4. Regarding the idea of drawing a defensive line across South Vietnam from Ban Me Thuot to Nha Trang, and the need to recapture Ban Me Thuot as per President Thieu's order, see Veith, *Black April*, 173.

5. For reference to house-to-house search operation of PAVN troops, and the start of civilian evacuation out of Ban Me Thuot, see Veith, *Black April*, 169.

6. Tran Thi Minh Canh, *The Book of Canh: Memoirs of a Vietnamese Woman, Physician, CIA Informant, People's Salvation Army Commander-in-Chief, and Prisoner of War* (Milford, CT: Self-Published, 1996), 71–72, as quoted in Veith, *Black April*, 351.

7. Alan Dawson, *55 Days: The Fall of South Vietnam* (1977), 186. Some South Vietnamese marines and ARVN troops did more than simply block civilian refugees from access to ships they also wanted to board. There were also reports of ARVN soldiers turning their weapons on civilians who had already come aboard American merchant ships, notably *Pioneer Contender*. See, for example, "Troops Kill 25 on Rescue Ships," *Newsday* (New York), April 1, 1975; "Death rides refugee ship," *The Times Union* (Albany, NY), April 1, 1975, 1.

8. Defense Attaché Smith's characterization of the decision by Thieu to give up Kontum and Pleiku is in Porter, *Vietnam*, Vol. 2, 660.

9. For descriptions of Route 7A between Pleiku and Thuy Hoa, and the evacuation that would take place along it in 1975, see Veith, *Black April*, 202–234; Clark Dougan, David Fulghum, et al., *The Vietnam Experience: The Fall of the South* (Boston: Boston Publishing Co., 1985), 56–63.

10. Contemporaneous reports on the evacuation out of Pleiku, which soon became known as the "Road of Blood and Tears," were filed in Saigon by Nguyen Tu, the only journalist to accompany the evacuation. See Veith, *Black April*, 231.

11. Veith, *Black April*, 234.

12. The civilian and military survivors of evacuation along Route 7A, minus much of the rolling stock and other equipment that had set out from Pleiku, began arriving at the coast, at Tuy Hoa, on March 25. From there, unable to escape seaward, many would make their way further to the south along Route 1 to Nha Trang. While ships of the South Vietnamese navy would take many of them on board for transit to other areas—and ultimately to American merchant ships for the longer transit to refugee camps on Guam and elsewhere—many would be left behind.

13. On April 1 the South Vietnamese Navy's LSM *Han Giang* (HQ-401), at the pier in Nha Trang, began to board civilian evacuees. According to one account: "The ship filled so rapidly that it began to list, forcing the captain to back away from the pier. Seeing the masses of clamoring civilians, and mindful of the terrible tragedy at Danang, the local Navy commander refused to allow any more of his ships to dock at Nha Trang. Soon they weighed anchor and sailed to Cam Ranh." See Veith, *Black April*, 351–352.

14. In his "Final Assessment" written only a few days after his own evacuation from Saigon on April 29, 1975, Major General H.D. Smith, the U.S. Defense Attaché, described the flawed decision-making and other factors—such as the "family syndrome" (proximity to family)—that contributed to ARVN desertions and set initial evacuations in motion out of Ban Me Thuot, Kontum, and Pleiku. See Porter, *Vietnam*, Vol. 2, 662.

15. Named for a lagoon near the mouth of the Perfume River, and based on Truan An Island there, what would become the Tan My Naval Support Activity (Detachment)—often commonly referred to as Tan My Docks—was constructed in 1967. After major dredging operations, it would eventually include shallow draft offloading ramps for four LSTs. It was to this area that civilian refugees, ARVN, and Vietnamese Marines would make their way ahead of the PAVN offensive against Hue in March 1975. Small landing craft—probably LCMs—would shuttle those fortunate enough to board them out to the LST *Can Tho* (HQ-801). As many as 6,000 civilians might have been evacuated in this manner on March 24. But, as in most other points of evacuation along the entire coastline of South Vietnam in subsequent weeks, many could

not be accommodated and would be left behind. For a description of the development of Tan My Support Activity, see Hooper, *Mobility, Support, Endurance*, 112–117. For the evacuations out of Tan My see Veith, *Black April*, 315–317.

16. The inability of Vietnamese Marines to board evacuation landing craft at Tan My and points along the coast to the south is described in Veith, *Black April*, 316–319. "As night fell on 26 March," he writes, "firefights with PAVN troops continued. The Marines had nowhere to hide, and the senior commanders decided they had no choice but to try and fight their way to the Tu Hien crossing [about half way between Tan My and the Hai Van Pass to the north of Da Nang]. Forming a column, the remaining troops moved south along the beach. Very few Marines made it to Tu Hien, and most were captured the next day. Many committed suicide with grenades rather than surrender. The 147th Marine Brigade died on the beach; only about one in four Marines were rescued." Veith, *Black April*, 318–319.

17. Evacuations out of Chu Lai, also a shallow-draft approach area, were largely accomplished by landing craft of the South Vietnamese Navy between March 25 and 26. Some 10,500 troops and civilians were evacuated, with most (6,000) taken to Cu Lao Re Island, about 18 miles east of Chu Lai, where they were disembarked on March 27. The remainder (about 4,000) were taken to Da Nang, to join thousands of other desperate refugees in the massive and chaotic evacuations soon to take place there with the involvement of American merchant ships and other MSC tug and barge assets. For the Chu Lai evacuations, see Veith, 319–320; Smith, "Final Report by the Defense Attaché, Saigon" in Porter, *Vietnam*, Vol. 2, 662.

18. "Final Report by the Defense Attaché."

19. Veith, *Black April*, 289.

20. Regarding the order to send assets to Da Nang to begin assisting with evacuations, Major General Smith states in his "Final Report" that he had previously "directed that all available Military Sealift Command (MSC) shipping in the area be moved to Da Nang to backhaul materiel. This resulted in two ships [*Pioneer Contender* and *Transnorthern*] plus other MSC-controlled ships joining the evacuation convoy. However, instead of materiel, they, of necessity, moved people." Porter, *Vietnam*, Vol. 2, 662.

21. Dawson, *55 Days*, 186; "Troops Kill 25 on Rescue Ship," *Newsday*, April 1, 1975; "Death rides refugee ship," *The Times Union*, April 1, 1975, 1.

22. *Sealift*, Military Sealift Command, June 1975, 4.

23. Snepp, *Decent Interval*, 248–249.

24. Snepp, *Decent Interval*, 249.

25. Snepp, *Decent Interval*.

26. Joseph Delehant letter to author, June 20, 1979. A 1970 graduate of the Maritime College, State University of New York, Delehant would

ship out for the first time in July 1970, and on two subsequent voyages to Vietnam as a junior officer, all in SS *Steel Vendor* (Isthmian), before shipping out again to Vietnam for the last time, on October 22, 1974, for the fateful voyage in *Pioneer Contender*. That voyage would finally end for him on May 29, 1975, two months to the day following the initial arrival of *Pioneer Contender* in Da Nang to evacuate refugees.

27. Located in the Gulf of Thailand off the coasts of Vietnam and Cambodia, Phu Quoc Island, now a national park and resort area, had once served the French and later South Vietnam as a penal colony. During the final evacuation phase in 1975 thousands of Vietnamese refugees would be put ashore there before boarding ships again for transit to Guam and elsewhere for processing and longer-term, but temporary, housing.

28. Delehant letter to author, June 20, 1979.

29. Alan Dawson, *55 Days: The Fall of South Vietnam*, 186; *Sealift Magazine*, June 1975, 4.

31. Dawson, *55 Days*, 186; For additional references to *Pioneer Commander*'s involvement in evacuation operations at this time, see *Sealift Magazine*, June 1975, 4, 7, 9, 10–11, 14; Veith, *Black April*, 354; Snepp, *Decent Interval*, 260.

32. For the role of USNS *Sgt. Miller* in Operation Passage to Freedom, see chapter 5, above.

33. For references to the role of USNS *Sgt. Andrew Miller* in 1975 evacuation operations, see *Sealift*, June 1975, 4, 7, 9–10, 12, 15–17, 20.

34. *Seafarers Log*, April 1975, 5.

35. *Sealift*, June 1975, 12, 24.

36. Charles Welch's letter was published in the May 1975 issue of *American Maritime Officer* (D2, MEBA), 1, 5; see Snepp, *Decent Interval*, 259.

37. *Sealift*, June 1975, 20.

38. *Sealift*, June 1975, 17.

39. Louis R. Granger, "How to Give a Cook an Ulcer," *Sealift*, December 1975, 4–6.

40. *Sealift*, June 1975, 12. Accounts of *Greenville Victory*'s role in evacuation operations also appear in Veith, *Black April*, 354–355, 529, n. 41; Schreadley, *From the Rivers to the Sea*, 384.

41. For reference to ARVN firing upon civilians aboard, or as they attempted to go aboard ships, see, for example, Dawson, *55 Days*, 186; "Troops Kill 25 on Rescue Ship," *Newsday*, April 1, 1975; "Death Rides refugee ship," *The Times Union*, April 1, 1975, 1.

42. *The New York Times*, April 10, 1975, 1; *Seafarers Log*, April 1975, 5.

43. Delehant, personal log, April 13, 1975.

44. C.A. Welch, letter to District 2 Chief Dispatcher Gabe Williamson and Headquarters Dispatcher John Lee, as appears in *American Maritime Officer*, May 1975.

45. The departure of Thieu from Saigon on April 25, 1975, was later described in some detail by CIA operative Frank Snepp, who drove the car that took Thieu to Ton Son Nhut for the flight out to Taiwan. See Snepp, *Decent Interval*, 433–437; Young, *The Vietnam Wars*, 297.

46. Before flights out of Tan Son Nhut by fixed-wing aircraft were stopped due to artillery and rocket attacks against the airport, some 50,493 civilians, including 2,678 orphans, were evacuated out between the early part of March and April 28, 1975. From that point on evacuations out of Saigon would be limited to those done by helicopters, ships, and an assortment of smaller watercraft.

47. The Interagency Task Force (IATF) for Indochina created by President Ford on April 16 was tasked to transport, process, receive, and resettle Vietnamese refugees. It would involve 12 agencies—including the Military Sealift Command—and ultimately be responsible for evacuating some 130,000 Vietnamese refugees by air and sea, 111,919 of which would be housed temporarily on Guam.

48. In April 1975 an estimated 130,000 Vietnamese were evacuated out of South Vietnam by sea and air, and from that number a reported 111,919 were transported, largely by ship, to Guam as part of Operation New Life. www. globalsecurity.org/military/ops/new_life.htm.

49. *Sealift*, June 1975, 8.

50. According to one MSC summary account, the *Green Wave* was ordered to Newport on April 25. See *Sealift*, June 1975, 8. Welch's reference to *Green Wave*'s arrival in Saigon/ Newport is in *American Maritime Officer*, May 1975, 5.

51. *Sealift*, June 1975, 8.

52. *Sealift*, June 1975.

53. Snepp, *Decent Interval*, 447.

54. Snepp, *Decent Interval*, 452.

55. *Pioneer Contractor*, a C4-S-57a hull type, was laid down as *American Contractor* at the Bethlehem Steel Fore River Shipyard, Quincy, Massachusetts in 1962 and delivered to U.S. Lines on July 24, 1963. The ship's name was changed to *Pioneer Contractor* on November 25, 1966. It would remain in service or reserve fleet status until sold for scrapping in Brownsville, Texas in January 2009.

56. Eugene Kauder, "Last Voyage to Vung Tau: A Vietnam Finale," *Radio Officers News*, June 1975, 1, 7.

57. Kauder, "Last Voyage to Vung Tau," 1.

58. Kauder, "Last Voyage to Vung Tau."

59. For details pertaining to the start of Frequent Wind from the perspective of CIA operatives on the ground in Saigon, see Snepp, *Decent Interval*, 508–509, 514–515, 520–521. For a brief overview of Frequent Wind from the perspective of the Military Sealift Command publicists, see *Sealift*, June 1975, 7–9.

60. Larry Thompson, *Refugee Workers in the Indochinese Exodus, 1975–1982* (Jefferson, NC: McFarland & Co., 2010); Daniel L. Haulman, "Vietnam Evacuation: Operation Frequent Wind," www.media.defense.gov.

61. Haulman, "Vietnam Evacuation: Operation Frequent Wind."

62. Regarding the initial proposal to use

barges for evacuations out of Saigon, see Snepp, *Decent Interval*, 452, 504.

63. Snepp, *Decent Interval*, 493.

64. For references to the tug *Chitose Maru*, including its earlier use during the Cam Ranh evacuations when it transported refugees out to *Greenville Victory*, see Veith, *Black April*, 355; *Sealift*, June 1975, 8.

65. The LST *Boo Heung Pioneer*, a Korean vessel under contract to MSC, was one of the last to leave Saigon with evacuees, on April 29. According to subsequent MSC summaries of this operation, *Boo Hung Pioneer* was responsible for transporting some 7,200 evacuees to ships waiting offshore. See *Sealift*, June 1975, 8, 24; Veith, *Black April*, 529, n41.

66. Snepp, *Decent Interval*, 524.

67. Snepp, *Decent Interval*, 530–531.

68. The provincial capital of Can Tho had been looked upon by some as a possible "final bastion" for the government of South Vietnam if Saigon were to be captured by PAVN forces; General Giap had suggested in Hanoi this might be so, and argued for planning to counter such a move. For additional discussion regarding this possibility within North Vietnam's senior military and political leadership see Veith, *Black April*, 474, 482. For one recollection of the Can Tho evacuation, see Santoli, *To Bear Any Burden*, 13.

69. Santoli, *To Bear Any Burden*, 15.

70. Santoli, *To Bear Any Burden*, 15–17.

71. Santoli, *To Bear Any Burden*.

72. The final advance of a PAVN tank column into Saigon early on the morning of April 30, via the Newport Bridge and ultimately to the presidential palace, is described in detail in Veith, *Black April*, 492–493.

73. *Sealift*, June 1975, 8–9.

74. *Sealift*, June 1975, 9, 12.

75. The total figure for Vietnamese, American, and third-country nationals lifted out by helicopter during Operation Frequent Wind is generally put at or just under 7,000. A breakdown of this figure is the following: 5,595 Vietnamese (and third-country nationals), 1,373 Americans. Most of the Vietnamese evacuees were subsequently transported by ships crewed by American merchant seamen to a temporary refugee center on Guam (some 8,000 were flown to Wake Island). See Bob Drury and Tom Clavin, *Last Men Out: The True Story of America's Heroic Final Hours in Vietnam* (New York: Simon and Schuster, 2011), 258; George R. Dunham, *U.S. Marines in Vietnam: The Bitter End, 1973–1975* (History and Museums Division Headquarters, U.S. Marine Corps, 1990), 221; Bruce R. Hoon, "A Wake Island Story," http://c141heaven.info/dotcom/tall_tales/a_wake_island_story.php.

76. Most Vietnamese evacuees—nearly 112,00 of an estimated total of 130,00, were evacuated out of South Vietnam between March and early May 1975—and would be transported to the temporary refugee camp developed for that purpose on Guam. Wanting to complete processing and temporary housing operations there before the anticipated arrival of the end-of-year monsoons, most of these refugees would be moved to the United States for permanent settlement by September. The program was officially ended on November 1, 1975. Wake Island would also handle more than 8,000 Vietnamese refugees—most brought in by C-141 aircraft—before they too were shifted largely to the United States. See Bruce R. Hoon, "A Wake Island Story," http://c141heaven.info/dotcom/tall_tales/a_wake_island_story.php.

77. For more on Operation New Life, see for example, Richard A. Mackie, *Operation Newlife: The Untold Story* (1998), and Larry Clinton Thompson, *Refugee Workers in the Indochina Exodus, 1975-1982* (Jefferson, NC: McFarland, 2010).

Chapter 18

1. Flink's grandfather, an Estonian national, was lost in the Baltic Sea in 1890. His father, Constantin Flink, was born in Estonia in 1887, and came to the United States inadvertently in 1916 when his ship, in route to Canada, was damaged in a storm and had to be towed to New York. He remained, became a U.S. citizen, and was later in command of the six-masted, steel-hulled schooner *Star of Scotland* during World War II when it was shelled and sunk by a German submarine between Cape Town and Brazil. Surviving a 20-day ordeal in a lifeboat, Flink resumed his career in the Merchant Marine. He passed away in Southern California at the age of 90, in 1976. See Walter E. Niilus, "Estonians in Southern California" at estonianhistory-SC.pdf. For more on the sinking of *Star of Scotland*, see Captain Arthur R. Moore, *A Careless Word, A Needless Sinking* (Kings Point, NY: American Merchant Marine Museum, 1983), 263.

2. For the sheer numbers involved, SS *Meredith Victory* had established a record during the Korean War in December 1950 when some 14,000 civilians were embarked during evacuations out of Hungnam before the Chinese offensive. That record stood for nearly 25 years until *Pioneer Contender* evacuated 16,600 out of Cam Ranh Bay in 1975. See J.H. Doyle and A.J. Mayer, "December 1950 at Hungnam," USNI *Proceedings*, April 1979, 44–45, Commander. J. Robert Lunney, *Proceedings*, July 1979, 93.

3. Launched as *American Contender* at Bethlehem Steel Company, Quincy, Massachusetts, in 1963, with name changed to *Pioneer Contender* in 1967, the C4-S-57a hull type, 22-knot cargo ship continued in service until 1981 when it entered the James River NDRF. It was sold for scrapping in 1987, and moved to breakers in Kaohsiung, Taiwan the next year.

4. The loss of *Badger State* with 26 members of her crew occurred after encountering a ferocious

storm in the Pacific while in route to Vietnam with a full load of ammunition, including 500- and 1,000-pound bombs. The shifting of cargo due to what was determined to be inadequate use of shoring materials, despite the heroic efforts by the crew, was ultimately believed to have caused the loss of ship and lives. This is described in chapter 13, above.

5. Located some seven miles down-channel from Saigon, and some miles above Nha Be, Cat Lai was developed principally for the receipt and handling of ammunition.

6. The use of defoliants, including one form shipped in steel drums marked with an orange band—known commonly as "Agent Orange"— was introduced in 1966 and subsequently used extensively to clear areas along navigation channels from which attacks were made against shipping.

7. The U.S. Department of State requested through the Defense attaché's office in Saigon on March 24 that assets be made available to assist with evacuations out of Da Nang. The order went out the next day to *Pioneer Contender*, and also *Transcolorado*, to cease cargo operations and proceed directly to Da Nang. *Pioneer Contender* would be the first to arrive, on March 28.

8. Da Nang, the second largest city in South Vietnam, had been considered of such strategic importance—in early war planning as well as for later defensive and even evacuation purposes, should it come to that—that a defensive "enclave" be established around it. However, the decision by President Trieu to withdraw airborne troops from positions south and west of Da Nang in mid-March seriously undermined the enclave strategy in that area, and ultimately contributed to the disorder and lack of security that would characterize evacuations out of Da Nang later in the month. See "Final Report by the Defense Attache, Saigon," in Porter, *Vietnam*, Vol. 2, 661–662; Snepp, *Decent Interval*, 202, 206, 209–210.

9. While Flink repeatedly uses this figure, official reports, contemporaneously published accounts, publications of the Military Sealift Command itself, as well as an account entered into the Congressional Record a few weeks after the evacuations, all put the figure at 16,600.

10. Joseph Delehant letter to author, June 20, 1979.

11. Joseph Delehant letter to author.

12. Made aware of the lack of security on the first ships involved in evacuation operations, President Gerald Ford issued orders on April 1, 1975, for U.S. Marines—groups of between 40 and 60—to be placed on ships as soon as practicable. The first American merchant ship to arrive in Da Nang on March 28, *Pioneer Contender* did have a small group of U.S. Marines, evacuated out of the American consulate with other evacuees, on board for the first run out of Da Nang down to Cam Ranh Bay. A larger detail was placed aboard

some days later. In a page-one article published in *The New York Times* on April 10, Marines are pictured boarding SS *Transcolorado* for the first time the day before.

13. In addition to references to panicked ARVN troops killing civilians to "make room" for themselves on ships involved in evacuation operations, there were contemporaneous reports of summary killings of assembled groups of civilians by ARVN and/or Vietnamese Marines on the decks of evacuation vessels. See, for example, "25 Refugees Reported Killed by Own Troops," *The New York Times*, 1 April 1975. With a byline given as "Aboard Pioneer Contender off South Vietnam, March 31 [1975]" this report refers to the execution of "Viet Cong" suspects on the fantail of SS *Pioneer Commander*.

14. See note 27, chapter 17, above.

15. One of the three ships of the Military Sealift Command's "nucleus" fleet crewed by American merchant seamen, and involved in the Vietnam evacuations at this time, USNS *Sgt. Andrew Miller* was the second ship, after *Pioneer Contender*, to arrive in support of those evacuations out of Da Nang on March 28. While and since U.S. Marines had not yet been detailed to go aboard *Miller* and other ships to provide security during these operations, and no doubt had to deal similarly with ARVN who had come aboard with their weapons, *Miller* does not appear to have been commandeered by disgruntled, and armed, evacuees as would be the case some days later with USNS *Greenville Victory*. See chapter 17, above.

16. Delehant letter to author.

17. These were the Landing Craft Mechanized (LCM), a smaller landing craft which were produced during World War II. Depending on the specific type, they generally measured between 50 and 75 feet in length, had a beam between 14 and 21 feet, and could carry, as with the larger LCM (8), one M48 (Patton) tank, or 200 troops. In addition to landing troops on beachheads, they would become logistical support and lighterage workhorses in shallow draft port areas, serve as liberty (shore leave) launches, and a variety of other functions as would become all too clear during evacuation operations in 1975.

18. These ships are not actually "aircraft carriers" in the traditional sense. USS *Blue Ridge*, the command vessel for the Vietnam evacuation operations, is an Amphibious Command and Control Ship (LCC), and as such was designed for accommodating helicopters but not fixed-wing aircraft. USS *Frederick* was actually an LST (1184), and as such not designed for aircraft operations; USS *Dubuque*, an Amphibious Transport Dock (LPD-8), was designed for support of landing craft and amphibious assault vehicles, and has a flight deck that can accommodate and store helicopters.

19. Operation Frequent Wind lasted only

18 hours, between April 29 and 30, 1975, ending when the last of the helicopters involved in the operation touched down on USS *Midway* with the remaining U.S. Marines assigned to the American Embassy. Thereafter, evacuations continued by sea craft as part of Operation New Home, begun in early April 1975. See Thomas Tobin, USAF Southeast Asia monograph 6: "Last Flight From Saigon" (USGPO, 1978).

20. Saigon was captured by PAVN forces early on April 30, 1975, thus ending Frequent Wind operations.

21. While it is not clear to which floating dry-dock Flink refers, it was no doubt one of 33 Auxiliary Floating Drydocks (ARD) built during World War II. While not built with engines, they were designed with shaped bows and equipped with rudders for easier towing but were not typically given names. The ARD-5, one of the few such floating drydocks operated in Vietnam, might well have been the one Captain Flink observed being towed in 1975. It was not until late the following year, and no longer in Vietnam, that it was actually given a name: USS *Waterford.*

22. Flink is probably referring here to the city of Can Tho, the largest city in the Delta area some 80 miles to the south of Saigon, and from which helicopter and river evacuations took place on April 30. Upon reaching the mouth of the Bassac River and proceeding offshore, one group of evacuees encountered and were taken aboard by *Pioneer Contender.* See Al Santoli, *To Bear Any Burden,* 11–17.

23. Final evacuations out of Vung Tau, actually occurring after the "fall" of Saigon, continued until May 2, 1975.

24. The three U.S. Lines ships in the staging area would have been *Pioneer Contender, Pioneer Commander,* and *American Challenger.* A fourth U.S. Lines ship, *American Racer,* was also involved in final-phase evacuations to a lesser extent, and a fifth U.S. Lines ship, *Pioneer Contractor,* arriving too late from the United States and unable to discharge much cargo prior to the fall of Saigon, was only able to embark about 100 refugees who had made their way out in small boats in the vicinity of Vung Tau. See chapter 17, above.

25. While most—more than 100,000—of the Vietnamese evacuees would be processed and temporarily housed on Guam, some 8,000 were airlifted to Wake Island, with the first planeload arriving on April 26, 1975. For more information, go to www.wakeisland1975.com.

26. *Congressional Record,* April 17, 1975, E 1812.

27. The evacuation of 14,000 refugees at one time out of Hungnam by the merchant ship *Meredith Victory* during the Korean War was unprecedented. It remained so until 1975 when some 16,600 Vietnamese refugees were evacuated out of Cam Ranh Bay by the SS *Pioneer Contender,* Capt. Edward Flink commanding. The author, seeking similar recognition for Pioneer Contender as had been given earlier to *Meredith Victory,* submitted a formal proposal to the U.S. Maritime Administration (MarAd) that *Pioneer Contender* be given the Gallant Ship Award. The proposal was acknowledged by MarAd but never acted upon.

Chapter 19

1. For a good contemporaneous account published while *Mayaguez* was still being held by the Cambodian Khmer Rouge, and containing a full list of its 39 crewmembers, see Peter J. Kumpa, "Cambodia seizes U.S. merchant ship," *The Baltimore Sun,* May 14, 1975.

2. For an excellent account containing comments by the Master of *Mayaguez,* Captain Charles T. Miller, soon after the incident, see Sydney H. Schanberg, "Mayaguez Captain Tells Story of Rescue," *The New York Times,* May 18, 1975, 1, 7. Schanberg, a Pulitzer Prize-winning journalist who would cover Cambodia extensively, would publish an extensive account of the rise of the Khmer Rouge, which in turn would become the basis for the film *The Killing Fields.*

3. Frank Conway interview with author, Piney Point, MD, January 1981.

4. "Mayaguez: After Three Days of Captivity—All Hands Safe," *Seafarers Log,* June 1975, 21.

5. Sydney H. Schanberg, "Mayaguez Captain Tells Story of Rescue," *The New York Times,* May 18, 1975, 7.

6. SS *Mayaguez* was launched as *White Falcon,* a Maritime Commission C2-S-AJ1 type merchant ship at North Carolina Shipbuilding Co., in April 1944. After World War II the ship was renamed *Santa Eliana,* and then SS *Sea,* before beginning service with Sea-Land Service, Inc. as *Mayaguez* in 1965.

7. Major Thomas E. Behuniak, "The Seizure and Recovery of the S.S. Mayaguez: Legal Analysis of United States Claims, Part 1," *Military Law Review,* Department of the Army, Fall 1978.

8. Jordan J. Paust, "More Revelations About Mayaguez (and its Secret Cargo)," *Boston College International and Comparative Law Review,* July 27, 2014.

9. Peter Maguire, "Leave No Man Behind: The Truth About the Mayaguez Incident," *The Diplomat,* June 19, 2018, https://thediplomat.co/2018/06/leave-n0-man-behind-the-truth-about-the-mayaguez-incident.

10. Bill Bellinger, "Seafarer Bellinger Tells It as It Happens," *Seafarers Log,* June 1975, 20.

11. Bill Bellinger, "On board the S.S. Mayaguez," *The Record,* June 9, 1975, 2.

12. Bellinger, "Seafarer Bellinger Tells It as It Happens," 20.

13. "Seafarer Bellinger Tells It as It Happens."

14. "Seafarer Bellinger Tells It as It Happens."

15. "Crew of Mayaguez Is Alive and Well," *Seafarers Log,* May 1975, 3.

16. Schanberg, "Mayaguez Captain Tells Story of Rescue," 1.

17. Bellinger, "Seafarer Bellinger Tells It as It Happens," 20.

18. "Seafarer Bellinger Tells It as It Happens."

19. Schanberg, "Mayaguez Captain Tells Story of Rescue," 1.

20. "MM&P Mates Accompany Marines On Mayaguez Rescue," *The Master, Mate & Pilot*, July 1975, 9.

21. *Sealift Magazine*, June 1975, 24.

22. "MM&P Mates Accompany Marines On Mayaguez Rescue."

23. Three Marines—Joseph Hargrove, Gary Hall, and Danny Marshall—who were accidentally left behind during the pullout from action on Koh Tang Island, and could not be recovered, were subsequently captured and executed by the Khmer Rouge. Their names were the last to be added in chronological order (far right) to the Vietnam Veterans Memorial in Washington, D.C., a fact that underscores the validity of referring to the *Mayaguez* Incident and action on Koh Tang Island collectively as the "last battle of the Vietnam War."

24. Schanberg, "Mayaguez Captain Tells Story of Rescue," 7.

25. "Mayaguez Captain Tells Story of Rescue."

26. Bellinger, "Seafarer Bellinger Tells It as It Happens."

27. "Seafarer Bellinger Tells It as It Happens."

28. Maguire, "Leave No Man Behind: The Truth About the Mayaguez Incident."

29. "Mayaguez: After Three Days of Captivity—All Hands Safe," *Seafarers Log*, June 1975, 21.

30. Bellinger, "Seafarer Bellinger Tells It as It Happens."

31. Schanberg, "Mayaguez Captain Tells Story of Rescue," 7.

32. Maguire, "Leave No Man Behind: The Truth About the Mayaguez Incident."

33. "Leave No Man Behind: The Truth About the Mayaguez Incident."

34. Peter Maguire has argued that Secretary of State Henry Kissinger "goaded" President Ford into believing the seizure of *Mayaguez* "provided an opportunity for the United States 'to prove that others will be worse off if they tackle us, and not that they can return to the status quo. It is not enough to get the ship's release.' One Pentagon official told *Newsweek* at the time, 'Henry Kissinger was determined to give the Khmer Rouge a bloody nose.'" See "Leave No Man Behind: The Truth About the Mayaguez Incident," *The Diplomat*, June 19, 2018.

35. Young, *The Vietnam Wars*, 301; 361, n. 1.

36. Maguire, "Leave No Man Behind."

37. "Leave No Man Behind."

38. Schanberg, "Mayaguez Captain Tells Story of Rescue," 7.

39. "Mayaguez Captain Tells Story of Rescue," 1.

40. "Mayaguez Captain Tells Story of Rescue," 7.

41. "Mayaguez Captain Tells Story of Rescue."

42. Kate Webb, "SS Mayaguez: Forgotten Ship Sails the Same Old Route," UPI, May 2, 1976.

43. Mayaguez, Captured by Cambodians, to Be Scrapped," *Seafarers Log*, May 1979, 38.

Chapter 20

1. Published initially in French in 2009, *Ru*—a word that means "lullaby" in Vietnamese, and also "a stream" in French—was subsequently published in English in 2012. Highly acclaimed, the novel is based largely on the experiences of its author, Kim Thuy, who became a "boat person" at the age of 10 in 1978, as part of the second "wave" of boat people to leave Vietnam. After a period of months in a Malaysian refugee camp, she and her family eventually settled in Grandy, East Quebec, Canada. Kim Thuy would go on to earn degrees in linguistics and translation, and a law degree. Since the publication of *Ru* she has published other books.

2. "217 Boat People Owe Lives to Sharp Eyes of Ch. Steward," *Seafarers Log*, February 1980, 4; *The Master, Mate & Pilot*, October 1979, 7. Launched at Todd Shipyard, San Francisco, California in 1974, the diesel-powered transport oiler T-AOT-1690 remained in service as an MSC nucleus fleet oiler until transferred in 1995 to Greek owners, operated under the Panamanian flag. The ship was scrapped in 2000.

3. *Seafarers Log*, February 1980, 4.

4. *Seafarers Log*.

5. While the type and dimensions of boats used by Vietnamese refugees was not always recorded by those coming upon them at sea, one major study of Vietnamese boat people for the period between 1975 and 1981 described them as "wooden coastal and river fishing craft, or other workhorses. Most were between 40 and 80 feet in length and had seen better days." This estimate for boat length can however be easily scaled down, since boats in the mid-30-foot range were not uncommon. As an example, one group of 62 Vietnamese refugees rescued by LNG *Virgo* in 1980 was in a boat estimated at 35 feet long. In another case 60 boat people were rescued, from a boat also estimated to be 35 feet long, by the crew of USNS *Sealift Antarctic* in April 1980. And to cite another example, it was reported that some 133 boat people were aboard a vessel estimated at 35 feet in length when they were rescued by the crew of SS *James Lykes* in the South China Sea on November 1, 1980. See "United Nations official cites rescue by SS *James Lykes* of 'boat people,'" *The NMU Pilot*, December 1980, 7. For a description of boats typically used by Vietnamese refugees, including some of the minimal modifications made to accommodate numbers of people well beyond the original design complements,

and to provide increased freeboard in some cases of fishing and other work boats, see Barry Wain, *The Refused: The Agony of the Indochina Refugees* (New York: Simon and Schuster, 1981), 88–89; See *The NMU Pilot*, June 1980, 13.

6. *Seafarers Log*, February 1980, 4.

7. Wain, *The Refused*, 81–83.

8. The greatest number of arrivals of Vietnamese refugees in the United States following the end of the Vietnam War—nearly half of which had been transported by ships crewed by American merchant seamen at some point—would occur in 1975, followed by a sharp decline in each of the next two years. The numbers began to rise again in 1978, reflecting the start of a second "wave" of departures by sea, which peaked again in 1980 as Vietnamese refugee arrivals in the U.S. approached 100,000. By 1983, though still well above the numbers recorded for 1976 and 1977, the totals had dropped again to just over 20,000. The next peak would occur in the mid-1990s, coinciding roughly with formal "normalization" of relations between Vietnam and the U.S. (1994), with numbers of arrivals from Vietnam nearing 40,000. That number would decline markedly again by the end of the decade—as the end of the Vietnam War was now more than 20 years in the past and another generation had begun to return or to visit the traditional homeland for the first time. The number of Vietnamese refugee arrivals would continue to decrease until, by the beginning of the second decade of the new millennium, they would scarcely register on charts reflecting such arrivals. See Linda W. Gordon, "Southeast Asian Refugee Migration to the United States," *Center for Migration Studies special issues* 5 (3): 153–173.

9. Young, *The Vietnam Wars*, 306. See also Charles Benoit, "Vietnam's 'Boat People,'" in David W.P. Elliot, ed., *Third Indochina Conflict* (1981), 139–162.

10. Wain, *The Refused*, 66.

11. For context and analysis of the Vietnamese incursion into Cambodia in 1978, and its role in ending the "killing fields" perpetrated by the Khmer Rouge against the Cambodian people, see for example Ben Kiernan, *How Pol Pot Came to Power: Colonialism, Nationalism, and Communism in Cambodia, 1930–1975* (New Haven, CT: Yale University Press, 1985); see also Young, *The Vietnam Wars*, 308–311.

12. "God Heard Our Plea, the Big Ship Came Closer," *The Master, Mate & Pilot*, February 1980, 4.

13. "God Heard Our Plea, the Big Ship Came Closer."

14. "God Heard Our Plea, the Big Ship Came Closer."

15. "NMU crew's heroic rescue saves 60 Vietnamese refugees," *The NMU Pilot*, June 1980, 13.

16. See Young, *The Vietnam Wars*, 306.

17. Young, *The Vietnam Wars*; Wain, *The Refused*.

18. Wain, *The Refused*, 142.

19. After initial large-scale evacuations of Vietnamese at the end of the Vietnam War, resulting in Vietnamese refugee arrivals in the United States in 1975 that surpassed 120,000, there was a sharp drop-off of such arrivals in 1976 and 1977 due to U.S. Government policy that denied entry except in cases of family reunification. The next major "wave" began in late 1978 due to "continuing political and ethnic conflicts within Southeast Asia," which included the Sino-Vietnamese border war and resultant heavy backlash against Vietnamese with Chinese ancestry (known as "Hoa"). Many of that demographic group became "boat people," which in turn resulted in Vietnamese refugee annual arrivals once again approaching 100,000 in the late 1970s and early 1980s. Thereafter Vietnamese refugee arrivals in the United States, including large numbers of "boat people," generally numbered between 20,000 and 30,000 in the mid-to late 1980s and early 1990s, with a spike again in 1994 that approached 40,000. The numbers dropped well below 20,000 per year in the late 1990s. And then, with normalization of relations between Vietnam and the United States (1994), and many formerly young "boat people" having moved into adulthood and raising families of their own, many Vietnamese began to return to Vietnam for visits, and to introduce the next generation to their ancestral homeland. Consequently, the arrival of Vietnamese refugees continued to fall to the point where, by the first decade of the new millennium, their numbers were relatively minuscule.

20. The second "wave" of Vietnamese boat people, comprised largely of ethnic Chinese (Hoa), is generally considered to have begun in late 1978. For discussion of the ethnic composition of this wave, see Wain, *The Refused*, 66–67; 77–81, 89; Young, *The Vietnam Wars*, 306.

21. For studies that have looked at Vietnamese refugee migration to the United States in what is described as four basic "waves" in the two decades following the end of the Vietnam War, see for example, Lan Cao and Himilce Novas, *Everything You Need to know about Asian American History* (New York: Plume, revised edition 2004); Linda Trinh Vo, "The Vietnamese American Experience From Dispersion to the Development of Post-Refugee Communities" in *Asian American Studies: A Reader*, Jean Yu-Wen, Shen Wu, and Min Song, eds. (Brunswick, NJ: Rutgers University Press, 2000), 290–305.

22. Regarding pirate attacks on Vietnamese boat people, see Wain, 42–43, 69–73, 202, 204, 228.

23. "Helping hands on the high seas," *The Master, Mate & Pilot*, December 1980, 8–9.

24. "Helping hands on the high seas," 8.

25. "Helping hands on the high seas."

26. "Helping hands on the high seas."

27. One of a series of new ships designed for transporting liquefied natural gas (LNG), LNG

Aires was built by General Dynamics, Quincy, MA and launched into service in 1977, just in time for engaging in a series of rescues of Vietnamese "boat people" along its regular shipping route through the South China Sea. Years later it would be sold foreign, operating under the flag of the Marshall Islands.

28. "What a Crew: Save Boat People, Deliver Baby," *Seafarers Log*, November 1980; David Hecht, prepared statement (unpublished) on behalf of crew, LNG *Aires*, September 1980.

29. Hecht, prepared statement.

30. *Seafarers Log*, November 1980.

31. *Seafarers Log*, July 1982.

32. *Seafarers Log*.

33. *Seafarers Log*, July 1982.

34. *Seafarers Log*, September 1989, 5.

35. Corey Kilgannon, "Decades Later, a Family of 'Boat People' Find Their Rescuers," *The New York Times*, November 7, 2017, www.nytimes. com (New York/Region); print version: "Vietnamese Refugees Find Their Rescuers," *The New York Times*, November 8, 2017, A20.

36. "Vietnamese Refugees Find Their Rescuers."

37. "Vietnamese Refugees Find Their Rescuers."

38. "Vietnamese Refugees Find Their Rescuers."

39. "Vietnamese Refugees Find Their Rescuers."

40. "Vietnamese Refugees Find Their Rescuers."

41. "Vietnamese Refugees Find Their Rescuers.

42. While estimates of the number of "boat people" departing Vietnam between 1975 and 1995 (800,000) and those believed to have been lost at sea in the process (200,000–400,000) would eventually become available, the number of those rescued by merchant and naval ships are more elusive. However, some figures of boat people actually rescued by American ships are available, as are estimates of others rescued by American ships. See note 47, below. The author had previously compiled a list of "boat people" rescues by ships crewed by American merchant seamen—ships owned and operated by private shipping companies, and government-owned ships of the Military Sealift Command's "nucleus" fleet—based on accounts published largely by maritime labor organizations representing seamen involved in those rescue operations. That list, which accounts for the rescues of nearly 2,000 Vietnamese boat people, does not claim to be complete for the period covered. While it does account for nearly 900 refugees rescued by the ships operated by one company alone—the LNG ships of Energy Transportation Corp (ETC)—a statement made by ETC some years later would claim to have been involved in the rescue of more than 2,000 boat people. All told, while accurate numbers are elusive, such rescues by privately owned and MSC-operated ships would no doubt approach a figure in the neighborhood of perhaps 5,000. This does not include, of course, additional perhaps thousands of Vietnamese rescued at sea by ships of the U.S. Navy crewed by naval personnel.

43. Launched in 1965 at Ingalls Shipbuilding, Pascagoula, MS, as a C6-s-60a-type break-bulk cargo ship, *Beaver State* was lengthened by Todd Shipyards, Galveston, TX in 1976 and converted to a partial containership. It was in that configuration that the ship would have been involved in this rescue of Vietnamese boat people. Years later, *Beaver State* was converted again to a C6-s-MA606-type crane ship, and was eventually placed in the Military Sealift Command's Ready Reserve.

44. *Seafarers Log*, June 1982, 16.

45. Bruce Sherman, "Tell them about my shipmates," *Seattle Post-Intelligencer*, June 8, 1981, B10.

46. From electrostatic copy of SS *Andrew Jackson* log entries hand-copied by Howard Bethell. Some of these entries also appear in the Sherman article cited above.

47. *Seattle Post-Intelligencer*, June 8, 1981, B10.

48. Howard Bethell's extensive recollections of his World War II service, including the torpedoing and loss of two of his ships, are recounted in my book *Merchant Marine Survivors of World War II: Oral Histories of Cargo Carrying Under Fire* (Jefferson, NC: McFarland & Co., 2015).

49. For an article about the ordeal of the Vuong family as "boat people," a reunion of members of the family in 2017 with some former crew members of LNG *Virgo*, and comments made by Joseph Cuneo, the former president of ETC regarding the choice between incurring additional voyage expenses and diverting ships to rescue boat people, see Corey Kilgannon, "Vietnamese Refugees Find Their Rescuers," *The New York Times*, November 8, 2017, A20.

50. "Vietnamese Refugees Find Their Rescuers."

51. "Vietnamese Refugees Find Their Rescuers."

52. "Vietnamese Refugees Find Their Rescuers." The first of two reunions with former crew members of LNG *Virgo* would take place in March 2016 at the home of Captain George Overstreet in Lakeland, Florida.

53. "Vietnamese Refugees Find Their Rescuers."

54. "Vietnamese Refugees Find Their Rescuers."

55. Jie Zong and Jeanne Batalova, Migration Information Source, June 8, 2016. See www. migrationpolicy.org/article/vietnamese-immigrants-united-states.

Chapter 21

1. AP, "U.S. Warship Docks In Saigon Port," November 19, 2000, www.cbsnews.com/news/us-warship-docks-in-saigon-port.

2. "U.S. Warship Docks In Saigon Port."

3. "U.S. Warship Docks In Saigon Port."

4. Linda D. Kozaryn, "Cohen to Visit Vietnam, Asian Allies," American Forces Press Service, March 8, 2000, archive.defense.gov/news/

newsarticle; "It's Time for U.S.-Vietnam Military Ties, Cohen says," DOD News, March 13, 2000, archive.defense.gov/news/newsarticle; Robert Burns, "Cohen Remains Hopeful on Building Vietnamese Ties," AP, March 14, 2000, https://greensboro.com/cohen-remains-hopeful-on-building-vietnamese-ties-during-a-visit-from-u-s-defense-secretary/article_068cf004-b1ed-5744-963c-617c07d10569.html.

5. The possibility of military-to-military cooperation between Vietnam and the United States—something unthinkable for decades following the end of the war—was at least broached in discussions during Secretary of Defense William Cohen's visit to Vietnam in 2000. It would not be long before such cooperation would begin to take place, but in the decades-long initial phase of such cooperation this would be restricted to "non-lethal" forms, such as search and rescue operations, communications, and meteorological and medical applications. With heightened tensions relating to territorial and resource claims, and China's active land reclamation and facilities construction in disputed areas of the South China Sea, the sale and transfer of military hardware with potentially lethal application—offshore patrol craft and coast guard cutters, for example—began to enter into military-to-military discussions and agreement between Vietnam and the United States.

6. For a good source providing historical context and analysis relating to China's active extension of sea power into the South China Sea and other areas within the so-called "first island chain" through the first decade of the twenty-first century, see Toshi Yoshuhara and James R. Holmes, *Red Star Over The Pacific: China's Rise and the Challenge to U.S. Maritime Strategy* (Annapolis, MD: Naval Institute Press, 2010).

7. Robert D. Kaplan, *Asia's Cauldron: The South China Sea and the End of a Stable Pacific* (New York: Random House, 2014), 82. See also, The Honorable Kevin Rudd, "Can China and the United States Avoid War?" U.S. Naval Institute *Proceedings*, December 2018, 20–27.

8. Yoshihara and Holmes, *Red Star Over The Pacific*.

9. Kathleen T. Rhem, American Forces Press Service, "Rumsfeld in Vietnam to Meet With Leaders, See MIA-Recovery Efforts," DOD News, June 4, 2006, archive.defense.gov/news/newsarticle.

10. China Institute of International Studies, "U.S.-Vietnam Security Cooperation: Development and Prospects," May 11, 2015; www.ciis.org.cn; Defense Security Cooperation Agency, International Military Education and Training (IMET), www.dsca.mil.

11. "U.S. and Vietnam Begin Naval Engagement Activities," *The Maritime Executive*, April 6, 2015.

12. Margie Mason, "U.S. Navy Ship Visits Port in former Saigon," AP, March 30, 2005, retrieved in *Rutland Herald*, August 29, 2020, www.rutlandherald.com.

13. "U.S. Navy Ship Visits Port in Former Saigon."

14. "U.S. Navy Ship Visits Port in Former Saigon."

15. "U.S. Navy Ship Visits Port in Former Saigon."

16. Matthew R. White, "Lassen Visits Vietnam in Storybook Return of Its Commander," public.navy.mil/surfor/ddg82/pages/lassenvisitsvietnam.aspx.

17. "Lassen Visits Vietnam in Storybook Return."

18. "Lassen Visits Vietnam in Storybook Return."

19. Adam R. Cole, USN, "U.S. Navy Ships Arrive in Vietnam for Port Visit," DOD News.

20. "U.S. Navy Ships Arrive in Vietnam for Port Visit."

21. "U.S. Navy Ships Arrive in Vietnam for Port Visit."

22. Regarding early discussions between the United States and Vietnam, and evolving geo-political context which gave rise to this, see note 5, above.

23. Regarding the five-year period of negotiations that resulted in the signing of a bilateral trade agreement between Vietnam and the United States in 2000, and specifics contained in the agreement, see, for example, Eleanor Albert, "The Evolution of U.S.-Vietnam Ties," Council on Foreign Relations. www.cfr.org/backgrounder/evolution-us-vietnam-ties.

24. U.S. Census Bureau. "Trade in Goods with Vietnam," www.census.gov/foreign-trade/balance/c5520.html.

25. See Michael F. Martin, "U.S.-Vietnam Economic and Trade Relations: Issues for the 111th Congress," www.fas.org/sgp/crs/row/R40755.pdf.

26. For background on Cooperation Afloat Readiness and Training (CARAT) exercises with Vietnam, see, for example, Prashanth Parameswaran, "U.S., Vietnam Kick Off First Naval Engagement Activity in Trump Era," *The Diplomat*, July 6, 2017, https://thediplomat.com/2017/07/us-vietnam-kick-off-first-naval-engagement-activity-in-trump-era.

27. Edward Baxter, "MSC Returns to Vietnam: Heezen Makes History in Vietnam," MSC.navy.mil.

28. "MSC Returns to Vietnam: Heezen Makes History in Vietnam."

29. How warships and other ships engaged in normal civilian commercial activities were regarded in the agreement on Ending the War in Vietnam, see for example, Agreement on Ending the War, Chapter 2, Articles 5 and 6; Protocol to the Cease-Fire Agreement, Article 2 (b); Article 3 a (1); George Aldrich, DOD legal briefing paper, 1973; in Porter, *Vietnam*, II, 602.

30. It is not clear when merchant ships began making their way once again in commercial service between Vietnam and the United States. One indicator, however, of ocean-borne commerce between the two countries is reflected in figures for "trade in goods" provided by the U.S. Census Bureau for the 10-year period between 1992 and 2011. There were no import figures reported for 1992 and 1993, attributable to the U.S. trade embargo on Vietnam, which would not be lifted until 1994. And export figures for those years were minuscule. With the lifting of the embargo, however, and restoration of diplomatic relations between the two countries soon after, things began to change. And by 2002, two years after the signing of a bilateral trade agreement between Vietnam and the U.S. (after five years of negotiations) the figure for exports had more than doubled again while imports of Vietnamese goods increased more than 10-fold. While it's understood that an undetermined percentage of goods moving between the two countries would have been transported in ships of other nations, it can be assumed that also moving between the U.S. and Vietnam would have been an increasing number of American-flag ships. However, the number of ships engaged in this commerce remains elusive. See U.S. Census Bureau, "Trade in Goods with Vietnam" www.census.gov/foreign-trade/balance/c5520.html.

31. "USNS Bruce C. Heezen to conduct search operations off the coast of Vietnam," U.S. Embassy Hanoi News Service, www.msc.navy.mil.

32. "USNS Bruce C. Heezen to conduct search operations."

33. "USNS Bruce C. Heezen to conduct search operations."

34. "USNS Bruce C. Heezen to conduct search operations."

35. msc.navy.com ; maritime-executive.com.

36. "USNS Bowditch Completes Joint U.S.-Vietnam Oceanographic Survey Mission," Maritime Executive, June 22, 2011.

37. "USNS Bowditch Completes Joint U.S.-Vietnam Oceanographic Survey Mission."

38. Erik Stavin, "POW/MIA team finds potential underwater crash sites off Vietnam's coast," Stars and Stripes, June 21, 2011. For one example of the process by which the underwater search for MIA remains proceeded over a period of years from initial search phase, to identification of aircraft, recovery of remains, identification of remains, eventual notifications of families involved, and public announcement of a successful search for the MIA are made, see "Naval Aviator Accounted For From Vietnam," Defense POW/MIA Accounting Agency, Release No: 18–120, August 28, 2018, dpaa.mil.

39. "USNS Safeguard Completes First U.S. Navy Voyage Repairs in Vietnam," September 19, 2009, www.defense-aerospace.com.

40. Regarding another subsequent visit by Safeguard to Vietnam, see, for example, "Safeguard hosts diving exchanges with Vietnam," Military Sealift Command, September 2011, www.navy.mil.

41. For further historical context relating to the arrival of USS Safeguard in Vietnam, see, for example, Yoshihara and Holmes, Red Star Over The Pacific: China's Rise and the Challenge to U.S. Maritime Strategy (2010), and Kaplan, Asia's Cauldron: The South China Sea and the End of a Stable Pacific (New York: Random House, 2014).

42. U.S. Department of State, 2009–2017, "Air Transport Agreements Between the U.S. and Vietnam," state.gov.

43. U.S. Department of Transportation, Maritime Administration, International Agreements, U.S.-Vietnamese Maritime Bilateral Agreement, March 15, 2007, www.maritime.dot.gov.

44. "USNS Safeguard Completes First U.S. Navy Voyage Repairs in Vietnam," September 19, 2009, www.defense-aerospace.com.

45. USNS Richard E. Byrd (T-AKE-4) has a length overall of 689 feet (654' waterline) and a service speed of 20 knots. For summary construction history and descriptive characteristics for USNS Richard E. Byrd, see www.marinetraffic.com.

46. Regarding USNS Richard E. Byrd, see also: https://military-history.fandom.com/wiki/USNS Richard E. Byrd (T-AKE-4); https://www.globalsecurity.org/military/library/news/2008/07/mil-080725-nns03.htm

47. "USNS Richard E. Byrd Completes First U.S. Navy Ship Visit to Vietnam Port in 38 years," www.offshore-energy.biz; Marine Link, "MSC Ship: First USN Ship Visit to Vietnam Port in 38 Years," www.marinelink.com/news/vietnam-first-visit340094. See also Carl Thayer, "Will Vietnam Lease Cam Ranh Bay to the United States?" The Diplomat, May 6, 2020, www.thediplomat.com/2020/05/will-vietnam-lease-cam-ranh-bay-to-the-united-states.

48. "USNS Richard E. Byrd Completes First U.S. Navy Ship Visit to Vietnam Port."

49. "USNS Richard E. Byrd Completes First U.S. Navy Ship Visit to Vietnam Port."

50. "USNS Richard E. Byrd Completes First U.S. Navy Ship Visit to Vietnam Port."

51. Patrick Goodenough, CNSNews, "Panetta, in Historic Vietnam Visit, Sees 'Tremendous Potential Here' for U.S. Naval Forces," csnsnews.com/news/article/panetta-historic-vietnam-visit-sees-tremendous-potential.

52. "Panetta, in Historic Vietnam Visit."

53. "Panetta, in Historic Vietnam Visit."

54. "Panetta, in Historic Vietnam Visit."

55. "Panetta, in Historic Vietnam Visit."

Epilogue

1. There were seven members of the 1993 PHAM mission group. This included me and four

others who had served in Vietnam during the war in one capacity or another, and for varying lengths of time. Two others, a counselor with the Veterans Administration and the PHAM chapter coordinator for New York, were traveling to Vietnam for the first time.

2. The Rung Sat Special Zone (RSSZ), so designated in the early 1960s, comprised a brain-shaped area of dense mangrove and jungle extending most of the length of the distance from Vung Tau at the coast to Saigon. The deep-draft shipping channel to Saigon ran through the heart of it.

3. Between 1991 and 1998 there were eight PHAM medical supply missions, including those in 1993 and 1998 in which the author participated, sent to Vietnam. See PHAM "Fact Sheet" from 1998.

4. Due to travel requirements PHAM missions to Vietnam were restricted to two large cartons of medical supplies per person in each mission group. Thus, in 1993 our group of seven travelled with a total of 14 cartons. The 1998 mission group of four travelled with only eight cartons. However, for that group an additional 10 cartons were sent ahead to Hanoi via FedEx; those cartons were retrieved soon after our arrival, allowing for typical distribution of supplies to a wide assortment of hospitals, clinics, and other facilities in-country during our 10-day visit.

5. The agreement by the United States to "contribute to healing the wounds of war" by assisting North Vietnam with postwar reconstruction assistance appears in the Paris Peace Accords "Ending the War and Restoring Peace in Vietnam" of January 27, 1973. See Gettleman, et al., *Vietnam and America*, 479. This pledge to assist North Vietnam with reconstruction aid was repeated in a letter from President Nixon to Pham Van Dong dated February 1, 1973. See Porter, *Vietnam*, Vol. 2: 599–600.

6. Young, *The Vietnam Wars*, 311.

7. After graduating from Oberlin College in Ohio Lady Borton was sent to Quang Nhai, South Vietnam in 1968 to work in the Quaker Service Rehabilitation Center there, thus beginning a long and remarkable relationship with Vietnam that included long periods of service there following the war. She returned in 1985 to work with Quaker Service—Vietnam in Hanoi, would serve as its interim director there from 1990 to 1991, and from 1993 as field director. In addition to her work with Quaker Service in Vietnam she is a teacher and writer. Notable among her published book-length works are *Sensing the Enemy: An American Woman Among the Boat People of Vietnam* (1984) and *After Sorrow: An American Among the Vietnamese* (1995), in which she describes her first 25 years working with and for the Vietnamese.

8. Five years after returning from Vietnam I received a Master's Degree in Asian History from St. John's University in New York. Some years later, in a doctoral program at New York University, I was a teaching assistant for Dr. Marilyn Young in a course she taught there about the Vietnam War. I subsequently taught a course on the Vietnam War at NYU, at Pace University (online), and for several years at Purchase College, SUNY in New York. I also taught Vietnamese history for several years as part of an East Asian History survey course at Pace University. Also reflecting my interest in Vietnam and the Vietnam War, I completed a doctoral dissertation at NYU in 1991 titled "Roots of Opposition: The Critical Response to U.S. Indochina Policy, 1945 to 1954."

9. The Majestic Hotel, located at 1 Dong Khoi Street (Rue Catinat during the French period), described as reflecting French Colonial as well as French Riviera style, was built in 1925 and contained 44 guest rooms in its original configuration. It was expanded in 1965 with the addition of two floors to the original three. The hotel's name was changed after the war to the Mekong Hotel (Khach San Cuu Long), but later restored.

10. This was the *Phong Chau*, a Vietnamese butane tanker. "NSA Fire Crews Quick To Subdue Ship Blaze," *The White Elephant News*, Vol. 3, No. 12, July 11, 1969.

11. Initial construction of the Tam Bao Pagoda dates to 1953.

12. The Indianized Kingdom of Champa dates to the first century, C.E. and lasted until the sixteenth century, until finally supplanted by the Vietnamese. At its height it occupied what is approximately the lower half of the current geographical range of modern-day Vietnam. The largest collection of Cham sculptures, heavily reflecting the Hindu influences of India, are on display in the Museum of Cham Sculpture in Da Nang, created in 1915 and known originally as the Musee Henri Parmentier.

13. The four-member 1998 PHAM mission group arrived in Hanoi on July 29, 1998, and departed from Hanoi again on August 6. Unlike most other mission groups, which checked all supply cartons on board aircraft in which they traveled, the 1998 group had its 19 cartons sent ahead for pickup in Hanoi by Federal Express.

14. The Hanoi Opera House was begun by the French Government in 1901 and completed in 1911. It is a quintessential example of neoclassical French architecture.

15. "The Truong Son Martyrs" Cemetery in Quang Tri Province contains the remains of some 10,000 Viet Minh, North Vietnamese, and NLF soldiers, as well as civilians who worked to construct and repair the "Ho Chi Minh Trail" logistical supply route. More than 90 percent of those interred there have not been identified.

Bibliography

Bodard, Lucien. *The Quicksand War*. New York: Little Brown & Co., 1967.

Bowles, Chester. *The New Dimensions of Peace*. New York: Harper & Bros., 1955.

Brown, Malcolm W. *The New Face of War*. New York: Bobbs-Merrill Co., Inc., 1965.

Buttinger, Joseph. *Vietnam: A Dragon Embattled*, 2 Vols. New York: Frederick A. Praeger, 1967.

Cogger, Captain Paul J. *Finished with Engine*. New York: Vantage Press, 1972.

Committee of Concerned Asian Scholars. *The Indochina Story: A Fully Documented Account*. New York: Bantam Books, 1970.

Cooper, Chester L. *The Lost Crusade: America in Vietnam*. Greenwich, CT: Fawcett Publications, 1972.

de Gaulle, Charles. *The War Memoirs of Charles de Gaulle: Salvation, 1944–1946*. Translated by Richard Howard. New York: Simon & Schuster, 1960.

Drachman, Edward R. *United States Policy Toward Vietnam, 1940–1945*. Rutherford, NJ: Fairleigh Dickinson University Press, 1970.

Duiker, William J. *Ho Chi Minh: A Life*. New York: Hyperion, 2000.

Fall, Bernard B. *The Two Viet-Nams: A Political and Military Analysis*. London: Pall Mall Press, 1963.

Frankum, Ronald Bruce. *Operation Passage to Freedom: The United States Navy in Vietnam, 1954–1955*. Lubbock: Texas Tech University Press, 2007.

Gettleman, Marvin E., Jane Franklin, Marilyn B. Young, and H. Bruce Franklin, eds. *Vietnam and America: The Most Comprehensive Documented History of the Vietnam War*. New York: Grove Press, 1995.

Hammer, Ellen. *The Struggle for Indochina*. Redwood City, CA: Stanford University Press, 1955.

Hanh, Thich Nhat. *Vietnam: Lotus in a Sea of Fire*. New York: Hill & Wang, 1967.

Hayes, Samuel P. *The Beginning of American Aid to Southeast Asia*. Lexington, MA: Heath Lexington Books, 1971.

Hilsman, Roger. *To Move a Nation*. New York: Doubleday, 1967.

Ho, Si Thanh. *The Commandos of Saigon: Untold Stories*. Hanoi: People's Army Publishing House, 2007.

Hooper, Edwin Bickford, Dean C. Allard, and Oscar P. Fitzgerald. *The United States Navy in the Vietnam Conflict*, Vol. 1, *The Setting of the Stage to 1959*. Washington, DC: Naval Historical Division, Department of the Navy, 1976.

Hooper, Vice Admiral Edwin Bickford. *Mobility, Support, Endurance: A Story of Naval Operational Logistics in the Vietnam War, 1965–1968*. Washington, DC: Naval and Historical Division, Department of the Navy, 1972.

Isaacs, Arnold R. *Without Honor: Defeat in Vietnam and Cambodia*. Baltimore, MD: Johns Hopkins University Press, 1983, 1998.

Kahin, George McT. *Intervention: How America Became Involved in Vietnam*. New York: Alfred A. Knopf, 1986.

Kaplan, Robert D. *Asia's Cauldron: The South China Sea and the End of a Stable Pacific*. New York: Random House, 2014.

Karnow, Stanley. *Vietnam: A History*. New York: Viking, 1983.

Lacouture, Jean. *Vietnam: Between Two Truces*. New York: Vintage, 1966.

Lamb, Helen B. *Vietnam's Will to Live*. London: Monthly Review Press, 1972.

Mansfield, Robert A., and William L. Worden. *Towboats to the Orient: A History of Alaska Barge and Transport in the South China Sea*. Seattle, WA: Pac Editions, 1970.

Marr, David G. *Vietnam 1945: The Quest for Power*. Berkeley: University of California Press, 1995.

Moore, Lieutenant General Harold G., and Joseph L. Galloway. *We Were Soldiers Once... And Young*. New York: Random House, 1992.

Patti, Archimedes L.A. *Why Vietnam? Prelude to America's Albatross*. Berkeley: University of California Press, 1980.

Ploger, Major General Robert B. *U.S. Army Engineers 1965–1970*. Washington, DC: Department of the Army, 1974.

Porter, Gareth. *Vietnam: The Definitive Documentation of Human Decisions*, 2 Vols. Stanfordville, NY: Earl M. Coleman, 1979.

Santoli, Al. *To Bear Any Burden: The Vietnam War and Its Aftermath in the Words of Americans and Southeast Asians*. New York: E.P. Dutton, 1983.

Sawyer, L.A., and W.H. Mitchell. *Victory Ships and*

Tankers: The History of the 'Victory' Type Cargo Ships and of the Tankers Built in the United States of America During World War II. Cambridge, MD: Cornell Maritime Press, Inc., 1974.

Schreadley, R.L. *From the Rivers to the Sea: The United States Navy in Vietnam.* Annapolis, MD: Naval Institute Press, 1992.

Shaplen, Robert. *The Lost Revolution.* New York: Harper & Row, 1965.

Sheehan, Neil, Hedrick Smith, E.W. Kenworthy, and Fox Butterfield. *The Pentagon Papers as Published by the New York Times.* New York: Quadrangle Books, 1971.

Sherwood, John Darrell. *War in the Shallows: U.S. Navy Coastal and Riverine Warfare in Vietnam, 1965–1968.* Washington, DC: Naval History and Heritage Command, 2015.

Simpson, Howard R. *Dien Bien Phu: The Epic Battle America Forgot.* Washington, DC: Brassey's, Inc., 1994.

Snepp, Frank. *Decent Interval.* New York: Random House, 1977.

Terzani, Tiziano. *Giai Phong! The Fall and Liberation of Saigon.* Translated by John Shepley. New York: St. Martin's Press, 1976.

Tregaskis, Richard. *Southeast Asia: Building the Bases: The History of Construction in Southeast Asia.* Port Hueneme, CA: U.S. Navy Seabee Museum, 1975.

U.S. Army, Department of Military History. Hale Report.

U.S. Department of State. Foreign Relations of the United States (FRUS), "Charles Bohlen's Minutes of the Roosevelt-Stalin Meeting at Livadia Palace, February 8, 1945," *The Conferences at Malta and Yalta, 1945.* Washington: USGPO, 1955.

U.S. House of Representatives, 89th Congress, 2nd session, Mar–Oct 1966, "Hearings, Maritime Manpower Shortage."

U.S. House of Representatives, 89th Congress, Hearings Before The Subcommittee on Merchant Marine. *Vietnam—Shipping Policy Review,* Parts 2 and 3. Washington: USGPO, 1966.

Veith, George J. *Black April: The Fall of South Vietnam 1973–75.* New York: Encounter Books, 2013.

Wain, Barry. *The Refused: The Agony of the Indo-China Refugees.* New York: Simon and Schuster, 1981.

Young, Marilyn. *The Vietnam Wars 1945–1990.* New York: HarperCollins, 1991.

Index

353